Toyota Camry Automotive Repair Manual

by Robert Maddox and John H Haynes

Member of the Guild of Motoring Writers

Models covered:

All Toyota Camry models
1992 through 1996

Does not include all-wheel drive information

(1A4 - 92006)

ABCDE
FGHIJ
KLMNO

Haynes Publishing Group
Sparkford Nr Yeovil
Somerset BA22 7JJ England

Haynes North America, Inc
861 Lawrence Drive
Newbury Park
California 91320 USA

Acknowledgements

We are grateful for the help and cooperation of the Toyota Motor Corporation for their assistance with technical information, certain illustrations and vehicle photos. Technical writers who contributed to this project include Mike Stubblefield, Jay Storer and Larry Warren.

A book in the Haynes Automotive Repair Manual Series

Printed in the U.S.A.

ISBN 1 56392 310 6

Library of Congress Catalog Card Number 98-84202

While every attempt is made to ensure that the information in this manual is correct, no liability can be accepted by the authors or publishers for loss, damage or injury caused by any errors in, or omissions from, the information given.

Contents

Haynes mechanic, author and photographer with 1995 Toyota Camry

About this manual

Its purpose

The purpose of this manual is to help you get the best value from your vehicle. It can do so in several ways. It can help you decide what work must be done, even if you choose to have it done by a dealer service department or a repair shop; it provides information and procedures for routine maintenance and servicing; and it offers diagnostic and repair procedures to follow when trouble occurs.

We hope you use the manual to tackle the work yourself. For many simpler jobs, doing it yourself may be quicker than arranging an appointment to get the vehicle into a shop and making the trips to leave it and pick it up. More importantly, a lot of money can be saved by avoiding the expense the shop must pass on to you to cover its labor and overhead costs. An added benefit is the sense of satisfaction and accomplishment that you feel after doing the job yourself.

Using the manual

The manual is divided into Chapters. Each Chapter is divided into numbered Sections, which are headed in bold type between horizontal lines. Each Section consists of consecutively numbered paragraphs.

At the beginning of each numbered Section you will be referred to any illustrations which apply to the procedures in that Section. The reference numbers used in illustration captions pinpoint the pertinent Section and the Step within that Section. That is, illustration 3.2 means the illustration refers to Section 3 and Step (or paragraph) 2 within that Section.

Procedures, once described in the text, are not normally repeated. When it's necessary to refer to another Chapter, the reference will be given as Chapter and Section number. Cross references given without use of the word "Chapter" apply to Sections and/or paragraphs in the same Chapter. For example, "see Section 8" means in the same Chapter.

References to the left or right side of the vehicle assume you are sitting in the driver's seat, facing forward.

Even though we have prepared this manual with extreme care, neither the publisher nor the author can accept responsibility for any errors in, or omissions from, the information given.

NOTE

A **Note** provides information necessary to properly complete a procedure or information which will make the procedure easier to understand.

CAUTION

A **Caution** provides a special procedure or special steps which must be taken while completing the procedure where the Caution is found. Not heeding a Caution can result in damage to the assembly being worked on.

WARNING

A **Warning** provides a special procedure or special steps which must be taken while completing the procedure where the Warning is found. Not heeding a Warning can result in personal injury.

Introduction to the Toyota Camry

Toyota Camry models are available in coupe, four-door sedan and station wagon body styles.

The transversely mounted inline four-cylinder and V6 engines used in these models are equipped with electronic fuel injection.

The engine drives the front wheels through either a five-speed manual or a four-speed automatic transaxle via independent driveaxles.

Independent suspension, featuring coil spring/strut damper units, is used on all four wheels. The power-assisted rack and pinion steering unit is mounted behind the engine.

The brakes are disc at the front with either drum or discs at the rear, depending on model, with power assist standard. Some models are equipped with Anti-lock brakes (ABS).

Vehicle identification numbers

Modifications are a continuing and unpublicized process in vehicle manufacturing. Since spare parts manuals and lists are compiled on a numerical basis, the individual vehicle numbers are essential to correctly identify the component required.

Vehicle Identification Number (VIN)

This very important identification number is stamped on a plate attached to the dashboard inside the windshield on the driver's side of the vehicle (see illustration). It can also be found on the certification label located on the driver's side door post. The VIN also appears on the Vehicle Certificate of Title and Registration. It contains information such as where and when the vehicle was manufactured, the model year and the body style.

Certification label

The Certification label is attached to the driver's side door. The plate contains the name of the manufacturer, the month and year of production, the Gross Vehicle Weight Rating (GVWR), the Gross Axle Weight Rating (GAWR) and the certification statement.

Engine identification numbers

The engine serial number can be found in a variety of locations, depending on engine type (see illustrations). These models can be equipped with any of three engines:

5S-FE four-cylinder (all years)
3VZ-FE V6 (1992 and 1993)
1MZ-FE V6 (1994 and later)

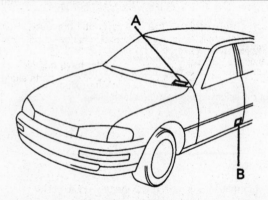

The Vehicle Identification Number (VIN) is located on a plate (A), on the top of the dash (visible through the windshield) and on the certification label (B), located on the drivers side door post

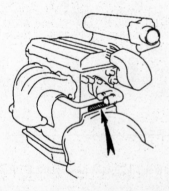

The engine serial number on the 5S-FE four-cylinder engine is located on the rear of the block below the cylinder head

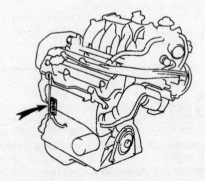

On the 3VZ-FE V6 engine, the serial number is found on the front side of the block, near the oil dipstick

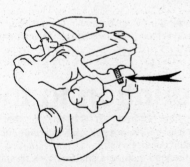

The 1MZ-FE V6 engine serial number is located on the front side of the block under the exhaust manifold

Buying parts

Replacement parts are available from many sources, which generally fall into one of two categories - authorized dealer parts departments and independent retail auto parts stores. Our advice concerning these parts is as follows:

Retail auto parts stores: Good auto parts stores will stock frequently needed components which wear out relatively fast, such as clutch components, exhaust systems, brake parts, tune-up parts, etc. These stores often supply new or reconditioned parts on an exchange basis, which can save a considerable amount of money. Discount auto parts stores are often very good places to buy materials and parts needed for general vehicle maintenance such as oil, grease, filters, spark plugs, belts, touch-up paint, bulbs, etc. They also usually sell tools and general accessories, have convenient hours, charge lower prices and can often be found not far from home.

Authorized dealer parts department: This is the best source for parts which are unique to the vehicle and not generally available elsewhere (such as major engine parts, transmission parts, trim pieces, etc.).

Warranty information: If the vehicle is still covered under warranty, be sure that any replacement parts purchased - regardless of the source - do not invalidate the warranty!

To be sure of obtaining the correct parts, have engine and chassis numbers available and, if possible, take the old parts along for positive identification.

Maintenance techniques, tools and working facilities

Maintenance techniques

There are a number of techniques involved in maintenance and repair that will be referred to throughout this manual. Application of these techniques will enable the home mechanic to be more efficient, better organized and capable of performing the various tasks properly, which will ensure that the repair job is thorough and complete.

Fasteners

Fasteners are nuts, bolts, studs and screws used to hold two or more parts together. There are a few things to keep in mind when working with fasteners. Almost all of them use a locking device of some type, either a lockwasher, locknut, locking tab or thread adhesive. All threaded fasteners should be clean and straight, with undamaged threads and undamaged corners on the hex head where the wrench fits. Develop the habit of replacing all damaged nuts and bolts with new ones. Special locknuts with nylon or fiber inserts can only be used once. If they are removed, they lose their locking ability and must be replaced with new ones.

Rusted nuts and bolts should be treated with a penetrating fluid to ease removal and prevent breakage. Some mechanics use turpentine in a spout-type oil can, which works quite well. After applying the rust penetrant, let it work for a few minutes before trying to loosen the nut or bolt. Badly rusted fasteners may have to be chiseled or sawed off or removed with a special nut breaker, available at tool stores.

If a bolt or stud breaks off in an assembly, it can be drilled and removed with a special tool commonly available for this purpose. Most automotive machine shops can perform this task, as well as other repair procedures, such as the repair of threaded holes that have been stripped out.

Flat washers and lockwashers, when removed from an assembly, should always be replaced exactly as removed. Replace any damaged washers with new ones. Never use a lockwasher on any soft metal surface (such as aluminum), thin sheet metal or plastic.

Fastener sizes

For a number of reasons, automobile manufacturers are making wider and wider use of metric fasteners. Therefore, it is important to be able to tell the difference between standard (sometimes called U.S. or SAE) and metric hardware, since they cannot be interchanged.

All bolts, whether standard or metric, are sized according to diameter, thread pitch and length. For example, a standard 1/2 - 13 x 1 bolt is 1/2 inch in diameter, has 13 threads per inch and is 1 inch long. An M12 - 1.75 x 25 metric bolt is 12 mm in diameter, has a thread pitch of 1.75 mm (the distance between threads) and is 25 mm long. The two bolts are nearly identical, and easily confused, but they are not interchangeable.

In addition to the differences in diameter, thread pitch and length, metric and standard bolts can also be distinguished by examining the bolt heads. To begin with, the distance across the flats on a standard bolt head is measured in inches, while the same dimension on a metric bolt is sized in millimeters (the same is true for nuts). As a result, a standard wrench should not be used on a metric bolt and a metric

wrench should not be used on a standard bolt. Also, most standard bolts have slashes radiating out from the center of the head to denote the grade or strength of the bolt, which is an indication of the amount of torque that can be applied to it. The greater the number of slashes, the greater the strength of the bolt. Grades 0 through 5 are commonly used on automobiles. Metric bolts have a property class (grade) number, rather than a slash, molded into their heads to indicate bolt strength. In this case, the higher the number, the stronger the bolt. Property class numbers 8.8, 9.8 and 10.9 are commonly used on automobiles.

Strength markings can also be used to distinguish standard hex nuts from metric hex nuts. Many standard nuts have dots stamped into one side, while metric nuts are marked with a number. The greater the number of dots, or the higher the number, the greater the strength of the nut.

Metric studs are also marked on their ends according to property class (grade). Larger studs are numbered (the same as metric bolts), while smaller studs carry a geometric code to denote grade.

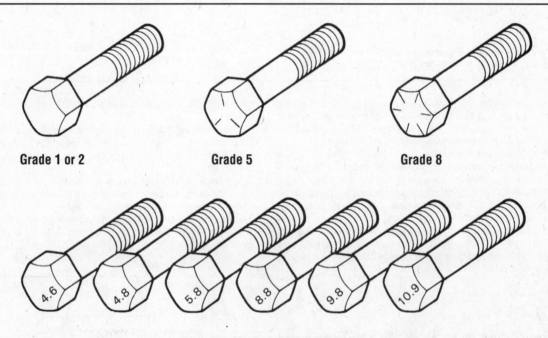

Bolt strength markings (top - standard/SAE/USS; bottom - metric)

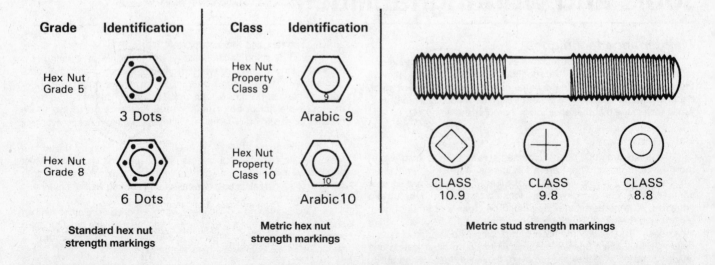

Standard hex nut strength markings

Metric hex nut strength markings

Metric stud strength markings

It should be noted that many fasteners, especially Grades 0 through 2, have no distinguishing marks on them. When such is the case, the only way to determine whether it is standard or metric is to measure the thread pitch or compare it to a known fastener of the same size.

Standard fasteners are often referred to as SAE, as opposed to metric. However, it should be noted that SAE technically refers to a non-metric fine thread fastener only. Coarse thread non-metric fasteners are referred to as USS sizes.

Since fasteners of the same size (both standard and metric) may have different strength ratings, be sure to reinstall any bolts, studs or nuts removed from your vehicle in their original locations. Also, when replacing a fastener with a new one, make sure that the new one has a strength rating equal to or greater than the original.

Tightening sequences and procedures

Most threaded fasteners should be tightened to a specific torque value (torque is the twisting force applied to a threaded component such as a nut or bolt). Overtightening the fastener can weaken it and cause it to break, while undertightening can cause it to eventually come loose. Bolts, screws and studs, depending on the material they are made of and their thread diameters, have specific torque values, many of which are noted in the Specifications at the beginning of each Chapter. Be sure to follow the torque recommendations closely. For fasteners not assigned a specific torque, a general torque value chart is presented here as a guide. These torque values are for dry (unlubricated) fasteners threaded into steel or cast iron (not aluminum). As was previously mentioned, the size and grade of a fastener determine the amount of torque that can safely be applied to it. The

Metric thread sizes	Ft-lbs	Nm
M-6	6 to 9	9 to 12
M-8	14 to 21	19 to 28
M-10	28 to 40	38 to 54
M-12	50 to 71	68 to 96
M-14	80 to 140	109 to 154
Pipe thread sizes		
1/8	5 to 8	7 to 10
1/4	12 to 18	17 to 24
3/8	22 to 33	30 to 44
1/2	25 to 35	34 to 47
U.S. thread sizes		
1/4 - 20	6 to 9	9 to 12
5/16 - 18	12 to 18	17 to 24
5/16 - 24	14 to 20	19 to 27
3/8 - 16	22 to 32	30 to 43
3/8 - 24	27 to 38	37 to 51
7/16 - 14	40 to 55	55 to 74
7/16 - 20	40 to 60	55 to 81
1/2 - 13	55 to 80	75 to 108

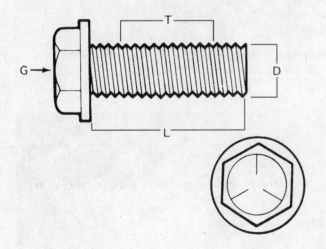

Standard (SAE and USS) bolt dimensions/grade marks

G   *Grade marks (bolt length)*
L   *Length (in inches)*
T   *Thread pitch (number of threads per inch)*
D   *Nominal diameter (in inches)*

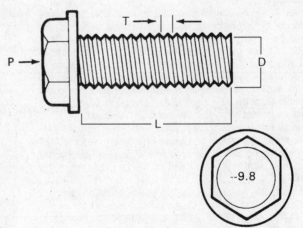

Metric bolt dimensions/grade marks

P   *Property class (bolt strength)*
L   *Length (in millimeters)*
T   *Thread pitch (distance between threads in millimeters)*
D   *Diameter*

figures listed here are approximate for Grade 2 and Grade 3 fasteners. Higher grades can tolerate higher torque values.

Fasteners laid out in a pattern, such as cylinder head bolts, oil pan bolts, differential cover bolts, etc., must be loosened or tightened in sequence to avoid warping the component. This sequence will normally be shown in the appropriate Chapter. If a specific pattern is not given, the following procedures can be used to prevent warping.

Initially, the bolts or nuts should be assembled finger-tight only. Next, they should be tightened one full turn each, in a criss-cross or diagonal pattern. After each one has been tightened one full turn, return to the first one and tighten them all one-half turn, following the same pattern. Finally, tighten each of them one-quarter turn at a time until each fastener has been tightened to the proper torque. To loosen and remove the fasteners, the procedure would be reversed.

Component disassembly

Component disassembly should be done with care and purpose to help ensure that the parts go back together properly. Always keep track of the sequence in which parts are removed. Make note of special characteristics or marks on parts that can be installed more than one way, such as a grooved thrust washer on a shaft. It is a good idea to lay the disassembled parts out on a clean surface in the order that they were removed. It may also be helpful to make sketches or take instant photos of components before removal.

When removing fasteners from a component, keep track of their locations. Sometimes threading a bolt back in a part, or putting the washers and nut back on a stud, can prevent mix-ups later. If nuts and bolts cannot be returned to their original locations, they should be kept in a compartmented box or a series of small boxes. A cupcake or muffin tin is ideal for this purpose, since each cavity can hold the bolts and nuts from a particular area (i.e. oil pan bolts, valve cover bolts, engine mount bolts, etc.). A pan of this type is especially helpful when working on assemblies with very small parts, such as the carburetor, alternator, valve train or interior dash and trim pieces. The cavities can be marked with paint or tape to identify the contents.

Whenever wiring looms, harnesses or connectors are separated, it is a good idea to identify the two halves with numbered pieces of masking tape so they can be easily reconnected.

Gasket sealing surfaces

Throughout any vehicle, gaskets are used to seal the mating surfaces between two parts and keep lubricants, fluids, vacuum or pressure contained in an assembly.

Many times these gaskets are coated with a liquid or paste-type gasket sealing compound before assembly. Age, heat and pressure can sometimes cause the two parts to stick together so tightly that they are very difficult to separate. Often, the assembly can be loosened by striking it with a soft-face hammer near the mating surfaces. A regular hammer can be used if a block of wood is placed between the hammer and the part. Do not hammer on cast parts or parts that could be easily damaged. With any particularly stubborn part, always recheck to make sure that every fastener has been removed.

Avoid using a screwdriver or bar to pry apart an assembly, as they can easily mar the gasket sealing surfaces of the parts, which must remain smooth. If prying is absolutely necessary, use an old broom handle, but keep in mind that extra clean up will be necessary if the wood splinters.

After the parts are separated, the old gasket must be carefully scraped off and the gasket surfaces cleaned. Stubborn gasket material can be soaked with rust penetrant or treated with a special chemical to soften it so it can be easily scraped off. A scraper can be fashioned from a piece of copper tubing by flattening and sharpening one end. Copper is recommended because it is usually softer than the surfaces to be scraped, which reduces the chance of gouging the part. Some gaskets can be removed with a wire brush, but regardless of the method used, the mating surfaces must be left clean and smooth. If for some reason the gasket surface is gouged, then a gasket sealer thick enough to fill scratches will have to be used during reassembly of the components. For most applications, a non-drying (or semi-drying) gasket sealer should be used.

Hose removal tips

Warning: *If the vehicle is equipped with air conditioning, do not disconnect any of the A/C hoses without first having the system depressurized by a dealer service department or a service station.*

Hose removal precautions closely parallel gasket removal precautions. Avoid scratching or gouging the surface that the hose mates against or the connection may leak. This is especially true for radiator hoses. Because of various chemical reactions, the rubber in hoses can bond itself to the metal spigot that the hose fits over. To remove a hose, first loosen the hose clamps that secure it to the spigot. Then, with slip-joint pliers, grab the hose at the clamp and rotate it around the spigot. Work it back and forth until it is completely free, then pull it off. Silicone or other lubricants will ease removal if they can be applied between the hose and the outside of the spigot. Apply the same lubricant to the inside of the hose and the outside of the spigot to simplify installation.

As a last resort (and if the hose is to be replaced with a new one anyway), the rubber can be slit with a knife and the hose peeled from the spigot. If this must be done, be careful that the metal connection is not damaged.

If a hose clamp is broken or damaged, do not reuse it. Wire-type clamps usually weaken with age, so it is a good idea to replace them with screw-type clamps whenever a hose is removed.

Tools

A selection of good tools is a basic requirement for anyone who plans to maintain and repair his or her own vehicle. For the owner who has few tools, the initial investment might seem high, but when compared to the spiraling costs of professional auto maintenance and repair, it is a wise one.

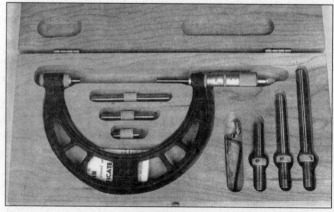

Micrometer set

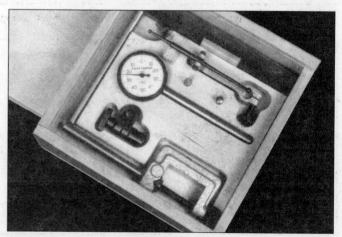

Dial indicator set

Dial caliper

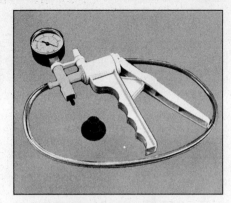

Hand-operated vacuum pump

Timing light

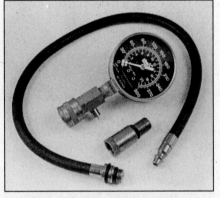

Compression gauge with spark plug hole adapter

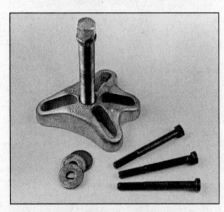

Damper/steering wheel puller

General purpose puller

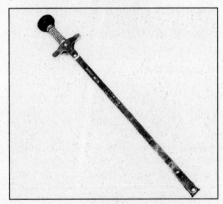

Hydraulic lifter removal tool

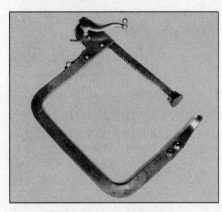

Valve spring compressor

Valve spring compressor

Ridge reamer

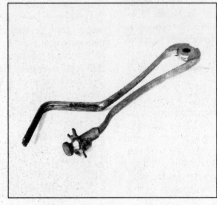

Piston ring groove cleaning tool

Ring removal/installation tool

Ring compressor

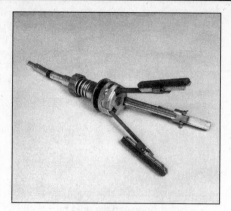

Cylinder hone

Brake hold-down spring tool

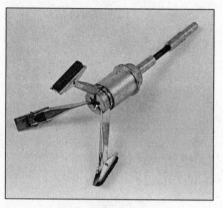

Brake cylinder hone

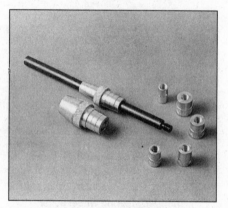

Clutch plate alignment tool

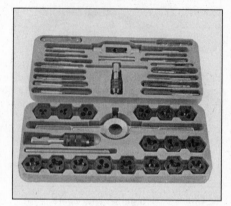

Tap and die set

To help the owner decide which tools are needed to perform the tasks detailed in this manual, the following tool lists are offered: *Maintenance and minor repair*, *Repair/overhaul* and *Special*.

The newcomer to practical mechanics should start off with the *maintenance and minor repair* tool kit, which is adequate for the simpler jobs performed on a vehicle. Then, as confidence and experience grow, the owner can tackle more difficult tasks, buying additional tools as they are needed. Eventually the basic kit will be expanded into the *repair and overhaul* tool set. Over a period of time, the experienced do-it-yourselfer will assemble a tool set complete enough for most repair and overhaul procedures and will add tools from the special category when it is felt that the expense is justified by the frequency of use.

Maintenance and minor repair tool kit

The tools in this list should be considered the minimum required for performance of routine maintenance, servicing and minor repair work. We recommend the purchase of combination wrenches (box-end and open-end combined in one wrench). While more expensive than open end wrenches, they offer the advantages of both types of wrench.

Combination wrench set (1/4-inch to 1 inch or 6 mm to 19 mm)
Adjustable wrench, 8 inch
Spark plug wrench with rubber insert
Spark plug gap adjusting tool
Feeler gauge set
Brake bleeder wrench
Standard screwdriver (5/16-inch x 6 inch)
Phillips screwdriver (No. 2 x 6 inch)
Combination pliers - 6 inch
Hacksaw and assortment of blades
Tire pressure gauge
Grease gun

Oil can
Fine emery cloth
Wire brush
Battery post and cable cleaning tool
Oil filter wrench
Funnel (medium size)
Safety goggles
Jackstands (2)
Drain pan

Note: *If basic tune-ups are going to be part of routine maintenance, it will be necessary to purchase a good quality stroboscopic timing light and combination tachometer/dwell meter. Although they are included in the list of special tools, it is mentioned here because they are absolutely necessary for tuning most vehicles properly.*

Repair and overhaul tool set

These tools are essential for anyone who plans to perform major repairs and are in addition to those in the maintenance and minor repair tool kit. Included is a comprehensive set of sockets which, though expensive, are invaluable because of their versatility, especially when various extensions and drives are available. We recommend the 1/2-inch drive over the 3/8-inch drive. Although the larger drive is bulky and more expensive, it has the capacity of accepting a very wide range of large sockets. Ideally, however, the mechanic should have a 3/8-inch drive set and a 1/2-inch drive set.

Socket set(s)
Reversible ratchet
Extension - 10 inch
Universal joint
Torque wrench (same size drive as sockets)
Ball peen hammer - 8 ounce
Soft-face hammer (plastic/rubber)
Standard screwdriver (1/4-inch x 6 inch)

Standard screwdriver (stubby - 5/16-inch)
Phillips screwdriver (No. 3 x 8 inch)
Phillips screwdriver (stubby - No. 2)
Pliers - vise grip
Pliers - lineman's
Pliers - needle nose
Pliers - snap-ring (internal and external)
Cold chisel - 1/2-inch
Scribe
Scraper (made from flattened copper tubing)
Centerpunch
Pin punches (1/16, 1/8, 3/16-inch)
Steel rule/straightedge - 12 inch
Allen wrench set (1/8 to 3/8-inch or 4 mm to 10 mm)
A selection of files
Wire brush (large)
Jackstands (second set)
Jack (scissor or hydraulic type)

Note: *Another tool which is often useful is an electric drill with a chuck capacity of 3/8-inch and a set of good quality drill bits.*

Special tools

The tools in this list include those which are not used regularly, are expensive to buy, or which need to be used in accordance with their manufacturer's instructions. Unless these tools will be used frequently, it is not very economical to purchase many of them. A consideration would be to split the cost and use between yourself and a friend or friends. In addition, most of these tools can be obtained from a tool rental shop on a temporary basis.

This list primarily contains only those tools and instruments widely available to the public, and not those special tools produced by the vehicle manufacturer for distribution to dealer service departments. Occasionally, references to the manufacturer's special tools are included in the text of this manual. Generally, an alternative method of doing the job without the special tool is offered. However, sometimes there is no alternative to their use. Where this is the case, and the tool cannot be purchased or borrowed, the work should be turned over to the dealer service department or an automotive repair shop.

Valve spring compressor
Piston ring groove cleaning tool
Piston ring compressor
Piston ring installation tool
Cylinder compression gauge
Cylinder ridge reamer
Cylinder surfacing hone
Cylinder bore gauge
Micrometers and/or dial calipers
Hydraulic lifter removal tool
Balljoint separator
Universal-type puller
Impact screwdriver
Dial indicator set
Stroboscopic timing light (inductive pick-up)
Hand operated vacuum/pressure pump
Tachometer/dwell meter
Universal electrical multimeter
Cable hoist
Brake spring removal and installation tools
Floor jack

Buying tools

For the do-it-yourselfer who is just starting to get involved in vehicle maintenance and repair, there are a number of options available when purchasing tools. If maintenance and minor repair is the extent of the work to be done, the purchase of individual tools is satisfactory. If, on the other hand, extensive work is planned, it would be a good idea to purchase a modest tool set from one of the large retail chain stores. A set can usually be bought at a substantial savings over the individual tool prices, and they often come with a tool box. As additional tools are needed, add-on sets, individual tools and a larger tool box can be purchased to expand the tool selection. Building a tool set gradually allows the cost of the tools to be spread over a longer period of time and gives the mechanic the freedom to choose only those tools that will actually be used.

Tool stores will often be the only source of some of the special tools that are needed, but regardless of where tools are bought, try to avoid cheap ones, especially when buying screwdrivers and sockets, because they won't last very long. The expense involved in replacing cheap tools will eventually be greater than the initial cost of quality tools.

Care and maintenance of tools

Good tools are expensive, so it makes sense to treat them with respect. Keep them clean and in usable condition and store them properly when not in use. Always wipe off any dirt, grease or metal chips before putting them away. Never leave tools lying around in the work area. Upon completion of a job, always check closely under the hood for tools that may have been left there so they won't get lost during a test drive.

Some tools, such as screwdrivers, pliers, wrenches and sockets, can be hung on a panel mounted on the garage or workshop wall, while others should be kept in a tool box or tray. Measuring instruments, gauges, meters, etc. must be carefully stored where they cannot be damaged by weather or impact from other tools.

When tools are used with care and stored properly, they will last a very long time. Even with the best of care, though, tools will wear out if used frequently. When a tool is damaged or worn out, replace it. Subsequent jobs will be safer and more enjoyable if you do.

Working facilities

Not to be overlooked when discussing tools is the workshop. If anything more than routine maintenance is to be carried out, some sort of suitable work area is essential.

It is understood, and appreciated, that many home mechanics do not have a good workshop or garage available, and end up removing an engine or doing major repairs outside. It is recommended, however, that the overhaul or repair be completed under the cover of a roof.

A clean, flat workbench or table of comfortable working height is an absolute necessity. The workbench should be equipped with a vise that has a jaw opening of at least four inches.

As mentioned previously, some clean, dry storage space is also required for tools, as well as the lubricants, fluids, cleaning solvents, etc. which soon become necessary.

Sometimes waste oil and fluids, drained from the engine or cooling system during normal maintenance or repairs, present a disposal problem. To avoid pouring them on the ground or into a sewage system, pour the used fluids into large containers, seal them with caps and take them to an authorized disposal site or recycling center. Plastic jugs, such as old antifreeze containers, are ideal for this purpose.

Always keep a supply of old newspapers and clean rags available. Old towels are excellent for mopping up spills. Many mechanics use rolls of paper towels for most work because they are readily available and disposable. To help keep the area under the vehicle clean, a large cardboard box can be cut open and flattened to protect the garage or shop floor.

Whenever working over a painted surface, such as when leaning over a fender to service something under the hood, always cover it with an old blanket or bedspread to protect the finish. Vinyl covered pads, made especially for this purpose, are available at auto parts stores.

Jacking and towing

Jacking

The jack supplied with the vehicle should only be used for raising the vehicle for changing a tire or placing jackstands under the frame. **Warning:** *Never crawl under the vehicle or start the engine when the jack is being used as the only means of support.*

All vehicles are supplied with a scissors-type jack. When jacking the vehicle, it should be engaged with the seam notch, between the two dimples **(see illustration).**

The vehicle should be on level ground with the wheels blocked and the transmission in Park (automatic) or Reverse (manual). Pry off the hub cap (if equipped) using the tapered end of the lug wrench. Loosen the lug nuts one-half turn and leave them in place until the wheel is raised off the ground.

Place the jack under the side of the vehicle in the indicated position. Use the supplied wrench to turn the jackscrew clockwise until the wheel is raised off the ground. Remove the lug nuts, pull off the wheel and replace it with the spare.

With the beveled side in, replace the lug nuts and tighten them until snug. Lower the vehicle by turning the jackscrew counterclockwise. Remove the jack and tighten the nuts in a diagonal pattern to the torque listed in the Chapter 1 Specifications. If a torque wrench is not available, have the torque checked by a service station as soon as possible. Replace the hubcap by placing it in position and using the heel of your hand or a rubber mallet to seat it.

Towing

Manual transmission-equipped vehicles can be towed with all four wheels on the ground. Automatic transmission-equipped models should only be towed with all four wheels on the ground if speeds do not exceed 35 mph and the distance is not over 50 miles, otherwise transmission damage can result.

The jack fits over the rocker panel flange, between the two notches (there are two jacking points on each side of the vehicle)

Towing equipment specifically designed for this purpose should be used and should be attached to the main structural members of the vehicle, not the bumper or brackets.

Safety is a major consideration when towing and all applicable state and local laws must be obeyed. A safety chain system must be used for all towing.

While towing, the parking brake should be released and the transmission should be in Neutral. The steering must be unlocked (ignition switch in the Off position). Remember that power steering and power brakes will not work with the engine off.

Booster battery (jump) starting

Observe these precautions when using a booster battery to start a vehicle:

a) *Before connecting the booster battery, make sure the ignition switch is in the Off position.*
b) *Turn off the lights, heater and other electrical loads.*
c) *Your eyes should be shielded. Safety goggles are a good idea.*
d) *Make sure the booster battery is the same voltage as the dead one in the vehicle.*
e) *The two vehicles MUST NOT TOUCH each other!*
f) *Make sure the transaxle is in Neutral (manual) or Park (automatic).*
g) *If the booster battery is not a maintenance-free type, remove the vent caps and lay a cloth over the vent holes.*

Connect the red jumper cable to the positive (+) terminals of each battery **(see illustration)**.

Connect one end of the black jumper cable to the negative (-) terminal of the booster battery. The other end of this cable should be connected to a good ground on the vehicle to be started, such as a bolt or bracket on the body.

Start the engine using the booster battery, then, with the engine running at idle speed, disconnect the jumper cables in the reverse order of connection.

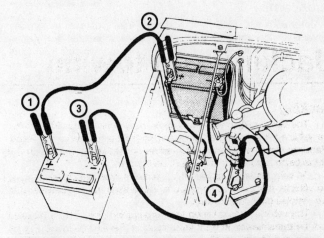

Make the booster battery cable connections in the numerical order shown (note that the negative cable of the booster battery is NOT attached to the negative terminal of the dead battery)

Stereo anti-theft system precaution

Stereo systems displaying ANTI-THEFT SYSTEM on the cassette tape slot cover have a built-in theft deterrent system designed to render the stereo inoperative should the stereo be stolen. If the power source to the stereo is cut, the anti-theft system will activate, so even if the power source is immediately reconnected the stereo will not function. If your vehicle is equipped with this anti-theft system, do not disconnect the cable from the negative terminal of the battery, remove the stereo or disconnect related components unless you have the individual ID (code) number for the stereo.

If you discover that the system is inoperative after disconnecting and reconnecting the power source, enter the ID number. If the wrong number is entered Err will appear on the display. You may make up to nine errors - a tenth error will activate the system and HELP will appear on the display. If this occurs, contact your local Toyota dealer service department.

Automotive chemicals and lubricants

A number of automotive chemicals and lubricants are available for use during vehicle maintenance and repair. They include a wide variety of products ranging from cleaning solvents and degreasers to lubricants and protective sprays for rubber, plastic and vinyl.

Cleaners

Carburetor cleaner and choke cleaner is a strong solvent for gum, varnish and carbon. Most carburetor cleaners leave a dry-type lubricant film which will not harden or gum up. Because of this film it is not recommended for use on electrical components.

Brake system cleaner is used to remove grease and brake fluid from the brake system, where clean surfaces are absolutely necessary. It leaves no residue and often eliminates brake squeal caused by contaminants.

Electrical cleaner removes oxidation, corrosion and carbon deposits from electrical contacts, restoring full current flow. It can also be used to clean spark plugs, carburetor jets, voltage regulators and other parts where an oil-free surface is desired.

Demoisturants remove water and moisture from electrical components such as alternators, voltage regulators, electrical connectors and fuse blocks. They are non-conductive, non-corrosive and non-flammable.

Degreasers are heavy-duty solvents used to remove grease from the outside of the engine and from chassis components. They can be sprayed or brushed on and, depending on the type, are rinsed off either with water or solvent.

Lubricants

Motor oil is the lubricant formulated for use in engines. It normally contains a wide variety of additives to prevent corrosion and reduce foaming and wear. Motor oil comes in various weights (viscosity ratings) from 5 to 80. The recommended weight of the oil depends on the season, temperature and the demands on the engine. Light oil is used in cold climates and under light load conditions. Heavy oil is used in hot climates and where high loads are encountered. Multi-viscosity oils are designed to have characteristics of both light and heavy oils and are available in a number of weights from 5W-20 to 20W-50.

Gear oil is designed to be used in differentials, manual transmissions and other areas where high-temperature lubrication is required.

Chassis and wheel bearing grease is a heavy grease used where increased loads and friction are encountered, such as for wheel bearings, balljoints, tie-rod ends and universal joints.

High-temperature wheel bearing grease is designed to withstand the extreme temperatures encountered by wheel bearings in disc brake equipped vehicles. It usually contains molybdenum disulfide (moly), which is a dry-type lubricant.

White grease is a heavy grease for metal-to-metal applications where water is a problem. White grease stays soft under both low and high temperatures (usually from -100 to +190-degrees F), and will not wash off or dilute in the presence of water.

Assembly lube is a special extreme pressure lubricant, usually containing moly, used to lubricate high-load parts (such as main and rod bearings and cam lobes) for initial start-up of a new engine. The assembly lube lubricates the parts without being squeezed out or washed away until the engine oiling system begins to function.

Silicone lubricants are used to protect rubber, plastic, vinyl and nylon parts.

Graphite lubricants are used where oils cannot be used due to contamination problems, such as in locks. The dry graphite will lubricate metal parts while remaining uncontaminated by dirt, water, oil or acids. It is electrically conductive and will not foul electrical contacts in locks such as the ignition switch.

Moly penetrants loosen and lubricate frozen, rusted and corroded fasteners and prevent future rusting or freezing.

Heat-sink grease is a special electrically non-conductive grease that is used for mounting electronic ignition modules where it is essential that heat is transferred away from the module.

Sealants

RTV sealant is one of the most widely used gasket compounds. Made from silicone, RTV is air curing, it seals, bonds, waterproofs, fills surface irregularities, remains flexible, doesn't shrink, is relatively easy to remove, and is used as a supplementary sealer with almost all low and medium temperature gaskets.

Anaerobic sealant is much like RTV in that it can be used either to seal gaskets or to form gaskets by itself. It remains flexible, is solvent resistant and fills surface imperfections. The difference between an anaerobic sealant and an RTV-type sealant is in the curing. RTV cures when exposed to air, while an anaerobic sealant cures only in the absence of air. This means that an anaerobic sealant cures only after the assembly of parts, sealing them together.

Thread and pipe sealant is used for sealing hydraulic and pneumatic fittings and vacuum lines. It is usually made from a Teflon compound, and comes in a spray, a paint-on liquid and as a wrap-around tape.

Chemicals

Anti-seize compound prevents seizing, galling, cold welding, rust and corrosion in fasteners. High-temperature ant-seize, usually made with copper and graphite lubricants, is used for exhaust system and exhaust manifold bolts.

Anaerobic locking compounds are used to keep fasteners from vibrating or working loose and cure only after installation, in the absence of air. Medium strength locking compound is used for small nuts, bolts and screws that may be removed later. High-strength locking compound is for large nuts, bolts and studs which aren't removed on a regular basis.

Oil additives range from viscosity index improvers to chemical treatments that claim to reduce internal engine friction. It should be noted that most oil manufacturers caution against using additives with their oils.

Gas additives perform several functions, depending on their chemical makeup. They usually contain solvents that help dissolve gum and varnish that build up on carburetor, fuel injection and intake parts. They also serve to break down carbon deposits that form on the inside surfaces of the combustion chambers. Some additives contain upper cylinder lubricants for valves and piston rings, and others contain chemicals to remove condensation from the gas tank.

Miscellaneous

Brake fluid is specially formulated hydraulic fluid that can withstand the heat and pressure encountered in brake systems. Care must be taken so this fluid does not come in contact with painted surfaces or plastics. An opened container should always be resealed to prevent contamination by water or dirt.

Weatherstrip adhesive is used to bond weatherstripping around doors, windows and trunk lids. It is sometimes used to attach trim pieces.

Undercoating is a petroleum-based, tar-like substance that is designed to protect metal surfaces on the underside of the vehicle from corrosion. It also acts as a sound-deadening agent by insulating the bottom of the vehicle.

Waxes and polishes are used to help protect painted and plated surfaces from the weather. Different types of paint may require the use of different types of wax and polish. Some polishes utilize a chemical or abrasive cleaner to help remove the top layer of oxidized (dull) paint on older vehicles. In recent years many non-wax polishes that contain a wide variety of chemicals such as polymers and silicones have been introduced. These non-wax polishes are usually easier to apply and last longer than conventional waxes and polishes.

Conversion factors

Length (distance)
Inches (in)	X	25.4	= Millimetres (mm)	X 0.0394	= Inches (in)
Feet (ft)	X	0.305	= Metres (m)	X 3.281	= Feet (ft)
Miles	X	1.609	= Kilometres (km)	X 0.621	= Miles

Volume (capacity)
Cubic inches (cu in; in^3)	X 16.387 = Cubic centimetres (cc; cm^3)	X 0.061	= Cubic inches (cu in; in^3)
Imperial pints (Imp pt)	X 0.568 = Litres (l)	X 1.76	= Imperial pints (Imp pt)
Imperial quarts (Imp qt)	X 1.137 = Litres (l)	X 0.88	= Imperial quarts (Imp qt)
Imperial quarts (Imp qt)	X 1.201 = US quarts (US qt)	X 0.833	= Imperial quarts (Imp qt)
US quarts (US qt)	X 0.946 = Litres (l)	X 1.057	= US quarts (US qt)
Imperial gallons (Imp gal)	X 4.546 = Litres (l)	X 0.22	= Imperial gallons (Imp gal)
Imperial gallons (Imp gal)	X 1.201 = US gallons (US gal)	X 0.833	= Imperial gallons (Imp gal)
US gallons (US gal)	X 3.785 = Litres (l)	X 0.264	= US gallons (US gal)

Mass (weight)
Ounces (oz)	X 28.35 = Grams (g)	X 0.035	Ounces (oz)
Pounds (lb)	X 0.454 = Kilograms (kg)	X 2.205	= Pounds (lb)

Force
Ounces-force (ozf; oz)	X 0.278 = Newtons (N)	X 3.6	= Ounces-force (ozf; oz)
Pounds-force (lbf; lb)	X 4.448 = Newtons (N)	X 0.225	= Pounds-force (lbf; lb)
Newtons (N)	X 0.1 = Kilograms-force (kgf; kg)	X 9.81	= Newtons (N)

Pressure
Pounds-force per square inch (psi; lbf/in^2; lb/in^2)	X 0.070 = Kilograms-force per square centimetre (kgf/cm^2; kg/cm^2)	X 14.223	= Pounds-force per square inch (psi; lbf/in^2; lb/in^2)
Pounds-force per square inch (psi; lbf/in^2; lb/in^2)	X 0.068 = Atmospheres (atm)	X 14.696	= Pounds-force per square inch (psi; lbf/in^2; lb/in^2)
Pounds-force per square inch (psi; lbf/in^2; lb/in^2)	X 0.069 = Bars	X 14.5	= Pounds-force per square inch (psi; lbf/in^2; lb/in^2)
Pounds-force per square inch (psi; lbf/in^2; lb/in^2)	X 6.895 = Kilopascals (kPa)	X 0.145	= Pounds-force per square inch (psi; lbf/in^2; lb/in^2)
Kilopascals (kPa)	X 0.01 = Kilograms-force per square centimetre (kgf/cm^2; kg/cm^2)	X 98.1	= Kilopascals (kPa)

Torque (moment of force)
Pounds-force inches (lbf in; lb in)	X 1.152 = Kilograms-force centimetre (kgf cm; kg cm)	X 0.868	= Pounds-force inches (lbf in; lb in)
Pounds-force inches (lbf in; lb in)	X 0.113 = Newton metres (Nm)	X 8.85	= Pounds-force inches (lbf in; lb in)
Pounds-force inches (lbf in; lb in)	X 0.083 = Pounds-force feet (lbf ft; lb ft)	X 12	= Pounds-force inches (lbf in; lb in)
Pounds-force feet (lbf ft; lb ft)	X 0.138 = Kilograms-force metres (kgf m; kg m)	X 7.233	= Pounds-force feet (lbf ft; lb ft)
Pounds-force feet (lbf ft; lb ft)	X 1.356 = Newton metres (Nm)	X 0.738	= Pounds-force feet (lbf ft; lb ft)
Newton metres (Nm)	X 0.102 = Kilograms-force metres (kgf m; kg m)	X 9.804	= Newton metres (Nm)

Power
Horsepower (hp)	X 745.7 = Watts (W)	X 0.0013	= Horsepower (hp)

Velocity (speed)
Miles per hour (miles/hr; mph)	X 1.609 = Kilometres per hour (km/hr; kph)	X 0.621	= Miles per hour (miles/hr; mph)

Fuel consumption*
Miles per gallon, Imperial (mpg)	X 0.354 = Kilometres per litre (km/l)	X 2.825	= Miles per gallon, Imperial (mpg)
Miles per gallon, US (mpg)	X 0.425 = Kilometres per litre (km/l)	X 2.352	= Miles per gallon, US (mpg)

Temperature
Degrees Fahrenheit = (°C x 1.8) + 32   Degrees Celsius (Degrees Centigrade; °C) = (°F - 32) x 0.56

It is common practice to convert from miles per gallon (mpg) to litres/100 kilometres (l/100km), where mpg (Imperial) x l/100 km = 282 and mpg (US) x l/100 km = 235

Safety first

Regardless of how enthusiastic you may be about getting on with the job at hand, take the time to ensure that your safety is not jeopardized. A moment's lack of attention can result in an accident, as can failure to observe certain simple safety precautions. The possibility of an accident will always exist, and the following points should not be considered a comprehensive list of all dangers. Rather, they are intended to make you aware of the risks and to encourage a safety conscious approach to all work you carry out on your vehicle.

Essential DOs and DON'Ts

DON'T rely on a jack when working under the vehicle. Always use approved jackstands to support the weight of the vehicle and place them under the recommended lift or support points.

DON'T attempt to loosen extremely tight fasteners (i.e. wheel lug nuts) while the vehicle is on a jack - it may fall.

DON'T start the engine without first making sure that the transmission is in Neutral (or Park where applicable) and the parking brake is set.

DON'T remove the radiator cap from a hot cooling system - let it cool or cover it with a cloth and release the pressure gradually.

DON'T attempt to drain the engine oil until you are sure it has cooled to the point that it will not burn you.

DON'T touch any part of the engine or exhaust system until it has cooled sufficiently to avoid burns.

DON'T siphon toxic liquids such as gasoline, antifreeze and brake fluid by mouth, or allow them to remain on your skin.

DON'T inhale brake lining dust - it is potentially hazardous (see *Asbestos* below).

DON'T allow spilled oil or grease to remain on the floor - wipe it up before someone slips on it.

DON'T use loose fitting wrenches or other tools which may slip and cause injury.

DON'T push on wrenches when loosening or tightening nuts or bolts. Always try to pull the wrench toward you. If the situation calls for pushing the wrench away, push with an open hand to avoid scraped knuckles if the wrench should slip.

DON'T attempt to lift a heavy component alone - get someone to help you.

DON'T rush or take unsafe shortcuts to finish a job.

DON'T allow children or animals in or around the vehicle while you are working on it.

DO wear eye protection when using power tools such as a drill, sander, bench grinder, etc. and when working under a vehicle.

DO keep loose clothing and long hair well out of the way of moving parts.

DO make sure that any hoist used has a safe working load rating adequate for the job.

DO get someone to check on you periodically when working alone on a vehicle.

DO carry out work in a logical sequence and make sure that everything is correctly assembled and tightened.

DO keep chemicals and fluids tightly capped and out of the reach of children and pets.

DO remember that your vehicle's safety affects that of yourself and others. If in doubt on any point, get professional advice.

Asbestos

Certain friction, insulating, sealing, and other products - such as brake linings, brake bands, clutch linings, torque converters, gaskets, etc. - contain asbestos. Extreme care must be taken to avoid inhalation of dust from such products, since it is hazardous to health. If in doubt, assume that they do contain asbestos.

Fire

Remember at all times that gasoline is highly flammable. Never smoke or have any kind of open flame around when working on a vehicle. But the risk does not end there. A spark caused by an electrical short circuit, by two metal surfaces contacting each other, or even by static electricity built up in your body under certain conditions, can ignite gasoline vapors, which in a confined space are highly explosive. Do not, under any circumstances, use gasoline for cleaning parts. Use an approved safety solvent.

Always disconnect the battery ground (-) cable at the battery before working on any part of the fuel system or electrical system. Never risk spilling fuel on a hot engine or exhaust component. It is strongly recommended that a fire extinguisher suitable for use on fuel and electrical fires be kept handy in the garage or workshop at all times. Never try to extinguish a fuel or electrical fire with water.

Fumes

Certain fumes are highly toxic and can quickly cause unconsciousness and even death if inhaled to any extent. Gasoline vapor falls into this category, as do the vapors from some cleaning solvents. Any draining or pouring of such volatile fluids should be done in a well ventilated area.

When using cleaning fluids and solvents, read the instructions on the container carefully. Never use materials from unmarked containers.

Never run the engine in an enclosed space, such as a garage. Exhaust fumes contain carbon monoxide, which is extremely poisonous. If you need to run the engine, always do so in the open air, or at least have the rear of the vehicle outside the work area.

If you are fortunate enough to have the use of an inspection pit, never drain or pour gasoline and never run the engine while the vehicle is over the pit. The fumes, being heavier than air, will concentrate in the pit with possibly lethal results.

The battery

Never create a spark or allow a bare light bulb near a battery. They normally give off a certain amount of hydrogen gas, which is highly explosive.

Always disconnect the battery ground (-) cable at the battery before working on the fuel or electrical systems.

If possible, loosen the filler caps or cover when charging the battery from an external source (this does not apply to sealed or maintenance-free batteries). Do not charge at an excessive rate or the battery may burst.

Take care when adding water to a non maintenance-free battery and when carrying a battery. The electrolyte, even when diluted, is very corrosive and should not be allowed to contact clothing or skin.

Always wear eye protection when cleaning the battery to prevent the caustic deposits from entering your eyes.

Household current

When using an electric power tool, inspection light, etc., which operates on household current, always make sure that the tool is correctly connected to its plug and that, where necessary, it is properly grounded. Do not use such items in damp conditions and, again, do not create a spark or apply excessive heat in the vicinity of fuel or fuel vapor.

Secondary ignition system voltage

A severe electric shock can result from touching certain parts of the ignition system (such as the spark plug wires) when the engine is running or being cranked, particularly if components are damp or the insulation is defective. In the case of an electronic ignition system, the secondary system voltage is much higher and could prove fatal.

Troubleshooting

Contents

This section provides an easy reference guide to the more common problems which may occur during the operation of your vehicle. These problems and their possible causes are grouped under headings denoting various components or systems, such as Engine, Cooling system, etc. They also refer you to the chapter and/or section which deals with the problem.

Remember that successful troubleshooting is not a mysterious art practiced only by professional mechanics. It is simply the result of the right knowledge combined with an intelligent, systematic approach to the problem. Always work by a process of elimination, starting with the simplest solution and working through to the most complex - and never overlook the obvious. Anyone can run the gas tank dry or leave the lights on overnight, so don't assume that you are exempt from such oversights.

Finally, always establish a clear idea of why a problem has occurred and take steps to ensure that it doesn't happen again. If the electrical system fails because of a poor connection, check the other connections in the system to make sure that they don't fail as well. If a particular fuse continues to blow, find out why - don't just replace one fuse after another. Remember, failure of a small component can often be indicative of potential failure or incorrect functioning of a more important component or system.

Engine

1   Engine will not rotate when attempting to start

1   Battery terminal connections loose or corroded (Chapter 1).
2   Battery discharged or faulty (Chapter 1).
3   Automatic transaxle not completely engaged in Park (Chapter 7) or clutch not completely depressed (Chapter 8).
4   Broken, loose or disconnected wiring in the starting circuit (Chapters 5 and 12).
5   Starter motor pinion jammed in flywheel ring gear (Chapter 5).
6   Starter solenoid faulty (Chapter 5).
7   Starter motor faulty (Chapter 5).
8   Ignition switch faulty (Chapter 12).
9   Starter pinion or flywheel teeth worn or broken (Chapter 5).

2   Engine rotates but will not start

1   Fuel tank empty.
2   Battery discharged (engine rotates slowly) (Chapter 5).
3   Battery terminal connections loose or corroded (Chapter 1).
4   Leaking fuel injector(s), faulty fuel pump, pressure regulator, etc. (Chapter 4).
5   Fuel not reaching fuel rail (Chapter 4).
6   Ignition components damp or damaged (Chapter 5).
7   Worn, faulty or incorrectly gapped spark plugs (Chapter 1).
8   Broken, loose or disconnected wiring in the starting circuit (Chapter 5).
9   Loose distributor is changing ignition timing (Chapter 5).
10   Broken, loose or disconnected wires at the ignition coil(s) or faulty coil(s) (Chapter 5).
11   Faulty camshaft or crankshaft position sensor (1MZ-FE engine) (Chapter 6).

3   Engine hard to start when cold

1   Battery discharged or low (Chapter 1).
2   Malfunctioning fuel system (Chapter 4).
3   Faulty cold start injector (Chapter 4).
4   Injector(s) leaking (Chapter 4).
5   Distributor rotor carbon tracked (Chapter 5).
6   Faulty coolant temperature sensor (Chapter 6).

4   Engine hard to start when hot

1   Air filter clogged (Chapter 1).
2   Fuel not reaching the fuel injection system (Chapter 4).
3   Corroded battery connections, especially ground (Chapter 1).

5   Starter motor noisy or excessively rough in engagement

1   Pinion or flywheel gear teeth worn or broken (Chapter 5).
2   Starter motor mounting bolts loose or missing (Chapter 5).

6   Engine starts but stops immediately

1   Loose or faulty electrical connections at distributor, coil(s) or alternator (Chapter 5).
2   Insufficient fuel reaching the fuel injector(s) (Chapters 1 and 4).
3   Vacuum leak at the gasket between the intake manifold/plenum and throttle body (Chapters 1 and 4).

7   Oil puddle under engine

1   Oil pan gasket and/or oil pan drain bolt washer leaking (Chapter 2).
2   Oil pressure sending unit leaking (Chapter 2).
3   Cylinder head covers leaking (Chapter 2).
4   Engine oil seals leaking (Chapter 2).
5   Oil pump housing leaking (Chapter 2).

8   Engine lopes while idling or idles erratically

1   Vacuum leakage (Chapters 2 and 4).
2   Leaking EGR valve (Chapter 6).
3   Air filter clogged (Chapter 1).
4   Fuel pump not delivering sufficient fuel to the fuel injection system (Chapter 4).
5   Leaking head gasket (Chapter 2).
6   Timing belt and/or pulleys worn (Chapter 2).
7   Camshaft lobes worn (Chapter 2).

9   Engine misses at idle speed

1   Spark plugs worn or not gapped properly (Chapter 1).
2   Faulty spark plug wires (Chapter 1).
3   Vacuum leaks (Chapter 1).
4   Incorrect ignition timing (Chapter 5).
5   Uneven or low compression (Chapter 2).

10   Engine misses throughout driving speed range

1   Fuel filter clogged and/or impurities in the fuel system (Chapter 1).
2   Low fuel output at the injector(s) (Chapter 4).
3   Faulty or incorrectly gapped spark plugs (Chapter 1).
4   Incorrect ignition timing (Chapter 5).
5   Cracked distributor cap, disconnected distributor wires or damaged distributor components (Chapters 1 and 5).
6   Leaking spark plug wires (Chapters 1 or 5).
7   Faulty emission system components (Chapter 6).

8   Low or uneven cylinder compression pressures (Chapter 2).
9   Weak or faulty ignition system (Chapter 5).
10 Vacuum leak in fuel injection system, intake manifold/plenum, air control valve or vacuum hoses (Chapter 4).

11   Engine stumbles on acceleration

1   Spark plugs fouled (Chapter 1).
2   Fuel injection system faulty (Chapter 4).
3   Fuel filter clogged (Chapters 1 and 4).
4   Incorrect ignition timing (Chapter 5).
5   Intake manifold or plenum air leak (Chapters 2 and 4).

12   Engine surges while holding accelerator steady

1   Intake air leak (Chapter 4).
2   Fuel pump faulty (Chapter 4).
3   Loose fuel injector wire harness connectors (Chapter 4).
4   Defective ECM or information sensor (Chapter 6).

13   Engine stalls

1   Idle speed incorrect (Chapter 1).
2   Fuel filter clogged and/or water and impurities in the fuel system (Chapters 1 and 4).
3   Distributor components damp or damaged (Chapter 5).
4   Faulty emissions system components (Chapter 6).
5   Faulty or incorrectly gapped spark plugs (Chapter 1).
6   Faulty spark plug wires (Chapter 1).
7   Vacuum leak in the fuel injection system, intake manifold or vacuum hoses (Chapters 2 and 4).
8   Valve clearances incorrectly set (Chapter 1).

14   Engine lacks power

1   Incorrect ignition timing (Chapter 5).
2   Excessive play in distributor shaft (Chapter 5).
3   Worn rotor, distributor cap or wires (Chapters 1 and 5).
4   Faulty or incorrectly gapped spark plugs (Chapter 1).
5   Fuel injection system malfunction (Chapter 4).
6   Faulty coil(s) (Chapter 5).
7   Brakes binding (Chapter 9).
8   Automatic transaxle fluid level incorrect (Chapter 1).
9   Clutch slipping (Chapter 8).
10 Fuel filter clogged and/or impurities in the fuel system (Chapters 1 and 4).
11 Emission control system not functioning properly (Chapter 6).
12 Low or uneven cylinder compression pressures (Chapter 2).
13 Obstructed exhaust system (Chapter 4).

15   Engine backfires

1   Emission control system not functioning properly (Chapter 6).
2   Ignition timing incorrect (Chapter 5).
3   Faulty secondary ignition system (cracked spark plug insulator, faulty plug wires, distributor cap and/or rotor) (Chapters 1 and 5).
4   Fuel injection system malfunction (Chapter 4).
5   Vacuum leak at fuel injector(s), intake manifold, air control valve or vacuum hoses (Chapters 2 and 4).
6   Valve clearances incorrectly set and/or valves sticking (Chapter 1).

16   Pinging or knocking engine sounds during acceleration or uphill

1   Incorrect grade of fuel.
2   Ignition timing incorrect (Chapter 5).
3   Fuel injection system faulty (Chapter 4).
4   Improper or damaged spark plugs or wires (Chapter 1).
5   Worn or damaged distributor components (Chapter 5).
6   EGR valve not functioning (Chapter 6).
7   Vacuum leak (Chapters 2 and 4).
8   Defective knock sensor (Chapter 6).

17   Engine runs with oil pressure light on

1   Low oil level (Chapter 1).
2   Idle rpm below specification (Chapter 4).
3   Short in wiring circuit (Chapter 12).
4   Faulty oil pressure sender (Chapter 2).
5   Worn engine bearings and/or oil pump (Chapter 2).

18   Engine diesels (continues to run) after switching off

1   Idle speed too high (Chapter 1).
2   Excessive engine operating temperature (Chapter 3).
3   Ignition timing in need of adjustment (Chapter 5).

Engine electrical system

19   Battery will not hold a charge

1   Alternator drivebelt defective or not adjusted properly (Chapter 1).
2   Battery electrolyte level low (Chapter 1).
3   Battery terminals loose or corroded (Chapter 1).
4   Alternator not charging properly (Chapter 5).
5   Loose, broken or faulty wiring in the charging circuit (Chapter 5).
6   Short in vehicle wiring (Chapter 12).
7   Internally defective battery (Chapters 1 and 5).

20   Alternator light fails to go out

1   Faulty alternator or charging circuit (Chapter 5).
2   Alternator drivebelt defective or out of adjustment (Chapter 1).
3   Alternator voltage regulator inoperative (Chapter 5).

21   Alternator light fails to come on when key is turned on

1   Warning light bulb defective (Chapter 12).
2   Fault in the printed circuit, dash wiring or bulb holder (Chapter 12).

Fuel system

22   Excessive fuel consumption

1   Dirty or clogged air filter element (Chapter 1).
2   Incorrectly set ignition timing (Chapter 5).
3   Emissions system not functioning properly (Chapter 6).
4   Fuel injection system not functioning properly (Chapter 4).
5   Low tire pressure or incorrect tire size (Chapter 1).

23 Fuel leakage and/or fuel odor

1 Leaking fuel feed or return line (Chapters 1 and 4).
2 Tank overfilled.
3 Evaporative canister filter clogged (Chapters 1 and 6).
4 Fuel injection system not functioning properly (Chapter 4).

Cooling system

24 Overheating

1 Insufficient coolant in system (Chapter 1).
2 Water pump defective (Chapter 3).
3 Radiator core blocked or grille restricted (Chapter 3).
4 Thermostat faulty (Chapter 3).
5 Electric coolant fan blades broken or cracked (Chapter 3).
6 Radiator cap not maintaining proper pressure (Chapter 3).
7 Ignition timing incorrect (Chapter 5).
8 Fault in the hydraulic cooling fan system (1992 and 1993 V6 models).

25 Overcooling

1 Faulty thermostat (Chapter 3).
2 Inaccurate temperature gauge sending unit (Chapter 3)

26 External coolant leakage

1 Deteriorated/damaged hoses; loose clamps (Chapters 1 and 3).
2 Water pump defective (Chapter 3).
3 Leakage from radiator core or coolant reservoir bottle (Chapter 3).
4 Engine drain or water jacket core plugs leaking (Chapter 2).

27 Internal coolant leakage

1 Leaking cylinder head gasket (Chapter 2).
2 Cracked cylinder bore or cylinder head (Chapter 2).

28 Coolant loss

1 Too much coolant in system (Chapter 1).
2 Coolant boiling away because of overheating (Chapter 3).
3 Internal or external leakage (Chapter 3).
4 Faulty radiator cap (Chapter 3).

29 Poor coolant circulation

1 Inoperative water pump (Chapter 3).
2 Restriction in cooling system (Chapters 1 and 3).
3 Water pump drivebelt defective/out of adjustment (Chapter 1).
4 Thermostat sticking (Chapter 3).

Clutch

30 Pedal travels to floor - no pressure or very little resistance

1 Master or release cylinder faulty (Chapter 8).

2 Hose/pipe burst or leaking (Chapter 8).
3 Connections leaking (Chapter 8).
4 No fluid in reservoir (Chapter 8).
5 If fluid level in reservoir rises as pedal is depressed, master cylinder center valve seal is faulty (Chapter 8).
6 If there is fluid on dust seal at master cylinder, piston primary seal is leaking (Chapter 8).
7 Broken release bearing or fork (Chapter 8).

31 Fluid in area of master cylinder dust cover and on pedal

Rear seal failure in master cylinder (Chapter 8).

32 Fluid on release cylinder

Release cylinder plunger seal faulty (Chapter 8).

33 Pedal feels spongy when depressed

Air in system (Chapter 8).

34 Unable to select gears

1 Faulty transaxle (Chapter 7).
2 Faulty clutch disc (Chapter 8).
3 Release lever and bearing not assembled properly (Chapter 8).
4 Faulty pressure plate (Chapter 8).
5 Pressure plate-to-flywheel bolts loose (Chapter 8).

35 Clutch slips (engine speed increases with no increase in vehicle speed)

1 Clutch plate worn (Chapter 8).
2 Clutch plate is oil soaked by leaking rear main seal (Chapter 8).
3 Clutch plate not seated. It may take 30 or 40 normal starts for a new one to seat.
4 Warped pressure plate or flywheel (Chapter 8).
5 Weak diaphragm spring (Chapter 8).
6 Clutch plate overheated. Allow to cool.

36 Grabbing (chattering) as clutch is engaged

1 Oil on clutch plate lining, burned or glazed facings (Chapter 8).
2 Worn or loose engine or transaxle mounts (Chapters 2 and 7).
3 Worn splines on clutch plate hub (Chapter 8).
4 Warped pressure plate or flywheel (Chapter 8).
5 Burned or smeared resin on flywheel or pressure plate (Chapter 8).

37 Transaxle rattling (clicking)

1 Release lever loose (Chapter 8).
2 Clutch plate damper spring failure (Chapter 8).
3 Low engine idle speed (Chapter 1).

38 Noise in clutch area

1 Fork shaft improperly installed (Chapter 8).
2 Faulty bearing (Chapter 8).

39 Clutch pedal stays on floor

1 Clutch master cylinder piston binding in bore (Chapter 8).
2 Broken release bearing or fork (Chapter 8).

40 High pedal effort

1 Piston binding in bore (Chapter 8).
2 Pressure plate faulty (Chapter 8).
3 Incorrect size master or release cylinder (Chapter 8).

Manual transaxle

41 Knocking noise at low speeds

1 Worn driveaxle constant velocity (CV) joints (Chapter 8).
2 Worn side gear shaft counterbore in differential case (Chapter 7A).*

42 Noise most pronounced when turning

Differential gear noise (Chapter 7A).*

43 Clunk on acceleration or deceleration

1 Loose engine or transaxle mounts (Chapters 2 and 7A).
2 Worn differential pinion shaft in case.*
3 Worn side gear shaft counterbore in differential case (Chapter 7A).*
4 Worn or damaged driveaxle inboard CV joints (Chapter 8).

44 Clicking noise in turns

Worn or damaged outboard CV joint (Chapter 8).

45 Vibration

1 Rough wheel bearing (Chapters 1 and 10).
2 Damaged driveaxle (Chapter 8).
3 Out of round tires (Chapter 1).
4 Tire out of balance (Chapters 1 and 10).
5 Worn CV joint (Chapter 8).

46 Noisy in neutral with engine running

1 Damaged input gear bearing (Chapter 7A).*
2 Damaged clutch release bearing (Chapter 8).

47 Noisy in one particular gear

1 Damaged or worn constant mesh gears (Chapter 7A).*
2 Damaged or worn synchronizers (Chapter 7A).*
3 Bent reverse fork (Chapter 7A).*
4 Damaged fourth speed gear or output gear (Chapter 7A).*
5 Worn or damaged reverse idler gear or idler bushing (Chapter 7A).*

48 Noisy in all gears

1 Insufficient lubricant (Chapters 1 and 7A).
2 Damaged or worn bearings (Chapter 7A).*
3 Worn or damaged input gear shaft and/or output gear shaft (Chapter 7A).*

49 Slips out of gear

1 Worn or improperly adjusted linkage (Chapter 7A).
2 Transaxle loose on engine (Chapter 7A).
3 Shift linkage does not work freely, binds (Chapter 7A).
4 Input gear bearing retainer broken or loose (Chapter 7A).*
5 Dirt between clutch cover and engine housing (Chapter 7A).
6 Worn shift fork (Chapter 7A).*

50 Leaks lubricant

1 Side gear shaft seals worn (Chapter 7).
2 Excessive amount of lubricant in transaxle (Chapters 1 and 7A).
3 Loose or broken input gear shaft bearing retainer (Chapter 7A).*
4 Input gear bearing retainer O-ring and/or lip seal damaged (Chapter 7A).*

51 Locked in gear

Lock pin or interlock pin missing (Chapter 7A).*
* Although the corrective action necessary to remedy the symptoms described is beyond the scope of this manual, the above information should be helpful in isolating the cause of the condition so that the owner can communicate clearly with a professional mechanic.

Automatic transaxle
Note: Due to the complexity of the automatic transaxle, it is difficult for the home mechanic to properly diagnose and service this component. For problems other than the following, the vehicle should be taken to a dealer or transaxle shop.

52 Fluid leakage

1 Automatic transaxle fluid is a deep red color. Fluid leaks should not be confused with engine oil, which can easily be blown onto the transaxle by air flow.
2 To pinpoint a leak, first remove all built-up dirt and grime from the transaxle housing with degreasing agents and/or steam cleaning. Then drive the vehicle at low speeds so air flow will not blow the leak far from its source. Raise the vehicle and determine where the leak is coming from. Common areas of leakage are:

a) Pan (Chapters 1 and 7)
b) Dipstick tube (Chapters 1 and 7)
c) Transaxle oil lines (Chapter 7)
d) Speed sensor (Chapter 7)
e) Differential drain plug (Chapters 1 and 7B)

53 Transaxle fluid brown or has a burned smell

Transaxle fluid overheated (Chapter 1).

54 General shift mechanism problems

1 Chapter 7, Part B, deals with checking and adjusting the shift

linkage on automatic transaxles. Common problems which may be attributed to poorly adjusted linkage are:

   a) *Engine starting in gears other than Park or Neutral.*
   b) *Indicator on shifter pointing to a gear other than the one actually being used.*
   c) *Vehicle moves when in Park.*

2   Refer to Chapter 7B for the shift linkage adjustment procedure.

55   Transaxle will not downshift with accelerator pedal pressed to the floor

Throttle valve cable out of adjustment (Chapter 7B).

56   Engine will start in gears other than Park or Neutral

Neutral start switch malfunctioning (Chapter 7B).

57   Transaxle slips, shifts roughly, is noisy or has no drive in forward or reverse gears

There are many probable causes for the above problems, but the home mechanic should be concerned with only one possibility - fluid level. Before taking the vehicle to a repair shop, check the level and condition of the fluid as described in Chapter 1. Correct the fluid level as necessary or change the fluid and filter if needed. If the problem persists, have a professional diagnose the cause.

Driveaxles

58   Clicking noise in turns

Worn or damaged outboard CV joint (Chapter 8).

59   Shudder or vibration during acceleration

1   Excessive toe-in (Chapter 10).
2   Incorrect spring heights (Chapter 10).
3   Worn or damaged inboard or outboard CV joints (Chapter 8).
4   Sticking inboard CV joint assembly (Chapter 8).

60   Vibration at highway speeds

1   Out of balance front wheels and/or tires (Chapters 1 and 10).
2   Out of round front tires (Chapters 1 and 10).
3   Worn CV joint(s) (Chapter 8).

Brakes

Note: *Before assuming that a brake problem exists, make sure that:*

   a) *The tires are in good condition and properly inflated (Chapter 1).*
   b) *The front end alignment is correct (Chapter 10).*
   c) *The vehicle is not loaded with weight in an unequal manner.*

61   Vehicle pulls to one side during braking

1   Incorrect tire pressures (Chapter 1).
2   Front end out of alignment (have the front end aligned).
3   Front, or rear, tires not matched to one another.

4   Restricted brake lines or hoses (Chapter 9).
5   Malfunctioning drum brake or caliper assembly (Chapter 9).
6   Loose suspension parts (Chapter 10).
7   Loose calipers (Chapter 9).
8   Excessive wear of brake shoe or pad material or disc/drum on one side.

62   Noise (high-pitched squeal when the brakes are applied)

Front and/or rear disc brake pads worn out. The noise comes from the wear sensor rubbing against the disc (does not apply to all vehicles). Replace pads with new ones immediately (Chapter 9).

63   Brake roughness or chatter (pedal pulsates)

1   Excessive lateral runout (Chapter 9).
2   Uneven pad wear (Chapter 9).
3   Defective disc (Chapter 9).

64   Excessive brake pedal effort required to stop vehicle

1   Malfunctioning power brake booster (Chapter 9).
2   Partial system failure (Chapter 9).
3   Excessively worn pads or shoes (Chapter 9).
4   Piston in caliper or wheel cylinder stuck or sluggish (Chapter 9).
5   Brake pads or shoes contaminated with oil or grease (Chapter 9).
6   New pads or shoes installed and not yet seated. It will take a while for the new material to seat against the disc or drum.

65   Excessive brake pedal travel

1   Partial brake system failure (Chapter 9).
2   Insufficient fluid in master cylinder (Chapters 1 and 9).
3   Air trapped in system (Chapters 1 and 9).

66   Dragging brakes

1   Incorrect adjustment of brake light switch (Chapter 9).
2   Master cylinder pistons not returning correctly (Chapter 9).
3   Restricted brakes lines or hoses (Chapters 1 and 9).
4   Incorrect parking brake adjustment (Chapter 9).

67   Grabbing or uneven braking action

1   Malfunction of proportioning valve (Chapter 9).
2   Malfunction of power brake booster unit (Chapter 9).
3   Binding brake pedal mechanism (Chapter 9).

68   Brake pedal feels spongy when depressed

1   Air in hydraulic lines (Chapter 9).
2   Master cylinder mounting bolts loose (Chapter 9).
3   Master cylinder defective (Chapter 9).

69   Brake pedal travels to the floor with little resistance

1   Little or no fluid in the master cylinder reservoir caused by leaking

caliper piston(s) (Chapter 9).
2   Loose, damaged or disconnected brake lines (Chapter 9).

70 Parking brake does not hold

Parking brake linkage improperly adjusted (Chapters 1 and 9).

Suspension and steering systems

Note: *Before attempting to diagnose the suspension and steering systems, perform the following preliminary checks:*

a) *Tires for wrong pressure and uneven wear.*
b) *Steering universal joints from the column to the rack and pinion for loose connectors or wear.*
c) *Front and rear suspension and the rack and pinion assembly for loose or damaged parts.*
d) *Out-of-round or out-of-balance tires, bent rims and loose and/or rough wheel bearings.*

71 Vehicle pulls to one side

1   Mismatched or uneven tires (Chapter 10).
2   Broken or sagging springs (Chapter 10).
3   Wheel alignment (Chapter 10).
4   Front brake dragging (Chapter 9).

72 Abnormal or excessive tire wear

1   Wheel alignment (Chapter 10).
2   Sagging or broken springs (Chapter 10).
3   Tire out of balance (Chapter 10).
4   Worn strut damper (Chapter 10).
5   Overloaded vehicle.
6   Tires not rotated regularly.

73 Wheel makes a thumping noise

1   Blister or bump on tire (Chapter 10).
2   Improper strut damper action (Chapter 10).

74 Shimmy, shake or vibration

1   Tire or wheel out-of-balance or out-of-round (Chapter 10).
2   Loose or worn wheel bearings (Chapters 1, 8 and 10).
3   Worn tie-rod ends (Chapter 10).
4   Worn lower balljoints (Chapters 1 and 10).
5   Excessive wheel runout (Chapter 10).
6   Blister or bump on tire (Chapter 10).

75 Hard steering

1   Lack of lubrication at balljoints, tie-rod ends and rack and pinion assembly (Chapter 10).
2   Front wheel alignment (Chapter 10).
3   Low tire pressure(s) (Chapters 1 and 10).

76 Poor returnability of steering to center

1   Lack of lubrication at balljoints and tie-rod ends (Chapter 10).
2   Binding in balljoints (Chapter 10).

3   Binding in steering column (Chapter 10).
4   Lack of lubricant in steering gear assembly (Chapter 10).
5   Front wheel alignment (Chapter 10).

77 Abnormal noise at the front end

1   Lack of lubrication at balljoints and tie-rod ends (Chapters 1 and 10).
2   Damaged strut mounting (Chapter 10).
3   Worn control arm bushings or tie-rod ends (Chapter 10).
4   Loose stabilizer bar (Chapter 10).
5   Loose wheel nuts (Chapters 1 and 10).
6   Loose suspension bolts (Chapter 10)

78 Wander or poor steering stability

1   Mismatched or uneven tires (Chapter 10).
2   Lack of lubrication at balljoints and tie-rod ends (Chapters 1 and 10).
3   Worn strut assemblies (Chapter 10).
4   Loose stabilizer bar (Chapter 10).
5   Broken or sagging springs (Chapter 10).
6   Wheels out of alignment (Chapter 10).

79 Erratic steering when braking

1   Wheel bearings worn (Chapter 10).
2   Broken or sagging springs (Chapter 10).
3   Leaking wheel cylinder or caliper (Chapter 10).
4   Warped rotors or drums (Chapter 10).

80 Excessive pitching and/or rolling around corners or during braking

1   Loose stabilizer bar (Chapter 10).
2   Worn strut dampers or mountings (Chapter 10).
3   Broken or sagging springs (Chapter 10).
4   Overloaded vehicle.

81 Suspension bottoms

1   Overloaded vehicle.
2   Worn strut dampers (Chapter 10).
3   Incorrect, broken or sagging springs (Chapter 10).

82 Cupped tires

1   Front wheel or rear wheel alignment (Chapter 10).
2   Worn strut dampers (Chapter 10).
3   Wheel bearings worn (Chapter 10).
4   Excessive tire or wheel runout (Chapter 10).
5   Worn balljoints (Chapter 10).

83 Excessive tire wear on outside edge

1   Inflation pressures incorrect (Chapter 1).
2   Excessive speed in turns.
3   Front end alignment incorrect (excessive toe-in). Have professionally aligned.
4   Suspension arm bent or twisted (Chapter 10).

84 Excessive tire wear on inside edge

1   Inflation pressures incorrect (Chapter 1).
2   Front end alignment incorrect (toe-out). Have professionally aligned.
3   Loose or damaged steering components (Chapter 10).

85 Tire tread worn in one place

1   Tires out of balance.
2   Damaged or buckled wheel. Inspect and replace if necessary.
3   Defective tire (Chapter 1).

86 Excessive play or looseness in steering system

1   Wheel bearing(s) worn (Chapter 10).
2   Tie-rod end loose (Chapter 10).
3   Steering gear loose (Chapter 10).
4   Worn or loose steering intermediate shaft (Chapter 10).

87 Rattling or clicking noise in steering gear

1   Steering gear loose (Chapter 10).
2   Steering gear defective.

Chapter 1
Tune-up and routine maintenance

Contents

Specifications

Recommended lubricants and fluids

Engine oil type	API grade SG or SG/CD multigrade and fuel efficient oil
Viscosity	See accompanying chart
Fuel	Unleaded gasoline, 87 octane or higher
Coolant	50 to 70-percent ethylene-glycol based antifreeze and water
Automatic transaxle fluid type	DEXRON II automatic transmission fluid
Automatic transaxle differential fluid type	DEXRON II automatic transmission fluid
Manual transaxle lubricant type	API GL-3, GL-4 or GL-5 75W-90 gear oil
Brake fluid type	DOT 3 brake fluid
Clutch fluid type	DOT 3 brake fluid
Power steering system fluid	DEXRON II automatic transmission fluid

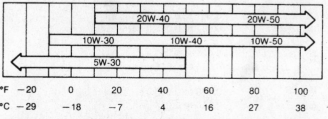

Engine oil viscosity chart

Capacities

Engine oil (including filter)
  5S-FE engine.. 3.8 qts
  3VZ-FE engine... 4.5 qts
  1MZ-FE engine... 5.0 qts
Coolant
  5S-FE engine.. 6.7 qts
  3VZ-FE engine... 8.9 qts
  1MZ-FE engine... 9.2 qts
Transaxle
  Automatic
    5S-FE engine
      Drain and refill.. 2.6 qts
      Differential .... 1.7 qts
    3VZ-FE engine
      Drain and refill.. 3.3 qts
      Differential .... 0.8 qts
    1MZ-FE engine
      Drain and refill.. 3.7 qts
      Differential .... 0.9 qts
  Manual... 2.7 qts

Ignition system

Spark plug type and gap
  5S-FE engine
    Type .... NGK BKR6EP-11 or equivalent
    Gap .... 0.043 inch
  3VZ-FE engine
    Type .... NGK BCPR6EP-11 or equivalent
    Gap .... 0.043 inch
  1MZ-FE engine
    Type .... NGK BKR6EP-11 or equivalent
    Gap .... 0.043 inch
Spark plug wire resistance .... Less than 25,000 ohms
Engine firing order
  5S-FE engine.. 1-3-4-2
  3VZ-FE engine... 1-2-3-4-5-6
  1MZ-FE engine... 1-2-3-4-5-6

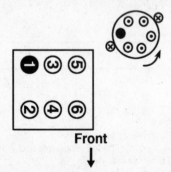
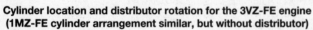

Cylinder location and distributor rotation for the 3VZ-FE engine
(1MZ-FE cylinder arrangement similar, but without distributor)

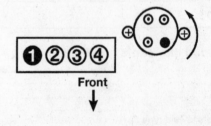

Cylinder location and distributor rotation for the 5S-FE engine

Valve clearance (engine cold)

5S-FE engine
  Intake.. 0.007 to 0.011 inch
  Exhaust... 0.011 to 0.015 inch
3VZ-FE engine
  Intake.. 0.005 to 0.009 inch
  Exhaust... 0.011 to 0.015 inch
1MZ-FE engine
  Intake.. 0.006 to 0.010 inch
  Exhaust... 0.010 to 0.014 inch

Cooling system

Thermostat rating	
Starts to open..	190-degrees F
Fully open...	212-degrees F
Accessory drivebelt tension (with Burroughs or Nippondenso tension gauge)	
5S-FE engine	
Alternator (with air conditioning)	
New belt	170 to 180 lbs
Used belt	120 to 140 lbs
Alternator (without air conditioning)	
New belt	100 to 150 lbs
Used belt	75 to 115 lbs
Power steering pump	
New belt	100 to 150 lbs
Used belt	60 to 100 lbs
3VZ-FE engine	
Alternator	
New belt	170 to 180 lbs
Used belt	95 to 135 lbs
Power steering pump	
New belt	150 to 185 lbs
Used belt	95 to 135 lbs
1MZ-FE engine	
Alternator	
New belt	170 to 180 lbs
Used belt	95 to 135 lbs
Power steering pump	
New belt	150 to 185 lbs
Used belt	95 to 135 lbs

Clutch

Clutch pedal freeplay...	7/32 to 5/8 inch
Pedal height	
5S-FE engine...	6-3/8 to 6-3/4 inches
3VZ-FE engine...	6-1/2 to 6-5/8 inches
1MZ-FE engine...	6-3/8 to 6-3/4 inches
Pushrod play at pedal top	3/64 to 13/64 inch

Brakes

Disc brake pad lining thickness (minimum)...	1/16 inch
Drum brake shoe lining thickness (minimum)......................	1/16 inch
Brake pedal	
Freeplay...	1/32 to 1/4 inch
Free height	5-3/4 inches
Brake light switch clearance	1/32 to 3/32 inch
Pedal reserve height..	2-3/4 inches
Parking brake adjustment	
Lever-type	5 to 8 clicks
Pedal-type	3 to 6 clicks

Suspension and steering

Steering wheel freeplay limit..	1-3/16 inches
Balljoint allowable movement	0 inch

Torque specifications

	Ft-lbs (unless otherwise indicated)
Automatic transaxle	
Pan bolts..	48 in-lbs
Strainer bolt...	96 in-lbs
Drain plug	36
Manual transaxle drain and filler plugs	36
Wheel lug nuts..	76
Chassis and body	
Front seat mounting bolt..	27
Front suspension lower crossmember-to-body bolt.........................	134
Rear suspension member-to-body bolt	
1992 and earlier..	83
1993 and later	38
Spark plugs...	13

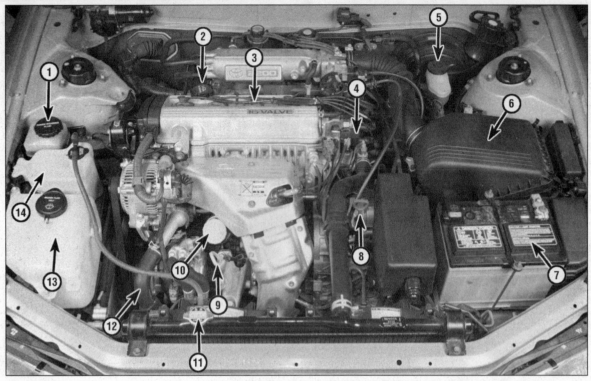

Typical four-cylinder engine compartment layout

1	Power steering fluid reservoir	6	Air filter housing	11	Radiator cap
2	Engine oil filler cap	7	Battery	12	Radiator hose
3	Spark plug	8	Automatic transaxle fluid dipstick	13	Windshield washer fluid reservoir
4	Distributor cap	9	Engine oil dipstick	14	Engine coolant reservoir
5	Brake master cylinder reservoir	10	Engine oil filter		

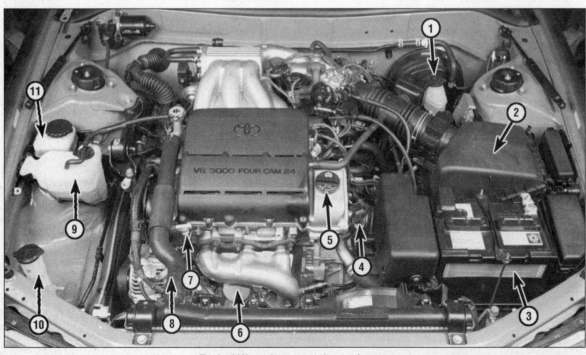

Typical V6 engine compartment layout

1	Brake master cylinder reservoir	5	Engine oil filler cap	9	Windshield washer fluid reservoir
2	Air filter housing	6	Engine oil filter	10	Engine coolant reservoir
3	Battery	7	Engine oil dipstick	11	Power steering fluid reservoir
4	Automatic transaxle fluid dipstick	8	Radiator hose		

Typical engine compartment underside components

1	Engine oil drain plug	4	Steering gear boot	7	Inner driveaxle boot
2	Front brake caliper	5	Automatic transaxle drain plug	8	Brake hose
3	Outer driveaxle boot	6	Exhaust pipe		

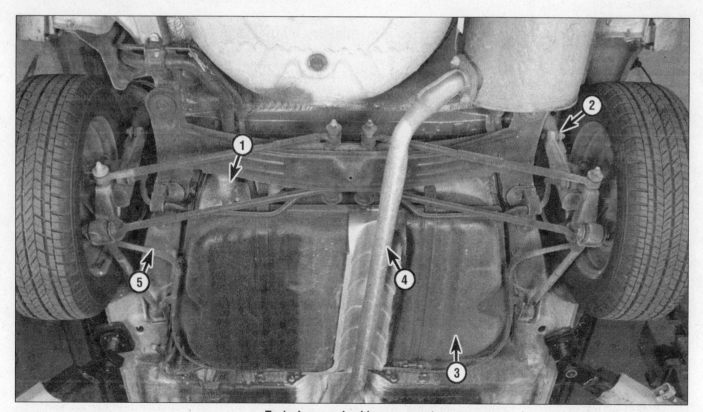

Typical rear underside components

1	Fuel pipe-to-tank hose	3	Fuel tank	5	Parking brake cable
2	Shock and spring assembly	4	Exhaust pipe		

1 Toyota Camry maintenance schedule

The maintenance intervals in this manual are provided with the assumption that you, not the dealer, will be doing the work. These are the minimum maintenance intervals recommended by the factory for Camrys that are driven daily. If you wish to keep your vehicle in peak condition at all times, you may wish to perform some of these procedures even more often. Because frequent maintenance enhances the efficiency, performance and resale value of your car, we encourage you to do so. If you drive in dusty areas, tow a trailer, idle or drive at low speeds for extended periods or drive for short distances (less than four miles) in below freezing temperatures, shorter intervals are also recommended.

When your vehicle is new, it should be serviced by a factory authorized dealer service department to protect the factory warranty. In many cases, the initial maintenance check is done at no cost to the

Every 250 miles or weekly, whichever comes first

Check the engine oil level (Section 4)
Check the engine coolant level (Section 4)
Check the windshield washer fluid level (Section 4)
Check the brake and clutch fluid levels (Section 4)
Check the tires and tire pressures (Section 5)

Every 3000 miles or 3 months, whichever comes first

All items listed above plus:
Check the power steering fluid level (Section 6)
Check the automatic transaxle fluid level (Section 7)
Change the engine oil and oil filter (Section 8)

Every 6000 miles or 6 months, whichever comes first

Inspect and replace if necessary the windshield wiper blades (Section 9)
Check the clutch pedal for proper freeplay and height (Section 10)
Check and service the battery (Section 11)
Check and adjust if necessary the engine drivebelts (Section 12)
Inspect and replace if necessary all underhood hoses (Section 13)
Check the cooling system (Section 14)
Rotate the tires (Section 15)

Every 15,000 miles or 12 months, whichever comes first

All items listed above plus:
Inspect the brake system (Section 16)*
Replace the air filter (Section 17)
Inspect the fuel system (Section 18)
Check the automatic transaxle differential lubricant level (Section 19)*
Check the manual transaxle lubricant level (Section 20)*
Inspect the suspension and steering components (Section 21)*
Check the driveaxle boots (Section 22)

Every 30,000 miles or 24 months, whichever comes first

All items listed above plus:
Replace the fuel filter (Section 23)
Service the cooling system (drain, flush and refill) (Section 24)
Inspect the evaporative emissions control system (Section 25)
Inspect the exhaust system (Section 26)
Change the automatic transaxle and differential fluid (Section 27) **
Change the manual transaxle lubricant (Section 28)
Check and tighten critical chassis and body fasteners (Section 29)
Replace the spark plugs (Section 30)
Inspect and replace if necessary the spark plug wires, distributor cap and rotor (Section 31)

Every 60,000 miles or 48 months, whichever comes first

Inspect and if necessary adjust the valve clearance (Section 32)
Replace the timing belt (Chapter 2A) ***
Replace the fuel tank cap gasket (Section 33)
Check and replace if necessary the PCV valve (Section 34)

This item is affected by "severe" operating conditions as described below. If your vehicle is operated under "severe" conditions, perform all maintenance indicated with an asterisk (*) at 3000 mile/3 month intervals. Severe conditions are indicated if you mainly operate your vehicle under one or more of the following conditions:

Operating in dusty areas
Towing a trailer
Idling for extended periods and/or low speed operation
Operating when outside temperatures remain below freezing and when most trips are less than 4 miles

** If operated under one or more of the following conditions, change the automatic transaxle fluid and differential lubricant every 15,000 miles:
In heavy city traffic where the outside temperature regularly reaches 90-degrees F (32-degrees C) or higher
In hilly or mountainous terrain
Frequent trailer pulling

*** Replace the timing belt at 60,000 miles only if operated under severe conditions.

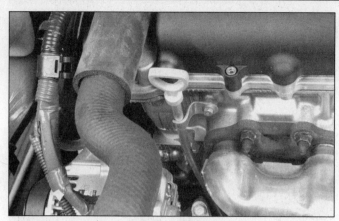

4.2 The engine oil dipstick is mounted on the front (radiator) side of the engine

2 Introduction

This chapter is designed to help the home mechanic maintain the Toyota Camry for peak performance, economy, safety and long life.

On the following pages is a master maintenance schedule, followed by sections dealing specifically with each item on the schedule. Visual checks, adjustments, component replacement and other helpful items are included. Refer to the accompanying illustrations of the engine compartment and the underside of the vehicle for the location of various components.

Servicing your Camry in accordance with the mileage/time maintenance schedule and the following Sections will provide it with a planned maintenance program that should result in a long and reliable service life. This is a comprehensive plan, so maintaining some items but not others at the specified service intervals will not produce the same results.

As you service your Camry, you will discover that many of the procedures can - and should - be grouped together because of the nature of the particular procedure you're performing or because of the close proximity of two otherwise unrelated components to one another.

For example, if the vehicle is raised for any reason, you should inspect the exhaust, suspension, steering and fuel systems while you're under the vehicle. When you're rotating the tires, it makes good sense to check the brakes and wheel bearings since the wheels are already removed.

Finally, let's suppose you have to borrow or rent a torque wrench. Even if you only need to tighten the spark plugs, you might as well check the torque of as many critical fasteners as time allows.

The first step of this maintenance program is to prepare yourself before the actual work begins. Read through all sections pertinent to the procedures you're planning to do, then make a list of and gather together all the parts and tools you will need to do the job. If it looks as if you might run into problems during a particular segment of some procedure, seek advice from your local parts man or dealer service department.

3 Tune-up general information

The term tune-up is used in this manual to represent a combination of individual operations rather than one specific procedure.

If, from the time the vehicle is new, the routine maintenance schedule is followed closely and frequent checks are made of fluid levels and high wear items, as suggested throughout this manual, the engine will be kept in relatively good running condition and the need for additional work will be minimized.

More likely than not, however, there will be times when the engine is running poorly due to lack of regular maintenance. This is even more likely if a used vehicle, which has not received regular and frequent maintenance checks, is purchased. In such cases, an engine tune-up will be needed outside of the regular routine maintenance intervals.

The first step in any tune-up or engine diagnosis to help correct a poor running engine would be a cylinder compression check. A check of the engine compression (Chapter 2 Part B) will give valuable information regarding the overall performance of many internal components and should be used as a basis for tune-up and repair procedures. If, for instance, a compression check indicates serious internal engine wear, a conventional tune-up will not help the running condition of the engine and would be a waste of time and money.

The following series of operations are those most often needed to bring a generally poor running engine back into a proper state of tune.

Minor tune-up

Clean, inspect and test the battery (Section 11)
Check all engine related fluids (Section 4)
Check and adjust the drivebelts (Section 12)
Replace the spark plugs (Section 30)
Inspect the distributor cap and rotor (Section 31)
Inspect the spark plug and coil wires (Section 31)
Check the air filter (Section 17)
Check the cooling system (Section 14)
Check all underhood hoses (Section 13)

Major tune-up

All items listed under Minor tune-up, plus . . .
Check the ignition system (Section 31)
Check the charging system (Chapter 5)
Check the fuel system (Section 18)
Replace the air filter (Section 17)
Replace the distributor cap and rotor (Section 31)
Replace the spark plug wires (Section 31)

4 Fluid level checks (every 250 miles or weekly)

1 Fluids are an essential part of the lubrication, cooling, brake, clutch and other systems. Because these fluids gradually become depleted and/or contaminated during normal operation of the vehicle, they must be periodically replenished. See *Recommended lubricants* and *fluids* and *capacities* at the beginning of this Chapter before adding fluid to any of the following components. **Note:** *The vehicle must be on level ground before fluid levels can be checked.*

Engine oil

Refer to illustrations 4.2, 4.4 and 4.6
2 The engine oil level is checked with a dipstick located at the front side of the engine **(see illustration)**. The dipstick extends through a metal tube from which it protrudes down into the engine oil pan.
3 The oil level should be checked before the vehicle has been driven, or about 15 minutes after the engine has been shut off. If the oil is checked immediately after driving the vehicle, some of the oil will remain in the upper engine components, producing an inaccurate reading on the dipstick.
4 Pull the dipstick from the tube and wipe all the oil from the end with a clean rag or paper towel. Insert the clean dipstick all the way back into its metal tube and pull it out again. Observe the oil at the end of the dipstick. At its highest point, the level should be between the L and F marks **(see illustration)**.

4.4 The oil level should be at the or near the F mark on the dipstick - if it isn't, add enough oil to bring the level to or near the F mark (it takes one quart to raise the level from the L to F mark)

4.6 The threaded oil filler cap is located on or near the valve cover - to prevent dirt from contaminating the engine, always make sure the area around this opening is clean before removing the cap

4.8 Make sure the coolant level is between the Full and Low lines - if it's below the Low line, add a sufficient quantity of the specified mixture of antifreeze and water

5   It takes one quart of oil to raise the level from the L mark to the F mark on the dipstick. Do not allow the level to drop below the L mark or oil starvation may cause engine damage. Conversely, overfilling the engine (adding oil above the F mark) may cause oil-fouled spark plugs, oil leaks or oil seal failures.

6   Remove the threaded cap from the valve cover to add oil **(see illustration)**. Use a funnel to prevent spills. After adding the oil, install the filler cap hand tight. Start the engine and look carefully for any small leaks around the oil filter or drain plug. Stop the engine and check the oil level again after it has had sufficient time to drain from the upper block and cylinder head galleys.

7   Checking the oil level is an important preventive maintenance step. A continually dropping oil level indicates oil leakage through damaged seals, from loose connections, or past worn rings or valve guides. If the oil looks milky in color or has water droplets in it, a cylinder head gasket may be blown. The engine should be checked immediately. The condition of the oil should also be checked. Each time you check the oil level, slide your thumb and index finger up the dipstick before wiping off the oil. If you see small dirt or metal particles clinging to the dipstick, the oil should be changed (see Section 8).

Engine coolant

Refer to illustration 4.8

Warning: *Do not allow antifreeze to come in contact with your skin or painted surfaces of the vehicle. Flush contaminated areas immediately with plenty of water. Don't store new coolant or leave old coolant lying around where it's accessible to children or pets – they're attracted by its sweet smell. Ingestion of even a small amount of coolant can be fatal! Wipe up garage floor and drip pan spills immediately. Keep antifreeze containers covered and repair cooling system leaks as soon as they're noticed.*

8   All vehicles covered by this manual are equipped with a pressurized coolant recovery system. A white coolant reservoir located in the front corner of the engine compartment is connected by a hose to the base of the coolant filler cap **(see illustration)**. If the coolant heats up during engine operation, coolant can escape through a pressurized filler cap, then through a connecting hose into the reservoir. As the engine cools, the coolant is automatically drawn back into the cooling system to maintain the correct level.

9   The coolant level should be checked regularly. It must be between the Full and Low lines on the tank. The level will vary with the temperature of the engine. When the engine is cold, the coolant level should be at or slightly above the Low mark on the tank. Once the engine has warmed up, the level should be at or near the Full mark. If it isn't, allow the fluid in the tank to cool, then remove the cap from the reservoir and add coolant to bring the level up to the Full line. Use only ethylene/glycol type coolant and water in the mixture ratio recom-

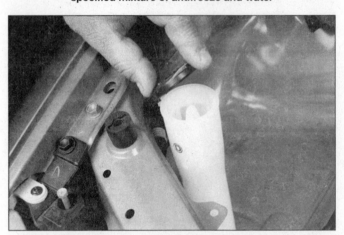

4.14 The windshield washer fluid reservoir is located at right front corner of the engine compartment - fluid can be added after flipping up the cap

mended by your owner's manual. Do not use supplemental inhibitors or additives. If only a small amount of coolant is required to bring the system up to the proper level, water can be used. However, repeated additions of water will dilute the recommended antifreeze and water solution. In order to maintain the proper ratio of antifreeze and water, it is advisable to top up the coolant level with the correct mixture. Refer to your owner's manual for the recommended ratio.

10   If the coolant level drops within a short time after replenishment, there may be a leak in the system. Inspect the radiator, hoses, engine coolant filler cap, drain plugs, air bleeder plugs and water pump. If no leak is evident, have the radiator cap pressure tested. **Warning:** *Never remove the radiator cap or the coolant recovery reservoir cap when the engine is running or has just been shut down, because the cooling system is hot. Escaping steam and scalding liquid could cause serious injury.*

11   If it is necessary to open the radiator cap, wait until the system has cooled completely, then wrap a thick cloth around the cap and turn it to the first stop. If any steam escapes, wait until the system has cooled further, then remove the cap.

12   When checking the coolant level, always note its condition. It should be relatively clear. If it is brown or rust colored, the system should be drained, flushed and refilled. Even if the coolant appears to be normal, the corrosion inhibitors wear out with use, so it must be replaced at the specified intervals.

13   Do not allow antifreeze to come in contact with your skin or painted surfaces of the vehicle. Flush contacted areas immediately with plenty of water.

4.15 On non-sealed batteries, keep the electrolyte level of all the cells in the battery between the upper and lower levels (arrow) - use only distilled water to replenish a cell and never overfill it or electrolyte may squirt out of the battery during periods of heavy charging

4.17 The brake fluid should be kept between the Min and Max marks on the reservoir - turn and lift up the cap to add fluid

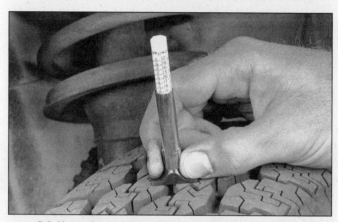

5.2 Use a tire tread depth gauge to monitor tire wear - they are available at auto parts stores and service stations and cost very little

Windshield washer fluid

Refer to illustration 4.14

14   Fluid for the windshield washer system is stored in a plastic reservoir which is located at the right front corner of the engine compartment **(see illustration)**. In milder climates, plain water can be used to top up the reservoir, but the reservoir should be kept no more than two-thirds full to allow for expansion should the water freeze. In colder climates, the use of a specially designed windshield washer fluid, available at your dealer and any auto parts store, will help lower the freezing point of the fluid. Mix the solution with water in accordance with the manufacturer's directions on the container. Do not use regular antifreeze. It will damage the vehicle's paint.

Battery electrolyte

Refer to illustration 4.15

15   On models not equipped with a sealed battery, check the electrolyte level of all six battery cells. It must be between the upper and lower levels **(see illustration)**. If the level is low, unscrew the filler/vent cap and add distilled water. Install and securely retighten the cap. **Caution:** *Overfilling the cells may cause electrolyte to spill over during periods of heavy charging, causing corrosion or damage.*

Brake and clutch fluid

Refer to illustration 4.17

16   The brake master cylinder is mounted on the front of the power booster unit in the engine compartment. The clutch cylinder used on manual transaxles is located next to the master cylinder.

17   To check the fluid level of the brake master cylinder reservoir, simply look at the MAX and MIN marks on the reservoir **(see illustration)**. To check the fluid level of the clutch master cylinder reservoir, note whether the fluid level is even with the maximum level line. The level should be within the specified distance from the maximum fill line for both reservoirs.

18   If the level is low for either reservoir, wipe the top of the reservoir cover with a clean rag to prevent contamination of the brake or clutch system before lifting the cover.

19   Add only the specified brake fluid to the brake or clutch reservoir (refer to *Recommended lubricants and fluids* at the front of this chapter or to your owner's manual). Mixing different types of brake fluid can damage the system. Fill the brake master cylinder reservoir only to the dotted line - this brings the fluid to the correct level when you put the cover back on. **Warning:** *Use caution when filling either reservoir - brake fluid can harm your eyes and damage painted surfaces. Do not use brake fluid that has been opened for more than one year or has been left open. Brake fluid absorbs moisture from the air. Excess moisture can cause a dangerous loss of braking.*

20   While the reservoir cap is removed, inspect the master cylinder reservoir for contamination. If deposits, dirt particles or water droplets are present, the system should be drained and refilled (see Chapter 8 for clutch reservoir or Chapter 9 for brake reservoir).

21   After filling the reservoir to the proper level, make sure the lid is properly seated to prevent fluid leakage and/or system pressure loss.

22   The brake fluid in the master cylinder will drop slightly as the brake pads at each wheel wear down during normal operation. If the master cylinder requires repeated replenishing to keep it at the proper level, this is an indication of leakage in the brake system, which should be corrected immediately. Check all brake lines and connections, along with the wheel cylinders and booster (see Section 16 for more information).

23   If, upon checking the master cylinder fluid level, you discover one or both reservoirs empty or nearly empty, the brake system should be bled (see Chapter 9).

5   Tire and tire pressure checks (every 250 miles or weekly)

Refer to illustrations 5.2, 5.3, 5.4a, 5.4b and 5.8

1   Periodic inspection of the tires may spare you from the inconvenience of being stranded with a flat tire. It can also provide you with vital information regarding possible problems in the steering and suspension systems before major damage occurs.

2   Normal tread wear can be monitored with a simple, inexpensive device known as a tread depth indicator **(see illustration)**. When the tread depth reaches the specified minimum, replace the tire(s).

Condition	Probable cause	Corrective action	Condition	Probable cause	Corrective action
Shoulder wear	• Underinflation (both sides wear) • Incorrect wheel camber (one side wear) • Hard cornering • Lack of rotation	• Measure and adjust pressure. • Repair or replace axle and suspension parts. • Reduce speed. • Rotate tires.	Feathered edge Toe wear	• Incorrect toe	• Adjust toe-in.
Center wear	• Overinflation • Lack of rotation	• Measure and adjust pressure. • Rotate tires.	Uneven wear	• Incorrect camber or caster • Malfunctioning suspension • Unbalanced wheel • Out-of-round brake drum • Lack of rotation	• Repair or replace axle and suspension parts. • Repair or replace suspension parts. • Balance or replace. • Turn or replace. • Rotate tires.

5.3 This chart will help you determine the condition of the tires, the probable cause(s) of abnormal wear and the corrective action necessary

5.4a If a tire looses air on a steady basis, check the valve core first to make sure it's snug (special inexpensive wrenches are commonly available at auto parts stores)

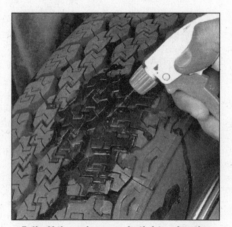

5.4b If the valve core is tight, raise the corner of the vehicle with the low tire and spray a soapy water solution onto the tread as the tire is turned slowly - leaks will cause small bubbles to appear

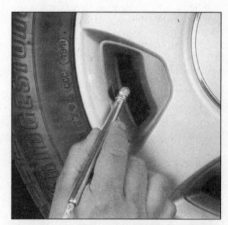

5.8 To extend the life of the tires, check the air pressure at least once a week with an accurate gauge (don't forget the spare)

3   Note any abnormal tread wear **(see illustration)**. Tread pattern irregularities such as cupping, flat spots and more wear on one side than the other are indications of front end alignment and/or balance problems. If any of these conditions are noted, take the vehicle to a tire shop or service station to correct the problem.

4   Look closely for cuts, punctures and embedded nails or tacks. Sometimes a tire will hold its air pressure for a short time or leak down very slowly even after a nail has embedded itself into the tread. If a slow leak persists, check the valve stem core to make sure it is tight **(see illustration)**. Examine the tread for an object that may have embedded itself into the tire or for a "plug" that may have begun to leak (radial tire punctures are repaired with a plug that is installed in a puncture). If a puncture is suspected, it can be easily verified by spraying a solution of soapy water onto the puncture area **(see illustration)**. The soapy solution will bubble if there is a leak. Unless the puncture is inordinately large, a tire shop or gas station can usually repair the punctured tire.

5   Carefully inspect the inner sidewall of each tire for evidence of brake fluid leakage. If you see any, inspect the brakes immediately.

6   Correct tire air pressure adds miles to the lifespan of the tires, improves mileage and enhances overall ride quality. Tire pressure cannot be accurately estimated by looking at a tire, particularly if it is a radial. A tire pressure gauge is therefore essential. Keep an accurate gauge in the glovebox. The pressure gauges fitted to the nozzles of air hoses at gas stations are often inaccurate.

7   Always check tire pressure when the tires are cold. "Cold," in this case, means the vehicle has not been driven over a mile in the three hours preceding a tire pressure check. A pressure rise of four to eight pounds is not uncommon once the tires are warm.

8   Unscrew the valve cap protruding from the wheel or hubcap and push the gauge firmly onto the valve **(see illustration)**. Note the reading on the gauge and compare this figure to the recommended tire pressure shown on the tire placard in the glovebox. Be sure to reinstall the valve cap to keep dirt and moisture out of the valve stem

6.4a The power steering fluid reservoir (arrow) is located on the right side of the engine compartment

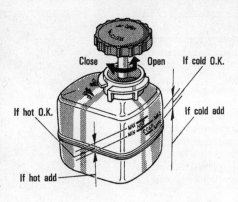

6.4b The reservoir is translucent so the fluid level can be checked either hot or cold without removing the cap

7.4a The automatic transaxle dipstick is located next to the battery

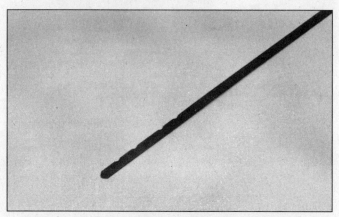

7.4b If the automatic transaxle fluid is cold, the level should be between the lower two notches; if it's at normal operating temperature, the level should be between the upper notches on the dipstick

mechanism. Check all four tires and, if necessary, add enough air to bring them up to the recommended pressure levels.

9   Don't forget to keep the spare tire inflated to the specified pressure (consult your owner's manual). Note that the air pressure specified for a compact spare is significantly higher than the pressure of the regular tires.

6   Power steering fluid level check (every 3000 miles or 3 months)

Refer to illustrations 6.4a and 6.4b

1   Unlike manual steering, the power steering system relies on fluid which may, over a period of time, require replenishing. On 1993 and earlier vehicles with V6 engines, the power steering fluid is also used to power a hydraulic cooling fan so checking this level is particularly important on these models.

2   The fluid reservoir for the power steering pump is located on the right (passenger side) inner fender panel near the front of the engine.

3   For the check, the front wheels should be pointed straight ahead and the engine should be off.

4   The reservoir is translucent plastic and the fluid level can be checked visually **(see illustrations)**.

5   If additional fluid is required, pour the specified type directly into the reservoir, using a funnel to prevent spills.

6   If the reservoir requires frequent fluid additions, all power steering hoses, hose connections, the power steering pump and the rack and pinion assembly should be carefully checked for leaks.

7   Automatic transaxle fluid level check (every 3000 miles or 3 months)

Refer to illustrations 7.4a and 7.4b

1   The level of the automatic transaxle fluid should be carefully maintained. Low fluid level can lead to slipping or loss of drive, while overfilling can cause foaming, loss of fluid and transaxle damage.

2   The transaxle fluid level should only be checked when the transaxle is hot (at its normal operating temperature). If the vehicle has just been driven over 10 miles (15 miles in a frigid climate), and the fluid temperature is 160 to 175-degrees F, the transaxle is hot. **Caution:** *If the vehicle has just been driven for a long time at high speed or in city traffic in hot weather, or if it has been pulling a trailer, an accurate fluid level reading cannot be obtained. Allow the fluid to cool down for about 30 minutes.*

3   If the vehicle has not been driven, park the vehicle on level ground, set the parking brake and start the engine. While the engine is idling, depress the brake pedal and move the selector lever through all the gear ranges, beginning and ending in Park.

4   With the engine still idling, remove the dipstick from its tube **(see illustration)**. Check the level of the fluid on the dipstick **(see illustration)** and note its condition.

5   Wipe the fluid from the dipstick with a clean rag and reinsert it back into the filler tube until the cap seats.

6   Pull the dipstick out again and note the fluid level. If the transaxle is cold, the level should be in the COLD or COOL range on the dipstick. If it is hot, the fluid level should be in the HOT range. If the level is at the low side of either range, add the specified automatic transmission fluid through the dipstick tube with a funnel.

7   Add just enough of the recommended fluid to fill the transaxle to the proper level. It takes about one pint to raise the level from the low mark to the high mark when the fluid is hot, so add the fluid a little at a time and keep checking the level until it is correct.

8   The condition of the fluid should also be checked along with the level. If the fluid at the end of the dipstick is black or a dark reddish brown color, or if it emits a burned smell, the fluid should be changed (see Section 27). If you are in doubt about the condition of the fluid, purchase some new fluid and compare the two for color and smell.

8   Engine oil and oil filter change (every 3000 miles or 3 months)

Refer to illustrations 8.2, 8.7, 8.13, and 8.15

1   Frequent oil changes are the best preventive maintenance the home mechanic can give the engine, because aging oil becomes diluted and contaminated, which leads to premature engine wear.

2   Make sure that you have all the necessary tools before you begin

this procedure **(see illustration)**. You should also have plenty of rags or newspapers handy for mopping up any spills.

3   Access to the underside of the vehicle is greatly improved if the vehicle can be lifted on a hoist, driven onto ramps or supported by jackstands. **Warning:** *Do not work under a vehicle which is supported only by a bumper, hydraulic or scissors-type jack.*

4   If this is your first oil change, get under the vehicle and familiarize yourself with the location of the oil drain plug. The engine and exhaust components will be warm during the actual work, so try to anticipate any potential problems before the engine and accessories are hot.

5   Park the vehicle on a level spot. Start the engine and allow it to reach its normal operating temperature (the needle on the temperature gauge should be at least above the bottom mark). Warm oil and sludge will flow out more easily. Turn off the engine when it's warmed up. Remove the filler cap.

6   Raise the vehicle and support it on jackstands. **Warning:** *To avoid personal injury, never get beneath the vehicle when it is supported by only by a jack. The jack provided with your vehicle is designed solely for raising the vehicle to remove and replace the wheels. Always use jackstands to support the vehicle when it becomes necessary to place your body underneath the vehicle.*

7   Being careful not to touch the hot exhaust components, place the drain pan under the drain plug in the bottom of the pan and remove the plug **(see illustration)**. You may want to wear gloves while unscrewing the plug the final few turns if the engine is really hot.

8   Allow the old oil to drain into the pan. It may be necessary to move the pan farther under the engine as the oil flow slows to a trickle. Inspect the old oil for the presence of metal shavings and chips.

9   After all the oil has drained, wipe off the drain plug with a clean rag. Even minute metal particles clinging to the plug would immediately contaminate the new oil.

10   Clean the area around the drain plug opening, reinstall the plug and tighten it securely, but do not strip the threads.

11   Move the drain pan into position under the oil filter.

12   Remove all tools, rags, etc. from under the vehicle, being careful not to spill the oil in the drain pan, then lower the vehicle.

13   Loosen the oil filter **(see illustration)** by turning it counterclockwise with the filter wrench. Any standard filter wrench will work. Once the filter is loose, use your hands to unscrew it from the block. Just as the filter is detached from the block, immediately tilt the open end up to prevent the oil inside the filter from spilling out. **Warning:** *The engine exhaust manifold may still be hot, so be careful.*

14   With a clean rag, wipe off the mounting surface on the block. If a residue of old oil is allowed to remain, it will smoke when the block is heated up. It will also prevent the new filter from seating properly. Also make sure that the none of the old gasket remains stuck to the

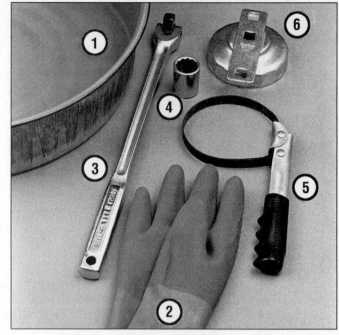

8.2 These tools are required when changing the engine oil and filter

1 **Drain pan** - *It should be fairly shallow in depth, but wide to prevent spills*

2 **Rubber gloves** - *When removing the drain plug and filter, you will get oil on your hands (the gloves will prevent burns)*

3 **Breaker bar** - *Sometimes the oil drain plug is tight, and a long breaker bar is needed to loosen it*

4 **Socket** - *To be used with the breaker bar or a ratchet (must be the correct size to fit the drain plug)*

5 **Filter wrench** - *This is a metal band-type wrench, which requires clearance around the filter to be effective*

6 **Filter wrench** - *This type fits on the bottom of the filter and can be turned with a ratchet or breaker bar (different-size wrenches are available for different types of filters)*

mounting surface. It can be removed with a scraper if necessary.

15   Compare the old filter with the new one to make sure they are the same type. Smear some engine oil on the rubber gasket of the new

8.7 Use the proper size box-end wrench or socket to remove the oil drain plug without rounding off the corners

8.13 The oil filter is mounted upside down on four-cylinder engines so it's a good idea to pack rags around it before removal to minimize the mess - since it usually on very tight, you'll need a special wrench for removal - DO NOT use the wrench to tighten the new filter

8.15 Lubricate the oil filter gasket with clean engine oil before installing the filter on the engine

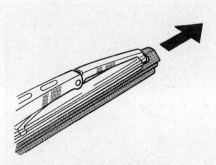

9.6 Pull the type A wiper element tabs out of the frame

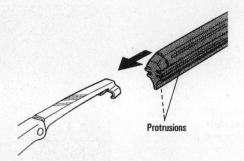

9.7 To install a new element, insert the end of the blade with the small protrusions into the frame

Protrusions

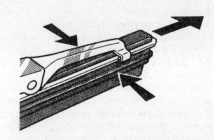

9.8 Squeeze the end of the type B wiper element and pull it straight out of the frame

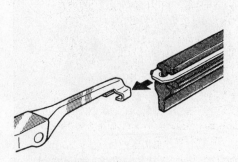

9.9 Insert the end without the cutout into the frame

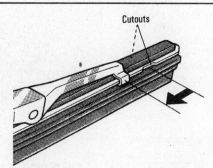

Cutouts

9.10 Slide the element into place until the cutouts seat into the locking claw

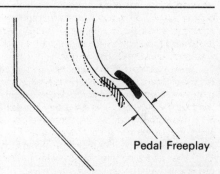

Pedal Freeplay

10.1 To check the clutch pedal freeplay, measure the distance between the natural resting place of the pedal and the point at which you encounter resistance

filter and screw it into place **(see illustration)**. Because overtightening the filter will damage the gasket, do not use a filter wrench to tighten the filter. Tighten it by hand until the gasket contacts the seating surface. Then seat the filter by giving it an additional 3/4-turn.

16   Add new oil to the engine through the oil filler cap in the valve cover. Use a spout or funnel to prevent oil from spilling onto the top of the engine. Pour three quarts of fresh oil into the engine. Wait a few minutes to allow the oil to drain into the pan, then check the level on the oil dipstick (see Section 4 if necessary). If the oil level is at or near the F mark, install the filler cap hand tight, start the engine and allow the new oil to circulate.

17   Allow the engine to run for about a minute. While the engine is running, look under the vehicle and check for leaks at the oil pan drain plug and around the oil filter. If either is leaking, stop the engine and tighten the plug or filter slightly.

18   Wait a few minutes to allow the oil to trickle down into the pan, then recheck the level on the dipstick and, if necessary, add enough oil to bring the level to the F mark.

19   During the first few trips after an oil change, make it a point to check frequently for leaks and proper oil level.

20   The old oil drained from the engine cannot be reused in its present state and should be discarded. Oil reclamation centers, auto repair shops and gas stations will normally accept the oil, which can be refined and used again. After the oil has cooled, it can be drained into a suitable container (capped plastic jugs, topped bottles, milk cartons, etc.) for transport to one of these disposal sites.

9   Windshield wiper blade inspection and replacement (every 6000 miles or 6 months)

Refer to illustrations 9.6, 9.7, 9.8, 9.9 and 9.10

1   The windshield wiper and blade assembly should be inspected periodically for damage, loose components and cracked or worn blade elements.

2   Road film can build up on the wiper blades and affect their efficiency, so they should be washed regularly with a mild detergent solution.

3   The action of the wiping mechanism can loosen bolts, nuts and fasteners, so they should be checked and tightened, as necessary, at the same time the wiper blades are checked.

4   If the wiper blade elements are cracked, worn or warped, or no longer clean adequately, they should be replaced with new ones.

5   Lift the arm assembly away from the glass for clearance.

Type A

6   Working from the end of the wiper closest to the arm, pull the rubber blade element from the frame and discard it **(see illustration)**.

7   To install a new rubber wiper element, insert the end with the small protrusions into the replacement hole and work the rubber along the slot in the blade frame **see illustration)**.

Type B

8   Squeeze the end of the wiper element and pull it out of the frame **(see illustration)**.

9   Insert the end of the new element without cutouts into the end of the frame **(see illustration)**.

10   Work the rubber along the slot in the blade frame until the cutouts are locked into place by wiper frame claw **(see illustration)**.

10   Clutch pedal freeplay and height check and adjustment (every 6000 miles or 6 months)

Refer to illustrations 10.1 and 10.2

1   Press down lightly on the clutch pedal and, with a small steel ruler, measure the distance that it moves freely before the clutch resistance is felt **(see illustration)**. The freeplay should be within the specified limits. If it isn't, it must be adjusted.

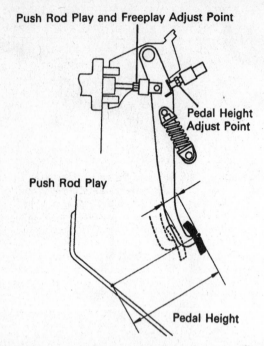

Push Rod Play and Freeplay Adjust Point

Pedal Height Adjust Point

Push Rod Play

Pedal Height

10.2 Clutch pedal pushrod play, freeplay and adjustment details

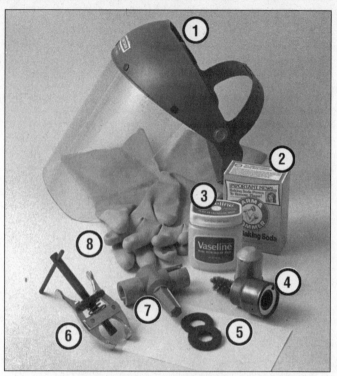

11.1 Tools and materials required for battery maintenance

1   *Face shield/safety goggles* - *When removing corrosion with a brush, the acidic particles can easily fly up into your eyes*

2   *Baking soda* - *A solution of baking soda and water can be used to neutralize corrosion*

3   *Petroleum jelly* - *A layer of this on the battery posts will help prevent corrosion*

4   *Battery post/cable cleaner* - *This wire brush cleaning tool will remove all traces of corrosion from the battery posts and cable clamps*

5   *Treated felt washers* - *Placing one of these on each post, directly under the cable clamps, will help prevent corrosion*

6   *Puller* - *Sometimes the cable clamps are very difficult to pull off the posts, even after the nut/bolt has been completely loosened. This tool pulls the clamp straight up and off the post without damage*

7   *Battery post/cable cleaner* - *Here is another cleaning tool which is a slightly different version of Number 4 above, but it does the same thing*

8   *Rubber gloves* - *Another safety item to consider when servicing the battery; remember that's acid inside the battery!*

2   Loosen the locknut on the pedal end of the clutch pushrod **(see illustration)**.
3   Turn the pushrod until pedal freeplay and pushrod freeplay are correct.
4   Tighten the locknut.
5   After adjusting the pedal freeplay, check the pedal height.
6   If pedal height is incorrect, loosen the locknut and turn the stopper bolt until the height is correct. Tighten the locknut.

11   Battery check, maintenance and charging (every 6000 miles or 6 months)

Refer to illustrations 11.1, 11.6a, 11.6b, 11.7a, 11.7b and 11.8
Warning: *Certain precautions must be followed when checking and servicing the battery. Hydrogen gas, which is highly flammable, is always present in the battery cells, so keep lighted tobacco and all other open flames and sparks away from the battery. The electrolyte inside the battery is actually dilute sulfuric acid, which will cause injury if splashed on your skin or in your eyes. It will also ruin clothes and painted surfaces. When removing the battery cables, always detach the negative cable first and hook it up last!*
Caution: *If the stereo in your vehicle is equipped with an anti-theft system, make sure you have the correct activation code before disconnecting the battery.*
Note: *On 1993 and later models, the airbag system will be disabled if the battery is disconnected for more than a brief period. If the airbag light comes on and stays on after the battery is reconnected, the vehicle must be taken to a dealer to have the system reset with a special tool.*
1   A routine preventive maintenance program for the battery in your vehicle is the only way to ensure quick and reliable starts. But before performing any battery maintenance, make sure that you have the proper equipment necessary to work safely around the battery **(see illustration)**.
2   There are also several precautions that should be taken whenever battery maintenance is performed. Before servicing the battery, always turn the engine and all accessories off and disconnect the cable from the negative terminal of the battery.

3   The battery produces hydrogen gas, which is both flammable and explosive. Never create a spark, smoke or light a match around the battery. Always charge the battery in a ventilated area.
4   Electrolyte contains poisonous and corrosive sulfuric acid. Do not allow it to get in your eyes, on your skin on your clothes. Never ingest it. Wear protective safety glasses when working near the battery. Keep children away from the battery.
5   Note the external condition of the battery. If the positive terminal and cable clamp on your vehicle's battery is equipped with a rubber protector, make sure that it's not torn or damaged. It should completely cover the terminal. Look for any corroded or loose connections, cracks in the case or cover or loose hold-down clamps. Also check the entire length of each cable for cracks and frayed conductors.
6   If corrosion, which looks like white, fluffy deposits **(see illustration)** is evident, particularly around the terminals, the battery should be removed for cleaning. Loosen the cable clamp bolts with a wrench, being careful to remove the ground cable first, and slide them off the

11.6a Battery terminal corrosion usually appears as light, fluffy powder

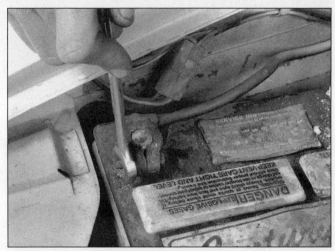

11.6b Removing the cable from a battery post with a wrench - sometimes special battery pliers are required for this procedure if corrosion has caused deterioration of the nut hex (always remove the ground cable first and hook it up last!)

11.7a When cleaning the cable clamps, all corrosion must be removed (the inside of the clamp is tapered to match the taper on the post, so don't remove too much material)

11.7b Regardless of the type of tool used on the battery posts, a clean, shiny surface should be the result

11.8 Make sure each battery hold-down nut (arrow) is tight

terminals **(see illustration)**. Then disconnect the hold-down clamp bolt and nut, remove the clamp and lift the battery from the engine compartment.

7   Clean the cable clamps thoroughly with a battery brush or a terminal cleaner and a solution of warm water and baking soda **(see illustration)**. Wash the terminals and the top of the battery case with the same solution but make sure that the solution doesn't get into the battery When cleaning the cables, terminals and battery top, wear safety goggles and rubber gloves to prevent any solution from coming in contact with your eyes or hands. Wear old clothes too - even diluted, sulfuric acid splashed onto clothes will burn holes in them. If the terminals have been extensively corroded, clean them up with a terminal cleaner **(see illustration)**. Thoroughly wash all cleaned areas with plain water.

8   Make sure that the battery tray is in good condition and the hold-down clamp bolt or nut is tight **(see illustration)**. If the battery is removed from the tray, make sure no parts remain in the bottom of the tray when the battery is reinstalled. When reinstalling the hold-down clamp bolt or nut, do not overtighten it.

9   Information on removing and installing the battery can be found in Chapter 5. Information on jump starting can be found at the front of this manual. For more detailed battery checking procedures, refer to the *Haynes Automotive Electrical Manual*.

Cleaning

10   Corrosion on the hold-down components, battery case and surrounding areas can be removed with a solution of water and baking soda. Thoroughly rinse all cleaned areas with plain water.

11   Any metal parts of the vehicle damaged by corrosion should be covered with a zinc-based primer, then painted.

Charging

Warning: *When batteries are being charged, hydrogen gas, which is very explosive and flammable, is produced. Do not smoke or allow open flames near a charging or a recently charged battery. Wear eye protection when near the battery during charging. Also, make sure the charger is unplugged before connecting or disconnecting the battery from the charger.*

12   Slow-rate charging is the best way to restore a battery that's discharged to the point where it will not start the engine. It's also a good way to maintain the battery charge in a vehicle that's only driven a few miles between starts. Maintaining the battery charge is particularly important in the winter when the battery must work harder to start the engine and electrical accessories that drain the battery are in greater use.

13   It's best to use a one or two-amp battery charger (sometimes

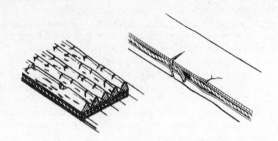

**12.3 Check a V-ribbed belt for signs of wear like these -
if the belt looks worn - replace it**

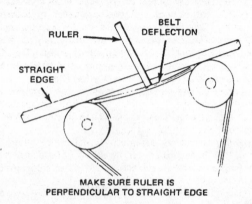

12.5 Measuring drivebelt deflection with a straightedge and ruler

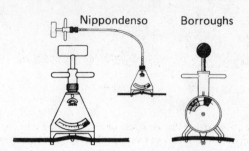

**12.4 If you're able to borrow either a Nippondenso or Burroughs
belt tension gauge, this his how it's installed on the belt -
compare the reading on the scale with the specified tension**

**12.6 After loosening the pivot bolt and the adjustment pinch bolt,
turn the adjustment bolt (arrow) clockwise to tighten the belt,
or counterclockwise to loosen the belt**

called a "trickle" charger). They are the safest and put the least strain on the battery. They are also the least expensive. For a faster charge, you can use a higher amperage charger, but don't use one rated more than 1/10th the amp/hour rating of the battery. Rapid boost charges that claim to restore the power of the battery in one to two hours are hardest on the battery and can damage batteries not in good condition. This type of charging should only be used in emergency situations.

14   The average time necessary to charge a battery should be listed in the instructions that come with the charger. As a general rule, a trickle charger will charge a battery in 12 to 16 hours.

12   Drivebelt check, adjustment and replacement (every 6000 miles or 6 months)

Refer to illustrations 12.3, 12.4, 12.5, 12.6 and 12.10

Check

1   The alternator and air conditioning compressor drivebelts, also referred to as V-ribbed belts or simply "fan" belts, are located at the right end of the engine. The good condition and proper adjustment of the alternator belt is critical to the operation of the engine. Because of their composition and the high stresses to which they are subjected, drivebelts stretch and deteriorate as they get older. They must therefore be periodically inspected.

2   The number of belts used on a particular vehicle depends on the accessories installed. One belt transmits power from the crankshaft to the alternator and air conditioning. If the vehicle is equipped with power steering, the pump is driven by it's own belt.

3   With the engine off, open the hood and locate the drivebelts at the left end of the engine. With a flashlight, check each belt for separation of the adhesive rubber on both sides of the core, core separation from

the belt side, a severed core, separation of the ribs from the adhesive rubber, cracking or separation of the ribs, and torn or worn ribs or cracks in the inner ridges of the ribs **(see illustration)**. Also check for fraying and glazing, which gives the belt a shiny appearance. Both sides of the belt should be inspected, which means you will have to twist the belt to check the underside. Use your fingers to feel the belt where you can't see it. If any of the above conditions are evident, replace the belt (go to Step 8).

4   To check the tension of each belt in accordance with factory specifications, install either a Nippondenso or Burroughs belt tension gauge on the belt **(see illustration)**. Measure the tension in accordance with the manufacturer's instructions and compare your measurement to the specified drivebelt tension for either a used or new belt. **Note:** *A "used" belt is defined as any belt which has been operated more than five minutes on the engine; a "new" belt is one that has been used for less than five minutes.*

5   If you don't have either of the above tools, and cannot borrow one, the following rule of thumb method is recommended: Push firmly on the belt with your thumb at a distance halfway between the pulleys and note how far the belt can be pushed (deflected). Measure this deflection with a ruler **(see illustration)**. The belt should deflect 1/4-inch if the distance from pulley center to pulley center is between 7 and 11 inches; the belt should deflect 1/2-inch if the distance from pulley center to pulley center is between 12 and 16 inches.

Adjustment

6   If the alternator/air conditioner compressor belt must be adjusted, loosen the alternator pivot bolt located on the front left corner of the block. Loosen the locking bolt and turn the adjusting bolt **(see**

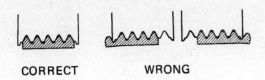

CORRECT   WRONG

12.10 When installing the V-ribbed belt, make sure it is centered on the pulley - it must not overlap either edge of the pulley

illustration). Measure the belt tension in accordance with one of the above methods. Repeat this step until the air conditioning compressor drivebelt is adjusted.

7   Adjust the power steering pump belt by loosening adjustment bolt that secures the pump to the slotted bracket and pivot the pump (away from the engine to tighten the belt, toward it to loosen it). Repeat the procedure until the drivebelt tension is correct and tighten the bolt.

Replacement

8   To replace a belt, follow the above procedures for drivebelt adjustment but slip the belt off the crankshaft pulley and remove it. If you are replacing the power steering pump belt, you will have to remove the air conditioning compressor belt first because of the way they are arranged on the crankshaft pulley. Because of this and because belts tend to wear out more or less together, it is a good idea to replace both belts at the same time. Mark each belt and its appropriate pulley groove so the replacement belts can be installed in their proper positions.

9   Take the old belts to the parts store in order to make a direct comparison for length, width and design.

10   After replacing the drivebelt, make sure that it fits properly in the ribbed grooves in the pulleys (see illustration). It is essential that the belt be properly centered.

11   Adjust the belt(s) in accordance with the procedure outlined above.

13   Underhood hose check and replacement (every 6000 miles or 6 months)

Caution: *Replacement of air conditioning hoses must be left to a dealer service department or air conditioning shop that has the equipment to depressurize the system safely. Never remove air conditioning components or hoses until the system has been depressurized.*

General

1   High temperatures in the engine compartment can cause the deterioration of the rubber and plastic hoses used for engine, accessory and emission systems operation. Periodic inspection should be made for cracks, loose clamps, material hardening and leaks.

2   Information specific to the cooling system hoses can be found in Section 14.

3   Some, but not all, hoses are secured to the fittings with clamps. Where clamps are used, check to be sure they haven't lost their tension, allowing the hose to leak. If clamps aren't used, make sure the hose has not expanded and/or hardened where it slips over the fitting, allowing it to leak.

Vacuum hoses

4   It's quite common for vacuum hoses, especially those in the emissions system, to be color coded or identified by colored stripes molded into them. Various systems require hoses with different wall thickness, collapse resistance and temperature resistance. When replacing hoses, be sure the new ones are made of the same material.

5   Often the only effective way to check a hose is to remove it

completely from the vehicle. If more than one hose is removed, be sure to label the hoses and fittings to ensure correct installation.

6   When checking vacuum hoses, be sure to include any plastic T-fittings in the check. Inspect the fittings for cracks and the hose where it fits over the fitting for distortion, which could cause leakage.

7   A small piece of vacuum hose (1/4-inch inside diameter) can be used as a stethoscope to detect vacuum leaks. Hold one end of the hose to your ear and probe around vacuum hoses and fittings, listening for the "hissing" sound characteristic of a vacuum leak. **Warning:** *When probing with the vacuum hose stethoscope, be very careful not to come into contact with moving engine components such as the drivebelts, cooling fan, etc.*

Fuel hose

Warning: *There are certain precautions which must be taken when inspecting or servicing fuel system components. Work in a well ventilated area and do not allow open flames (cigarettes, appliance pilot lights, etc.) or bare light bulbs near the work area. Mop up any spills immediately and do not store fuel soaked rags where they could ignite.*

8   Check all rubber fuel lines for deterioration and chafing. Check especially for cracks in areas where the hose bends and just before fittings, such as where a hose attaches to the fuel filter.

9   High quality fuel line, usually identified by the word *Fluroelastomer* printed on the hose, should be used for fuel line replacement. Never, under any circumstances, use unreinforced vacuum line, clear plastic tubing or water hose for fuel lines.

10   Spring-type clamps are commonly used on fuel lines. These clamps often lose their tension over a period of time, and can be "sprung" during removal. Replace all spring-type clamps with screw clamps whenever a hose is replaced.

Metal lines

11   Sections of metal line are often used for fuel line between the fuel pump and fuel injection unit. Check carefully to be sure the line has not been bent or crimped and that cracks have not started in the line.

12   If a section of metal fuel line must be replaced, only seamless steel tubing should be used, since copper and aluminum tubing don't have the strength necessary to withstand normal engine vibration.

13   Check the metal brake lines where they enter the master cylinder and brake proportioning unit (if used) for cracks in the lines or loose fittings. Any sign of brake fluid leakage calls for an immediate thorough inspection of the brake system.

14   Cooling system check (every 6000 miles or 6 months)

Refer to illustration 14.4

1   Many major engine failures can be attributed to a faulty cooling system. If the vehicle is equipped with an automatic transaxle, the cooling system also cools the transaxle fluid and thus plays an important role in prolonging transaxle life.

2   The cooling system should be checked with the engine cold. Do this before the vehicle is driven for the day or after the engine has been shut off for at least three hours.

3   Remove the radiator cap by turning it to the left until it reaches a stop. If you hear a hissing sound (indicating there is still pressure in the system), wait until it stops. Now press down on the cap with the palm of your hand and continue turning to the left until the cap can be removed. Thoroughly clean the cap, inside and out, with clean water. Also clean the filler neck on the radiator. All traces of corrosion should be removed. The coolant inside the radiator should be relatively transparent. If it's rust colored, the system should be drained and refilled (see Section 24). If the coolant level isn't up to the top, add additional antifreeze/coolant mixture (see Section 4).

4   Carefully check the large upper and lower radiator hoses along with the smaller diameter heater hoses which run from the engine to the firewall. Inspect each hose along its entire length, replacing any hose which is cracked, swollen or shows signs of deterioration. Cracks may become more apparent if the hose is squeezed (see illustration).

1

Regardless of condition, it's a good idea to replace hoses with new ones every two years.

5　Make sure that all hose connections are tight. A leak in the cooling system will usually show up as white or rust colored deposits on the areas adjoining the leak. If wire-type clamps are used at the ends of the hoses, it may be a good idea to replace them with more secure screw-type clamps.

6　Use compressed air or a soft brush to remove bugs, leaves, etc. from the front of the radiator or air conditioning condenser. Be careful not to damage the delicate cooling fins or cut yourself on them.

7　Every other inspection, or at the first indication of cooling system problems, have the cap and system pressure tested. If you don't have a pressure tester, most gas stations and repair shops will do this for a minimal charge.

15　Tire rotation (every 6000 miles or 6 months)

Refer to illustration 15.2

1　The tires should be rotated at the specified intervals and whenever uneven wear is noticed. Since the vehicle will be raised and the tires removed anyway, check the brakes (see Section 16) at this time.

2　Radial tires must be rotated in a specific pattern **(see illustration)**.

3　Refer to the information in *Jacking and towing* at the front of this manual for the proper procedures to follow when raising the vehicle and changing a tire. If the brakes are to be checked, do not apply the parking brake as stated. Make sure the tires are blocked to prevent the vehicle from rolling.

4　Preferably, the entire vehicle should be raised at the same time. This can be done on a hoist or by jacking up each corner and then lowering the vehicle onto jackstands placed under the frame rails. Always use four jackstands and make sure the vehicle is firmly supported.

5　After rotation, check and adjust the tire pressures as necessary and be sure to check the lug nut tightness.

6　For further information on the wheels and tires, refer to Chapter 10.

16　Brake check (every 15,000 miles or 12 months)

Note: *For detailed photographs of the brake system, refer to Chapter 9.*

1　In addition to the specified intervals, the brakes should be inspected every time the wheels are removed or whenever a defect is suspected. Any of the following symptoms could indicate a potential brake system defect: The vehicle pulls to one side when the brake pedal is depressed; the brakes make squealing or dragging noises when applied; brake travel is excessive; the pedal pulsates; brake fluid leaks, usually onto the inside of the tire or wheel.

ALWAYS CHECK hose for chafed or burned areas that may cause an untimely and costly failure.

SOFT hose indicates inside deterioration. This deterioration can contaminate the cooling system and cause particles to clog the radiator.

HARDENED hose can fail at any time. Tightening hose clamps will not seal the connection or stop leaks.

SWOLLEN hose or oil soaked ends indicate danger and possible failure from oil or grease contamination. Squeeze the hose to locate cracks and breaks that cause leaks.

14.4　Hoses, like drivebelts, have a habit of failing at the worst possible time - to prevent the inconvenience of a blown radiator or heater hose, inspect them carefully as shown here

2　The disc brake pads have built-in wear indicators which should make a high pitched squealing or scraping noise when they are worn to the replacement point. When you hear this noise, replace the pads immediately or expensive damage to the discs can result.

3　Loosen the wheel lug nuts.

4　Raise the vehicle and place it securely on jackstands.

5　Remove the wheels (see *Jacking and towing* at the front of this book, or your owner's manual, if necessary).

Disc brakes

Refer to illustration 16.6

6　There are two pads - an outer and an inner - in each caliper. The pads are visible through inspection holes in each caliper **(see illustration)**.

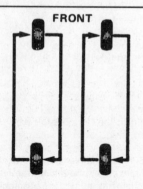

15.2　The recommended tire rotation pattern for these models

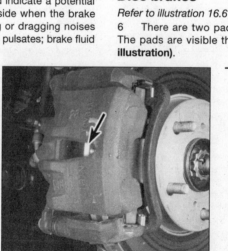

16.6　You'll find an inspection hole like this in each caliper that you can view the inner and outer brake pad lining through

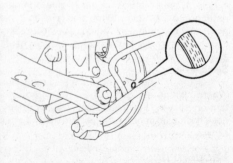

16.13　A quick check of the remaining drum brake shoe lining material can be made by removing the rubber plug in the backing plate and looking through the inspection hole

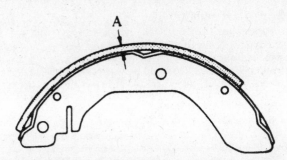

16.16 If the lining is bonded to the brake shoe, measure the lining thickness from the outer surface to the metal shoe, as shown here; if the lining is riveted to the shoe, measure from the lining outer surface to the rivet head

7   Check the pad thickness by looking at each end of the caliper and through the inspection hole in the caliper body. If the lining material is less than the thickness listed in this Chapter's Specifications, replace the pads. **Note:** *Keep in mind that the lining material is riveted or bonded to a metal backing plate and the metal portion is not included in this measurement.*

8   If it is difficult to determine the exact thickness of the remaining pad material by the above method, or if you are at all concerned about the condition of the pads, remove the caliper(s), then remove the pads from the calipers for further inspection (refer to Chapter 9).

9   Once the pads are removed from the calipers, clean them with brake cleaner and remeasure them with a small steel pocket ruler or a vernier caliper.

10   Measure the disc thickness with a micrometer to make sure that it still has service life remaining. If any disc is thinner than the specified minimum thickness, replace it (refer to Chapter 9). Even if the disc has service life remaining, check its condition. Look for scoring, gouging and burned spots. If these conditions exist, remove the disc and have it resurfaced (see Chapter 9).

11   Before installing the wheels, check all brake lines and hoses for damage, wear, deformation, cracks, corrosion, leakage, bends and twists, particularly in the vicinity of the rubber hoses at the calipers. Check the clamps for tightness and the connections for leakage. Make sure that all hoses and lines are clear of sharp edges, moving parts and the exhaust system. If any of the above conditions are noted, repair, reroute or replace the lines and/or fittings as necessary (see Chapter 9).

12   Some models are equipped with disc brakes on the rear wheels which incorporate drum-type parking brakes into the rear discs. The inspection procedure for these parking brakes is the same as for the rear drum brakes described below.

Rear drum brakes

Refer to illustrations 16.13, 16.16 and 16.18

13   To check the brake shoe lining thickness without removing the brake drums, remove the rubber plug from the backing plate and use a flashlight to inspect the linings **(see illustration)**. For a more thorough brake inspection, follow the procedure below.

14   Refer to Chapter 9 and remove the rear brake drums.

15   **Warning:** *Brake dust produced by lining wear and deposited on brake components contains asbestos, which is hazardous to your health. DO NOT blow it out with compressed air and DO NOT inhale it! DO NOT use gasoline or solvents to remove the dust. Brake system cleaner should be used to flush the dust into a drain pan. After the brake components are wiped clean with a damp rag, dispose of the contaminated rag(s) and solvent in a covered and labeled container. Try to use non-asbestos replacement parts whenever possible.*

16   Note the thickness of the lining material on the rear brake shoes **(see illustration)** and look for signs of contamination by brake fluid and grease. If the lining material is within 1/16-inch of the recessed rivets or metal shoes, replace the brake shoes with new ones. The shoes should also be replaced if they are cracked, glazed (shiny lining

16.18 Carefully peel back the wheel cylinder boot and check for leaking fluid indicating that the cylinder must be replaced or rebuilt

surfaces) or contaminated with brake fluid or grease. See Chapter 9 for the replacement procedure.

17   Check the shoe return and hold-down springs and the adjusting mechanism to make sure they're installed correctly and in good condition. Deteriorated or distorted springs, if not replaced, could allow the linings to drag and wear prematurely.

18   Check the wheel cylinders for leakage by carefully peeling back the rubber boots **(see illustration)**. If brake fluid is noted behind the boots, the wheel cylinders must be replaced (see Chapter 9).

19   Check the drums for cracks, score marks, deep scratches and hard spots, which will appear as small discolored areas. If imperfections cannot be removed with emery cloth, the drums must be resurfaced by an automotive machine shop (see Chapter 9 for more detailed information).

20   Refer to Chapter 9 and install the brake drums.

21   Install the wheels and snug the wheel lug nuts finger tight.

22   Remove the jackstands and lower the vehicle.

23   Tighten the wheel lug nuts to the torque listed in this Chapter's Specifications.

Brake booster check

24   Sit in the driver's seat and perform the following sequence of tests.

25   With the engine stopped, depress the brake pedal several times - the travel distance should not change.

26   With the brake fully depressed, start the engine - the pedal should move down a little when the engine starts.

27   Depress the brake, stop the engine and hold the pedal in for about 30 seconds - the pedal should neither sink nor rise.

28   Restart the engine, run it for about a minute and turn it off. Then firmly depress the brake several times - the pedal travel should decrease with each application.

29   If your brakes do not operate as described above when the preceding tests are performed, the brake booster is either in need of repair or has failed. Refer to Chapter 9 for the removal procedure.

Parking brake

30   Slowly pull up on the parking brake handle or push down on the parking brake pedal and count the number of clicks you hear until the handle is up (or the pedal down) as far as it will go. The adjustment is correct if you hear the specified number of clicks. If you hear more or fewer clicks, it's time to adjust the parking brake (refer to Chapter 9).

31   An alternative method of checking the parking brake is to park the vehicle on a steep hill with the parking brake set and the transmission in Neutral. If the parking brake cannot prevent the vehicle from rolling, it is in need of adjustment (see Chapter 9).

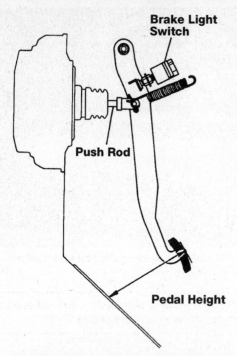

Brake Light
Switch

Push Rod

Pedal Height

16.32 Brake pedal height adjustment details

Brake pedal height and freeplay check and adjustment

Brake pedal height

Refer to illustrations 16.32 and 16.36

32   With the brake pedal fully released, measure the distance from the top of the pad to the floor **(see illustration)**.
33   If the height is not as listed in the Specifications Section at the beginning of this Chapter it must be adjusted.
34   Remove the brake light switch (Chapter 9) and loosen the locknut on the brake booster pushrod.
35   Turn the pushrod until the pedal height is correct and tighten the locknut.
36   Install the brake light switch and measure the clearance (freeplay) between the pedal stopper and the tip of the brake light switch **(see illustration)**.
37   If the clearance isn't as listed in the Specifications Section at the beginning of this Chapter, adjust it by loosening the locknut on the switch. Rotate the switch to achieve the specified freeplay and tighten the locknut. After checking and adjusting (if necessary) the pedal height, check the pedal freeplay.

Brake pedal freeplay

Refer to illustration 16.38

38   Press down lightly on the brake pedal and, with a small steel ruler, measure the distance that it moves freely before resistance is felt **(see illustration)**. The freeplay should be within the specified limits. If it isn't, check the brake light switch clearance and adjust as necessary.

Brake pedal reserve height

Refer to illustration 16.40

39   After checking and, if necessary, adjusting the pedal height and freeplay, the pedal depressed height must be checked.
40   With the engine running, press the brake pedal fully and measure the pedal pad-to-floor distance **(see illustration)**.
41   If the minimum pedal reserve height is below that listed in the Specifications Section listed at the beginning of this Chapter, check the brake system for leaks or other damage.

---

17   Air filter replacement (every 15,000 miles or 12 months)

Refer to illustrations 17.1 and 17.2

1   The air filter is located inside a housing at the left (drivers) side of the engine compartment. To remove the air filter, release the four spring clips retaining the two halves of the air cleaner housing **(see illustration)**.
2   Lift the cover up and remove the air filter element **(see illustration)**.
3   Inspect the outer surface of the filter element. If it is dirty, replace it. If it is only moderately dusty, it can be reused by blowing it clean from the back to the front surface with compressed air. Because it is a pleated paper type filter, it cannot be washed or oiled. If it cannot be cleaned satisfactorily with compressed air, discard and replace it. **Caution:** *Never drive the vehicle with the air cleaner removed. Excessive engine wear could result and backfiring could even cause a fire under the hood.*
4   Installation is the reverse of removal.

---

18   Fuel system check (every 15,000 miles or 12 months)

Refer to illustration 18.5

Warning: *Certain precautions should be observed when inspecting or servicing the fuel system components. Work in a well ventilated area and do not allow open flames (cigarettes, appliance pilot lights, etc.) near the work area. Mop up spills immediately and do not store fuel soaked rags where they could ignite. It is a good idea to keep a dry chemical (Class B) fire extinguisher near the work area any time the fuel system is being serviced.*

1   If you smell gasoline while driving or after the vehicle has been sitting in the sun, inspect the fuel system immediately.

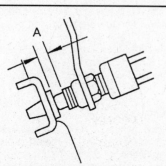

A

16.36 Brake light switch clearance (A) adjustment details

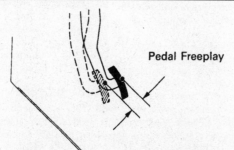

Pedal Freeplay

16.38 Check the brake pedal freeplay by measuring the distance from the resting place of the pedal to the point where you encounter resistance

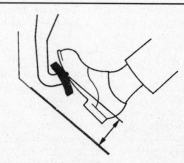

16.40 Brake pedal reserve height details

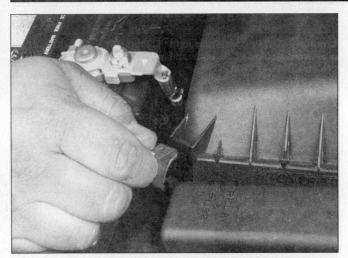

17.1 Detach the four air cleaner housing clips

17.2 Lift the cover up and remove the filter

2   Remove the fuel filler cap and inspect if for damage and corrosion. The gasket should have an unbroken sealing imprint. If the gasket is damaged or corroded, remove it and install a new one (Section 33).

3   Inspect the fuel feed and return lines for cracks. Make sure that the threaded flare nut type connectors which secure the metal fuel lines to the fuel injection system and the banjo bolts which secure the banjo fittings to the in-line fuel filter are tight.

4   Since some components of the fuel system - the fuel tank and part of the fuel feed and return lines, for example - are underneath the vehicle, they can be inspected more easily with the vehicle raised on a hoist. If that's not possible, raise the vehicle and support it securely on jackstands.

5   With the vehicle raised and safely supported, inspect the gas tank and filler neck for punctures, cracks and other damage. The connection between the filler neck and the tank is particularly critical. Sometimes a rubber filler neck will leak because of loose clamps or deteriorated rubber **(see illustration)**. These are problems a home mechanic can usually rectify. **Warning:** *Do not, under any circumstances, try to repair a fuel tank (except rubber components). A welding torch or any open flame can easily cause fuel vapors inside the tank to explode.*

6   Carefully check all rubber hoses and metal lines leading away from the fuel tank. Check for loose connections, deteriorated hoses, crimped lines and other damage. Carefully inspect the lines from the tank to the fuel injection system. Repair or replace damaged sections as necessary (see Chapter 4).

1

19   Automatic transaxle differential lubricant level check (every 15,000 miles or 12 months)

Refer to illustration 19.2

1   The automatic transaxle differential has a separate lubricant supply with a check/fill plug which must be removed to check the level. If the vehicle is raised to gain access to the plug, be sure to support it safely on jackstands - DO NOT crawl under the vehicle when it's supported only by the jack.

2   Remove the check/fill plug from the front of the differential **(see illustration)**.

3   Use your little finger as a dipstick to make sure the lubricant level is even with the bottom of the plug hole. If not, use a syringe or a gear oil pump to add the recommended lubricant (see this Chapter's Specifications) until it just starts to run out of the opening.

4   Install the plug and tighten it securely.

20   Manual transaxle lubricant level check (every 15,000 miles or 12 months)

Refer to illustration 20.1

1   The manual transaxle does not have a dipstick. To check the fluid level, raise the vehicle and support it securely on jackstands. On the lower front side of the transaxle housing, you will see a plug **(see illustration)**. Remove it. If the lubricant level is correct, it should be up to

18.5 Check the fuel tank filler hose connection (arrow) for leaks and damage

19.2 The automatic transaxle check/fill plug (arrow) is located on the driver's side of the transaxle

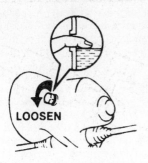

20.1 Use your finger as a dipstick to check the manual transaxle lubricant level

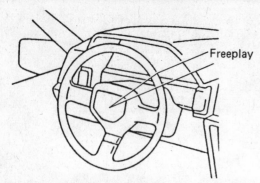

21.1 Steering wheel freeplay is the amount of travel between the initial steering input and the point at which the front wheels begin to turn (indicated by slight resistance)

the lower edge of the hole.

2   If the transaxle needs more lubricant (if the level is not up to the hole), use a syringe or a gear oil pump to add more. Stop filling the transaxle when the lubricant begins to run out the hole.

3   Install the plug and tighten it securely. Drive the vehicle a short distance, then check for leaks.

21 Steering and suspension check (every 15,000 miles or 12 months)

Refer to illustrations 21.1, 21.7 and 21.8
Note: *For detailed illustrations of the steering and suspension components, refer to Chapter 10.*

With the wheels on the ground

1   With the vehicle stopped and the front wheels pointed straight ahead, rock the steering wheel gently back and forth. If freeplay **(see illustration)** is excessive, a front wheel bearing, main shaft yoke, intermediate shaft yoke, lower arm balljoint or steering system joint is worn or the steering gear is out of adjustment or broken. Refer to Chapter 10 for the appropriate repair procedure.

2   Other symptoms, such as excessive vehicle body movement over rough roads, swaying (leaning) around corners and binding as the steering wheel is turned, may indicate faulty steering and/or suspension components.

3   Check the shock absorbers by pushing down and releasing the vehicle several times at each corner. If the vehicle does not come back to a level position within one or two bounces, the shocks/struts are worn and must be replaced. When bouncing the vehicle up and down, listen for squeaks and noises from the suspension components. Additional information on suspension components can be found in Chapter 10.

Under the vehicle

4   Raise the vehicle with a floor jack and support it securely on jackstands. See *Jacking and towing* at the front of this book for the proper jacking points.

5   Check the tires for irregular wear patterns and proper inflation. See Section 5 in this Chapter for information regarding tire wear and Chapter 10 for the wheel bearing replacement procedures.

6   Inspect the universal joint between the steering shaft and the steering gear housing. Check the steering gear housing for lubricant leakage or oozing. Make sure that the dust seals and boots are not damaged and that the boot clamps are not loose. Check the steering linkage for looseness or damage. Check the tie-rod ends for excessive play. Look for loose bolts, broken or disconnected parts and deteriorated rubber bushings on all suspension and steering components. While an assistant turns the steering wheel from side to side, check the steering components for free movement, chafing and binding. If the steering components do not seem to be reacting with the movement of the steering wheel, try to determine where the slack is located.

21.7 To check the balljoints attempt to move the lower arm up and down with a prybar to make sure here is no play in the balljoint (if there is, replace it)

7   Check the balljoints for wear by placing a wood block under each tire. Lower the jack until there is about half a load on the coil spring and place jackstands under the subframe. Make sure that the front wheels are in a straight forward position and block the wheel with chocks. Try to move each lower arm up and down with a prybar **(see illustration)** to ensure that its balljoint has no play. If any balljoint does have play, replace it. See Chapter 10 for the front balljoint replacement procedure.

8   Inspect the balljoint boots for damage and leaking grease **(see illustration)**. Replace the balljoints with new ones if they are damaged (see Chapter 10).

22 Driveaxle boot check (every 15,000 miles or 12 months)

Refer to illustration 22.2

1   The driveaxle boots are very important because they prevent dirt, water and foreign material from entering and damaging the constant velocity (CV) joints. Oil and grease can cause the boot material to deteriorate prematurely, so it's a good idea to wash the boots with soap and water.

2   Inspect the boots for tears and cracks as well as loose clamps **(see illustration)**. If there is any evidence of cracks or leaking lubricant, they must be replaced as described in Chapter 8.

23 Fuel filter replacement (every 30,000 miles or 24 months)

Refer to illustration 23.3

1   Disconnect the negative battery cable. **Caution:** *If the stereo in your vehicle is equipped with an anti-theft system, make sure you have the correct activation code before disconnecting the battery.* **Note:** *On 1993 and later models, the airbag system will be disabled if the battery is disconnected for more than a brief period. If the airbag light comes on and stays on after the battery is reconnected, the vehicle must be taken to a dealer to have the system reset with a special tool.*

2   If necessary for access, remove the air cleaner assembly (see Chapter 4) and evaporative canister (see Chapter 6).

3   Using a backup wrench to steady the filter, remove the threaded banjo bolt at the top and loosen the fitting at the bottom of the fuel filter (use a flare nut wrench if possible) **(see illustration)**

4   Remove both bracket bolts from the firewall and remove the old filter and the filter support bracket assembly.

5   Note that the inlet and outlet pipes are clearly labeled on their respective ends of the filter and that the flanged end of the filter faces down. Make sure the new filter is installed so that it's facing the proper

21.8 Push on the balljoint boot to check for tears and grease leaks

22.2 Flex the driveaxle boots by hand to check for tears, cracks and leaking grease

23.3 Using a backup wrench, remove the banjo bolt (arrow) at the top and bottom of the fuel filter

24.4 On most models you will have to remove a cover for access to the radiator drain fitting located at the bottom of the radiator (arrow)

24.5a On four-cylinder engines, the coolant drain plug is located on the back side of the engine block (arrow)

direction as noted above. When correctly installed, the filter should be installed so that the outlet pipe faces up and the inlet pipe faces down.

6   Using the new sealing washers provided by the filter manufacturer, install the inlet and outlet banjo fittings and tighten them securely.

7   The remainder of installation is the reverse of the removal procedure.

24 Cooling system servicing (draining, flushing and refilling) (every 30,000 miles or 24 months)

Warning: *Do not allow engine coolant (antifreeze) to come in contact with your skin or painted surfaces of the vehicle. Rinse off spills immediately with plenty of water. Antifreeze is highly toxic if ingested. Never leave antifreeze laying around in an open container or in puddles on the floor; children and pets are attracted by it's sweet smell and may drink it. Check with local authorities about disposing of used antifreeze. Many communities have collection centers which will see that antifreeze is disposed of safely.*

1   Periodically, the cooling system should be drained, flushed and refilled to replenish the antifreeze mixture and prevent formation of rust and corrosion, which can impair the performance of the cooling system and cause engine damage. When the cooling system is serviced, all hoses and the radiator cap should be checked and replaced if necessary.

Draining

Refer to illustrations 24.4, 24.5a, 24.5b and 24.5c

2   Apply the parking brake and block the wheels. If the vehicle has

just been driven, wait several hours to allow the engine to cool down before beginning this procedure.

3   Once the engine is completely cool, remove the radiator cap.

4   Move a large container under the radiator drain to catch the coolant. Attach a 3/8-inch inner diameter hose to the drain fitting to direct the coolant into the container (some models are already equipped with a hose), then open the drain fitting (a pair of pliers may be required to turn it) **(see illustration)**.

5   After the coolant stops flowing out of the radiator, move the container under the engine block drain plug **(see illustrations)**. Loosen the plug and allow the coolant in the block to drain.

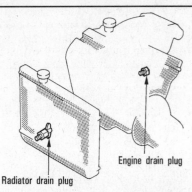

Engine drain plug

Radiator drain plug

24.5b On the 3MZ-FE V6 engine, the coolant drain plug is located on the back side of the block

24.5c The 1MZ-FE engine has a coolant drain like this (arrow) located on both sides of the block

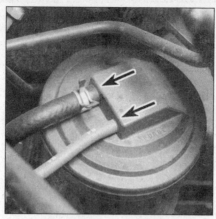

25.2 Check the charcoal canister for damage and the hose connections (arrows) for cracks and damage

26.2 Check the exhaust system rubber hangers (arrow) for damage

6　While the coolant is draining, check the condition of the radiator hoses, heater hoses and clamps (refer to Section 13 if necessary).

7　Replace any damaged clamps or hoses (see Chapter 3).

Flushing

8　Once the system is completely drained, flush the radiator with fresh water from a garden hose until water runs clear at the drain. The flushing action of the water will remove sediments from the radiator but will not remove rust and scale from the engine and cooling tube surfaces.

9　These deposits can be removed by the chemical action of a cleaner. Follow the procedure outlined in the manufacturer's instructions. If the radiator is severely corroded, damaged or leaking, it should be removed (see Chapter 3) and taken to a radiator repair shop.

10　Remove the overflow hose from the coolant recovery reservoir. Drain the reservoir and flush it with clean water, then reconnect the hose.

Refilling

11　Close and tighten the radiator drain. Install and tighten the block drain plug.

12　Place the heater temperature control in the maximum heat position.

13　Slowly add new coolant (a 50/50 mixture of water and antifreeze) to the radiator until it's full. Add coolant to the reservoir up to the lower mark.

14　Leave the radiator cap off and run the engine in a well-ventilated area until the thermostat opens (coolant will begin flowing through the radiator and the upper radiator hose will become hot).

15　Turn the engine off and let it cool. Add more coolant mixture to bring the level back up to the lip on the radiator filler neck.

16　Squeeze the upper radiator hose to expel air, then add more coolant mixture if necessary. Replace the radiator cap.

17　Start the engine, allow it to reach normal operating temperature and check for leaks.

25　Evaporative emissions control system check (every 30,000 miles or 24 months)

Refer to illustration 25.2

1　The function of the evaporative emissions control system is to draw fuel vapors from the gas tank and fuel system, store them in a charcoal canister and then burn them during normal engine operation.

2　The most common symptom of a fault in the evaporative emissions system is a strong fuel odor in the engine compartment. If a fuel odor is detected, inspect the charcoal canister, located at the front of the engine compartment. Check the canister and all hoses for damage and deterioration **(see illustration)**.

3　The evaporative emissions control system is explained in more detail in Chapter 6.

26　Exhaust system check (every 30,000 miles or 24 months)

Refer to illustration 26.2

1　With the engine cold (at least three hours after the vehicle has been driven), check the complete exhaust system from its starting point at the engine to the end of the tailpipe. This should be done on a hoist where unrestricted access is available.

2　Check the pipes and connections for evidence of leaks, severe corrosion or damage. Make sure that all brackets and hangers are in good condition and tight **(see illustration)**.

3　At the same time, inspect the underside of the body for holes, corrosion, open seams, etc. which may allow exhaust gases to enter the passenger compartment. Seal all body openings with silicone or body putty.

4　Rattles and other noises can often be traced to the exhaust system, especially the mounts and hangers. Try to move the pipes, muffler and catalytic converter. If the components can come in contact with the body or suspension parts, secure the exhaust system with new mounts.

5　Check the running condition of the engine by inspecting inside the end of the tailpipe. The exhaust deposits here are an indication of engine state-of-tune. If the pipe is black and sooty or coated with white deposits, the engine is in need of a tune-up, including a thorough fuel system inspection.

27　Automatic transaxle fluid/differential lubricant change and strainer cleaning (every 30,000 miles or 24 months)

Refer to illustrations 27.7, 27.8a, 27.8b, 27.9, 27.12 and 27.14

1　At the specified time intervals, the automatic transaxle and differential fluid should be drained and replaced.

Note: *Although the manufacturer doesn't specify it, it is a good idea to periodically clean the transaxle fluid strainer periodically to remove accumulated dirt and metal particles.*

2　Before beginning work, purchase the specified transmission fluid (see *Recommended fluids and lubricants* at the front of this chapter).

3　Other tools necessary for this job include jackstands to support the vehicle in a raised position, a 10 mm Allen wrench, a drain pan capable of holding at least eight pints, newspapers and clean rags.

Draining fluid

4　The fluid should be drained immediately after the vehicle has been driven. Hot fluid is more effective than cold fluid at removing built up sediment. **Warning:** *Fluid temperature can exceed 350-degrees F in a hot transaxle. Wear protective gloves.*

27.7 Use a 10 mm hex bit or Allen wrench to remove the automatic transaxle drain plug

27.8a After loosening the front bolts, remove the rear pan bolts and . . .

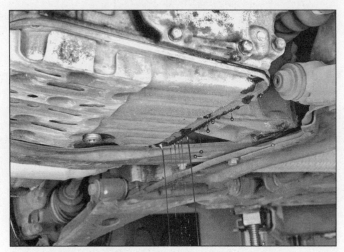

27.8b . . . allow the remaining fluid to drain out

27.9 Remove the strainer bolts and lower the strainer (be careful, there will be some residual fluid)

5   After the vehicle has been driven to warm up the fluid, raise it and place it on jackstands for access to the transaxle and differential drain plugs.
6   Move the necessary equipment under the vehicle, being careful not to touch any of the hot exhaust components.
7   Place the drain pan under the drain plug in the transaxle pan and remove the drain plug with the Allen wrench **(see illustration)**. Be sure the drain pan is in position, as fluid will come out with some force. Once the fluid is drained, reinstall the drain plug securely. If you aren't going to clean the strainer, proceed to Step 14.

Strainer cleaning

8   Remove the front transaxle pan bolts, then loosen the rear bolts and carefully pry the pan loose with a screwdriver and allow the remaining fluid to drain **(see illustrations)**. Once the fluid had drained, remove the bolts and lower the pan.
9   Remove the strainer retaining bolts, disconnect the clip (some models) and lower the strainer from the transaxle **(see illustration)**. Be careful when lowering the strainer as it contains residual fluid.
10   Wash the strainer thoroughly in clean transmission fluid.
11   Place the strainer in position, connect the clip (if equipped) and install the bolts. Tighten the bolts to the torque listed in this Chapter's Specifications.
12   Carefully clean the gasket surfaces of the fluid pan, removing all traces of old gasket material. Noting their location, remove the magnets, wash the pan in clean solvent and dry it with compressed air.

27.12 Noting their locations, remove the magnets and wash them and the pan in solvent before installing them

Be sure to clean and reinstall the magnets in the pan **(see illustration)**.
13   Install a new gasket, place the fluid pan in position and install the bolts in their original positions. Tighten the bolts to the torque listed in this Chapter's Specifications.

27.14 Remove the automatic transaxle differential drain plug with a hex bit or Allen wrench

29.1a Periodically check the tightness of the nuts and bolts on the front seats as well as . . .

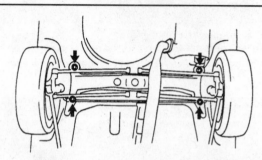

29.1c . . . and rear suspension mounts

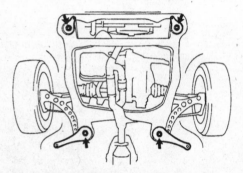

29.1b . . . the front suspension member . . .

Differential fluid replacement

14   Find the differential drain plug. Place the drain pan underneath the plug, remove it with an Allen wrench and drain the fluid **(see illustration)**. When the differential fluid has drained, reinstall the plug securely.

15   Referring to Section 19, add new fluid to the differential until it begins to run out of the filler hole (see *Recommended lubricants and fluids* at the beginning of this Chapter for the specified fluid type and capacity). **Caution:** *Do not overfill. The automatic transaxle and the differential are separate units.*

16   Lower the vehicle.

Adding transaxle fluid

17   With the engine off, add new fluid to the transaxle through the dipstick tube (see *Recommended fluids and lubricants* for the recommended fluid type and capacity). Use a funnel to prevent spills. It is best to add a little fluid at a time, continually checking the level with the dipstick (see Section 7). Allow the fluid time to drain into the pan.

18   Start the engine and shift the selector into all positions from P through L, then shift into P and apply the parking brake.

19   With the engine idling, check the fluid level. Add fluid up to the Cool level on the dipstick.

28   Manual transaxle lubricant change (every 30,000 miles or 24 months)

1   Remove the drain plug(s) and drain the fluid.
2   Reinstall the drain plug(s) securely.
3   Add new fluid until it begins to run out of the filler hole (Section 20). See *Recommended lubricants and fluids* for the specified lubricant type.

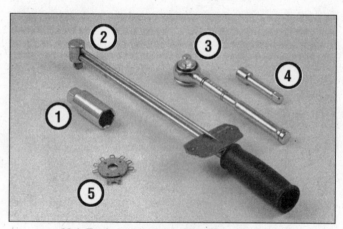

30.1 Tools required for changing spark plugs

1   **Spark plug socket** - *This will have special padding inside to protect the spark plug's porcelain insulator*
2   **Torque wrench** - *Although not mandatory, using this tool is the best way to ensure the plugs are tightened properly*
3   **Ratchet** - *Standard hand tool to fit the spark plug socket*
4   **Extension** - *Depending on model and accessories, you may need special extensions and universal joints to reach one or more of the plugs*
5   **Spark plug gap gauge** - *This gauge for checking the gap comes in a variety of styles. Make sure the gap for your engine is included*

29   Chassis and body fastener check (every 30,000 miles or 24 months)

Refer to illustrations 29.1a, 29.1b and 29.1c

1   Tighten the following parts to the torque values listed in this Chapter's Specifications: front seat mounting bolts and both front and rear suspension member-to-body mounting bolts and nuts (left and right sides) **(see illustrations)**.

30.4a Spark plug manufacturers recommend using a wire-type gauge when checking the gap - if the wire does not slide between the electrodes with a slight drag, adjustment is required

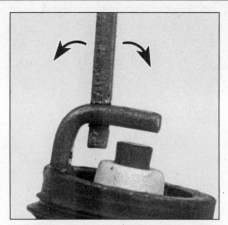

30.4b To change the gap, bend the side electrode only, as indicated by the arrows, and be very careful not to crack or chip the porcelain insulator surrounding the center electrode

30.6 On V6 engines, remove the screws and detach the cover over the front bank spark plugs

30.7a On the 1MZ-FE distributorless engine, remove the retaining bolt . . .

30.7b . . . and detach the coil

30.7c The access to the rear bank spark plugs on distributorless 1MZ-FE engines is very tight and the job may be made easier by removing the intake plenum as shown here

30 Spark plug check and replacement (every 30,000 miles or 24 months)

Refer to illustrations 30.1, 30.4a, 30.4b, 30.6, 30.7a, 30.7b, 30.7c, 30.8, 30.10, 30.12a and 30.12b

1   Spark plug replacement requires a spark plug socket which fits onto a ratchet wrench. This socket is lined with a rubber grommet to protect the porcelain insulator of the spark plug and to hold the plug while you insert it into the spark plug hole. You will also need a wire-type feeler gauge to check and adjust the spark plug gap and a torque wrench to tighten the new plugs to the specified torque **(see illustration)**.

2   If you are replacing the plugs, purchase the new plugs, adjust them to the proper gap and then replace each plug one at a time. **Note:** *The manufacturer specifies that only platinum-tipped spark plugs be used on these models. When buying new spark plugs, it's essential that you obtain the correct plugs for your specific vehicle. This information can be found in the Specifications Section at the beginning of this Chapter, on the Vehicle Emissions Control Information (VECI) label located on the underside of the hood or in the owner's manual. If these sources specify different plugs, purchase the spark plug type specified on the VECI label because that information is provided specifically for your engine.*

3   Inspect each of the new plugs for defects. If there are any signs of cracks in the porcelain insulator of a plug, don't use it.

4   Check the electrode gaps of the new plugs. Check the gap by inserting the wire gauge of the proper thickness between the electrodes at the tip of the plug **(see illustration)**. The gap between the electrodes should be identical to that listed in this Chapter's Specifications or on the VECI label. If the gap is incorrect, use the notched adjuster on the feeler gauge body to bend the curved side electrode slightly **(see illustration)**.

5   If the side electrode is not exactly over the center electrode, use the notched adjuster to align them. **Caution:** *If the gap of a new plug must be adjusted, bend only the base of the ground electrode - do not touch the tip.*

Removal

6   On V6 engines, use a 5 mm Allen wrench to remove the two bolts and detach the engine V-bank spark plug cover **(see illustration)**. For access to the rear bank plugs on V6 engines, disconnect any hoses or components that would interfere with access and move them out of the way.

7   On distributorless models, remove the bolt and detach the coil/wire assembly from the spark plug **(see illustrations)**. The rear bank spark plugs on distributorless models are a very tight fit. Even though it may mean more work initially, the job may actually be made easier in the long run by removing the intake plenum (Chapter 4) **(see illustration)**.

30.8 When removing spark plug wires, pull only on the boot using a twisting/pulling motion

30.10 Because they are deeply recessed, the proper spark plug socket and an extension will be required when removing or installing the spark plugs

30.12a A light coat of anti-seize compound applied to the threads of the spark plugs will keep the threads in the cylinder head from being damaged the next time the plugs are removed

8   To prevent the possibility of mixing up spark plug wires on models with distributors, work on one spark plug at a time. Remove the wire and boot from one spark plug. Grasp the boot - not the cable - as shown, give it a half twisting motion and pull straight up **(see illustration)**.

9   If compressed air is available, blow any dirt or foreign material away from the spark plug area before proceeding (a common bicycle pump will also work).

10   Remove the spark plug **(see illustration)**.

11   Whether you are replacing the plugs at this time or intend to re-use the old plugs, compare each old spark plug with those shown on the inside of the back cover to determine the overall running condition of the engine.

Installation

12   Apply a small amount of anti-seize compound to the spark plug threads **(see illustration)**. It's often difficult to insert spark plugs into their holes without cross-threading them. To avoid this possibility, fit a short piece of 3/8-inch ID rubber hose over the end of the spark plug **(see illustration)**. The flexible hose acts as a universal joint to help align the plug with the plug hole. Should the plug begin to cross-thread, the hose will slip on the spark plug, preventing thread damage. Tighten the plug to the torque listed in this Chapter's Specifications.

13   Attach the plug wire to the new spark plug, again using a twisting motion on the boot until it is firmly seated on the end of the spark plug.

14   Follow the above procedure for the remaining spark plugs, replacing them one at a time to prevent mixing up the spark plug wires.

31   Spark plug wire, distributor cap and rotor check and replacement (every 30,000 miles or 24 months)

Refer to illustrations 31.11, 31.12 and 31.13
Note: *On models without a distributor, the only check possible is of the coil wiring and spark plug connection.*

1   The spark plug wires should be checked whenever new spark plugs are installed.

2   Begin this procedure by making a visual check of the spark plug wires while the engine is running. In a darkened garage (make sure there is ventilation) start the engine and observe each plug wire. Be careful not to come into contact with any moving engine parts. If there is a break in the wire, you will see arcing or a small spark at the damaged area. If arcing is noticed, make a note to obtain new wires, then allow the engine to cool and check the distributor cap and rotor.

3   The spark plug wires should be inspected one at a time to prevent mixing up the order, which is essential for proper engine operation. Each original plug wire should be numbered to help identify its location. If the number is illegible, a piece of tape can be marked with

30.12b A piece of 3/8-inch rubber hose will aid in getting the spark plug started in the hole

the correct number and wrapped around the plug wire.

4   Disconnect the plug wire from the spark plug. A removal tool can be used for this purpose or you can grasp the rubber boot, twist the boot half a turn and pull the boot free. Do not pull on the wire itself.

5   Check inside the boot for corrosion, which will look like a white crusty powder.

6   Push the wire and boot back onto the end of the spark plug. It should fit tightly onto the end of the plug. If it doesn't, remove the wire and use pliers to carefully crimp the metal connector inside the wire boot until the fit is snug.

7   Using a clean rag, wipe the entire length of the wire to remove built-up dirt and grease. Once the wire is clean, check for burns, cracks and other damage. Do not bend the wire sharply, because the conductor might break.

8   Disconnect the wire from the distributor. Again, pull only on the rubber boot. Check for corrosion and a tight fit. Replace the wire in the distributor.

9   Inspect the remaining spark plug wires, making sure that each one is securely fastened at the distributor and spark plug when the check is complete.

10   If new spark plug wires are required, purchase a set for your specific engine model. Pre-cut wire sets with the boots already installed are available. Remove and replace the wires one at a time to avoid mix-ups in the firing order.

11   Detach the distributor cap by removing the two cap retaining bolts (see the distributor exploded views in Chapter 5 if necessary). Look inside it for cracks, carbon tracks and worn, burned or loose contacts **(see illustration)**.

12   Pull the rotor off the distributor shaft and examine it for cracks and carbon tracks **(see illustration)**. Replace the cap and rotor if any damage or defects are noted.

13   It is common practice to install a new cap and rotor whenever new spark plug wires are installed, but if you wish to continue using the old cap, check the resistance between the spark plug wires and the

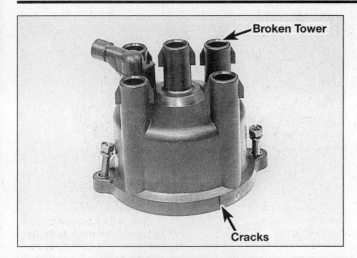

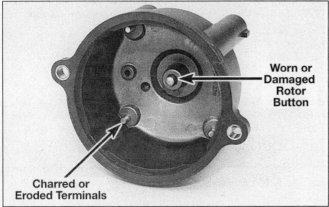

31.11 Shown here are some of the common defects to look for when inspecting the distributor cap (if in doubt about its condition, install a new one)

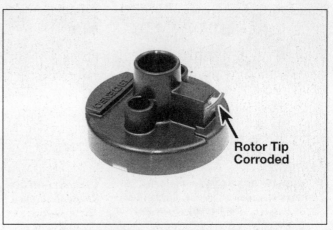

31.12 The ignition rotor should be checked for wear and corrosion as indicated here (if in doubt about its condition, buy a new one)

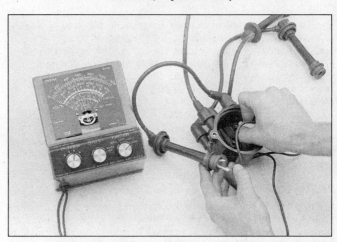

31.13 Measure the resistance value of the distributor cap and the spark plug wires - if it exceeds the specified maximum value, replace either the cap, or the wires, or both

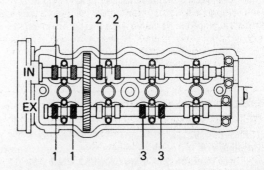

32.7a On four-cylinder engines, when the no. 1 piston is at TDC on the compression stroke, the valve clearance for the no. 1 and no. 3 cylinder exhaust valves and the no. 1 and no. 2 cylinder intake valves can be measured

cap first **(see illustration)**. If the indicated resistance is more than the maximum value listed in this Chapter's Specifications, replace the cap and/or wires.

14   When installing a new cap, remove the wires from the old cap one at a time and attach them to the new cap in the exact same location - do not simultaneously remove all the wires from the old cap or firing order mix-ups may occur.

32   Valve clearance check and adjustment (every 60,000 miles or 48 months)

Refer to illustrations 32.7a, 32.7b, 32.7c, 32.7d, 32.8, 32.9a, 32.9b, 32.9c, 32.9d, 32.11a, 32.11b, 32.11c and 32.12
Note: *The following procedure requires the use of a special valve lifter tool. It is impossible to perform this task without it.*
1   Disconnect the negative cable from the battery. **Caution:** *If the stereo in your vehicle is equipped with an anti-theft system, make sure you have the correct activation code before disconnecting the battery.* **Note:** *On 1993 and later models, the airbag system will be disabled if the battery is disconnected for more than a brief period. If the airbag light comes on and stays on after the battery is reconnected, the vehicle must be taken to a dealer to have the system reset with a special tool.*
2   On four-cylinder models, disconnect the spark plug wires (Section 31) and remove any other components that will interfere with valve cover removal.
3   On V6 engines, drain the coolant (Section 24), remove the air cleaner assembly and air intake plenum (Chapter 4) and any other components that will interfere with valve cover removal.
4   Blow out the recessed area between the camshafts with

compressed air, if available, to remove any debris that might fall into the cylinders, then remove the spark plugs (see Section 30).
5   Remove the valve cover(s) (refer to Chapter 2).
6   Refer to Chapter 2 and position the number 1 piston at TDC on the compression stroke.
7   Measure the clearance of the indicated valves with a feeler gauge of the specified thickness **(see illustrations)**. Record the measurements which are out of specification. They will be used later to determine the required replacement shims.

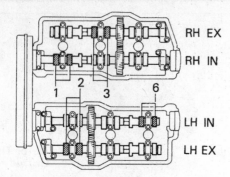

32.7b On the 3VZ-FE V6 engine, when the no. 1 piston is at TDC on the compression stroke, the valve clearance of the valves indicated can be measured

32.7d Measure the clearance for each valve with a feeler gauge of the specified thickness - if the clearance is correct, you should feel a slight drag on the gauge as you pull it out

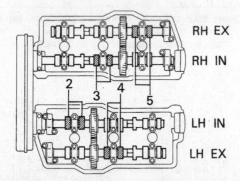

32.9a Rotate the 3VZ-FE V6 engine 240-degrees from TDC for the no. 1 piston on the compression stroke, and measure the clearance of the valves indicated

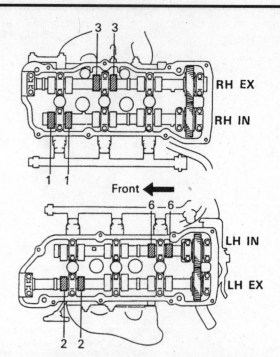

32.7c On the 1MZ-FE V6 engine, when the no. 1 piston is at TDC on the compression stroke, the clearance of the indicated valves can be measured

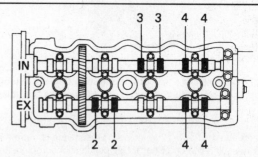

32.8 On four-cylinder engines, when the no. 4 piston is at TDC on the compression stroke, the valve clearance for the no. 2 and no. 4 exhaust valves and the no. 3 and no. 4 intake valves can be measured

8   On four-cylinder engines, turn the crankshaft one complete revolution and realign the timing marks. Measure the remaining valves **(see illustration).**

9   On V6 engines, turn the crankshaft 2/3-turn (240-degrees) clockwise. Measure the valve clearance on the valves shown **(see illustrations)**. Rotate the crankshaft a further 2/3-turn and measure the clearance on the remaining valves **(see illustrations).**

10   After all the valves have been measured, turn the crankshaft pulley until the camshaft lobe above the first valve which you intend to adjust is pointing upward, away from the shim.

11   Position the notch in the valve lifter toward the spark plug. Then depress the valve lifter with the special valve lifter tools **(see illustrations)**. Place the special valve lifter tool in position as shown, with the

longer jaw of the tool gripping the lower edge of the cast lifter boss and the upper, shorter jaw gripping the upper edge of the lifter itself. Depress the valve lifter by squeezing the handles of the valve lifter tool together, then hold the lifter down with the smaller tool and remove the larger one. Remove the adjusting shim with a small screwdriver or a pair of tweezers **(see illustrations)**. Note that the wire hook on the end of some valve lifter tool handles can be used to clamp both handles together to keep the lifter depressed while the shim is removed.

12   Measure the thickness of the shim with a micrometer **(see illustration)**. To calculate the correct thickness of a replacement shim that will place the valve clearance within the specified value, use the following formula:

$$N = T + (A - V)$$

T = thickness of the old shim
A = valve clearance measured
N = thickness of the new shim

V = desired valve clearance (see this Chapters Specifications)

13   Select a shim with a thickness as close as possible to the valve clearance calculated. Shims, which are available in 17 sizes in increments of 0.0020-inch (0.050 mm), range in size from 0.0984-inch (2.500 mm) to 0.1299-inch (3.300 mm). **Note:** *Through careful analysis*

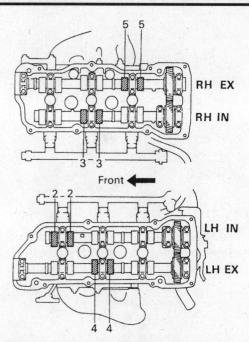

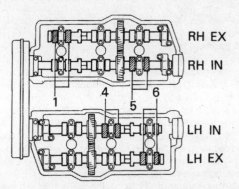

32.9c On the 3VZ-FE V6 engine, rotate the crankshaft and additional 2/3 of a revolution (240-degrees) and measure the clearance of the remaining valves

32.9b After the 1MZ-FE V6 engine has been rotated 240-degrees from TDC for the no. 1 piston, on the compression stroke, measure the clearance of the indicated valves

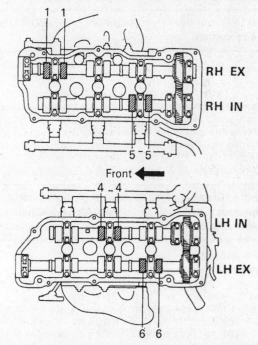

32.9d On the 1MZ-FE V6 engine, rotate the crankshaft an additional 2/3 of a revolution (240-degrees) and measure the clearance of the remaining valves

32.11a Install the valve lifter tool as shown and squeeze the handles together to depress the valve lifter, then hold the lifter down with the smaller tool so the shim can be removed

32.11b Keep pressure on the lifter with the smaller tool and remove the shim with a small screwdriver . . .

32.11c . . . a pair of tweezers or a magnet as shown here

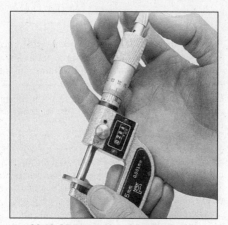

32.12 Measure the shim thickness with a micrometer

1

of the shim sizes needed to bring the out-of-specification valve clearance within specification, it is often possible to simply move a shim that has to come out anyway to another valve lifter requiring a shim of that particular size, thereby reducing the number of new shims that must be purchased.

14   Place the special valve lifter tool in position as shown in illustration 32.11a, with the longer jaw of the tool gripping the lower edge of the cast lifter boss and the upper, shorter jaw gripping the upper edge of the lifter itself, press down the valve lifter by squeezing the handles of the valve lifter tool together and install the new adjusting shim (note that the wire hook on the end of one valve lifter tool handle can be used to clamp the handles together to keep the lifter depressed while the shim is inserted). Measure the clearance with a feeler gauge to make sure that your calculations are correct.

15   Repeat this procedure until all the valves which are out of clearance have been corrected.

16   Installation of the spark plugs, valve cover, spark plug wires and boots, accelerator cable bracket, etc. is the reverse of removal.

33   Fuel tank cap gasket replacement (every 60,000 miles or 48 months)

Refer to illustration 33.2

1   Obtain a new gasket.

2   Remove the tank cap and carefully pry the old gasket out of the recess **(see illustration)**. Be very careful not to damage the sealing surface inside the cap.

3   Work the new gasket into the cap recess.

4   Install the cap, then remove it and make sure the gasket seals all the way around.

34   Positive Crankcase Ventilation (PCV) valve and hose check and replacement (every 60,000 miles or 48 months)

Refer to illustration 34.4

1   The PCV valve and hose is located in the valve cover.

2   Disconnect the hose, pull the PCV valve from the cover, then reconnect the hose.

3   With the engine idling at normal operating temperature, place your finger over the valve opening. If there's no vacuum at the valve, check for a plugged hose or valve. Replace any plugged or deteriorated hoses.

4   Turn off the engine. Remove the PCV valve from the hose. Blow

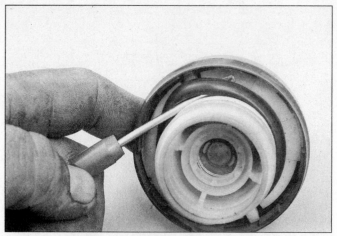

33.2 Use a small screwdriver to carefully pry out the old gasket - take care not to damage the cap

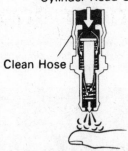

Cylinder Head Side

Clean Hose

34.4 To check the PCV valve, first attach a clean section of hose to the cylinder head side of the valve and blow through it - air should pass through easily - then blow through the opposite side of the valve and verify that air doesn't pass through it

through the valve from the valve cover (cylinder head) end. If air will not pass through the valve in this direction, replace it with a new one **(see illustration)**.

5   When purchasing a replacement PCV valve, make sure it's for your particular vehicle and engine size. Compare the old valve with the new one to make sure they're the same.

Chapter 2 Part A
Four-cylinder engine

Contents

Specifications

General

Engine type

5S-FE	DOHC, inline four-cylinder, four valves per cylinder
Cylinder numbers (drivebelt end-to-transaxle end)	1-2-3-4
Firing order	1-3-4-2

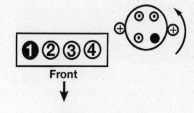

Cylinder location and distributor rotation

Cylinder head

Warpage limits

Cylinder head-to-block surface	0.020 inch
Intake and exhaust manifolds	0.0118 inch

Timing belt

Idler pulley spring free length	1.811 inches

Camshaft

Journal diameter (all)	1.0614 to 1.0620 inches

Bearing oil clearance

Standard	0.0010 to 0.0024 inch
Service limit	0.0039 inch
Runout limit	0.0016 inch

Camshaft (continued)

Lobe height	
Intake camshaft	
Standard	1.6539 to 1.6579 inches
Service limit	1.6496 inches
Exhaust camshaft	
Standard	1.5722 to 1.5811 inches
Service limit	1.5728 inches
Camshaft thrust clearance (endplay)	
Intake camshaft	
Standard	0.0018 to 0.0039 inch
Service limit	0.0047 inch
Exhaust camshaft	
Standard	0.0012 to 0.0033 inch
Service limit	0.0039 inch
Camshaft gear spring free length	0.886 to 0.902 inch
Camshaft gear backlash	
Standard	0.0008 to 0.0079 inch
Service limit	0.0188 inch
Valve lifter	
Diameter	1.2191 to 1.2195 inches
Bore diameter	1.2205 to 1.2212 inches
Lifter oil clearance	
Standard	0.0009 to 0.0020 inch
Service limit	0.0028 inch

Oil pump

Driven rotor-to-case clearance	
Standard	0.0039 to 0.0063 inch
Service limit	0.0079 inch
Rotor tip clearance	
Standard	0.0016 to 0.0063 inch
Service limit	0.0079 inch

Torque specifications

	Ft-lbs (unless otherwise indicated)
Intake manifold nuts/bolts	14
Intake manifold brace bolts	
at manifold	16
at block	31
Exhaust manifold nuts/bolts	36
Crankshaft pulley-to-crankshaft bolt	80
Flywheel/driveplate bolts	
Flywheel (manual transaxle)	65
Driveplate (automatic transaxle)	61
Idler pulley bolts	31
Cylinder head bolts	
Step 1	36
Step 2	Turn an additional 90-degrees (1/4 turn)
Camshaft bearing cap bolts	14
Camshaft sprocket bolt	40
Oil pump bolts	82 in-lbs
Oil pump sprocket nut	21
Oil pick-up (strainer) nuts/bolts	48 in-lbs
Oil pan-to-block bolts	48 in-lbs
Spark plug tube nuts	29
Rear crankshaft oil seal retainer bolts	82 in-lbs

1   General information

This Part of Chapter 2 is devoted to in-vehicle repair procedures for the four-cylinder engines. All information concerning engine removal and installation and engine block and cylinder head overhaul can be found in Part C of this Chapter.

The following repair procedures are based on the assumption that the engine is installed in the vehicle. If the engine has been removed from the vehicle and mounted on a stand, many of the steps outlined in this Part of Chapter 2 will not apply.

The Specifications included in this Part of Chapter 2 apply only to the procedures contained in this Part. Part C of Chapter 2 contains the Specifications necessary for cylinder head and engine block rebuilding.

During the years covered by this manual, the four-cylinder engine in the Camry is designated the 5S-FE, which is a slightly larger and improved version of the four-cylinder engine in previous models. The engine design includes dual overhead camshafts (DOHC) and four valves per cylinder.

2 Repair operations possible with the engine in the vehicle

Many major repair operations can be accomplished without removing the engine from the vehicle.

Clean the engine compartment and the exterior of the engine with some type of degreaser before any work is done. It will make the job easier and help keep dirt out of the internal areas of the engine.

Depending on the components involved, it may be helpful to remove the hood to improve access to the engine as repairs are performed (refer to Chapter 11 if necessary). Cover the fenders to prevent damage to the paint. Special pads are available, but an old bedspread or blanket will also work.

If vacuum, exhaust, oil or coolant leaks develop, indicating a need for gasket or seal replacement, the repairs can generally be made with the engine in the vehicle. The intake and exhaust manifold gaskets, oil pan gasket, crankshaft oil seals and cylinder head gasket are all accessible with the engine in place.

Exterior engine components, such as the intake and exhaust manifolds, the oil pan, the oil pump, the water pump, the starter motor, the alternator, the distributor and the fuel system components can be removed for repair with the engine in place.

Since the cylinder head can be removed without pulling the engine, camshaft and valve component servicing can also be accomplished with the engine in the vehicle. Replacement of the timing belt and pulleys is also possible with the engine in the vehicle.

In extreme cases caused by a lack of necessary equipment, repair or replacement of piston rings, pistons, connecting rods and rod bearings is possible with the engine in the vehicle. However, this practice is not recommended because of the cleaning and preparation work that must be done to the components involved.

3 Top Dead Center (TDC) for number one piston - locating

Refer to illustration 3.8

Note: *The following procedure is based on the assumption that the distributor is correctly installed. If you are trying to locate TDC to install the distributor correctly, piston position must be determined by feeling for compression at the number one spark plug hole, then aligning the ignition timing marks as described in step 8.*

1 Top Dead Center (TDC) is the highest point in the cylinder that each piston reaches as it travels up the cylinder bore. Each piston reaches TDC on the compression stroke and again on the exhaust stroke, but TDC generally refers to piston position on the compression stroke.

2 Positioning the piston(s) at TDC is an essential part of many procedures such as camshaft and timing belt/pulley removal and distributor removal.

3 Before beginning this procedure, be sure to place the transmission in Neutral and apply the parking brake or block the rear wheels. Also, disable the ignition system by detaching the coil wire from the center terminal of the distributor cap and grounding it on the block with a jumper wire. Remove the spark plugs (see Chapter 1).

4 In order to bring any piston to TDC, the crankshaft must be turned using one of the methods outlined below. When looking at the front of the engine, normal crankshaft rotation is clockwise.

a) *The preferred method is to turn the crankshaft with a socket and ratchet attached to the bolt threaded into the front of the crankshaft. Apply pressure on the bolt in a clockwise direction only. Never turn the bolt counterclockwise.*

b) *A remote starter switch, which may save some time, can also be used. Follow the instructions included with the switch. Once the piston is close to TDC, use a socket and ratchet as described in the previous paragraph.*

3.8 Align the crankshaft drivebelt pulley notch (arrow) with the 0 (zero) on the timing plate

c) *If an assistant is available to turn the ignition switch to the Start position in short bursts, you can get the piston close to TDC without a remote starter switch. Make sure your assistant is out of the vehicle, away from the ignition switch, then use a socket and ratchet as described in Paragraph a) to complete the procedure.*

5 Note the position of the terminal for the number one spark plug wire on the distributor cap. If the terminal isn't marked, follow the plug wire from the number one cylinder spark plug to the cap.

6 Use a felt-tip pen or chalk to make a mark on the distributor body directly under the number one terminal.

7 Detach the cap from the distributor and set it aside (see Chapter 1 if necessary).

8 Turn the crankshaft until the notch in the crankshaft pulley is aligned with the 0 on the timing plate located at the front of the engine **(see illustration)**.

9 Look at the distributor rotor - it should be pointing directly at the mark you made on the distributor body.

10 If the rotor is 180-degrees off, the number one piston is at TDC on the exhaust stroke.

11 To get the piston to TDC on the compression stroke, turn the crankshaft one complete turn (360-degrees) clockwise. The rotor should now be pointing at the mark on the distributor. When the rotor is pointing at the number one spark plug wire terminal in the distributor cap and the ignition timing marks are aligned, the number one piston is at TDC on the compression stroke. **Note:** *If it's impossible to align the ignition timing marks when the rotor is pointing at the mark on the distributor body, the timing belt may have jumped the teeth on the pulleys or may have been installed incorrectly.*

12 After the number one piston has been positioned at TDC on the compression stroke, TDC for any of the remaining pistons can be located by turning the crankshaft and following the firing order. Mark the remaining spark plug wire terminal locations on the distributor body just like you did for the number one terminal, then number the marks to correspond with the cylinder numbers. As you turn the crankshaft, the rotor will also turn. When it's pointing directly at one of the marks on the distributor, the piston for that particular cylinder is at TDC on the compression stroke.

4 Valve cover - removal and installation

Refer to illustrations 4.4, 4.5a, 4.5b and 4.7

Removal

1 Disconnect the negative cable from the battery. **Caution:** *If the stereo in your vehicle is equipped with an anti-theft system, make sure you have the correct activation code before disconnecting the battery.*

Note: *On 1993 and later models, the airbag system will be disabled if the battery is disconnected for more than a brief period. If the airbag light comes on and stays on after the battery is reconnected, the vehicle must be taken to a dealer to have the system reset with a special tool.*

2   Detach the breather hose from the valve cover.

3   Remove the spark plug wires from the spark plugs, handling them by the boots, not pulling on the wires.

4   Remove or partly unscrew two of the upper timing belt cover bolts to allow the engine wiring harness **(see illustration)** to be pulled up out

4.4 Retract two of the upper timing belt cover bolts, allowing the wiring harness to be pulled up and clear of the valve cover

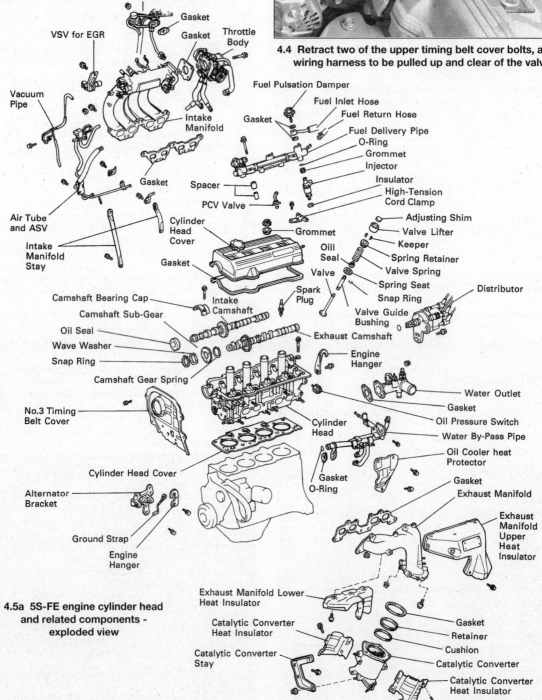

4.5a 5S-FE engine cylinder head and related components - exploded view

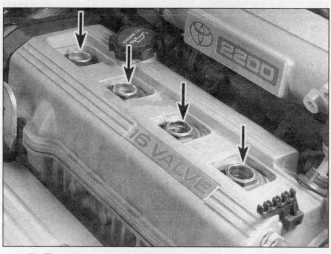

4.5b The valve cover is held in place by the large spark plug tube nuts (arrows)

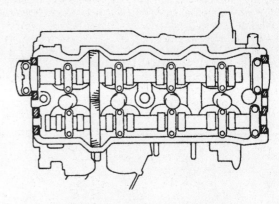

4.7 Apply sealant to the eight points indicated by the shaded areas before installing the valve cover

of the way.

5   Remove the spark plug tube nuts, then detach the cover and gasket from the head. The spark plug tube nuts are used to hold the cover in place **(see illustrations)**. If the cover is stuck to the head, bump the end with a block of wood and a hammer to jar it loose. If that doesn't work, try to slip a flexible putty knife between the head and cover to break the seal. **Caution:** *Don't pry at the cover-to-head joint or damage to the sealing surfaces may occur, leading to oil leaks after the cover is reinstalled.*

Installation

6   The mating surfaces of the housing or cylinder head and cover must be clean when the cover is installed. Use a gasket scraper to remove all traces of sealant and old gasket material, then clean the mating surfaces with lacquer thinner or acetone. If there's residue or oil on the mating surfaces when the cover is installed, oil leaks may develop.

7   Apply RTV sealant to the gasket/seal joints **(see illustration)**. Install the spark plug tube grommets in the valve cover with the index marks facing the timing belt end of the engine.

8   Position a new gasket on the cylinder head, then install the valve cover and nuts.

9   Tighten the nuts to the specified torque in three or four equal steps.

10   Reinstall the remaining parts, run the engine and check for oil leaks.

5   Intake manifold - removal and installation

Refer to illustrations 5.4a, 5.4b, and 5.8

Removal

1   Disconnect the negative cable from the battery. **Caution:** *If the stereo in your vehicle is equipped with an anti-theft system, make sure you have the correct activation code before disconnecting the battery.* **Note:** *On 1993 and later models, the airbag system will be disabled if the battery is disconnected for more than a brief period. If the airbag light comes on and stays on after the battery is reconnected, the vehicle must be taken to a dealer to have the system reset with a special tool.*

2   Drain the cooling system (see Chapter 1).

3   Loosen the air cleaner hose clamp at the throttle body and remove the air cleaner top (four clamps), resonator and hose.

4   Label and detach any wire harness, control cables or hoses connected to the intake manifold **(see illustrations)**.

5   Carefully lift the wire harness over the manifold.

6   Unbolt any braces still in place.

7   Remove the mounting nuts/bolts, then detach the manifold from the engine.

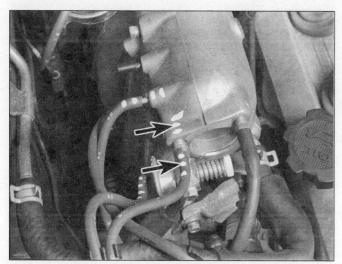

5.4a The various hoses should be marked to ensure correct reinstallation

5.4b Press in on the clips to release the wiring harness retainers

2A

5.8 Remove all traces of old gasket material and sealant with a scraper - be careful not to gouge the aluminum manifold

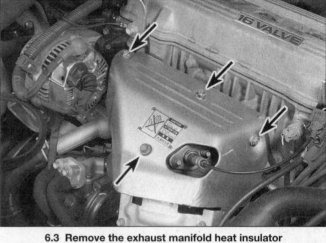

6.3 Remove the exhaust manifold heat insulator bolts (arrows)

Installation

8   Use a scraper to remove all traces of old gasket material and sealant from the manifold and cylinder head **(see illustration)**, then clean the mating surfaces with lacquer thinner or acetone. If the gasket was leaking, have the manifold checked for warpage at an automotive machine shop and resurfaced if necessary.

9   Install a new gasket, then position the manifold on the head and install the nuts/bolts.

10   Tighten the nuts/bolts in three or four equal steps to the torque listed in this Chapter's Specifications. Work from the center out towards the ends to avoid warping the manifold.

11   Install the remaining parts in the reverse order of removal.

12   Before starting the engine, check the throttle linkage for smooth operation.

13   Run the engine and check for coolant and vacuum leaks.

14   Road test the vehicle and check for proper operation of all accessories, including the cruise control system.

6   Exhaust manifold - removal and installation

Refer to illustrations 6.3 and 6.7

Warning: *The engine must be completely cool before beginning this procedure.*

Removal

1   Disconnect the negative cable from the battery. **Caution:** *If the stereo in your vehicle is equipped with an anti-theft system, make sure you have the correct activation code before disconnecting the battery.* **Note:** *On 1993 and later models, the airbag system will be disabled if the battery is disconnected for more than a brief period. If the airbag light comes on and stays on after the battery is reconnected, the vehicle must be taken to a dealer to have the system reset with a special tool.*

2   Unplug the oxygen sensor wire harness. If you're installing a new manifold, remove the sensor (see Chapter 6).

3   Remove the upper heat insulator from the manifold **(see illustration)**.

4   Apply penetrating oil to the exhaust manifold mounting nuts/bolts.

5   Disconnect the catalytic converter from the exhaust manifold (see Chapter 4).

6   Remove the exhaust manifold brace (some models have two braces), ground strap, and lower heat insulator.

7   Remove the nuts/bolts and detach the manifold and gasket **(see illustration)**.

6.7 Remove the exhaust manifold nuts - remove the oil filter for better access to the two exhaust nuts above the oil filter boss

Installation

8   Use a scraper to remove all traces of old gasket material and carbon deposits from the manifold and cylinder head mating surfaces. If the gasket was leaking, have the manifold checked for warpage at an automotive machine shop and resurfaced if necessary.

9   Position a new gasket over the cylinder head studs. **Note:** *The marks on the gasket should face out (away from the head) and the arrow should point toward the rear (transaxle end) of the engine.*

10   Install the manifold and thread the mounting nuts/bolts into place.

11   Working from the center out, tighten the nuts/bolts to the torque listed in this Chapter's Specifications in three or four equal steps.

12   Reinstall the remaining parts in the reverse order of removal.

13   Run the engine and check for exhaust leaks.

7   Timing belt and sprockets - removal, inspection and installation

Removal

Refer to illustrations 7.9a, 7.9b, 7.11, 7.12, 7.13, 7.14, 7.15a, 7.15b, 7.16, 7.17, 7.18a and 7.18b

1   Disconnect the negative cable from the battery. **Caution:** *If the stereo in your vehicle is equipped with an anti-theft system, make sure you have the correct activation code before disconnecting the battery.* **Note:** *On 1993 and later models, the airbag system will be disabled if*

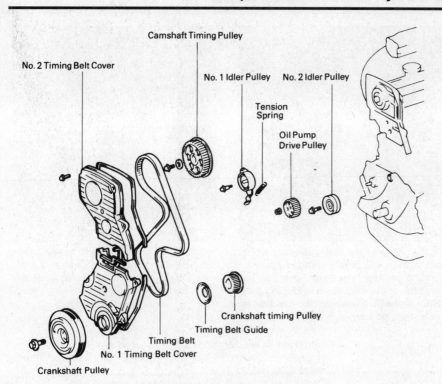

7.9a Four-cylinder engine timing belt components

7.9b Support the engine and remove the right engine mount

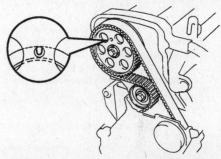

7.11 Align the upper camshaft sprocket timing marks with the number 1 cylinder at TDC

2A

the battery is disconnected for more than a brief period. If the airbag light comes on and stays on after the battery is reconnected, the vehicle must be taken to a dealer to have the system reset with a special tool.

2   Block the rear wheels and set the parking brake.

3   Loosen the lug nuts on the right front wheel and raise the vehicle. Support the front of the vehicle securely on jackstands.

4   Remove the right front wheel and fender apron seal (see Chapter 11).

5   Remove the coolant overflow tank (see Chapter 3).

6   Remove the spark plugs and drivebelts (see Chapter 1).

7   Remove the alternator and bracket (see Chapter 5).

8   Unbolt the power steering reservoir and cruise control actuator (if equipped) and set them aside.

9   Support the engine from underneath with a jack (use a wood block on the jack and don't place the block under the oil pan drain plug) and remove the right engine mount and engine support rod **(see illustrations)**. Note: *If you're planning on removing the oil pan in addition to the timing belt, support the engine with a hoist from above (see Chapter 2C - engine removal).*

10   Remove the upper timing belt cover screws, pull up the wiring harness (see Section 4) and remove the upper (no. 2) timing belt cover and gaskets (see Section 4).

11   Position the number one piston at TDC on the compression stroke (see Section 3). Make sure the small hole in the camshaft pulley is aligned with the TDC mark on the cam bearing cap **(see illustration)**.

12   If you plan to re-use the timing belt, apply match marks on the sprocket and belt and an arrow indicating direction of travel on the belt **(see illustration)**.

13   Loosen the upper (no. 1) idler pulley set bolt and unhook the spring **(see illustration)**. Slip the timing belt off the sprocket. If you're

7.12 If you intend to re-use the timing belt, apply match marks on the sprocket and belt (arrow)

7.13 Loosen the upper idler pulley set bolt (arrow) and unhook the spring

7.14 Remove the valve cover and hold the camshaft with a large wrench on the raised hex as the sprocket bolt is loosened - DO NOT use the timing belt tension to keep the sprocket from turning!

7.15a Remove the flywheel/driveplate cover and use a prybar wedged against the ring gear teeth or a converter bolt to hold the crankshaft while loosening the pulley bolt with a breaker bar - the bolt is very tight, so use the appropriate tools

7.15b Often the crankshaft pulley can be removed with even applications of a pry bar - if you use a puller, it should be the type that attaches to the hub only (do not use a jaw-type puller)

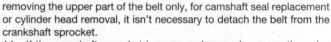

7.16 Remove the lower timing belt cover bolts (arrows) and slip the cover and gaskets off the engine

removing the upper part of the belt only, for camshaft seal replacement or cylinder head removal, it isn't necessary to detach the belt from the crankshaft.

14　If the camshaft sprocket is worn or damaged, remove the valve cover, hold the rear (intake) camshaft with a large wrench and remove the bolt, then detach the sprocket (see illustration).

15　Remove the crankshaft pulley bolt. Wedge a large screwdriver into the flywheel/driveplate ring gear teeth or against a converter bolt to keep the engine from turning. Use a breaker bar and socket to loosen the pulley bolt (see illustration). Remove the bolt and detach the pulley with prybars or a vibration damper puller (see illustration). Do not use a gear puller! Before the pulley is removed completely, double-check that the crankshaft is still at TDC.

16　Remove the lower (no. 1) timing belt cover and gaskets (see illustration) and slip the belt guide off the crankshaft.

17　If you plan to re-use the timing belt, apply match marks on the sprocket and belt (see illustration).

18　Slip the timing belt off the sprocket and remove it. If the sprocket is worn or damaged, or if you need to replace the crankshaft front oil seal, remove the sprocket from the crankshaft (see illustrations).

Inspection

Refer to illustrations 7.19, 7.21, 7.22 and 7.23

Caution: Do not bend, twist or turn the timing belt inside out. Do not allow it to come in contact with oil, coolant or fuel. Do not utilize timing

7.17 If you plan to re-use the timing belt, apply match marks (arrow) on the belt and sprocket

7.18a The crankshaft sprocket should slide off the crankshaft easily

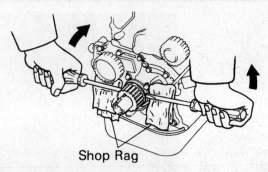

7.18b If the crankshaft sprocket is stuck, protect the oil pump case with rags and pry the sprocket off with two screwdrivers

7.21 Check the timing belt for cracked and missing teeth

belt tension to keep the camshaft or crankshaft from turning when installing the sprocket bolt(s). Do not turn the crankshaft or camshaft more than a few degrees (if necessary for tooth alignment) while the timing belt is removed.

19   Remove the idler pulleys and check the bearings for smooth operation and excessive play. Inspect the spring for damage and compare the free length to this Chapter's Specifications **(see illustration)**.

20   If the timing belt broke during engine operation, the belt may have been contaminated or overtightened.

21   If the belt teeth are cracked or missing **(see illustration)**, the distributor, water pump, oil pump or camshaft(s) may have seized. **Caution:** *If the timing belt broke during engine operation, the valves may have come in contact with the pistons, causing damage. Check the valve clearance (see Chapter 1) - bent valves usually will have excessive clearance, indicating damage that will require head removal to repair.*

22   If there is noticeable wear or cracks on the face of the belt, check to see if there are nicks or burrs on the idler pulleys **(see illustration)**.

23   If there is wear or damage on only one side of the belt, check the belt guide and the alignment of the sprockets **(see illustration)**.

24   Replace the timing belt with a new one if obvious wear or damage is noted or if it is the least bit questionable. Correct any problems which contributed to belt failure prior to belt installation. **Note:** *Professionals recommend replacing the belt whenever it is removed, since belt failure can lead to expensive engine damage. The factory recommends changing the belt at 60,000-mile intervals.*

Installation

Refer to illustrations 7.29, 7.31 and 7.34

25   Remove all dirt, oil and grease from the timing belt area at the front of the engine.

26   If they were removed, install the idler pulleys and tension spring. The upper (no. 1) idler should be pulled back against spring tension as far as possible and the bolt temporarily tightened.

27   Recheck the camshaft and crankshaft timing marks to be sure

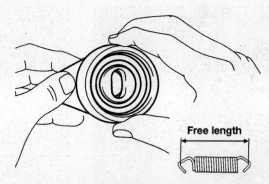

7.19 Check the idler pulley bearing for smooth operation and measure the free length of the tension spring for comparison to this Chapter's Specifications

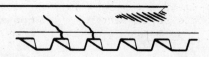

7.22 If the face of the belt is cracked or worn, check the idler pulleys for nicks or burrs

7.23 Wear on one side of the belt indicates sprocket misalignment problems

they are properly aligned (see Step 11).

28   Install the timing belt on the crankshaft, oil pump, water pump and idler pulleys. If the original belt is being reinstalled, align the marks made during removal.

29   Slip the belt guide onto the crankshaft with the cupped side facing out **(see illustration)**.

30   Reinstall the lower timing belt cover and crankshaft pulley and recheck the TDC marks.

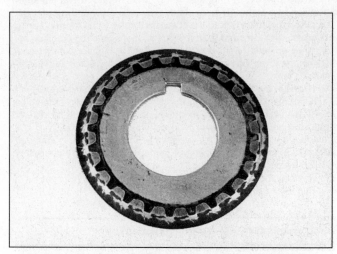

7.29 The belt guide should be installed with the tooth marks in contact with the timing belt and the cupped side facing out

2A

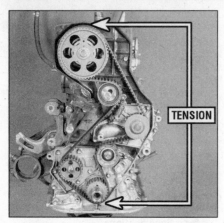

7.31 There should be moderate tension on the side of the belt facing the front of the vehicle

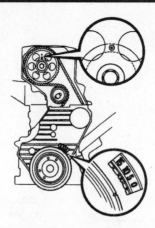

7.34 The marks should align as shown at Top Dead Center

8.2a Wrap tape around the screwdriver tip and carefully work the crankshaft front oil seal out of the bore - DO NOT nick or scratch the crankshaft in the process!

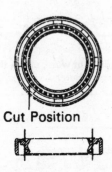

8.2b The seal may be removed more easily by carefully cutting the lip as indicated

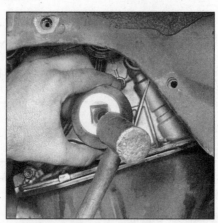

8.4 Gently drive the new seal into place with the spring side installed into the engine

9.3 Carefully pry the camshaft seal out of the bore - DO NOT nick or scratch the camshaft journal

31   Slip the timing belt over the camshaft sprocket. Keep tension on the side nearest the front of the vehicle **(see illustration)**. If the original belt is being reinstalled, align the marks made during removal.

32   Loosen the upper (no. 1) idler pulley bolt 1/2-turn, allowing the spring to apply pressure to the idler pulley.

33   If the tension spring was silver, slowly turn the crankshaft clockwise two complete revolutions (720-degrees), and tighten the idler pulley mounting bolt to the specified torque. If the tension spring was green, turn the crankshaft 1-7/8 revolutions until the crank pulley mark lines up with the 45-degree BTDC (before TDC for number one) mark on the lower belt cover, then tighten the idler pulley to Specifications.

34   Recheck the timing marks **(see illustration)**. With the crankshaft at TDC for number one cylinder, the camshaft sprocket hole must line up with the timing mark. If the marks are not aligned exactly as shown, repeat the belt installation procedure. **Caution:** *DO NOT start the engine until you're absolutely certain that the timing belt is installed correctly. Serious and costly engine damage could occur if the belt is installed wrong.*

35   Reinstall the remaining parts in the reverse order of removal.

36   Run the engine and check for proper operation.

8   Crankshaft front oil seal - replacement

Refer to illustrations 8.2a, 8.2b and 8.4

1   Remove the timing belt and crankshaft sprocket (see Section 7).

2   Note how far the seal is recessed in the bore, then carefully pry it out of the oil pump housing with a screwdriver or seal removal tool **(see illustration)**. Don't scratch the housing bore or damage the crankshaft in the process (if the crankshaft is damaged, the new seal will end up leaking). **Note:** *The seal may be easier to remove if the old seal lip is cut with a sharp utility knife first* **(see illustration)**.

3   Clean the bore in the housing and coat the outer edge of the new seal with engine oil or multi-purpose grease. Apply moly-base grease to the seal lip.

4   Using a socket with an outside diameter slightly smaller than the outside diameter of the seal, carefully drive the new seal into place with a hammer **(see illustration)**. Make sure it's installed squarely and driven in to the same depth as the original. If a socket isn't available, a short section of large diameter pipe will also work. Check the seal after installation to make sure the spring didn't pop out of place.

5   Reinstall the crankshaft sprocket and timing belt (see Section 7).

6   Run the engine and check for oil leaks at the front seal.

9   Camshaft oil seal - replacement

Refer to illustration 9.3

1   Remove the timing belt, upper idler pulley, and camshaft sprocket (see Section 7).

2   Remove the upper timing belt rear cover.

3   Note how far the seal is seated in the bore, then carefully pry it out with a small screwdriver **(see illustration)**. Don't scratch the bore

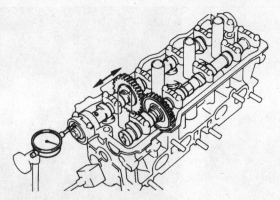

10.4 Mount a dial indicator as shown to measure camshaft endplay

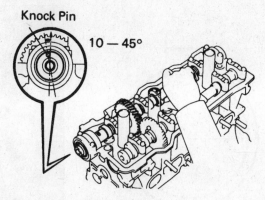

10.5 Turn the INTAKE camshaft until the knock pin is 10 to 45-degrees to the left of vertical (12 o'clock position)

10.6 Install a service bolt through the sub-gear, into the main gear (arrow)

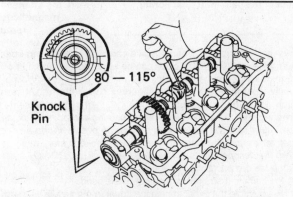

10.11 Turn the intake camshaft until the knock pin is 80 to 115-degrees to the left of vertical (12 o'clock position)

or damage the camshaft in the process (if the camshaft is damaged, the new seal will end up leaking).

4   Clean the bore and coat the outer edge of the new seal with engine oil or multi-purpose grease. Apply multi-purpose grease to the seal lip.

5   Using a socket with an outside diameter slightly smaller than the outside diameter of the seal, carefully drive the new seal into place with a hammer. Make sure it's installed squarely and driven in to the same depth as the original. If a socket isn't available, a short section of pipe will also work.

6   Reinstall the timing belt rear cover, camshaft sprocket, and timing belt (see Section 7).

7   Run the engine and check for oil leaks at the camshaft seal.

10   Camshafts and valve lifters - removal, inspection and installation

Note: *Before beginning this procedure, obtain two 6 x 1.0 mm bolts 16 to 20 mm long. They will be referred to as service bolts in the text.*

Removal

Refer to illustrations 10.4, 10.5, 10.6 and 10.11

1   Remove the valve cover as described in Section 4.

2   Remove the distributor (see Chapter 5).

3   Remove the timing belt, camshaft sprocket, and upper rear belt cover (see Sections 7 and 9).

4   Measure the camshaft thrust clearance (endplay) with a dial

indicator **(see illustration)**. If the clearance is greater than the service limit, replace the camshaft and/or the cylinder head.

Exhaust camshaft

5   Position the knock pin in the INTAKE camshaft at 10 to 45-degrees left of vertical **(see illustration)**. This will position the exhaust camshaft lobes so the camshaft will be pushed out evenly by the valve spring pressure.

6   Secure the exhaust camshaft sub-gear to the main gear by installing one of the service bolts into a threaded hole **(see illustration)**.

7   Remove the rear (transaxle end) exhaust camshaft bearing cap bolts and detach the bearing cap.

8   Loosen the number 1, 2 and 4 exhaust camshaft bearing cap bolts in 1/4-turn increments until the bolts can be removed by hand. Lift off the first, second and fourth bearing caps.

9   Finally, loosen the number 3 bearing cap bolts in 1/4-turn increments until they can be removed by hand, then detach the center (no. 3) cap. **Caution:** *As the center bearing cap bolts are being loosened, make sure the camshaft is moving up evenly. If one end or the other stops moving and the cam gets cocked, start over by reinstalling the bearing caps and resetting the knock pin. DO NOT try to pry or force the camshaft out.*

10   Lift the camshaft straight up and out of the head.

Intake camshaft

11   Position the knock pin in the intake camshaft at 80 to 115-degrees left of vertical **(see illustration)**.

12   Remove the front (timing belt end) intake camshaft bearing cap bolts and detach the bearing cap and oil seal. **Caution:** *Do not pry the cap off. If it doesn't come loose easily, leave it in place without bolts.*

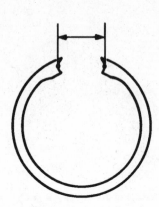

10.20 Measure the distance between the ends of the camshaft gear spring

10.21 Wipe the oil off the valve shims and mark the intakes I and the exhausts E - a magnetic tool works well for removing lifters

10.22 Wipe off the oil and inspect each lifter for wear and scuffing

13   Loosen the number 1, 3 and 4 intake camshaft bearing cap bolts in 1/4-turn increments until the bolts can be removed by hand. Lift off the first, third and fourth bearing caps.

14   Finally, loosen the number 2 bearing cap bolts in 1/4-turn increments until they can be removed by hand, then detach the center (no. 2) bearing cap. **Caution:** *As the center bearing cap bolts are being loosened, make sure the camshaft is moving up evenly. If one end or the other stops moving and the cam gets cocked, start over by reinstalling the bearing caps and resetting the knock pin. DO NOT try to pry or force the camshaft out.*

15   Lift the camshaft straight up and out of the head.

16   To disassemble the exhaust camshaft gear, mount it in a vise with the jaws gripping the large hex on the shaft.

17   Install a second service bolt in the unthreaded hole in the camshaft sub-gear. Using a screwdriver positioned against the service bolt just installed, rotate the sub-gear clockwise and remove the first service bolt from the threaded hole.

18   Remove the sub-gear snap-ring.

19   The wave washer, sub-gear and camshaft gear spring can now be removed from the camshaft.

Inspection

Refer to illustrations 10.20, 10.21, 10.22, 10.26, 10.27, 10.28a, 10.28b and 10.30

20   Measure the free length (distance between the ends) of the camshaft gear spring **(see illustration)** and compare it to this Chapter's Specifications. If not as specified, replace the spring.

21   Carefully label, then remove the valve lifters and shims **(see illustration)**.

22   Inspect each lifter for scuffing and score marks **(see illustration)**.

23   Measure the outside diameter of each lifter and the corresponding lifter bore inside diameter. Subtract the lifter diameter from the lifter bore diameter to determine the oil clearance. Compare it to this Chapter's Specifications. If the oil clearance is excessive, a new head and/or new lifters will be required.

24   Store the lifters in a clean box, separated from each other, so they won't be damaged. Make sure the shims stay with the lifters (don't mix them up).

25   Visually examine the cam lobes and bearing journals for score marks, pitting, galling and evidence of overheating (blue, discolored areas). Look for flaking away of the hardened surface layer of each lobe.

26   Using a micrometer, measure the height of each camshaft lobe **(see illustration)**. Compare your measurements with this Chapter's Specifications. If the height for any one lobe is less than the specified minimum, replace the camshaft.

27   Using a micrometer, measure the diameter of each journal at several points **(see illustration)**. Compare your measurements with this Chapter's Specifications. If the diameter of any one journal is less than specified, replace the camshaft.

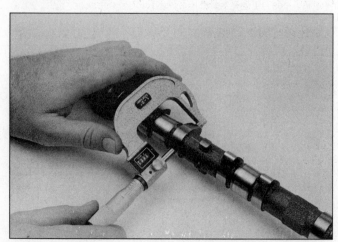

10.26 Measure the lobe heights on each camshaft - if any lobe height is less than the specified allowable minimum, replace that camshaft

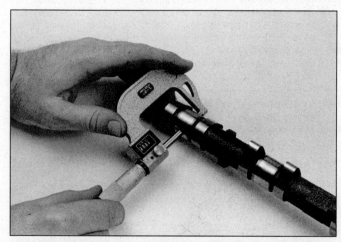

10.27 Measure each journal diameter with a micrometer (if any journal measures less than the specified limit, replace the camshaft)

10.28a Lay a strip of Plastigage on each camshaft journal

10.28b Compare the width of the crushed Plastigage to the scale on the envelope to determine the oil clearance

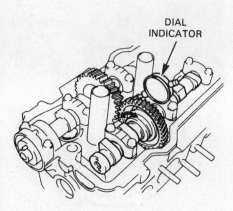

10.30 Position a dial indicator as shown here to measure gear backlash

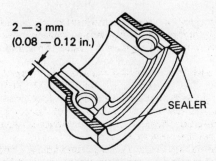

10.34 Apply sealer to the shaded areas of the front intake camshaft bearing cap

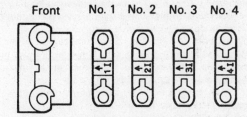

10.35 Intake camshaft bearing cap arrangement - the arrows point toward the front or timing belt end of the engine

28 Check the oil clearance for each camshaft journal as follows:

a) Clean the bearing caps and the camshaft journals with lacquer thinner or acetone.

b) Carefully lay the camshaft(s) in place in the head. Don't install the lifters and don't use any lubrication.

c) Lay a strip of Plastigage on each journal (see illustration).

d) Install the bearing caps with the arrows pointing toward the front (timing belt end) of the engine.

e) Tighten the bolts to the specified torque in 1/4-turn increments. **Note:** Don't turn the camshaft while the Plastigage is in place.

f) Remove the bolts and detach the caps.

g) Compare the width of the crushed Plastigage (at its widest point) to the scale on the Plastigage envelope (see illustration).

h) If the clearance is greater than specified, replace the camshaft and/or cylinder head.

i) Scrape off the Plastigage with your fingernail or the edge of a credit card - don't scratch or nick the journals or bearing caps.

29 Temporarily install the camshafts without installing the lifters or exhaust camshaft sub-gear.

30 Measure the gear backlash (the free play between the gear teeth) with a dial indicator (see illustration) and compare it to this Chapter's Specifications.

Installation

Refer to illustrations 10.34, 10.35, 10.36, 10.43, 10.45 and 10.46

Intake camshaft

31 Apply moly-base grease or engine assembly lube to the lifters, then install them in their original locations. Make sure the valve adjustment shims are in place in the lifters.

32 Apply moly-base grease or engine assembly lube to the camshaft lobes and bearing journals.

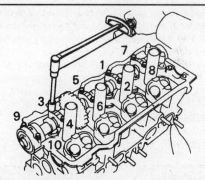

10.36 INTAKE camshaft bearing cap bolt tightening sequence

33 Position the intake camshaft in the cylinder head with the knock pin 80-degrees to the left of vertical (see illustration 10.11).

34 Apply a thin coat of RTV sealant to the outer edge of the front bearing-cap-to-cylinder-head mating surface (see illustration). **Note:** *The cap must be installed immediately or the sealer will dry prematurely.*

35 Install the bearing caps in numerical order with the arrows pointing toward the timing belt end of the engine (see illustration).

36 Following the recommended tightening sequence (see illustration), tighten the bearing cap bolts in 1/4-turn increments to the torque listed in this Chapter's Specifications.

37 Refer to Section 9 and install a new camshaft oil seal.

Exhaust camshaft

38 Reassemble the exhaust camshaft gear. Install the cam gear spring, sub-gear and wave washer in the gear. Secure them with the snap-ring.

10.43 Align the camshaft timing gears as shown here

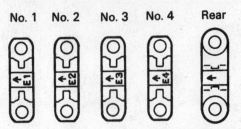

10.45 Exhaust camshaft bearing cap arrangement - the arrows point toward the front or timing belt end of the engine

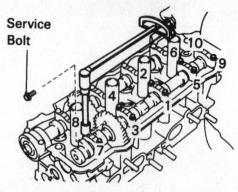

10.46 EXHAUST camshaft bearing cap bolt tightening sequence

39   Reinstall the service bolt in the unthreaded hole, turn the sub-gear with a screwdriver and install the second service bolt in the threaded hole. Tighten it to clamp the sub-gear to the camshaft gear, then remove the first bolt.

40   Apply moly-base grease or engine assembly lube to the lifters, then install them in their original locations. Make sure the valve adjustment shims are in place in the lifters.

41   Apply moly-base grease or engine assembly lube to the camshaft lobes and bearing journals.

42   Rotate the INTAKE camshaft until the knock pin is positioned 10-degrees to the left of vertical **(see illustration 10.5)**.

43   Align the exhaust camshaft gear with the intake camshaft gear by matching up the timing marks on the gears **(see illustration)**. **Caution:** *There are also assembly reference marks on each gear, above the timing marks - do not mistake them for the timing marks.*

44   Roll the exhaust camshaft down into position. Turn the intake camshaft back and forth a little until the exhaust camshaft sits in the bearings evenly.

45   Install the bearing caps in numerical order with the arrows pointing toward the timing belt end of the engine **(see illustration)**.

46   Following the recommended sequence **(see illustration)**, tighten the bearing cap bolts in 1/4-turn increments to the torque listed in this Chapter's Specifications.

47   Remove the service bolt from the camshaft gear.

48   Install the timing belt pulley on the intake camshaft and tighten the bolt to the torque listed in this Chapter's Specifications. Prevent the camshaft from turning by holding it with a wrench on the large hex **(see illustration 7.14)**.

49   Install the timing belt (see Section 7).

50   The remainder of installation is the reverse of the removal procedure.

11   Cylinder head - removal and installation

Note: *The engine must be completely cool before beginning this procedure.*

Removal

Refer to illustration 11.14

1   Disconnect the negative cable from the battery. **Caution:** *If the stereo in your vehicle is equipped with an anti-theft system, make sure you have the correct activation code before disconnecting the battery.* **Note:** *On 1993 and later models, the airbag system will be disabled if the battery is disconnected for more than a brief period. If the airbag light comes on and stays on after the battery is reconnected, the*

vehicle must be taken to a dealer to have the system reset with a special tool.

2   Drain the coolant from the engine block and radiator (see Chapter 1).

3   Drain the engine oil and remove the oil filter (see Chapter 1).

4   Remove the throttle body, fuel injectors and fuel rail (see Chapter 4).

5   Remove the intake manifold (see Section 5).

6   Remove the exhaust manifold (see Section 6).

7   Remove the timing belt, camshaft sprocket and upper idler pulley (see Section 7).

8   Remove the upper rear (no. 3) timing belt cover **(see illustration 4.4)**.

9   Remove the camshafts and lifters (see Section 10).

10   Remove the alternator and distributor (see Chapter 5).

11   Unbolt the power steering pump and set it aside without disconnecting the hoses.

12   Label and remove any remaining items, such as coolant fittings, tubes, cables, hoses or wires **(see illustration 5.4a)**. At this point the head should be ready for removal.

13   Using an 8 mm hex head socket bit and a breaker bar, loosen the cylinder head bolts in 1/4-turn increments until they can be removed by hand. Loosen the cylinder head bolts opposite of the recommended tightening sequence **(see illustration 11.25)** to avoid warping or cracking the head.

14   Lift the cylinder head off the engine block. If it's stuck, very carefully pry up at the transaxle end, beyond the gasket surface **(see illustration)**.

15   Remove all external components from the head to allow for thorough cleaning and inspection. See Chapter 2, Part C, for cylinder head servicing procedures.

Installation

Refer to illustrations 11.17 and 11.25

16   The mating surfaces of the cylinder head and block must be perfectly clean when the head is installed.

11.14 If the head is stuck, pry only at the overhang, not between the mating surfaces

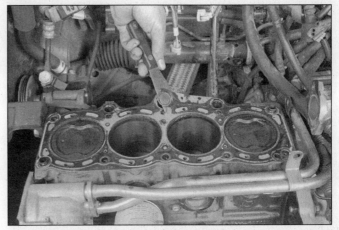

11.17 Remove all traces of old gasket material - the cylinder head and block mating surfaces must be perfectly clean to ensure a good gasket seal

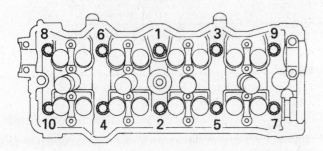

11.25 Cylinder head bolt TIGHTENING sequence

17   Use a gasket scraper to remove all traces of carbon and old gasket material **(see illustration)**, then clean the mating surfaces with lacquer thinner or acetone. If there's oil on the mating surfaces when the head is installed, the gasket may not seal correctly and leaks could develop. When working on the block, stuff the cylinders with clean shop rags to keep out debris. Use a vacuum cleaner to remove material that falls into the cylinders.

18   Check the block and head mating surfaces for nicks, deep scratches and other damage. If damage is slight, it can be removed with a file; if it's excessive, machining may be the only alternative.

19   Use a tap of the correct size to chase the threads in the cylinder head bolt holes, then clean the holes with compressed air - make sure that nothing remains in the holes. **Warning:** *Wear eye protection when using compressed air!*

20   Mount each bolt in a vise and run a die down the threads to remove corrosion and restore the threads. Dirt, corrosion, sealant and damaged threads will affect torque readings.

21   Install the components that were removed from the head.

22   Position the new gasket over the dowel pins in the block.

23   Carefully set the head on the block without disturbing the gasket.

24   Before installing the head bolts, apply a small amount of clean engine oil to the threads.

25   Install the bolts in their original locations and tighten them finger tight. Following the recommended sequence, tighten the bolts in several steps to the torque listed in this Chapter's Specifications **(see illustration)**.

26   The remaining installation steps are the reverse of removal.

27   Check and adjust the valves as necessary (see Chapter 1).

28   Refill the cooling system, install a new oil filter and add oil to the engine (see Chapter 1).

29   Run the engine and check for leaks. Set the ignition timing (see Chapter 5) and road test the vehicle.

12   Oil pan - removal and installation

Refer to illustrations 12.8, 12.9 and 12.14

2A

Removal

1   Disconnect the negative cable from the battery. **Caution:** *If the stereo in your vehicle is equipped with an anti-theft system, make sure you have the correct activation code before disconnecting the battery.* **Note:** *On 1993 and later models, the airbag system will be disabled if the battery is disconnected for more than a brief period. If the airbag light comes on and stays on after the battery is reconnected, the vehicle must be taken to a dealer to have the system reset with a special tool.*

2   Set the parking brake and block the rear wheels.

3   Raise the front of the vehicle and support it securely on jackstands.

4   Remove the splash shields under the engine, if equipped.

5   Drain the engine oil and remove the oil filter (see Chapter 1). Remove the oil dipstick.

6   Disconnect the three nuts holding the front exhaust pipe to the engine-side catalytic converter, then the two bolts/nuts connecting the pipe to the rear of the exhaust system.

7   Unbolt the two bolts and remove the support bracket, then remove the front exhaust pipe.

8   Remove the block-to-transaxle brace **(see illustration)**.

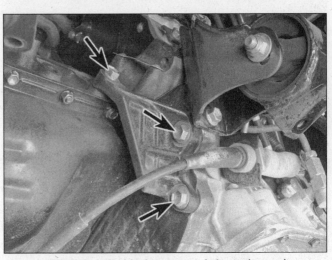

12.8 Unbolt the block-to-transaxle brace (arrows)

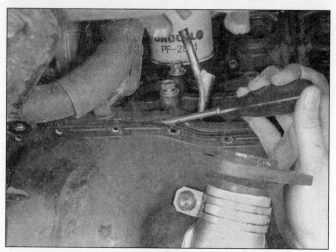

12.9 Carefully pry the oil pan away from the block - if the mating surfaces are damaged, oil leaks could develop

9   Remove the bolts and detach the oil pan. If it's stuck, pry it loose very carefully with a small screwdriver or putty knife **(see illustration)**. Don't damage the mating surfaces of the pan and block or oil leaks could develop.

Installation

10   Use a scraper to remove all traces of old gasket material and sealant from the block and oil pan. Clean the mating surfaces with lacquer thinner or acetone.

11   Make sure the threaded bolt holes in the block are clean.

12   Check the oil pan flange for distortion, particularly around the bolt holes. If necessary, place the pan on a block of wood and use a hammer to flatten and restore the gasket surface.

13   Inspect the oil pump pick-up tube assembly for cracks and a blocked strainer. If the pick-up was removed, clean it thoroughly and install it now, using a new O-ring or gasket. Tighten the nuts/bolts to the torque listed in this Chapter's Specifications.

14   Apply a 5 mm wide bead of RTV sealant to the oil pan flange **(see illustration)**. **Note:** *The oil pan must be installed within 5 minutes once the sealer has been applied.*

15   Carefully position the oil pan on the engine block and install the bolts. Working from the center out, tighten them to the torque listed in this Chapter's Specifications in three or four steps.

16   The remainder of installation is the reverse of removal. Be sure to add oil and install a new oil filter. Use new "doughnut" gaskets on each

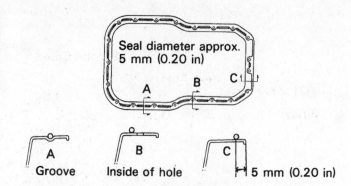

12.14 Apply a bead of RTV sealant to the oil pan flange

end of the front exhaust pipe.

17   Run the engine and check for oil pressure and leaks.

13   Oil pump - removal, inspection and installation

Removal

Refer to illustrations 13.2, 13.4, 13.5a, 13.5b, 13.6 and 13.8

1   Remove the oil pan (see Section 12).

2   Remove the nuts/bolts and detach the oil pick-up tube assembly **(see illustration)**.

3   Support the engine securely from above and remove the lower idler pulley, crankshaft pulley, timing belt, and crankshaft sprocket (see Section 7).

4   Remove the 12 bolts and detach the oil pump case from the engine **(see illustration)**. You may have to pry carefully between the front main bearing cap and the pump case with a screwdriver.

5   Remove the two remaining bolts **(see illustration)** and separate the pump body from the case. Lift out the driven rotor and remove the O-ring **(see illustration)**.

6   Clamp the pump sprocket in a well padded vise **(see illustration)** and remove the sprocket nut and sprocket. Remove the drive rotor.

7   Use a scraper to remove all traces of sealant and old gasket material from the pump case and engine block, then clean the mating surfaces with lacquer thinner or acetone.

8   Remove the oil pressure relief valve snap-ring **(see illustration)**, retainer, spring and piston. **Warning:** *The spring is tightly compressed - be careful and wear eye protection.*

13.2 The oil pick-up assembly and baffle plate are held in place with two nuts and two bolts (arrows)

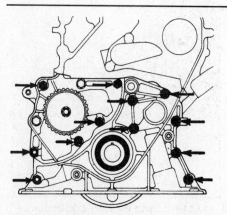

13.4 Remove the oil pump case-to-block bolts (arrows)

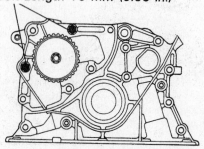

13.5a Remove the oil pump body-to-oil pump case bolts

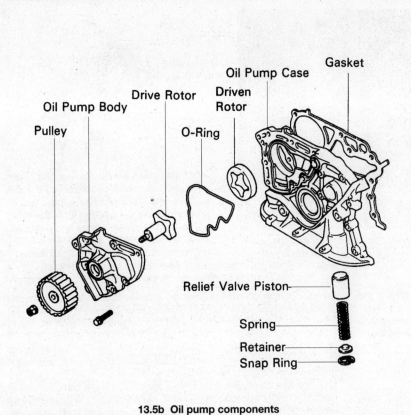

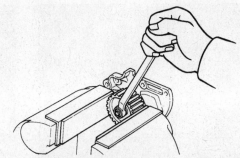

13.6 Hold the oil pump sprocket in a well-padded vise while the retaining nut is removed

13.5b Oil pump components

13.8 Remove the snap-ring to disassemble the oil pressure relief valve

2A

Inspection

Refer to illustrations 13.11a and 13.11b

9   Clean all components with solvent, then inspect them for wear and damage.

10   Check the oil pressure relief valve piston sliding surface and valve spring. If either the spring or the valve is damaged, they must be replaced as a set.

11   Check the driven rotor-to-case and drive rotor tip clearance with feeler gauges **(see illustrations)** and compare the results to this Chapter's Specifications. If the clearance is excessive, replace the rotors as a set. If necessary, replace the oil pump case and body.

Installation

Refer to illustrations 13.14

12   Pry the old drive rotor shaft seal out with a screwdriver. Using a deep socket and a hammer, carefully drive a new seal into place. Apply multi-purpose grease to the seal lip.

13   Install a new crankshaft seal using the same procedure as outlined in the previous step. Apply multi-purpose grease to the seal lip.

14   Install a new O-ring, then lubricate the driven rotor with clean engine oil and place it in the pump case with the mark facing out **(see illustration)**.

15   Lubricate the shaft and install the drive rotor in the pump body,

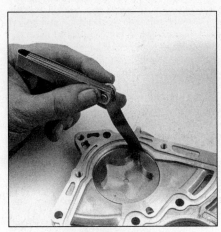

13.11a Measure the driven rotor-to-case clearance . . .

13.11b . . . and the rotor tip clearance with a feeler gauge

13.14 Oil pump case ready for pump body installation - Note that the seal is in place, the O-ring is in place and the mark on the driven rotor is facing out (arrow)

14.3 Mark the flywheel/driveplate and the crankshaft so they can be reassembled in the same relative positions

14.5 On vehicles equipped with a spacer plate, Note the position of the locating pin (arrow)

15.2 The quick way to replace the rear crankshaft oil seal is to simply pry the old one out with a screwdriver, lubricate the crankshaft journal and the lip of the new seal with moly-base grease and push the new seal into place - the seal lip is very stiff and can be easily damaged during installation if you're not careful

then reinstall the pulley and tighten the nut to the torque listed in this Chapter's Specifications.

16   Pack the pump cavity with petroleum jelly and attach the pump body to the case with the 16 mm-long bolts (see illustration 13.5a).

17   Lubricate the oil pressure relief valve piston with clean engine oil and reinstall the valve components in the pump case.

18   Place a new gasket on the engine block (the dowel pins should hold it in place).

19   Position the pump case against the block and install the mounting bolts.

20   Tighten the bolts to the torque listed in this Chapter's Specifications in three or four steps. Follow a criss-cross pattern to avoid warping the case.

21   Using a new gasket, install the oil pick-up tube assembly and baffle plate. Tighten the fasteners to the torque listed in this Chapter's Specifications.

22   Reinstall the remaining parts in the reverse order of removal.

23   Add oil, start the engine and check for oil pressure and leaks.

24   Recheck the engine oil level.

14   Flywheel/driveplate - removal and installation

Refer to illustrations 14.3 and 14.5

Removal

1   Raise the vehicle and support it securely on jackstands, then refer to Chapter 7 and remove the transaxle. If it's leaking, now would be a very good time to replace the front pump seal/O-ring (automatic transaxle only).

2   Remove the pressure plate and clutch disc (Chapter 8) (manual transaxle equipped vehicles). Now is a good time to check/replace the clutch components and pilot bearing.

3   Use a center punch or paint to make alignment marks on the flywheel/driveplate and crankshaft to ensure correct alignment during reinstallation (see illustration).

4   Remove the bolts that secure the flywheel/driveplate to the crankshaft. If the crankshaft turns, wedge a screwdriver in the ring gear teeth to jam the flywheel.

5   Remove the flywheel/driveplate from the crankshaft. Since the flywheel is fairly heavy, be sure to support it while removing the last bolt. Automatic transaxle equipped vehicles have spacers on both sides of the driveplate (see illustration). Keep them with the driveplate.

Installation

6   Clean the flywheel to remove grease and oil. Inspect the surface

for cracks, rivet grooves, burned areas and score marks. Light scoring can be removed with emery cloth. Check for cracked and broken ring gear teeth. Lay the flywheel on a flat surface and use a straightedge to check for warpage.

7   Clean and inspect the mating surfaces of the flywheel/driveplate and the crankshaft. If the crankshaft rear seal is leaking, replace it before reinstalling the flywheel/driveplate.

8   Position the flywheel/driveplate against the crankshaft. Be sure to align the marks made during removal. Note that some engines have an alignment dowel or staggered bolt holes to ensure correct installation. Before installing the bolts, apply thread locking compound to the threads.

9   Wedge a screwdriver in the ring gear teeth to keep the flywheel/driveplate from turning and tighten the bolts to the torque listed in this Chapter's Specifications. Follow a criss-cross pattern and work up to the final torque in three or four steps.

10   The remainder of installation is the reverse of the removal procedure.

15   Rear main oil seal - replacement

Refer to illustrations 15.2, 15.5 and 15.6

1   The transaxle must be removed from the vehicle for this procedure (see Chapter 7).

2   The seal can be replaced without removing the oil pan or removing the seal retainer. However, this method is not recommended because the lip of the seal is quite stiff and it's possible to cock the seal in the retainer bore or damage it during installation. If you want to take the chance, pry out the old seal with a screwdriver (see illustration). Apply multi-purpose grease to the crankshaft seal journal and the lip of the new seal and carefully push the new seal into place. The lip is stiff so carefully work it onto the seal journal of the crankshaft with a smooth object like the end of an extension as you tap the seal into place. Don't rush it or you may damage the seal.

3   The following method is recommended but requires removal of the oil pan (see Section 12) and the seal retainer.

4   After the oil pan has been removed, remove the bolts, detach the seal retainer and remove all the old gasket material.

5   Position the seal and retainer assembly between two wood blocks on a workbench and drive the old seal out from the back side with a screwdriver (see illustration).

6   Drive the new seal into the retainer with a block of wood (see illustration) or a section of pipe slightly smaller in diameter than the outside diameter of the seal.

7   Lubricate the crankshaft seal journal and the lip of the new seal with multi-purpose grease. Position a new gasket on the engine block.

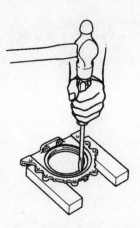

15.5 After removing the retainer assembly from the block, support it between two wood blocks and drive out the old seal with a screwdriver and hammer

15.6 Drive the new seal into the retainer with a block of wood or a section of pipe, if you have one large enough - make sure that you don't cock the seal in the retainer bore

2A

8   Slowly and carefully push the seal onto the crankshaft. The seal lip is stiff, so work it onto the crankshaft with a smooth object such as the end of an extension as you push the retainer against the block.
9   Install and tighten the retainer bolts to the torque listed in this Chapter's Specifications. The bottom sealing flange of the retainer must not extend below the bottom sealing flange (oil pan rail) of the block.
10   The remaining steps are the reverse of removal.

16 Engine mounts - check and replacement

Refer to illustration 16.4
1   Engine mounts seldom require attention, but broken or deteriorated mounts should be replaced immediately or the added strain placed on the driveline components may cause damage or wear.

Check

2   During the check, the engine must be raised slightly to remove the weight from the mounts.
3   Raise the vehicle and support it securely on jackstands, then position a jack under the engine oil pan. Place a large block of wood between the jack head and the oil pan, then carefully raise the engine just enough to take the weight off the mounts. Do not position the wood block under the drain plug. **Warning:** *DO NOT place any part of your body under the engine when it's supported only by a jack!*
4   Check the mounts **(see illustration)** to see if the rubber is cracked, hardened or separated from the metal plates. Sometimes the rubber will split right down the center.
5   Check for relative movement between the mount plates and the engine or frame (use a large screwdriver or pry bar to attempt to move the mounts). If movement is noted, lower the engine and tighten the mount fasteners.
6   Rubber preservative should be applied to the mounts to slow deterioration.

Replacement

7   Disconnect the negative battery cable from the battery, then raise the vehicle and support it securely on jackstands (if not already done). Support the engine as described in Step 3. **Caution:** *If the stereo in your vehicle is equipped with an anti-theft system, make sure you have the correct activation code before disconnecting the battery.* **Note:** *On 1993 and later models, the airbag system will be disabled if the battery is disconnected for more than a brief period. If the airbag light comes on and stays on after the battery is reconnected, the vehicle must be*

taken to a dealer to have the system reset with a special tool.
8   To remove the right engine mount, remove the nut and withdraw the through-bolt from the frame bracket.

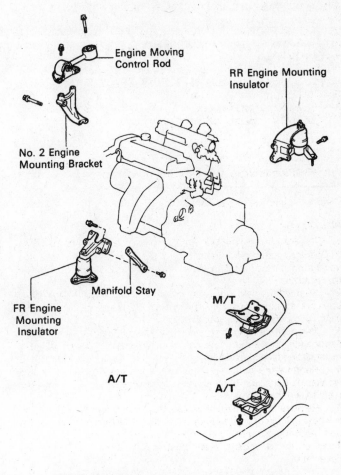

16.4 Typical 4-cylinder engine mount components

9   Remove the mount-to-bracket nuts and detach the mount.

10   To remove the rear engine mount, pull the rubber plugs from the chassis to access the three nuts.

11   To remove the front engine mount, remove the nut holding the insulator to the engine bracket, then the three nuts holding the insulator to the chassis.

12   Installation is the reverse of removal. Use thread locking compound on the mount bolts/nuts and be sure to tighten them securely.

13   See Chapter 7 for transaxle mount replacement.

Chapter 2 Part B
V6 engines

Contents

Specifications

General

Cylinder numbers (timing belt end-to-transaxle end)	
Right (firewall) side	1-3-5
Left (radiator) side	2-4-6
Firing order	1-2-3-4-5-6

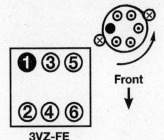

Front

Cylinder location and distributor rotation

3VZ-FE

Cylinder head

Warpage limits
  3VZ-FE engine (1992 and 1993)
    Cylinder head.. 0.0039 inch
    Intake manifold .... 0.0039 inch
    Exhaust manifolds .... 0.0394 inch
  1MZ-FE engine (1994 on)
    Cylinder head.. 0.0039 inch
    Intake manifold .... 0.0031 inch
    Exhaust manifolds .... 0.0196 inch

Camshaft and related components

Valve clearance (engine cold)
  Intake .... 0.005 to 0.009 inch
  Exhaust.. 0.011 to 0.015 inch
Bearing journal diameter... 1.0610 to 1.0616 inches
Bearing oil clearance
  Standard.. 0.0014 to 0.0028 inch
  Service limit .... 0.0039 inch
Lobe height
  Intake
    3VZ-FE engine (1992 and 1993)
      Standard.. 1.6598 to 1.6638 inches
      Service Limit .... 1.6539 inches
    1MZ-FE engine (1994 on)
      Standard.. 1.6579 to 1.6618 inches
      Service Limit .... 1.6520 inches
  Exhaust
    Standard.. 1.6520 to 1.6559 inches
    Service limit.. 1.6461 inches
Thrust clearance (endplay)
  Standard
    3VZ-FE engine (1992 and 1993) .... 0.0013 to 0.0031 inch
    1MZ-FE engine (1994 on) .... 0.0016 to 0.0035 inch
  Service limit .... 0.0047 inch
Runout limit (total indicator reading)............................ 0.0024 inch
Camshaft gear backlash
  Standard.. 0.0008 to 0.0079 inch
  Service limit .... 0.0188 inch
Camshaft gear spring free distance .... 0.712 to 0.740 inch
Timing belt tensioner protrusion.................................... 0.394 to 0.425 inch
Lifters
  Outside diameter... 1.2191 to 1.2195 inch
  Bore diameter.. 1.2204 to 1.2212 inch
  Lifter-to-bore (oil) clearance
    Standard .... 0.0009 to 0.0020 inch
    Service limit.. 0.0031 inch

Oil pump

Driven rotor-to-pump body clearance
  Standard.. 0.0039 to 0.0069 inch
  Service limit .... 0.0118 inch
Rotor tip clearance
  Standard.. 0.0043 to 0.0094 inch
  Service limit .... 0.0138 inch
Rotor side clearance
  Standard.. 0.0012 to 0.0035 inch
  Service limit .... 0.0059 inch

Torque specifications   **Ft-lbs** (unless otherwise indicated)

3VZ-FE engine (1992 and 1993)

Intake manifold bolts/nuts .... 156 in-lbs
Exhaust manifold nuts 29
Crankshaft pulley bolt... 181
Timing belt cover bolts (no. 3) .... 65 in-lbs
Idler pulley bolts
  No. 1 25
  No. 2 29
Timing belt tensioner bolts 20

Valve cover nuts	52 in-lbs
Camshaft pulley bolts	80
Camshaft bearing cap bolts	144 in-lbs
Cylinder head bolts	
Step 1	25
Step 2	Turn an additional 90-degrees (1/4-turn)
Step 3	Turn an additional 90-degrees (1/4-turn)
Cylinder head bolt (recessed)	156 in-lbs
Oil pan bolts	65 in-lbs
Oil pump mounting bolts	
12 mm bolt head	168 in-lbs
14 mm bolt head	30
Oil pick-up tube mounting bolts	65 in-lbs
Flywheel/driveplate bolts*	61
Rear crankshaft oil seal retainer mounting bolts	69 in-lbs

Apply thread locking compound to the threads prior to installation

1MZ-FE engine (1994 on)

Intake manifold bolts/nuts	132 in-lbs
Exhaust manifold nuts	36
Crankshaft pulley bolt	159
Timing belt cover bolts (no. 3)	74 in-lbs
Idler pulley bolts	
No. 1	25
No. 2	32
Timing belt tensioner bolts	20
Cylinder head cover nuts	69 in-lbs
Camshaft pulley bolts	94
Camshaft bearing cap bolts	144 in-lbs
Cylinder head bolts	
Step 1	40
Step 2	Turn an additional 90-degrees (1/4-turn)
Cylinder head bolt (recessed)	156 in-lbs
Oil pan bolts	
aluminum section	168 in-lbs
steel section	69 in-lbs
Oil pump mounting bolts	
10 mm bolt head	69 in-lbs
12 mm bolt head	168 in-lbs
Oil pick-up tube mounting bolts	69 in-lbs
Flywheel/driveplate bolts*	61
Rear crankshaft oil seal retainer mounting bolts	69 in-lbs

Apply thread locking compound to the threads prior to installation

1   General information

The Camry models covered by this manual are equipped with either one of two V6 engines; the 3VZ-FE used in 1992 and 1993 models, and the 1MZ-FE used in 1994 and later models. Both V6 engines are a 3.0-liter, DOHC (double-overhead-cam) design with four valves per cylinder (24 in all), but the 1MZ-FE features an aluminum engine block, distributorless ignition, two-piece oil pan and several other changes from the previous engine.

This Part of Chapter 2 is devoted to in-vehicle repair procedures for the V6 engines. All information concerning engine removal and installation and engine block and cylinder head overhaul can be found in Part C of this Chapter.

The following repair procedures are based on the assumption that the engine is installed in the vehicle. If the engine has been removed from the vehicle and mounted on a stand, many of the steps outlined in this Part of Chapter 2 will not apply.

The Specifications included in this Part of Chapter 2 apply only to the procedures contained in this Part. Part C of Chapter 2 contains the Specifications necessary for cylinder head and engine block rebuilding.

2   Repair operations possible with the engine in the vehicle

Refer to illustration 2.4

Many major repair operations can be accomplished without removing the engine from the vehicle.

1   Clean the engine compartment and the exterior of the engine with some type of degreaser before any work is done. It will make the job easier and help keep dirt out of the internal areas of the engine.

2   Depending on the components involved, it may be helpful to remove the hood to improve access to the engine as repairs are performed (refer to Chapter 11 if necessary). Cover the fenders to prevent damage to the paint. Special pads are available, but an old bedspread or blanket will also work.

3   If vacuum, exhaust, oil or coolant leaks develop, indicating a need for gasket or seal replacement, the repairs can generally be made with the engine in the vehicle. The intake and exhaust manifold gaskets, oil pan gasket, crankshaft oil seals and cylinder head gaskets are all accessible with the engine in place.

4   Exterior engine components, such as the intake and exhaust manifolds, the oil pan, the oil pump, the water pump, the starter motor,

the alternator, the distributor and the fuel system components can be removed for repair with the engine in place **(see illustration)**.

5   Since the cylinder heads can be removed without pulling the engine, valve component servicing can also be accomplished with the engine in the vehicle. Replacement of the camshafts, timing belt and pulleys is also possible with the engine in the vehicle.

6   In extreme cases caused by a lack of necessary equipment, repair or replacement of piston rings, pistons, connecting rods and rod bearings is possible with the engine in the vehicle. However, this practice is not recommended because of the cleaning and preparation work that must be done to the components involved.

3   Top Dead Center (TDC) for number one piston - locating

Refer to illustrations 3.5, 3.8, 3.13 and 3.14

Note: *The following procedure is based on the assumption that the distributor is correctly installed (3VZ-FE engine only). If you are trying to locate TDC to install the distributor correctly, piston position must be determined by feeling for compression at the number one spark plug hole, then aligning the ignition timing marks as described in step 8.*

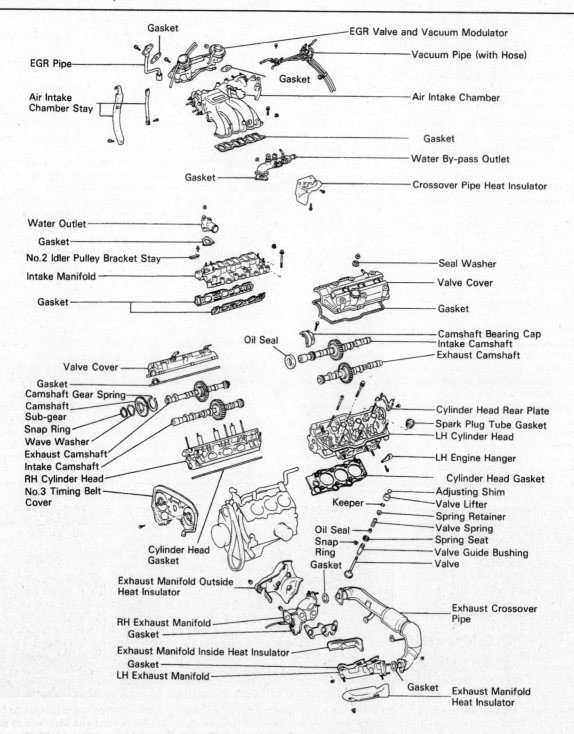

2.4 Cylinder heads and related components (typical)

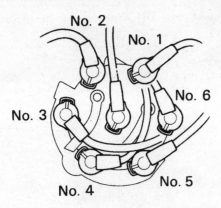

3.5 Make a mark on the distributor body, directly below the no. 1 spark plug wire terminal

1   Top Dead Center (TDC) is the highest point in the cylinder that each piston reaches as it travels up the cylinder bore. Each piston reaches TDC on the compression stroke and again on the exhaust stroke, but TDC generally refers to piston position on the compression stroke.

2   Positioning the piston(s) at TDC is an essential part of many procedures such as valve timing, camshaft and timing belt/pulley removal and distributor removal.

3   Before beginning this procedure, be sure to place the transaxle in Neutral and apply the parking brake or block the rear wheels. Also, disable the ignition system by detaching the coil wire from the center terminal of the distributor cap and grounding it on the block with a jumper wire. Remove the spark plugs (see Chapter 1).

4   In order to bring any piston to TDC, the crankshaft must be turned using one of the methods outlined below. When looking at the front of the engine, normal crankshaft rotation is clockwise.

  a) *The preferred method is to turn the crankshaft with a socket and ratchet attached to the bolt threaded into the front of the crankshaft. Apply pressure on the bolt in a clockwise direction only. Never turn the bolt counterclockwise.*

  b) *A remote starter switch, which may save some time, can also be used. Follow the instructions included with the switch. Once the piston is close to TDC, use a socket and ratchet as described in the previous paragraph.*

  c) *If an assistant is available to turn the ignition switch to the Start position in short bursts, you can get the piston close to TDC without a remote starter switch. Make sure your assistant is out of the vehicle, away from the ignition switch, then use a socket and ratchet as described in Paragraph (a) to complete the procedure.*

3VZ-FE engine

5   Note the position of the terminal for the number one spark plug wire on the distributor cap (see illustration). If the terminal isn't marked, follow the plug wire from the number one cylinder spark plug to the cap.

6   Use a felt-tip pen or chalk to make a mark on the distributor body directly under the terminal.

7   Detach the cap from the distributor and set it aside (see Chapter 1 if necessary).

8   Turn the crankshaft (see Paragraph 3 above) until the notch in the crankshaft pulley is aligned with the 0 on the timing plate (located at the front of the engine) (see illustration).

9   Look at the distributor rotor - it should be pointing directly at the mark you made on the distributor body.

10   If the rotor is 180-degrees off, the number one piston is at TDC on the exhaust stroke.

11   To get the piston to TDC on the compression stroke, turn the crankshaft one complete turn (360-degrees) clockwise. The rotor should now be pointing at the mark on the distributor. When the rotor is pointing at the number one spark plug wire terminal in the distributor cap and the ignition timing marks are aligned, the number one piston is at TDC on the compression stroke.

12   After the number one piston has been positioned at TDC on the compression stroke, TDC for any of the remaining pistons can be located by turning the crankshaft and following the firing order. Mark the remaining spark plug wire terminal locations on the distributor body just like you did for the number one terminal, then number the marks to correspond with the cylinder numbers. As you turn the crankshaft, the rotor will also turn. When it's pointing directly at one of the marks on the distributor, the piston for that particular cylinder is at TDC on the compression stroke.

1MZ-FE engine

13   The 1MZ-FE engine does not have a distributor, but rather a separate coil for each spark plug, fired in sequence by signals from the computer. To find TDC on the compression stroke for the number one cylinder, remove the number one coil and spark plug (see illustration) and detach the electrical connector from the number one coil.

14   Mount a compression pressure gauge in the number one spark plug hole (refer to Chapter 2C). It should be a gauge with a screw-in fitting and a hose at least six inches long (see illustration).

15   Rotate the crankshaft using one of the methods described above while observing the compression gauge. When TDC for the compression stroke of number one cylinder is reached, compression pressure will show on the gauge as the marks are beginning to line up. If you go past the marks, release the gauge pressure and rotate the crankshaft around two more revolutions. **Note:** *The most positive method for finding TDC on the 1MZ-FE engine is to examine the*

2B

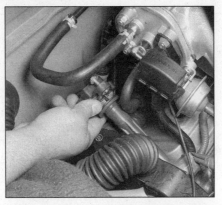

3.13 The coil for the number one spark plug can be removed with the intake plenum in place - disconnect the wire harness from the coil and remove the spark plug

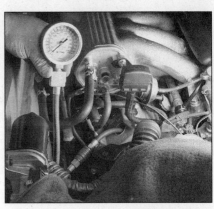

3.14 A compression gauge can be used in the number one plug hole to assist in finding TDC on 1MZ-FE engines

3.8 Turn the crankshaft until the notch in the pulley (arrow) aligns with the zero (0) on the timing plate

4.3 Remove the spark plug wires, the breather hose and the retaining nuts (arrows) to detach the valve cover

crankshaft timing marks and camshaft sprocket timing marks (see Section 7).

4   Valve covers - removal and installation

3VZ-FE engine
Removal
Refer to illustrations 4.3, 4.4, 4.5, and 4.6

1   Disconnect the negative cable from the battery. **Caution:** *If the stereo in your vehicle is equipped with an anti-theft system, make sure you have the correct activation code before disconnecting the battery.* **Note:** *On 1993 and later models, the airbag system will be disabled if the battery is disconnected for more than a brief period. If the airbag light comes on and stays on after the battery is reconnected, the vehicle must be taken to a dealer to have the system reset with a special tool.*

2   Remove the V-bank cover with a 5 mm hex wrench. If you're removing the rear (firewall side) cover, remove the air cleaner assembly, throttle body and air intake chamber (see Chapter 4).

3   If you're working on the front (radiator side) or both covers, remove the spark plug connectors and wires from the spark plugs **(see illustration)**.

4   Detach the front engine wiring harness **(see illustration)** and the following electrical connectors:

  a) *Three left-hand injectors*
  b) *Oil pressure switch*
  c) *Air-conditioning compressor (if equipped)*
  d) *Alternator connector*
  e) *Water temperature sensor*

5   Detach the rear engine wiring harness **(see illustration)** and the following electrical connectors:

  a) *Three right-hand injectors*
  b) *Water temperature sender gauge*
  c) *Oxygen sensor*
  d) *Power steering pump*

6   Remove the retaining nuts and sealing washers **(see illustration)**, then detach the cover(s). If the cover is stuck to the head, bump the end with a wood block and a hammer to jar it loose. If that doesn't work, try to slip a flexible putty knife between the head and cover to break the seal. **Caution:** *Don't pry at the cover-to-head joint or damage to the sealing surfaces may occur, leading to oil leaks after the cover is reinstalled.*

Installation
Refer to illustration 4.8

7   The mating surfaces of the cylinder head and cover must be clean when the cover is installed. Use a gasket scraper to remove all traces of sealant and old gasket material, then clean the mating surfaces with

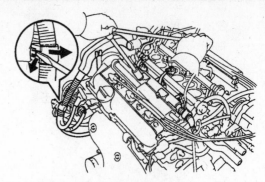

4.4 Disconnect the five clamps and pull the front engine harness out of the way

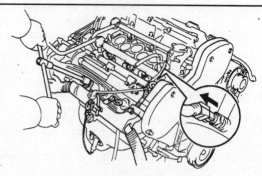

4.5 Disconnect the two clamps, remove two bolts, and pull the rear engine harness out of the way

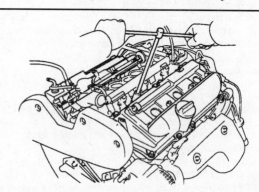

4.6 Remove the six nuts and sealing washers and remove the valve cover

lacquer thinner or acetone. If there's residue or oil on the mating surfaces when the cover is installed, oil leaks may develop.

8   Position the semi-circular seals in the cylinder head cutouts with new RTV sealant, then apply a thin, uniform layer of RTV sealant to the gasket/seal joints **(see illustration)**.

9   Install new spark plug tube seals.

10   Position a new gasket on the valve cover, then install the cover, sealing washers and nuts.

11   Tighten the nuts to the torque listed in this Chapter's Specifications in three or four equal steps.

12   Reinstall the remaining parts, run the engine and check for oil leaks.

1MZ-FE engine
Removal
Refer to illustrations 4.15, 4.16a, 4.16b, and 4.17

13   Disconnect the negative cable from the battery. **Caution:** *If the stereo in your vehicle is equipped with an anti-theft system, make sure you have the correct activation code before disconnecting the battery.*

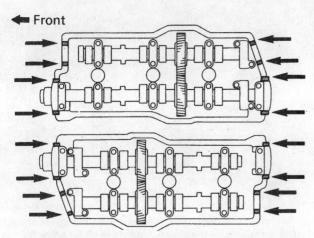

4.8 Apply RTV sealant to the shaded areas (arrows) before installing the gasket and cylinder head cover

4.15 Disconnect the spark plug coils from the harness and remove the coils

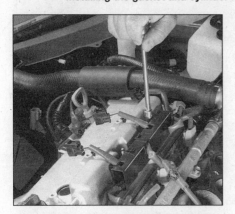

4.16a Remove two nuts and disconnect the left-hand engine harness . . .

4.16b . . . disconnect the wire clips at the timing belt cover and the five bolts retaining the right-hand harness, then move the harness away from the rear valve cover

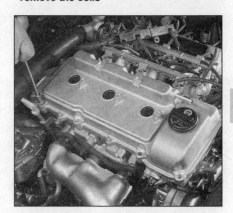

4.17 Remove the bolts and sealing washers and remove the valve cover

2B

Note: *On 1993 and later models, the airbag system will be disabled if the battery is disconnected for more than a brief period. If the airbag light comes on and stays on after the battery is reconnected, the vehicle must be taken to a dealer to have the system reset with a special tool.*

14   Remove the V-bank cover with a 5 mm hex wrench.

If you're removing the rear (firewall side) cover, remove the air cleaner assembly, throttle body and air intake chamber (see Chapter 4).

15   If you're working on the front (radiator side) or both covers, remove the coil connectors, coils and spark plugs **(see illustration)**.

16   Detach the engine wiring harness from the left side of the engine, the number 3 timing belt cover, the rear of the engine and right-hand side **(see illustrations)**.

17   Remove the retaining nuts and sealing washers, then detach the cover(s) **(see illustration)**. If the cover is stuck to the head, bump the end with a wood block and a hammer to jar it loose. If that doesn't work, try to slip a flexible putty knife between the head and cover to break the seal. **Caution:** *Don't pry at the cover-to-head joint or damage to the sealing surfaces may occur, leading to oil leaks after the cover is reinstalled.*

Installation

Refer to illustration 4.20

18   The mating surfaces of the cylinder head and cover must be clean when the cover is installed. Use a gasket scraper to remove all traces of sealant and old gasket material, then clean the mating surfaces with lacquer thinner or acetone. If there's residue or oil on the mating

surfaces when the cover is installed, oil leaks may develop.

19   Install new spark plug tube seals.

20   Apply RTV sealant to the gasket/seal joints at the front and rear camshaft-to-head mounts and install the valve cover with a new gasket **(see illustration)**.

4.20 Apply RTV sealant to the areas indicated (arrows) and install the cover with a new gasket

5.6 Remove the bolts and sealing washers and remove the intake manifold

5.7 This water transfer hose (arrow) on 1MZ-FE engines should be replaced whenever the intake manifold is off for other repairs

21   Tighten the nuts to the torque listed in this Chapter's Specifications in three or four equal steps.
22   Reinstall the remaining parts, run the engine and check for oil leaks.

5   Intake manifold - removal and installation

Removal

Refer to illustrations 5.6 and 5.7

1   Disconnect the negative cable from the battery. **Caution:** *If the stereo in your vehicle is equipped with an anti-theft system, make sure you have the correct activation code before disconnecting the battery.* **Note:** *On 1993 and later models, the airbag system will be disabled if the battery is disconnected for more than a brief period. If the airbag light comes on and stays on after the battery is reconnected, the vehicle must be taken to a dealer to have the system reset with a special tool.*
2   Drain the coolant into a clean container (see Chapter 1).
3   Remove the air cleaner assembly, throttle body, fuel injectors and air intake chamber (see Chapter 4). **Note:** *The intake manifold can be removed with the injectors and fuel rails in place or removed, depending on the work to be done.*
4   Remove the upper (no. 2) idler pulley bracket stay **(see illustration 2.4)**.
5   Clearly label, then detach all remaining wires, hoses and brackets still attached to the intake manifold and coolant outlets. On 3VZ-FE engines, remove the water bypass outlet.
6   Remove the eight mounting nuts/bolts, then detach the manifold from the engine **(see illustration)**. If it's stuck, don't pry between the gasket mating surfaces or damage may result.
7   On 1MZ-FE engines, there is a water transfer hose **(see illustration)** that is exposed only when the intake manifold is removed. Because of the difficulty in getting at this hose for replacement, we recommend that it be replaced with a new hose if the intake manifold is removed for other work.

Installation

Refer to illustration 5.9

8   Use a scraper to remove all traces of old gasket material and sealant from the manifold and cylinder heads, then clean the mating surfaces with lacquer thinner or acetone.
9   Install new gaskets, then position the manifold on the engine. Make sure the gaskets haven't shifted and install the nuts/bolts **(see illustration)**.
10   Tighten the nuts/bolts, in three or four equal steps, to the torque listed in this Chapter's Specifications. Work from the center out

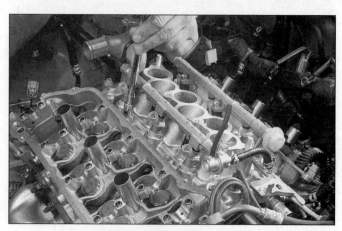

5.9 Install the manifold with new gaskets and torque to specifications

towards the ends to avoid warping the manifold.
11   Install the remaining parts in the reverse order of removal.
12   Refill the cooling system. Run the engine and check for fuel, vacuum and coolant leaks.

6   Exhaust manifolds - removal and installation

Refer to illustrations 6.4a, 6.4b, 6.5 and 6.6
Warning: *The engine must be completely cool before beginning this procedure.*
1   Disconnect the negative cable from the battery. **Caution:** *If the stereo in your vehicle is equipped with an anti-theft system, make sure you have the correct activation code before disconnecting the battery.* **Note:** *On 1993 and later models, the airbag system will be disabled if the battery is disconnected for more than a brief period. If the airbag light comes on and stays on after the battery is reconnected, the vehicle must be taken to a dealer to have the system reset with a special tool.*
2   Spray penetrating oil on the exhaust manifold fasteners and allow it to soak in.
3   Remove the heated oxygen sensors from the front and rear manifolds.
4   Remove the EGR pipe from the exhaust manifold **(see illustrations)**.
5   On the 3VZ-FE engine, remove the heat insulators from the manifold(s) **(see illustration)**.
6   Unbolt the exhaust manifolds from the cylinder heads and slip them off the mounting studs.

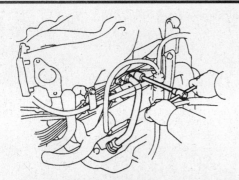

6.4a Remove the EGR pipe (3VZ-FE engine)

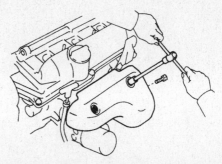

6.5 On 3VZ-FE engines, remove the exhaust heat shield

6.4b Remove the EGR pipe (1MZ-FE engine) from the rear manifold at each end (arrows)

7   Carefully inspect the manifolds and fasteners for cracks and damage.

8   Use a scraper to remove all traces of old gasket material and carbon deposits from the manifolds and cylinder head mating surfaces. If the gasket was leaking, have the manifolds checked for warpage at an automotive machine shop and resurfaced if necessary.

9   Position new gaskets over the cylinder head studs.

10   Install the manifolds and thread the mounting nuts into place.

11   Working from the center out, tighten the nuts to the torque listed in this Chapter's Specifications in three or four equal steps.

12   Reinstall the remaining parts in the reverse order of removal. Use new gaskets when connecting the exhaust pipes.

13   Run the engine and check for exhaust leaks.

7   Timing belt and sprockets - removal, inspection and installation

Removal

Refer to illustrations 7.9, 7.11a, 7.11b, 7.13, 7.14, 7.15, 7.17, 7.19, 7.21, 7.23, 7.26 and 7.28

1   Disconnect the negative cable from the battery. **Caution:** *If the stereo in your vehicle is equipped with an anti-theft system, make sure you have the correct activation code before disconnecting the battery.* **Note:** *On 1993 and later models, the airbag system will be disabled if the battery is disconnected for more than a brief period. If the airbag light comes on and stays on after the battery is reconnected, the vehicle must be taken to a dealer to have the system reset with a special tool.*

2   Remove the coolant overflow tank and windshield washer tank (see Chapter 3).

3   Remove the cruise control actuator and vacuum pump, if equipped.

4   Remove the drivebelts from the alternator and power steering pump (see Chapter 1).

5   Loosen the lug nuts on the right front wheel, but don't remove them.

6   Raise the front of the vehicle and support it securely on jackstands. Apply the parking brake and block the rear wheels. Remove the right front wheel.

7   Remove the right front inner fender apron (see Chapter 11).

8   On the 3VZ-FE engine, remove the power steering fluid reservoir without disconnecting the hoses and secure it aside.

9   Support the engine with a jack from below and remove the right engine mount, braces, bracket and engine movement control rod **(see illustration)**. Use a wood block on the jack and do not place the jack

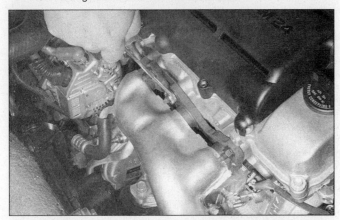

6.6 Unbolt the exhaust manifold from the cylinder head (the heat shield is not removable on the 1MZ-FE engine shown here)

7.9 Remove the engine movement control rod and front engine mount

2B

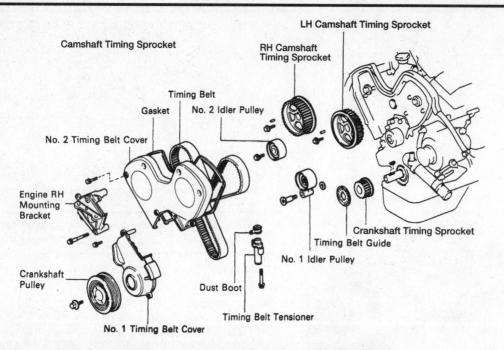

7.11b Remove the number 2 timing belt cover

7.13 If you intend to re-use the belt and the original installation marks are obscured or missing, make new ones

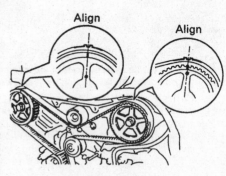

7.14 Both camshaft sprocket timing marks should align with the marks on the rear cover

7.15 Remove the two bolts and detach the timing belt tensioner

directly under the oil pan drain plug.

10   Remove the spark plugs (see Chapter 1).

11   Remove the upper (no. 2) timing belt cover and gasket **(see illustrations)**.

12   Position the number one cylinder at TDC (see Section 3).

13   Check to see if there are installation marks on the timing belt - If you intend to re-use the belt and the marks have been obscured, make new ones **(see illustration)**.

14   Make sure the camshaft pulley timing marks are properly aligned **(see illustration)**.

15   Remove the timing belt tensioner **(see illustration)**. Be sure to remove the rubber boot as well, it may stick in the tensioner recess.

16   Relieve the tension between the rear (right-hand) and front (left-hand) camshaft sprockets by turning the rear sprocket slightly clockwise **(see illustration 7.11a)**.

17   If you plan to re-use the timing belt and the marks were worn off, place a new mark on the belt at the edge of the lower (no. 1) timing belt cover **(see illustration)**. **Note:** *This is necessary only on the 3VZ-FE engine, because there are no internal alignment marks to go by once the lower cover is removed.*

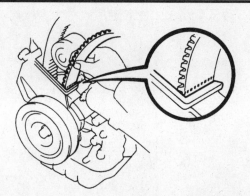

7.17 If you intend to re-use the belt and this mark is worn off, make a new one

7.19 If the camshaft sprockets are damaged, or the cams are to be removed, hold the hex portion of the camshaft (arrow) with a wrench while removing the sprocket bolt

7.21 Remove the flywheel/driveplate cover and use a prybar (arrow) wedged against the ring gear teeth or a converter bolt to hold the crankshaft while loosening the pulley bolt with a breaker bar - the bolt is very tight, so use the appropriate tools

screwdriver into the flywheel/driveplate ring gear teeth or against a converter bolt to keep the engine from turning. Use a breaker bar and socket to loosen the pulley bolt **(see illustration)**.

22   When the crankshaft pulley bolt is loosened, the TDC position of the crankshaft may be disturbed. Check and align again, if necessary **(see illustration 3.8)**. **Note:** *On the 1MZ-FE engine, the crankshaft timing belt sprocket has a TDC alignment mark that lines up with a mark on the oil pump housing, making it easy to check the TDC alignment even after the crankshaft pulley and lower timing belt cover are removed.*

23   The crankshaft pulley should come off with strong hand pressure **(see illustration)** if not, use two prybars behind it to lever it off. Do not use a jaw-type puller.

24   Remove the lower (no. 1) timing belt cover and gasket **(see illustration 7.11a)**.

25   Slip the timing belt guide off the crankshaft.

26   If you're re-using the belt, check for a mark on the belt adjacent to the drilled mark on the crankshaft sprocket **(see illustration)**. If the original mark is gone, make a new one, then slip the belt off the sprocket.

27   Using a 10 mm Allen wrench, remove the no. 1 idler pulley and plate washer **(see illustration 7.11a)**.

28   If it's worn or damaged, or if you're replacing the crankshaft front oil seal, the crankshaft sprocket can now be removed. If it won't come off by hand, lever it off with two screwdrivers **(see illustration)**. On 1MZ-FE engines, a steering wheel type puller may be needed to remove the sprocket. Be careful not to damage the crankshaft sensor

18   Remove the timing belt from the camshaft sprockets.

19   The camshaft sprockets can be removed at this point, if they are worn or damaged. Remove the cylinder head cover(s) (see Section 4) and hold the camshaft with a wrench on the cast-in hex while loosening the sprocket bolt **(see illustration)**. Remove the bolt and detach the sprocket.

20   Remove the upper (no. 2) idler pulley **(see illustration 7.11a)**.

21   Remove the crankshaft (drivebelt) pulley bolt. Wedge a large

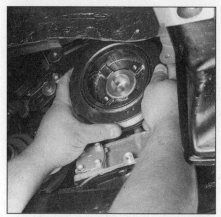

7.23 A puller should not be necessary to remove the crankshaft pulley - if it is stuck use two prybars behind it

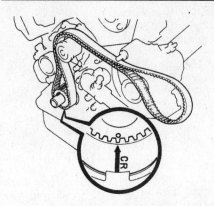

7.26 There should be a mark on the belt next to the drilled mark on the sprocket

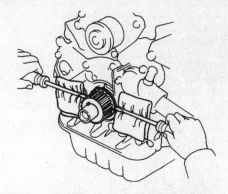

7.28 Pad the front of the engine when prying off the crankshaft sprocket

7.31 Check the tensioner for signs of leakage and test for leakdown by forcing it against an immovable object

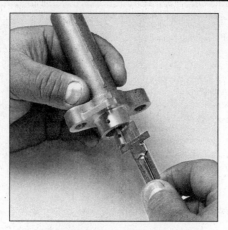

7.32 Measure the tensioner pushrod protrusion and compare it to the Specifications

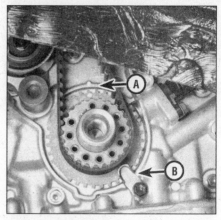

7.35 On 1MZ-FE engines, align the marks on the crankshaft timing sprocket with the marks on the oil pump case (arrow A), and replace the sprocket retainer (arrow B) and bolt

portion of the sprocket during the removal process. If necessary, remove the lower sprocket retainer **(see illustration 7.35)**.

Inspection

Refer to illustrations 7.31 and 7.32

29   Refer to Chapter 2, Part A for the timing belt inspection procedures.

30   Check the belt tensioner for visible oil leakage. If there's only a faint trace of oil on the pushrod side, the tensioner seal is in satisfactory condition.

31   Hold the tensioner in both hands and push it forcefully against an immovable object **(see illustration)**. If the pushrod moves, replace the tensioner.

32   Measure the protrusion of the pushrod from the housing end **(see illustration)**. Compare your measurement to this Chapter's Specifications. If the protrusion is not as specified, replace the tensioner.

33   Check that the idler pulleys turn smoothly.

Installation

Refer to illustrations 7.35 and 7.50

34   Remove all dirt, oil and grease from the timing belt area at the front of the engine.

35   Align the crankshaft timing sprocket keyway with the crankshaft key and install the sprocket with the flange side up against the engine **(see illustration 7.11a)**. On 1MZ-FE engines, be careful not to damage the crankshaft sensor portion of the crankshaft sprocket. Check the alignment of the TDC marks on the sprocket and the oil pump housing, and reinstall the retainer and bolt **(see illustration)**.

36   Apply thread locking compound to the first two or three threads on the lower (no. 1) idler pulley bolt, then position the idler pulley and washer and install the bolt. Tighten the bolt to the torque listed in this Chapter's Specifications.

37   Install the timing belt, starting at the crankshaft sprocket. If you're re-using the original belt, align the marks on the belt with the marks on the sprockets and covers. Install the belt over the lower (no. 1) idler and water pump pulleys.

38   Slip the belt guide over the crankshaft with the cupped side facing out.

39   Install the lower (no. 1) timing belt cover and gasket **(see illustration 7.11a)**.

40   Slip the crankshaft (drivebelt) sprocket onto the crankshaft, aligning the pulley keyway with the crankshaft key. Install the bolt and tighten it to the torque listed in this Chapter's Specifications. Use the method described in Step 21 to keep the crankshaft from turning.

41   Install the upper (no. 2) idler pulley. Tighten the bolt to the torque listed in this Chapter's Specifications. Make sure the pulley turns smoothly.

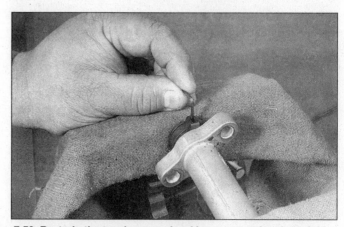

7.50 Restrain the tensioner pushrod by compressing the unit in a vise and inserting a pin approximately 0.050-inch (1.27 mm) in diameter - make sure the rubber boot is in place

42   Install the front (left-hand) camshaft sprocket (if it was removed) on the camshaft with the flange side facing OUT. Align the pin hole in the sprocket with the pin in the end of the camshaft.

43   Install the retaining bolt and tighten it to the torque listed in this Chapter's Specifications. Use the method described in Step 19 to keep the camshaft from turning.

44   Recheck the timing marks to be sure the crankshaft hasn't turned **(see illustration 3.8)**. If you're re-using the original belt, the installation mark should line up as it did in Step 18. If not, change the position of the timing belt on the crankshaft sprocket. The mark on the front (left-hand) camshaft sprocket should be at the top (12 o'clock position), aligned with the mark on the rear (no. 3) timing cover.

45   The rear (right-hand) camshaft knock pin hole should be at the top (12 o'clock position). If necessary, remove the valve cover and turn the camshaft slightly with a wrench to align the sprocket with the mark on the rear (no. 3) cover **(see illustration 7.14)**.

46   Turn the front (left-hand) camshaft sprocket clockwise slightly (about one tooth) with a pin spanner. If the special tool isn't available, grip the hex on the camshaft with a wrench and turn it **(see illustration 7.19)**. If you're re-using the original belt, align the installation mark with the camshaft timing mark. Slip the belt onto the sprocket, then turn the camshaft counterclockwise, back to its original position. There should now be slight tension on the belt.

47   Install the rear (right-hand) camshaft sprocket (if it was removed) on the camshaft with the flange side facing IN. Align the pin hole in the

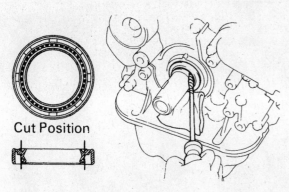

8.3 Cut away the crankshaft seal lip, wrap a screwdriver tip with tape and pry out the seal

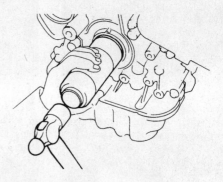

8.5 Lubricate the seal lip and drive the new crankshaft seal into place with a large socket or piece of pipe and a hammer

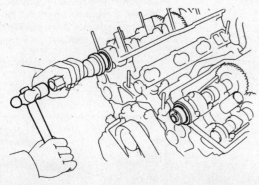

9.5 Lubricate the seal lip and tap the new camshaft seal into place with a large socket or piece of pipe and a hammer

sprocket with the knock pin in the end of the camshaft.

48 Install the retaining bolt and tighten it to the torque listed in this Chapter's Specifications. Use the method described in Step 19 to keep the camshaft from turning. Be sure the timing mark is still aligned with the rear (no. 3) cover.

49 Slip the belt onto the sprocket. If you're re-using the original belt, align the installation marks.

50 Using a press or vise, slowly compress the timing belt tensioner pushrod **(see illustration)**. Insert a metal pin, drill bit or Allen wrench through the holes in the pushrod and housing. Release the pressure from the press or vise.

51 Install the timing belt tensioner and tighten the bolts to the torque listed in this Chapter's Specifications. Remove the retaining pin.

52 Using a socket and breaker bar on the crankshaft pulley bolt, turn the crankshaft slowly through two complete revolutions (720-degrees). Recheck the timing marks **(see illustrations 3.8 and 7.14)**. **Caution:** *If the timing marks are not aligned exactly as shown, repeat the timing belt installation procedure. DO NOT start the engine until you're absolutely certain that the timing belt is installed correctly. Serious and costly engine damage could occur if the belt is installed wrong.*

53 Reinstall the right engine mounting bracket.

54 Install the upper (no. 2) timing belt cover and gasket.

55 Install the right engine mount and braces and tighten the bolts securely.

56 Reinstall the remaining parts in the reverse order of removal.

8 Crankshaft front oil seal - replacement

Refer to illustrations 8.3 and 8.5

1 Remove the timing belt and crankshaft timing belt sprocket (see Section 7).

2 Note how far the seal is recessed in the bore, then cut away the

seal lip with a razor knife.

3 Carefully pry the seal out of the engine with a screwdriver or seal removal tool **(see illustration)**. If you use a screwdriver, wrap tape around the tip - don't scratch the housing bore or damage the crankshaft (if the crankshaft is damaged, the new seal will end up leaking).

4 Clean the bore in the engine and coat the outer edge of the new seal with engine oil or multi-purpose grease. Apply the same grease to the seal lip.

5 Using a socket with an outside diameter slightly smaller than the outside diameter of the seal, carefully drive the new seal into place with a hammer **(see illustration)**. Make sure it's installed squarely and driven in to the same depth as the original. If a socket isn't available, a short section of large diameter pipe will also work. Check the seal after installation to make sure the spring didn't pop out of place.

6 Reinstall the crankshaft timing sprocket and timing belt (see Section 7). On 1MZ-FE engines, be careful not to scratch the crankshaft sensor portion of the sprocket.

7 Run the engine and check for oil leaks at the front seal.

9 Camshaft oil seals - replacement

Refer to illustration 9.5

1 Remove the timing belt and camshaft sprocket(s) (see Section 7).

2 Remove the bolts and detach the rear (no. 3) timing belt cover.

3 Note how far the seal is seated in the bore, then carefully pry it out with a straight-slot screwdriver. Wrap the screwdriver tip with tape - don't scratch the bore or damage the camshaft (if the camshaft is damaged, the new seal will end up leaking).

4 Clean the bore and coat the outer edge of the new seal with engine oil or multi-purpose grease. Apply multi-purpose grease to the seal lip.

5 Using a socket with an outside diameter slightly smaller than the outside diameter of the seal, carefully drive the new seal into place with a hammer. Make sure it's installed squarely and driven in to the same depth as the original. If a socket isn't available, a short section of pipe will also work **(see illustration)**.

6 Reinstall the rear timing belt cover and tighten the bolts.

7 Reinstall the camshaft sprocket(s) and timing belt (see Section 7).

8 Run the engine and check for oil leaks at the camshaft seal.

10 Camshafts and lifters - removal, inspection and installation

Note: *Before beginning this procedure, obtain two 6 x 1.0 mm bolts 16 to 20 mm long. They will be referred to as service bolts in the text. The basic procedure below is the same for both V6 engines, although the camshaft gears are at the back of the cylinder heads on the 1MZ-FE engine, not the middle as on the 3VZ-FE engine.*

2B

10.3 Align the timing marks (arrow) on the camshaft gears

10.4 Install a service bolt through the sub-gear into the main gear

10.10 Mark up a cardboard box to store the lifters/shims and camshaft bearing caps - use a separate box for each set to avoid mix-ups and mark the FRONT, INTAKE and EXHAUST orientation

10.12 With the hex portion of the camshaft held in a vise, use a two-pin spanner to remove the tension from the subgear and remove the service bolt, then release the subgear

10.13 Remove the snap-ring with a pair of snap-ring pliers

Removal

Refer to illustrations 10.3, 10.4, 10.10, 10.12, 10.13 and 10.14

1   Remove the valve covers (see Section 4) and the timing belt (see Section 7).

2   On 3VZ-FE engines, remove the distributor (see Chapter 5).

3   The following steps apply to the removal of each of the four camshafts. On each head, the exhaust camshaft subgear is secured first, the exhaust cam removed, then the intake camshaft. Align the cam timing marks on the drive and driven gears **(see illustration)**. Turn the camshaft with a wrench if necessary.

4   Secure the exhaust camshaft sub-gear to the driven gear with a service bolt installed in the threaded hole **(see illustration)**. **Caution:** *Since the camshaft thrust clearance is minimal, the camshafts must be held level as they are being removed. If they aren't, the portion of the cylinder head next to the cam gears may crack or be damaged by the gear leverage. Before lifting a camshaft out of the head, make certain that the torsional spring force of the sub-gear has been eliminated by the service bolt.*

5   Loosen the camshaft bearing cap bolts in 1/4-turn increments until they can be removed by hand. Follow the reverse of the recommended tightening sequence **(see illustration 10.29)**.

6   Remove the bearing caps and gently lift out the exhaust camshaft. Be sure to keep it level.

7   Loosen the intake camshaft bearing cap bolts in 1/4-turn increments until they can be removed by hand. Follow the reverse of the recommended tightening sequence **(see illustration 10.24)**.

8   Remove the intake bearing caps and oil seal and gently lift out the intake camshaft. Be sure to keep it level.

9   Repeat the steps for the left-hand (front) cylinder head.

10   Store the bearing caps in the correct order. **Note:** *If necessary, the valve lifters and shims can now be removed with a magnetic tool. Be sure to store them separately so they can be reinstalled in their original locations* **(see illustration)**.

11   To disassemble an exhaust camshaft gear, mount the cam in a vise with the jaws gripping the large hex on the shaft.

12   Install a second service bolt in the unthreaded hole in the camshaft sub-gear. Using a screwdriver positioned against the service bolt just installed, rotate the sub-gear clockwise and remove the first service bolt. The second bolt isn't needed if you have a two-pin spanner **(see illustration)**.

13   Remove the sub-gear snap-ring **(see illustration)**.

14   The wave washer, sub-gear and camshaft gear spring can now be removed from the camshaft **(see illustration)**. Be sure to keep the parts from the left side camshaft separate from the right side.

Inspection

15   Refer to Chapter 2, Part A for camshaft, lifter and related component inspection procedures. Be sure to use the Specifications in this Part of Chapter 2 for the V6 engines.

10.14 Remove the wave washer (1), the camshaft subgear (2) and the gear spring (3)

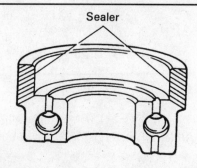

10.22 Apply RTV sealant to the shaded areas on the bearing cap

Installation

Refer to illustrations 10.21, 10.22, 10.23, 10.24 and 10.29

16   Reassemble the exhaust camshaft gear(s) by installing the camshaft gear spring, sub-gear, wave washer and snap-ring.

17   Mount the camshaft in a padded vise.

18   Insert a service bolt into the unthreaded hole in the camshaft subgear. Using a screwdriver, align the holes of the camshaft driven gear and sub-gear by turning the camshaft sub-gear clockwise. Install a second service bolt in the threaded hole, tightening it to clamp the gears together. Remove the service bolt from the unthreaded hole. Repeat the procedure for the other camshaft.

19   Apply moly-base grease or engine assembly lube to the lifters, then install them in their original locations in the cylinder heads. Make sure the valve adjustment shims are in place in the lifters, and that all lifters are installed in their original bores.

Intake camshaft in rear (right-hand) cylinder head

20   Apply moly-base grease or engine assembly lube to the camshaft lobes, bearing journals and gear thrust faces.

21   Set the intake camshaft in place in the rear cylinder head with the timing marks (two dots) facing the exhaust camshaft side of the head **(see illustration)**.

22   Apply a thin coat of RTV sealant to the outer edges of the front bearing cap cylinder head mating surfaces **(see illustration)**.

23   Install the bearing caps in numerical order with the arrows pointing toward the front (timing belt end) of the engine **(see illustration)**.

24   Tighten the bearing cap bolts in 1/4-turn increments to the torque listed in this Chapter's Specifications. Follow the recommended sequence **(see illustration)**.

25   Refer to Section 9 and install a new camshaft oil seal.

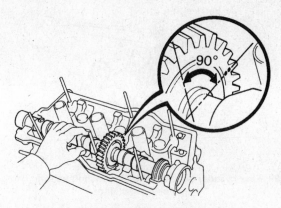

10.21 Set the rear cylinder head intake camshaft into place with the two dots at the 3 o'clock position (facing the exhaust camshaft)

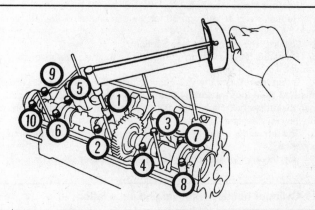

10.23 Install the rear cylinder head INTAKE camshaft bearing caps as shown with the arrows pointing toward the timing belt end of the engine

Exhaust camshaft in rear (right-hand) cylinder head

26   Apply moly-base grease or engine assembly lube to the camshaft lobes, bearing journals and gear thrust faces.

27   Set the exhaust camshaft in place in the rear cylinder head with the timing marks (two dots) aligned with the intake camshaft timing marks **(see illustration 10.3)**.

28   Install the bearing caps in numerical order with the arrows pointing toward the front (timing-belt end) of the engine.

29   Tighten the bearing cap bolts in 1/4-turn increments to the torque

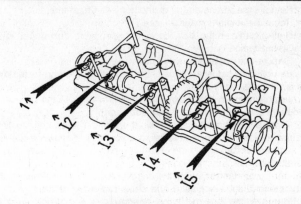

10.24 Rear cylinder head INTAKE camshaft bearing cap bolt tightening sequence

2B

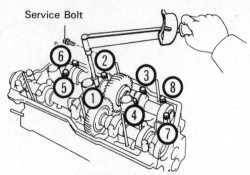

10.29 Rear cylinder head EXHAUST camshaft bearing cap bolt tightening sequence

11.10 Remove the recessed bolts with an 8 mm hex bit socket

listed in this Chapter's Specifications. Follow the recommended sequence **(see illustration)**.

30   Remove the service bolt.

31   Repeat steps 16 through 30 for the camshafts on the left-hand (front) cylinder head.

32   Reinstall the timing belt (see Section 7).

33   Reinstall the remaining components in the reverse order of removal.

34   Before reinstalling the valve covers, use RTV sealant in the areas indicated **(see illustrations 4.8 and 4.20)**. On the 1MZ-FE engine, clean the rubber half-circle plugs for the back of the heads and reinstall with new RTV sealant.

35   The remainder of the installation is the reverse of the disassembly sequence.

36   Run the engine, then check for leaks and proper operation.

11   Cylinder heads - removal and installation

Removal

Refer to illustration 11.10

1   Disconnect the negative cable from the battery. **Caution:** *If the stereo in your vehicle is equipped with an anti-theft system, make sure you have the correct activation code before disconnecting the battery.* **Note:** *On 1993 and later models, the airbag system will be disabled if the battery is disconnected for more than a brief period. If the airbag light comes on and stays on after the battery is reconnected, the vehicle must be taken to a dealer to have the system reset with a special tool.*

2   Drain the cooling system, including the block (see Chapter 1).

3   Remove the air intake chamber, fuel delivery pipes and injectors (see Chapter 4).

4   Remove the exhaust manifold(s) (see Section 6).

5   Remove the alternator and distributor (see Chapter 5).

6   Remove the intake manifold (see Section 5).

7   Remove the timing belt, camshaft sprockets and upper idler pulley (see Section 7).

8   Remove the upper timing belt cover 3.

9   Remove the camshaft(s) from the head(s) you intend to remove (see Section 10).

10   Using an 8 mm hex bit or Allen wrench, remove the recessed head bolts (one in each head) **(see illustration)**.

11   Using a 12-point socket, loosen the cylinder head bolts in 1/4-turn increments until they can be removed by hand. Follow the reverse order of the factory recommended tightening sequence **(see illustration 11.22)**.

12   Lift the cylinder head off the engine block. If the head is stuck, place a wood block against it and strike the wood with a hammer. **Caution:** *Don't pry between the head and block. The gasket surfaces may be damaged and leaks could result.*

13   Repeat the procedure for the other head.

11.19 Be sure the new head gaskets are positioned right side up (check all holes and coolant passages for correct alignment) and over the block dowels

Installation

Refer to illustrations 11.19 and 11.22

14   The mating surfaces of the cylinder heads and block must be perfectly clean when the heads are installed.

15   Use a gasket scraper to remove all traces of carbon and old gasket material, then clean the mating surfaces with lacquer thinner or acetone. If there's oil on the mating surfaces when the head is installed, the gasket may not seal correctly and leaks could develop. When working on the block, stuff the cylinders with clean shop rags to keep out debris. Use a vacuum cleaner to remove material that falls into the cylinders.

16   Check the block and head mating surfaces for nicks, deep scratches and other damage. If damage is slight, it can be removed with a file; if it's excessive, machining may be the only alternative.

17   Use a tap of the correct size to chase the threads in the cylinder head bolt holes, then clean the holes with compressed air - make sure that nothing remains in the holes. **Warning:** *Wear eye protection when using compressed air!*

18   Mount each bolt in a vise and run a die down the threads to remove corrosion and restore the threads. Dirt, corrosion, sealant and damaged threads will affect torque readings.

19   Position the new gaskets over the dowel pins in the block **(see illustration)**.

20   Carefully set the head on the block without disturbing the gasket.

21   Before installing the head bolts, apply a small amount of clean engine oil to the threads.

22   Install the bolts in their original locations and tighten them finger tight. Following the recommended sequence, tighten the bolts to the

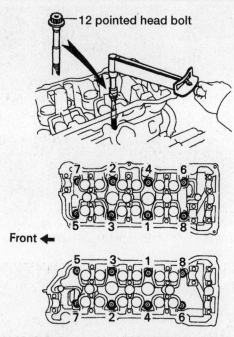

11.22 Cylinder head bolt TIGHTENING sequence

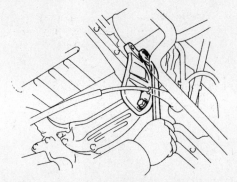

12.8 Unbolt the engine stiffener plate at the bellhousing

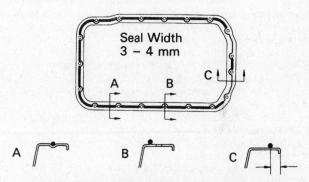

12.14 Apply RTV sealant to the oil pan as shown and install immediately

torque listed in this Chapter's Specifications (see illustration). Don't tighten the recessed bolt at this time.

23 Mark the front of each bolt head with paint. You can also mark the socket you are using. Place the socket over the 12-point bolt so that you can observe the mark, and reference Step 24.

24 Following the same sequence, tighten each bolt an additional 1/4-turn (90-degrees) (see illustration 11.22).

25 On the 3VZ-FE engine only, tighten each bolt yet another 1/4-turn (90-degrees) following the same sequence. The paint marks should now all be 180-degrees from the starting point.

26 Tighten the recessed bolt to the torque listed in this Chapter's Specifications.

27 Repeat the entire procedure to install the other cylinder head.

28 The remaining installation steps are the reverse of removal.

29 Refill the cooling system, change the oil and filter (see Chapter 1), run the engine and check for leaks.

12 Oil pan - removal and installation

3VZ-FE engine

Removal

Refer to illustration 12.8

1 Remove the hood (see Chapter 11).

2 Disconnect the negative cable from the battery. **Caution:** *If the stereo in your vehicle is equipped with an anti-theft system, make sure you have the correct activation code before disconnecting the battery.* **Note:** *On 1993 and later models, the airbag system will be disabled if the battery is disconnected for more than a brief period. If the airbag light comes on and stays on after the battery is reconnected, the vehicle must be taken to a dealer to have the system reset with a special tool.*

3 Raise the vehicle and support it securely on jackstands.

4 Remove the engine splash shields.

5 Drain the engine oil.

6 remove the oil filter.

7 Disconnect the front exhaust pipe from the catalytic converter, the two bolts and the support bracket, and the nuts holding the pipe to the front and rear exhaust manifolds (see Chapter 4).

8 Remove the engine stiffener plate (see illustration).

9 Remove the bolts and detach the oil pan. If it's stuck, pry it loose very carefully with a small screwdriver or putty knife. Don't damage the mating surfaces of the pan and block or oil leaks could develop.

Installation

Refer to illustration 12.14

10 Use a scraper to remove all traces of old sealant from the block and oil pan. Clean the mating surfaces with lacquer thinner or acetone.

11 Make sure the threaded bolt holes in the block are clean.

12 Check the oil pan flange for distortion, particularly around the bolt holes. If necessary, place the pan on a wood block and use a hammer to flatten and restore the gasket surface.

13 Inspect the oil pump pick-up tube assembly for cracks and a blocked strainer. If the pick-up was removed, clean it with solvent or thinner and install it now, using a new gasket. Tighten the fasteners to the torque listed in this Chapter's Specifications.

14 Apply a 3 to 4 mm wide bead of RTV sealant to the oil pan flange (see illustration). **Note:** *The oil pan must be installed within 5 minutes once the sealer has been applied.*

15 Carefully position the oil pan on the engine block and install the bolts. Working from the center out, tighten them to the torque listed in this Chapter's Specifications in three or four steps.

16 The remainder of installation is the reverse of removal. Be sure to add oil and install a new oil filter.

17 Run the engine and check for oil pressure and leaks.

1MZ-FE engine

Removal

Refer to illustrations 12.24, 12.25, 12.26 and 12.28

18 Remove the hood (see Chapter 11).

19 Disconnect the negative cable from the battery. **Caution:** *If the stereo in your vehicle is equipped with an anti-theft system, make sure you have the correct activation code before disconnecting the battery.*

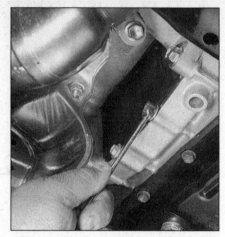

12.24 Remove two bolts and the flywheel housing cover

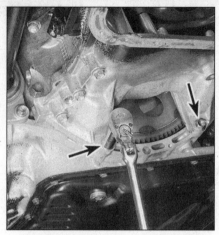

12.25 Remove the two bolts (arrows) securing the aluminum upper pan to the transaxle

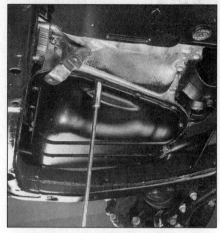

12.26 Remove the steel section of the oil pan

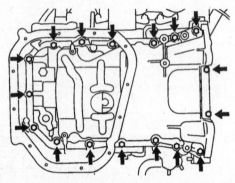

12.28 Remove all 17 of the bolts retaining the aluminum portion of the pan

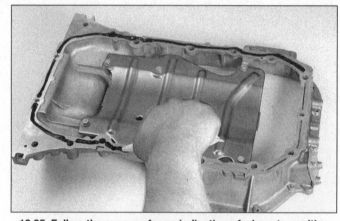

12.35 Follow the grooves for an indication of where to position the bead of new RTV sealant on the aluminum pan section and install the pan

Note: *On 1993 and later models, the airbag system will be disabled if the battery is disconnected for more than a brief period. If the airbag light comes on and stays on after the battery is reconnected, the vehicle must be taken to a dealer to have the system reset with a special tool.*

20   Raise the vehicle and support it securely on jackstands.
21   Remove the engine splash shields.
22   Drain the engine oil and remove the oil filter.
23   Disconnect the front exhaust pipe from the catalytic converter, the two bolts and the support bracket, and the nuts holding the pipe to the front and rear exhaust manifolds (see Chapter 4).
24   Remove the flywheel housing cover **(see illustration)**.
25   Remove the two bolts holding the aluminum oil pan section to the transaxle **(see illustration)**.
26   Remove the 10 bolts and two nuts securing the steel oil pan section, and detach the steel pan **(see illustration)**. If it's stuck, pry it loose very carefully with a small screwdriver or putty knife. Don't damage the mating surfaces of the pan or oil leaks could develop.
27   Remove the oil pump strainer/pickup.
28   Remove the 17 bolts securing the aluminum oil pan section to the block **(see illustration)**. **Note:** *Some bolts are within the area formerly covered by the steel pan section.*
29   Remove the oil pan baffle plate, if necessary.

Installation

Refer to illustration 12.35 and 12.39

30   Use a scraper to remove all traces of old sealant from the block and oil pan. Clean the mating surfaces with lacquer thinner or acetone.
31   Make sure the threaded bolt holes in the block are clean.
32   Check the flange of the steel pan section for distortion, partic-

ularly around the bolt holes. If necessary, place the pan on a wood block and use a hammer to flatten and restore the gasket surface.
33   If the baffle had been removed, reinstall it now.
34   Clean the mating surfaces of the aluminum block and aluminum pan section, being careful not to gouge the soft metal, which could lead to leaks.
35   Apply RTV sealant to the aluminum pan section, following the

12.39 Install the steel section and tighten the bolts evenly to avoid warping the pan flange

13.4 The oil pick-up tube is held in place with three fasteners (arrows)

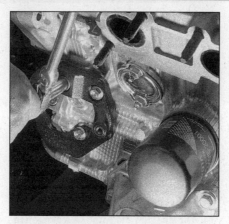

13.7 Unbolt the air conditioning compressor bracket from the block

13.8 Remove the power steering pump adjuster bar and pry the pump away from the oil pump body

13.9 Using a 10 mm hex bit or Allen wrench, remove the lower timing belt idler pulley

13.11 Remove the oil pressure relief plug, spring and valve

13.12 Use a large Phillips screwdriver or bit to remove the screws retaining the pump cover

2B

grooves, which indicates where to apply the bead of sealant inside and outside the bolts **(see illustration)**.

36   Install the aluminum pan section within 5 minutes and uniformly tighten the bolts to the torque listed in this Chapter's Specifications in several passes.

37   Inspect the oil pump pick-up/strainer assembly for cracks and a blocked strainer. If the pick-up was removed, clean it with solvent or thinner and install it now, using a new gasket. Tighten the fasteners to the torque listed in this Chapter's Specifications.

38   Apply a 3 to 4 mm wide bead of RTV sealant to the flange of the steel oil pan section. **Note:** *The steel pan section must be installed within 5 minutes once the sealant has been applied.*

39   Carefully position the oil pan on the engine block and install the bolts. Working from the center out, tighten them to the torque listed in this Chapter's Specifications in three or four steps **(see illustration)**.

40   The remainder of installation is the reverse of removal. Be sure to add oil and install a new oil filter.

41   Run the engine and check for oil pressure and leaks.

13   Oil pump - removal, inspection and installation

Removal

Refer to illustrations 13.4, 13.7, 13.8, 13.9, 13.11 and 13.12

1   Remove the oil pan (see Section 12).

2   Remove the timing belt (see Section 7) and lower timing belt idler pulley.

3   Remove the crankshaft timing sprocket (see Section 7).

4   Remove the oil pick-up tube **(see illustration)**.

5   Remove the alternator (see Chapter 5).

6   Unbolt the air conditioning compressor and set it aside without disconnecting the refrigerant lines.

7   Remove the compressor bracket **(see illustration)**.

8   Remove the power steering adjusting bar and pry the pump away from the oil pump body **(see illustration)**.

9   Remove the lower timing belt idler pulley **(see illustration)**.

10   Remove the bolts and detach the oil pump from the engine. You may have to pry carefully between the front main bearing cap and the pump body with a screwdriver.

11   Remove the O-ring. Remove the oil pressure relief valve snap-ring, retainer, spring and valve **(see illustration)**. **Warning:** *The spring is tightly compressed - be careful and wear eye protection.*

12   Use a large Phillips screwdriver to remove the eight screws retaining the body cover to the rear of the oil pump **(see illustration)**.

13   Lift the cover off and remove the pump rotors.

14   Use a scraper to remove all traces of sealant and old gasket material from the pump body and engine block, then clean the mating surfaces with lacquer thinner or acetone.

Inspection

Refer to illustrations 13.17a, 13.17b and 13.17c

15   Clean all components with solvent, then inspect them for wear and damage.

16   Check the oil pressure relief valve sliding surface and valve spring. If either the spring or the valve is damaged, they must be replaced as a set.

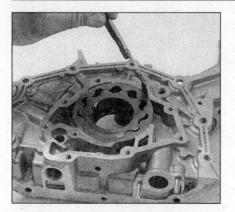

13.17a Measure the driven rotor-to-body clearance with a feeler gauge

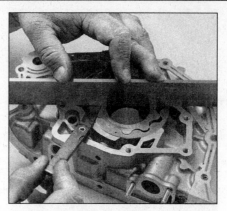

13.17b Measure the rotor side clearance with a precision straightedge and feeler gauge

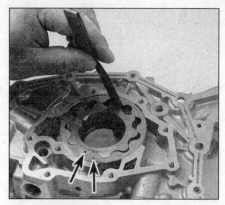

13.17c Measure the rotor tip clearance with a feeler gauge - note the rotor marks are facing out (when the pump body cover is installed, the marks will be against the cover)

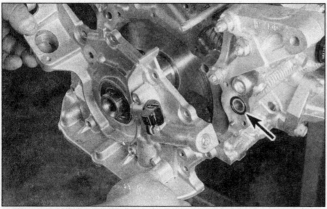

13.26 Be sure to align the drive rotor and the crankshaft as the oil pump is installed, and install a new O-ring (arrow) on the block

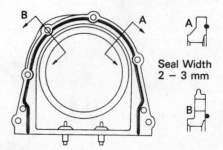

15.1 Apply sealant to the oil seal retainer-to-block mating surface

Seal Width 2 – 3 mm

17   Check the clearance of the following components with a feeler gauge and compare the measurements to this Chapter's Specifications (**see illustrations**):

 a) *Driven rotor-to-oil pump body*
 b) *Rotor side clearance*
 c) *Rotor tip clearance*

Installation

Refer to illustration 13.26

18   Pry the old crankshaft seal out with a screwdriver.

19   Apply multi-purpose grease or engine oil to the outer edge of the new seal and carefully drive it into place with a deep socket and a hammer. Also apply multi-purpose grease to the seal lip.

20   Place the drive and driven rotors into the pump body with the marks facing out (**see illustration 13.17c**).

21   Pack the pump cavity with petroleum jelly and install the cover. Tighten the screws securely following a criss-cross pattern.

22   Lubricate the oil pressure relief valve with engine oil and install the valve components in the pump body.

23   Use acetone or lacquer thinner and a clean rag to remove all traces of oil from the gasket surfaces.

24   Apply a 2 to 3 mm wide bead of RTV sealant to the oil pump. Avoid using an excessive amount of sealer, especially around oil passages and bolt holes. Assembly must be completed within five minutes of sealant application, otherwise the material must be removed and reapplied.

25   Position a new O-ring on the block.

26   Engage the spline teeth on the oil pump drive rotor with the large teeth on the crankshaft and slide the pump into place (**see illustration**).

27   Install the oil pump mounting bolts in their original locations and tighten them to the torque listed in this Chapter's Specifications in a criss-cross pattern.

28   Using a new gasket, install the oil pick-up tube and tighten the fasteners to the torque listed in this Chapter's Specifications.

29   Reinstall the remaining parts in the reverse order of removal.

30   Add oil, start the engine and check for oil leaks.

31   Recheck the engine oil level.

14   Flywheel/driveplate - removal and installation

Refer to Chapter 2, Part A for this procedure, but be sure to use the torque specifications in this Part of Chapter 2 for the V6 engine.

15   Rear main oil seal - replacement

Refer to illustration 15.1

1   Refer to Chapter 2, Part A for this procedure, but note that the V6 engine doesn't have a gasket between the seal retainer and the engine block. Instead, apply a 2 to 3 mm wide bead of RTV sealant to the retainer flange (**see illustration**) before attaching the retainer to the block. Also, be sure to use the torque specifications in this Part of Chapter 2 for the V6 engine.

16   Engine mounts - check and replacement

Refer to Chapter 2, Part A, but note that the V6 engine mounts are slightly different in ways that don't significantly affect the check and replacement procedures.

Chapter 2 Part C
General engine overhaul procedures

Contents

2C

Specifications

5S-FE four-cylinder engine

General

Displacement	134 cubic inches (2.2 liters)
Cylinder compression pressure	
Standard	178 psi
Minimum	142 psi
Oil pressure (engine warm)	
At idle	4.3 psi minimum
At 3000 rpm	36 to 71 psi

Cylinder head

Warpage limits	
Block surface	0.0020 inch
Manifold surfaces	0.0031 inch

Valves and related components

Valve margin width	
Standard	0.031 to 0.047 inch
Minimum	0.020 inch
Valve stem diameter	
Intake	0.2350 to 0.2356 inch
Exhaust	0.2348 to 0.2354 inch
Valve stem-to-guide clearance	
Intake	
Standard	0.0010 to 0.0024 inch
Service limit	0.0031 inch
Exhaust	
Standard	0.0012 to 0.0026 inch
Service limit	0.0039 inch
Valve spring	
Out-of-square limit	0.079 inch
Free length	1.6520 to 1.6531 inches
Installed height	1.366 inches

5S-FE four-cylinder engine (continued)

Valves and related components (continued)

Valve lifter
   Diameter .... 1.2191 to 1.2195 inches
   Lifter bore diameter .... 1.2204 to 1.2212 inch
   Lifter-to-bore clearance
      Standard .... 0.0009 to 0.0020 inch
      Service limit .... 0.0028 inch

Crankshaft and connecting rods

Connecting rod journal
   Diameter .... 2.0466 to 2.0472 inches
   Taper and out-of-round limits .... 0.0008 inch
   Bearing oil clearance
      Standard .... 0.0009 to 0.0022 inch
      Service limit .... 0.0031 inch
Connecting rod side clearance (endplay)
   Standard .... 0.0063 to 0.0123 inch
   Service limit .... 0.0138 inch
Main bearing journal
   Diameter .... 2.1653 to 2.1655 inches
   Taper and out-of-round limits .... 0.0008 inch
   Runout limit .... 0.0024 inch
   Bearing oil clearance (standard)
      No. 3 (center) main .... 0.0010 to 0.0017 inch
      All others .... 0.0006 to 0.0013 inch
      Service limit .... 0.0031 inch
Crankshaft endplay
   Standard .... 0.0008 to 0.0087 inch
   Service limit .... 0.0118 inch
   Thrust washer thickness .... 0.0961 to 0.0980 inch

Balancer assembly

Balance shaft no.1-to-balance shaft no. 2 backlash (off-engine)
   Position 1 .... 0.0008 to 0.0030 inch
   Position 2 .... 0.0002 to 0.0030 inch
   Position 3 .... 0.0002 to 0.0022 inch
Balance shaft no. 1-to-crankshaft backlash (on-engine) .... 0.0010 to 0.0035 inch
Balance shaft endplay (thrust clearance)
   Standard .... 0.0026 to 0.0043 inch
   Service Limit .... 0.0043 inch

Engine block

Deck warpage limit .... 0.0020 inch
Cylinder bore diameter
   Standard
      Mark 1 .... 3.4252 to 3.4256 inches
      Mark 2 .... 3.4256 to 3.4260 inches
      Mark 3 .... 3.4260 to 3.4264 inches
   Service limit .... 3.4342 inches
Taper and out-of-round limits .... 0.0008 inch

Pistons and rings

Piston diameter
   Mark 1 .... 3.4193 to 3.4197 inches
   Mark 2 .... 3.4197 to 3.4201 inches
   Mark 3 .... 3.4201 to 3.4205 inches
Piston-to-bore clearance
   Standard .... 0.0055 to 0.0063 inch
   Service limit .... 0.0071 inch
Piston ring end gap
   No. 1 (top) compression ring
      Standard .... 0.0106 to 0.0197 inch
      Service limit .... 0.0433 inch
   No. 2 (middle) compression ring
      Standard .... 0.0138 to 0.0234 inch
      Service limit .... 0.0472 inch
   Oil ring
      Standard .... 0.0079 to 0.0217 inch
      Service limit .... 0.0453 inch

Piston ring groove clearance
No. 1 (top) compression ring .... 0.0016 to 0.0031 inch
No. 2 (middle) compression ring .... 0.0012 to 0.0028 inch

Torque specifications*

Ft-lbs (unless otherwise indicated)

Main bearing cap bolts 43
Connecting rod cap nuts
Step 1 18
Step 2 .... turn an additional 90-degrees (1/4-turn)
Engine balancer assembly to block 36

* **Note:** *Refer to Part A for additional torque specifications.*

3VZ-FE V6 engine

General

Displacement .... 183 cubic inches (3.0 liters)
Cylinder compression pressure at 250 rpm
Standard .... 178 psi
Minimum .... 142 psi
Oil pressure (engine hot)
At 3000 rpm .... 43 to 78 psi
At idle .... 4.3 psi minimum

Cylinder head

Warpage limit .... 0.0039 inch

Valves and related components

Valve margin width
Standard .... 0.0394 inch
Minimum .... 0.0197 inch
Valve stem diameter
Intake .... 0.2350 to 0.2356 inch
Exhaust .... 0.2348 to 0.2354 inch
Valve stem-to-guide clearance
Intake
Standard .... 0.001 to 0.0024 inch
Service limit .... 0.0031 inch
Exhaust
Standard .... 0.0012 to 0.0026 inch
Service limit .... 0.0039 inch
Valve spring
Out-of-square limit .... 0.075 inch
Free length .... 1.630 inches
Installed height .... 1.311 inches
Valve lifter
Diameter .... 1.2191 to 1.2195 inches
Lifter bore diameter .... 1.2204 to 1.2212 inches
Lifter-to-bore clearance
Standard .... 0.0009 to 0.0020 inch
Service limit .... 0.0031 inch

Crankshaft and connecting rods

Connecting rod journal
Diameter .... 2.1648 to 2.1654 inches
Taper and out-of-round limits .... 0.0008 inch
Bearing oil clearance
Standard .... 0.0011 to 0.0026 inch
Service limit .... 0.0031 inch
Connecting rod side clearance (endplay)
Standard .... 0.0059 to 0.0130 inch
Service limit .... 0.0150 inch
Main bearing journal
Diameter .... 2.5191 to 2.5197 inches
Taper and out-of-round limits .... 0.0008 inch
Bearing oil clearance
Standard .... 0.0011 to 0.0022 inch
Service limit .... 0.0031 inch
Crankshaft endplay
Standard .... 0.0008 to 0.0087 inch
Service limit .... 0.0118 inch
Thrust washer thickness .... 0.0961 to 0.0980 inch

3VZ-FE V6 engine (continued)

Engine block

Deck warpage limit	0.0020 inch
Cylinder bore diameter	
Standard	
Mark 1	3.4449 to 3.4453 inches
Mark 2	3.4453 to 3.4457 inches
Mark 3	3.4457 to 3.4461 inches
Service limit	3.4539 inches

Pistons and rings

Piston diameter (standard)	
Mark 1	3.4394 to 3.4398 inches
Mark 2	3.4398 to 3.4402 inches
Mark 3	3.4402 to 3.4405 inches
Piston-to-bore clearance	
Standard	0.0051 to 0.0059 inch
Service limit	0.0067 inch
Piston ring end gap	
No. 1 (top) compression ring	
Standard	0.0011 to 0.0197 inch
Service limit	0.0433 inch
No. 2 (middle) compression ring	
Standard	0.0150 to 0.0236 inch
Service limit	0.0472 inch
Oil ring	
Standard	0.0059 to 0.0224 inch
Service limit	0.0461 inch
Piston ring groove clearance	
No. 1 (top) compression ring	0.0004 to 0.0031 inch
No. 2 (middle) compression ring	0.0012 to 0.0028 inch

Torque specifications*

	Ft-lbs (unless otherwise indicated)
Main bearing cap assembly bolts	
Step 1	45
Step 2	Turn an additional 90-degrees (1/4-turn)
Connecting rod cap nuts	
Step 1	18
Step 2	Turn an additional 90-degrees (1/4-turn)

* **Note:** *Refer to Part B for additional torque specifications.*

1MZ-FE V6 engine

General

Displacement	183 cubic inches (3.0 liters)
Cylinder compression pressure at 250 rpm	
Standard	218 psi
Minimum	145 psi
Oil pressure (engine hot)	
At 3000 rpm	43 to 78 psi
At idle	4.3 psi minimum

Cylinder head

Warpage limit	0.0039 inch

Valves and related components

Valve margin width	
Standard	0.039 inch
Minimum	0.020 inch
Valve stem diameter	
Intake	0.2154 to 0.2159 inch
Exhaust	0.2152 to 0.22157 inch
Valve stem-to-guide clearance	
Intake	
Standard	0.001 to 0.0024 inch
Service limit	0.0031 inch
Exhaust	
Standard	0.0012 to 0.0026 inch
Service limit	0.0039 inch

Valve spring
 Out-of-square limit .... 0.079 inch
 Free length .... 1.7913 inches
 Installed height .... 1.331 inches
Valve lifter
 Diameter .... 1.2191 to 1.2195 inches
 Lifter bore diameter .... 1.2205 to 1.2211 inches
 Lifter-to-bore clearance
  Standard .... 0.0009 to 0.0020 inch
  Service limit .... 0.0028 inch

Crankshaft and connecting rods

Connecting rod journal
 Diameter .... 2.0864 to 2.0866 inches
 Taper and out-of-round limits .... 0.0008 inch
 Bearing oil clearance
  Standard .... 0.0015 to 0.0025 inch
  Service limit .... 0.0031 inch
Connecting rod side clearance (endplay)
 Standard... 0.0059 to 0.0118 inch
 Service limit .... 0.0138 inch
Main bearing journal
 Diameter .... 2.4011 to 2.4016 inches
 Taper and out-of-round limits .... 0.0008 inch
 Bearing oil clearance
  Standard .... 0.0010 to 0.0018 inch
  Service limit .... 0.0031 inch
Crankshaft endplay
 Standard .... 0.0016 to 0.0095 inch
 Service limit .... 0.0138 inch
 Thrust washer thickness .... 0.0760 to 0.0780 inch

Engine block

Deck warpage limit .... 0.0028 inch
Cylinder bore diameter
 Standard .... 3.4449 to 3.4453 inches
 Service limit .... 3.4457 inches

Pistons and rings

Piston diameter (standard) .... 3.4412 to 3.4416 inches
Piston-to-bore clearance
 Standard... 0.0033 to 0.0042 inch
 Service limit .... 0.0051 inch
Piston ring end gap
 No. 1 (top) compression ring
  Standard .... 0.0098 to 0.0138 inch
  Service limit .... 0.0374 inch
 No. 2 (middle) compression ring
  Standard .... 0.0138 to 0.0177 inch
  Service limit .... 0.0413 inch
 Oil ring
  Standard .... 0.0059 to 0.0157 inch
  Service limit .... 0.0394 inch
Piston ring groove clearance
 No. 1 (top) compression ring .... 0.0008 to 0.0028 inch
 No. 2 (middle) compression ring .... 0.0008 to 0.0024 inch

Torque specifications*   **Ft-lbs** (unless otherwise indicated)

Main bearing cap assembly bolts
 12-point bolts
  Step 1.. 16
  Step 2.. Turn an additional 90-degrees (1/4-turn)
 6-point bolts 20
Connecting rod cap nuts
 Step 1 18
 Step 2 .... Turn an additional 90-degrees (1/4-turn)

* **Note:** *Refer to Part B for additional torque specifications*

2C

2.4a The oil pressure can be checked by removing the sending unit and installing a pressure gauge in its place (5S-FE model shown)

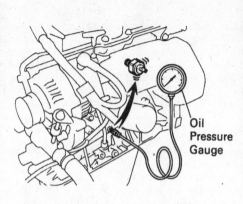

2.4b On 3VZ-FE models, the oil pressure sending unit is located in the left front corner of the engine block, near the oil filter

2.4c On 1MZ-FE models, the sending unit is located at the front of the engine, below the alternator mount (arrow)

1   General information

Included in this portion of Chapter 2 are the general overhaul procedures for the cylinder head(s) and internal engine components.

The information ranges from advice concerning preparation for an overhaul and the purchase of replacement parts to detailed, step-by-step procedures covering removal and installation of internal engine components and the inspection of parts.

The following Sections have been written based on the assumption that the engine has been removed from the vehicle. For information concerning in-vehicle engine repair, as well as removal and installation of the external components necessary for the overhaul, see Part A or B of this Chapter and Section 8 of this Part.

The Specifications included in this Part are only those necessary for the inspection and overhaul procedures which follow. Refer to Parts A and B for additional Specifications.

2   Engine overhaul - general information

Refer to illustrations 2.4a, 2.4b and 2.4c

It's not always easy to determine when, or if, an engine should be completely overhauled, as a number of factors must be considered.

High mileage is not necessarily an indication that an overhaul is needed, while low mileage doesn't preclude the need for an overhaul. Frequency of servicing is probably the most important consideration. An engine that's had regular and frequent oil and filter changes, as well as other required maintenance, will most likely give many thousands of miles of reliable service. Conversely, a neglected engine may require an overhaul very early in its life.

Excessive oil consumption is an indication that piston rings, valve seals and/or valve guides are in need of attention. Make sure that oil leaks aren't responsible before deciding that the rings and/or guides are bad. Perform a cylinder compression check to determine the extent of the work required (see Section 3).

Check the oil pressure with a gauge installed in place of the oil pressure sending unit **(see illustrations)** and compare it to this Chapter's Specifications. If it's extremely low, the bearings and/or oil pump are probably worn out.

Loss of power, rough running, knocking or metallic engine noises, excessive valve train noise and high fuel consumption rates may also point to the need for an overhaul, especially if they're all present at the same time. If a complete tune-up doesn't remedy the situation, major mechanical work is the only solution.

An engine overhaul involves restoring the internal parts to the specifications of a new engine. During an overhaul, the piston rings are replaced and the cylinder walls are reconditioned (rebored and/or honed). If a rebore is done by an automotive machine shop, new oversize pistons will also be installed. The main bearings, connecting rod bearings and camshaft bearings are generally replaced with new ones and, if necessary, the crankshaft may be reground to restore the journals. Generally, the valves are serviced as well, since they're usually in less-than-perfect condition at this point. While the engine is being overhauled, other components, such as the distributor, starter and alternator, can be rebuilt as well. The end result should be a like new engine that will give many trouble free miles. **Note:** *Critical cooling system components such as the hoses, drivebelts, thermostat and water pump should be replaced with new parts when an engine is overhauled. The radiator should be checked carefully to ensure that it isn't clogged or leaking (see Chapter 3). If you purchase a rebuilt engine or short block, some rebuilders will not warranty their engines unless the radiator has been professionally flushed. Also, we don't recommend overhauling the oil pump - always install a new one when an engine is rebuilt.*

Before beginning the engine overhaul, read through the entire procedure to familiarize yourself with the scope and requirements of the job. Overhauling an engine isn't difficult, but it is time consuming. Plan on the vehicle being tied up for a minimum of two weeks, especially if parts must be taken to an automotive machine shop for repair or reconditioning. Check on availability of parts and make sure that any necessary special tools and equipment are obtained in advance. Most work can be done with typical hand tools, although a number of precision measuring tools are required for inspecting parts to determine if they must be replaced. Often an automotive machine shop will handle the inspection of parts and offer advice concerning reconditioning and replacement. **Note:** *Always wait until the engine has been completely disassembled and all components, especially the engine block, have been inspected before deciding what service and repair operations must be performed by an automotive machine shop.* Since the block's condition will be the major factor to consider when determining whether to overhaul the original engine or buy a rebuilt one, never purchase parts or have machine work done on other components until the block has been thoroughly inspected. As a general rule, time is the primary cost of an overhaul, so it doesn't pay to install worn or substandard parts.

As a final note, to ensure maximum life and minimum trouble from a rebuilt engine, everything must be assembled with care in a spotlessly clean environment.

3   Vacuum gauge diagnostic checks

A vacuum gauge provides valuable information about what is going on in the engine at a low-cost. You can check for worn rings or cylinder walls, leaking head or intake manifold gaskets, incorrect carburetor adjustments, restricted exhaust, stuck or burned valves, weak valve springs, improper ignition or valve timing and ignition problems.

Unfortunately, vacuum gauge readings are easy to misinterpret, so they should be used in conjunction with other tests to confirm the diagnosis.

Both the absolute readings and the rate of needle movement are important for accurate interpretation. Most gauges measure vacuum in inches of mercury (in-Hg). As a point of reference, normal atmospheric pressure at sea level is about 30 in-Hg. As vacuum increases (or atmospheric pressure decreases), the reading will decrease. Also, for every 1,000 foot increase in elevation above sea level; the gauge readings will decrease about one inch of mercury.

Connect the vacuum gauge directly to intake manifold vacuum, not to ported (carburetor) vacuum. Be sure no hoses are left disconnected during the test or false readings will result.

Before you begin the test, allow the engine to warm up completely. Block the wheels and set the parking brake. With the transmission in neutral (or Park, on automatics), start the engine and allow it to run at normal idle speed. **Warning:** *Carefully inspect the fan blades for cracks or damage before starting the engine. Keep your hands and the vacuum tester clear of the fan and do not stand in front of the vehicle or in line with the fan when the engine is running.*

Read the vacuum gauge; an average, healthy engine should normally produce between 17 and 22 inches of vacuum with a fairly steady needle.

Refer to the following vacuum gauge readings and what they indicate about the engines condition:

1   A low steady reading usually indicates a leaking gasket between the intake manifold and carburetor or throttle body, a leaky vacuum hose, late ignition timing or incorrect camshaft timing. Check ignition timing with a timing light and eliminate all other possible causes, utilizing the tests provided in this Chapter before you remove the timing belt cover to check the timing marks.

2   If the reading is three to eight inches below normal and it fluctuates at that low reading, suspect an intake manifold gasket leak at an intake port or a faulty injector.

3   If the needle has regular drops of about two to four inches at a steady rate the valves are probably leaking. Perform a compression or leak-down test to confirm this.

4   An irregular drop or down-flick of the needle can be caused by a sticking valve or an ignition misfire. Perform a compression or leak-down test and read the spark plugs.

5   A rapid vibration of about four in-Hg vibration at idle combined with exhaust smoke indicates worn valve guides. Perform a leak-down test to confirm this. If the rapid vibration occurs with an increase in engine speed, check for a leaking intake manifold gasket or head gasket, weak valve springs, burned valves or ignition misfire.

6   A slight fluctuation, say one inch up and down, may mean ignition problems. Check all the usual tune-up items and, if necessary, run the engine on an ignition analyzer.

7   If there is a large fluctuation, perform a compression or leak-down test to look for a weak or dead cylinder or a blown head gasket.

8   If the needle moves slowly through a wide range, check for a clogged PCV system, incorrect idle fuel mixture, carburetor/throttle body or intake manifold gasket leaks.

9   Check for a slow return after revving the engine by quickly snapping the throttle open until the engine reaches about 2,500 rpm and let it shut. Normally the reading should drop to near zero, rise above normal idle reading (about 5 in.-Hg over) and then return to the previous idle reading. If the vacuum returns slowly and doesn't peak when the throttle is snapped shut, the rings may be worn. If there is a long delay, look for a restricted exhaust system (often the muffler or catalytic converter). An easy way to check this is to temporarily disconnect the exhaust ahead of the suspected part and redo the test.

4   Cylinder compression check

Refer to illustration 4.6

1   A compression check will tell you what mechanical condition the upper end (pistons, rings, valves, head gasket[s]) of your engine is in. Specifically, it can tell you if the compression is down due to leakage caused by worn piston rings, defective valves and seats or a blown head gasket. **Note:** *The engine must be at normal operating temperature and the battery must be fully charged for this check.*

2   Begin by cleaning the area around the spark plugs before you remove them (compressed air should be used, if available, otherwise a small brush or even a bicycle tire pump will work). The idea is to prevent dirt from getting into the cylinders as the compression check is being done.

3   Remove all of the spark plugs from the engine (see Chapter 1).

4   Block the throttle wide open.

5   Detach the coil wire from the center of the distributor cap and ground it on the engine block. Use a jumper wire with alligator clips on each end to ensure a good ground. **Caution:** *On 1MZ-FE V6 engine, number and disconnect the harness plugs from each coil, do not crank the engine over with the coils removed but still connected, or they may be damaged. The fuel pump circuit should also be disabled (see Chapter 4).*

6   Install the compression gauge in the spark plug hole **(see illustration)**.

7   Crank the engine over at least seven compression strokes and watch the gauge. The compression should build up quickly in a healthy engine. Low compression on the first stroke, followed by gradually increasing pressure on successive strokes, indicates worn piston rings. A low compression reading on the first stroke, which doesn't build up during successive strokes, indicates leaking valves or a blown head gasket (a cracked head could also be the cause). Deposits on the undersides of the valve heads can also cause low compression. Record the highest gauge reading obtained.

8   Repeat the procedure for the remaining cylinders and compare the results to this Chapter's Specifications.

9   Add some engine oil (about three squirts from a plunger-type oil can) to each cylinder, through the spark plug hole, and repeat the test.

10   If the compression increases after the oil is added, the piston rings are definitely worn. If the compression doesn't increase significantly, the leakage is occurring at the valves or head gasket. Leakage past the valves may be caused by burned valve seats and/or faces or warped, cracked or bent valves.

11   If two adjacent cylinders have equally low compression, there's a strong possibility that the head gasket between them is blown. The

4.6 A compression gauge with a threaded fitting for the spark plug hole is preferred over the type that requires hand pressure to maintain the seal - be sure to open the throttle valve as far as possible during the compression check!

appearance of coolant in the combustion chambers or the crankcase would verify this condition.

12   If one cylinder is 20 percent lower than the others, and the engine has a slightly rough idle, a worn exhaust lobe on the camshaft could be the cause.

13   If the compression is unusually high, the combustion chambers are probably coated with carbon deposits. If that's the case, the cylinder head(s) should be removed and decarbonized.

14   If compression is way down or varies greatly between cylinders, it would be a good idea to have a leak-down test performed by an automotive repair shop. This test will pinpoint exactly where the leakage is occurring and how severe it is.

5   Engine removal - methods and precautions

If you've decided that an engine must be removed for overhaul or major repair work, several preliminary steps should be taken.

Locating a suitable place to work is extremely important. Adequate work space, along with storage space for the vehicle, will be needed. If a shop or garage isn't available, at the very least a flat, level, clean work surface made of concrete or asphalt is required.

Cleaning the engine compartment and engine before beginning the removal procedure will help keep tools clean and organized.

An engine hoist or A-frame will also be necessary. Make sure the equipment is rated in excess of the combined weight of the engine and transaxle. Safety is of primary importance, considering the potential hazards involved in lifting the engine out of the vehicle.

If the engine is being removed by a novice, a helper should be available. Advice and aid from someone more experienced would also be helpful. There are many instances when one person cannot simultaneously perform all of the operations required when lifting the engine out of the vehicle.

Plan the operation ahead of time. Arrange for or obtain all of the tools and equipment you'll need prior to beginning the job. Some of the equipment necessary to perform engine removal and installation safely and with relative ease are (in addition to an engine hoist) a heavy duty floor jack, complete sets of wrenches and sockets as described in the front of this manual, wooden blocks and plenty of rags and cleaning solvent for mopping up spilled oil, coolant and gasoline. If the hoist must be rented, make sure that you arrange for it in advance and perform all of the operations possible without it beforehand. This will save you money and time.

Plan for the vehicle to be out of use for quite a while. A machine shop will be required to perform some of the work which the do-it-yourselfer can't accomplish without special equipment. These shops often have a busy schedule, so it would be a good idea to consult them before removing the engine in order to accurately estimate the amount of time required to rebuild or repair components that may need work.

Always be extremely careful when removing and installing the

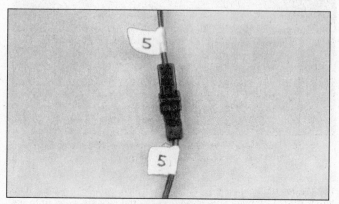

6.7 Label both ends of each wire and hose before disconnecting it

engine. Serious injury can result from careless actions. Plan ahead, take your time and a job of this nature, although major, can be accomplished successfully.

6   Engine - removal and installation

Refer to illustrations 6.7, 6.16, 6.18, 6.20, 6.21, 6.26a, 6.26b and 6.27
Note: *Read through the entire Section before beginning this procedure. The factory recommends removing the engine and transaxle from the top as a unit, then separating the engine from the transaxle on the shop floor. If the transaxle is not being serviced, it is possible to leave the transaxle in the vehicle and remove the engine from the top by itself, by removing the front crank pulley and tilting up the timing belt end of the engine for clearance.*

Removal

Warning: *These models are equipped with airbags. The airbag is armed and can deploy (inflate) anytime the battery is connected. To prevent accidental deployment (and possible injury), turn the ignition key to LOCK and disconnect the negative battery cable whenever working near airbag components. After the battery is disconnected, wait at least 90 seconds before beginning work (the system has a back-up capacitor that must fully discharge). For more information see Chapter 12.*
Note: *On 1993 and later models, the airbag system will be disabled if the battery is disconnected for more than a brief period. If the airbag light comes on and stays on after the battery is reconnected, the vehicle must be taken to a dealer to have the system reset with a special tool.*

1   Relieve the fuel system pressure (see Chapter 4).

2   Disconnect the negative cable from the battery. **Caution:** *If the stereo in your vehicle is equipped with an anti-theft system, make sure you have the correct activation code before disconnecting the battery.*

3   Remove the battery and battery tray.

4   Place protective covers on the fenders and cowl and remove the hood (see Chapter 11).

5   Remove the air cleaner assembly (see Chapter 4).

6   Raise the vehicle and support it securely on jackstands. Drain the cooling system and engine oil and remove the drivebelts (see Chapter 1).

7   Clearly label, then disconnect all vacuum lines, coolant and emissions hoses, wiring harness connectors, ground straps and fuel lines. Masking tape and/or a touch up paint applicator work well for marking items **(see illustration)**. Take instant photos or sketch the locations of components and brackets.

8   Remove the windshield washer tank and coolant reservoir tank.

9   Remove the cooling fan(s), shroud(s) and radiator (see Chapter 3).

10   Disconnect the heater hoses.

11   Release the residual fuel pressure in the tank by removing the gas cap, then undo the fuel lines connecting the engine to the chassis (see Chapter 4). Plug or cap all open fittings.

12   Disconnect the throttle linkage, transmission Throttle Valve (TV) linkage and speed control cable, if equipped, from the engine (see Chapter 4).

13   Disconnect the engine harness plugs and clips from the front and left side of the engine.

14   Disconnect the wire harness clips at the transaxle end of the engine and pull back the wiring on all sides to clear the engine.

15   On power steering equipped vehicles, unbolt the power steering pump. If clearance allows, tie the pump aside without disconnecting the hoses. If necessary, remove the pump (see Chapter 10).

16   On air-conditioned models, unbolt the compressor and set it aside **(see illustration)**. Do not disconnect the refrigerant hoses.

17   Detach the exhaust pipe(s) from the manifold(s) (see Chapter 4).

18   On four-cylinder models equipped with a oil cooler (small canister mounted between the oil filter and the block), remove the oil filter, hoses connected to the cooler, and the oil cooler **(see illustration)**.

19   Attach a lifting sling to the engine. Position a hoist and connect

6.16 Unbolt the A/C compressor and use wire or rope to tie it out of the way

6.18 On models equipped with an oil cooler, remove the oil filter, cooler (arrow) and the cooler hoses

6.20 Remove the passenger-side driveaxle (A), the engine mount through-bolt (B), and the firewall-side engine mount bracket (C)

6.21 Remove the radiator-side engine mount bolt (A) - If the transaxle is coming out with the engine, unbolt the engine shock absorber (B)

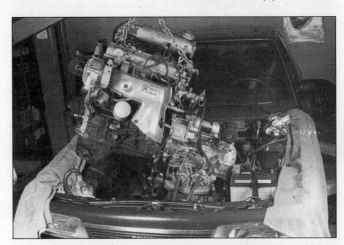

6.26a Lift the engine/transaxle high enough to clear the vehicle, then move it away and lower the hoist - this four-cylinder is being removed with the transaxle still attached

2C

6.26b This 1MZ-FE V6 is being removed with the transaxle remaining in the car

the sling to it. Take up the slack until there is slight tension on the hoist.

20 Remove the passenger-side driveaxle (see Chapter 8), and remove the firewall-side engine mount bracket from the block and the throughbolt from the engine mount. **Note:** *On some models, the right driveaxle passes through the engine mount bracket* **(see illustration)**

21 Remove the bolt securing the radiator-side engine mount to the chassis **(see illustration)**.

22 On automatic transaxle equipped models, detach the torque converter dust shield from the lower bellhousing. Remove the torque converter-to-driveplate fasteners (see Chapter 7B) and push the converter back slightly into the bellhousing.

23 Remove the engine-to-transaxle bolts and separate the engine from the transaxle. The torque converter should remain in the transaxle. **Note:** *If the transaxle is to be removed at the same time, the driver's side engine mount should be disconnected, along with any wires, cables or hoses connected to the transaxle. The engine-to-transaxle bolts should remain in place at this time.*

24 Recheck to be sure nothing except the mounts are still connecting the engine to the vehicle or to the transaxle. Disconnect and label anything still remaining.

25 Support the transaxle with a floor jack. Place a block of wood on the jack head to prevent damage to the transaxle. Remove the bolts from the engine mounts, leaving those attached to the transaxle in place. **Warning:** *Do not place any part of your body under the engine/transaxle when it's supported only by a hoist or other lifting device.*

26 Slowly lift the engine (or engine/transaxle) out of the vehicle **(see illustrations)**. It may be necessary to pry the mounts away from the frame brackets.

27 Move the engine away from the vehicle and carefully lower the

6.27 Lower the engine outside of the vehicle, remove the driveplate, and attach the engine to a suitable workstand

hoist until the engine can be set on the floor; or remove the flywheel/driveplate and mount the engine on an engine stand **(see illustration)**. **Note:** *On automatic transaxle-equipped models, mark the front and rear spacer plates and keep them with the driveplate.*

Installation

28   Check the engine/transaxle mounts. If they're worn or damaged, replace them.

29   On manual transaxle equipped models, inspect the clutch components (see Chapter 8) and on automatic models inspect the converter seal and bushing.

30   On manual transaxle equipped vehicles, apply a dab of high temperature grease to the pilot bearing. On automatic transaxle equipped models, apply a dab of grease to the nose of the converter.

31   Carefully guide the transaxle into place, following the procedure outlined in Chapter 7B. **Caution:** *Do not use the bolts to force the engine and transaxle into alignment. It may crack or damage major components.*

32   Install the engine-to-transaxle bolts and tighten them securely.

33   Attach the hoist to the engine and carefully lower the engine/transaxle assembly into the engine compartment. **Note:** *If the engine was removed with the transaxle remaining in the car, lower the engine into the car until an assistant can help you line up the dowels pins on the block with the transaxle. Some twisting and angling of the engine and/or the transaxle will be necessary to secure proper alignment of the two.*

34   Install the mount bolts and tighten them securely.

35   Reinstall the remaining components and fasteners in the reverse order of removal.

36   Add coolant, oil, power steering and transmission fluids as needed (see Chapter 1).

37   Run the engine and check for proper operation and leaks. Shut off the engine and recheck the fluid levels.

7   Engine rebuilding alternatives

The do-it-yourselfer is faced with a number of options when performing an engine overhaul. The decision to replace the engine block, piston/connecting rod assemblies and crankshaft depends on a number of factors, with the number one consideration being the condition of the block. Other considerations are cost, access to machine shop facilities, parts availability, time required to complete the project and the extent of prior mechanical experience on the part of the do-it-yourselfer.

Some of the rebuilding alternatives include:

Individual parts - If the inspection procedures reveal that the engine block and most engine components are in reusable condition, purchasing individual parts may be the most economical alternative.

The block, crankshaft and piston/connecting rod assemblies should all be inspected carefully. Even if the block shows little wear, the cylinder bores should be surface honed.

Short block - A short block consists of an engine block with a crankshaft and piston/connecting rod assemblies already installed. All new bearings are incorporated and all clearances will be correct. The existing camshaft, valve train components, cylinder head(s) and external parts can be bolted to the short block with little or no machine shop work necessary.

Long block - A long block consists of a short block plus an oil pump, oil pan, cylinder head(s), valve cover(s), camshaft and valve train components, timing sprockets and chain or gears and timing cover. All components are installed with new bearings, seals and gaskets incorporated throughout. The installation of manifolds and external parts is all that's necessary.

Give careful thought to which alternative is best for you and discuss the situation with local automotive machine shops, auto parts dealers and experienced rebuilders before ordering or purchasing replacement parts.

8   Engine overhaul - disassembly sequence

Refer to illustrations 8.5a and 8.5b

1   It's much easier to disassemble and work on the engine if it's mounted on a portable engine stand. A stand can often be rented quite cheaply from an equipment rental yard. Before the engine is mounted on a stand, the flywheel/driveplate and rear oil seal retainer should be removed from the engine.

2   If a stand isn't available, it's possible to disassemble the engine with it blocked up on the floor. Be extra careful not to tip or drop the engine when working without a stand.

3   If you're going to obtain a rebuilt engine, all external components must come off first, to be transferred to the replacement engine, just as they will if you're doing a complete engine overhaul yourself. These include:

    Alternator and brackets
    Emissions control components
    Distributor, spark plug wires and spark plugs
    Thermostat and housing cover
    Water pump
    EFI components
    Intake/exhaust manifolds
    Oil filter
    Engine mounts
    Clutch and flywheel/driveplate
    Engine rear plate

Note: *When removing the external components from the engine, pay close attention to details that may be helpful or important during installation. Note the installed position of gaskets, seals, spacers, pins, brackets, washers, bolts and other small items.*

4   If you're obtaining a short block, which consists of the engine block, crankshaft, pistons and connecting rods all assembled, then the cylinder head(s), oil pan and oil pump will have to be removed as well. See *Engine rebuilding alternatives* for additional information regarding the different possibilities to be considered.

5   If you're planning a complete overhaul, the engine must be disassembled and the internal components removed in the following order **(see illustrations)**.

    Intake and exhaust manifolds
    Valve cover(s)
    Timing belt covers
    Timing belt and sprockets
    Cylinder head(s)
    Oil pan
    Oil pump
    Engine balancer assembly (5S-FE engines)
    Piston/connecting rod assemblies
    Crankshaft rear oil seal retainer
    Crankshaft and main bearings

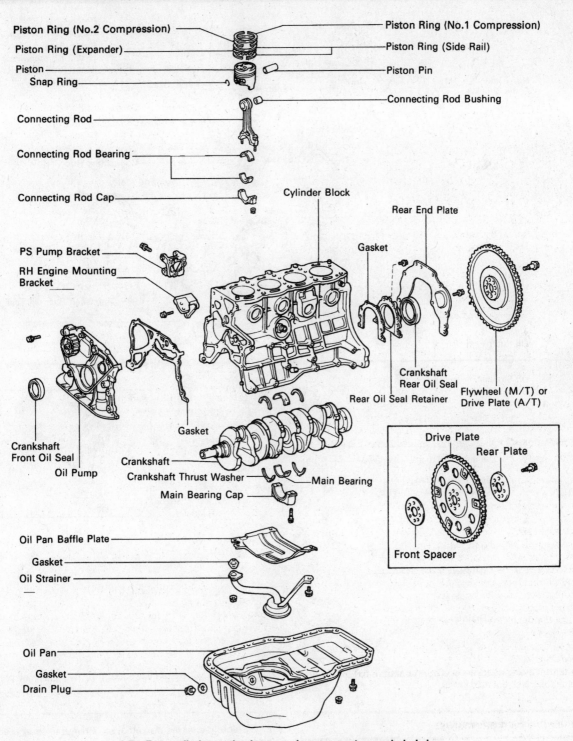

Piston Ring (No.2 Compression)

Piston Ring (Expander)

Piston

Snap Ring

Connecting Rod

Connecting Rod Bearing

Connecting Rod Cap

Piston Ring (No.1 Compression)

Piston Ring (Side Rail)

Piston Pin

Connecting Rod Bushing

Cylinder Block

Rear End Plate

Gasket

PS Pump Bracket

RH Engine Mounting Bracket

Crankshaft Front Oil Seal

Oil Pump

Crankshaft

Crankshaft Thrust Washer

Main Bearing Cap

Gasket

Main Bearing

Crankshaft Rear Oil Seal

Rear Oil Seal Retainer

Flywheel (M/T) or Drive Plate (A/T)

Drive Plate

Rear Plate

Front Spacer

Oil Pan Baffle Plate

Gasket

Oil Strainer

Oil Pan

Gasket

Drain Plug

8.5a Four-cylinder engine lower end components - exploded view

6   Before beginning the disassembly and overhaul procedures, make sure the following items are available. Also, refer to Section 22 for a list of tools and materials needed for engine reassembly.

Common hand tools
Small cardboard boxes or plastic bags for storing parts
Gasket scraper
Ridge reamer
Vibration damper puller
Micrometers
Telescoping gauges

Dial indicator set
Valve spring compressor
Cylinder surfacing hone
Piston ring groove cleaning tool
Electric drill motor
Tap and die set
Wire brushes
Oil gallery brushes
Cleaning solvent

2C

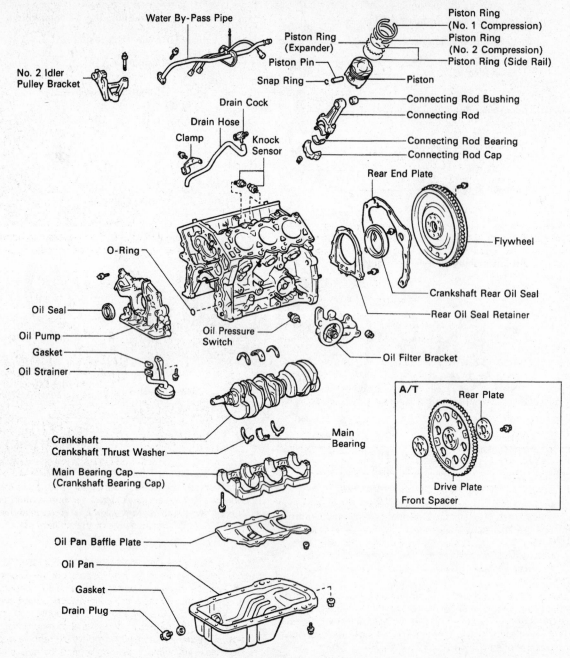

8.5b V6 engine lower end components - exploded view (3MZ-FE shown, 1MZ-FE similar except for two-piece oil pan and separate main caps)

9   Cylinder head - disassembly

Refer to illustrations 9.2 and 9.3

Note: *New and rebuilt cylinder heads are commonly available for most engines at dealerships and auto parts stores. Due to the fact that some specialized tools are necessary for the disassembly and inspection procedures, and replacement parts may not be readily available, it may be more practical and economical for the home mechanic to purchase replacement head(s) rather than taking the time to disassemble, inspect and recondition the original(s).*

1   Cylinder head disassembly involves removal of the intake and exhaust valves and related components. It's assumed that the lifters or rocker arms and camshaft(s) have already been removed (see Part A or B as needed).

2   Before the valves are removed, arrange to label and store them, along with their related components, so they can be kept separate and reinstalled in the same valve guides they are removed from **(see illustration)**.

3   Compress the springs on the first valve with a spring compressor and remove the keepers **(see illustration)**. Carefully release the valve spring compressor and remove the retainer, the spring and the spring seat (if used). **Caution:** *Be very careful not to nick or otherwise damage the lifter bores when compressing the valve springs.* **Note:** *If your spring compressor does not have an end such as the one shown with cutouts on the side, an adapter is available to use with a standard spring compressor.*

4   Pull the valve out of the head, then remove the oil seal from the guide. If the valve binds in the guide (won't pull through), push it back

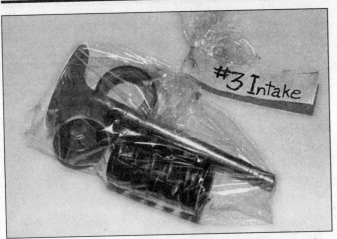

9.2 A small plastic bag, with an appropriate label, can be used to store the valve train components so they can be kept together and reinstalled in the correct guide

9.3 Compress the spring until the keepers can be removed with a small magnetic screwdriver or needle-nose pliers

2C

into the head and deburr the area around the keeper groove with a fine file or whetstone.

5 Repeat the procedure for the remaining valves. Remember to keep all the parts for each valve together so they can be reinstalled in the same locations.

6 Once the valves and related components have been removed and stored in an organized manner, the head should be thoroughly cleaned and inspected. If a complete engine overhaul is being done, finish the engine disassembly procedures before beginning the cylinder head cleaning and inspection process.

10 Cylinder head - cleaning and inspection

10.12 Check the cylinder head gasket surfaces for warpage by trying to slip a feeler gauge under the precision straightedge (see the Specifications for the maximum warpage allowed and use a feeler gauge of that thickness)

Refer to illustrations 10.12, 10.14, 10.16, 10.17 and 10.18

1 Thorough cleaning of the cylinder head(s) and related valve train components, followed by a detailed inspection, will enable you to decide how much valve service work must be done during the engine overhaul. **Note:** *If the engine was severely overheated, the cylinder head is probably warped (see Step 12).*

Cleaning

2 Scrape all traces of old gasket material and sealing compound off the head gasket, intake manifold and exhaust manifold sealing surfaces. Be very careful not to gouge the cylinder head. Special gasket removal solvents that soften gaskets and make removal much easier are available at auto parts stores.

3 Remove all built up scale from the coolant passages.

4 Run a stiff wire brush through the various holes to remove deposits that may have formed in them. If there are heavy rust deposits in the water passages, the bare head should be professionally cleaned at a machine shop.

5 Run an appropriate size tap into each of the threaded holes to remove corrosion and thread sealant that may be present. If compressed air is available, use it to clear the holes of debris produced by this operation. **Warning:** *Wear eye protection when using compressed air!*

6 Clean the exhaust and intake manifold stud threads with a wire brush.

7 Clean the cylinder head with solvent and dry it thoroughly. Compressed air will speed the drying process and ensure that all holes and recessed areas are clean. **Note:** *Decarbonizing chemicals are available and may prove very useful when cleaning cylinder heads and valve train components. They are very caustic and should be used with caution. Be sure to follow the instructions on the container.*

8 Clean the lifters with solvent and dry them thoroughly (don't mix

them up during the cleaning process). Compressed air will speed the drying process and can be used to clean out the oil passages.

9 Clean all the valve springs, spring seats, keepers and retainers with solvent and dry them thoroughly. Work on the components from one valve at a time to avoid mixing up the parts.

10 Scrape off any heavy deposits that may have formed on the valves, then use a motorized wire brush to remove deposits from the valve heads and stems. Again, make sure the valves don't get mixed up.

Inspection

Note: *Be sure to perform all of the following inspection procedures before concluding that machine shop work is required. Make a list of the items that need attention. The inspection procedures for the lifters and the camshafts, can be found in Part A or B.*

Cylinder head

11 Inspect the head very carefully for cracks, evidence of coolant leakage and other damage. If cracks are found, check with an automotive machine shop concerning repair. If repair isn't possible, a new cylinder head should be obtained.

12 Using a straightedge and feeler gauge, check the head gasket mating surface for warpage **(see illustration)**. If the warpage exceeds the limit found in this Chapter's Specifications, it can be resurfaced at an automotive machine shop. **Note:** *If the V6 engine heads are resurfaced, the intake manifold flanges may also require machining.*

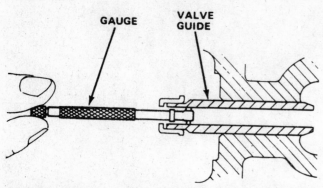

10.14 Use a small hole gauge to determine the inside diameter of the valve guides (the gauge is then measured with a micrometer)

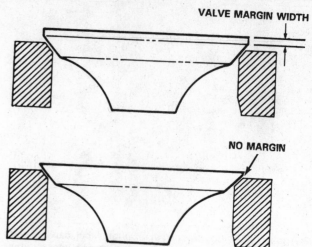

10.16 The margin width on each valve must be as specified (if no margin exists, the valve cannot be re-used)

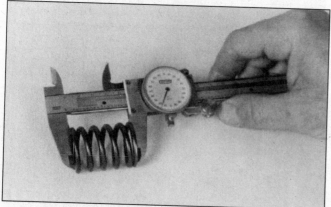

10.17 Measure the free length of each valve spring with a dial or vernier caliper

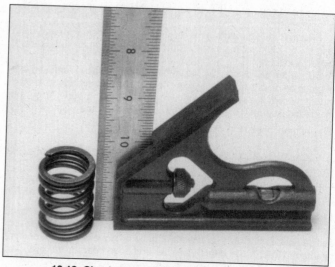

10.18 Check each valve spring for squareness

13   Examine the valve seats in each of the combustion chambers. If they're pitted, cracked or burned, the head will require valve service that's beyond the scope of the home mechanic.

14   Check the valve stem-to-guide clearance with a small hole gauge and micrometer **(see illustration)**. Also, check the valve stem deflection with a dial indicator attached securely to the head. The valve must be in the guide and approximately 1/16-inch off the seat. The total valve stem movement indicated by the gauge needle must be noted, then divided by two to obtain the actual clearance value. If it exceeds the stem-to-guide clearance limit found in this Chapter's Specifications, the valve guides should be replaced. After this is done, if there's still some doubt regarding the condition of the valve guides they should be checked by an automotive machine shop (the cost should be minimal).

Valves

15   Carefully inspect each valve face for uneven wear, deformation, cracks, pits and burned areas. Check the valve stem for scuffing and galling and the neck for cracks. Rotate the valve and check for any obvious indication that it's bent. Look for pits and excessive wear on the end of the stem. The presence of any of these conditions indicates the need for valve service by an automotive machine shop.

16   Measure the margin width on each valve **(see illustration)**. Any valve with a margin narrower than that listed in this Chapter's Specifications will have to be replaced with a new one.

Valve components

17   Check each valve spring for wear (on the ends) and pits. Measure the free length and compare it to this Chapter's Specifications **(see illustration)**. Any springs that are shorter than specified have sagged and should not be re-used. The tension of all springs should be pressure checked with a special fixture before deciding that they're suitable for use in a rebuilt engine (take the springs to an automotive

machine shop for this check).

18   Stand each spring on a flat surface and check it for squareness **(see illustration)**. If any of the springs are distorted or sagged, replace all of them with new parts.

19   Check the spring retainers and keepers for obvious wear and cracks. Any questionable parts should be replaced with new ones, as extensive damage will occur if they fail during engine operation.

20   Any damaged or excessively worn parts must be replaced with new ones.

21   If the inspection process indicates that the valve components are in generally poor condition and worn beyond the limits specified, which is usually the case in an engine that's being overhauled, reassemble the valves in the cylinder head and refer to Section 12 for valve servicing recommendations.

11   Valves - servicing

1   Because of the complex nature of the job and the special tools and equipment needed, servicing of the valves, the valve seats and the valve guides, commonly known as a valve job, should be done by a professional.

2   The home mechanic can remove and disassemble the head(s), do

12.3 Gently tap the valve seals (arrow) into place with a deep socket and hammer

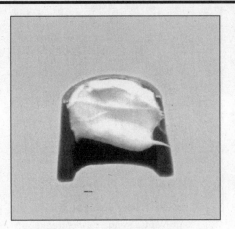

12.6 The small valve stem keepers are easier to position when coated with grease

13.2 A ridge reamer is required to remove the ridge from the top of each cylinder - do this before removing the pistons!

the initial cleaning and inspection, then reassemble and deliver them to a dealer service department or an automotive machine shop for the actual service work. Doing the inspection will enable you to see what condition the head(s) and valvetrain components are in and will ensure that you know what work and new parts are required when dealing with an automotive machine shop.

3   The dealer service department, or automotive machine shop, will remove the valves and springs, recondition or replace the valves and valve seats, recondition the valve guides, check and replace the valve springs, spring retainers and keepers (as necessary), replace the valve seals with new ones, reassemble the valve components and make sure the installed spring height is correct. The cylinder head gasket surface will also be resurfaced if it's warped.

4   After the valve job has been performed by a professional, the head(s) will be in like new condition. When the heads are returned, be sure to clean them again before installation on the engine to remove any metal particles and abrasive grit that may still be present from the valve service or head resurfacing operations. Use compressed air, if available, to blow out all the oil holes and passages.

12 Cylinder head - reassembly

Refer to illustrations 12.3, 12.6

1   Regardless of whether or not the head was sent to an automotive machine shop for valve servicing, make sure it's clean before beginning reassembly.

2   If the head was sent out for valve servicing, the valves and related components will already be in place. Begin the reassembly procedure with Step 8.

3   Install new seals on each of the valve guides. **Note:** *Intake and exhaust valves require different seals - DO NOT mix them up!* Gently tap each intake valve seal into place until it's seated on the guide **(see illustration). Caution:** *Don't hammer on the valve seals once they're seated or you may damage them. Don't twist or cock the seals during installation or they won't seat properly on the valve stems.*

4   Beginning at one end of the head, lubricate and install the first valve. Apply moly-base grease or clean engine oil to the valve stem.

5   Drop the spring seat or shim(s) over the valve guide and set the valve spring and retainer in place.

6   Compress the springs with a valve spring compressor and carefully install the keepers in the upper groove, then slowly release the compressor and make sure the keepers seat properly. Apply a small dab of grease to each keeper to hold it in place if necessary **(see illustration)**.

7   Repeat the procedure for the remaining valves. Be sure to return the components to their original locations - don't mix them up!

8   Check the valve spring installed height with a dial or vernier caliper.

13 Pistons/connecting rods - removal

Refer to illustrations 13.2, 13.4, 13.5 and 13.7

Note: *Prior to removing the piston/connecting rod assemblies, remove the cylinder head(s), the oil pan and the oil pump pick-up tube by referring to the appropriate Sections in Chapter 2A or 2B.*

1   On 5S-FE engines only, remove the engine balancer assembly, loosening the bolts opposite the tightening sequence in several steps **(see illustration 27.4)**. Keep the spacers with the balancer assembly by securing them with wire or twist-ties.

2   Use your fingernail to feel if a ridge has formed at the upper limit of ring travel (about 1/4-inch down from the top of each cylinder). If carbon deposits or cylinder wear have produced ridges, they must be completely removed with a special tool **(see illustration)**. Follow the manufacturer's instructions provided with the tool. Failure to remove the ridges before attempting to remove the piston/connecting rod assemblies may result in piston damage.

3   After the cylinder ridges have been removed, turn the engine upside-down so the crankshaft is facing up.

4   Before the connecting rods are removed, check the endplay with feeler gauges. Slide them between the first connecting rod and the crankshaft throw until the play is removed **(see illustration)**. The endplay is equal to the thickness of the feeler gauge(s). If the endplay exceeds the specified service limit, new connecting rods will be required. If new rods (or a new crankshaft) are installed, the endplay may fall under the service limit (if it does, the rods will have to be machined to restore it - consult an automotive machine shop for advice if necessary). Repeat the procedure for the remaining connecting rods.

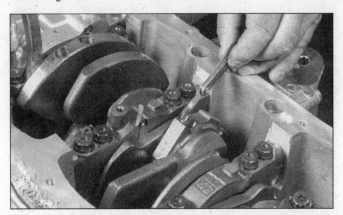

13.4 Check the connecting rod side clearance with a feeler gauge as shown here

2C

13.5 The connecting rods and caps should be marked to indicate which cylinder they're installed in - if they aren't, mark them with a center punch to avoid confusion during reassembly - do not confuse the markings shown here as rod numbers; these are bearing size identifications

13.7 To prevent damage to the crankshaft journals and cylinder walls, slip sections of hose over the rod bolts before removing the pistons

14.1 Checking crankshaft endplay with a dial indicator

14.3 Checking crankshaft endplay with a feeler gauge

5   Check the connecting rods and caps for identification marks. If they aren't plainly marked, use a small center punch to make the appropriate number of indentations on each rod and cap (1, 2, 3, etc., depending on the engine type and cylinder they're associated with) **(see illustration)**.

6   Loosen each of the connecting rod cap nuts 1/2-turn at a time until they can be removed by hand. Remove the number one connecting rod cap and bearing insert. Don't drop the bearing insert out of the cap.

7   Slip a short length of plastic or rubber hose over each connecting rod cap bolt to protect the crankshaft journal and cylinder wall as the piston is removed **(see illustration)**.

8   Remove the bearing insert and push the connecting rod/piston assembly out through the top of the engine. Use a wooden hammer handle to push on the upper bearing surface in the connecting rod. If resistance is felt, double-check to make sure that all of the ridge was removed from the cylinder.

9   Repeat the procedure for the remaining cylinders. **Note:** *Turn the crankshaft as needed to put the rod to be removed close to parallel with the cylinder bore, i.e. don't try to drive it out while at a large angle to the bore.*

10   After removal, reassemble the connecting rod caps and bearing inserts in their respective connecting rods and install the cap nuts finger tight. Leaving the old bearing inserts in place until reassembly will help prevent the connecting rod bearing surfaces from being accidentally nicked or gouged.

11   Don't separate the pistons from the connecting rods (see Section 18 for additional information).

14   Crankshaft - removal

Refer to illustrations 14.1, 14.3 and 14.5

Note: *The crankshaft can be removed only after the engine has been removed from the vehicle. It's assumed that the flywheel or driveplate, vibration damper, timing belt, oil pan, oil pick-up tube, oil pump and piston/connecting rod assemblies have already been removed. The rear main oil seal and retainer must be removed from the block before proceeding with crankshaft removal.*

1   Before the crankshaft is removed, check the endplay. Mount a dial indicator with the stem in line with the crankshaft and just touching one of the crank throws **(see illustration)**.

2   Push the crankshaft all the way to the rear and zero the dial indicator. Next, pry the crankshaft to the front as far as possible and

check the reading on the dial indicator. The distance that it moves is the endplay. If it's greater than specified, check the crankshaft thrust surfaces for wear. If no wear is evident, new thrust washers should correct the endplay.

3   If a dial indicator isn't available, feeler gauges can be used. Gently pry or push the crankshaft all the way to the front of the engine. Slip feeler gauges between the crankshaft and the front face of the thrust main bearing to determine the clearance **(see illustration)**. The thrust bearing on four-cylinder engines is the number three (center) bearing, while on the V6 engines it's the number two journal.

4   On four-cylinder engines, check the main bearing caps to see if they're marked to indicate their locations. They should be numbered consecutively from the front of the engine to the rear. If they aren't, mark them with number stamping dies or a center punch. Main bearing caps generally have a cast-in arrow, which points to the front of the engine. Loosen the main bearing cap bolts 1/4-turn at a time each, in the reverse order of the recommended tightening sequence **(see illustrations 24.12a, 24.12b and 24.12c)**, until they can be removed by hand. The main bearing caps on the 3VZ-FE V6 engine are a one-piece assembly which may have to be carefully pried away from the block. **Note:** *The 1MZ-FE V6 has main cap bolts along the sides of the block. Remove those first (with their sealing washers) in the reverse order of the tightening sequence (see illustration 24.12d). Then remove the rest of the main cap bolts in the reverse order of the tightening sequence (see illustration 24.12c).* Note if any stud bolts are used and make sure they're returned to their original locations when the crankshaft is reinstalled.

5   Gently tap the caps with a soft-face hammer, then separate them from the engine block. If necessary, use the bolts as levers to remove

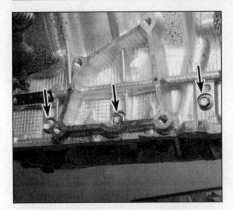

14.5 The 1MZ-FE engine has side bolts (arrows) into the main caps (rear bolt on this side not seen here) - the engine mount must be removed to access the bolt in the center of this photo

15.1a A hammer and a large punch can be used to knock the core plugs sideways in their bores

15.1b Pull the core plugs from the block with pliers

15.1c The equivalent of a core plug on the 1MZ-FE engine is this bolted-on plate, sealed with sealant

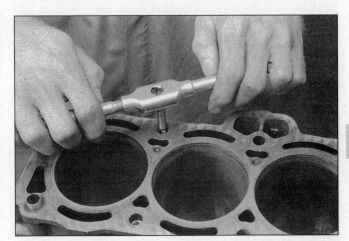

15.8 All bolt holes in the block - particularly the main bearing cap and head bolt holes - should be cleaned and restored with a tap (be sure to remove debris from the holes after this is done)

2C

the caps. Try not to drop the bearing inserts if they come out with the caps.

6   Carefully lift the crankshaft out of the engine. It may be a good idea to have an assistant available, since the crankshaft is quite heavy. With the bearing inserts in place in the engine block and main bearing caps or cap assembly, return the caps to their respective locations on the engine block and tighten the bolts finger tight.

15 Engine block - cleaning

Refer to illustrations 15.1a, 15.1b, 15.1c, 15.8 and 15.10
Caution: *The core plugs (also known as freeze or soft plugs) may be difficult or impossible to retrieve if they're driven completely into the block coolant passages.*

1   Using the blunt end of a punch, tap in on the outer edge of the core plug to turn the plug sideways in the bore. Then using pliers, pull the core plug from the engine block **(see illustrations)**. **Note:** *The 1MZ-FE engine does not have conventional core plugs in its aluminum block, but rather bolted on plates with RTV sealant* **(see illustration)**.
2   Using a gasket scraper, remove all traces of gasket material from the engine block. Be very careful not to nick or gouge the gasket sealing surfaces.
3   Remove the main bearing caps or cap assembly and separate the bearing inserts from the caps and the engine block. Tag the bearings, indicating which cylinder they were removed from and whether they were in the cap or the block, then set them aside.

4   Remove all of the threaded oil gallery plugs from the block. The plugs are usually very tight - they may have to be drilled out and the holes retapped. Use new plugs when the engine is reassembled.
5   If the engine is extremely dirty, it should be taken to an automotive machine shop to be steam cleaned or hot tanked.
6   After the block is returned, clean all oil holes and oil galleries one more time. Brushes specifically designed for this purpose are available at most auto parts stores. Flush the passages with warm water until the water runs clear, dry the block thoroughly and wipe all machined surfaces with a light, rust preventive oil. If you have access to compressed air, use it to speed the drying process and to blow out all the oil holes and galleries. **Warning:** *Wear eye protection when using compressed air!*
7   If the block isn't extremely dirty or sludged up, you can do an adequate cleaning job with hot soapy water and a stiff brush. Take plenty of time and do a thorough job. Regardless of the cleaning method used, be sure to clean all oil holes and galleries very thoroughly, dry the block completely and coat all machined surfaces with light oil.
8   The threaded holes in the block must be clean to ensure accurate torque readings during reassembly. Run the proper size tap into each of the holes to remove rust, corrosion, thread sealant or sludge and restore damaged threads **(see illustration)**. If possible, use compressed air to clear the holes of debris produced by this operation. Now is a good time to clean the threads on the head bolts and the main bearing cap bolts as well.

15.10　A large socket on an extension can be used to drive the new core plugs into the bores

9　Reinstall the main bearing caps and tighten the bolts finger tight.

10　After coating the sealing surfaces of the new core plugs with Permatex no. 2 sealant, install them in the engine block **(see illustration)**. Make sure they're driven in straight and seated properly or leakage could result. Special tools are available for this purpose, but a large socket, with an outside diameter that will just slip into the core plug, a 1/2-inch drive extension and a hammer will work just as well.

11　Apply non-hardening sealant (such as Permatex no. 2 or Teflon pipe sealant) to the new oil gallery plugs and thread them into the holes in the block. Make sure they're tightened securely.

12　If the engine isn't going to be reassembled right away, cover it with a large plastic trash bag to keep it clean.

16　Engine block - inspection

Refer to illustrations 16.4a, 16.4b, 16.4c and 16.12

1　Before the block is inspected, it should be cleaned as described in Section 15.

2　Visually check the block for cracks, rust and corrosion. Look for stripped threads in the threaded holes. It's also a good idea to have the block checked for hidden cracks by an automotive machine shop that has the special equipment to do this type of work, especially if the vehicle had a history of overheating or using coolant. If defects are found, have the block repaired, if possible, or replaced.

3　Check the cylinder bores for scuffing and scoring.

4　Measure the diameter of each cylinder at the top (just under the ridge area), center and bottom of the cylinder bore, parallel to the crankshaft axis **(see illustrations)**.

5　Next, measure each cylinder's diameter at the same three

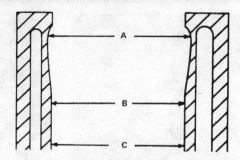

16.4a　Measure the diameter of each cylinder just under the wear ridge (A), at the center (B) and at the bottom (C)

16.4b　The ability to "feel" when the telescoping gauge is at the correct point will be developed over time, so work slowly and repeat the check until you're satisfied that the bore measurement is accurate

locations across the crankshaft axis. Compare the results to this Chapter's Specifications.

6　If the required precision measuring tools aren't available and there isn't a tool rental facility nearby, the piston-to-cylinder clearances can be obtained, though not quite as accurately, using feeler gauge stock. Feeler gauge stock comes in 12-inch lengths and various thickness and is generally available at auto parts stores.

7　To check the clearance with feeler stock, select a feeler gauge and slip it into the cylinder along with the matching piston. The piston must be positioned exactly as it normally would be. The feeler gauge must be between the piston and cylinder on one of the thrust faces (90-degrees to the piston pin bore).

8　The piston should slip through the cylinder (with the feeler gauge in place) with moderate pressure.

9　If it falls through or slides through easily, the clearance is

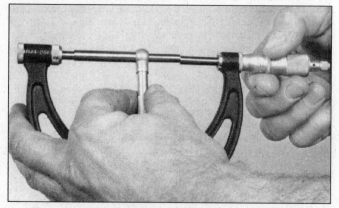

16.4c　The gauge is then measured with a micrometer to determine the bore size

16.12　Check the block deck (both banks on a V6 engine) for distortion with a precision straightedge and feeler gauges

17.3a A "bottle brush" hone will produce better results if you have never done cylinder honing before

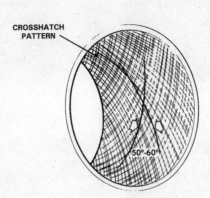

17.3b The cylinder hone should leave a smooth, crosshatch pattern with the lines intersecting at approximately a 60-degree angle

18.4a The piston ring grooves can be cleaned with a special tool, as shown here . . .

excessive and a new piston will be required. If the piston binds at the lower end of the cylinder and is loose toward the top, the cylinder is tapered. If tight spots are encountered as the piston/feeler gauge is rotated in the cylinder, the cylinder is out-of-round.

10   Repeat the procedure for the remaining pistons and cylinders.

11   If the cylinder walls are badly scuffed or scored, or if they're out-of-round or tapered beyond the limits given in this Chapter's Specifications, have the engine block rebored and honed at an automotive machine shop. If a rebore is done, oversize pistons and rings will be required.

12   Using a precision straightedge and feeler gauge, check the block deck (the surface that mates with the cylinder head[s]) for distortion **(see illustration)**. If it's distorted beyond the specified limit, it can be resurfaced by an automotive machine shop.

13   If the cylinders are in reasonably good condition and not worn to the outside of the limits, and if the piston-to-cylinder clearances can be maintained properly, then they don't have to be rebored. Honing is all that's necessary (refer to Section 17).

17   Cylinder honing

Refer to illustrations 17.3a and 17.3b

1   Prior to engine reassembly, the cylinder bores must be honed so the new piston rings will seat correctly and provide the best possible combustion chamber seal. **Note:** *If you don't have the tools or don't want to tackle the honing operation, most automotive machine shops will do it for a reasonable fee.*

2   Before honing the cylinders, install the main bearing caps or cap assembly (without bearing inserts) and tighten the bolts to the specified torque.

3   Two types of cylinder hones are commonly available - the flex hone or "bottle brush" type and the more traditional surfacing hone with spring-loaded stones. Both will do the job, but for the less experienced mechanic the "bottle brush" hone will probably be easier to use. You'll also need some kerosene or honing oil, rags and an electric drill motor. The drill motor should be operated at a steady, slow speed. Use a large 1/2-inch drill or a 3/8-inch variable-speed drill. Proceed as follows:

a) *Mount the hone in the drill motor, compress the stones and slip it into the first cylinder* **(see illustration)**. **Warning:** *Be sure to wear safety goggles or a face shield!*

b) *Lubricate the cylinder with plenty of honing oil, turn on the drill and move the hone up-and-down in the cylinder at a pace that will produce a fine crosshatch pattern on the cylinder walls. Ideally, the crosshatch lines should intersect at approximately a 60-degree angle* **(see illustration)**. *Be sure to use plenty of lubricant and don't take off any more material than is absolutely necessary to produce the desired finish.* **Note:** *Piston ring manufacturers*

may specify a smaller crosshatch angle than the traditional 60-degrees - read and follow any instructions included with the new rings.

c) *Don't withdraw the hone from the cylinder while it's running. Instead, shut off the drill and continue moving the hone up-and-down in the cylinder until it comes to a complete stop, then compress the stones and withdraw the hone. If you're using a "bottle brush" type hone, stop the drill motor, then turn the chuck in the normal direction of rotation while withdrawing the hone from the cylinder.*

d) *Wipe the oil out of the cylinder and repeat the procedure for the remaining cylinders.*

4   After the honing job is complete, chamfer the top edges of the cylinder bores with a small file so the rings won't catch when the pistons are installed. Be very careful not to nick the cylinder walls with the end of the file.

5   The entire engine block must be washed again very thoroughly with warm, soapy water to remove all traces of the abrasive grit produced during the honing operation. **Note:** *The bores can be considered clean when a lint-free white cloth - dampened with clean engine oil - used to wipe them out doesn't pick up any more honing residue, which will show up as gray areas on the cloth. Be sure to run a brush through all oil holes and galleries and flush them with running water.*

6   After rinsing, dry the block and apply a coat of light rust preventive oil to all machined surfaces. Wrap the block in a plastic trash bag to keep it clean and set it aside until reassembly.

18   Pistons/connecting rods - inspection

Refer to illustrations 18.4a, 18.4b, 18.10 and 18.11

1   Before the inspection process can be carried out, the piston/connecting rod assemblies must be cleaned and the original piston rings removed from the pistons. **Note:** *Always use new piston rings when the engine is reassembled.*

2   Using a piston ring installation tool, carefully remove the rings from the pistons. Be careful not to nick or gouge the pistons in the process.

3   Scrape all traces of carbon from the top of the piston. A hand-held wire brush or a piece of fine emery cloth can be used once the majority of the deposits have been scraped away. Do not, under any circumstances, use a wire brush mounted in a drill motor to remove deposits from the pistons. The piston material is soft and may be eroded away by the wire brush.

4   Use a piston ring groove-cleaning tool to remove carbon deposits from the ring grooves. If a tool isn't available, a piece broken off the old ring will do the job. Be very careful to remove only the carbon deposits - don't remove any metal and do not nick or scratch the sides of the

2C

18.4b . . . or a section of a broken ring

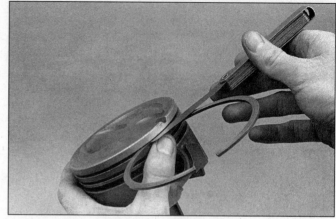

18.10 Check the ring groove clearance with a feeler gauge at several points around the groove

ring grooves **(see illustrations)**.

5   Once the deposits have been removed, clean the piston/rod assemblies with solvent and dry them with compressed air (if available). Make sure the oil return holes in the back sides of the ring grooves and the oil hole in the lower end of each rod are clear.

6   If the pistons and cylinder walls aren't damaged or worn excessively, and if the engine block is not rebored, new pistons won't be necessary. Normal piston wear appears as even vertical wear on the piston thrust surfaces and slight looseness of the top ring in its groove. New piston rings, however, should always be used when an engine is rebuilt.

7   Carefully inspect each piston for cracks around the skirt, at the pin bosses and at the ring lands.

8   Look for scoring and scuffing on the thrust faces of the skirt, holes in the piston crown and burned areas at the edge of the crown. If the skirt is scored or scuffed, the engine may have been suffering from overheating and/or abnormal combustion, which caused excessively high operating temperatures. The cooling and lubrication systems should be checked thoroughly. A hole in the piston crown is an indication that abnormal combustion (preignition) was occurring. Burned areas at the edge of the piston crown are usually evidence of spark knock (detonation). If any of the above problems exist, the causes must be corrected or the damage will occur again. The causes may include intake air leaks, incorrect air/fuel mixture, incorrect ignition timing and EGR system malfunctions.

9   Corrosion of the piston, in the form of small pits, indicates that coolant is leaking into the combustion chamber and/or the crankcase. Again, the cause must be corrected or the problem may persist in the rebuilt engine.

10   Measure the piston ring groove clearance by laying a new piston ring in each ring groove and slipping a feeler gauge in beside it **(see illustration)**. Check the clearance at three or four locations around each groove. Be sure to use the correct ring for each groove - they are different. If the clearance is greater than that listed in this Chapter's Specifications, new pistons will have to be used.

11   Check the piston-to-bore clearance by measuring the bore (see Section 16) and the piston diameter. Make sure the pistons and bores are correctly matched. Measure the piston across the skirt, at a 90-degree angle to the piston pin **(see illustration)**. Subtract the piston diameter from the bore diameter to obtain the clearance. If it's greater than specified, the block will have to be rebored and new pistons and rings installed.

12   Check the piston-to-rod clearance by twisting the piston and rod in opposite directions. Any noticeable play indicates excessive wear, which must be corrected.

13   If the pistons must be removed from the connecting rods for any reason, the rods should be taken to an automotive machine shop, to be checked for bend and twist, since automotive machine shops have special equipment for this purpose.

14   Check the connecting rods for cracks and other damage. Temporarily remove the rod caps, lift out the old bearing inserts, wipe the rod and cap bearing surfaces clean and inspect them for nicks, gouges and scratches. After checking the rods, replace the old bearings, slip the caps into place and tighten the nuts finger tight. **Note:** *If the engine is being rebuilt because of a connecting rod knock, be sure to install new rods.*

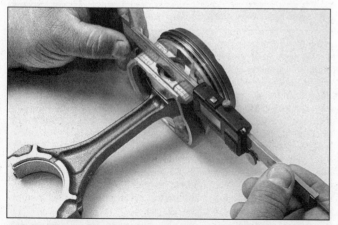

18.11 Measure the piston diameter at a 90-degree angle to the piston pin, at the bottom of the piston pin area - a precision caliper may be used if a micrometer isn't available

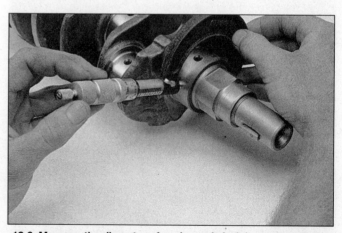

19.6 Measure the diameter of each crankshaft journal at several points to detect taper and out-of-round conditions

19 Crankshaft - inspection

Refer to illustration 19.6

1   Clean the crankshaft with solvent and dry it with compressed air (if available). Be sure to clean the oil holes with a stiff brush and flush them with solvent.

2   Check the main and connecting rod bearing journals for uneven wear, scoring, pits and cracks.

3   Rub a penny across each journal several times. If a journal picks up copper from the penny, it's too rough and must be reground.

4   Remove all burrs from the crankshaft oil holes with a stone, file or scraper.

5   Check the rest of the crankshaft for cracks and other damage. It should be magnafluxed to reveal hidden cracks - an automotive machine shop will handle the procedure.

6   Using a micrometer, measure the diameter of the main and connecting rod journals and compare the results to this Chapter's Specifications **(see illustration)**. By measuring the diameter at a number of points around each journal's circumference, you'll be able to determine whether or not the journal is out-of-round. Take the measurement at each end of the journal, near the crank throws, to determine if the journal is tapered. Crankshaft runout should be checked also, but large V-blocks and a dial indicator are needed to do it correctly. If you don't have the equipment, have a machine shop check the runout.

7   If the crankshaft journals are damaged, tapered, out-of-round or worn beyond the limits given in the Specifications, have the crankshaft reground by an automotive machine shop. Be sure to use the correct size bearing inserts if the crankshaft is reconditioned.

8   Check the oil seal journals at each end of the crankshaft for wear and damage. If the seal has worn a groove in the journal, or if it's nicked or scratched, the new seal may leak when the engine is reassembled. In some cases, an automotive machine shop may be able to repair the journal by pressing on a thin sleeve. If repair isn't feasible, a new or different crankshaft should be installed.

9   Refer to Section 20 and examine the main and rod bearing inserts.

20 Main and connecting rod bearings - inspection and selection

Inspection

Refer to illustration 20.1

1   Even though the main and connecting rod bearings should be replaced with new ones during the engine overhaul, the old bearings should be retained for close examination, as they may reveal valuable information about the condition of the engine **(see illustration)**.

2   Bearing failure occurs because of lack of lubrication, the presence of dirt or other foreign particles, overloading the engine and corrosion. Regardless of the cause of bearing failure, it must be corrected before the engine is reassembled to prevent it from happening again.

3   When examining the bearings, remove them from the engine block, the main bearing caps, the connecting rods and the rod caps and lay them out on a clean surface in the same general position as their location in the engine. This will enable you to match any bearing problems with the corresponding crankshaft journal.

4   Dirt and other foreign particles get into the engine in a variety of ways. It may be left in the engine during assembly, or it may pass through filters or the PCV system. It may get into the oil, and from there into the bearings. Metal chips from machining operations and normal engine wear are often present. Abrasives are sometimes left in engine components after reconditioning, especially when parts are not thoroughly cleaned using the proper cleaning methods. Whatever the source, these foreign objects often end up embedded in the soft bearing material and are easily recognized. Large particles will not

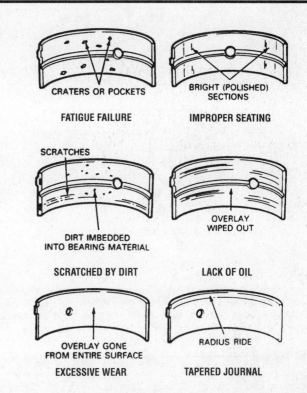

20.1 When inspecting the main and connecting rod bearings, look for these problems

2C

embed in the bearing and will score or gouge the bearing and journal. The best prevention for this cause of bearing failure is to clean all parts thoroughly and keep everything spotlessly clean during engine assembly. Frequent and regular engine oil and filter changes are also recommended.

5   Lack of lubrication (or lubrication breakdown) has a number of interrelated causes. Excessive heat (which thins the oil), overloading (which squeezes the oil from the bearing face) and oil leakage or throw off (from excessive bearing clearances, worn oil pump or high engine speeds) all contribute to lubrication breakdown. Blocked oil passages, which usually are the result of misaligned oil holes in a bearing shell, will also oil starve a bearing and destroy it. When lack of lubrication is the cause of bearing failure, the bearing material is wiped or extruded from the steel backing of the bearing. Temperatures may increase to the point where the steel backing turns blue from overheating.

6   Driving habits can have a definite effect on bearing life. Driving habits can have a definite effect on bearing life. Low speed operation in too high a gear (lugging the engine) puts very high loads on bearings, which tends to squeeze out the oil film. These loads cause the bearings to flex, which produces fine cracks in the bearing face (fatigue failure). Eventually the bearing material will loosen in pieces and tear away from the steel backing. Short trip driving leads to corrosion of bearings because insufficient engine heat is produced to drive off the condensed water and corrosive gases. These products collect in the engine oil, forming acid and sludge. As the oil is carried to the engine bearings, the acid attacks and corrodes the bearing material.

7   Incorrect bearing installation during engine assembly will lead to bearing failure as well. Tight-fitting bearings leave insufficient bearing oil clearance and will result in oil starvation. Dirt or foreign particles trapped behind a bearing insert result in high spots on the bearing which lead to failure.

Selection

Refer to illustrations 20.10a, 20.10b, 20.10c and 20.11

8   If the original bearings are worn or damaged, or if the oil

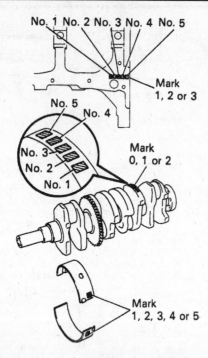

20.10a   If the number on the original main bearing is not clear, install a new bearing with a number that matches the number stamped into the block - different journals may require different size bearings (5S-FE grade number locations shown)

20.10c   Grade numbers on the 1MZ-FE V6 are located on the front of the block above the crankshaft (A); and crankshaft journal grades are on the side of the first counterweight (B)

clearances are incorrect (see Sections 24 or 26), the following procedures should be used to select the correct new bearings for engine reassembly. However, if the crankshaft has been reground, new undersize bearings must be installed - the following procedure should not be used if undersize bearings are required! The automotive machine shop that reconditions the crankshaft will provide or help you select the correct size bearings. Regardless of how the bearing sizes are determined, use the oil clearance, measured with Plastigage, as a guide to ensure the bearings are the right size.

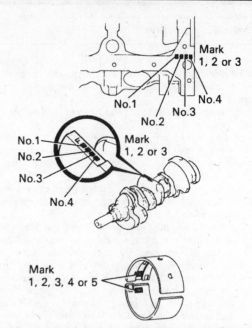

20.10b   Bearing numbers on the 3VZ-FE V6 are inside the bearing shells, and the crank journal gradings are on a different counterweight than the four-cylinder engines

	Total number " ": Number mark				
Cylinder block (A) + Crankshaft (B) =	0 – 5	6 – 11	12 – 17	18 – 23	24 – 28
Use bearing	"1"	"2"	"3"	"4"	"5"

EXAMPLE: Cylinder block "06" (A)
               + Crankshaft "08" (B)
               = Total number 14 (Use bearing "3")

20.11   Select the proper bearings for the 1MZ-FE engine based on this chart - add the crank and block numbers and select the bearing size listed underneath

Main bearings

9   If you need to use a STANDARD size main bearing, install one that has the same number as the original bearing **(see illustrations 20.10a and 20.10b for the bearing number locations)**. There are five sizes of main bearings.

10   If the number on the original main bearing has been obscured, locate the main journal grade numbers stamped into the oil pan mating surface on the engine block and the crankshaft counterweights **(see illustrations)**. On the 1MZ-FE V6 engine, the block numbers are on the front of the block, just above the first main bearing, and the crankshaft numbers are on the first counterweight **(see illustration)**.

11   Adding the block number to the crank number for a particular journal will give the recommended bearing size for the 5S-FE and 3VZ-FE engines. Use the accompanying chart to determine the correct bearings for each journal on the 1MZ-FE engine **(see illustration)**.

Connecting rod bearings

12   If you need to use a STANDARD size rod bearing, install one that has the same number as the number stamped into the connecting rod cap **(see illustration 13.5)**.

All bearings

13   Remember, the oil clearance is the final judge when selecting new bearing sizes. If you have any questions or are unsure which bearings to use, get help from a Toyota dealer parts or service department.

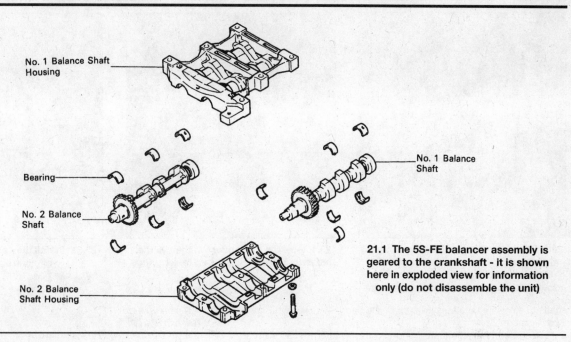

No. 1 Balance Shaft Housing

Bearing

No. 2 Balance Shaft

No. 2 Balance Shaft Housing

No. 1 Balance Shaft

21.1 The 5S-FE balancer assembly is geared to the crankshaft - it is shown here in exploded view for information only (do not disassemble the unit)

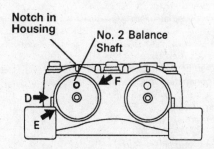

Notch in Housing

No. 2 Balance Shaft

D

E

F

21.2a The balancer shafts have punch marks and the number 2 housing has alignment notches - start with the shafts aligned as shown . . .

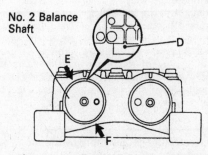

No. 2 Balance Shaft

D

E

F

21.2b . . . then turn until mark D lines up with the notch in the housing

21 Balancer assembly - backlash check (5S-FE engine only)

Refer to illustrations 21.1, 21.2a, 21.2b, 21.3a and 21.3b
Note: *This procedure checks the internal condition of the balancer assembly for worn gears, bearings and/or shafts. For balancer assembly installation and crankshaft-to-balancer backlash checks, see Section 27.*

1   The engine balancer assembly consists of two shafts contained in an upper and lower aluminum housing assembly. The shafts are geared together, and one of the shafts is geared to the crankshaft **(see illustration)**. The following procedure applies only with the balancer assembly removed from the engine.
2   Start with the punch marks on the number 2 shaft lined up as indicated **(see illustration)**, then align the number 2 shaft so that mark D is aligned with the housing **(see illustration)**.
3   Using locking pliers to hold the number 2 shaft from turning, measure the backlash on the number 1 gear with a dial indicator **(see illustrations)**, while keeping forward pressure on the rear of both

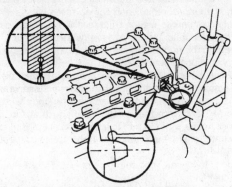

21.3a Set the dial indicator up as shown . . .

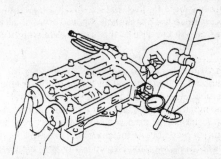

21.3b . . . and measure the backlash while applying mild hand pressure on the rear of both shafts

2C

23.3 When checking piston ring end gap, the ring must be square in the cylinder bore (this is done by pushing the ring down with the top of a piston as shown)

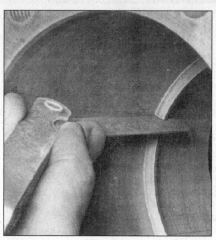

23.4 With the ring square in the cylinder, measure the end gap with a feeler gauge

23.9a Install the spacer/expander in the oil control ring groove

shafts to eliminate thrust play. Compare the backlash to this Chapter's Specifications.

4   Remove the dial indicator, and turn the number 2 shaft so that punch mark E now aligns with the case. Measure backlash again as in Step 3 and compare the results with this Chapter's Specifications.

5   Remove the dial indicator again, and turn the number 2 shaft so that punch mark F now aligns with the case. Measure backlash again as in Step 3 and compare the results with this Chapter's Specifications. **Note:** *If any of the three measurements exceeds the Specifications, it is suggested that the engine balance assembly be taken to a Toyota dealer or other qualified service facility for further disassembly and repair.*

22   Engine overhaul - reassembly sequence

1   Before beginning engine reassembly, make sure you have all the necessary new parts, gaskets and seals as well as the following items on hand:

Common hand tools
A 1/2-inch drive torque wrench
Piston ring installation tool
Piston ring compressor
*Short lengths of rubber or plastic hose
   to fit over connecting rod bolts*
Plastigage
Feeler gauges
A fine-tooth file
New engine oil
Engine assembly lube or moly-base grease
Gasket sealer
Thread locking compound

2   In order to save time and avoid problems, engine reassembly must be done in the following general order:

Four-cylinder engines

Piston rings (Part C)
Crankshaft and main bearings (Part C)
Piston/connecting rod assemblies (Part C)
Rear main (crankshaft) oil seal (Part C)
Engine balancer assembly (Part C)
Cylinder head and lifters (Part A)
Camshafts (Part A)
Timing belt and sprockets (Part A)
Timing belt covers (Part A)
Oil pump (Part A)

Oil pick-up (Part A)
Oil pan (Part A)
Intake and exhaust manifolds (Part A)
Valve cover (Part A)
Flywheel/driveplate (Part A)

V6 engines

Piston rings (Part C)
Crankshaft and main bearings (Part C)
Piston/connecting rod assemblies (Part C)
Rear main oil seal/retainer (Part C)
Oil pump (Part B)
Oil pan (Part B)
Cylinder heads (Part B)
Camshafts and lifters (Part B)
Timing belt and sprockets (Part B)
Timing belt covers (Part B)
Valve covers (Part B)
Intake and exhaust manifolds (Part B)
Flywheel/driveplate (Part B)

23   Piston rings - installation

Refer to illustrations 23.3, 23.4, 23.9a, 23.9b and 23.12

1   Before installing the new piston rings, the ring end gaps must be checked. It's assumed that the piston ring groove clearance has been checked and verified correct (see Section 18).

2   Lay out the piston/connecting rod assemblies and the new ring sets so the ring sets will be matched with the same piston and cylinder during the end gap measurement and engine assembly.

3   Insert the top (number one) ring into the first cylinder and square it up with the cylinder walls by pushing it in with the top of the piston **(see illustration)**. The ring should be near the bottom of the cylinder, at the lower limit of ring travel.

4   To measure the end gap, slip feeler gauges between the ends of the ring until a gauge equal to the gap width is found **(see illustration)**. The feeler gauge should slide between the ring ends with a slight amount of drag. Compare the measurement to that found in this Chapter's Specifications. If the gap is larger or smaller than specified, double-check to make sure you have the correct rings before proceeding.

5   If the gap is too small, replace the rings - DO NOT file the ends to increase the clearance.

6   Excess end gap isn't critical unless it's greater than 0.040-inch. Again, double-check to make sure you have the correct rings for your engine.

23.9b DO NOT use a piston ring installation tool when installing the oil ring side rails

7 Repeat the procedure for each ring that will be installed in the first cylinder and for each ring in the remaining cylinders. Remember to keep rings, pistons and cylinders matched up.

8 Once the ring end gaps have been checked/corrected, the rings can be installed on the pistons.

9 The oil control ring (lowest one on the piston) is usually installed first. It's composed of three separate components. Slip the spacer/expander into the groove **(see illustration)**. If an anti-rotation tang is used, make sure it's inserted into the drilled hole in the ring groove. Next, install the lower side rail. Don't use a piston ring installation tool on the oil ring side rails, as they may be damaged. Instead, place one end of the side rail into the groove between the spacer/expander and the ring land, hold it firmly in place and slide a finger around the piston while pushing the rail into the groove **(see illustration)**. Next, install the upper side rail in the same manner.

10 After the three oil ring components have been installed, check to make sure that both the upper and lower side rails can be turned smoothly in the ring groove.

11 The number two (middle) ring is installed next. It's usually stamped with a mark which must face up, toward the top of the piston. **Note:** *Always follow the instructions printed on the ring package or box - different manufacturers may require different approaches. Do not mix up the top and middle rings, as they have different cross sections.*

12 Use a piston ring installation tool and make sure the ring's identification mark is facing the top of the piston, then slip the ring into the middle groove on the piston **(see illustration)**. Don't expand the ring any more than necessary to slide it over the piston.

13 Install the number one (top) ring in the same manner. Make sure the mark is facing up. Be careful not to confuse the number one and number two rings.

14 Repeat the procedure for the remaining pistons and rings.

---

24 Crankshaft - installation and main bearing oil clearance check

Refer to illustrations 24.10, 24.12a, 24.12b, 24.12c, 24.12d, 24.12e, 24.14, 24.19a, 24.19b and 24.20

1 Crankshaft installation is the first major step in engine reassembly. It's assumed at this point that the engine block and crankshaft have been cleaned, inspected and repaired or reconditioned.

2 Position the engine with the bottom facing up.

3 Remove the main bearing cap bolts and lift out the caps or cap assembly. Lay the caps out in the proper.

4 If they're still in place, remove the old bearing inserts from the block and the main bearing caps. Wipe the main bearing surfaces of the block and caps with a clean, lint free cloth. They must be kept spotlessly clean!

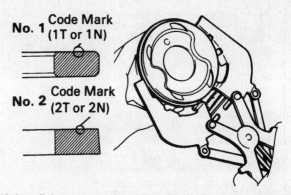

23.12 Install the compression rings with a ring expander - the mark must face up (four-cylinder engine shown - on V6 engines, top rings are marked 1R or T, second rings are marked 2R or T2)

24.10 Lay the Plastigage strips (arrow) on the main bearing journals, parallel to the crankshaft centerline

Main bearing oil clearance check

5 Clean the back sides of the new main bearing inserts and lay the bearing half with the oil groove in each main bearing saddle in the block. Lay the other bearing half from each bearing set in the corresponding main bearing cap. Make sure the tab on each bearing insert fits into the recess in the block or cap. Also, the oil holes in the block must line up with the oil holes in the bearing insert. **Caution:** *Do not hammer the bearings into place and don't nick or gouge the bearing faces. No lubrication should be used at this time.*

6 If you're working on a V6 engine, the thrust bearings (washers) must be installed in the number two cap and saddle. On four-cylinder engines, the thrust bearings (washers) must be installed in the number three (center) cap.

7 Clean the faces of the bearings in the block and the crankshaft main bearing journals with a clean, lint free cloth. Check or clean the oil holes in the crankshaft, as any dirt here can go only one way - straight through the new bearings.

8 Once you're certain the crankshaft is clean, carefully lay it in position in the main bearings.

9 Before the crankshaft can be permanently installed, the main bearing oil clearance must be checked.

10 Trim several pieces of the appropriate size Plastigage (they must be slightly shorter than the width of the main bearings) and place one piece on each crankshaft main bearing journal, parallel with the journal axis **(see illustration)**.

11 Clean the faces of the bearings in the caps and install the caps in their respective positions (don't mix them up) with the arrows pointing toward the front of the engine. If you're working on a 3VZ-FE engine,

2C

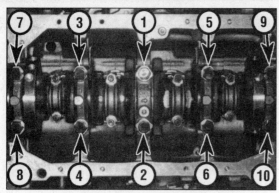

24.12a Main bearing cap bolt tightening sequence - four-cylinder engines

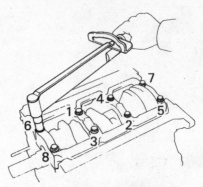

24.12b Main bearing cap assembly bolt tightening sequence - 3VZ-FE engine

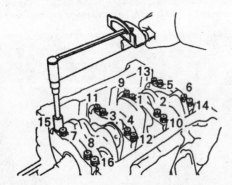

24.12c Main bearing cap bolt tightening sequence - 1MZ-FE engine

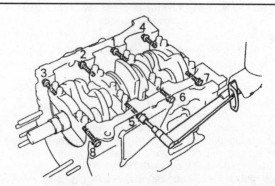

24.12d Main bearing cap side bolt tightening sequence - 1MZ-FE engine (tighten side bolts after tightening cap bolts)

carefully lay the main bearing cap assembly in place. Don't disturb the Plastigage. Apply a light coat of oil to the bolt threads and the undersides of the bolt heads, then install them.

12   Following the recommended sequence **(see illustrations)**, tighten the main bearing cap bolts, in three steps, to the torque listed in this Chapter's Specifications. Don't rotate the crankshaft at any time during this operation! **Note:** *On V6 engines only, after reaching the specified torque on all of the bolts, tighten each bolt in sequence an additional 90-degrees (except the six-point bolts on the 1MZ-FE engine)* **(see illustration)**.

13   Remove the bolts and carefully lift off the main bearing caps or cap assembly. Keep them in order. Don't disturb the Plastigage or rotate the crankshaft. If any of the main bearing caps are difficult to remove, tap them gently from side-to-side with a soft-face hammer to loosen them.

14   Compare the width of the crushed Plastigage on each journal to the scale printed on the Plastigage envelope to obtain the main bearing oil clearance **(see illustration)**. Check the Specifications to make sure it's correct.

15   If the clearance is not as specified, the bearing inserts may be the wrong size (which means different ones will be required - see Section 20). Before deciding that different inserts are needed, make sure that no dirt or oil was between the bearing inserts and the caps or block when the clearance was measured. If the Plastigage is noticeably wider at one end than the other, the journal may be tapered (see Section 19).

16   Carefully scrape all traces of the Plastigage material off the main bearing journals and/or the bearing faces. Don't nick or scratch the bearing faces.

Final crankshaft installation

17   Carefully lift the crankshaft out of the engine. Clean the bearing faces in the block, then apply a thin, uniform layer of clean moly-base grease or engine assembly lube to each of the bearing surfaces. Coat

24.12e On V6 engines only, after reaching the specified torque, mark the front side of each bolt with paint as shown here, plus a paint mark on the socket, then turn the bolts an additional 1/4-turn - the paint marks should now be 90-degrees from their original position

the thrust washers as well.

18   Lubricate the crankshaft surfaces that contact the oil seals with moly-base grease, engine assembly lube or clean engine oil.

19   Make sure the crankshaft journals are clean, then lay the crankshaft back in place in the block. Clean the faces of the bearings in the caps or cap assembly, then apply lubricant to them. Install the caps in their respective positions with the arrows pointing toward the front of the engine. **Note:** *Be sure to install the thrust washers. On four-cylinder engines, the thrust washers go with the number 3 main journal, and the number 2 main journal on V6 engines.* The upper (block side) thrust washers can be rotated into position around the crank with the crank in the block, with the thrust washer grooves facing OUT. The

24.14 Compare the width of the crushed Plastigage to the scale on the envelope to determine the main bearing oil clearance (always take the measurement at the widest point of the Plastigage) - be sure to use the correct scale; standard and metric scales are included

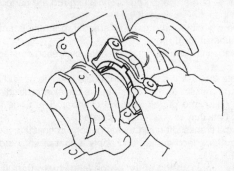

24.19b On four-cylinder engines, install the thrust washer in the number three cap with the oil grooves facing OUT, and on V6 engines, the tangs should fit into the slots on the caps

24.19a Rotate the thrust washer into position with the oil grooves facing OUT

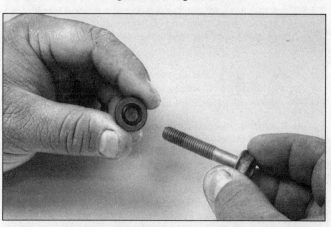

24.20 The 1MZ-FE engine uses hex-headed bolts that secure the sides of the main caps - when rebuilding this engine use new sealing washers on these bolts

25.3 After removing the retainer from the block, support it on a couple of wood blocks and drive out the old seal with a punch or screwdriver and hammer

tanged lower thrust washers should be placed on the caps with their grooves OUT and the tangs fitting into the cap slots **(see illustrations)**.

20   Apply a light coat of oil to the bolt threads and the under sides of the bolt heads, then install them. Tighten all main bearing cap bolts to the torque listed in this Chapter's Specifications, following the recommended sequence. **Note:** *On the 1MZ-FE V6, install the inner (closest to the crankshaft) 12-point bolts first, tap the caps down lightly with a plastic-faced hammer, then install the outer 12-point bolts and begin the torque sequence. The six-point (hex-head) bolts are not installed and tightened until all of the 12-point bolts have been tightened to the proper torque **(see illustrations 24.12c and 24.12d)**. Be sure to use new sealing washers on the hex-head bolts.* **(see illustration)**.

21   On manual transmission equipped models, install a new pilot bearing in the end of the crankshaft.

22   Rotate the crankshaft a number of times by hand to check for any obvious binding.

23   Check the crankshaft endplay with a feeler gauge or a dial indicator as described in Section 14. The endplay should be correct if the crankshaft thrust faces aren't worn or damaged and new thrust washers have been installed.

24   Install a new rear main oil seal, then bolt the retainer to the block (see Section 25).

25   Rear main oil seal installation

Refer to illustrations 25.3 and 25.5

1   The crankshaft must be installed first and the main bearing caps

or cap assembly bolted in place, then the new seal should be installed in the retainer and the retainer bolted to the block.

2   Check the seal contact surface on the crankshaft very carefully for scratches and nicks that could damage the new seal lip and cause oil leaks. If the crankshaft is damaged, the only alternative is a new or different crankshaft.

3   The old seal can be removed from the retainer by driving it out from the back side with a hammer and punch **(see illustration)**. Be

25.5 Drive the new seal into the retainer with a wood block or a section of pipe, if you have one large enough - make sure you don't cock the seal in the retainer bore

sure to note how far it's recessed into the bore before removing it; the new seal will have to be recessed an equal amount. Be very careful not to scratch or otherwise damage the bore in the retainer or oil leaks could develop.

4   Make sure the retainer is clean, then apply a thin coat of engine oil to the outer edge of the new seal. The seal must be pressed squarely into the bore, so hammering it into place isn't recommended. If you don't have access to a press, sandwich the housing and seal between two smooth pieces of wood and press the seal into place with the jaws of a large vise. The pieces of wood must be thick enough to distribute the force evenly around the entire circumference of the seal. Work slowly and make sure the seal enters the bore squarely.

5   As a last resort, the seal can be tapped into the retainer with a hammer. Use a block of wood to distribute the force evenly and make sure the seal is driven in squarely **(see illustration)**.

6   The seal lips must be lubricated with clean engine oil or moly-based grease before the seal/retainer is slipped over the crankshaft and bolted to the block. On four-cylinder engines, use a new gasket - and sealant- and make sure the dowel pins are in place before installing the retainer. On V6 engines, no gasket is required. Instead, apply a 2 mm wide bead of RTV sealant to the retainer-to-block surface.

7   Tighten the bolts a little at a time to the torque listed in Chapter 2A or 2B Specifications.

26 Pistons/connecting rods - installation and rod bearing oil clearance check

Refer to illustrations 26.3, 26.5, 26.9, 26.11, 26.13, 26.15 and 26.17

1   Before installing the piston/connecting rod assemblies, the cylinder walls must be perfectly clean, the top edge of each cylinder must be chamfered, and the crankshaft must be in place.

2   Remove the cap from the end of the number one connecting rod (refer to the marks made during removal). Remove the original bearing inserts and wipe the bearing surfaces of the connecting rod and cap with a clean, lint-free cloth. They must be kept spotlessly clean.

Connecting rod bearing oil clearance check

3   Clean the back side of the new upper bearing insert, then lay it in place in the connecting rod. Make sure the tab on the bearing fits into the recess in the rod so the oil holes line up **(see illustration)**. Don't hammer the bearing insert into place and be very careful not to nick or gouge the bearing face. Don't lubricate the bearing at this time.

4   Clean the back side of the other bearing insert and install it in the rod cap. Again, make sure the tab on the bearing fits into the recess in the cap, and don't apply any lubricant. It's critically important that the mating surfaces of the bearing and connecting rod are perfectly clean and oil free when they're assembled.

5   Position the piston ring gaps at staggered intervals around the piston **(see illustration)**.

6   Slip a section of plastic or rubber hose over each connecting rod cap bolt.

7   Lubricate the piston and rings with clean engine oil and attach a piston ring compressor to the piston. Leave the skirt protruding about 1/4-inch to guide the piston into the cylinder. The rings must be compressed until they're flush with the piston.

8   Rotate the crankshaft until the number one connecting rod journal is at BDC (bottom dead center) and apply a coat of engine oil to the cylinder wall.

9   With the dimple on top of the piston **(see illustration)** facing the front of the engine, gently insert the piston/connecting rod assembly into the number one cylinder bore and rest the bottom edge of the ring compressor on the engine block.

10   Tap the top edge of the ring compressor to make sure it's contacting the block around its entire circumference.

11   Gently tap on the top of the piston with the end of a wooden hammer handle **(see illustration)** while guiding the end of the connecting rod into place on the crankshaft journal. The piston rings may try to pop out of the ring compressor just before entering the cylinder bore, so keep some downward pressure on the ring compressor. Work slowly, and if any resistance is felt as the piston enters the cylinder, stop immediately. Find out what's hanging up and

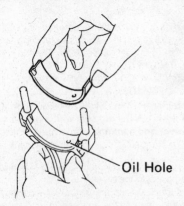

26.3 Align the oil hole in the bearing with the oil hole in the rod

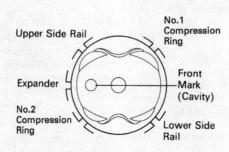

26.5 Stagger the ring end gaps around the piston, as shown, before installing the pistons

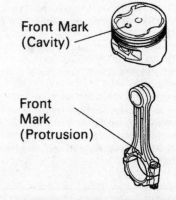

26.9 Check to be sure both the mark on the piston and the mark on the connecting rod are aligned as shown

26.11 The piston can be driven (gently) into the cylinder bore with the end of a wooden or plastic hammer handle

26.13 Lay the Plastigage strips on each rod bearing journal, parallel to the crankshaft centerline

26.15 Install the connecting rod caps with the front mark (arrow) facing the timing belt end of the engine, and torque to Specifications - for the 90-degree second step, use an angle gauge as shown, or use paint reference marks on the rod nuts and the socket

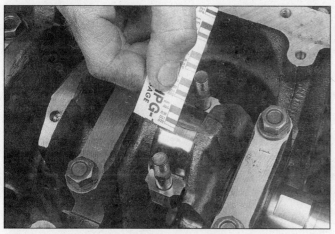

26.17 Measure the width of the crushed Plastigage to determine the rod bearing oil clearance (be sure to use the correct scale - standard and metric scales are included)

fix it before proceeding. **Caution:** *Do not, for any reason, force the piston into the cylinder - you might break a ring and/or the piston.*

12   Once the piston/connecting rod assembly is installed, the connecting rod bearing oil clearance must be checked before the rod cap is permanently bolted in place.

13   Cut a piece of the appropriate size Plastigage slightly shorter than the width of the connecting rod bearing and lay it in place on the number one connecting rod journal, parallel with the journal axis **(see illustration)**.

14   Clean the connecting rod cap bearing face, remove the protective hoses from the connecting rod bolts and install the rod cap. Make sure the mating mark on the cap is on the same side as the mark on the connecting rod. Check the cap to make sure the front mark is facing the timing belt end of the engine.

15   Apply a light coat of oil to the under sides of the nuts, then install and tighten them to the torque listed in this Chapter's Specifications, working up to it in three steps. Use a thin-wall socket to avoid erroneous torque readings that can result if the socket is wedged between the rod cap and nut. If the socket tends to wedge itself between the nut and the cap, lift up on it slightly until it no longer contacts the cap. Do not rotate the crankshaft at any time during this operation. **Note:** *After reaching the specified torque, tighten each nut an additional 90-degrees (1/4-turn)***(see illustration)**.

16   Remove the nuts and detach the rod cap, being very careful not to disturb the Plastigage.

17   Compare the width of the crushed Plastigage to the scale printed on the Plastigage envelope to obtain the oil clearance **(see**

illustration)**. Compare it to this Chapter's Specifications to make sure the clearance is correct.

18   If the clearance is not as specified, the bearing inserts may be the wrong size (which means different ones will be required). Before deciding that different inserts are needed, make sure that no dirt or oil was between the bearing inserts and the connecting rod or cap when the clearance was measured. Also, recheck the journal diameter. If the Plastigage was wider at one end than the other, the journal may be tapered (refer to Section 19).

Final connecting rod installation

19   Carefully scrape all traces of the Plastigage material off the rod journal and/or bearing face. Be very careful not to scratch the bearing, use your fingernail or the edge of a credit card to remove the Plastigage.

20   Make sure the bearing faces are perfectly clean, then apply a uniform layer of clean moly-base grease or engine assembly lube to both of them. You'll have to push the piston higher into the cylinder to expose the face of the bearing insert in the connecting rod, be sure to slip the protective hoses over the rod bolts first.

21   Slide the connecting rod back into place on the journal, remove the protective hoses from the rod cap bolts, install the rod cap and tighten the nuts to the torque listed in this Chapter's Specifications. Again, work up to the torque in three steps.

22   Repeat the entire procedure for the remaining pistons/connecting rods.

23   The important points to remember are:

a)   *Keep the back sides of the bearing inserts and the insides of the connecting rods and caps perfectly clean when assembling them.*

b)   *Make sure you have the correct piston/rod assembly for each cylinder.*

c)   *The dimple on the piston must face the front of the engine.*

d)   *Lubricate the cylinder walls with clean oil.*

e)   *Lubricate the bearing faces when installing the rod caps after the oil clearance has been checked.*

24   After all the piston/connecting rod assemblies have been properly installed, rotate the crankshaft a number of times by hand to check for any obvious binding.

25   As a final step, the connecting rod endplay must be checked. Refer to Section 13 for this procedure.

26   Compare the measured endplay to this Chapter's Specifications to make sure it's correct. If it was correct before disassembly and the original crankshaft and rods were reinstalled, it should still be right. If new rods or a new crankshaft were installed, the endplay may be inadequate. If so, the rods will have to be removed and taken to an automotive machine shop for resizing.

2C

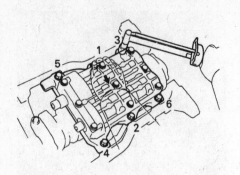

27.4 With the balance shafts aligned with the case, apply hand pressure as shown while tightening the bolts in sequence

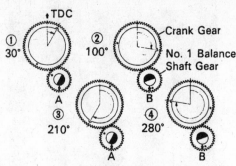

27.6 Check the balancer shaft gear-to-crankshaft gear backlash at the four locations shown

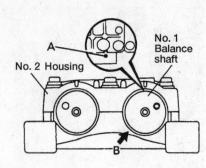

27.8 Check backlash with the balance shaft number 1 aligned as shown

27   Balancer assembly installation (5S-FE engines only)

Refer to illustrations 27.4, 27.6, 27.8 and 27.9

1   After the crankshaft and pistons/rods have all been installed, torqued and checked, clean the surface of the block and the balancer assembly spacers, then place the spacers on the block.

2   Turn the crankshaft until number 1 piston is at TDC (see Section 13).

3   Align the punch marks on the balance shafts with their corresponding marks on the housing **(see illustration 21.2a)**. Place the balancer assembly on the block and install the bolts.

4   Apply hand pressure on the center of the assembly in the direction indicated and tighten the bolts to the torque listed in this Chapter's Specifications, in several steps, in the sequence shown **(see illustration)**.

5   Position a dial indicator against the end of the number 1 balance shaft and check the shaft endplay while pushing the shaft back and forth by hand. Repeat the check for the number 2 balance shaft and compare your readings to this Chapter's Specifications. If the endplay is excessive, remove the balancer assembly and take it to a Toyota dealership or other qualified service facility for repair.

6   Because the backlash between the crankshaft gear and the number 1 balance shaft varies with rotation, backlash must be checked at the four locations indicated **(see illustration)**.

7   Rotate the crankshaft several revolutions and return to TDC for number 1 piston. Check that the punch marks are still aligned **(see illustration 21.2a)**.

8   Rotate the engine clockwise until punch mark A lines up with the notch in the balancer housing **(see illustration)**. Position a lever-type dial indicator on the side of a tooth of the number 1 shaft gear **(see illustration 21.3a)**. Lightly twist the number 1 shaft back and forth a few times by hand and, while pressing on the rear of the shaft to take up the endplay, lightly twist the shaft while observing the dial indicator. Compare the results to on-engine balancer backlash in this Chapter's Specifications.

9   Remove the dial indicator and rotate the engine clockwise until punch mark B on balance shaft 1 lines up with the notch in the housing **(see illustration)**. Measure backlash at this position as in Step 8 and compare the results to on-engine balancer backlash in this Chapter's Specifications.

10   Repeat Steps 7 and 8 (punch mark A) and compare the results to on-engine balancer backlash in this Chapter's Specifications.

11   Repeat Step 9 (punch mark B) and compare the results to on-engine balancer backlash in this Chapter's Specifications.

12   If any of the readings exceed Specifications, change the spacer between the block and the balance assembly to obtain proper backlash. To increase backlash, select a thicker spacer; select a thinner spacer to reduce backlash. Changing the spacer by 0.0008-inch changes the backlash by 0.0006-inch. **Note:** *Various size spacers are available at your Toyota Dealership.*

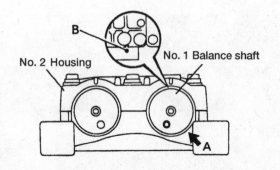

27.9 The second and fourth positions for checking balancer backlash are with the balance shaft number 1 aligned as shown

28   Initial start-up and break-in after overhaul

Warning: *Have a fire extinguisher handy when starting the engine for the first time.*

1   Once the engine has been installed in the vehicle, double-check the engine oil and coolant levels.

2   With the spark plugs out of the engine and the ignition system and fuel pump disabled (see Section 3), crank the engine until oil pressure registers on the gauge or the light goes out.

3   Install the spark plugs, hook up the plug wires and restore the ignition system and fuel pump functions (see Section 3).

4   Start the engine. It may take a few moments for the fuel system to build up pressure, but the engine should start without a great deal of effort.

5   After the engine starts, it should be allowed to warm up to normal operating temperature. While the engine is warming up, make a thorough check for fuel, oil and coolant leaks.

6   Shut the engine off and recheck the engine oil and coolant levels.

7   Drive the vehicle to an area with minimum traffic, accelerate from 30 to 50 mph, then allow the vehicle to slow to 30 mph with the throttle closed. Repeat the procedure 10 or 12 times. This will load the piston rings and cause them to seat properly against the cylinder walls. Check again for oil and coolant leaks.

8   Drive the vehicle gently for the first 500 miles (no sustained high speeds) and keep a constant check on the oil level. It is not unusual for an engine to use oil during the break-in period.

9   At approximately 500 to 600 miles, change the oil and filter.

10   For the next few hundred miles, drive the vehicle normally. Do not pamper it or abuse it.

11   After 2000 miles, change the oil and filter again and consider the engine broken in.

Chapter 3 Cooling, heating and air conditioning systems

Contents

Specifications

General

Radiator cap pressure rating	
5S-FE four-cylinder engine	10.7 to 14.9 psi
3VZ-FE V6 engine	
on radiator..	13.5 to 17.8 psi
on water outlet	12.1 to 16.4 psi
1MZ-FE V6 engine..	12.1 to 16.4 psi
Thermostat rating	See Chapter 1

Torque specifications

Ft-lbs (unless otherwise indicated)

Thermostat housing bolts	
5S-FE four-cylinder engine	78 in-lbs
3VZ-FE V6 engine	14
1MZ-FE V6 engine..	69 in-lbs
Water pump-to-block bolts	
5S-FE four-cylinder engine	82 in-lbs
3VZ-FE V6 engine	14
1MZ-FE V6 engine..	53 in-lbs

1.1 Typical cooling system details

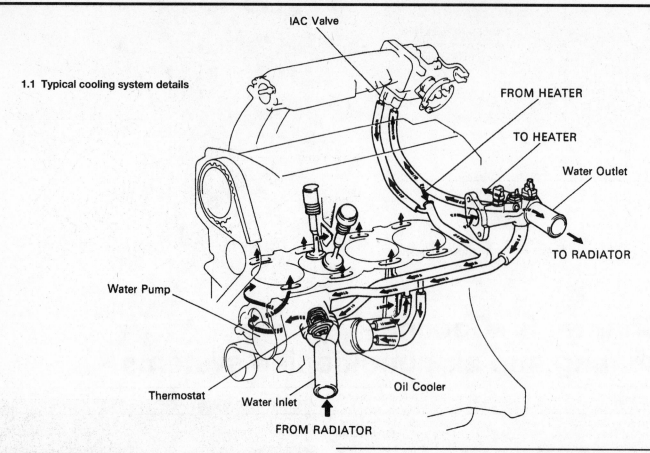

IAC Valve

FROM HEATER

TO HEATER

Water Outlet

TO RADIATOR

Water Pump

Thermostat   Water Inlet   Oil Cooler

FROM RADIATOR

1   General information

Engine cooling system

Refer to illustration 1.1

All vehicles covered by this manual employ a pressurized engine cooling system with thermostatically controlled coolant circulation (**see illustration**). An impeller type water pump mounted on the front of the block pumps coolant through the engine. The coolant flows around each cylinder and toward the rear of the engine. Cast-in coolant passages direct coolant around the intake and exhaust ports, near the spark plug areas and in proximity to the exhaust valve guides.

A wax pellet type thermostat is located in the thermostat housing near the front of the engine. During warm up, the closed thermostat prevents coolant from circulating through the radiator. When the engine reaches normal operating temperature, the thermostat opens and allows hot coolant to travel through the radiator, where it is cooled before returning to the engine.

The cooling system is sealed by a pressure type radiator cap. This raises the boiling point of the coolant, and the higher boiling point of the coolant increases the cooling efficiency of the radiator. If the system pressure exceeds the cap pressure relief value, the excess pressure in the system forces the spring-loaded valve inside the cap off its seat and allows the coolant to escape through the overflow tube into a coolant reservoir. When the system cools, the excess coolant is automatically drawn from the reservoir back into the radiator.

The coolant reservoir does double duty as both the point at which fresh coolant is added to the cooling system to maintain the proper fluid level and as a holding tank for overheated coolant.

This type of cooling system is known as a closed design because coolant that escapes past the pressure cap is saved and reused.

Heating system

The heating system consists of a blower fan and heater core located within the heater box, the inlet and outlet hoses connecting the heater core to the engine cooling system and the heater/air conditioning control head on the dashboard. Hot engine coolant is circulated through the heater core. When the heater mode is activated, a flap door opens to expose the heater box to the passenger compartment. A fan switch on the control head activates the blower motor, which forces air through the core, heating the air.

Air conditioning system

The air conditioning system consists of a condenser mounted in front of the radiator, an evaporator mounted adjacent to the heater core, a compressor mounted on the engine, a filter-drier (accumulator) which contains a high pressure relief valve and the plumbing connecting all of the above.

A blower fan forces the warmer air of the passenger compartment through the evaporator core (sort of a radiator-in-reverse), transferring the heat from the air to the refrigerant. The liquid refrigerant boils off into low pressure vapor, taking the heat with it when it leaves the evaporator. The compressor keeps refrigerant circulating through the system, pumping the warmed coolant through the condenser where it is cooled and then circulated back to the evaporator.

2   Antifreeze - general information

Warning: *Do not allow antifreeze to come in contact with your skin or painted surfaces of the vehicle. Rinse off spills immediately with plenty of water. Antifreeze is highly toxic if ingested. Never leave antifreeze lying around in an open container or in puddles on the floor; children and pets are attracted by it's sweet smell and may drink it. Check with local authorities about disposing of used antifreeze. Many communities have collection centers which will see that antifreeze is disposed of safely. Never dump used antifreeze on the ground or into drains.*

The cooling system should be filled with a water/ethylene-glycol based antifreeze solution, which will prevent freezing down to at least -20 degrees F, or lower if local climate requires it. It also provides protection against corrosion and increases the coolant boiling point.

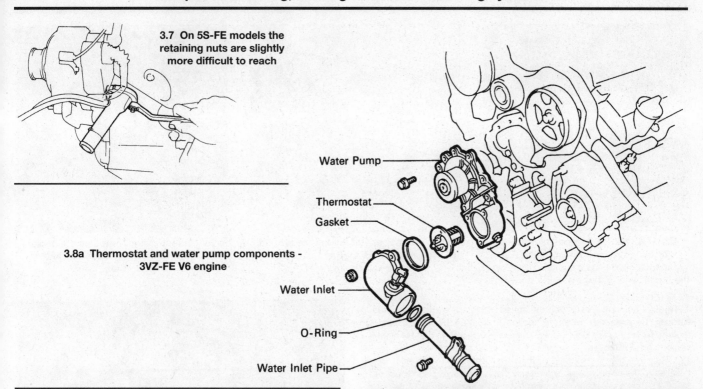

3.7 On 5S-FE models the retaining nuts are slightly more difficult to reach

3.8a Thermostat and water pump components - 3VZ-FE V6 engine

Water Pump

Thermostat

Gasket

Water Inlet

O-Ring

Water Inlet Pipe

The cooling system should be drained, flushed and refilled at least every other year (see Chapter 1). The use of antifreeze solutions for periods of longer than two years is likely to cause damage and encourage the formation of rust and scale in the system. If your tap water is "hard", i.e. contains a lot of dissolved minerals, use distilled water with the antifreeze.

Before adding antifreeze to the system, check all hose connections, because antifreeze tends to search out and leak through very minute openings. Engines do not normally consume coolant. Therefore, if the level goes down find the cause and correct it.

The exact mixture of antifreeze-to-water which you should use depends on the relative weather conditions. The mixture should contain at least 50 percent antifreeze, but should never contain more than 70 percent antifreeze. Consult the mixture ratio chart on the antifreeze container before adding coolant. Hydrometers are available at most auto parts stores to test the ratio of antifreeze to water. Use antifreeze which meets the vehicle manufacturer's specifications.

3   Thermostat - check and replacement

Warning: *Do not attempt to remove the radiator cap, coolant or thermostat until the engine has cooled completely.*

Check

1   Before assuming the thermostat is responsible for a cooling system problem, check the coolant level (Chapter 1), drivebelt tension (Chapter 1) and temperature gauge (or light) operation.
2   If the engine takes a long time to warm up (as indicated by the temperature gauge or heater operation), the thermostat is probably stuck open. Replace the thermostat with a new one.
3   If the engine runs hot, use your hand to check the temperature of the lower radiator hose. If the hose is not hot, but the engine is, the thermostat is probably stuck in the closed position, preventing the coolant inside the engine from escaping to the radiator. Replace the thermostat. **Caution:** *Do not drive the vehicle without a thermostat. The computer may stay in open loop and emissions and fuel economy will suffer.*
4   If the lower radiator hose is hot, it means that the coolant is flowing and the thermostat is open. Consult the Troubleshooting Section at the front of this manual for further diagnosis.

3.8b On 1MZ-FE V6 models, unbolt the water inlet pipe (arrow) from the cylinder head and remove it from the thermostat housing

Replacement

Refer to illustrations 3.7, 3.8a, 3.8b, 3.9 and 3.11

5   Disconnect the negative cable from the battery. **Caution:** *If the stereo in your vehicle is equipped with an anti-theft system, make sure you have the correct activation code before disconnecting the battery.* **Note:** *On 1993 and later models, the airbag system will be disabled if the battery is disconnected for more than a brief period. If the airbag light comes on and stays on after the battery is reconnected, the vehicle must be taken to a dealer to have the system reset with a special tool.*
6   Drain the coolant from the radiator (see Chapter 1).
7   On four-cylinder models remove the water inlet pipe from the thermostat housing (located on the water pump housing) **(see illustration)**. **Note:** *For easier access to the lower bolt, remove the oil filter.*
8   On V6 models, unbolt the water inlet pipe and remove the pipe and O-ring **(see illustrations)**.
9   Remove the fasteners and electrical connectors from the

3

3.9 The 1MZ-FE thermostat housing (arrow) is at the back of the intake manifold, above the transaxle - remove the hoses, wiring plugs and the three nuts

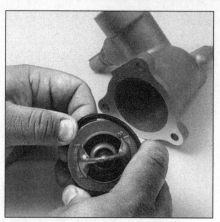

3.11 The thermostat gasket fits around the edge of the thermostat like a grooved sealing ring

4.1a On four-cylinder models the coolant temperature switch is located in the lower radiator tank

thermostat housing and detach the housing from the engine **(see illustration)**. Be prepared for some coolant to spill as the gasket seal is broken. **Note:** *Access on 1MZ-FE engines is easier with the air cleaner cap and hose removed.*

10   Remove the thermostat, noting the direction in which it was installed in the housing, and thoroughly clean the sealing surfaces.

11   Fit a new gasket onto the thermostat **(see illustration)**. Make sure it is evenly fitted all the way around.

12   Install the thermostat and housing, positioning the jiggle pin at the highest point.

13   Tighten the housing fasteners to the torque listed in this Chapter's Specifications and reinstall the remaining components in the reverse order of removal. On V6 models, use a new O-ring on the water inlet pipe and lubricate the O-ring with soapy water.

14   Refill the cooling system and on V6 models, bleed the air from the system (see Chapter 1). Run the engine and check for leaks and proper operation.

4   Engine cooling fan and relay - check and replacement

Warning: *To avoid possible injury, keep clear of the fan blades, as they may start turning at any time!*

Check

Refer to illustrations 4.1a, 4.1b, 4.2 and 4.4

1   If the radiator fan won't shut off when the engine is cool, disconnect the wiring connector from the coolant temperature switch **(see illustrations)** and bridge the connector. If this shuts off the fan, replace the switch. **Note:** *On four-cylinder engines the switch is in the lower tank of the radiator, and on the 1MZ-FE V6, there are two on the thermostat housing (for the 3VZ-FE V6 fan check, see Section 5).*

2   On four-cylinder engines and the 1MZ-FE V6 engine, test the number 1 ECT (engine coolant temperate switch) for continuity with an ohmmeter. When the engine is cold (below 190-degrees F) there should be continuity **(see illustration)**. When the engine is warm (above 208-degrees F), there should be NO continuity.

3   Check the number 2 ECT with an ohmmeter also. It should exhibit NO continuity when below 181-degrees F, and there should be continuity when above 190-degrees F. If either ECT fails these test replace the defective switch.

4   To test an inoperative fan motor (one that doesn't come on when the engine gets hot or when the air conditioner is on), first check the fuses and/or fusible links (see Chapter 12). Then disconnect the electrical connector at the motor and use fused jumper wires to connect the fan directly to the battery **(see illustration)**. If the fan still does not work, replace the fan motor. **Warning:** *Do not allow the test*

4.1b On 1MZ-FE V6 models, the number 1 (A) and number 2 (B) water temperature switches are on the thermostat housing at the driver's side of the intake manifold

clips to contact each other or any metallic part of the vehicle.

5   If the motor tested OK in the previous test but is still inoperative, then the fault lies in the relays, wiring or the cooling fan ECU. The fan relay and main engine relay can be tested as described below.

Relay check

Refer to illustrations 4.6a, 4.6b, 4.7 and 4.8

6   Locate the main relay box (located in the engine compartment, on the driver's side) **(see illustrations)**. Only air-conditioning-equipped models will have a cooling fan relay number 2, and not all will have a number 3 relay. If your vehicle has them, test them.

7   Remove the cooling fan no.1 relay, and using an ohmmeter, test for continuity as shown **(see illustration)**.There should be continuity between terminals 1 and 2, and between 3 and 4. When battery voltage is applied across terminals 1 and 2, there should be NO continuity between terminals 3 and 4.

8   If the fan relays check OK, remove the main engine relay and test it as shown **(see illustration)**. There should be continuity between terminals 3 and 5, and between 2 and 4. There should be NO continuity between terminals 1 and 2. With battery voltage applied across terminals 3 and 5, there should be continuity between 1 and 2, and NO continuity between 2 and 4. If both relays test OK, we recommend you take the vehicle to a dealer or other qualified repair facility for further diagnosis, due to the complexity and variety of the circuits involved.

4.2 Test the two ECT switches for continuity - number 1 ECT should show continuity only when cold

4.4 Disconnect the fan wiring connector and connect jumper wires directly to the positive and negative terminals of the battery

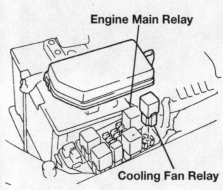

4.6a Main relay box - main engine relay and fan relay locations (5S-FE models)

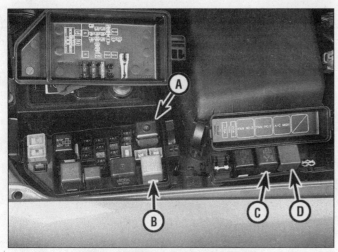

4.6b 1MZ-FE model relay locations

| a | Main engine relay | c | No. 2 cooling fan relay |
| b | No. 1 cooling fan relay | d | No. 3 cooling fan relay |

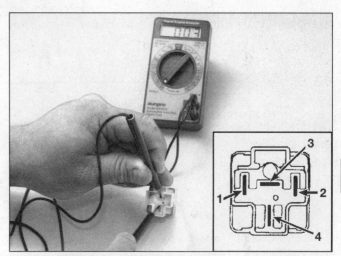

4.7 Test the cooling fan relay number 1 for continuity

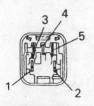

4.8 Test the main engine relay for continuity

4.11 Remove the fasteners (arrows) and cruise control actuator cover

Replacement

Refer to illustrations 4.11, 4.12, 4.13 and 4.14

9   Disconnect the negative battery cable. **Caution:** *If the stereo in your vehicle is equipped with an anti-theft system, make sure you have the correct activation code before disconnecting the battery.* **Note:** *On 1993 and later models, the airbag system will be disabled if the battery is disconnected for more than a brief period. If the airbag light comes on and stays on after the battery is reconnected, the vehicle must be taken to a dealer to have the system reset with a special tool.*

10   Disconnect the wiring connector at the fan motor. **Note:** *Models equipped with air-conditioned have two cooling fans. The one on the passenger side of the radiator is cooling fan no. 2, which provides additional cooling when the air-conditioning is on. This fan and its relay can be tested and removed/replaced with the same procedures as the engine cooling fan no. 1.*

11   On models with cruise control, remove the cruise control actuator cover for easier fan removal **(see illustration)**.

12   Unbolt the fan shroud from the radiator and lift the fan/shroud assembly from the vehicle **(see illustration)**. On models with

4.12 Unbolt the fan and shroud and remove the assembly from the radiator

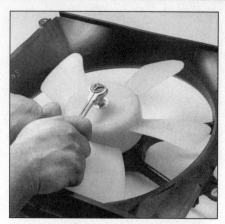

4.13 Remove the fan from the motor

4.14 Remove the motor from the shroud

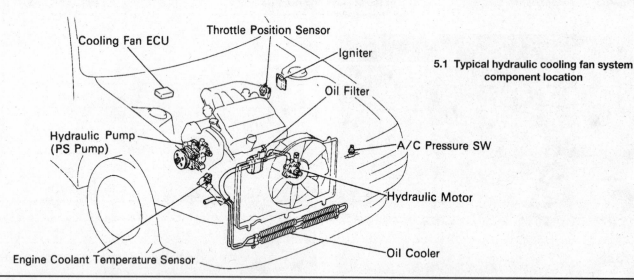

5.1 Typical hydraulic cooling fan system component location

air-conditioning, the condenser fan may have to be removed first to allow room for removal of the main engine cooling fan.

13   Hold the fan blades and remove the fan retaining nut (and spacer, if equipped) **(see illustration)**. **Note:** *On 1MZ-FE engines, the number 2 cooling fan blade is retained by a clip, not a nut.*

14   Unbolt the fan motor from the shroud **(see illustration)**.

15   Installation is the reverse of removal.

5   Hydraulic cooling fan (1992 through 1994 V6 models) - check and replacement

Refer to illustrations 5.1, 5.2, 5.5 and 5.10

1   On 1992 through 1994 V6 models, the main engine cooling fan is hydraulically-driven. The power steering pump on these models has two extra hoses which direct power steering fluid to and from the fan. The fan is controlled by the cooling fan Electronic Control Unit (ECU) and a solenoid valve that adjusts the volume of fluid flow **(see illustration)**. After fluid leaves the cooling fan, it is routed through an oil cooler mounted under and in front of the radiator. A reservoir tank is mounted in the engine compartment, serving both the power steering pump and the hydraulic fan system.

Check

2   Connect a jumper wire to the check connector between terminals E1 and OP1 **(see illustration)**. The cooling fan should run at approximately 1100 rpm.

3   Start the engine and hold the engine speed at approximately 2000 rpm until the fluid reaches normal operating temperature (158

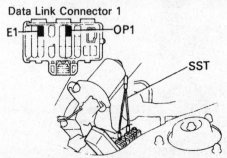

5.2 Connect a jumper wire between terminals E1 and OP1 on the check connector to test the cooling fan operation

to 195-degrees F). Check that there is no foaming of the fluid in the reservoir. Stop the engine and if necessary, add fluid to bring the level to the HOT mark. Remove the jumper from the check connector.

4   The cooling fan ECU is located under the glove compartment. To test the ECU circuits, remove the instrument panel lower cover and glove compartment and disconnect the harness connector at the ECU.

5   Check the circuits on the harness connector according to the chart **(see illustration)**. If the circuits test OK and a problem exists with the cooling fan cycling on and off, the ECU is probably defective. Reconnect the connector to the ECU.

6   To check the coolant temperature sensor, disconnect the connector at the coolant temperature sensor, located in the inlet at the passenger-side of the engine, and remove the sensor. Place the sensor

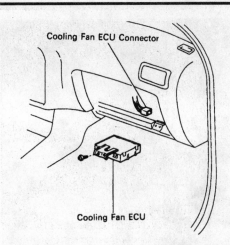

Cooling Fan ECU Connector

Cooling Fan ECU

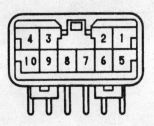

Check for	Tester connection	Condition	Specified value
Voltage	1 – Ground	Ignition switch ON	Battery voltage
Resistance	2 – 3	Solenoid valve at cold (25°C (77°F))	7.6 – 8.0 Ω
Continuity	4 – Ground	–	Continuity
Continuity	5 – Ground	Throttle valve open	No continuity
		Throttle valve closed	Continuity
Continuity	8 – Ground	A/C pressure SW connector disconnected	No continuity
		A/C pressure SW connector connected	Continuity
Resistance	9 – 10	Engine coolant temperature at 80°C (176°F)	1.48 – 1.58 kΩ

5.5 Locate the cooling fan ECU under the glove box, disconnect the connector and test the circuits on the harness connector as shown

3

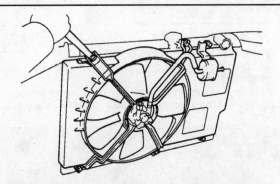

5.10 Remove the fan and shroud from the radiator as a unit, then separate the hydraulic motor for service

in a pan of hot water and connect an ohmmeter to the two terminals on the sensor. Resistance should be 1480 to 1580 ohms at 176-degrees F.

7   To test the solenoid valve, disconnect the harness connector (at the rear of the power steering pump) and connect an ohmmeter to the two terminals of the connector on the solenoid. Resistance should be 7.6 to 8.0 ohms at 77-degrees F.

Replacement

8   To replace the fan or fan motor, drain the cooling system and remove the upper radiator hose.

9   Remove the union bolt and disconnect the pressure hose from the fan motor, catching any fluid in a small drain container.

10   Disconnect the return hose, remove the six bolts retaining the fan shroud to the radiator and remove the fan and shroud (see illustration).

11   Holding the fan blades, loosen the fan-blade nut clockwise (left-hand thread) and remove the fan from the motor.

12   Remove the three bolts holding the fan motor to the shroud and remove the motor. Repairs to the fan motor should be referred to a Toyota dealership or other qualified repair facility.

13   Installation is basically the reverse of the disassembly procedure. Be sure to use new gaskets when reconnecting the pressure hose to the fan motor.

14   After initial operation, recheck the fluid level in the reservoir.

6   Radiator and coolant resevoir - removal and installation

Refer to illustrations 6.6, 6.7 and 6.8

Warning: *Do not start this procedure until the engine is completely cool. Do not allow antifreeze to come in contact with your skin or painted surfaces of the vehicle. Rinse off spills immediately with plenty of water. Antifreeze is highly toxic if ingested. Never leave antifreeze lying around in an open container or in puddles on the floor; children and pets are attracted by it's sweet smell and may drink it. Check with local authorities about disposing of used antifreeze. Many communities have collection centers which will see that antifreeze is disposed of safely. Never dump used antifreeze on the ground or into drains.*

Removal

1   Disconnect the negative battery cable. **Caution:** *If the stereo in your vehicle is equipped with an anti-theft system, make sure you have the correct activation code before disconnecting the battery.* **Note:** *On 1993 and later models, the airbag system will be disabled if the battery is disconnected for more than a brief period. If the airbag light comes*

6.6 Remove the automatic transaxle cooler lines (arrows)

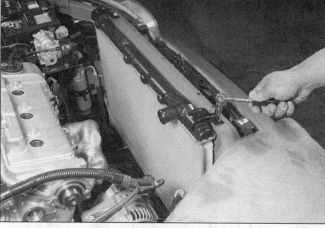

6.7 Remove the hold-down clamps from each end of the radiator

on and stays on after the battery is reconnected, the vehicle must be taken to a dealer to have the system reset with a special tool.
2   Drain the coolant into a container (see Chapter 1).
3   Remove both the upper and lower radiator hoses.
4   Disconnect the reservoir hose from the radiator filler neck.
5   Remove the cooling fan (see Sections 4 or 5).
6   If equipped with an automatic transaxle, disconnect the cooler lines from the radiator **(see illustration)**. Place a drip pan to catch the fluid and cap the fittings.
7   Remove the bolts that attach the radiator to its support **(see illustration)**.
8   Lift out the radiator **(see illustration)**. Be aware of dripping fluids and the sharp fins.
9   With the radiator removed, it can be inspected for leaks, damage and internal blockage. If in need of repairs, have a professional radiator shop or dealer service department perform the work as special techniques are required.
10   Bugs and dirt can be cleaned from the radiator with compressed air and a soft brush. Don't bend the cooling fins as this is done. **Warning:** *Wear eye protection*.

Installation

11   Installation is the reverse of the removal procedure. Be sure the rubber mounts are in place.

12   After installation, fill the cooling system with the proper mixture of antifreeze and water. Refer to Chapter 1 if necessary.
13   Start the engine and check for leaks. Allow the engine to reach normal operating temperature, indicated by the upper radiator hose becoming hot. Recheck the coolant level and add more if required.
14   On automatic transmission equipped models, check and add fluid as needed.

Coolant reservoir, removal and installation

Refer to illustration 6.15
15   On most models, the coolant reservoir simply pulls up and out of the bracket on the fenderwell **(see illustration)**.
17   Pour the coolant into a container. Wash out and inspect the reservoir for cracks and chafing. Replace it if damaged.
18   Installation is the reverse of removal.

7   Water pump - check

1   A failure in the water pump can cause serious engine damage due to overheating.
2   With the engine running and warmed to normal operating temperature, squeeze the upper radiator hose. If the water pump is working

6.8 Remove the radiator carefully, and do not lose the rubber mounts - they must be in place when the radiator is reinstalled

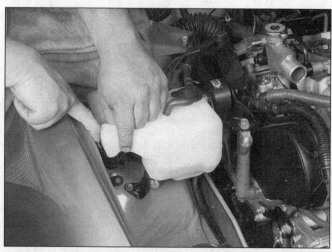

6.15 Typical coolant reservoir removal

properly, a pressure surge should be felt as the hose is released. **Warning:** *Keep hands away from fan blades!*

3   Water pumps are equipped with weep or vent holes. If a failure occurs in the pump seal, coolant will leak from this hole. In most cases it will be necessary to use a flashlight to find the hole on the water pump by looking through the space behind the pulley just below the water pump shaft.

4   If the water pump shaft bearings fail there may be a howling sound at the front of the engine while it is running. Bearing wear can be felt if the water pump pulley is rocked up and down. Do not mistake drivebelt slippage, which causes a squealing sound, for water pump failure. Spray automotive drivebelt dressing on the belts to eliminate the belt as a possible cause of the noise.

8   Water pump - removal and installation

Warning: *Do not start this procedure until the engine is completely cool. Do not allow antifreeze to come in contact with your skin or painted surfaces of the vehicle. Rinse off spills immediately with plenty of water. Antifreeze is highly toxic if ingested. Never leave antifreeze lying around in an open container or in puddles on the floor; children and pets are attracted by it's sweet smell and may drink it. Check with local authorities about disposing of used antifreeze. Many communities have collection centers which will see that antifreeze is disposed of safely. Never dump used antifreeze on the ground or into drains.*

Four-cylinder engines

Refer to illustrations 8.3, 8.4, 8.6, 8.9a and 8.9b

1   Disconnect the negative battery cable and drain the cooling system. **Caution:** *If the stereo in your vehicle is equipped with an anti-theft system, make sure you have the correct activation code before disconnecting the battery.* **Note:** *On 1993 and later models, the airbag system will be disabled if the battery is disconnected for more than a*

8.3 Remove the alternator adjusting bar (arrow)

brief period. If the airbag light comes on and stays on after the battery is reconnected, the vehicle must be taken to a dealer to have the system reset with a special tool.

2   Remove the timing belt, number 1 and number 2 idler pulleys (see Chapter 2A).

3   Remove the alternator adjusting bar **(see illustration)**.

4   Remove the bolts from the water pump **(see illustration)**, noting the locations of the different length bolts. Remove the pump and gasket. If necessary, tap the pump loose with a soft-face hammer.

5   It isn't necessary to remove to remove the pump cover (housing), but a thorough job would include removing it to replace the gaskets and O-rings.

3

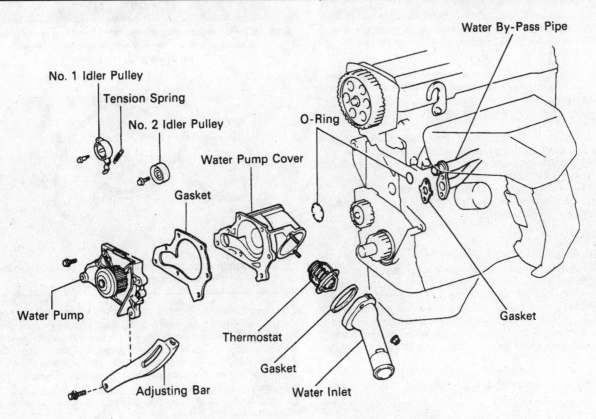

8.4 Typical four-cylinder engine water pump components

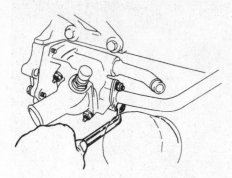

8.6 Disconnect the coolant bypass hose from the water neck (arrow) - the heater pipe is attached with two nuts

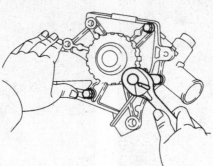

8.9a Install these bolts first . . .

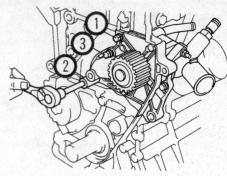

8.9b . . . then tighten these bolts in the order shown

8.14 Release the three wiring harness clips (arrows), pull the harness back and remove the number three belt cover

8.15 1MZ-FE model water pumps have two long studs (arrow) - at least one must be removed with a small wrench to allow water pump removal

6   Disconnect the coolant bypass hose from the water neck, then remove the two nuts and heater pipe **(see illustration)** and lift out the pump cover (housing).

7   Thoroughly clean all sealing surfaces, removing all traces of old gaskets, sealer and O-rings.

8   Be sure to use new O-rings between the pump cover and engine block and also a new gasket between the heater pipe and cover.

9   Using a new gasket, install the pump and bolts **(see illustrations)** and tighten them to the torque listed in this Chapter's Specifications.

10   Install the remaining parts in the reverse order of removal.

11   Refill the cooling system (see Chapter 1), run the engine and check for leaks and proper operation.

V6 engines

Refer to illustrations 8.14, 8.15, 8.17a and 8.17b

12   Disconnect the negative battery cable and drain the cooling system. **Caution:** *If the stereo in your vehicle is equipped with an anti-theft system, make sure you have the correct activation code before disconnecting the battery.* **Note:** *On 1993 and later models, the airbag system will be disabled if the battery is disconnected for more than a brief period. If the airbag light comes on and stays on after the battery is reconnected, the vehicle must be taken to a dealer to have the system reset with a special tool.*

13   Remove the timing belt (see Chapter 2B).

14   Remove the bolt retaining the water inlet pipe to the alternator adjuster and remove the water inlet pipe and thermostat (see Section 3). On 1MZ-FE models, remove the number 3 timing belt cover **(see illustration)**.

15   Remove the water pump retaining bolts/nuts and separate the

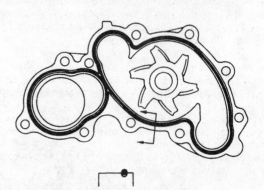

8.17a Apply a 2 to 3 mm wide bead of RTV sealant to the water pump flange groove

pump from the engine. **Note:** *On the 1MZ-FE model, there are two long studs (some engines may have bolts) that hold the engine mounting bracket and the water pump. The studs have a small hex-head that is used to remove the stud* **(see illustration)**. *If it is stuck, remove the stud with locking pliers and replace the stud with a new bolt of the same length. At least one of these long studs must be removed to allow the water pump to be removed.*

16   Thoroughly clean all sealing surfaces, removing all traces of old gaskets, sealer and O-rings. Remove any traces of oil with acetone or lacquer thinner and a clean rag.

17   On all except 1MZ-FE models, apply RTV sealant to the pump

8.17b On 1MZ-FE models, a new metal/rubber gasket (arrow) is used when installing a water pump

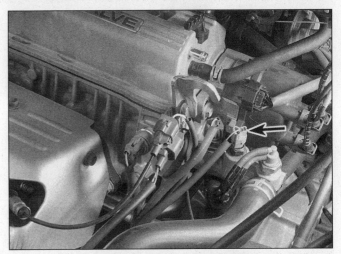

9.3a Coolant temperature sending unit location - 4-cylinder engine

9.3b On the 3VZ-FE V6 engine, the coolant temperature sensor is located under the bypass housing, above the exhaust crossover pipe - remove the heat shield bolts (arrows) and detach the shield for access

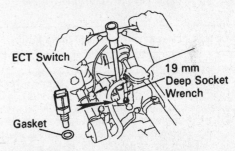

9.3c The ECT sensor (arrow) on the 1MZ-FE engine is located in the water outlet at the passenger-side of the engine - use a deep socket to remove it

3

groove using a nozzle cut to a 2 to 3 mm opening. 1MZ-FE models use a metal and rubber gasket instead of sealant **(see illustrations)**. **Note:** *Assembly must be completed within five minutes to prevent the sealer from setting up.*

18   Reinstall the pump and the remaining parts in the reverse order of removal. Tighten the water pump bolts in several steps to the torque listed in this Chapter's Specifications.

19   Refill the cooling system (see Chapter 1) and run the engine, checking for leaks and proper operation.

9   Coolant temperature sending unit - check and replacement

Warning: *Do not start this procedure until the engine is completely cool. Do not allow antifreeze to come in contact with your skin or painted surfaces of the vehicle. Rinse off spills immediately with plenty of water. Antifreeze is highly toxic if ingested. Never leave antifreeze lying around in an open container or in puddles on the floor; children and pets are attracted by it's sweet smell and may drink it. Check with local authorities about disposing of used antifreeze. Many communities have collection centers which will see that antifreeze is disposed of safely. Never dump used antifreeze on the ground or into drains.*
Note: *The following procedure applies only to the standard analog*

instruments. *The optional digital panel diagnosis requires special equipment the home mechanic is not likely to have.*

Check

Refer to illustrations 9.3a, 9.3b and 9.3c

1   If the coolant temperature gauge is inoperative, check the fuses first (see Chapter 12).

2   If the temperature gauge indicates excessive temperature after running a while, see the Troubleshooting Section in the front of the manual.

3   If the temperature gauge indicates Hot as soon as the engine is started cold, disconnect the wire at the coolant temperature sensor **(see illustrations)**. If the gauge reading drops, replace the sending unit. If the reading remains high, the wire to the gauge may be shorted to ground or the gauge is faulty.

4   If the coolant temperature gauge fails to show any indication after the engine has been warmed up, (approx. 10 minutes) and the fuses checked out OK, shut off the engine. Disconnect the wire at the sending unit and, using a jumper wire, connect the wire to a clean ground on the engine. Briefly turn on the ignition without starting the engine. If the gauge now indicates Hot, replace the sending unit.

5   If the gauge fails to respond, the circuit may be open or the gauge may be faulty - see Chapter 12 for additional information.

Replacement

6   Drain the coolant (see Chapter 1).

7   Disconnect the wiring connector from the sending unit.

8   Using a deep socket or a wrench, remove the sending unit.

9   Install the new unit and tighten it securely. Do not use thread sealer as it may electrically insulate the sending unit.

10   Reconnect the wiring connector, refill the cooling system and check for coolant leakage and proper gauge function.

10.3 On most models, remove the glove compartment liner, the glove compartment door and the right lower dash panel to gain access to the blower unit

10   Blower unit - check, removal and installation

Refer to illustrations 10.3, 10.4, 10.5 and 10.6

Warning: *These models are equipped with airbags. The airbag is armed and can deploy (inflate) anytime the battery is connected. To prevent accidental deployment (and possible injury), turn the ignition key to LOCK and disconnect the negative battery cable whenever working near airbag components. After the battery is disconnected, wait at least 90 seconds before beginning work (the system has a back-up capacitor that must fully discharge). For more information see Chapter 12.*

1   Disconnect the negative cable from the battery. **Caution:** *If the stereo in your vehicle is equipped with an anti-theft system, make sure you have the correct activation code before disconnecting the battery.* **Note:** *On 1993 and later models, the airbag system will be disabled if the battery is disconnected for more than a brief period. If the airbag light comes on and stays on after the battery is reconnected, the vehicle must be taken to a dealer to have the system reset with a special tool.*

2   The blower unit is located in the passenger compartment above the right front footwell.

3   Remove the glove compartment liner, the glove compartment door and the right lower dash panel **(see illustration)**.

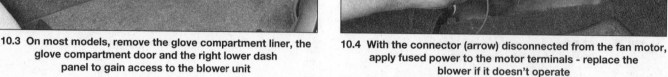

10.4 With the connector (arrow) disconnected from the fan motor, apply fused power to the motor terminals - replace the blower if it doesn't operate

4   Disconnect the flexible tube and wiring connector from the blower unit, then attach a fused source of battery power to terminal 2 and ground terminal 1 with a jumper wire **(see illustration)**. If the motor does not operate, replace the motor.

5   If the fan operated in step 4, momentarily connect the battery cable, turn on the ignition switch and the fan switch and check for voltage with a test light at the harness connector **(see illustration)**.

6   To remove the blower, remove the blower unit retaining screws and lower the unit from the housing. **Note:** *On 1MZ-FE models, remove the two screws and the wiring harness connector for better access to the blower* **(see illustration)**.

7   If the motor is being replaced, transfer the fan to the new motor prior to installation.

8   Installation is the reverse of removal. Check for proper operation.

Blower motor resistor

Refer to illustrations 10.9 and 10.10

9   The blower resistor is located to the right of the accelerator pedal, attached to the back of the heater/air conditioning unit **(see illustration)**. Disconnect the harness connector from the resistor, remove the screws and remove the resistor.

10   Using a self-powered continuity tester, check for continuity in the resistor terminals **(see illustration)**. If continuity is not as specified, replace the resistor.

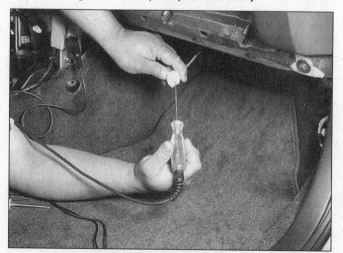

10.5 Check for power at the blower motor connector with a test light

10.6 On 1MZ-FE models, remove the two screws (arrows) and lower this connector to access the blower motor

11 Heater core - removal and installation

Refer to illustrations 11.5, 11.6 and 11.7

Warning 1: *These models are equipped with airbags. The airbag is armed and can deploy (inflate) anytime the battery is connected. To prevent accidental deployment (and possible injury), turn the ignition key to LOCK and disconnect the negative battery cable whenever working near airbag components. After the battery is disconnected, wait at least 90 seconds before beginning work (the system has a back-up capacitor that must fully discharge). For more information see Chapter 12.*

Warning 2: *Do not allow antifreeze to come in contact with your skin or painted surfaces of the vehicle. Rinse off spills immediately with plenty of water. Antifreeze is highly toxic if ingested. Never leave antifreeze lying around in an open container or in puddles on the floor; children and pets are attracted by it's sweet smell and may drink it. Check with local authorities about disposing of used antifreeze. Many communities have collection centers which will see that antifreeze is disposed of safely. Never dump used antifreeze on the ground or into drains.*

1   Disconnect the negative cable from the battery. **Caution:** *If the stereo in your vehicle is equipped with an anti-theft system, make sure you have the correct activation code before disconnecting the battery.* **Note:** *On 1993 and later models, the airbag system will be disabled if the battery is disconnected for more than a brief period. If the airbag light comes on and stays on after the battery is reconnected, the vehicle must be taken to a dealer to have the system reset with a special tool.*

2   Drain the cooling system (see Chapter 1).

3   Working in the engine compartment, disconnect the heater hoses where they enter the firewall (below the heater valve).

4   Pull back the carpeting from the driver's side of the console area.

5   Remove the two clips and the heater protector plate **(see illustration)**.

10.9 On the driver's side, to the right of the gas pedal, disconnect the wires and mounting fasteners to remove the blower resistor (arrow) for testing

6   Remove the three screws and clamps and disconnect the heater pipes **(see illustration)**.

7   Pull the heater core out of the heater/air conditioning unit **(see illustration)**. **Note:** *Keep plenty of towels or rags on the carpeting to catch any coolant that may drip.*

8   Installation is the reverse order of removal.

9   Refill the cooling system, reconnect the battery and run the engine. Check for leaks and proper system operation.

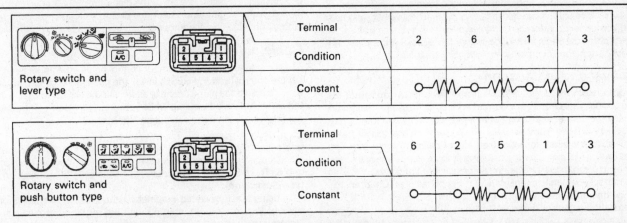

	Terminal		2	6	1	3
Rotary switch and lever type	Condition					
	Constant					

	Terminal		6	2	5	1	3
Rotary switch and push button type	Condition						
	Constant						

10.10 Continuity diagrams for blower motor resistors

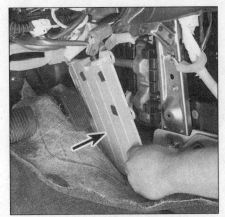

11.5 Pull back the carpeting on the driver's side, and remove the heater protector (arrow)

11.6 Disconnect the heater pipes at the junctions (arrows)

11.7 Slide the heater core out of heater/air conditioning unit

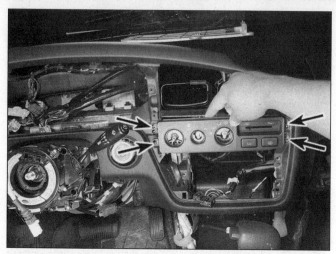

12.4 Remove these screws (arrows) to release the control panel

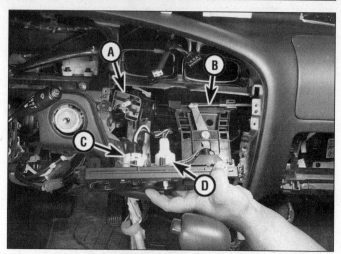

12.5 Heater/air conditioning control panel components:

     a   *Temperature control shaft*
     b   *Air inlet damper control cable*
     c   *Blower speed connector*
     d   *Mode control connector*

12 Heater and air conditioning control assembly - removal and installation, cable adjustment and electrical checks

Refer to illustrations 12.4, 12.5, 12.9, 12.10, 12.11 and 12.12

Warning: *These models are equipped with airbags. The airbag is armed and can deploy (inflate) anytime the battery is connected. To prevent accidental deployment (and possible injury), turn the ignition key to LOCK and disconnect the negative battery cable whenever working near airbag components. After the battery is disconnected, wait at least 90 seconds before beginning work (the system has a back-up capacitor that must fully discharge). For more information see Chapter 12.*

Removal and installation

1   Disconnect the negative cable from the battery. **Caution:** *If the stereo in your vehicle is equipped with an anti-theft system, make sure you have the correct activation code before disconnecting the battery.* **Note:** *On 1993 and later models, the airbag system will be disabled if the battery is disconnected for more than a brief period. If the airbag light comes on and stays on after the battery is reconnected, the vehicle must be taken to a dealer to have the system reset with a special tool.*

2   Remove the instrument cluster trim panel (see Chapter 11). Remove the radio (see Chapter 12).

3   Pull off the control knobs.

4   Remove the mounting screws located on the front of the control

assembly **(see illustration)**.

5   Pull the control out slightly. Push the temperature control shaft through and leave it in position as the control panel is pulled forward **(see illustration)**.

6   Installation is the reverse of the disassembly procedure.

7   Run the engine and check for proper functioning of the heater (and air conditioning, if equipped).

Cable adjustment

8   To adjust the air inlet damper control cable **(see illustration 12.5)** set the control lever to FRESH, install the cable and clamp it in place.

9   To adjust the air mix control cable, set the air mix to COOL, install the cable and lock the clamp while applying slight pressure (away from the firewall) on the outer cable **(see illustration)**.

Electrical checks

10   Check the air-conditioning switch continuity between terminals 2 and 5. There should be continuity when the switch is pushed in (ON) **(see illustration)**.

11   Using a self-powered continuity tester, test the terminals on the back of the control unit, starting with the mode control switch **(see illustration)**.

12.9 The air mix control cable (arrow) should be attached when the control is in the COOL position

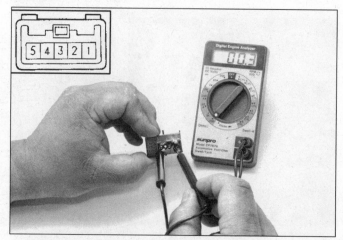

12.10 With the switch pushed IN, there should be continuity between terminals 2 and 5 on the air-conditioning switch

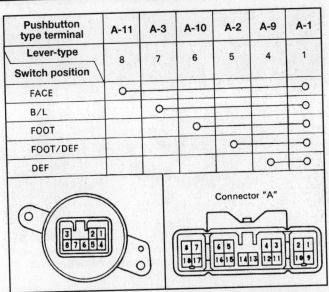

Pushbutton type terminal	A-11	A-3	A-10	A-2	A-9	A-1
Lever-type Switch position	8	7	6	5	4	1
FACE	O					O
B/L		O				O
FOOT			O			O
FOOT/DEF				O		O
DEF					O	O

Connector "A"

12.11 The pushbutton and lever-type controls have different connectors, but the continuity tests are the same

12 Test the blower speed control switch for continuity (see illustration). Any tests which do not meet specifications indicate the control unit should be replaced.

13 Air conditioning and heating system - check and maintenance

Air conditioning system

Refer to illustrations 13.1, 13.5 and 13.17

Warning: *The air conditioning system is under high pressure. Do not loosen any hose fittings or remove any components until the system has been discharged. Air conditioning refrigerant should be properly discharged into an EPA-approved recovery/recycling unit by a dealer service department or an automotive air conditioning repair facility. Always wear eye protection when disconnecting air conditioning system fittings.*

1   The following maintenance checks should be performed on a regular basis to ensure that the air conditioner continues to operate at peak efficiency **(see illustration)**.

  a) *Inspect the condition of the compressor drivebelt. If it is worn or deteriorated, replace it (see Chapter 1).*

  b) *Check the drivebelt tension and, if necessary, adjust it (see Chapter 1).*

3

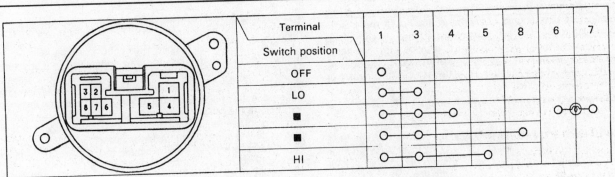

Terminal Switch position	1	3	4	5	8	6	7
OFF	O						
LO	O	O					
■	O	O	O				
■	O	O			O		
HI	O	O		O			

12.12 Continuity tests for the blower speed selector switch

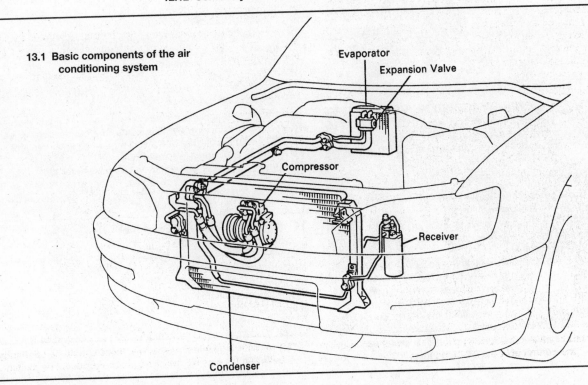

13.1 Basic components of the air conditioning system

Evaporator

Expansion Valve

Compressor

Receiver

Condenser

c) *Inspect the system hoses. Look for cracks, bubbles, hardening and deterioration. Inspect the hoses and all fittings for oil bubbles or seepage. If there is any evidence of wear, damage or leakage, replace the hose(s).*

d) *Inspect the condenser fins for leaves, bugs and any other foreign material that may have embedded itself in the fins. Use a "fin comb" or compressed air to remove debris from the condenser.*

e) *Make sure the system has the correct refrigerant charge.*

2   It's a good idea to operate the system for about ten minutes at least once a month. This is particularly important during the winter months because long term non-use can cause hardening, and subsequent failure, of the seals.

3   Because of the complexity of the air conditioning system and the special equipment necessary to service it, in-depth troubleshooting and repairs are beyond the scope of this manual. However, simple component replacement procedures are provided in this Chapter.

4   The most common cause of poor cooling is simply a low system refrigerant charge. If a noticeable drop in system cooling ability occurs, one on the following quick checks will help you determine whether the refrigerant level is low.

5   Inspect the sight glass **(see illustration)**. If the refrigerant looks foamy when running, it's low. When ambient temperatures are very hot, bubbles may show in the sight glass even with the proper amount of refrigerant. With the proper amount of refrigerant, when the air conditioning is turned off, the sight glass should show refrigerant that foams, then clears.

6   If there is no sight glass, feel the inlet and outlet pipes at the compressor. One side should be cold and one hot. If there is no perceptible difference between the two pipes, there is something wrong with the compressor or the system. It might be a low charge - it might be something else. Further testing of this type of system is beyond the scope of this manual. Take the vehicle to a dealer or automotive air-conditioning shop.

Adding refrigerant (all systems)

Caution 1: *Refrigerant has changed from the use of R-12, through 1993 models, to the "environmentally friendly" R-134a used in 1994 and later models. The two refrigerants are NOT compatible. Even after purging and evacuating an R-12 system, there is enough residual oil and refrigerant in the hoses and components that simply filling the system with R-134a cannot be done. Special fittings and manifold gauge sets are used on the different refrigerant types so that an accidental hook-up of the two systems cannot be made.*

Caution 2: *When replacing entire components, additional refrigerant oil should be added equal to the amount that is removed with the component being replaced. Refrigerant oils, just like refrigerant R-12 vs. R-134a, are not compatible. Be sure to read the can before adding any oil to the system, to make sure it is compatible with the type of system being repaired.*

Note: *Because of recent Federal regulations by the Environmental Protection Agency, 14-ounce cans of refrigerant , of either R-12 or R-134, may not be available in your area. If this is the case, it will be necessary to take your vehicle to a licensed air conditioning technician for charging.*

Heating systems

7   If the air coming out of the heater vents isn't hot, the problem could stem from any of the following causes:

a) *The thermostat is stuck open, preventing the engine coolant from warming up enough to carry heat to the heater core. Replace the thermostat (see Section 3).*

b) *A heater hose is blocked, preventing the flow of coolant through the heater core. Feel both heater hoses at the firewall. They should be hot. If one of them is cold, there is an obstruction in one of the hoses or in the heater core, or the heater control valve is shut. Detach the hoses and back flush the heater core with a water hose. If the heater core is clear but circulation is impeded, remove the two hoses and flush them out with a water hose.*

c) *If flushing fails to remove the blockage from the heater core, the core must be replaced. (see Section 11).*

13.5 The sight glass is located on the top of the receiver/drier (arrow) in the left front corner below the battery

8   If the blower motor speed does not correspond to the setting selected on the blower switch, the problem could be a bad fuse, circuit, switch, blower motor resistor or motor.

9   Before checking the blower motor or circuit, always check the fuse first.

10   Using a test light or voltmeter, check the voltage available to the motor.

11   Pull the heating/air conditioning control assembly (see Section 12) out far enough from the dash to verify - with a test light or voltmeter - that current is reaching the blower switch on the control assembly. If the switch is not getting current, troubleshoot the circuit between the battery and the switch (see wiring diagrams at the end of this manual).

12   Locate the blower motor resistor behind the heater/air conditioning unit **(see illustration 10.9)**. Check the resistor to make sure that it's getting current from the blower switch.

13   If the resistor is not getting current, check the circuit wiring. If the circuit is good, replace the switch (see Section 10).

14   Using a test light or voltmeter, verify that the blower motor is getting current (see Section 10). If the blower motor is not getting current, replace the resistor.

15   If there isn't any air coming out of the vents:

a) *Turn the ignition ON and activate the fan control. Place your ear at the heating/air conditioning register (vent) and listen. Most motors are audible. Can you hear the motor running?*

b) *If you can't (and have already verified that the blower switch and the blower motor resistor are good), the blower motor itself is probably bad (see Section 10).*

16   If the carpet under the heater core is damp, or if antifreeze vapor or steam is coming through the vents, the heater core is leaking. Remove it (see Section 11) and install a new unit (most radiator shops will not repair a leaking heater core).

17   Pulling back the carpeting on the passenger side around the heater/air conditioning unit reveals a rubber drain hose **(see illustration)** going down through the floor pan, make sure it is not clogged.

---

14   Air conditioning receiver/drier - removal and installation

Refer to illustration 14.3

Warning: *The air conditioning system is under high pressure. Do not loosen any hose fittings or remove any components until the system has been discharged. Air conditioning refrigerant should be properly discharged into an EPA-approved recovery/recycling unit by a dealer service department or an automotive air conditioning repair facility. Always wear eye protection when disconnecting air conditioning system fittings.*

1   Have the refrigerant discharged by an air conditioning technician.

13.17 This drain hose from the heater/air conditioning unit should be kept clear to allow drainage of condensation

14.3 After the system has been discharged, unbolt the two refrigerant lines from the receiver/drier and cap them

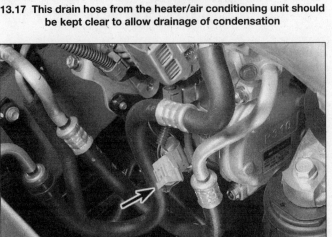

15.4 Disconnect the wiring harness connector (arrow) at the compressor

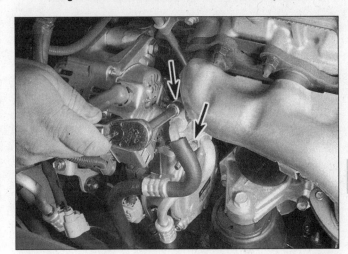

15.5 Unbolt the flanges (arrows) and detach the refrigerant lines

3

2   Remove the battery, ignitor bracket (see Chapter 5) and coolant reservoir (see Section 6) as necessary to obtain access. **Caution:** *If the stereo in your vehicle is equipped with an anti-theft system, make sure you have the correct activation code before disconnecting the battery.* **Note:** *On 1993 and later models, the airbag system will be disabled if the battery is disconnected for more than a brief period. If the airbag light comes on and stays on after the battery is reconnected, the vehicle must be taken to a dealer to have the system reset with a special tool.*

3   Disconnect the refrigerant lines **(see illustration)** from the receiver/drier and cap the open fittings to prevent entry of moisture.

4   Loosen the pinch bolt and slip the receiver/drier out of the bracket.

5   Installation is the reverse of removal.

6   Have the system evacuated, charged and leak tested by the shop that discharged it. If the receiver was replaced, have them add about 15 cc (0.5 oz.) refrigeration oil to the compressor. Use only the refrigeration oil compatible with the refrigerant of your system (R-12 or R-134a).

15 Air conditioning compressor - removal and installation

Refer to illustrations 15.4 and 15.5

Warning: *The air conditioning system is under high pressure. Do not loosen any hose fittings or remove any components until the system has been discharged. Air conditioning refrigerant should be properly*

discharged into an EPA-approved recovery/recycling unit by a dealer service department or an automotive air conditioning repair facility. Always wear eye protection when disconnecting air conditioning system fittings.

1   Have the refrigerant discharged by an automotive air conditioning technician.

2   Disconnect the negative cable from the battery. **Caution:** *If the stereo in your vehicle is equipped with an anti-theft system, make sure you have the correct activation code before disconnecting the battery.* **Note:** *On 1993 and later models, the airbag system will be disabled if the battery is disconnected for more than a brief period. If the airbag light comes on and stays on after the battery is reconnected, the vehicle must be taken to a dealer to have the system reset with a special tool.*

3   Remove the drivebelt from the compressor (see Chapter 1).

4   Detach the wiring connector **(see illustration)**.

5   Disconnect the refrigerant lines **(see illustration)**.

6   Unbolt the compressor and lift it from the vehicle.

7   If a new or rebuilt compressor is being installed, follow the directions which come with it regarding the proper level of oil prior to installation.

8   Installation is the reverse of removal. Replace any O-rings with new ones specifically made for the purpose and lubricate them with refrigerant oil.

9   Have the system evacuated, recharged and leak tested by the shop that discharged it.

**16.4 Disconnect the refrigerant lines by reaching through the
grille opening with a socket and long extension (arrow)**

**16.5 Remove the bolt and condenser hold-down bracket
on each side (arrow)**

16   Air conditioning condenser - removal and installation

Refer to illustrations 16.4 and 16.5

Warning: *The air conditioning system is under high pressure. Do not
loosen any hose fittings or remove any components until the system
has been discharged. Air conditioning refrigerant should be properly
discharged into an EPA-approved recovery/recycling unit by a dealer
service department or an automotive air conditioning repair facility.
Always wear eye protection when disconnecting air conditioning
system fittings.*

1   Have the refrigerant discharged by an air conditioning technician.
2   Remove the radiator as described in Section 6.
3   Remove the battery and ignitor bracket, if necessary. **Caution:** *If
the stereo in your vehicle is equipped with an anti-theft system, make
sure you have the correct activation code before disconnecting the*
battery. **Note:** *On 1993 and later models, the airbag system will be
disabled if the battery is disconnected for more than a brief period. If
the airbag light comes on and stays on after the battery is reconnected,
the vehicle must be taken to a dealer to have the system reset with a
special tool.*

4   Remove the grille for access (see Chapter 11) and disconnect the
inlet and outlet fittings **(see illustration)**. Cap the open fittings immediately to keep moisture and dirt out of the system.
5   Remove the brackets **(see illustration)** and lift the condenser out.
6   Install the condenser, brackets and bolts, making sure the rubber
cushions fit on the mounting points properly.
7   Reconnect the refrigerant lines, using new O-rings where needed.
8   Reinstall the remaining parts in the reverse order of removal.
9   Have the system evacuated, charged and leak tested by the shop
that discharged it.

Chapter 4
Fuel and exhaust systems

Contents

4

Specifications

Fuel system

Fuel pressure
 Ignition ON, engine not running .... 38 to 44 psi
 Engine idling
  Vacuum sensing hose detached .... 38 to 44 psi
  Vacuum sensing hose attached .... 30 to 36 psi
 Fuel system hold pressure .... 21 psi
Fuel injector resistance .... 13.4 to 14.2 ohms
Cold start valve resistance .... 2 to 4 ohms
Idle Air Control (IAC) valve resistance
 Four-cylinder engine .... 19 to 23 ohms
 V6 engines
  3VZ-FE .... 10 to 30 ohms
  1MZ-FE .... 17 to 28.5 ohms
Idle-up valve solenoid resistance .... 30 to 34 ohms

Idle Speed

Automatic transmission .... 750 rpm
Manual transmission .... 700 rpm

Torque specification

Ft-lbs

Throttle body mounting bolts 14
Fuel rail mounting bolts 14

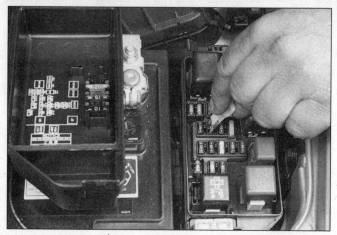

2.3 Remove the 30 amp fuse (AM2) to disable the fuel pump

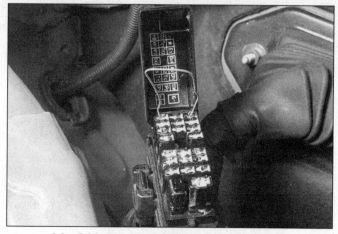

**3.2a Bridge terminals FP and +B using a jumper
wire or paper clip**

1   General information

The fuel system consists of a fuel tank, an electric fuel pump (located in the fuel tank), an EFI/ fuel pump relay, fuel injectors, an air cleaner assembly and a throttle body unit. The fuel injection components are all equipped with the Multi Point Fuel Injection (MPFI) system.

Multi Point Fuel Injection (MPFI) system

Multi point fuel injection uses timed impulses to sequentially inject the fuel directly into the intake port of each cylinder. The injectors are controlled by the Electronic Control Module (ECM). The ECM monitors various engine parameters and delivers the exact amount of fuel, in the correct sequence, into the intake ports. The throttle body serves only to control the amount of air passing into the system. Because each cylinder is equipped with an injector mounted immediately adjacent to the intake valve, much better control of the fuel/air mixture ratio is possible.

Fuel pump and lines

Fuel is circulated from the fuel tank to the fuel injection system, and back to the fuel tank, through a pair of metal lines running along the underside of the vehicle. An electric fuel pump is attached to the fuel sending unit inside the fuel tank. A vapor return system routes all vapors and hot fuel back to the fuel tank through a separate return line.

The fuel pump will operate as long as the engine is cranking or running and the ECM is receiving ignition reference pulses from the electronic ignition system (see Chapter 5). If there are no reference pulses, the fuel pump will shut off after 2 or 3 seconds.

Exhaust system

The exhaust system includes an exhaust manifold fitted with an exhaust oxygen sensor, a catalytic converter, an exhaust pipe, and a muffler.

The catalytic converter is an emission control device added to the exhaust system to reduce pollutants. A single-bed converter is used in combination with a three-way (reduction) catalyst. Refer to Chapter 6 for more information regarding the catalytic converter.

2   Fuel pressure relief

Refer to illustration 2.3
Warning: *Gasoline is extremely flammable, so take extra precautions when you work on any part of the fuel system. Don't smoke or allow open flames or bare light bulbs near the work area, and don't work in a garage where a natural gas-type appliance (such as a water heater or a clothes dryer) with a pilot light is present. Since gasoline is carcinogenic, wear latex gloves when there's a possibility of being exposed to fuel, and, if you spill any fuel on your skin, rinse it off immediately with*

soap and water. Mop up any spills immediately and do not store fuel-soaked rags where they could ignite. The fuel system is under constant pressure, so, if any fuel lines are to be disconnected, the fuel pressure in the system must be relieved first. When you perform any kind of work on the fuel system, wear safety glasses and have a Class B type fire extinguisher on hand.
1   Before servicing any fuel system component, you must relieve the fuel pressure to minimize the risk of fire or personal injury.
2   Remove the fuel filler cap - this will relieve any pressure built up in the tank.
3   Remove the 30 amp fuel pump fuse (AM2) from the main fuse panel **(see illustration)**. **Note:** *Consult your owner's manual for the exact location of the fuel pump fuse if the information is not stamped under the fuse cover.*
4   Start the engine and wait for the engine to stall, then turn the ignition key to Off.
5   The fuel system is now depressurized. **Note:** *Place a rag around the fuel line before removing any hose clamp or fitting to prevent any residual fuel from spilling onto the engine.*

3   Fuel pump/fuel pressure - check

Warning: *Gasoline is extremely flammable, so take extra precautions when you work on any part of the fuel system. Don't smoke or allow open flames or bare light bulbs near the work area, and don't work in a garage where a natural gas-type appliance (such as a water heater or a*

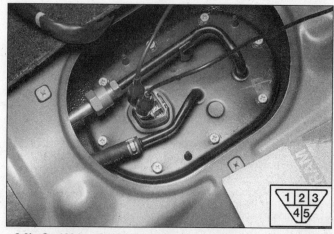

**3.2b On 1994 and 1995 V6 engines, apply battery voltage using
jumper wires to terminals 4 and 5 on the fuel pump electrical
connector and listen for fuel pump activity**

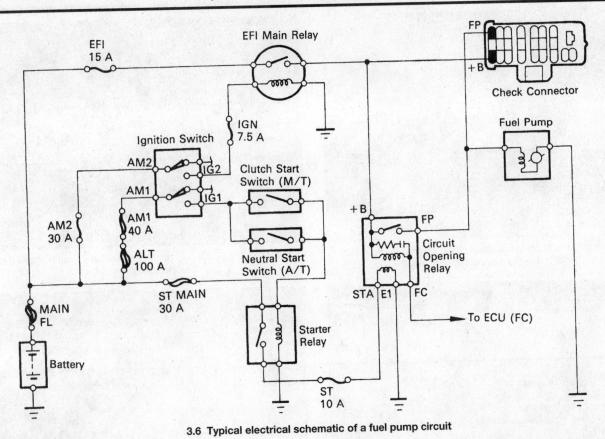

3.6 Typical electrical schematic of a fuel pump circuit

clothes dryer) with a pilot light is present. Since gasoline is carcinogenic, wear latex gloves when there's a possibility of being exposed to
fuel, and, if you spill any fuel on your skin, rinse it off immediately with
soap and water. Mop up any spills immediately and do not store fuel-
soaked rags where they could ignite. The fuel system is under constant
pressure, so, if any fuel lines are to be disconnected, the fuel pressure
in the system must be relieved first. When you perform any kind of work
on the fuel system, wear safety glasses and have a Class B type fire
extinguisher on hand.

Fuel pump operation check

Refer to illustrations 3.2a, 3.2b and 3.6

1   Turn ON the ignition switch (but do not start the engine).

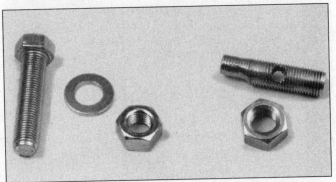

**3.7 Cut the head off the bolt (12 mm diameter/1.25 thread pitch)
and drill a hole directly through the center. Grind the end to form
a slight taper and drill a vertical hole to allow system pressure to
flow. It is important that the vertical hole is drilled in the correct
location. The easiest method is to use the banjo bolt that was
removed from the fuel filter and place it directly next to the tool
for the correct alignment of the vertical passage for fuel flow**

2   Bridge terminals +B and Fp of the SST test terminal connector
with a jumper wire (see illustration). Note: On 1994 and later models
equipped with the 1MZ-FE V6 engine, it is not possible to power the
fuel pump using the SST test terminal. On these models, apply battery
voltage directly to the fuel pump (see illustration) and listen for fuel
pump operation.

3   The fuel pump is now activated. Listen for fuel pump noises from
the fuel tank (under rear seat) and verify that there is pressure in the
hose from the fuel filter.

4   Remove the jumper wire. Close the cap on the service electrical
connector.

5   Turn the ignition switch OFF.

6   If the fuel pump did not operate, inspect the following electrical
components: the EFI 15-amp fuse and the ignition switch 30-amp fuse
(AM2) (see illustration) and/or the EFI main relay and the circuit opening
relay, (see Steps 32 through 47), the fuel pump; and the wiring and
electrical connectors (see the wiring diagrams at the end of the book).

Fuel pressure check

Refer to illustrations 3.7 and 3.11

7   A fuel pressure gauge, capable of measuring a minimum of 50-
psi, equipped with a banjo fitting on the end of the hose (Toyota
special service tool no. SST 09268-45012) is required for the following
procedure. There are a couple of alternatives if you are unable to
obtain the special Toyota fuel pressure gauge set:

a) Obtain a 12 mm banjo fitting that will adapt to your fuel pressure
    gauge hose with a hose clamp.

b) If you can't find the correct size banjo fitting, obtain a 12 mm bolt
    with 1.25 mm thread pitch, cut the head off and drill a hole
    through the center. Add a locknut with the same thread pitch and
    seal the threads with teflon tape (see illustration).

8   Remove the fuel tank cap.

9   Verify that the battery voltage is 12 volts or more (see Chapter 5).

10   Relieve the fuel pressure (see Section 2).

3.11 Install the fuel pressure gauge to the top of the fuel filter (located in the engine compartment)

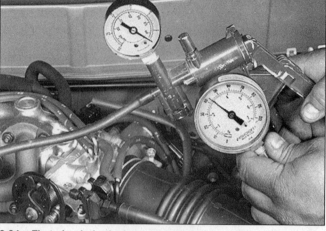

3.24a First check the fuel pressure without vacuum applied to the fuel pressure regulator

3.24b Next, apply vacuum to the fuel pressure regulator. Fuel pressure should DECREASE as vacuum INCREASES

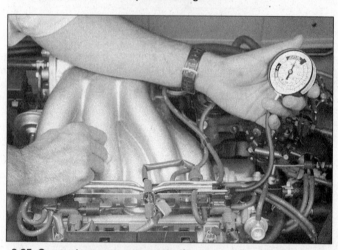

3.25 Connect a vacuum gauge to the vacuum line leading to the fuel pressure regulator and check the vacuum source

11   There are two methods possible for testing the fuel pressure:

a) *If you have the special banjo fitting (Toyota tool number SST 09268-45012) required to attach the fuel pressure gauge, remove the fuel rail bolt and install the special tool into the fuel rail.*

b) *If you have constructed the drilled-out bolt and locknut tool, detach one side of the fuel filter (see illustration) and install the fuel pressure gauge at this point.*

12   To attach the fuel pressure gauge:

a) *If you are using the factory setup, use the special banjo fitting on the fuel rail to attach the fuel pressure gauge to the fuel rail. Be sure to use crush washers on both sides of the banjo fitting.*

b) *If you are using a drilled-out 12 mm bolt, working in the engine compartment, attach the bolt to the fuel filter, tighten the locknut and attach the fuel pressure gauge hose with a hose clamp.*

13   Wipe off any gasoline that has leaked out of the fuel rail.

14   Place the transmission in Neutral (manual) or Park (automatic) and apply the parking brake.

15   Bridge terminals +B and Fp of the check electrical connector **(see illustration 3.2a)**. **Note:** *Models equipped with the 1MZ-FE engine will require battery voltage applied directly to the fuel pump connector* **(see illustration 3.2b)**.

16   Turn the ignition to ON (engine not running). Measure the fuel pressure and compare it to the fuel pressure listed in this Chapter's Specifications.

a) *If the pressure is high, check for a restricted fuel return line. If the line is clear, replace the pressure regulator.*

b) *If the pressure is low, pinch the fuel return line. If the pressure goes up, replace the fuel pressure regulator. If the pressure does not increase, check the fuel feed line, the fuel pump and the fuel filter.*

17   Remove the jumper wire from the service electrical connector or fuel pump connector.

18   Start the engine.

a) *Measure the fuel pressure at idle and compare your reading to the fuel pressure listed in this Chapter's Specifications.*

b) *If the pressure is not as specified, check the vacuum sensing hose and fuel pressure regulator (see Steps 24 through 31).*

19   Stop the engine and verify that the fuel pressure remains at 21 psi or more for five minutes after the engine is turned off.

20   Carefully remove the fuel pressure gauge. Be sure to cover the fitting with a rag before loosening it.

21   Using new crush washers, reattach the pipe banjo fitting to the fuel rail.

22   Be sure to wipe up any spilled gasoline.

23   Start the engine and check for leaks.

Fuel pressure regulator check

Refer to illustrations 3.24a, 3.24b, 3.25, 3.26a and 3.26b

24   Disconnect and plug the vacuum hose from the fuel pressure regulator and connect a hand-held vacuum pump to the regulator. Start the engine and read the fuel pressure gauge without vacuum applied to the fuel pressure regulator **(see illustrations)**. Apply

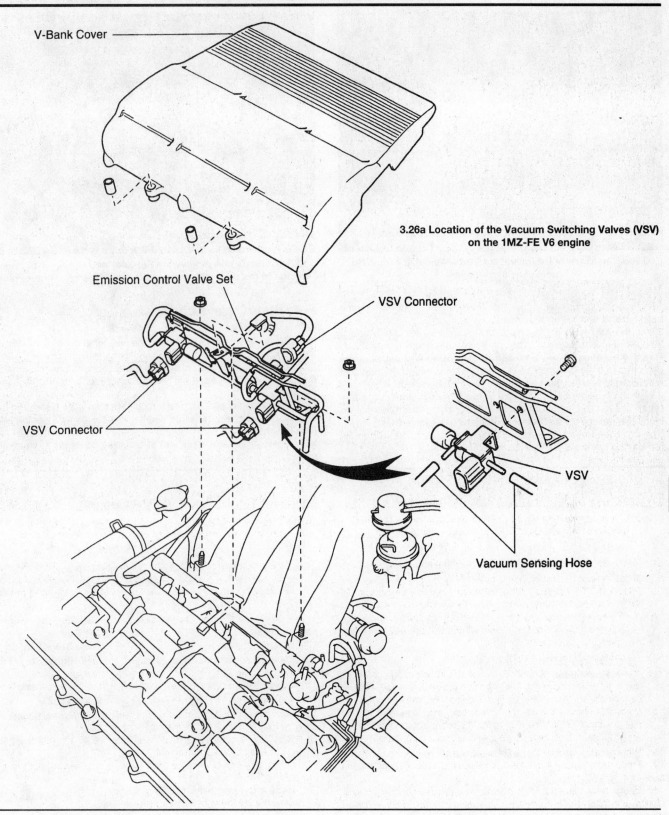

V-Bank Cover

**3.26a Location of the Vacuum Switching Valves (VSV)
on the 1MZ-FE V6 engine**

Emission Control Valve Set

VSV Connector

VSV Connector

VSV

Vacuum Sensing Hose

vacuum to the regulator and check the fuel pressure again. The fuel pressure should decrease as vacuum increases. Compare your readings with the values listed in this Chapter's Specifications.
25   Reconnect the vacuum hose to the regulator and check the fuel pressure at idle, comparing your reading with the value listed in this Chapter's Specifications. Disconnect the hose and watch the gauge - the pressure should jump up to the maximum specified pressure as

soon as the hose is disconnected. If the pressure at idle was too high (with the hose disconnected), connect a vacuum gauge to the hose and check for vacuum **(see illustration)**. If there is no reading on the gauge, check the Vacuum Switching Valve (VSV).
26   Locate the VSV used for fuel pressure control and using an ohmmeter, measure the resistance between the terminals **(see illustrations)**. It should be between 30 to 40 ohms.

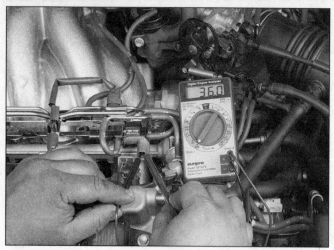

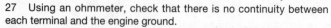

3.26b Check the resistance of the VSV solenoid. It should be between 30 to 40 ohms.

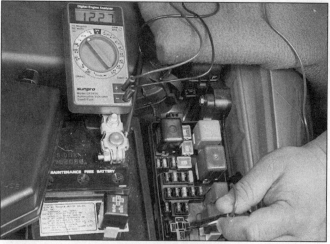

3.33a Locate and remove the EFI relay and check for battery voltage to the relay with the ignition key ON (engine not running)

27　Using an ohmmeter, check that there is no continuity between each terminal and the engine ground.

28　If the test results are incorrect, replace the VSV with a new part.

29　If the fuel pressure is LOW, pinch the fuel return line shut and watch the gauge. If the pressure doesn't rise, the fuel pump is defective or there is a restriction in the fuel feed line. If the pressure rises sharply, replace the fuel pressure regulator (see Section 13).

30　If the indicated fuel pressure is too high, disconnect the fuel return line and blow through it to check for blockage. If there is no blockage, replace the fuel pressure regulator (see Section 13).

31　If the fuel pressure does not fluctuate as described in Step 29, replace the fuel pressure regulator (see Section 13).

Fuel pump relays check

Refer to illustrations 3.33a, 3.33b, 3.34a and 3.34b

32　There are two relays involved in the fuel pump circuit. First, test for battery voltage to the EFI main relay and then the circuit opening relay.

33　Remove the EFI main relay from the electrical connector and with the ignition key ON (engine not running), check for battery voltage **(see illustrations)**.

34　If battery voltage is present, insert the relay back into the connector and check for battery voltage at the circuit opening relay **(see illustrations)**.

35　If battery voltage is present at the relay connectors, check the relays.

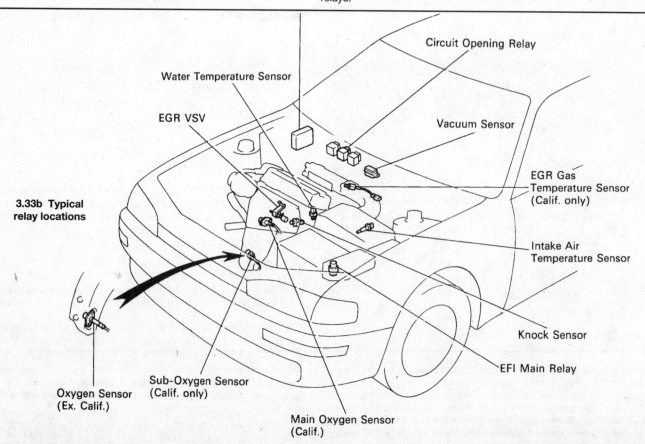

3.33b Typical relay locations

Circuit Opening Relay

Water Temperature Sensor

EGR VSV

Vacuum Sensor

EGR Gas Temperature Sensor (Calif. only)

Intake Air Temperature Sensor

Knock Sensor

EFI Main Relay

Oxygen Sensor (Ex. Calif.)

Sub-Oxygen Sensor (Calif. only)

Main Oxygen Sensor (Calif.)

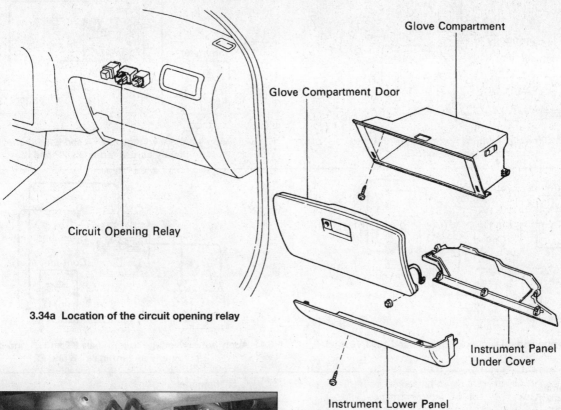

3.34a Location of the circuit opening relay

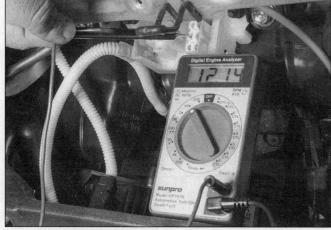

3.34b Remove the circuit opening relay and check
for battery voltage

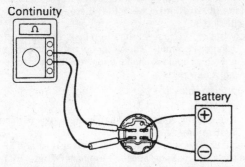

3.37 Apply battery voltage to the EFI main relay terminals 1 and 3
and check for continuity across terminals 2 and 4

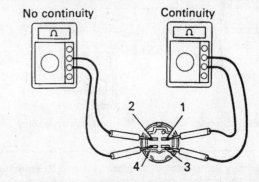

3.36 Checking the EFI main relay, continuity should exist across
terminals 1 and 3 but not terminals 2 and 4

1992 and 1993 models

EFI main relay

Refer to illustrations 3.36 and 3.37

36   Using an ohmmeter, check for continuity across terminals 1 and 3
(see illustration). Check that there is no continuity across terminals 2
and 4.

37   Apply battery voltage across terminals 1 and 3 **(see illustration)**.
Using an ohmmeter, check for continuity across terminals 2 and 4.
Continuity should exist. If the test results are incorrect, replace the
relay with a new part.

Circuit opening relay (Four cylinder models)

Refer to illustrations 3.38 and 3.39

38   Using an ohmmeter, check for continuity across terminals STA
and E1 **(see illustration)**. Also, check for continuity across +B and FC.
Check that there is no continuity across terminals +B and FP.

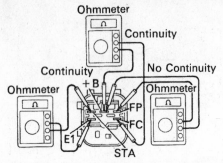

3.38 Circuit opening relay checks on 1992 and 1993 four cylinder models

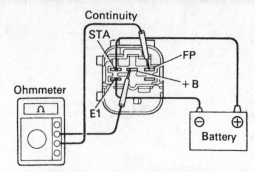

3.39 Apply battery voltage to STA and E1 and check for continuity across terminals FP and B

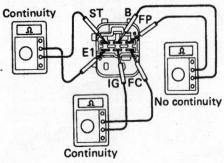

3.40 Circuit opening relay checks on 1992 and 1993 V6 models

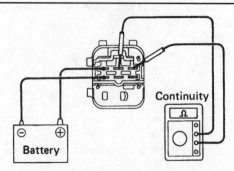

3.41 Apply battery voltage to terminals ST and E1 and check for continuity on terminals +B and FP

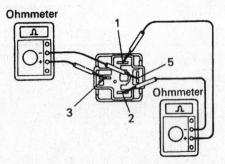

3.42 EFI main relay checks on Nippondenso style relay

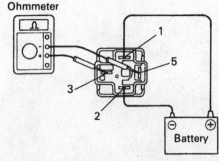

3.43 Apply battery voltage to terminals 1 and 2 and check for continuity between terminals 3 and 5

39   Apply battery voltage across terminals STA and E1 **(see illustration)**. Using an ohmmeter, check for continuity across terminals +B and FP. Continuity should exist. If the test results are incorrect, replace the relay with a new part.

Circuit opening relay (V6 models)
Refer to illustrations 3.40 and 3.41

40   Using an ohmmeter, check for continuity across terminals ST and E1 **(see illustration)**. Also, check for continuity across IG and IC. Check that there is no continuity across terminals B and FP.

41   Apply battery voltage across terminals ST and E1 **(see illustration)**. Using an ohmmeter, check for continuity across terminals B and FP. Continuity should exist. If the test results are incorrect, replace the relay with a new part.

1994 and 1995 models
EFI main relay (Nippondenso type)
Refer to illustrations 3.42 and 3.43

42   Using an ohmmeter, check for continuity across terminals 1 and 2 **(see illustration)**. Check that there is no continuity across terminals 3 and 5.

43   Apply battery voltage across terminals 1 and 2 **(see illustration)**.

Using an ohmmeter, check for continuity across terminals 3 and 5. Continuity should exist. If the test results are incorrect, replace the relay with a new part.

EFI main relay (Bosch type)
Refer to illustrations 3.44 and 3.45

44   Using an ohmmeter, check for continuity across terminals 86 and 85 **(see illustration)**. Check that there is no continuity across terminals 87 and 30.

45   Apply battery voltage across terminals 86 and 85 **(see illustration)**. Using an ohmmeter, check for continuity across terminals 87 and 30. Continuity should exist. If the test results are incorrect, replace the relay with a new part.

Circuit opening relay
Refer to illustrations 3.46 and 3.47

46   Using an ohmmeter, check for continuity across terminals ST and E1 **(see illustration)**. Also, check for continuity across +B and FC. Check that there is no continuity across terminals +B and FP.

47   Apply battery voltage across terminals ST and E1 **(see illustration)**. Using an ohmmeter, check for continuity across terminals +B and FP. Continuity should exist. If the test results are incorrect, replace the relay with a new part.

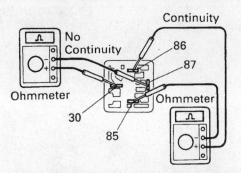

3.44 EFI main relay checks on Bosch style relay

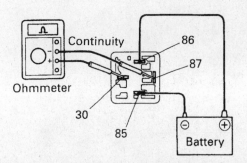

3.45 Apply battery voltage to terminals 85 and 86 and observe that continuity exists across terminals 87 and 30

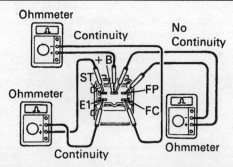

3.46 Circuit opening relay checks on 1994 and 1995 models

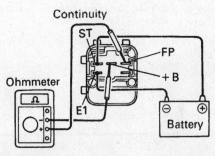

3.47 Apply battery voltage to ST and E1 and check for continuity across terminals FP and +B

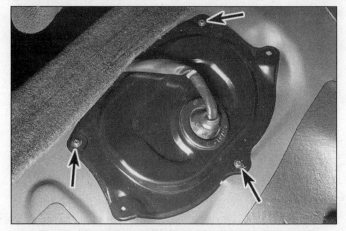

4.4 Remove the fuel pump/fuel level sending unit access cover screws (arrows) and separate the cover from the body

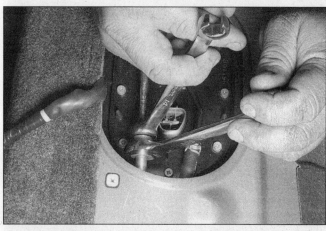

4.5 Use a flare-nut wrench and a back-up wrench to remove the fuel feed line - remove the clamp and hose from the fuel return line fitting

4   Fuel pump - removal and installation

Refer to illustrations 4.4, 4.5, 4.6, 4.7 and 4.13

Warning: *Gasoline is extremely flammable, so take extra precautions when you work on any part of the fuel system. Don't smoke or allow open flames or bare light bulbs near the work area, and don't work in a garage where a natural gas-type appliance (such as a water heater or a clothes dryer) with a pilot light is present. Since gasoline is carcinogenic, wear latex gloves when there's a possibility of being exposed to fuel, and, if you spill any fuel on your skin, rinse it off immediately with soap and water. Mop up any spills immediately and do not store fuel-soaked rags where they could ignite. The fuel system is under constant pressure, so, if any fuel lines are to be disconnected, the fuel pressure in the system must be relieved first. When you perform any kind of work on the fuel system, wear safety glasses and have a Class B type fire extinguisher on hand.*

1   Remove the fuel tank cap.

2   Disconnect the cable from the negative terminal of the battery. **Caution:** *If the stereo in your vehicle is equipped with an anti-theft system, make sure you have the correct activation code before disconnecting the battery.* **Note:** *On 1993 and later models, the airbag system will be disabled if the battery is disconnected for more than a brief period. If the airbag light comes on and stays on after the battery is reconnected, the vehicle must be taken to a dealer service department to have the system reset with a special tool.*

3   Remove the rear seat from inside the passenger compartment (see Chapter 11).

4   Remove the fuel pump/sending unit access cover **(see illustration)**.

5   Disconnect the electrical connector. Disconnect the fuel lines **(see illustration)**.

6   Remove the fuel pump/sending unit retaining bolts **(see illustration)**.

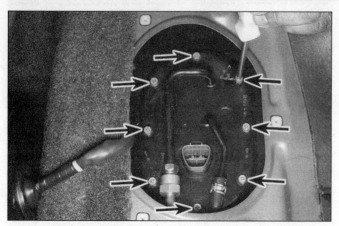

4.6 Remove the fuel pump/sending unit assembly mounting bolts (arrows)

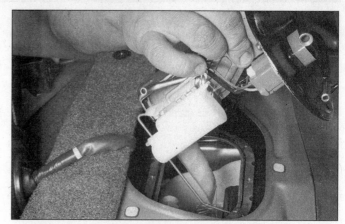

4.7 Lift the fuel pump/sending unit assembly from the fuel tank at an angle so as not to damage the inlet screen or float arm

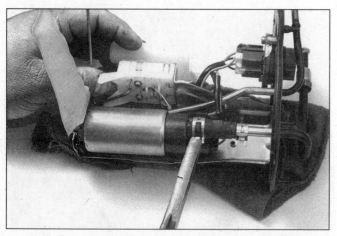

4.13 Remove the clamp from the fuel pump outlet hose

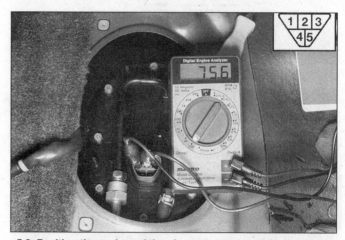

5.3 Position the probes of the ohmmeter onto terminals 1 and 2 and observe the fuel level sending unit resistance

7   Carefully withdraw the fuel pump/fuel level sending unit assembly from the fuel tank **(see illustration)**.

8   Pull the lower end of the fuel pump loose from the bracket.

9   Remove the rubber cushion from the lower end of the fuel pump.

10   Remove the clip securing the inlet screen to the pump.

11   Remove the screen and inspect it for contamination. If it is dirty, replace it.

12   If you are only replacing the fuel pump inlet screen, install the new screen, the clip and the rubber cushion, push the lower end of the pump back into the bracket and install the pump/sending unit assembly in the fuel tank.

13   If you are replacing the fuel pump, remove the hose clamp at the upper end of the pump and disconnect the pump from the hose **(see illustration)**.

14   Disconnect the wires from the pump terminals and remove the pump.

15   Installation is the reverse of removal.

5   Fuel level sending unit - check and replacement

Warning: *Gasoline is extremely flammable, so take extra precautions when you work on any part of the fuel system. Don't smoke or allow open flames or bare light bulbs near the work area, and don't work in a garage where a natural gas-type appliance (such as a water heater or a clothes dryer) with a pilot light is present. Since gasoline is carcinogenic, wear latex gloves when there's a possibility of being exposed to fuel, and, if you spill any fuel on your skin, rinse it off immediately with soap and water. Mop up any spills immediately and do not store fuel-*

soaked rags where they could ignite. The fuel system is under constant pressure, so, if any fuel lines are to be disconnected, the fuel pressure in the system must be relieved first. When you perform any kind of work on the fuel system, wear safety glasses and have a Class B type fire extinguisher on hand.

Check

Refer to illustrations 5.3 and 5.8

1   Before performing any tests on the fuel level sending unit, completely fill the tank with fuel.

2   Remove the rear seat and the fuel pump/sending unit access cover **(see illustration 4.4)**.

3   Disconnect the fuel level sending unit electrical connector **(see illustration)** located on top of the fuel tank.

4   Position the ohmmeter probes onto the electrical connector terminals (terminals number 1 and number 2) and check for resistance. Use the 200 scale on the ohmmeter.

5   With the fuel tank completely full, the resistance should be about 2.0 to 3.0 ohms.

6   Reconnect the electrical connector and drive it until the tank is nearly empty.

7   Check the resistance. The resistance of the sending unit should be about 110 to 115 ohms.

8   If the readings are incorrect, replace the sending unit. **Note:** *The test can also be performed with the fuel level sending unit removed from the fuel tank. Using an ohmmeter, check the resistance of the sending unit with the swing arm completely down (tank empty) and with the arm up (tank full)* **(see illustration)**. *The resistance should change steadily from 110 ohms to approximately 2.0 to 3.0 ohms.*

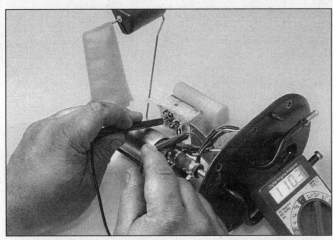

5.8 An accurate check of the sending unit can be made by removing it from the fuel tank and observing the resistance with the float down (empty) and then extended (full)

Replacement

9   Remove the fuel pump/fuel level sending unit assembly from the fuel tank (see Section 4).

10   Carefully angle the sending unit out of the opening without damaging the fuel level float located at the bottom of the assembly **(see illustration 4.7)**.

11   Disconnect the electrical connectors from the sending unit.

12   Remove the screw from the side of the sending unit bracket and separate the sending unit from the assembly.

13   Installation is the reverse of removal.

6   Fuel lines and fittings - inspection and replacement

Warning: *Gasoline is extremely flammable, so take extra precautions when you work on any part of the fuel system. Don't smoke or allow open flames or bare light bulbs near the work area, and don't work in a garage where a natural gas-type appliance (such as a water heater or a clothes dryer) with a pilot light is present. Since gasoline is carcinogenic, wear latex gloves when there's a possibility of being exposed to fuel, and, if you spill any fuel on your skin, rinse it off immediately with soap and water. Mop up any spills immediately and do not store fuel-soaked rags where they could ignite. The fuel system is under constant pressure, so, if any fuel lines are to be disconnected, the fuel pressure in the system must be relieved first. When you perform any kind of work on the fuel system, wear safety glasses and have a Class B type fire extinguisher on hand.*

Inspection

1   Once in a while, you will have to raise the vehicle to service or replace some component (an exhaust pipe hanger, for example). Whenever you work under the vehicle, always inspect fuel lines and all fittings and connections for damage or deterioration.

2   Check all hoses and pipes for cracks, kinks, deformation or obstructions.

3   Make sure all hoses and pipe clips attach their associated hoses or pipes securely to the underside of the vehicle.

4   Verify all hose clamps attaching rubber hoses to metal fuel lines or pipes are snug enough to assure a tight fit between the hoses and pipes.

Replacement

Refer to illustration 6.6

5   If you must replace any damaged sections, use original equipment replacement hoses or pipes constructed from exactly the same material as the section you are replacing. Do not install substitutes constructed from inferior or inappropriate material or you could

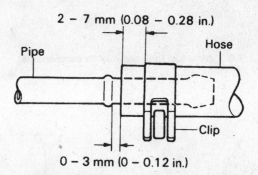

6.6 When attaching a section of rubber hose to a metal fuel line, be sure to overlap the hose as shown, secure it to the line with a new hose clamp of the proper type

cause a fuel leak or a fire.

6   Always, before detaching or disassembling any part of the fuel line system, note the routing of all hoses and pipes and the orientation of all clamps and clips to assure that replacement sections are installed in exactly the same manner. When attaching hoses to metal lines, overlap them as shown **(see illustration)**.

7   Before detaching any part of the fuel system, be sure to relieve the fuel line and tank pressure by removing the fuel tank cap and disconnecting the battery. Cover the fitting being disconnected with a rag to absorb any fuel that may spray out.

8   While you're under the vehicle, it's a good idea to check the condition of the fuel filter - make sure that it's not clogged or damaged (see Chapter 1).

7   Fuel tank - removal and installation

Refer to illustrations 7.6, 7.9 and 7.10

Warning: *Gasoline is extremely flammable, so take extra precautions when you work on any part of the fuel system. Don't smoke or allow open flames or bare light bulbs near the work area, and don't work in a garage where a natural gas-type appliance (such as a water heater or a clothes dryer) with a pilot light is present. Since gasoline is carcinogenic, wear latex gloves when there's a possibility of being exposed to fuel, and, if you spill any fuel on your skin, rinse it off immediately with soap and water. Mop up any spills immediately and do not store fuel-soaked rags where they could ignite. The fuel system is under constant pressure, so, if any fuel lines are to be disconnected, the fuel pressure in the system must be relieved first. When you perform any kind of work on the fuel system, wear safety glasses and have a Class B type fire extinguisher on hand.*

1   This procedure is much easier to perform if the fuel tank is empty. Some models may have a drain plug for this purpose. If for some reason the drain plug can't be removed, postpone the job until the tank is empty or siphon the fuel into an approved container using a siphoning kit (available at most auto parts stores). **Warning:** *Do not start the siphoning action by mouth!*

2   Remove the fuel filler cap to relieve fuel tank pressure.

3   Detach the cable from the negative terminal of the battery. **Caution:** *If the stereo in your vehicle is equipped with an anti-theft system, make sure you have the correct activation code before disconnecting the battery.* **Note:** *On 1993 and later models, the airbag system will be disabled if the battery is disconnected for more than a brief period. If the airbag light comes on and stays on after the battery is reconnected, the vehicle must be taken to a dealer service department to have the system reset with a special tool.*

4   If the tank is full or nearly full, drain the fuel into an approved container.

5   Raise the vehicle and place it securely on jackstands.

6   Familiarize yourself with the layout of the fuel tank assembly before proceeding **(see illustration)**.

7   Support the fuel tank with a floor jack. Place a sturdy plank

4

The location of Fuel Tank Cushion

7.6 Typical fuel tank and related components

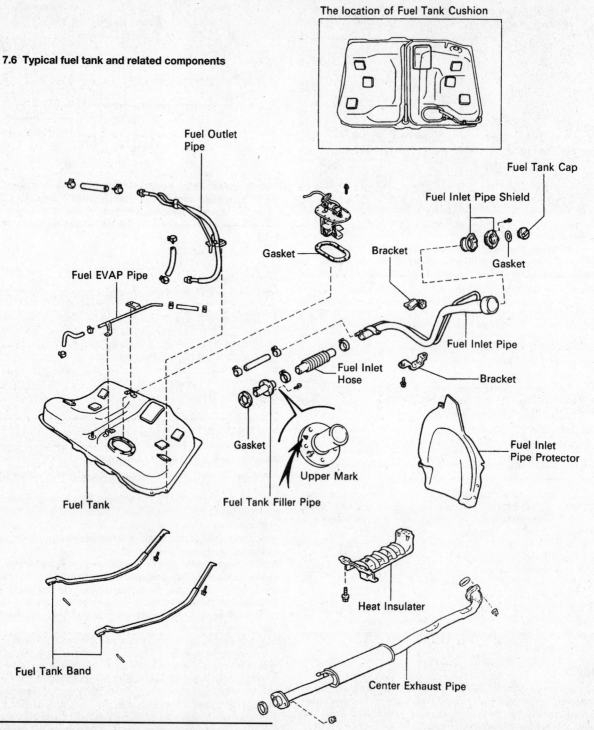

Fuel Outlet Pipe

Fuel Tank Cap

Fuel Inlet Pipe Shield

Gasket

Bracket

Gasket

Fuel EVAP Pipe

Fuel Inlet Pipe

Fuel Inlet Hose

Bracket

Gasket

Fuel Inlet Pipe Protector

Gasket

Upper Mark

Fuel Tank

Fuel Tank Filler Pipe

Heat Insulater

Fuel Tank Band

Center Exhaust Pipe

between the jack head and the fuel tank to protect the tank.

8   Detach the exhaust system from the center exhaust pipe completely to the rear of the vehicle.

9   Disconnect the fuel lines, the vapor return line and the fuel inlet pipe **(see illustration)**. Note: *Be sure to plug the hoses to prevent leakage and contamination of the fuel system.*

10   Remove the bolts from the fuel tank retaining straps **(see illustration)**.

11   Lower the tank enough to disconnect the electrical connector and ground strap from the fuel pump/fuel gauge sending unit, if you have not already done so.

12   Remove the tank from the vehicle.

13   Installation is the reverse of removal.

8   Fuel tank cleaning and repair - general information

1   Any repairs to the fuel tank or filler neck should be carried out by a professional who has experience in this critical and potentially dangerous work. Even after cleaning and flushing of the fuel system, explosive fumes can remain and ignite during repair of the tank.

2   If the fuel tank is removed from the vehicle, it should not be placed in an area where sparks or open flames could ignite the fumes coming out of the tank. Be especially careful inside garages where a natural gas-type appliance is located, because the pilot light could cause an explosion.

7.9 Remove the fuel inlet hose and the vapor return line from the fuel tank (arrows)

7.10 Remove the tank strap bolt (arrow) from the body

9.2 Loosen the air intake duct clamps

9 Air cleaner assembly - removal and installation

Refer to illustrations 9.2 and 9.3

1   Detach the clips and remove the air filter/air flow meter cover and the filter element (see Chapter 1).
2   Disconnect the air intake hose from the assembly (**see illustration**).
3   Remove the three bolts and remove the air cleaner assembly from the engine compartment (**see illustration**).
4   Installation is the reverse of removal.

10 Accelerator cable - removal, installation and adjustment

Refer to illustrations 10.2, 10.3 and 10.4

Removal

1   Detach the cable from the negative terminal of the battery. **Caution:** *If the stereo in your vehicle is equipped with an anti-theft system, make sure you have the correct activation code before disconnecting the battery.* **Note:** *On 1993 and later models, the airbag system will be disabled if the battery is disconnected for more than a brief period. If the airbag light comes on and stays on after the battery is reconnected, the vehicle must be taken to a dealer service department to have the system reset with a special tool.*

9.3 Remove the three bolts (arrows) from the air cleaner assembly and lift the assembly from the compartment

2   Loosen the locknut on the threaded portion of the throttle cable at the throttle body (**see illustration**).
3   Rotate the throttle lever, then slip the throttle cable end out of the slot in the lever (**see illustration**).
4   Detach the throttle cable from the accelerator pedal (**see illustration**).
5   From inside the vehicle, pull the cable through the cable tubing.

10.2 Loosen the locknuts on the accelerator cable

10.3 Rotate the throttle lever and remove the cable end from the slot

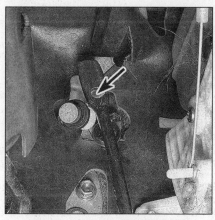

10.4 Separate the cable from the accelerator pedal assembly and slide the cable end out of the slot (arrow) in the housing

4

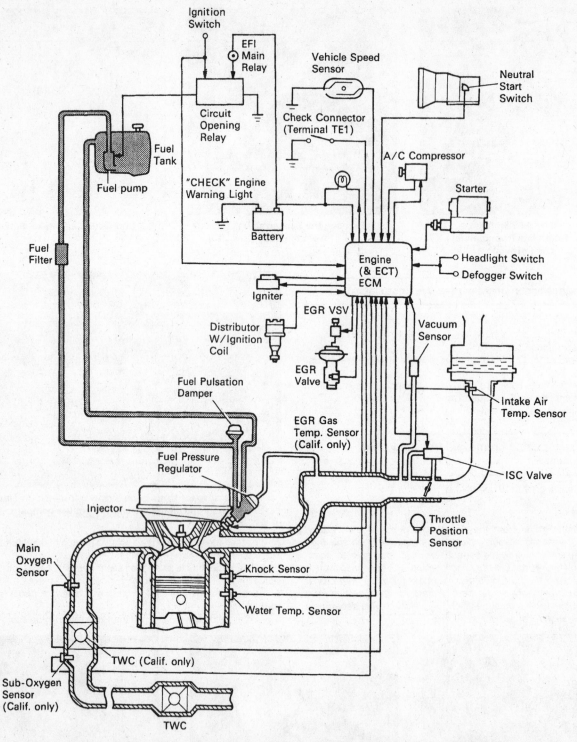

11.1a Schematic of a typical Toyota Computer Control System (TCCS) (four cylinder engine)

Installation and adjustment

6   Installation is the reverse of removal.
7   To adjust the cable, fully depress the accelerator pedal and check that the throttle is fully opened.
8   If not fully opened, loosen the locknuts, depress accelerator pedal and adjust the cable until the throttle is fully open.
9   Tighten the locknuts and recheck the adjustment. Make sure the throttle closes fully when the pedal is released.

11   Electronic Fuel Injection (EFI) system - general information

Refer to illustrations 11.1a and 11.1b

1   These models are equipped with an Electronic Fuel Injection (EFI) system. The EFI system is composed of three basic sub systems: fuel system, air induction system and electronic control system **(see illustrations)**.

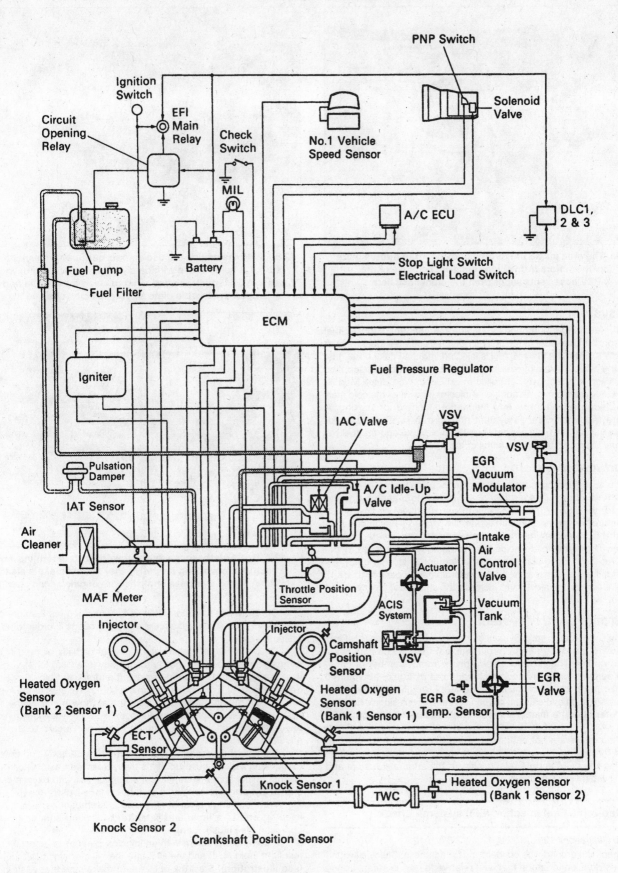

11.1b Schematic of a typical Toyota Computer Control System (TCCS) (V6 engine)

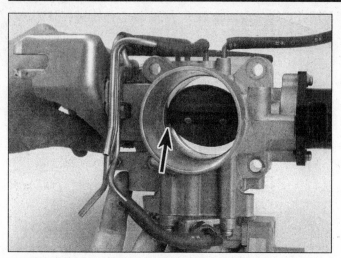

12.6a The area inside the throttle body near the throttle plate (arrow) suffers from sludge build-up because of the PCV hose vents vapor from the crankcase here

12.6b With the engine off, use aerosol carburetor cleaner (make sure it is safe for use with catalytic converters and oxygen sensors), a toothbrush and a rag to clean the throttle body - open the throttle plate so you can clean behind it

Fuel system

2   An electric fuel pump located inside the fuel tank supplies fuel under constant pressure to the fuel rail, which distributes fuel evenly to all injectors. From the fuel rail, fuel is injected into the intake ports, just above the intake valves, by fuel injectors. The amount of fuel supplied by the injectors is precisely controlled by an Electronic Control Module (ECM). On some models, an additional injector, known as the cold start injector, supplies extra fuel into the intake manifold for starting. A pressure regulator controls system pressure in relation to intake manifold vacuum. A fuel filter between the fuel pump and the fuel rail filters fuel to protect the components of the system.

Air induction system

3   The air system consists of an air filter housing, an air flow meter and a throttle body. The air flow meter is an information gathering device for the ECM. A potentiometer measures intake air flow and a temperature sensor measures intake air temperature. This information helps the ECM determine the amount of fuel to be injected by the injectors. The throttle plate inside the throttle body is controlled by the driver. As the throttle plate opens, the amount of air that can pass through the system increases, so the potentiometer opens further and the ECM signals the injectors to increase the amount of fuel delivered to the intake ports.

Electronic control system

4   The Computer Control System controls the EFI and other systems by means of an Electronic Control Module (ECM), which employs a microcomputer. The ECM receives signals from a number of information sensors which monitor such variables as intake air volume, intake air temperature, coolant temperature, engine rpm, acceleration/deceleration and exhaust oxygen content. These signals help the ECM determine the injection duration necessary for the optimum air/fuel ratio. Some of these sensors and their corresponding ECM-controlled relays are not contained within EFI components, but are located throughout the engine compartment. For further information regarding the ECM and its relationship to the engine electrical and ignition system, see Chapter 6.

12   Electronic Fuel Injection (EFI) system - check

Refer to illustrations 12.6a, 12.6b, 12.7, 12.8 and 12.9

1   Check the ground wire connections for tightness. Check all wiring and electrical connectors that are related to the system. Loose electrical connectors and poor grounds can cause many problems that resemble more serious malfunctions.

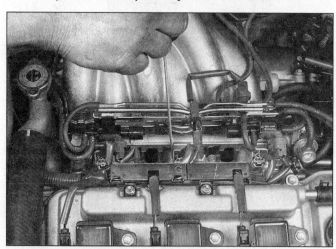

12.7 Use a stethoscope or a screwdriver to determine if the injectors are working properly - they should make a steady clicking sound that rises and falls with engine speed changes

2   Check to see that the battery is fully charged, as the control unit and sensors depend on an accurate supply voltage in order to properly meter the fuel.

3   Check the air filter element - a dirty or partially blocked filter will severely impede performance and economy (see Chapter 1).

4   If a blown fuse is found, replace it and see if it blows again. If it does, search for a grounded wire in the harness related to the system.

5   Check the air intake duct from the air flow meter to the intake manifold for leaks, which will result in an excessively lean mixture. Also check the condition of the vacuum hoses connected to the intake manifold.

6   Remove the air intake duct from the throttle body and check for carbon and residue build-up. If it's dirty, clean with aerosol carburetor cleaner (make sure the can says it's safe for use with oxygen sensors and catalytic converters) and a toothbrush **(see illustrations)**.

7   With the engine running, place a stethoscope against each injector, one at a time, and listen for a clicking sound, indicating operation **(see illustration)**.

8   If there is a problem with an injector, purchase a special injector test light (noid light) and install it into the injector electrical connector **(see illustration)**. Start the engine and make sure that each injector connector flashes the noid light. This will test for the proper voltage signal to the injector.

12.8 Install the "noid" light into the fuel injector electrical connector and check to see that it blinks with the engine running

12.9 Using an ohmmeter, measure the resistance across both terminals of the injector.

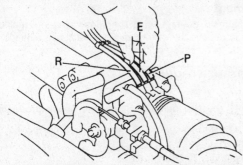

Port name	At idle	Other than ide
P	No vacuum	Vacuum
E	No vacuum	Vacuum
R	No vacuum	No vacuum

13.2a Throttle body vacuum port guide and table - four cylinder engines

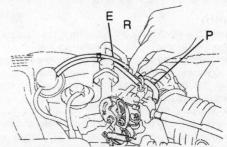

Port name	At idle	3,000 rpm or more
P	No vacuum	Vacuum
E	No vacuum	Vacuum
R	No vacuum	Vacuum

13.2b Throttle body vacuum port guide and table - V6 engines

9 With the engine OFF and the fuel injector electrical connectors disconnected, measure the resistance of each injector **(see illustration)**. Each injector should measure about 13.4 to 14.2 ohms. If not, the injector is probably faulty.
10 The remainder of the system checks should be left to a Toyota service department or other qualified repair shop, as there is a chance that the control unit may be damaged if not performed properly.

13 Electronic Fuel Injection (EFI) system - component check and replacement

Warning: *Gasoline is extremely flammable, so take extra precautions when you work on any part of the fuel system. Don't smoke or allow open flames or bare light bulbs near the work area, and don't work in a garage where a natural gas-type appliance (such as a water heater or a clothes dryer) with a pilot light is present. Since gasoline is carcinogenic, wear latex gloves when there's a possibility of being exposed to fuel, and, if you spill any fuel on your skin, rinse it off immediately with soap and water. Mop up any spills immediately and do not store fuel-soaked rags where they could ignite. The fuel system is under constant pressure, so, if any fuel lines are to be disconnected, the fuel pressure in the system must be relieved first. When you perform any kind of work on the fuel system, wear safety glasses and have a Class B type fire*

extinguisher on hand.
Caution: *If the stereo in your vehicle is equipped with an anti-theft system, make sure you have the correct activation code before disconnecting the battery.*
Note: *On 1993 and later models, the airbag system will be disabled if the battery is disconnected for more than a brief period. If the airbag light comes on and stays on after the battery is reconnected, the vehicle must be taken to a dealer service department to have the system reset with a special tool.*

Throttle body
Refer to illustrations 13.2a, 13.2b, 13.10 and 13.11
Check
1 Verify that the throttle linkage operates smoothly.
2 Start the engine, detach each vacuum hose and, using your finger, check the vacuum at each port on the throttle body with the engine at idle and above idle, then compare your observations with the vacuum table **(see illustrations)**.
Replacement
3 Detach the cable from the negative terminal of the battery *(see* **Caution** *and* **Note** *at the beginning of this Section).*
4 Drain the radiator (see Chapter 1).
5 Loosen the hose clamps and remove the air intake duct.
6 Detach the accelerator cable from the throttle lever (see

Section 10), then detach the throttle cable bracket and set it aside (it's not necessary to detach the throttle cable from the bracket).

7   If your vehicle is equipped with an automatic transmission, detach the throttle valve (TV) cable from the throttle linkage (see Chapter 7B), detach the TV cable brackets from the engine and set the cable and brackets aside.

8   Clearly label, then detach, all vacuum and coolant hoses from the throttle body.

9   Disconnect the electrical connector from the throttle position sensor (TPS).

10   Remove the four throttle body mounting bolts **(see illustration)**.

11   Detach the throttle body and gasket **(see illustration)** from the intake manifold.

12   Using a soft brush and carburetor cleaner, thoroughly clean the throttle body casting, then blow out all passages with compressed air. **Caution:** *Do not clean the throttle position sensor with anything. Just wipe it off carefully with a clean, soft cloth.*

13   Installation of the throttle body is the reverse of removal.

14   Be sure to tighten the throttle body mounting bolts to the torque listed in this Chapter's Specifications.

Throttle position sensor (TPS)

Refer to illustrations 13.16, 13.17a and 13.17b

Check

15   Disconnect the electrical connector from the throttle position sensor (TPS) and apply vacuum to the throttle positioner.

16   Insert a feeler gauge of the specified thickness between the throttle stop screw and the stop lever **(see illustration)**.

17   Using an ohmmeter, measure the resistance, between the indicated terminal pairs **(see illustrations)**.

18   If the resistance is not as specified, insert a 0.70 mm (0.028 in.) feeler gauge between the throttle stop screw and lever, and connect the ohmmeter to terminals IDL and E2. Loosen the TPS mounting screws and slowly rotate the sensor clockwise until the ohmmeter reads infinity.

19   Tighten the mounting screws, and using the proper feeler gauge, recheck the continuity between the specified terminals.

13.10 A typical throttle body is retained by four bolts/nuts (arrows)

Replacement

20   If adjustment doesn't bring the sensor within specifications, disconnect it, remove the screws and replace it with a new one, then adjust it as described in Step 18.

Fuel pressure regulator

Check

21   Refer to the fuel pump/fuel pressure check procedure (see Section 3).

Replacement

Refer to illustrations 13.26 and 13.27

22   Relieve the fuel pressure (see Section 2) and detach the cable from the negative terminal of the battery *(see **Caution** and **Note** at the*

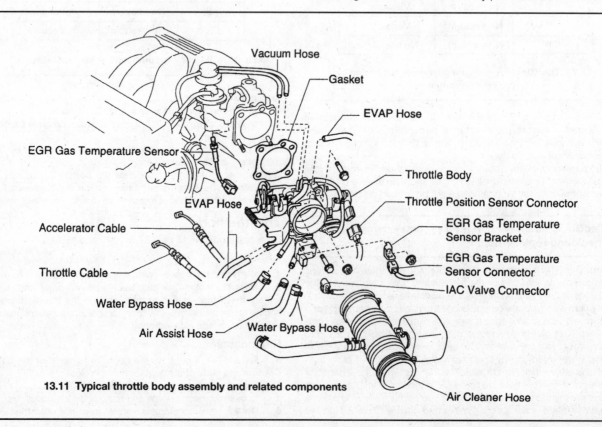

13.11 Typical throttle body assembly and related components

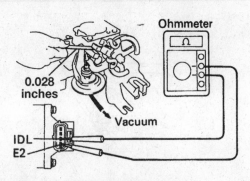

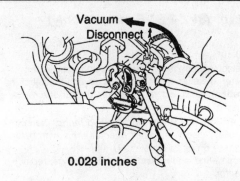

4 cylinder engines   **V6 engines**

13.16 To check the throttle position sensor (TPS), insert a feeler gauge of the specified thickness between the throttle stop screw and the stop lever, then measure the resistance between the proper terminals

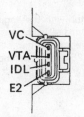
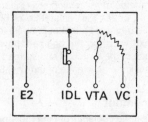

Clearance between lever and stop screw	Between terminals	Resistance
0 mm (0 in.)	VTA – E2	0.2 – 5.7 kΩ
0.50 mm (0.020 in.)	IDL – E2	2.3 kΩ or less
0.70 mm (0.028 in.)	IDL – E2	Infinity
Throttle valve fully open	VTA – E2	2.0 – 10.2 kΩ
—	VC – E2	2.5 – 5.9 kΩ

13.17a Use the terminal guide and the continuity table to check the TPS on four cylinder engines

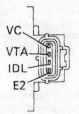
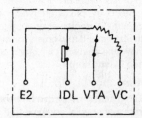

Clearance between lever and stop screw	Between terminals	Resistance
0 mm (0 in.)	VTA – E2	0.28 – 6.4 kΩ
0.35 mm (0.014 in.)	IDL – E2	0.5 kΩ or less
0.70 mm (0.028 in.)	IDL – E2	Infinity
Throttle valve fully open	VTA – E2	2.0 – 11.6 kΩ
—	VC – E2	2.7 – 7.7 kΩ

13.17b Use the terminal guide and the continuity table to check the TPS on V6 engines

beginning of this Section).
23 Detach the vacuum sensing hose from the regulator.
24 Place a metal container or shop towel under the fuel return hose.
25 Slide the clamp down the hose and remove the fuel return hose

from the regulator.
26 Remove the pressure regulator mounting bolts **(see illustration)** and detach the pressure regulator from the fuel rail.
27 Use a new O-ring and make sure that the pressure regulator is installed properly on the fuel rail **(see illustration)**.
28 The remainder of installation is the reverse of removal.

13.26 To remove the fuel pressure regulator from the fuel rail, detach the fuel return hose, remove the two regulator bolts (arrows) and separate the regulator from the fuel rail

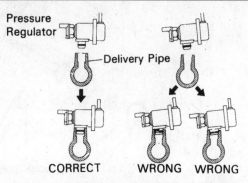

13.27 If the fuel pressure regulator is cocked during installation, it will not seal properly

Cold start injector (3VZ-FE V6 models only)

Check

Refer to illustration 13.30

29   Disconnect the electrical connector from the cold start injector.

30   Using an ohmmeter, measure the resistance between the injector terminals **(see illustration)**. Compare your measurement to the resistance listed in this Chapter's Specifications.

a) *If the indicated resistance is within the specified range, the cold start injector is okay. Check the start injector time switch for correct operation (see Steps 38 through 41).*

b) *If the indicated resistance isn't within the specified range, replace the cold start injector.*

31   Connect the cold start injector electrical connector.

Removal

Refer to illustration 13.35

32   Relieve the fuel pressure (see Section 2). Disconnect the cable from the negative terminal of the battery *(see **Caution** and **Note** at the beginning of this Section).*

33   Disconnect the cold start injector electrical connector.

34   Place a metal container or shop towel under the banjo fitting and remove the banjo bolt and crush washers. Discard the washers.

35   Remove the cold start injector mounting nuts, the injector and the gasket **(see illustration)**.

Bench test

36   The cold start injector can be bench tested (for spray pattern) but the test requires special equipment. If you are in any doubt as to the status of the cold start injector, take it to a dealer service department or other repair shop and have it tested.

Installation

37   Installation of the cold start injector is the reverse of removal. Be sure to use new crush washers on each side of the banjo fitting.

Cold start injector time switch (3VZ-FE V6 models only)

Check

38   Disconnect the electrical connector from the start injector time switch and using an ohmmeter, check the resistance between each terminal. **Note:** *The cold start injector time switch is located next to the*

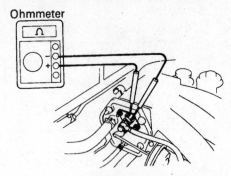

13.30 To check the resistance of the cold start injector, disconnect the electrical connector and measure the resistance between the terminals

coolant temperature sensor (see Chapter 6).

39   First, check the resistance of the switch with the engine cold (below 59 degrees F). It should be 25 to 45 ohms resistance.

40   Next, warm up the engine (above 86 degrees F) and check the resistance of the switch. It should read 65 to 85 ohms resistance.

41   Check the resistance of terminal STA to ground. It should read 25 to 85 ohms.

Replacement

42   Drain the coolant from the radiator (see Chapter 1).

43   Use a deep socket and remove the sensor from the engine.

44   Installation is the reverse of removal.

Idle air control (IAC) valve

Note: *The minimum idle speed is pre-set at the factory and should not require adjustment under normal operating conditions; however if the throttle body has been replaced or you suspect the minimum idle speed has been tampered with (for example, if the idle speed screw was removed from the throttle body) have the vehicle checked by a dealer service department or a qualified automotive repair shop.*

Check

Refer to illustrations 13.45, 13.46, 13.50a, 13.50b and 13.50c

45   Apply the parking brake, shift the transaxle to Neutral (manual) or

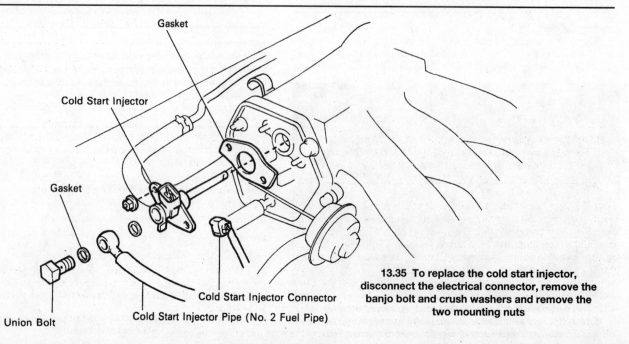

13.35 To replace the cold start injector, disconnect the electrical connector, remove the banjo bolt and crush washers and remove the two mounting nuts

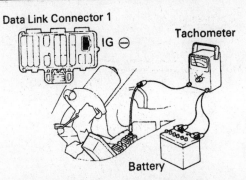

13.45 Install the test lead from the tachometer into the IG (-) terminal of the SST test terminal located in the corner of the engine compartment

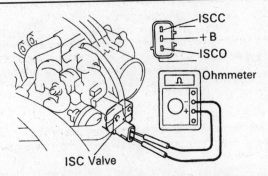

13.50a Using an ohmmeter, check resistance between +B and ISCC or ISCO - four cylinder engine

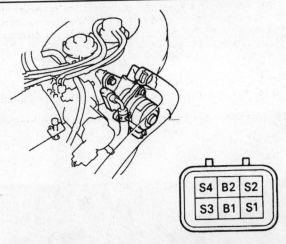

13.50c Terminal designations on the 3VZ-FE V6 engine - check the resistance between B1 and S1 or S3, also check the resistance between B2 and S2 or S4

Park (automatic) and block the drive wheels. Install a tachometer in accordance with the manufacturer's instructions. **Note:** Install the lead from the tachometer into the IG (—) terminal on the check electrical connector **(see illustration)**. Start the engine and allow it to reach normal operating temperature. Check the idle speed and compare it to the idle speed listed in this Chapter's Specifications.

46 Using a jumper wire, bridge terminals TE1 and E1 of the check electrical connector **(see illustration)**.

47 The engine speed should increase to approximately 1,000 to 1,200 rpm for five seconds then return to normal idle speed. **Note:** On 3VZ-FE models the idle speed may not increase, instead listen for a

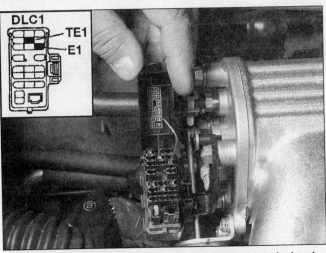

13.46 To test the IAC motor, locate the SST test terminal and using a jumper wire or paper clip, bridge terminals TE1 and E1

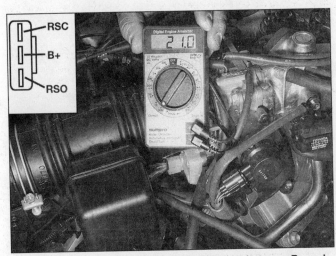

13.50b Using an ohmmeter, check resistance between B+ and RSC or RSO - 1MZ-FE V6 engine

clicking sound from the IAC valve, indicating operation.
a) If the engine speed changes as described, the IAC valve is okay.
b) If the engine speed does not change as described, measure the IAC valve resistance.

48 Remove the jumper wire.
49 Disconnect the IAC valve electrical connector.
50 Measure the resistance between the middle terminal and each of the other two outer terminals **(see illustrations)**. Compare your results to the IAC valve resistance in this Chapter's Specifications.
a) If the resistance is as specified, the IAC valve is okay (but there may be a problem with the wiring or the ECM).
b) If the resistance is not as specified, replace the IAC valve.
51 Connect the IAC valve electrical connector.

Replacement
Refer to illustrations 13.53a and 13.53b
52 Remove the throttle body (see Steps 4 through 14). **Note:** The IAC valve and assembly are difficult to reach, therefore it is recommended to remove the throttle body so that the new IAC valve assembly can be installed properly.
53 Remove the mounting screws and detach the IAC valve and gasket **(see illustrations)**.

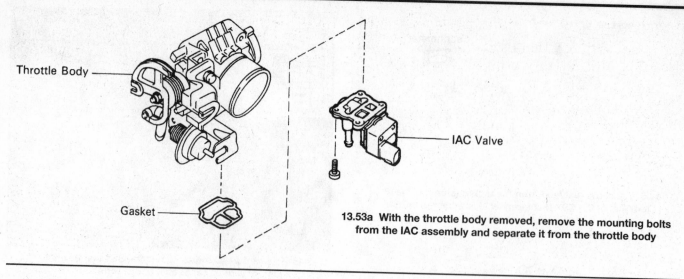

Throttle Body

IAC Valve

Gasket

13.53a With the throttle body removed, remove the mounting bolts from the IAC assembly and separate it from the throttle body

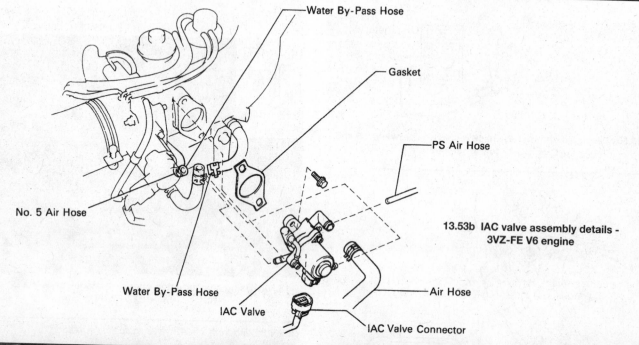

Water By-Pass Hose

Gasket

PS Air Hose

No. 5 Air Hose

13.53b IAC valve assembly details - 3VZ-FE V6 engine

Water By-Pass Hose

IAC Valve

Air Hose

IAC Valve Connector

13.60a Remove the two screws (arrows) and . . .

13.60b . . . position the VSV assembly off to the side

13.63 Remove the fuel lines from the fuel rail

13.64 Remove the fuel rail mounting bolts

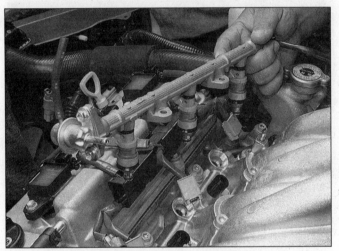

13.65a Carefully lift the fuel rail/injector assembly out of the engine compartment. Beware of any fuel that may spill out of the fuel pressure regulator while you are lifting it out

13.65b Remove the air intake plenum to gain access to the rear fuel rail assembly bolts (arrows)

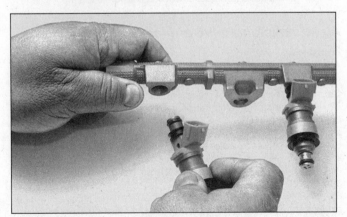

13.66 Simultaneously twist and pull the injector to remove it from the fuel rail

54   If the IAC assembly was replaced, be sure to install the Temperature Vacuum Valve (TVV) from the original assembly into the new unit (if equipped).

55   Installation of the IAC valve is the reverse of removal for all vehicles. Be sure to use a new gasket when installing the IAC valve.

Fuel rail and fuel injectors

Check

56   Refer to the fuel injection system checking procedure (see Section 12).

Replacement

Refer to illustrations 13.60a, 13.60b, 13.63, 13.64, 13.65a, 13.65b, 13.66, and 13.67

57   Relief the fuel pressure (see Section 2).

58   Detach the cable from the negative terminal of the battery *(see* **Caution** *and* **Note** *at the beginning of this Section).*

59   Remove the PCV hose from the cylinder head and intake manifold.

60   Remove the assembly that retains the Vacuum Switching Valve (VSV) control solenoids **(see illustrations)**.

61   Disconnect the fuel injector electrical connectors and set the injector wire harness aside.

62   Detach the vacuum sensing hose from the fuel pressure regulator.

63   Disconnect the fuel lines from the fuel pressure regulator and the fuel rail **(see illustration)**

64   Remove the fuel rail mounting bolts **(see illustration)**.

65   Remove the fuel rail with the fuel injectors attached **(see illustration)**. **Note:** *On V6 engines, it will be necessary to remove the air intake plenum to gain access to the rear (right bank) fuel rail* **(see illustration).**

66   Remove the fuel injector(s) from the fuel rail **(see illustration)** and set them aside in a clearly labeled storage container.

4

13.67 If you plan to reinstall the original injectors, remove and discard the O-rings and grommets and replace them with new ones

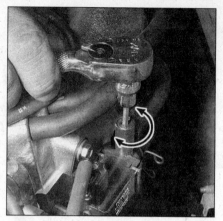

13.72 If the air conditioning idle-up valve exceeds the normal idle by more than 100 rpm adjust the valve using a hex socket

13.75 Check the resistance of the air conditioning idle-up valve solenoid

67   If you are replacing the injector(s), discard the old injector. If you intend to re-use the same injectors, replace the grommets and O-rings **(see illustration)**.
68   Installation of the fuel injectors is the reverse of removal.
69   Tighten the fuel rail mounting bolts to the torque listed in this Chapter's Specifications.

Air conditioning idle-up valve

Check

Refer to illustrations 13.72, 13.75 and 13.78

70   Apply the parking brake, shift the transaxle to Neutral (manual) or Park (automatic) and block the drive wheels. Install a tachometer in accordance with the manufacturer's instructions. **Note:** *Install the lead from the tachometer into the IG (—) terminal on the check electrical connector* **(see illustration 13.45)**. Start the engine and allow it to reach normal operating temperature and idle speed, turn the air conditioning system ON.
71   Using a jumper wire, bridge terminals TE1 and E1 of the check electrical connector **(see illustration 13.46)**.
72   Verify that the engine speed increases to approximately 1,000 to 1,200 rpm for approximately three seconds after engaging the test terminals, then returns to normal. After 15 seconds check the idle speed again, it should be approximately 100 rpm greater than normal.

  a) *If the engine speed changes as described, the air conditioning idle-up valve is okay.*
  b) *If the rpm increases more than 100 rpm, adjust the rpm range by turning the adjustment screw accordingly* **(see illustration)**.
  c) *If the engine speed does not change or decreases, measure the A/C idle-up valve resistance.*

73   Remove the jumper wire.
74   Disconnect the air conditioning idle-up valve electrical connector.
75   Measure the resistance between the terminals **(see illustration)**. It should be between 30 and 34 ohms.

  a) *If the resistance is as specified, the air conditioning idle-up valve is okay (but there may be a problem with the wiring or the ECM).*
  b) *If the resistance is not as specified, replace the valve (see below).*

76   Apply battery voltage across the terminals and check that air flows from port E to port F . **Note:** *Port E is the top port and port F is the bottom port.* Remove battery voltage and observe that air does not flow from port E through port F.
77   If the test results are incorrect, replace the air conditioning idle-up valve.

Replacement

78   Remove the mounting screws and detach the idle-up valve and gasket **(see illustration)**.

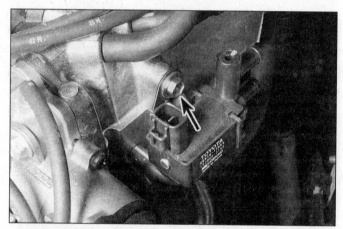

13.78 Remove the retaining bolt (arrow) from the air conditioning idle-up valve and separate it from the air intake plenum

79   Installation of the idle-up valve is the reverse of removal.
80   Be sure to use a new gasket when installing the idle-up valve.

Air intake plenum (V6 engines only)

Removal

Refer to illustrations 13.85, 13.87, 13.89 and 13.90

81   Detach the cable from the negative terminal of the battery *(see* **Caution** *and* **Note** *at the beginning of this Section).*
82   Disconnect the electrical connectors at the IAC valve, throttle position sensor (TPS), MAF sensor and EGR\EVAP canister control solenoid.
83   Detach the accelerator cable (see Section 10) and transmission linkage (see Chapter 7) from the throttle body assembly.
84   Remove the accelerator cable from the intake manifold (see Section 10).
85   Clearly label, then detach, the vacuum lines from air intake plenum, the EGR valve, the ACIS valve and the fuel pressure regulator **(see illustration)**.
86   Detach the PCV system by disconnecting the hose from the fitting on the air intake plenum.
87   Remove the plenum bracket and bolt **(see illustration)**.
88   If equipped, detach the coolant hoses from the throttle body. **Note:** *It will be necessary to drain the coolant from the radiator (see Chapter 1).*
89   Remove the air intake plenum retaining bolts **(see illustration)** and the lower (side) retaining bolts.

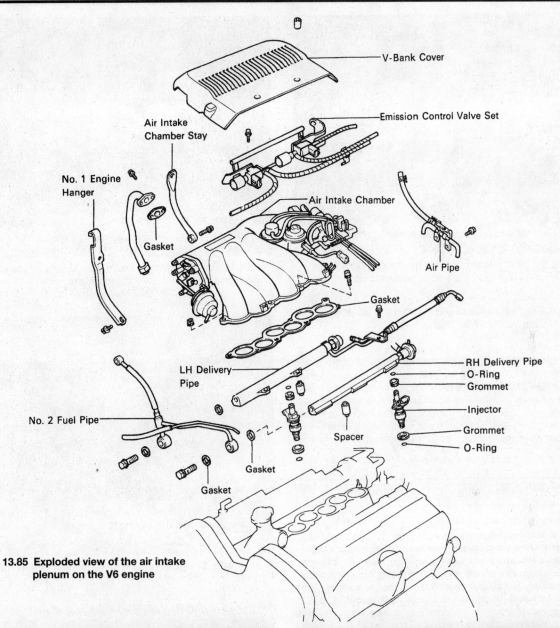

V-Bank Cover

Emission Control Valve Set

Air Intake
Chamber Stay

Air Intake Chamber

No. 1 Engine
Hanger

Gasket

Air Pipe

Gasket

LH Delivery
Pipe

RH Delivery Pipe

O-Ring

Grommet

No. 2 Fuel Pipe

Injector

Spacer

Grommet

O-Ring

Gasket

Gasket

13.85 Exploded view of the air intake plenum on the V6 engine

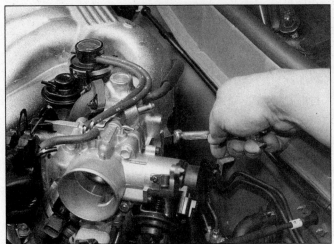

13.87 Remove the bolt and bracket from the backside of the air intake plenum

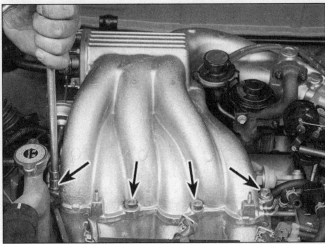

13.89 Remove the air intake plenum-to-intake manifold bolts (arrows)

4

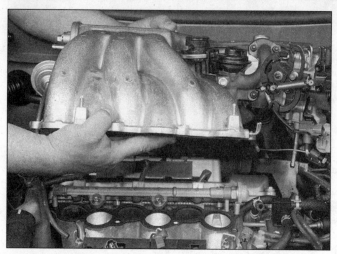

13.90 Lift the air intake plenum and the throttle body as a complete unit from the engine compartment

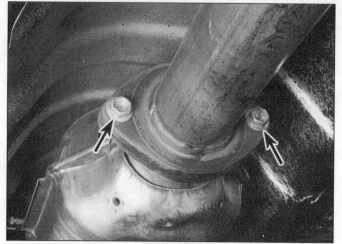

14.1a Be sure to lubricate the flange nuts on the catalytic converter (arrows) before attempting to remove them from the exhaust system

90   Remove the air intake plenum and throttle body as an assembly from the lower intake manifold **(see illustration)**.

Installation

91   Be sure to clean and inspect the mounting surface of the lower intake manifold (see Chapter 2A) and the air intake plenum before positioning the new gasket onto the lower intake mounting face. Install the air intake plenum and throttle body assembly onto the intake manifold. Ensure the gasket remains in place. Install the upper intake manifold retaining bolts and tighten the bolts to the torque listed in this Chapter's Specifications. Installation is otherwise the reverse of removal.

14   Exhaust system servicing - general information

Refer to illustrations 14.1a and 14.1b
Warning: *Inspection and repair of exhaust system components should be done only after the system components have cooled completely.*
1   The exhaust system consists of the exhaust manifold, catalytic converter, the muffler, the tailpipe and all connecting pipes, brackets, hangers and clamps. The exhaust system is attached to the body with mounting brackets and rubber hangers **(see illustration)**. If any of these parts are damaged or deteriorated, excessive noise and vibration will be transmitted to the body.
2   Conducting regular inspections of the exhaust system will keep it safe and quiet. Look for any damaged or bent parts, open seams, holes, loose connections, excessive corrosion or other defects which could allow exhaust fumes to enter the vehicle. Deteriorated exhaust system components should not be repaired - they should be replaced with new parts.
3   If the exhaust system components are extremely corroded or rusted together, they will probably have to be cut from the exhaust system. The convenient way to accomplish this is to have a muffler repair shop remove the corroded sections with a cutting torch. If, however, you want to save money by doing it yourself and you don't have an oxy/acetylene welding outfit with a cutting torch, simply cut off the old components with a hack-saw. If you have compressed air, special pneumatic cutting chisels can also be used. If you do decide to tackle the job at home, be sure to wear eye protection to protect your eyes from metal chips and work gloves to protect your hands.

14.1b Flange nuts on the rear section of the muffler

4   Here are some simple guidelines to apply when repairing the exhaust system:

 a) *Work from the back to the front when removing exhaust system components.*
 b) *Apply penetrating oil to the exhaust system component fasteners to make them easier to remove.*
 c) *Use new gaskets, hangers and clamps when installing exhaust system components.*
 d) *Apply anti-seize compound to the threads of all exhaust system fasteners during reassembly.*
 e) *Be sure to allow sufficient clearance between newly installed parts and all points on the underbody to avoid overheating the floor pan and possibly damaging the interior carpet and insulation. Pay particularly close attention to the catalytic converter and its heat shield.* **Warning:** *The catalytic converter operates at very high temperatures and takes a long time to cool. Wait until it's completely cool before attempting to remove the converter. Failure to do so could result in serious burns.*

Chapter 5
Engine electrical systems

Contents

Specifications

Ignition timing (all models)

With test terminals TE1 and E1 grounded	10 degrees BTDC
Without test terminals TE1 and E1 grounded	12 to 22 degrees BTDC

Ignition coil

Internal coil type distributor
Primary resistance	0.4 to 0.5 ohms
Secondary resistance	10.0 to 14.3 K-ohms

External coil type distributor
5S-FE engine
Primary resistance	0.3 to 0.55 ohms
Secondary resistance	9.0 to 15.4 K-ohms

3VZ-FE engine
Primary resistance	0.2 to 0.32 ohms
Secondary resistance	6.4 to 10.7 K-ohms

Distributorless ignition coil
Primary resistance	0.5 to 0.85 ohms

Distributor

Air gap
Internal coil type distributor	0.008 to 0.016 inch
External coil type distributor	0.008 to 0.020 inch

Pick-up coil resistance
External coil type distributor
Ne to G- terminals	155 to 250 ohms
G1 to G- terminals	125 to 200 ohms
G2 to G- terminals	125 to 200 ohms

Internal coil type distributor
Through 1995
Ne+ to Ne- terminals	370 to 550 ohms
G+ to G- terminals	185 to 275 ohms
1996	135 to 220 ohms

5

Charging system

Charging voltage	13.9 to 15.1 volts
Standard amperage	
All lights and accessories turned off	less than 10 amps
Headlights (hi-beam) and heater blower motor turned on	30 amps or more
Alternator brush length	
Standard	0.413 inch
Minimum	0.059 inch

1 General information

The engine electrical systems include all ignition, charging and starting components. Because of their engine related functions, these components are discussed separately from chassis electrical devices such as the lights, the instruments, etc. (which are included in Chapter 12).

Always observe the following precautions when working on the electrical systems:

a) *Be extremely careful when servicing engine electrical components. They are easily damaged if checked, connected or handled improperly.*

b) *Never leave the ignition switch on for long periods of time (10 minutes maximum) with the engine off.*

c) *Don't disconnect the battery cables while the engine is running.*

d) *Maintain correct polarity when connecting a battery cable from another vehicle during jump starting.*

e) *Always disconnect the negative cable first and hook it up last or the battery may be shorted by the tool being used to loosen the cable clamps.*

It's also a good idea to review the safety-related information regarding the engine electrical systems located in the *Safety first* section near the front of this manual before beginning any operation included in this Chapter.

2 Battery - emergency jump starting

Refer to the *Booster battery (jump) starting* procedure at the front of this manual.

3 Battery - removal and installation

Refer to illustration 3.2

1   Starting with the negative battery terminal, disconnect both cables from the battery terminals. **Caution:** *If the stereo in your vehicle is equipped with an anti-theft system, make sure you have the correct activation code before disconnecting the battery.* **Note:** *On 1993 and later models, the airbag system will be disabled if the battery is disconnected for more than a brief period. If the airbag light comes on and stays on after the battery is reconnected, the vehicle must be taken to a dealer service department to have the system reset with a special tool.*

2   Remove the battery hold-down clamp **(see illustration)**.

3   Lift out the battery. Be careful, it's heavy.

4   While the battery is out, inspect the carrier (tray) for corrosion.

5   If you are replacing the battery, make sure that you get one that's identical, with the same dimensions, amperage rating, cold cranking rating, etc as the original.

6   Installation is the reverse of removal.

4 Battery cables - check and replacement

Caution: *If the stereo in your vehicle is equipped with an anti-theft system, make sure you have the correct activation code before disconnecting the battery.*
Note: *On 1993 and later models, the airbag system will be disabled if the battery is disconnected for more than a brief period. If the airbag*

3.2 To remove the battery, detach the negative battery cable first, then the positive cable, remove the hold-down strap nuts (arrows) and remove the hold-down strap

light comes on and stays on after the battery is reconnected, the vehicle must be taken to a dealer service department to have the system reset with a special tool.

1   Periodically inspect the entire length of each battery cable for damage, cracked or burned insulation and corrosion. Poor battery cable connections can cause starting problems and decreased engine performance.

2   Check the cable-to-terminal connections at the ends of the cables for cracks, loose wire strands and corrosion. The presence of white, fluffy deposits under the insulation at the cable terminal connection is a sign that the cable is corroded and should be replaced. Check the terminals for distortion, missing mounting bolts and corrosion.

3   When removing the cables, always disconnect the negative cable first and hook it up last or the battery may be shorted by the tool used to loosen the cable clamps. Even if only the positive cable is being replaced, be sure to disconnect the negative cable from the battery first (see Chapter 1 for further information regarding battery cable removal).

4   Disconnect the old cables from the battery, then trace each of them to their opposite ends and detach them from the starter solenoid and ground terminals. Note the routing of each cable to ensure correct installation.

5   If you are replacing either or both of the old cables, take them with you when buying new cables. It is vitally important that you replace the cables with identical parts. Cables have characteristics that make them easy to identify: positive cables are usually red, larger in cross-section and have a larger diameter battery post clamp; ground cables are usually black, smaller in cross-section and have a slightly smaller diameter clamp for the negative post.

6   Clean the threads of the solenoid or ground connection with a wire brush to remove rust and corrosion. Apply a light coat of battery terminal corrosion inhibitor, or petroleum jelly, to the threads to prevent future corrosion.

7   Attach the cable to the solenoid or ground connection and tighten the mounting nut/bolt securely.

8   Before connecting a new cable to the battery, make sure that it reaches the battery post without having to be stretched.

9   Connect the positive cable first, followed by the negative cable.

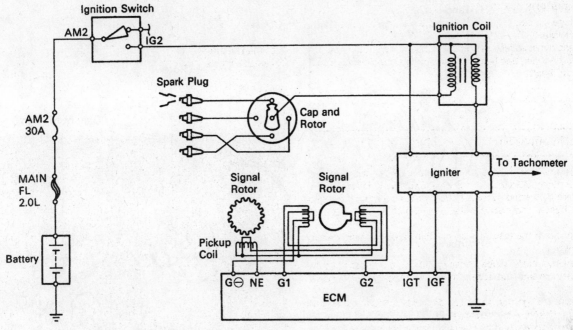

5.2a Schematic of the breakerless electronic ignition system on four-cylinder engines

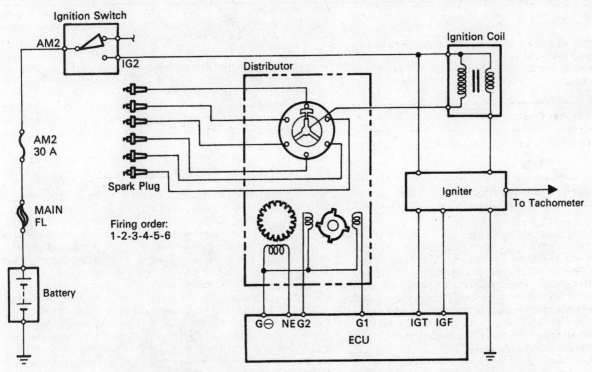

5.2b Schematic of the breakerless electronic ignition system on the 3VZ-FE V6 engine

5   Ignition system - general information and precautions

Refer to illustrations 5.2a, 5.2b, 5.3a, 5.3b and 5.4

1   There are two types of ignition systems equipped on the models covered by this manual. Four-cylinder engines (5S-FE) and 1992 and 1993 V6 engines (3VZ-FE) are equipped with a breakerless type electronic ignition. 1994 and later V6 engines (1MZ-FE) are equipped with a Distributorless Ignition System (DIS).

Breakerless ignition systems

2   The breakerless ignition system includes the ignition switch, the battery, the igniter, the pick-up coil, the ignition coil, the primary (low voltage) and secondary (high voltage) wiring circuits, the distributor and the spark plugs **(see illustrations)**. The ignition system is controlled by the Electronic Control Module (ECM). Using data provided by information sensors which monitor various engine functions (such as rpm, intake air volume, engine temperature, etc.),

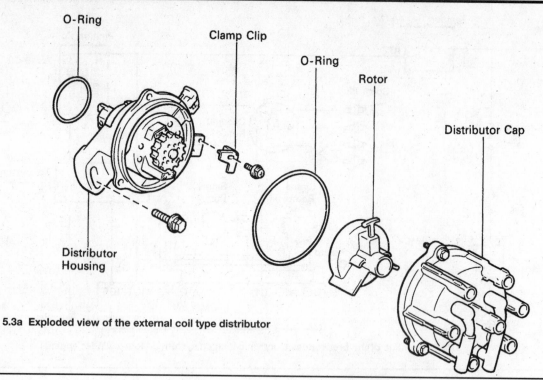

5.3a Exploded view of the external coil type distributor

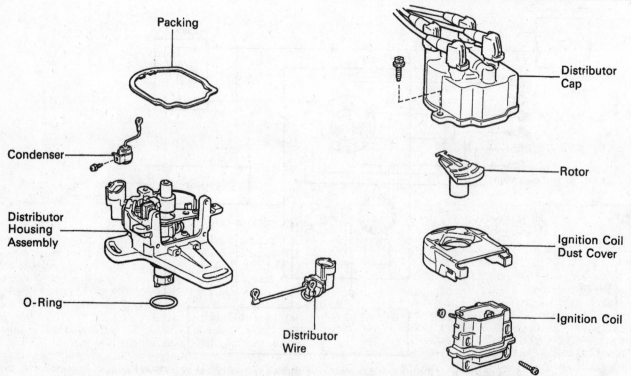

5.3b Exploded view of the internal coil type distributor

the ECM ensures a perfectly timed spark under all conditions. This system is known as Electronic Spark Advance (ESA).

3   The breakerless ignition systems are divided into two groups; external coil type distributors and internal coil type distributors **(see illustrations)**. When replacing these units be sure to make all the necessary ignition system checks before replacing the distributor as these units are expensive and can only be replaced as a single component.

Distributorless ignition system

4   The DIS system **(see illustration)** includes the camshaft position sensor, the crankshaft position sensor, six coils (one at each cylinder) and the igniter. The ECM (computer) generates cylinder identification signals which allow the igniter to trigger the correct coil while cranking the engine. The igniter distributes the signal to the proper coil driver circuit and determines dwell period based on coil primary current flow.

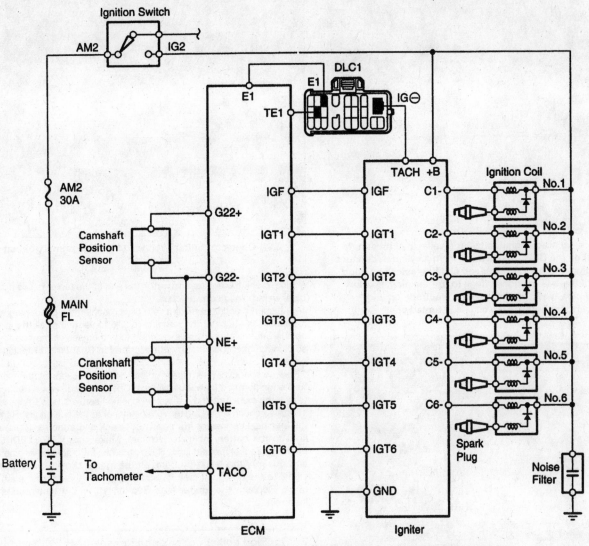

5.4 Schematic of the distributorless ignition system on the 1MZ-FE V6 engine

Each cylinder is fired independently and in the proper sequence as dictated by the ECM.

5   When working on the ignition system, take the following precautions:

a) *Do not keep the ignition switch on for more than 10 seconds if the engine will not start.*

b) *Always connect a tachometer in accordance with the manufacturer's instructions. Some tachometers may be incompatible with this ignition system. Consult a dealer service department before buying a tachometer for use with this vehicle.*

c) *Never allow the ignition coil terminals to touch ground. Grounding the coil could result in damage to the igniter and/or the ignition coil.*

d) *Do not disconnect the battery when the engine is running.*

e) *Make sure that the igniter is properly grounded.*

6   Ignition system - check

Warning: *Because of the high voltage generated by the ignition system, extreme care should be taken whenever an operation is performed involving ignition components. This not only includes the igniter, coil, distributor and spark plug wires, but related components such as plug connectors, tachometer and other test equipment also.*

Breakerless ignition systems

1   If the engine turns over but won't start, disconnect the spark plug wire from any spark plug and attach it to a calibrated tester (available at most auto parts stores). Connect the clip on the tester to a bolt or metal bracket on the engine. If you're unable to obtain a calibrated ignition tester, remove the wire from one of the spark plugs and using an insulated tool, pull back the boot and hold the end of the wire about 1/4-inch from a good ground.

2   Crank the engine and watch the end of the tester or spark plug wire to see if bright blue, well-defined sparks occur.

3   If sparks occur, sufficient voltage is reaching the plug to fire it (repeat the check at the remaining plug wires to verify that the distributor cap and rotor are OK). However, the plugs themselves may be fouled, so remove and check them as described in Chapter 1.

4   If no sparks or intermittent sparks occur, remove the distributor cap and check the cap and rotor as described in Chapter 1. If moisture is present, dry out the cap and rotor, then reinstall the cap and repeat the spark test.

5   If there's still no spark, detach the coil secondary wire from the distributor cap and hook it up to the tester (reattach the plug wire to the spark plug), then repeat the spark check. Again, if you don't have a tester, hold the end of the wire about 1/4-inch from a good ground.

6   If sparks now occur, the distributor cap, rotor or plug wire(s) may be defective.

6.9 To use a calibrated ignition tester (available at most auto parts stores) on the DIS, remove a coil from a cylinder, connect the spark plug boot to the tester and clip the tester to a good ground - if there is enough voltage to fire the plug, sparks will be clearly visible between the electrode tip and the tester body as the engine is turned over

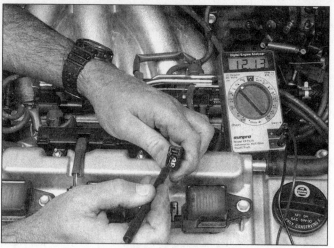

6.12 Check for battery voltage to the coil primary circuit

engine, crank the engine and watch the end of the tester to see if bright blue, well-defined sparks occur.

11   If sparks occur, sufficient voltage is reaching the spark plug to fire it (repeat the check at the remaining coils to verify that all the ignition coils are functioning). However, the plugs themselves may be fouled, so remove and check them as described in Chapter 1 or install new ones.

12   If no sparks or intermittent sparks occur, check for battery voltage to the ignition coil **(see illustration)**. Check the coils (see Section 7). Check the camshaft and crankshaft position sensors (see Chapter 6).

13   Also check for an igniter voltage signal to the coil packs. Remove the electrical connector from each coil pack and attach a 12 volt test light to the battery positive terminal. Make sure it is a LED (Light Emitting Diode) type test light. Have an assistant crank the engine over and observe the test light blink as the igniter provides the voltage signal to the coil pack **(see illustration)**. Make this test for each coil pack. Replace the igniter (see Section 10) if the test results are incorrect.

6.13 Install the LED test light to the positive battery terminal, crank the engine over and observe the light flash as the igniter signals the coil to fire

7   If no sparks occur, check the primary wire connections at the coil to make sure they're clean and tight. Check for voltage to the coil on the primary circuit from the ignition switch. Check the ignition coil (see Section 7) and the distributor pick-up coil (see Section 11). Make any necessary repairs, then repeat the check again.

8   If there's still no spark, the coil-to-cap wire may be bad (check the resistance with an ohmmeter and compare it to the spark plug wire resistance Specifications found in Chapter 1). If a known good wire doesn't make any difference in the test results, the igniter may be defective.

Distributorless Ignition system

Refer to illustrations 6.9, 6.12 and 6.13

9   If the engine turns over but won't start, disconnect the coil pack from any spark plug and attach it to a calibrated ignition tester (available at most auto parts stores) **(see illustration)**. Make sure the tester is designed for distributorless ignition systems if a universal tester isn't available.

10   Connect the clip on the tester to a bolt or metal bracket on the

7   Ignition coil(s) - check and replacement

Caution: *If the stereo in your vehicle is equipped with an anti-theft system, make sure you have the correct activation code before disconnecting the battery.*

Note: *On 1993 and later models, the airbag system will be disabled if the battery is disconnected for more than a brief period. If the airbag light comes on and stays on after the battery is reconnected, the vehicle must be taken to a dealer service department to have the system reset with a special tool.*

Breakerless ignition systems

External Coil type

Check

Refer to illustrations 7.4a and 7.4b

1   Detach the cable from the negative terminal of the battery (see **Caution** and **Note** above).

2   Disconnect the electrical connector and the coil wire from the coil.

3   Remove the coil mounting bolts and place the coil on the bench for testing.

4   Using an ohmmeter, check the coil:

a)   *Measure the resistance between the positive and negative terminals* **(see illustration)**. *Compare your reading with the specified coil primary resistance listed in this Chapter's Specifications.*

7.4a To check the primary resistance of the coil, measure the resistance between the positive and the negative terminals

7.4b To check the secondary resistance of the coil, measure the resistance between the positive terminal and the high tension terminal

7.12a On internal coil type distributors, remove the screws (arrows) and . . .

7.12b . . . separate the heat shield from the coil

7.13 Remove the nuts from the coil terminals (arrows)

7.14a To check the primary resistance of the coil, measure the resistance between the positive and the negative terminals

5

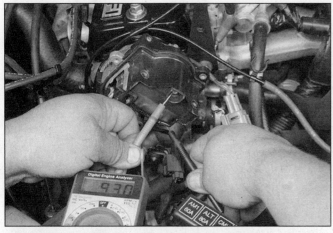

7.14b To check the secondary resistance of the coil, measure the resistance between the positive terminal and the high tension terminal

b) *Measure the resistance between the positive terminal and the high tension terminal* **(see illustration)**. *Compare your reading with the specified coil secondary resistance listed in this Chapter's Specifications.*

5   If either of the above tests yield resistance values outside the specified amount, replace the coil.

Replacement

6   Detach the cable from the negative terminal of the battery (see **Caution** and **Note** above).

7   If equipped, remove the heat shield from the coil.

8   Remove the coil mounting bolts.

9   Label and disconnect the electrical wires from the coil terminals.

10   Installation is the reverse of removal.

Internal Coil type

Check

Refer to illustrations 7.12a, 7.12b, 7.13, 7.14a and 7.14b

11   Detach the cable from the negative terminal of the battery (see **Caution** and **Note** above).

12   Remove the heat shield from the coil **(see illustrations)**.

13   Remove the mounting bolts from the coil electrical connectors **(see illustration)**.

14   Using an ohmmeter, check the coil:

a) *Measure the resistance between the positive and negative terminals* **(see illustration)**. *Compare your reading with the specified coil primary resistance listed in this Chapter's Specifications.*

b) *Measure the resistance between the positive terminal and the high tension terminal* **(see illustration)**. *Compare your reading with the specified coil secondary resistance listed in this Chapter's Specifications.*

15   If either of the above tests yield resistance values outside the specified amount, replace the coil.

7.19a Remove the retaining screws (arrows) . . .

7.19b . . . and lift the coil from the distributor housing

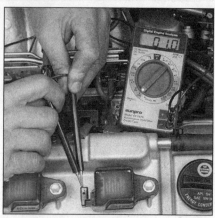

7.21 Checking the coil primary resistance on a DIS coil

8.5a Paint or scribe a mark (arrow) on the edge of the distributor housing immediately below the rotor tip to ensure that the rotor is pointing in the same direction when the distributor is reinstalled

8.5b Paint or scribe another mark across the cylinder head and the distributor body (arrows) to ensure that the distributor is aligned correctly when it is reinstalled

Replacement

Refer to illustrations 7.19a and 7.19b

16 Detach the cable from the negative terminal of the battery (see **Caution** and **Note** above).
17 Remove the heat shield from the coil.
18 Label and disconnect the electrical wires from the coil terminals.
19 Remove the coil mounting bolts **(see illustrations)**.
20 Installation is the reverse of removal.

Distributorless Ignition System

Check

Refer to illustration 7.21

21 With the ignition key OFF, disconnect the electrical harness connector(s) from each coil. Connect an ohmmeter across the coil primary terminals **(see illustration)**. The resistance should be as listed in this Chapter's Specifications. If not, replace the coil.

Replacement

22 Disconnect the negative cable from the battery (see **Caution** and **Note** above).
23 Remove the V-bank cover.
24 Disconnect the ignition coil harness electrical connector(s) from each individual coil pack. Label each connector so they don't get mixed up.

25 Remove the bolts securing the ignition coil to the mounting bracket on the engine and remove the coil.
26 Installation is the reverse of the removal procedure.

---

8   Distributor - removal and installation

Removal

Refer to illustrations 8.5a, 8.5b and 8.7

1 Detach the cable from the negative battery terminal. **Caution:** *If the stereo in your vehicle is equipped with an anti-theft system, make sure you have the correct activation code before disconnecting the battery.* **Note:** *On 1993 and later models, the airbag system will be disabled if the battery is disconnected for more than a brief period. If the airbag light comes on and stays on after the battery is reconnected, the vehicle must be taken to a dealer service department to have the system reset with a special tool.*
2 Disconnect the electrical connectors from the distributor.
3 Look for a raised "1" on the distributor cap. This marks the location for the number one cylinder spark plug wire terminal. If the cap does not have a mark for the number one terminal, locate the number one spark plug and trace the wire back to the terminal on the cap.
4 Remove the distributor cap (see Chapter 1) and turn the engine over until the rotor is pointing toward the number one spark plug

8.7 Remove the hold-down bolt from the distributor body and pull the distributor straight out

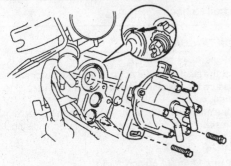

8.9 Install the distributor with the coupling on the distributor collar aligned with the cutout in the engine block

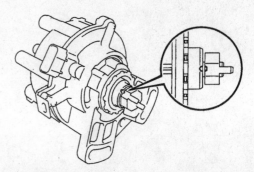

8.8 If you have set the engine at TDC compression for number one cylinder, align the cut-out portion of the coupling with the groove in the distributor housing

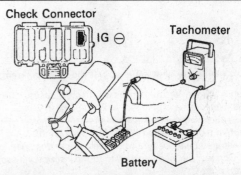

9.1 Install the tachometer lead onto the IG terminal located on the SST Check Connector

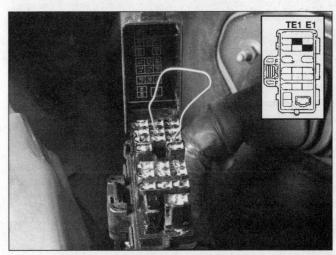

9.2 Attach a jumper between terminals E1 and TE1 on the SST test connector

terminal (see locating TDC procedure in Chapter 2A).

5   Make a mark on the edge of the distributor base directly below the rotor tip and in line with it. Also, mark the distributor base and the engine block to ensure that the distributor is installed correctly **(see illustrations)**.

6   If equipped with collar bolts, loosen but do not remove the two bolts in the distributor collar. This will give the distributor shaft clearance.

7   Remove the distributor hold-down bolt **(see illustration)**, then pull the distributor straight out to remove it. **Caution:** *DO NOT turn the crankshaft while the distributor is out of the engine, or the alignment marks will be useless.*

Installation

Refer to illustrations 8.8 and 8.9

Note: *If the crankshaft has been moved while the distributor is out, locate Top Dead Center (TDC) for the number one piston (see Chapter 2A) and position the distributor and the rotor accordingly.*

8   Align the cut-out portion of the coupling with the groove in the housing **(see illustration)**.

9   Insert the distributor into the engine in exactly the same relationship to the block that it was in when removed **(see illustration)**.

10   If the distributor does not seat completely, recheck the alignment marks between the distributor base and the block to verify that the distributor is in the same position it was in before removal. Also check the rotor to see if it's aligned with the mark you made on the edge of the distributor base.

11   Loosely install the distributor hold-down bolt(s).

12   Installation is the reverse of removal.

13   Check the ignition timing (see Section 9) and tighten the distributor hold-down bolt securely.

9   Ignition timing - check and adjustment

Refer to illustrations 9.1, 9.2, 9.3, 9.4 and 9.5

Note: *The following ignition timing procedure should apply to most models covered by this manual. However, if the procedure specified on the VECI label of your vehicle differs from this one, use the procedure found on the VECI label.*

Note: *The ignition timing is not adjustable on the 1MZ-FE V6 engine.*

1   Connect a tachometer according to the manufacturer's specifications **(see illustration)**.

2   Locate the diagnostic electrical connector and insert a jumper wire between terminals E1 and TE1 **(see illustration)**.

5

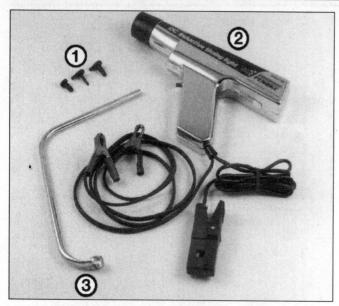

9.3 Tools needed to check and adjust the ignition timing

1   *Vacuum plugs* - *Vacuum hoses will, in most cases, have to be disconnected and plugged. Molded plugs in various shapes and sizes are available for this*
2   *Inductive pick-up timing light* - *Flashes a bright, concentrated beam of light when the number one spark plug fires. Connect the leads according to the instructions supplied with the light*
3   *Distributor wrench* - *On some models, the hold-down bolt for the distributor is difficult to reach and turn with conventional wrenches or sockets. A special wrench like this must be used*

3   With the ignition switch off, connect a timing light according to the manufacturer's specifications **(see illustration)**. Most timing lights are powered by the battery . Also, an inductive style pick-up is installed onto the number one cylinder spark plug wire.
4   Locate the timing marks on the timing cover and the crankshaft pulley **(see illustration)**.
5   Start the engine and allow it to warm up to normal operating temperature (upper radiator hose hot). Verify that the engine idle is correct (750 rpm with an automatic transaxle and 700 rpm with a manual transaxle). Aim the timing light at the timing scale on the front engine cover **(see illustration)**. The mark on the crankshaft pulley should line up with the S mark on the scale. If necessary, loosen the distributor hold-down bolt and slowly rotate the distributor until the timing marks align. Tighten the hold-down bolt and recheck the timing.

6   Remove the jumper wire from the diagnostic connector and observe the ignition timing advance to 12 to 22 degrees BTDC.
7   Turn the engine off and remove the tachometer and the timing light.

10   Igniter - replacement

Refer to illustration 10.3
1   Detach the cable from the negative terminal of the battery. **Caution:** *If the stereo in your vehicle is equipped with an anti-theft system, make sure you have the correct activation code before disconnecting the battery.* **Note:** *On 1993 and later models, the airbag system will be disabled if the battery is disconnected for more than a brief period. If the airbag light comes on and stays on after the battery is reconnected, the vehicle must be taken to a dealer service department to have the system reset with a special tool.*
2   Disconnect the electrical connector from the igniter.
3   Remove the bolts from the bracket assembly and pull the igniter/bracket assembly out of the engine compartment **(see illustration)**.
4   Installation is the reverse of removal.

11   Pick-up coil - check

Pick-up coil check

Refer to illustrations 11.1a and 11.1b
1   Disconnect the electrical connector at the distributor and using an ohmmeter, measure the resistance between the pick-up coil terminals **(see illustrations)**.
2   Compare the measurements to those listed in this Chapter's Specifications. If the resistance is not as specified, replace the distributor.

Air gap check

Refer to illustrations 11.5a, 11.5b and 11.5c
3   Detach the cable from the negative terminal of the battery. **Caution:** *If the stereo in your vehicle is equipped with an anti-theft system, make sure you have the correct activation code before disconnecting the battery.* **Note:** *On 1993 and later models, the airbag system will be disabled if the battery is disconnected for more than a brief period. If the airbag light comes on and stays on after the battery is reconnected, the vehicle must be taken to a dealer service department to have the system reset with a special tool.*
4   Remove the distributor from the engine (see Section 8).
5   Using a brass feeler gauge, measure the gap between the signal rotor and the pick-up coil projection **(see illustrations)**. Compare your measurement to the air gap listed in this Chapter's Specifications. If the air gap is not as specified, replace the distributor, as the air gap is not adjustable.

9.4 The timing marks are clearly stamped onto the front timing cover

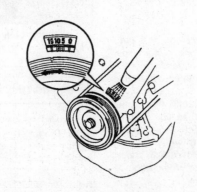

9.5 Point the timing light onto the timing marks with the engine at idle

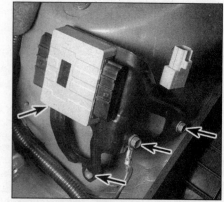

10.3 Remove the igniter bracket bolts (arrows) and lift the igniter unit from the engine compartment (V6 engine shown)

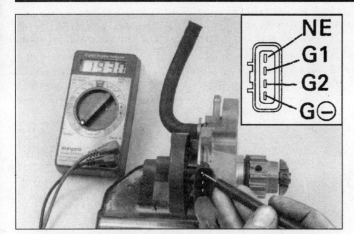

11.1a Check the resistance between terminals NE and G- on the pick-up coil (external coil type distributor). Follow the terminal designations and the resistance values for the remaining terminals listed in this Chapter's Specifications

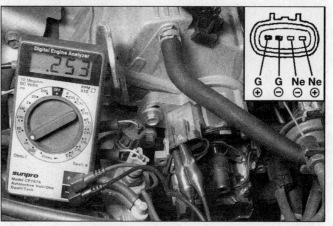

11.1b Check resistance on terminals G+ and G- on the pick-up coil (internal coil type distributor)

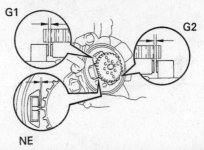

11.5b On the external coil type distributor there are three pick-up coils in the distributor housing. Because G1 and G2 are located under the rotor, it may be necessary to use a special service tool or modified feeler gauge to check the air gap

11.5a Measure the air gap between the signal rotor and the pick-up coil projection - if the gap is not within specification, replace the distributor (internal coil type distributor shown)

12 Charging system - general information and precautions

Refer to illustrations 12.1 and 12.3

The charging system includes the alternator, an internal voltage regulator, a charge indicator, the battery, a fusible link and the wiring between all the components **(see illustration)**. The charging system

5

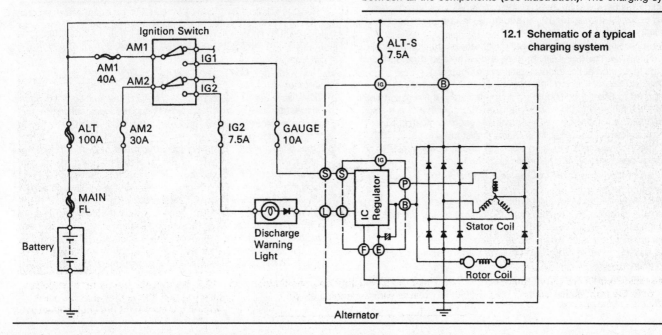

12.1 Schematic of a typical charging system

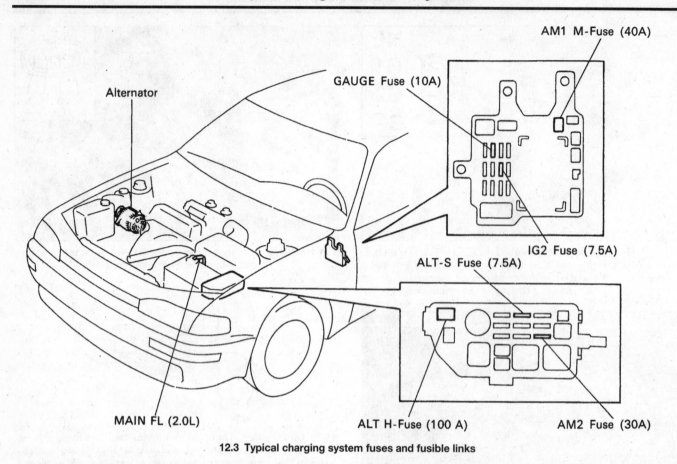

12.3 Typical charging system fuses and fusible links

---

supplies electrical power for the ignition system, the lights, the radio, etc. The alternator is driven by a drivebelt at the front of the engine.

The purpose of the voltage regulator is to limit the alternator's voltage to a preset value. This prevents power surges, circuit overloads, etc., during peak voltage output.

The fusible link is a short length of insulated wire integral with the engine compartment wiring harness **(see illustration)**. The link is several wire gauges smaller in diameter than the circuit it protects. Production fusible links and their identification flags are identified by the flag color. See Chapter 12 for additional information regarding fusible links.

The charging system doesn't ordinarily require periodic mainte- nance. However, the drivebelt, battery and wires and connections should be inspected at the intervals outlined in Chapter 1.

The dashboard warning light should come on when the ignition key is turned to Start, then should go off immediately. If it remains on, there is a malfunction in the charging system. Some vehicles are also equipped with a voltage gauge. If the voltage gauge indicates abnor- mally high or low voltage, check the charging system (see Section 13).

Be very careful when making electrical circuit connections to a vehicle equipped with an alternator and note the following:

a) *When reconnecting wires to the alternator from the battery, be sure to note the polarity.*

b) *Before using arc welding equipment to repair any part of the vehicle, disconnect the wires from the alternator and the battery terminals.*

c) *Never start the engine with a battery charger connected.*

d) *Always disconnect both battery leads before using a battery charger.*

e) *The alternator is driven by an engine drivebelt which could cause serious injury if your hand, hair or clothes become entangled in it with the engine running.*

f) *Because the alternator is connected directly to the battery, it could arc or cause a fire if overloaded or shorted out.*

g) *Wrap a plastic bag over the alternator and secure it with rubber bands before steam cleaning the engine.*

13 Charging system - check

Refer to illustrations 13.7 and 13.8

1   If a malfunction occurs in the charging circuit, don't automatically assume that the alternator is causing the problem. First check the following items:

a) *Check the drivebelt tension and its condition. Replace it if worn or deteriorated.*

b) *Make sure the alternator mounting and adjustment bolts are tight.*

c) *Inspect the alternator wiring harness and the electrical connectors at the alternator and voltage regulator. They must be in good condition and tight.*

d) *Check the fusible link (if equipped) located between the starter solenoid and the alternator or the large main fuses in the engine compartment. If it's burned, determine the cause, repair the circuit and replace the link or fuse (the vehicle won't start and/or the accessories won't work if the fusible link or fuse blows).*

e) *Check all the fuses that are in series with the charging system circuit* **(see illustration 12.3)**. *The location of these fuses and fusible links may vary from year and model but the designations are the same; main fusible link 2.0L, Alt H fuse (100 amp), AM1 (40 amp), AM2 (30 amp), IG2 (7.5 amp), Gauge 10A, and ALT (7.5 amp).*

f) *Start the engine and check the alternator for abnormal noises (a shrieking or squealing sound indicates a bad bushing).*

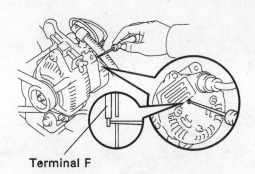

Terminal F

13.7 If the alternator is putting out less than standard voltage, ground terminal F, start the engine and check the voltage at the battery - if the reading is greater than standard voltage, replace the regulator; if the reading is less than standard, check the alternator or have it checked by a dealer

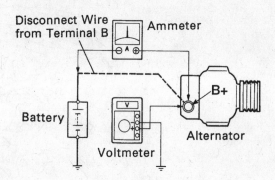

13.8 Hook up an ammeter as shown to check alternator output

a) *If the voltmeter reading is greater than standard voltage, replace the regulator.*

b) *If the voltmeter reading is less than standard voltage, check the alternator (or have it checked by a dealer service department if you do not have an ammeter).*

8   If you have an ammeter, hook it up to the charging system as shown **(see illustration)**. If you don't have a professional ammeter, you can also use an inductive-type current indicator. This device is inexpensive, readily available at auto parts stores and accurate enough to perform simple amperage checks like the following test.

9   With the engine running at 2,000 rpm, check the reading on the ammeter with all accessories and lights off, then again with the high-beam headlights on and the heater blower switch turned to the HI position. Compare your readings to the standard amperage listed in this Chapter's Specifications.

10   If the ammeter reading is less than standard amperage, repair or replace the alternator.

14   Alternator - removal and installation

Refer to illustrations 14.3, 14.8a and 14.8b

1   Detach the cable from the negative terminal of the battery. **Caution:** *If the stereo in your vehicle is equipped with an anti-theft system, make sure you have the correct activation code before disconnecting the battery.* **Note:** *On 1993 and later models, the airbag system will be disabled if the battery is disconnected for more than a brief period. If the airbag light comes on and stays on after the battery is reconnected, the vehicle must be taken to a dealer service department to have the system reset with a special tool.*

2   Detach the electrical connectors from the alternator.

3   Loosen the alternator adjustment and pivot bolts **(see illustration)** and detach the drivebelt.

4   Remove the adjustment and pivot bolts from the alternator adjustment bracket.

5   Remove the two bracket-to-water pump bolts and separate the alternator and bracket from the engine.

6   If you are replacing the alternator, take the old alternator with you when purchasing a replacement unit. Make sure that the new/rebuilt unit is identical to the old alternator. Look at the terminals - they should be the same in number, size and locations as the terminals on the old alternator. Finally, look at the identification markings - they will be stamped in the housing or printed on a tag or plaque affixed to the housing. Make sure that these numbers are the same on both alternators.

7   Many new/rebuilt alternators do not have a pulley installed, so you may have to switch the pulley from the old unit to the new/rebuilt one. When buying an alternator, find out the shop's policy regarding installation of pulleys - some shops will perform this service free of charge.

5

14.3 First loosen pivot bolt (A) and then turn the adjustment bolt (B) counterclockwise to release the tension on the drivebelt

g) *Check the specific gravity of the battery electrolyte. If it's low, charge the battery (doesn't apply to maintenance free batteries).*

h) *Make sure that the battery is fully charged (one bad cell in a battery can cause overcharging by the alternator).*

i) *Disconnect the battery cables (negative first, then positive).* **Caution:** *If the stereo in your vehicle is equipped with an anti-theft system, make sure you have the correct activation code before disconnecting the battery. Inspect the battery posts and the cable clamps for corrosion. Clean them thoroughly if necessary (see Section 4 and Chapter 1). Reconnect the positive cable, then the negative cable.*

2   Using a voltmeter, check the battery voltage with the engine off. It should be approximately 12 volts.

3   Start the engine and check the battery voltage again. It should now be approximately 13.5 to 15.1 volts.

4   Turn on the headlights. The voltage should drop and then come back up, if the charging system is working properly.

5   If the voltage reading is greater than the specified charging voltage, replace the voltage regulator (see Section 15).

6   If the voltmeter reading is less than standard voltage, check the regulator and alternator as follows.

7   Remove the rear cover from the alternator. Ground terminal F **(see illustration)**, start the engine, check the voltage at the battery and compare your reading to the standard voltage.

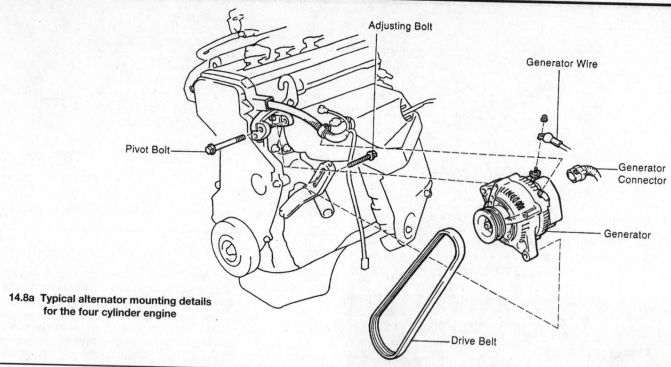

14.8a Typical alternator mounting details for the four cylinder engine

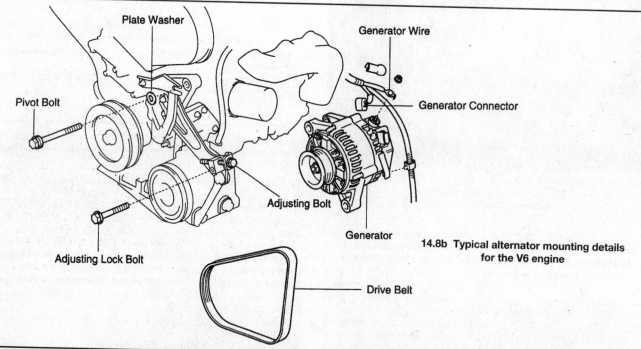

14.8b Typical alternator mounting details for the V6 engine

8   Installation is the reverse of removal **(see illustrations)**.

9   After the alternator is installed, adjust the drivebelt tension (see Chapter 1).

10   Check the charging voltage to verify proper operation of the alternator (see Section 13).

15   Alternator components - check and replacement

Disassembly

Refer to illustrations 15.2a, 15.2b, 15.2c, 15.3, 15.4a, 15.4b, 15.5 and 15.7

1   Remove the alternator (see Section 14) and place it on a clean workbench.

2   Remove the rear cover nuts, the nut and terminal insulator and the rear cover **(see illustrations)**.

3   Remove the five voltage regulator and brush holder mounting screws **(see illustration)**.

4   Remove the brush holder and the regulator from the rear end frame **(see illustrations)**. If you are only replacing the regulator, proceed to Step 8, install the new unit, reassemble the alternator and install it on the engine (see Section 14). If you are going to replace the brushes, proceed with the next Step.

5   Measure the exposed length of each brush **(see illustration)** and compare it to the minimum length listed in this Chapter's Specifications. If the length of either brush is less than the specified minimum, replace the brushes and brush holder assembly. **Note:** *On some models, it may be necessary to solder the new brushes in place.*

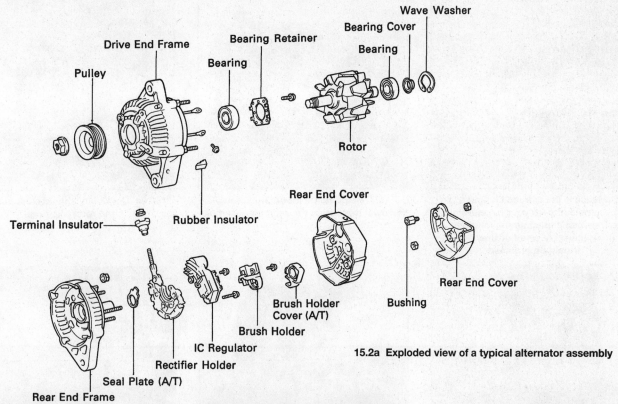

15.2a Exploded view of a typical alternator assembly

15.2b Remove the three nuts from the rear cover

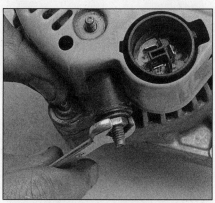

15.2c Take the nut, washer and insulator off terminal B and remove the alternator end cover

15.3 Once the rear cover is removed, remove the five screws (arrows) that retain the voltage regulator and the brush holder

15.4a Remove the brush holder

15.4b Remove the regulator

15.5 Measure the exposed length of the brushes and compare your measurements to the specified minimum length to determine whether they should be replaced

15.7 Remove the mounting screws (arrows) that retain the rectifier assembly

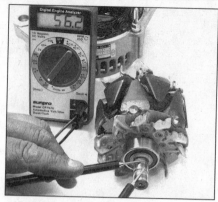

15.12a Continuity should exist between the rotor slip rings

15.12b Check the continuity between the rotor and the slip rings. There should be NO continuity

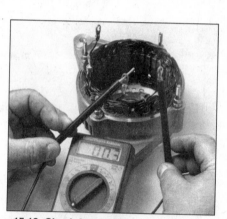

15.13 Check for continuity between the stator windings

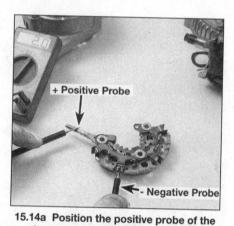

15.14a Position the positive probe of the ohmmeter onto the diode assembly positive post and the negative probe to ground. Continuity should exist

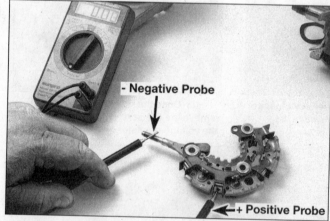

15.14b Switch the polarity of the ohmmeter probes and observe that now there is NO continuity within the diodes. Check each diode (four total) individually

6   Make sure that each brush moves smoothly in the brush holder.

7   Remove the rectifier assembly **(see illustration)**. Remove the four rubber insulators and the seal plate.

8   Scribe or paint marks on the front and rear end frame housings of the alternator to facilitate reassembly.

9   Remove the nut retaining the pulley to the rotor shaft and remove the pulley.

10   Remove the four nuts retaining the front and rear end frames

together, then separate the rear end frame assembly from the front end frame **(see illustration 15.2a)**.

11   Remove the thrust washer and remove the rotor from the front end frame.

Component checks

Refer to illustrations 15.12a, 15.12b, 15.13, 15.14a and 15.14b

12   Check for an open between the two slip rings **(see illustration)**. There should be 2 to 4 ohms resistance between the slip rings. Check for grounds between each slip ring and the rotor **(see illustration)**. There should be no continuity (infinite resistance) between the rotor and either slip ring. If the rotor fails either test, or if the slip rings are excessively worn, the rotor is defective.

13   Check for opens between each end terminal of the stator windings **(see illustration)**. If either reading is high (infinite resistance), the stator is defective. Check for a grounded stator winding between each stator terminal and the frame. If there's continuity between any stator winding and the frame the stator is defective.

14   Start the checks on the diode assembly by touching the positive probe of the ohmmeter onto the diode terminal and the negative probe onto one of the other designated diode terminals **(see illustration)**. Then reverse the probes and check again **(see illustration)**. The diode should have continuity with the ohmmeter one way and no continuity when the probes are reversed. Check each of the terminals in this manner. If any of the diodes fail the test, the diode assembly is defective.

Reassembly

Refer to illustration 15.16

15   Install the components in the reverse order of removal, noting the

following:

16   Install the brush holder by depressing each brush with a small screwdriver to clear the shaft **(see illustration)**.

17   Install the voltage regulator and brush holder screws into the rear frame.

18   Install the rear cover and tighten the three nuts securely.

19   Install the terminal insulator and tighten it with the nut.

20   Install the alternator (see Section 14).

16   Starting system - general information and precautions

Refer to illustration 16.2

The sole function of the starting system is to turn over the engine quickly enough to allow it to start.

The starting system consists of the battery, the starter motor, the starter solenoid and the electrical circuit connecting the components. The solenoid is mounted directly on the starter motor **(see illustration)**.

15.16 To facilitate installation of the brush holder, depress each brush with a small screwdriver to clear the shaft

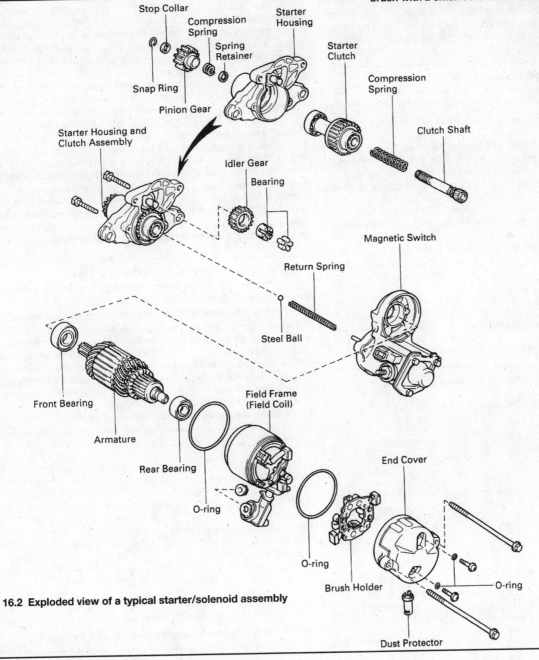

16.2 Exploded view of a typical starter/solenoid assembly

5

The solenoid/starter motor assembly is installed on the upper part of the engine, next to the transaxle bellhousing.

When the ignition key is turned to the START position, the starter solenoid is actuated through the starter control circuit. The starter solenoid then connects the battery to the starter. The battery supplies the electrical energy to the starter motor, which does the actual work of cranking the engine.

The starter motor on a vehicle equipped with a manual transaxle can be operated only when the clutch pedal is depressed; the starter on a vehicle equipped with an automatic transaxle can be operated only when the transaxle selector lever is in Park or Neutral.

Always observe the following precautions when working on the starting system:

a) *Excessive cranking of the starter motor can overheat it and cause serious damage. Never operate the starter motor for more than 15 seconds at a time without pausing to allow it to cool for at least two minutes.*

b) *The starter is connected directly to the battery and could arc or cause a fire if mishandled, overloaded or short circuited.*

c) *Always detach the cable from the negative terminal of the battery before working on the starting system.* **Caution:** *If the stereo in your vehicle is equipped with an anti-theft system, make sure you have the correct activation code before disconnecting the battery.*

17   Starter motor - testing in vehicle

Refer to illustration 17.5

Note: *Before diagnosing starter problems, make sure that the battery is fully charged.*

1   If the starter motor does not turn at all when the switch is operated, make sure that the shift lever is in Neutral or Park (automatic transaxle) or that the clutch pedal is depressed (manual transaxle).

2   Make sure that the battery is charged and that all cables, both at the battery and starter solenoid terminals, are clean and secure.

3   If the starter motor spins but the engine is not cranking, the overrunning clutch in the starter motor is slipping and the starter motor must be replaced.

4   If, when the switch is actuated, the starter motor does not operate at all but the solenoid clicks, then the problem lies with either the battery, the main solenoid contacts or the starter motor itself (or the engine is seized).

5   If the solenoid plunger cannot be heard when the switch is actuated, the battery is bad, the fusible link is burned (the circuit is open), the starter relay **(see illustration)** is defective or the starter solenoid itself is defective.

6   To check the solenoid, connect a jumper lead between the

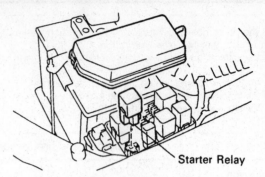

17.5 Check the starter relay for electrical opens or shorts

battery (+) and the ignition switch terminal (the small terminal) on the solenoid. If the starter motor now operates, the solenoid is OK and the problem is in the ignition switch, Neutral start switch or in the wiring.

7   If the starter motor still does not operate, remove the starter/solenoid assembly for disassembly, testing and repair.

8   If the starter motor cranks the engine at an abnormally slow speed, first make sure that the battery is charged and that all terminal connections are tight. If the engine is partially seized, or has the wrong viscosity oil in it, it will crank slowly.

9   Run the engine until normal operating temperature is reached, then disconnect the coil wire from the distributor cap and ground it on the engine.

10   Connect a voltmeter positive lead to the battery positive post and connect the negative lead to the negative post.

11   Crank the engine and take the voltmeter readings as soon as a steady figure is indicated. Do not allow the starter motor to turn for more than 15 seconds at a time. A reading of nine volts or more, with the starter motor turning at normal cranking speed, is normal. If the reading is nine volts or more but the cranking speed is slow, the motor is faulty. If the reading is less than nine volts and the cranking speed is slow, the solenoid contacts are probably burned, the starter motor is bad, the battery is discharged or there is a bad connection.

18   Starter motor - removal and installation

Refer to illustrations 18.5a and 18.5b

1   Detach the cable from the negative terminal of the battery. **Caution:** *If the stereo in your vehicle is equipped with an anti-theft system, make sure you have the correct activation code before disconnecting the battery.* **Note:** *On 1993 and later models, the airbag system will be disabled if the battery is disconnected for more than a brief period. If the airbag light comes on and stays on after the battery is reconnected, the vehicle must be taken to a dealer service department to have the system reset with a special tool.*

2   Remove the battery from the engine compartment.

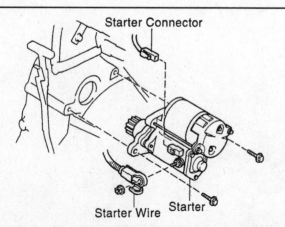

18.5a To remove the starter motor/solenoid assembly, detach the cable from the negative terminal of the battery, disconnect the electrical connectors and remove the mounting bolts (four cylinder engine shown)

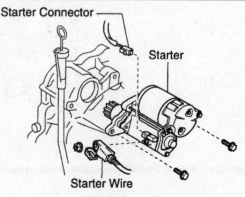

18.5b Starter/solenoid assembly on a V6 engine

19.2 Before disassembling the starter motor, solenoid and gear reduction assembly, scribe or paint an alignment mark across the starter motor and the gear reduction assembly

3   Disconnect and remove the cruise control assembly from the engine compartment (see Chapter 12).
4   Detach the electrical connectors from the starter/solenoid assembly.

5   Remove the starter motor mounting bolts **(see illustrations)**.
6   Remove the bracket from the upper section of the starter/solenoid assembly. **Note:** *It is necessary to loosen one or two of the bracket bolts to allow the starter/solenoid assembly to partially drop down to gain access to the remaining bracket assembly bolts and hardware.*
7   Installation is the reverse of removal.

19   Starter solenoid - removal and installation

Refer to illustrations 19.2, 19.3, 19.4, 19.5, 19.6a and 19.6b
1   Remove the starter motor (see Section 18).
2   Scribe or paint a mark across the starter motor and gear reduction assembly **(see illustration)**.
3   Disconnect the strap from the solenoid to the starter motor terminal **(see illustration)**.
4   Remove the screws **(see illustration)** which secure the gear reduction assembly to the solenoid.
5   Remove the through-bolts **(see illustration)** which secure the starter motor to the gear reduction assembly.
6   Separate the motor from the gear reduction and solenoid assembly then remove the solenoid from the gear reduction assembly **(see illustrations)**.
7   Installation is the reverse of removal. Be sure to align the paint or scribe mark.

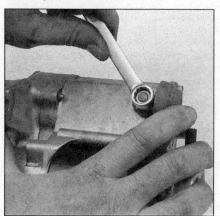

19.3 To disconnect the strap that connects the starter to the solenoid, remove this nut

19.4 To detach the solenoid from the starter motor, remove the screws (arrows) which secure the gear reduction assembly to the solenoid . . .

19.5 . . . then remove the through-bolts (arrows) which secure the starter motor to the gear reduction assembly

5

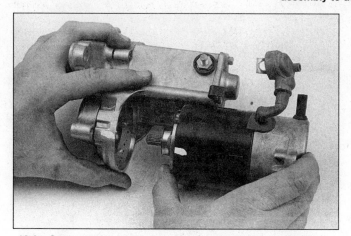

19.6a Separate the starter from the gear reduction assembly . . .

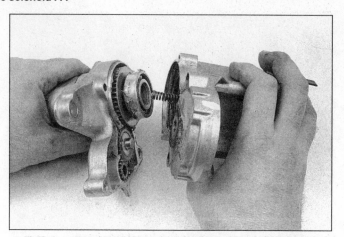

19.6b . . . then separate the solenoid from the gear reduction assembly (note the return spring protruding from the solenoid assembly - make sure that this spring is installed before reassembling the solenoid and the gear reduction assembly)

Notes

Chapter 6
Emissions and engine control systems

Contents

Specifications

EGR gas temperature sensor resistance

112 degrees F	69 to 89 K-ohms
212 degrees F	11 to 15 K-ohms
302 degrees F	2 to 4 K-ohms

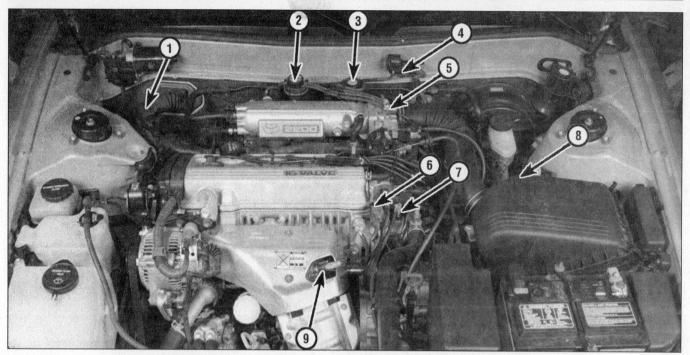

1.1a Emission and engine control components on the four-cylinder engine

1	Diagnostic test connector	4	MAP sensor	7	Distributor
2	EGR vacuum modulator	5	TPS (behind throttle body)	8	Igniter (behind air cleaner housing)
3	EGR valve	6	Coolant temperature sensor	9	Oxygen sensor

1.1b Emission and engine control components on the V6 engine

1	Intake air control valve	5	TPS (behind throttle body)	8	Camshaft position sensor
2	Diagnostic test connector	6	Igniter	9	Oxygen sensor
3	EGR vacuum modulator	7	MAF sensor	10	DIS coil (located under V-Bank cover)
4	EGR valve				

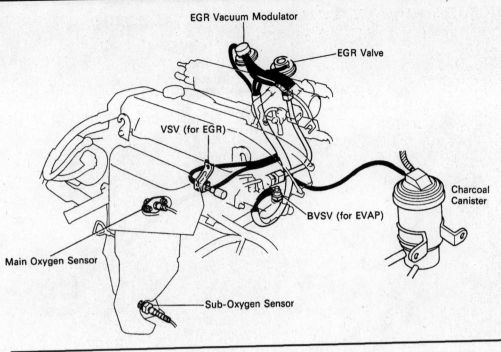

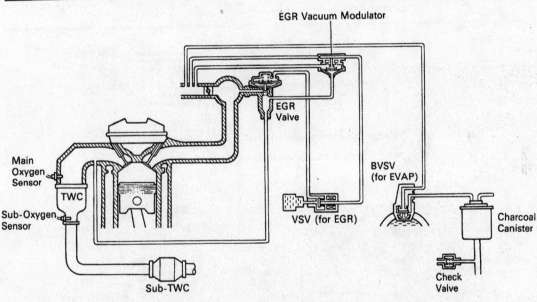

1.4a Typical vacuum hose routing diagram - four-cylinder engine

1 General information

Refer to illustrations 1.1a, 1.1b, 1.4a, 1.4b, 1.4c, 1.6a and 1.6b

To minimize pollution of the atmosphere from incompletely burned and evaporating gases and to maintain good driveability and fuel economy, a number of emission control systems are used on these vehicles **(see illustrations)**. They include the:

Positive Crankcase Ventilation (PCV) system
Evaporative Emission Control (EVAP) system
Exhaust Gas Recirculation (EGR) system
Three-way catalytic converter (TWC) system
Electronic Fuel Injection (EFI) system
Intake air induction system (V6 engines only)

The sections in this chapter include general descriptions, checking procedures within the scope of the home mechanic and component replacement procedures (when possible) for each of the systems listed above.

Before assuming an emissions control system is malfunctioning, check the fuel and ignition systems carefully (see Chapters 4 and 5). The diagnosis of some emission control devices requires specialized tools, equipment and training. If checking and servicing become too difficult or if a procedure is beyond the scope of your skills, consult your dealer service department or other repair shop.

This doesn't mean, however, that emission control systems are particularly difficult to maintain and repair. You can quickly and easily perform many checks and do most of the regular maintenance at home with common tune-up and hand tools. **Note**: *The most frequent cause of emissions problems is simply a loose or broken electrical connector or vacuum hose, so always check the electrical connectors and vacuum hoses first* **(see illustration)**.

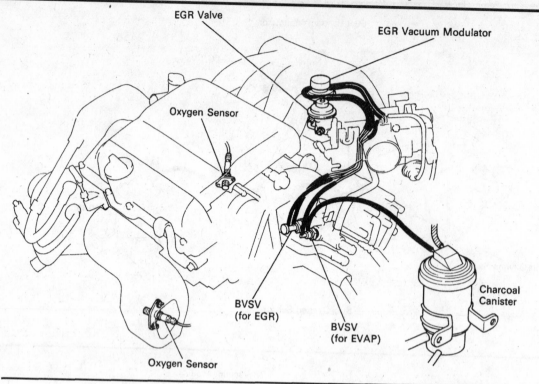

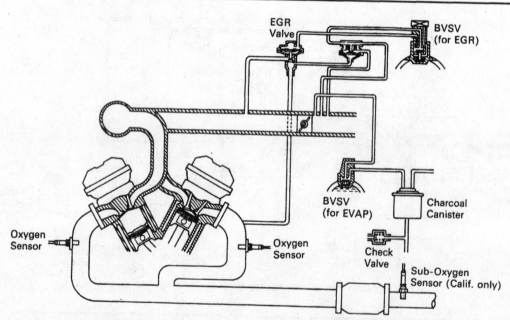

1.4b Typical vacuum hose routing diagram - 3VZ-FE V6 engine

Pay close attention to any special precautions outlined in this chapter. It should be noted that the illustrations of the various systems may not exactly match the system installed on your vehicle because of changes made by the manufacturer during production or from year-to-year.

The Vehicle Emissions Control Information (VECI) label and a vacuum hose diagram are located on the hood **(see illustrations)**. These contain important emissions specifications and setting procedures, and a vacuum hose schematic with emissions components identified. When servicing the engine or emissions systems, the VECI label in your particular vehicle should always be checked for up-to-date information.

2   Electronic control system and ECM - removal and installation

TCCS general information

1   The Toyota Computer Control System (TCCS) controls the fuel injection system by means of a microcomputer known as the Electronic Control Module (ECM).

2   The ECM receives signals from various sensors which monitor changing engine operating conditions such as intake air volume, intake air temperature, coolant temperature, engine rpm, acceleration/deceleration, exhaust oxygen content, etc. These signals are utilized by the

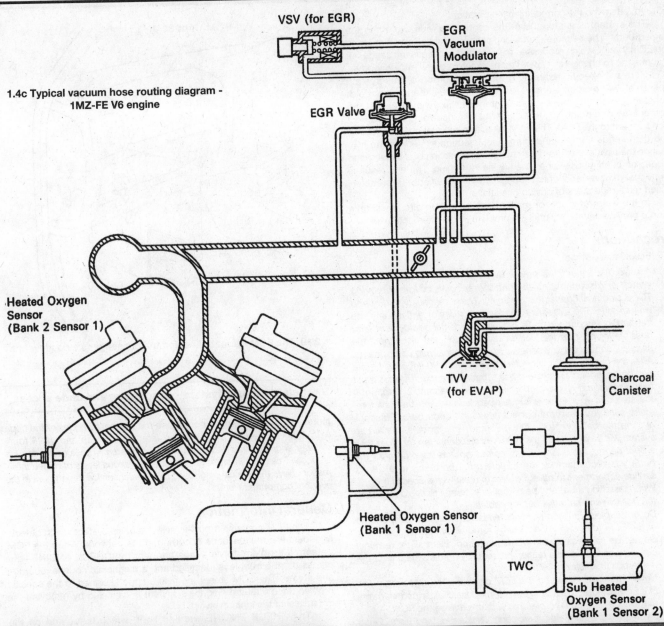

1.4c Typical vacuum hose routing diagram - 1MZ-FE V6 engine

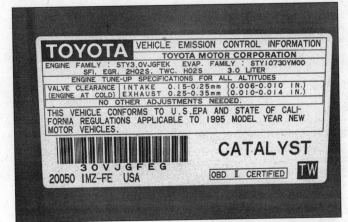

1.6a The Vehicle Emissions Control Information (VECI) label contains such essential information as the types of emission control systems installed on the engine and the idle speed and ignition timing specifications

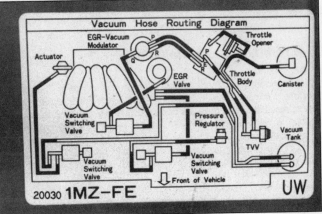

1.6b This is the other section of the VECI label that contains the vacuum hose routing

6

ECM to determine the correct injection duration.

3   The system is analogous to the central nervous system in the human body: The sensors (nerve endings) constantly relay signals to the ECM (brain), which processes the data and, if necessary, sends out a command to change the operating parameters of the engine (body).

4   Here's a specific example of how one portion of this system operates: An oxygen sensor, located in the exhaust manifold, constantly monitors the oxygen content of the exhaust gas. If the percentage of oxygen in the exhaust gas is incorrect, an electrical signal is sent to the ECM. The ECM takes this information, processes it and then sends a command to the fuel injection system telling it to change the air/fuel mixture. This happens in a fraction of a second and it goes on continuously when the engine is running. The end result is an air/fuel mixture ratio which is constantly maintained at a predetermined ratio, regardless of driving conditions.

5   In the event of a sensor malfunction, a backup circuit will take over to provide driveability until the problem is identified and fixed.

Precautions

6   Follow these steps:

a) *Always disconnect the power by either turning off the ignition switch or disconnecting the battery terminals before removing TCCS electrical connectors. Warning: These models are equipped with airbags. The airbag is armed and can deploy (inflate) anytime the battery is connected. To prevent accidental deployment (and possible injury), turn the ignition key to LOCK and disconnect the negative battery cable whenever working near airbag components. After the battery is disconnected, wait at least 90 seconds before beginning work. This system has a back-up capacitor that must fully discharge. For more information, see Chapter 12. Caution: If the stereo in your vehicle is equipped with an anti-theft system, make sure you have the correct activation code before disconnecting the battery. Note: On 1993 and later models, the airbag system will be disabled if the battery is disconnected for more than a brief period. If the airbag light comes on and stays on after the battery is reconnected, the vehicle must be taken to a dealer service department to have the system reset with a special tool.*

b) *When installing a battery, be particularly careful to avoid reversing the positive and negative battery cables.*

c) *Do not subject EFI components, emissions-related components or the ECM to severe impact during removal or installation.*

d) *Do not be careless during troubleshooting. Even slight terminal contact can invalidate a testing procedure and damage one of the numerous transistor circuits.*

e) *Never attempt to work on the ECM or open the ECM cover. The ECM is protected by a government-mandated extended warranty that will be nullified if you tamper with or damage the ECM.*

f) *If you are inspecting electronic control system components during rainy weather, make sure that water does not enter any part. When washing the engine compartment, do not spray these parts or their electrical connectors with water.*

ECM removal and installation

Refer to illustration 2.10

7   Disconnect the negative cable from the battery (see Chapter 5). **Caution:** *If the stereo in your vehicle is equipped with an anti-theft system, make sure you have the correct activation code before disconnecting the battery.* **Note:** *On 1993 and later models, the airbag system will be disabled if the battery is disconnected for more than a brief period. If the airbag light comes on and stays on after the battery is reconnected, the vehicle must be taken to a dealer service department to have the system reset with a special tool.*

8   Remove the lower instrument panel on the passenger side under the glove compartment (see Chapter 11).

9   Remove the glove compartment from the passenger compartment (see Chapter 11).

10   Remove the bolts from the ECM brackets **(see illustration).**

11   Lift the ECM from the vehicle.

12   Installation is the reverse of removal.

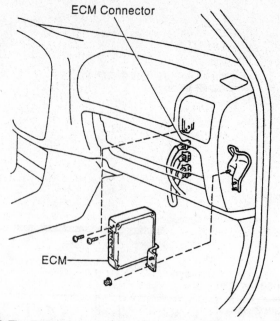

2.10 The ECM is located behind the passenger's side glovebox

---

3   Self Diagnosis system - description and code access

Note: *This procedure does not include the diagnostic codes or the code extracting procedure for 1994 and later V6 engines and 1996 four-cylinder engines equipped with the OBD II system. These codes require a special Scan tool in order to read out the various levels of coded information. Have the vehicle diagnosed by a dealer service department in the event of computer failure.*

General information

The ECM contains a built-in self-diagnosis system which detects and identifies malfunctions occurring in the network. When the ECM detects a problem, three things happen: the CHECK ENGINE light comes on, the trouble is identified and a diagnostic code is recorded and stored. The ECM stores the failure code assigned to the specific problem area until the diagnosis system is canceled by removing the EFI fuse with the ignition switch off.

The CHECK ENGINE warning light, which is located on the instrument panel, comes on when the ignition switch is turned to ON and the engine is not running. When the engine is started, the warning light should go out. If the light remains on, the self diagnosis system has detected a malfunction in the system.

Obtaining diagnostic code output

Refer to illustration 3.3

1   To obtain an output of diagnostic codes, verify first that the battery voltage is above 11 volts, the throttle is fully closed, the transaxle is in Neutral, the accessory switches are off and the engine is at normal operating temperature.

2   Turn the ignition switch to ON (engine not running). Do not start the engine.

3   Use a jumper wire to bridge terminals TE1 and E1 of the service electrical connector **(see illustration). Note:** *The self diagnosis system can be accessed by using either test terminal number 1 (engine compartment) or test terminal number 2 (under driver's dash).*

4   Read the diagnosis code as indicated by the number of flashes of the "CHECK ENGINE" light on the dash. Normal system operation is indicated by Code No. 1 (no malfunctions) for all models. The "CHECK ENGINE" light displays a Code No. 1 by blinking once every 0.25 seconds. Each code will be displayed by first blinking the first digit of

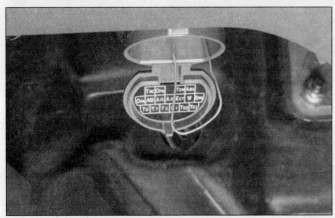

3.3 To access the self diagnosis system, locate the test terminal under the driver's dash and using a jumper wire or paper clip, bridge terminals TE1 and E1

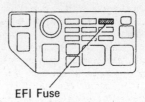

EFI Fuse

3.7 Typical location of the 15A EFI fuse

the code, then pause, and blink the second digit of the code. For example; Code 24 (IAT sensor) will flash two times, pause, and then flash four times. Each flash will be the exact same length but the distinction will be the pause that separates the digits of the code. Only code 1 (normal operation) will flash continuously without a pause.

5   If there are any malfunctions in the system, their corresponding trouble codes are stored in computer memory and the light will blink the requisite number of times for the indicated trouble codes. If there's more than one trouble code in the memory, they'll be displayed in numerical order (from lowest to highest) with a pause interval between each one. After the code with the largest number of flashes has been displayed, there will be another pause and then the sequence will begin all over again. **Note**: *The diagnostic trouble codes 25, 26, 27 and 71 use a special diagnostic capability called "two-trip detection logic". With this system, when a malfunction is first detected, it is temporarily stored into the ECM on the first test drive or "trip". The engine must be turned off and the vehicle taken on another test drive "trip" to allow the malfunction to be stored permanently in the ECM. This will distinguish a true problem from a false alarm on vehicles with these particular*

codes entered into the ECM. Normally the self-diagnosis system will detect the malfunctions, but in the event the home mechanic wants to double-check the diagnosis by canceling the codes and rechecking, then it will be necessary to go on two test drives to confirm any malfunctions with these particular codes.

6   To ensure correct interpretation of the flashing "CHECK ENGINE" light, watch carefully for the interval between the end of one code and the beginning of the next; otherwise, you will become confused by the apparent number of flashes and misinterpret the display (the length of this interval varies with the model year).

Canceling a diagnostic code

Refer to illustration 3.7

7   After the malfunctioning component has been repaired/replaced, the trouble code(s) stored in computer memory must be canceled. To accomplish this, simply remove the 15A EFI fuse **(see illustration)** for at least 10 seconds with the ignition switch off.

8   A stored code can also be canceled by removing the cable from the battery negative terminal, but other memory systems (such as the clock and radio presets) will also be canceled. **Caution**: *If the stereo in your vehicle is equipped with an anti-theft system, make sure you have the correct activation code before disconnecting the battery.*

9   If the diagnosis code is not canceled, it will be stored by the ECM and appear with any new codes in the event of future trouble.

10   Should it become necessary to work on engine components requiring removal of the battery terminal, always check to see if a diagnostic code has been recorded before disconnecting the battery.

6

Code	Circuit or system	Diagnosis	Trouble area
Code 1 1 flash, pause, 1 flash	Normal	This appears when none of the other codes are identified	
Code 12 1 flash, pause, 2 flashes	RPM signal	*No "Ne" signal to the ECM within several seconds after the engine is cranked. *No "G" signal to the ECM two times in succession when engine speed is between 500 rpm and 4,000 rpm	* Distributor circuit * Distributor * Igniter * Igniter circuit * Starter circuit * ECM
Code 13 1 flash, pause, 3 flashes	RPM signal	No "Ne" signal to the ECM engine speed is above 1,500 rpm	* Distributor circuit * Distributor * Igniter circuit * Igniter * ECM
Code 14 1 flash, pause, 4 flashes	Ignition signal	No "IGF" signal to the ECM 8 times in succession	* Igniter circuit * Igniter * ECM
Code 16 1 flash, pause, 6 flashes	A/T control signal	Problem between the engine CPU and A/T CPU in the ECM	* ECM
Code 21 2 flashes, pause, 1 flash	Main oxygen sensor	Problem in the main oxygen sensor circuit	* Main oxygen sensor circuit * ECM
	Main oxygen sensor heater	Open or short in circuit of main oxygen sensor heater circuit	* Main oxygen sensor heater

Code	Circuit or system	Diagnosis	Trouble area
Code 22 2 flashes, pause, 2 flashes	Coolant temperature	Open or short in the coolant sensor temperature sensor circuit	* Coolant temperature sensor circuit * Coolant temperature sensor * ECM
Code 24 2 flashes, pause, 4 flashes	Intake air temperature sensor	Open or short in the intake air sensor circuit	* Intake air temperature sensor * Intake air temperature sensor circuit * ECM
Code 25 2 flashes, pause, 5 flashes	Air/fuel ratio lean malfunction	The air/fuel ratio feedback correction value or adaptive control value continues at the upper (lean) or lower (rich) limit for a certain period of time	* Injector or injector circuit * Oxygen sensor or circuit * ECM * Fuel line pressure (injector blockage or leakage) * Coolant temperature sensor or circuit * Air temperature sensor or circuit * Air leak * Airflow meter * Air intake system * Ignition system
Code 26 2 flashes, pause, 6 flashes	Air/fuel ratio rich malfunction	The air/fuel ratio is overly rich Open or short circuit in the oxygen sensor	* Injector or injector circuit * Coolant temperature sensor or circuit * Air temperature sensor or circuit * Airflow meter * Oxygen sensor or circuit * Cold start injector * ECM
Code 27 2 flashes, pause, 7 flashes	Sub-oxygen sensor	Open or shorted circuit in the sub-oxygen sensor circuit	* Sub-oxygen sensor or circuit * ECM
Code 31 3 flashes, pause, 1 flash	Airflow meter	Open or short circuit in Vc to E2	* Airflow meter or circuit (V6 engine)
Code 31 3 flashes, pause, 1 flash	MAP sensor	Open or short in MAP sensor circuit	* MAP sensor circuit
Code 32 3 flashes, pause, 2 flashes	Airflow meter (V6 engine)	Open or short circuit in Vs to Vc or E2	* Airflow meter or circuit * ECM
Code 41 4 flashes, pause, 1 flash	Throttle position sensor	Open or short in the throttle position sensor circuit	* Throttle position sensor or circuit * ECM
Code 42 4 flashes, pause, 2 flashes	Vehicle speed sensor	No "SPD" signal for 8 seconds when the engine speed is between 3,100 and 5,000 rpm	* Vehicle speed sensor or circuit * ECM
Code 43 4 flashes, pause, 3 flashes	Starter signal	No "STA" signal to the ECM until engine speed reaches 800 rpm with the vehicle not moving	* Starter signal circuit * Ignition switch * Main relay switch * ECM
Code 51 5 flashes, pause, 1 flashes	Switch condition signal	No IDL signal or no NSW signal or A/C signal to the ECM when the test connector E1 and TE1 are connected	* A/C switch or circuit * A/C amplifier * Neutral Start switch (A/T) * Throttle Position sensor * ECM
Code 52 5 flashes, pause 2 flashes	Knock sensor signal	Open or short circuit in knock sensor circuit	* Knock sensor circuit * ECM
Code 53 5 flashes, pause 3 flashes	Knock control signal	Problem with knock control system in ECM	* ECM
Code 55 5 flashes, pause 5 flashes	Knock control signal (V6 engine RH bank)	Problem with knock control system in ECM	* ECM
Code 71 7 flashes, pause, 1 flash	EGR	EGR gas temperature signal is too low	* EGR system (EGR valve, hoses, etc.) * EGR gas temperature sensor or circuit * Vacuum switching valve for the EGR circuit * ECM

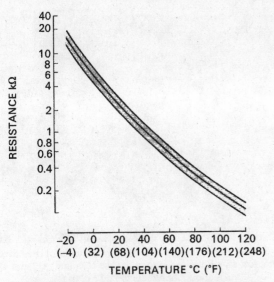

4.1 Compare the indicated resistance values specified on this graph - note that as the temperature increases (as the engine warms up) the resistance decreases

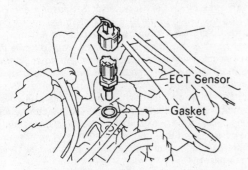

4.2b Coolant temperature sensor location on the four-cylinder engine

4.2a To check the coolant temperature sensor, use an ohmmeter to measure the resistance between the two sensor terminals

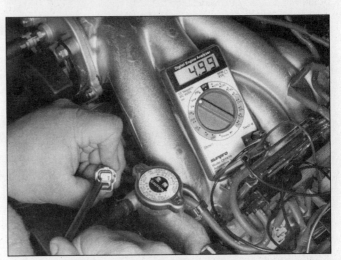

4.3 Use a voltmeter and probe the coolant temp sensor harness connector terminal for reference voltage with the ignition key ON (engine not running). It should be approximately 5.0 volts

4   Information sensors

Note 1: *Most of the components described in this section are protected by a Federally-mandated extended warranty. See your dealer for the details regarding your vehicle.*
Note 2: *Refer to Chapters 4 and 5 for additional information on the location and the diagnostic procedures for the information sensors that are not directly covered in this section.*

Coolant temperature sensor

General description

Refer to illustration 4.1

1   The coolant temperature sensor is a thermistor (a resistor which varies the value of its voltage output in accordance with temperature changes). As the sensor temperature DECREASES, the resistance values will INCREASE. As the sensor temperature INCREASES, the resistance values will DECREASE **(see illustration)**. A failure in this sensor circuit should set a Code 22. This code indicates a failure in the coolant temperature sensor circuit, so in most cases the appropriate solution to the problem will be either repair of a connector or wire, or replacement of the sensor.

Check

Refer to illustrations 4.2a, 4.2b and 4.3

2   To check the sensor, measure its resistance value **(see illustrations)** while it is completely cold (50 to 80 degrees F = 2,200 to 2,700 ohms). Next, start the engine and warm it up until it reaches operating temperature. The resistance should be lower (180 to 200 degrees F = 280 to 350 ohms). **Note**: *Limited access to the coolant temperature sensor makes it difficult to position electrical probes on the terminals. If necessary, remove the sensor and perform the tests in a pan of heated water to simulate the conditions. Compare the resistance values with the accompanying graph.*

3   If the resistance values of the coolant temperature sensor are correct, check the circuit for the proper signal voltage. Turn the ignition key ON (engine not running) and check for reference voltage **(see illustration)**. It should be approximately 5 volts.

Replacement

4   To remove the sensor, depress the locking tabs, unplug the electrical connector, then carefully unscrew the sensor. **Caution**: *Handle the coolant sensor with care. Damage to this sensor will affect the operation of the entire fuel injection system.*
5   Before installing the new sensor, wrap the threads with Teflon sealing tape to prevent leakage and thread corrosion.
6   Installation is the reverse of removal.

Oxygen sensor

General description

7   These models are equipped with either a single oxygen sensor system or a dual-stage oxygen sensor system. On dual-stage systems,

6

the main oxygen sensor is mounted ahead of the front catalytic converter and monitors the exhaust gases before they are changed. The sub oxygen sensor monitors the exhaust gases after they have passed through the front catalytic converter. The rear catalytic converter is not monitored. Each oxygen sensor monitors the oxygen content of the exhaust gas stream. The oxygen content in the exhaust reacts with the oxygen sensor to produce a voltage output which varies from 0.1-volt (high oxygen, lean mixture) to 0.9-volts (low oxygen, rich mixture). The ECM constantly monitors this variable voltage output to determine the ratio of oxygen to fuel in the mixture. The ECM alters the air/fuel mixture ratio by controlling the pulse width (open time) of the fuel injectors. A mixture ratio of 14.7 parts air to 1 part fuel is the ideal mixture ratio for minimizing exhaust emissions, thus allowing the catalytic converter to operate at maximum efficiency. It is this ratio of 14.7 to 1 which the ECM and the oxygen sensor attempt to maintain at all times.

8   The oxygen sensor produces no voltage when it is below its normal operating temperature of about 600-degrees F. During this initial period before warm-up, the ECM operates in open loop mode.

9   If the engine reaches normal operating temperature and/or has been running for two or more minutes, and if the main oxygen sensor is producing a steady signal voltage below 0.45-volts at 1,500 or more rpm, the ECM will set a Code 21. Code 21 will also set if there is a problem with the oxygen sensor heater circuit. Code 27 will indicate a problem with the sub oxygen sensor.

10   When there is a problem with the oxygen sensor or its circuit, the ECM operates in the open loop mode - that is, it controls fuel delivery in accordance with a programmed default value instead of feedback information from the oxygen sensor.

11   The proper operation of the oxygen sensor depends on four conditions:

a) *Electrical - The low voltages generated by the sensor depend upon good, clean connections which should be checked whenever a malfunction of the sensor is suspected or indicated.*

b) *Outside air supply - The sensor is designed to allow air circulation to the internal portion of the sensor. Whenever the sensor is removed and installed or replaced, make sure the air passages are not restricted.*

c) *Proper operating temperature - The ECM will not react to the sensor signal until the sensor reaches approximately 600-degrees F. This factor must be taken into consideration when evaluating the performance of the sensor.*

d) *Unleaded fuel - The use of unleaded fuel is essential for proper operation of the sensor. Make sure the fuel you are using is of this type.*

12   In addition to observing the above conditions, special care must be taken whenever the sensor is serviced.

a) *The oxygen sensor has a permanently attached pigtail and electrical connector which should not be removed from the sensor. Damage to or removal of the pigtail or electrical connector can adversely affect operation of the sensor.*

b) *Grease, dirt and other contaminants should be kept away from the electrical connector and the louvered end of the sensor.*

c) *Do not use cleaning solvents of any kind on the oxygen sensor.*

d) *Do not drop or roughly handle the sensor.*

e) *The silicone boot must be installed in the correct position to prevent the boot from being melted and to allow the sensor to operate properly.*

Check

Refer to illustrations 4.13a, 4.13b, 4.15, 4.18a and 4.18b

13   Locate the oxygen sensor electrical connector and inspect the oxygen sensor heater. Disconnect the oxygen sensor electrical connector and connect an ohmmeter between the +B and HT terminals **(see illustration)**. It should measure approximately 11.0 to 17.0 ohms. **Note:** *Four-cylinder engines are not equipped with an oxygen sensor heater. This will be indicated by a single wire from the oxygen sensor. V6 engines with heated oxygen sensors will be equipped with a four wire electrical connector. Later model four-cylinder engines are equipped*

4.13a To test the oxygen sensor heater, disconnect the harness connector, check the resistance across terminals HT and +B. It should between 11 to 17 ohms

with a main oxygen sensor located in the exhaust manifold and a sub oxygen sensor located after the catalytic converter. V6 engines are equipped with three oxygen sensors. Bank 1, Sensor 1 and Bank 2, Sensor 1 are both situated in the exhaust system before the catalytic converter. Bank 1, Sensor 2 is located after the catalytic converter. On V6 engines, it will be necessary to remove the front seats to locate the rear oxygen sensor electrical connector **(see illustration)**. **Note:** *On 1992 and 1993 V6 engines, the oxygen sensor after the catalytic converter is referred to as the sub-oxygen sensor.*

14   Also, check for proper supply voltage to the oxygen sensor heater. Measure the voltage with the harness connector connected. Insert two long pins into the backside of the electrical connector on the correct wire colors. With the ignition key ON (engine not running), check for battery voltage. There should be approximately 12 volts at the following terminals:

1992 and 1993 V6 engines

Sub-oxygen sensor	Black/orange wire (positive [+]) and brown wire (negative [-])
Main number 1	Not applicable (no heater)
Main number 2	Not applicable (no heater)

1994 and later V6 engines

Bank 1, Sensor 1	Black/orange wire (positive [+]) and brown wire (negative [-])
Bank 2, Sensor 1	Black/orange wire (positive [+]) and brown wire (negative [-])
Bank 1, Sensor 2	Black/orange wire (positive [+]) and brown wire (negative [-])

15   Next, check for a millivolt signal from the oxygen sensor. Locate the oxygen sensor electrical connector and insert a long pin into the oxygen sensor connector **(see illustration)**. Install the positive probe of a voltmeter onto the correct terminal and the negative probe to ground. Observe the sensor millivolt signal on the following terminals:

Four-cylinder engines

Main oxygen sensor	White wire
Sub oxygen sensor	Red/blue wire

1992 and 1993 V6 engines

Main number 1	White wire
Main number 2	Red/blue wire
Sub-oxygen sensor	White wire

1994 and later V6 engines

Bank 1, Sensor 1	White wire
Bank 2, Sensor 1	Red/blue wire
Bank 1, Sensor 2	Black wire

16   Monitor the voltage signal (millivolts) as the engine goes from cold to warm.

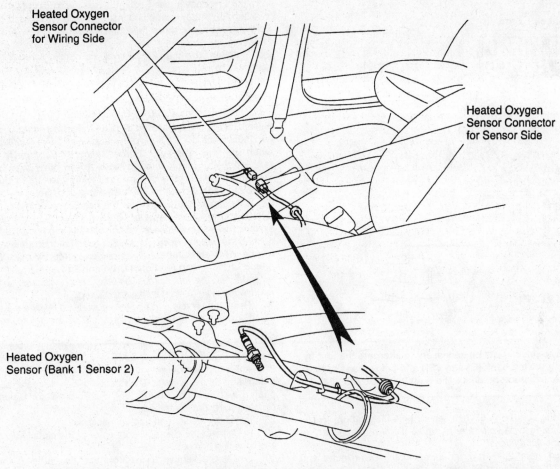

Heated Oxygen
Sensor Connector
for Wiring Side

Heated Oxygen
Sensor Connector
for Sensor Side

Heated Oxygen
Sensor (Bank 1 Sensor 2)

**4.13b On V6 engines, it will be necessary to remove the front passenger seat to gain access to the
rear oxygen sensor electrical connector**

17   The oxygen sensor will produce a steady voltage signal at first (open loop) of approximately 0.1 to 0.2 volts with the engine cold. After a period of approximately two minutes, the engine will reach operating temperature and the oxygen sensor will start to fluctuate between 0.1 to 0.9 volts (closed loop). If the oxygen sensor fails to reach the closed loop mode or there is a very long period of time until it does switch into closed loop mode, replace the oxygen sensor with a new part.

18   On 1992 and 1993 engines, inspect the feedback voltage. With the engine completely warmed up and the oxygen sensor connected, connect a voltmeter to the test connector VF1 (positive probe +) and E1 (negative probe -) **(see illustration).** On V6 engines, terminals VF1 (+) and E1 (-) will inspect the left bank oxygen sensor and then VF2 (+)

**4.15 Install a pin into the backside of the oxygen sensor
connector into the correct terminal and check for a millivolt
output signal generated by the sensor as it warms up**

**4.18a Install the probes of the voltmeter on terminals VF1 (+) and
E1 (-), raise the engine speed to 2,500 rpm and jump terminals
TE1 and E1 with a jumper wire or paper clip.**

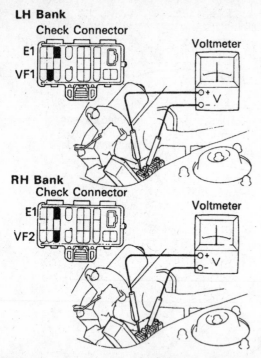

4.18b On V6 engines, it will be necessary to alternate the test by first checking the left bank (E1 and VF1) and then when the test results are satisfactory, check the right bank (E1 and VF2)

and E1 (-) for the right bank oxygen sensor **(see illustration)**. **Note:** *Use only an analog type voltmeter because it will be necessary to watch the needle fluctuations.*

19   Run the engine at 2,500 rpm for approximately two minutes and then jump terminals TE1 and E1 **(see illustration 4.18a)**. Check the number of times the needle fluctuates in 10 seconds. It should fluctuate eight times or more. If it does not, warm the engine up again and repeat the test.

20   If the voltmeter still does not fluctuate eight times or more, remove the jumper wire from terminals TE1 and E1 of the test connector. Maintain engine speed at 2,500 rpm and measure the voltage between terminals VF1 and E1. If the voltage reading is more than 0 volts, then replace the oxygen sensor with a new part. If the voltage reading is 0 volts, access the self diagnostic codes (see Section 3) and check for any malfunctions.

21   If codes 21, 25 or 26 are obtained, then remove the PCV hose

from the valve cover (see Section 8) and measure the voltage between VF1 and E1. If the voltage is 0 volts, replace the oxygen sensor. If the voltage reading is more than 0 volts, repair the over-rich running condition.

22   If codes other than 21, 25 or 26 are obtained, repair the particular sensor or circuit.

Replacement

Refer to illustrations 4.26a, 4.26b and 4.26c

Note: *Because it is installed in the exhaust manifold or pipe, which contracts when cool, the oxygen sensor may be very difficult to loosen when the engine is cold. Rather than risk damage to the sensor (assuming you are planning to reuse it in another manifold or pipe), start and run the engine for a minute or two, then shut it off. Be careful not to burn yourself during the following procedure.*

23   Disconnect the cable from the negative terminal of the battery. **Caution:** *If the stereo in your vehicle is equipped with an anti-theft system, make sure you have the correct activation code before disconnecting the battery.* **Note:** *On 1993 and later models, the airbag system will be disabled if the battery is disconnected for more than a brief period. If the airbag light comes on and stays on after the battery is reconnected, the vehicle must be taken to a dealer service department to have the system reset with a special tool.*

24   Raise the vehicle and place it securely on jackstands.

25   Carefully disconnect the electrical connector from the sensor pigtail lead.

26   Remove the oxygen sensor from the exhaust system **(see illustrations)**. **Caution:** *Excessive force may damage the threads.*

27   Anti-seize compound must be used on the threads of the sensor to facilitate future removal. The threads of new sensors will already be coated with this compound, but if an old sensor is removed and reinstalled, recoat the threads.

28   Install the sensor and tighten it securely.

29   Reconnect the electrical connector of the pigtail lead to the main engine wiring harness.

30   Lower the vehicle and reconnect the cable to the negative terminal of the battery.

Throttle Position Sensor (TPS)

General description

31   The Throttle Position Sensor (TPS) is located on the end of the throttle shaft on the throttle body (see Chapter 4). By monitoring the output voltage from the TPS, the ECM can alter fuel delivery based on throttle valve angle (driver demand). A broken or loose TPS can cause intermittent bursts of fuel from the injector and an unstable idle because the ECM thinks the throttle is moving. All the checks and replacement procedures are covered in Chapter 4.

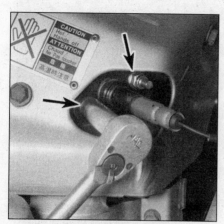

4.26a Remove the retaining nuts from the main oxygen sensor on a four-cylinder engine

4.26b Slotted sockets are available for easing oxygen sensor removal

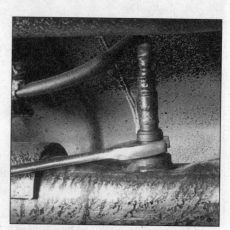

4.26c The sub-oxygen sensor is mounted in the lower exhaust pipe

Airflow Meter (3VZ-FE V6 models only)

General description

32 The airflow meter is located on the air cleaner housing. The airflow meter measures the amount of air entering the engine. The ECM uses this information to control fuel delivery. A large deflection of the measuring plate indicates acceleration, while a small deflection of the plate indicates deceleration or idle. Any malfunctions with the airflow meter will be recorded as Code 31 or 32.

Check

Refer to illustration 4.36

33 Remove the airflow meter (see Steps 39 through 43).
34 Check the airflow meter for cracks or any obvious damage.
35 Verify that the measuring plate moves freely.
36 Measure the resistance at the indicated airflow meter terminals **(see illustration)**.
37 Carefully move the measuring plate from fully closed to fully open and check the terminals for the proper resistance.
38 If the resistance readings are incorrect, replace the airflow meter.

Removal and installation

39 Remove the air filter (see Chapter 1).
40 Disconnect the harness electrical connector.
41 Loosen the hose clamp.
42 Remove the nuts that retain the airflow meter to the housing.
43 Separate the airflow meter from the air cleaner housing.
44 Installation is the reverse of removal.

Mass Airflow (MAF) sensor (1MZ-FE V6 models)

General Information

Refer to illustrations 4.46, 4.47, 4.49, 4.51 and 4.52

45 The Mass Airflow Sensor (MAF) is located on the air intake duct. This sensor uses a hot wire sensing element to measure the amount of air entering the engine. The air passing over the hot wire causes it to cool. Consequently, this change in temperature can be converted into an analog voltage signal to the ECM which in turn calculates the required fuel injector pulse width.

Check

46 Check for power to the MAF sensor. Disconnect the MAF sensor electrical connector. Working on the harness side with the ignition ON (engine not running), check for battery voltage on the black/orange wire **(see illustration)**.
47 Reconnect the electrical connector and backprobe the MAF sensor terminals VG- and VG **(see illustration)** with the voltmeter. The voltage should be less than 1.0 volt with the ignition switch ON (engine

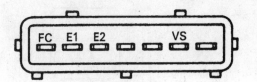

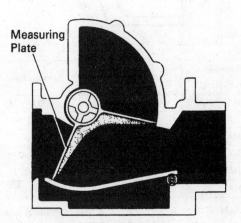

Measuring Plate

Between terminals	Resistsnce (Ω)	Measuring plate opening
FC — E1	Infinity	Fully closed
FC — E1	Zero	Other than closed
VS — E2	200 — 600	Fully closed
VS — E2	20 — 1,200	Fully open

4.36 Airflow meter terminal guide and continuity chart - 3VZ-FE V6 engine

not running). Raise the engine rpm. The signal voltage from the MAF sensor should increase to about 2.0 volts. It is impossible to simulate load conditions in the driveway but it is necessary to observe the voltmeter for a fluctuation in voltage as the engine speed is raised. The vehicle will not be under load conditions but it should manage to vary slightly.
48 If the voltage readings are correct, check the wiring harness for open circuits or a damaged harness (see Chapter 12).

6

4.46 Check for battery voltage to the MAF sensor on the black/orange wire

4.47 Probe terminals VG- and VG and check for voltage signal changes on the MAF sensor

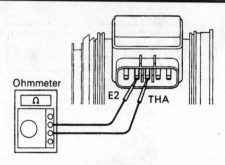

Between terminals	Resistance	Temperature
THA — E2	10 — 20 kΩ	−20°C (−4°F)
THA — E2	4 — 7 kΩ	0°C (32°F)
THA — E2	2 — 3 kΩ	20°C (68°F)
THA — E2	0.9 — 1.3 kΩ	40°C (104°F)
THA — E2	0.4 — 0.7 kΩ	60°C (140°F)
THA — E2	0.2 — 0.4 kΩ	80°C (176°F)

4.49 MAF sensor terminal guide and continuity chart - 1MZ-FE V6 engine

49 Also, check the resistance between terminals THA and E2 **(see illustration)**. There should be a steady fluctuation in resistance from cold to warm as the engine temperatures increase.

Replacement

50 Disconnect the electrical connector from the MAF sensor.
51 Remove the air cleaner assembly **(see illustration)**.
52 Remove the four bolts **(see illustration)** and lift the MAF sensor from the engine compartment.
53 Installation is the reverse of removal.

MAP sensor (four-cylinder models)

Refer to illustrations 4.55, 4.57 and 4.58

General Information

54 The MAP sensor monitors the intake manifold pressure changes resulting from changes in engine load and speed and converts the information into a voltage output. The ECM uses the MAP sensor to control fuel delivery and ignition timing. The ECM will receive information as a voltage signal. This signal can be detected using a voltmeter. The voltage will vary from 4.0 volts without engine vacuum to 0.5 volts with 25 in-Hg vacuum.

4.51 Remove the clamp and slide the air intake duct off the MAF sensor

4.52 Remove the bolts from the bracket retaining the MAF sensor to the air cleaner housing

Check

55 Turn the ignition On (engine not running). Check the reference voltage from the MAP sensor. Backprobe the red wire and check for approximately 5.0 volts **(see illustration)**.
56 Remove the vacuum hose from the MAP sensor and install a hand held vacuum pump.
57 Disconnect the electrical connector from the MAP sensor.

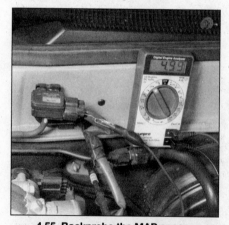

4.55 Backprobe the MAP sensor connector using a pin or paper clip into the red wire and check for reference voltage. It should be approximately 5.0 volts

4.57 Install a vacuum pump to the MAP sensor and check for signal voltage on the black/yellow wire without vacuum applied. It should be 3.5 to 5.0 volts

4.58 Now apply vacuum to the MAP sensor an observe that the voltage decreases to approximately 0.5 to 1.5 volts

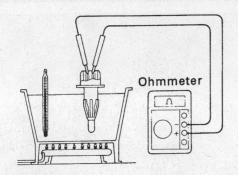

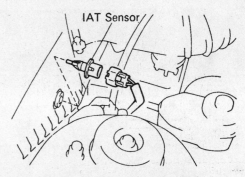

4.61 Location of the IAT sensor

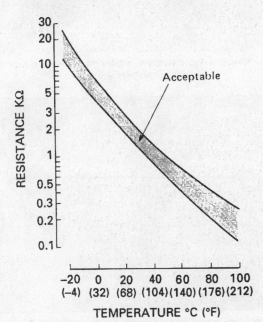

4.60 The air intake temperature sensor resistance will DECREASE when the temperature of the air INCREASES

Backprobe the MAP sensor harness connector using pins to the designated terminals **(see illustration)**. Using a voltmeter, check for signal voltage from the MAP sensor on the black/yellow wire. Without vacuum, the sensor voltage should be approximately 4.0 volts.

58   Use the hand-held vacuum pump and apply 25 in-Hg of vacuum

4.66 Disconnect the EGR gas temperature sensor connector and check the resistance of the sensor

to the MAP sensor and observe the voltage readings. The voltmeter should read approximately 0.5 volts **(see illustration)**.

59   If the test results are incorrect, replace the MAP sensor.

Intake Air Temperature (IAT) sensor

General description

Refer to illustrations 4.60 and 4.61

60   The intake air temperature sensor is located inside the air cleaner housing. This sensor acts as a resistor which changes value according to the temperature of the air entering the engine. Low temperatures produce a high resistance value (for example, at 68 degrees F the resistance is 2.2 to 2.6 K-ohms) while high temperatures produce low resistance values (at 176 degrees F the resistance is 300 to 330 ohms **(see illustration)**. The ECM supplies approximately 5-volts (reference voltage) to the air temperature sensor. The voltage will change according to the temperature of the incoming air. The voltage will be high when the air temperature is cold and low when the air temperature is warm. Any problems with the air temperature sensor will usually set a code 24.

Check

61   To check the air temperature sensor, disconnect the two prong electrical connector **(see illustration)** and turn the ignition key ON but do not start the engine.

62   Measure the voltage (reference voltage). The VOM should read approximately 5-volts.

63   If the voltage signal is not correct, have the ECM diagnosed by a dealer service department or other repair shop.

64   Measure the resistance across the air temperature sensor terminals. The resistance should be HIGH when the air temperature is LOW. Next, start the engine and let it idle. Wait awhile and let the engine reach operating temperature. Turn the ignition OFF, disconnect the air temperature sensor and measure the resistance across the terminals. The resistance should be LOW when the air temperature is HIGH. If the sensor does not exhibit this change in resistance, replace it with a new part.

EGR gas temperature sensor

General Description

65   The EGR gas temperature sensor is mounted near the EGR valve. This sensor detects the temperature of the exhaust as it moves through the EGR valve. The information is sent to the ECM and in turn the EGR on/off time is regulated precisely and more efficiently. Any malfunction with the EGR gas temperature sensor will set a code 71.

Check

Refer to illustration 4.66

66   Disconnect the harness connector for the EGR gas temperature sensor **(see illustration)** and measure the resistance of the sensor at the various temperatures. Refer to the Specifications listed in this Chapter for a list of the temperatures and the resistance values.

6

4.67 Remove the EGR gas temperature sensor using an open end wrench

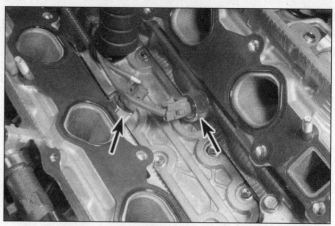

4.72 The knock sensors (arrows) on the V6 engine are located under the intake manifold

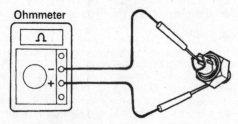

4.73 Check that NO continuity exists on the sensor terminal to the body of the sensor

4.76 Check the resistance of the camshaft sensor. It should be between 835 and 1,600 ohms

Removal and installation

Refer to illustration 4.67

67   Disconnect the harness connector for the EGR gas temperature sensor and using an open-end wrench, remove the sensor from the intake manifold **(see illustration)**.
68   Installation is the reverse of removal.

Vehicle speed sensor

General description

69   The Vehicle Speed Sensor (VSS) is located on the tail-section of the transmission (see Chapter 7B). The sensor is electronically controlled and sends a pulsing voltage signal to the ECM, which the ECM converts to miles per hour.
70   Any problems with the VSS and its circuit will set a code 42. Have the vehicle speed sensor, circuit and the ECM diagnosed by a dealership service department.

Knock sensor (V6 models only)

General Description

71   Irregular octane levels in modern gasoline can cause detonation in an engine. Detonation is sometimes referred to as "spark knock". The knock sensor sends a voltage signal to the ECM when no spark knock is occurring and the ECM provides normal advance. When the knock sensor detects abnormal vibration (spark knock), it turns off the circuit to the ECM, and distributor timing is retarded until the knock is eliminated. Any problems with the knock sensor or sensor circuit will set a code 52. Any problems with the knock control system in the ECM will set a code 53.

Check

Refer to illustrations 4.72 and 4.73

72   The knock sensors are located in the intake manifold **(see illustration)**. It will be necessary to remove the air intake plenum (see Chapter 4) and the intake manifold (see Chapter 2A) to gain access to the knock sensor.

73   Using an ohmmeter, check that there is no continuity between the terminal on the knock sensor and the body **(see illustration)**.
74   If continuity exists, replace the sensor with a new part.

Camshaft Position Sensor (1MZ-FE V6 models only)

Refer to illustrations 4.76 and 4.77

75   The camshaft position sensor is located in the cylinder head near the timing chain cover. As the camshaft turns, a magnet on the camshaft activates the Hall Effect switch in the sensor. This creates the signal that is sent to the ECM to indicate the exact angle (position) of the camshaft.

Check

76   Using an ohmmeter, measure the resistance of the camshaft position sensor **(see illustration)**. It should be between 835 to 1,600 ohms depending upon the temperature. If the resistance is not within the specified range, replace the sensor with a new part.
77   To replace the sensor, disconnect the electrical connector and remove the bolts **(see illustration)** from the camshaft position sensor.

Crankshaft Position Sensor (1MZ-FE V6 models only)

Refer to illustration 4.78

78   The crankshaft position sensor is located in the front timing cover near the crankshaft pulley **(see illustration)**. The crankshaft position sensor relays a signal to the ECM to indicate the exact position (angle) of the crankshaft.

4.77 Remove the camshaft sensor bolts (arrows)

Check

79   Using an ohmmeter, measure the resistance of the crankshaft position sensor. It should be between 1,630 to 3,225 ohms depending upon the temperature; the warmer the temperature of the sensor, the higher the resistance value. If the resistance is not within the specified range, replace the sensor with a new part.

80   To replace the sensor, disconnect the electrical connector and remove the bolts from the crankshaft position sensor.

5   Acoustic Control Induction System (ACIS) (V6 models only)

General information

Refer to illustration 5.1

1   The Acoustic Control Induction System (ACIS) allows the intake manifold to divert the path of intake air into the combustion chamber **(see illustration)**. Two air intake paths are provided in the intake manifold to allow the option of the intake volume most favorable for the particular engine speed. Optimum performance is achieved by switching the intake air control valve from either the closed position (for high torque at low RPM) or the open position (for maximum horsepower at high RPM).

2   The actuator mechanism is controlled by vacuum from the intake manifold. Any failure with the actuator or solenoid can lead to problems with the system, resulting in poor driveability. Follow the simple checks to help diagnose any system defects. **Note:** *The ACIS does not have any self diagnostic codes directly relating to this system.*

4.78 The crankshaft position sensor is located in the timing belt cover near the front pulley

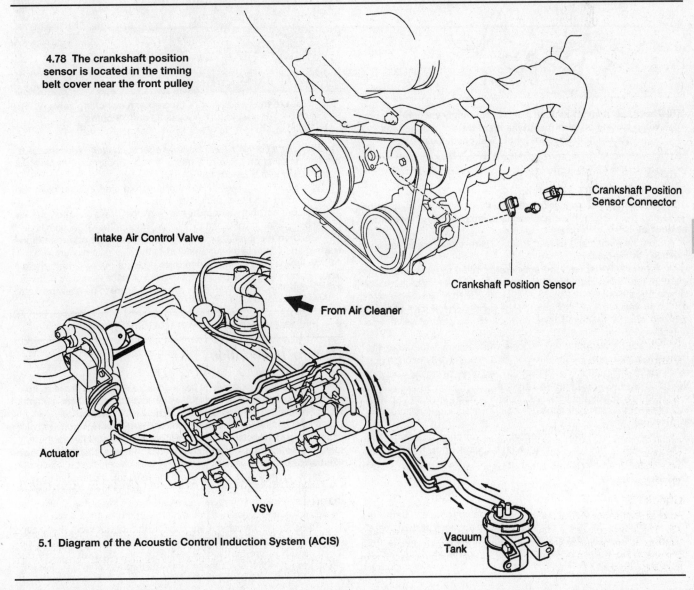

5.1 Diagram of the Acoustic Control Induction System (ACIS)

Intake Air Control Valve

From Air Cleaner

Actuator

VSV

Crankshaft Position Sensor Connector

Crankshaft Position Sensor

Vacuum Tank

6

5.3 Using a vacuum-T, install a vacuum gauge between the vacuum actuator and the vacuum source and observe that vacuum increases slightly with an increase in the engine rpm

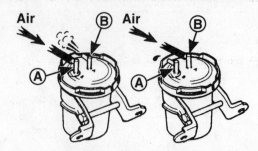

5.7 Check the vacuum tank by applying air pressure to port B and observe that air flows through B and out port A but does NOT flow through A and out port B

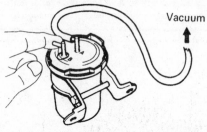

5.8 Check the vacuum tank for a tight seal. Apply vacuum to port A while closing off port B with the tip of the finger. The tank should hold vacuum for at least one minute

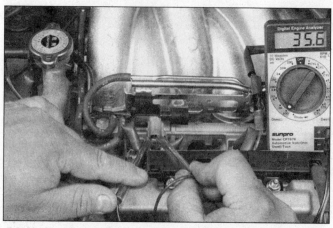

5.9 Measure the resistance of the vacuum switching valve (VSV). It should be between 33 and 39 ohms

Check

Refer to illustrations 5.3, 5.7, 5.8 and 5.9

3   Connect a three-way connector between the intake air control valve and the vacuum hose and install a vacuum gauge **(see illustration)** into the T-connector.

4   Start the engine and allow it to idle. There should be no vacuum indicated by the gauge.

5   Momentarily depress the accelerator pedal to wide open and observe that the gauge reads approximately 8 in-Hg. The actuator should pull the rod in.

6   If no vacuum was indicated by the gauge, check for a blocked vacuum port, a collapsed vacuum hose to the control valve or a defective VSV (see Step 9).

7   Inspect the vacuum tank. Locate the vacuum tank under the battery tray and apply pressure to port B. Air should pass through port B out port A. Apply air pressure to port A and observe that air does not pass through into port B **(see illustration)**.

8   Plug port B with the tip of the finger and apply vacuum to port A and observe that vacuum does not leak down after one minute **(see illustration)**.

9   Check the VSV. Install the probes of an ohmmeter onto the terminals and check the resistance **(see illustration)**. It should be between 33 and 39 ohms.

Replacement

Refer to illustration 5.13

10   Disconnect the negative cable from the battery terminal. **Caution:** *If the stereo in your vehicle is equipped with an anti-theft system, make sure you have the correct activation code before disconnecting the battery.* **Note:** *On 1993 and later models, the airbag system will be disabled if the battery is disconnected for more than a brief period. If*

the airbag light comes on and stays on after the battery is reconnected, the vehicle must be taken to a dealer service department to have the system reset with a special tool.

11   On 3VZ-FE engines, disconnect the cold start injector electrical connector and fuel hose (see Chapter 5).

12   Disconnect the vacuum hoses from the brake booster, the air conditioning idle-up valve and the intake air control valve vacuum hose.

13   Remove the intake air control valve retaining bolts **(see illustration)** and separate the assembly from the air intake plenum.

14   Scrape all remaining traces of the gasket material from the air intake plenum and valve body without damaging the aluminum material.

15   Installation is the reverse of removal. Be sure to use new gaskets.

6   Evaporative Emission Control (EVAP) system

General description

Refer to illustration 6.2

1   This system is designed to trap and store fuel that evaporates from the fuel tank, throttle body and intake manifold that would normally enter the atmosphere in the form of hydrocarbon (HC) emissions.

2   The Evaporative Emission Control (EVAP) system consists of a charcoal-filled canister, the lines connecting the canister to the fuel tank, the Temperature Vacuum Valve (TVV) and a check valve **(see illustration)**.

3   Fuel vapors are transferred from the fuel tank and throttle body to a canister where they're stored when the engine isn't running. When the engine is running, the fuel vapors are purged from the canister by intake airflow and consumed in the normal combustion process.

4   The charcoal canister is equipped with a check valve that incorporates three check balls. Depending upon the running conditions and the pressure in the fuel tank, the check balls open and close the passageways to the TVV (consequently the throttle body) and fuel tank.

5.13 Intake air control valve installation details

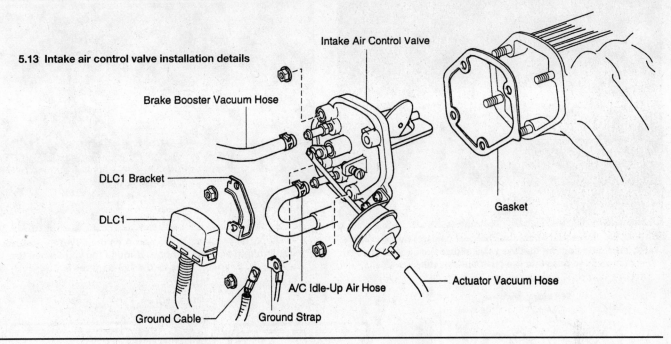

6.2 Typical EVAP system and operation chart

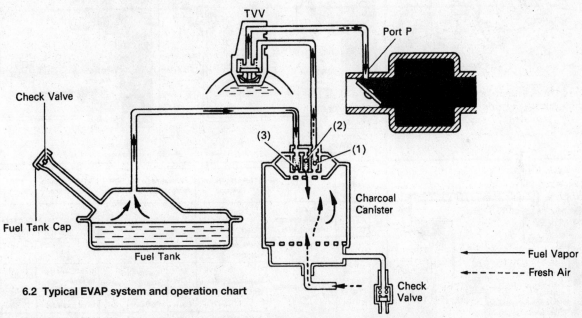

Coolant Temp.	TVV	Throttle Valve Opening	Canister Check Valve			Check Valve in Cap	Evaporated Fuel (HC)
			(1)	(2)	(3)		
Below 35°C (95°F)	CLOSED	–	–	–	–	–	HC from tank is absorbed into the canister
Above 54°C (129°F)	OPEN	Positioned below port P	CLOSED	–	–	–	
		Positioned above port P	OPEN	–	–	–	HC from canister is led into air intake chamber.
High pressure in tank	–	–	–	OPEN	CLOSED	CLOSED	HC from tank is absorbed into the canister.
High vacuum in take	–	–	–	CLOSED	OPEN	OPEN	Air is led into the fuel tank.

6.10 Apply air pressure into the charcoal canister purge control valve (inlet) and confirm that the valve allows the air (fuel vapors) to pass into the charcoal canister

6.11 Apply air pressure to the port A on the TVV (top port) and confirm that air does not pass through the valve when the temperature is below 129-degrees F.

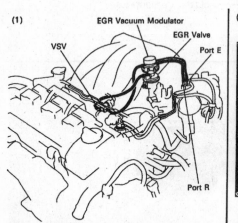

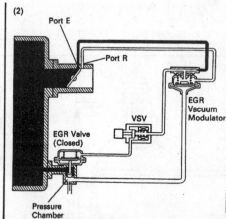

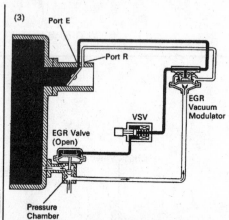

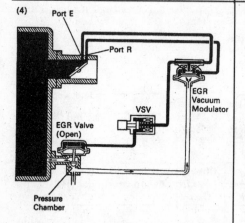

Engine Coolant Temp.	VSV	Throttle Valve Position	Pressure in the EGR Valve Pressure Chamber		EGR Vacuum Modulator	EGR Valve	Exhaust Gas
Below 55°C (131°F)	ON OPENS passage to atmosphere	–	–		–	CLOSED	Not recirculated
Above 60°C (140°F)	OFF CLOSED passage to atmosphere	Positioned below port E	–		–	CLOSED	Not recirculated
		Positioned between port E and port R	(1) LOW	*Pressure constantly alternating between low and high	OPENS passage to atmosphere	CLOSED	Not recirculated
			(2) HIGH		CLOSES passage to atmosphere	OPEN	Recirculated
		Positioned above port R	(3) HIGH	**	CLOSES passage to atmosphere	OPEN	Recirculated (increase)

* Pressure increase → Modulator closes → EGR valve opens → Pressure drops
EGR valve closes ← Modulator opens ←
** When the throttle valve is positioned above port R, the EGR vacuum modulator will close the atmosphere passage and open the EGR valve to increase the EGR gas, even if the exhaust pressure is insufficiently low.

7.1 Typical EGR system and operation chart

Check

Refer to illustrations 6.10 and 6.11

5   Poor idle, stalling and poor driveability can be caused by an inoperative check valve, a damaged canister, split or cracked hoses or hoses connected to the wrong fittings. Check the fuel filler cap for a damaged or deformed gasket (see Chapter 1).

6   Evidence of fuel loss or fuel odor can be caused by liquid fuel leaking from fuel lines, a cracked or damaged canister, an inoperative check valve, disconnected, misrouted, kinked, deteriorated or damaged vapor or control hoses.

7   Inspect each hose attached to the canister for kinks, leaks and cracks along its entire length. Repair or replace as necessary.

8   Look for fuel leaking from the bottom of the canister. If fuel is leaking, replace the canister and check the hoses and hose routing.

9   Inspect the canister. If it's cracked or damaged, replace it.

10   Check for a clogged filter or a stuck check valve. Using low pressure compressed air, blow into the canister tank pipe **(see illustration)**. Air should flow freely from the other pipes. If a problem is

7.4 Apply vacuum to the EGR valve and observe that the valve opens and allows exhaust gases to circulate. Once it is activated, the EGR valve should hold steady (no loss in vacuum)

7.7a To remove the EGR vacuum modulator filters for cleaning, remove the cap . . .

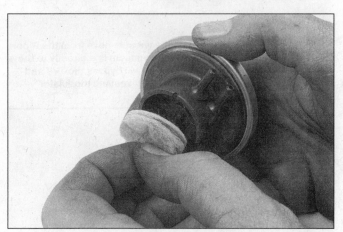

7.7b . . . then pull out the two filters and blow them out with compressed air - be sure the coarse side of the outer filter faces the atmosphere (out) when reinstalling the filters

7.9 Install a vacuum gauge between the vacuum switching valve (VSV) and the EGR valve using a three way adapter

found, replace the canister.
11   Check the operation of the TVV. With the engine completely cold, use a hand-held pump and direct air into port A **(see illustration)**. Air should not pass through the TVV. Now warm the engine to operating temperature (above 129-degrees F) and observe that air passes through the TVV. Replace the valve if the test results are incorrect.

Charcoal canister replacement

12   Clearly label, then detach the vacuum hoses from the canister.
13   Remove the mounting clamp bolts, lower the canister with the bracket, disconnect the hoses from the check valve and remove it from the vehicle.
14   Installation is the reverse of removal.

7   Exhaust Gas Recirculation (EGR) system

General description

Refer to illustration 7.1
1   To reduce oxides of nitrogen emissions, some of the exhaust gases are recirculated through the EGR valve to the intake manifold to lower combustion temperatures **(see illustration)**.
2   The EGR system consists of the EGR valve, the EGR modulator, vacuum switching valve (VSV), the Electronic Control Module (ECM) and the EGR gas temperature sensor.

Check

EGR valve

Refer to illustration 7.4
3   Start the engine and allow it to idle.
4   Detach the vacuum hose from the EGR valve and attach a hand vacuum pump in its place **(see illustration)**.
5   Apply vacuum to the EGR valve. Vacuum should remain steady and the engine should run poorly.
 a) *If the vacuum doesn't remain steady and the engine doesn't run poorly, replace the EGR valve and recheck it.*
 b) *If the vacuum remains steady but the engine doesn't run poorly, remove the EGR valve and check the valve and the intake manifold for blockage. Clean or replace parts as necessary and recheck.*

EGR vacuum modulator filter

Refer to illustrations 7.7a and 7.7b
6   Remove the valve (see Step 13 below).
7   Pull the cover off and check the filters **(see illustrations)**.
8   Clean them with compressed air, reinstall the cover and the modulator.

EGR system

Refer to illustrations 7.9, 7.10a, 7.10b, 7.11a and 7.11b
9   Disconnect the hose from the EGR valve and install a three-way union and vacuum gauge between the EGR valve and the Vacuum Switching Valve (VSV) **(see illustration)**.

6

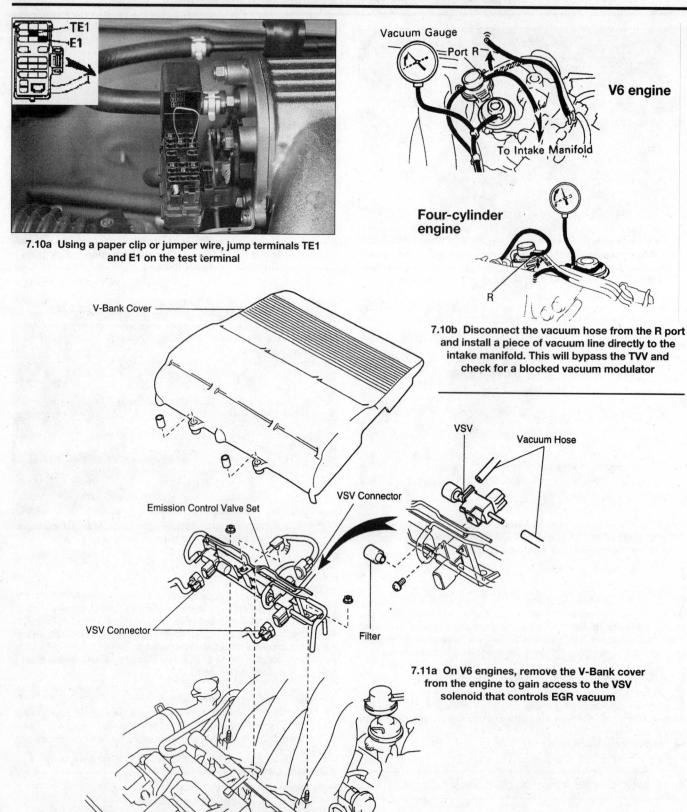

7.10a Using a paper clip or jumper wire, jump terminals TE1 and E1 on the test terminal

7.10b Disconnect the vacuum hose from the R port and install a piece of vacuum line directly to the intake manifold. This will bypass the TVV and check for a blocked vacuum modulator

7.11a On V6 engines, remove the V-Bank cover from the engine to gain access to the VSV solenoid that controls EGR vacuum

7.11b Check the resistance on the EGR VSV using an ohmmeter. It should be between 33 and 39 ohms

7.12a Remove the nuts (arrows) that retain the EGR pipe to the EGR valve and the exhaust system

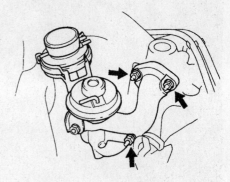

7.12b Remove the nuts (arrows) that retain the EGR valve assembly to the engine

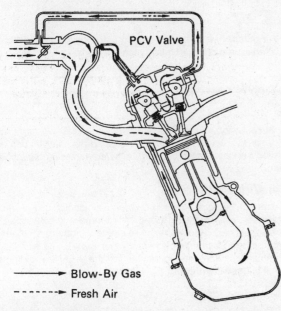

PCV Valve

→ Blow-By Gas
- - -→ Fresh Air

8.1a Diagram of the PCV system - four-cylinder engine

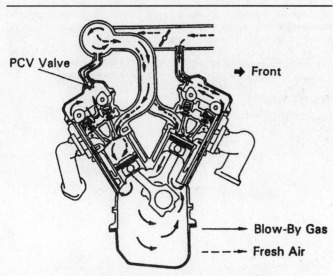

PCV Valve

→ Front

→ Blow-By Gas
- - -→ Fresh Air

8.1b Diagram of the PCV system - V6 engine

10   Start the engine and connect terminals TE1 and E1 on the test terminal **(see illustration).**

a) *With the coolant temperature below 131-degrees F (cold), verify that the vacuum gauge indicates zero (no vacuum) at 2,500 rpm.* **Note:** *California models with automatic transaxles and ECT models are set at 140-degrees.*

b) *With the engine warm, verify that the vacuum gauge indicates low vacuum at 2,500 rpm.*

c) *Disconnect the vacuum hose from the R port of the EGR vacuum modulator and connect the R port directly to the intake manifold using an extension* **(see illustration).** *Raise the rpm to 2,500 and observe the vacuum gauge indicate high vacuum.*

11   Check the operation of the VSV.

a) *On V6 engines, remove the V Bank cover to expose the vacuum solenoids* **(see illustration).** *The VSV on four-cylinder engines is located on the intake manifold.*

b) *Check the resistance of the VSV. It should be between 33 and 39 ohms* **(see illustration).**

c) *If the tests are incorrect, replace the VSV with a new part.*

Component replacement

EGR valve

Refer to illustrations 7.12a and 7.12b

12   Detach the vacuum hose, disconnect the fitting that attaches the EGR pipe to the EGR valve **(see illustration),** remove the EGR valve mounting bolts **(see illustration),** remove the EGR valve from the intake manifold and check it for sticking and heavy carbon deposits. If the valve is sticking or clogged with deposits, clean or replace it.

13   Installation is the reverse of removal.

EGR vacuum modulator valve

14   Label and disconnect the vacuum hoses and remove the EGR vacuum modulator from it's bracket.

15   Installation is the reverse of removal.

8   Positive Crankcase Ventilation (PCV) system

General information

Refer to illustrations 8.1a and 8.1b

1   The Positive Crankcase Ventilation (PCV) system reduces hydrocarbon emissions by scavenging crankcase vapors. It does this by circulating fresh air from the air cleaner through the crankcase, where it mixes with blow-by gases and is then rerouted through a PCV valve to the intake manifold **(see illustrations).**

2   The main components of the PCV system are the PCV valve, a fresh air intake and the vacuum hoses connecting these components with the engine.

6

9.2 The catalytic converter and the exhaust system can be removed from the vehicle as a complete unit

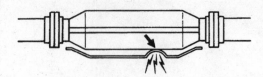

9.4 Periodically inspect the shield for dents and other damage - if a dent is deep enough to touch the surface of the converter, replace the shield

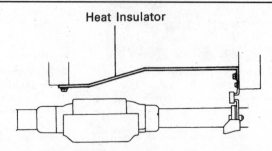

Heat Insulator

9.5 Periodically inspect the heat insulator to make sure there's adequate clearance between it and the converter

3   To maintain idle quality, the PCV valve restricts the flow when the intake manifold vacuum is high. If abnormal operating conditions (such as piston ring problems) arise, the system is designed to allow excessive amounts of blow-by gases to flow back through the crankcase vent tube into the air cleaner to be consumed by normal combustion.

4   This system directs the blow-by into the throttle body which, over time, can cause an oily residue build up in the area near the throttle plate. Consequently, it's a good idea to periodically clean this residue from the throttle body. Refer to Chapter 4 for this cleaning procedure.

Check

5   To check the valve, first pull it out of the grommet in the valve cover and shake the valve. It should rattle, indicating that it's not clogged with deposits. If the valve does not rattle, replace it with a new one.

6   Start the engine and allow it to idle, then place your finger over the valve opening. If vacuum is felt, the PCV valve is working properly. If no vacuum is felt, the PCV valve may be bad or the hose may be plugged. Also, check for vacuum leaks at the valve, filler cap and all the hoses.

Replacement

7   Pull straight up on the valve to remove it. Check the rubber grommet for cracks and distortion. If it's damaged, replace it.

8   If the valve is clogged, the hose is also probably plugged. Remove the hose and clean it with solvent.

9   After cleaning the hose, inspect it for damage, wear and deterioration. Make sure it fits snugly on the fittings.

10   If necessary, install a new PCV valve.

11   Install the clean PCV hose. Make sure that the PCV valve and hose are secure.

9   Catalytic converter

Refer to illustrations 9.2, 9.4 and 9.5

Note: *Because of a federally-mandated extended warranty which covers emissions-related components such as the catalytic converter, check with a dealer service department before replacing the converter at your own expense.*

General description

1   To reduce hydrocarbon, carbon monoxide and oxides of nitrogen emissions, all vehicles are equipped with a three-way catalyst system which oxidizes and reduces these chemicals, converting them into harmless nitrogen, carbon dioxide and water.

2   The catalytic converter is mounted in the exhaust system much like a muffler **(see illustration)**.

Check

3   Periodically inspect the catalytic converter-to-exhaust pipe mating flanges and bolts. Make sure that there are no loose bolts and no leaks between the flanges.

4   Look for dents in or damage to the catalytic converter protector **(see illustration)**. If any part of the protector is damaged or dented enough to touch the converter, repair or replace it.

5   Inspect the heat insulator for damage. Make sure that there is adequate clearance between the heat insulator and the catalytic converter **(see illustration)**.

Replacement

6   To replace the catalytic converter, refer to Chapter 4.

Chapter 7 Part A
Manual transaxle

Contents

Specifications

General
Shift lever preload .... 0.1 to 0.3 lbs

Torque specifications
Ft-lbs (unless otherwise indicated)

Back-up light switch
    1992 and 1993 30
    1994 and later 33
Transaxle-to-engine bolts
    10 mm bolts 34
    12 mm bolts 47

1 General information

The vehicles covered by this manual are equipped with either a 5-speed manual or a 4-speed automatic transaxle. Information on the manual transaxle is included in this Part of Chapter 7. Service procedures for the automatic transaxle are contained in Chapter 7, Part B.

The manual transaxle is a compact, two-piece, lightweight aluminum alloy housing containing both the transmission and differential assemblies.

Because of the complexity, unavailability of replacement parts and special tools necessary, internal repair procedures for the manual transaxle are not recommended for the home mechanic. For readers who wish to tackle a transaxle rebuild, exploded views and a brief *Manual transaxle overhaul - general information* Section are provided. The bulk of information in this Chapter is devoted to removal and installation procedures.

2 Shift and select cables - replacement

Refer to illustrations 2.3a and 2.3b

1   Remove the center console (see Chapter 11).
2   Raise the vehicle and support it securely on jackstands.
3   Remove the retaining clips and washers from the cable ends at the transaxle **(see illustrations)**.

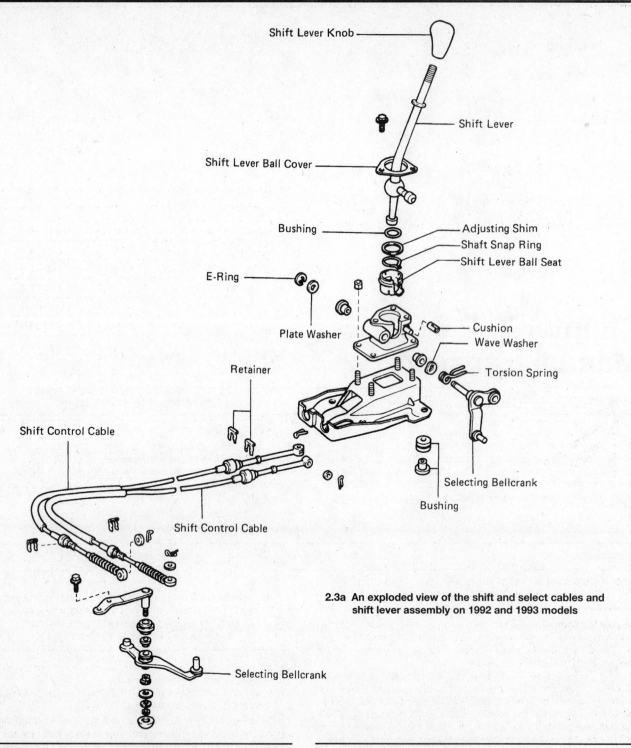

Shift Lever Knob

Shift Lever

Shift Lever Ball Cover

Bushing

E-Ring

Plate Washer

Retainer

Shift Control Cable

Shift Control Cable

Adjusting Shim
Shaft Snap Ring
Shift Lever Ball Seat

Cushion
Wave Washer

Torsion Spring

Selecting Bellcrank

Bushing

Selecting Bellcrank

2.3a   An exploded view of the shift and select cables and shift lever assembly on 1992 and 1993 models

4   Remove the large clip-type cable retainers that retain the shift and select cables to the bracket on the transaxle.

5   Remove the screws that attach the cable retainer, if applicable, to the engine side of the firewall. Remove the outer retainer and grommet.

6   Remove the clips and washers that attach the shift and select cables to the shift lever.

7   Remove the large clip-type cable retainers that attach the cables to the bracket at the forward end of the shift lever base.

8   Remove the inner retainer and grommet from the passenger side of the firewall.

9   Pull the cable out through the firewall from the engine side.

10   Installation is the reverse of removal.

3   Shift lever assembly - removal, installation, preload check and adjustment

Refer to illustrations 3.5 and 3.6

1   Remove the center console (see Chapter 11).

2   Remove the shift and select cable retainers and disconnect both cables from the shift lever (see Section 2).

3   Remove the retaining bolts and detach the shift lever assembly **(see illustrations 2.3a or 2.3b)**.

4   Installation is the reverse of removal.

5   Before installing the console on 1992 and 1993 models, check the shift lever preload by connecting a spring scale to the top of the shift

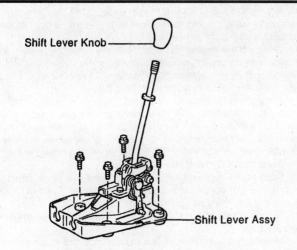

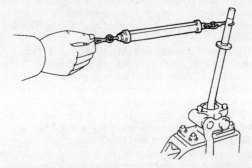

3.5 You'll need a spring scale like this to check shift lever preload

Mark	Thickness mm (in.)	Mark	Thickness mm (in.)
A	0.5 (0.020)	H	1.2 (0.047)
B	0.6 (0.024)	J	1.3 (0.051)
C	0.7 (0.028)	K	1.4 (0.055)
D	0.8 (0.031)	L	1.5 (0.059)
E	0.9 (0.035)	M	1.6 (0.063)
F	1.0 (0.039)	N	1.7 (0.067)
G	1.1 (0.043)		

**3.6 Shift lever preload adjustment shims
(1992 and 1993 models only)**

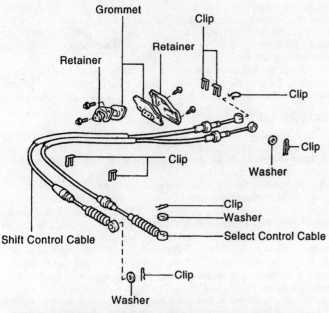

**2.3b An exploded view of the shift and select cables and shift
lever assembly on 1994 and 1995 models**

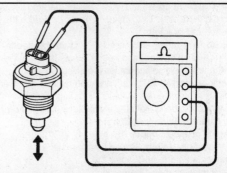

**4.2 To check the back-up light switch, verify that there's
continuity between the switch connector terminals
with the switch plunger depressed, and no
continuity with the plunger released**

lever **(see illustration)**. Pull lightly on the spring scale to make sure the initial pressure required to move the lever is within the range listed in this Chapter's Specifications. **Note:** *Preload adjustment isn't necessary on 1994 and later models.*

6   If the preload is not within specification, remove the lever **(see illustration 2.3a)** and install the proper adjusting shim. Shims are available in various thicknesses **(see illustration)** at any dealer parts department. The thicker the shim, the greater the preload. So, if the initial shift lever preload measurement indicates that the preload is too light, you would need a shim thicker than the one already installed; conversely, if the preload is too heavy, you would want a shim thinner than the one already installed. After you have exchanged shims, be sure to recheck the preload again.

7   The remainder of installation is the reverse of removal.

4   Back-up light switch - check and replacement

Refer to illustration 4.2

1   With the ignition key in the On position, place the shift lever in Reverse. The back-up lights should come on.

a) *If the lights don't come on, check the ignition switch, the GAUGE fuse, the bulbs and the wire harness (see Chapter 12).*

b) *If the lights remain on all the time, even when the shift lever is not in Reverse, check the wire harness.*

c) *If only one light comes on, but not the other, check the bulb for that light and check the harness.*

2   To check the operation of the back-up light switch itself, disconnect the electrical connector and remove the switch from the top of the transaxle, then use an ohmmeter to verify that there's continuity when the plunger is depressed, and no continuity when the plunger is released **(see illustration)**.

3   If the switch doesn't operate as described, replace it.

5   Manual transaxle - removal and installation

Removal

Note: *Read through the entire Section before beginning this procedure. The manufacturer recommends detaching the engine cradle and removing the transaxle from below. However, that method is difficult and dangerous without a vehicle hoist. We recommend*

7A

removing the engine and transaxle out the top as a unit, then separating the transaxle from the engine on the shop floor.

1   Place protective covers on the fenders and cowl and remove the hood (see Chapter 11).

2   Relieve the fuel system pressure (see Chapter 4).

3   Disconnect the negative cable from the battery. **Caution:** *If the stereo in your vehicle is equipped with an anti-theft system, make sure you have the correct activation code before disconnecting the battery.* **Note:** *On 1993 and later models, the airbag system will be disabled if the battery is disconnected for more than a brief period. If the airbag light comes on and stays on after the battery is reconnected, the vehicle must be taken to a dealer to have the system reset with a special tool.*

4   Remove the cruise control actuator cover, unplug the electrical connector for the actuator and remove the actuator (it's secured by three bolts on 1992 and 1993 models, by three nuts on 1994 and 1995 models).

5   Remove the battery and the battery tray (see Chapter 5).

6   Remove the air intake duct and the air cleaner housing (see Chapter 4).

7   Release the residual fuel pressure in the tank by removing the gas cap, then disconnect the fuel lines connecting the engine to the chassis (see Chapter 4). Plug or cap all open fittings.

8   Remove the fuel filter and fuel filter mounting bracket (see Chapter 1).

9   Remove the charcoal canister and the canister mounting bracket (see Chapter 6).

10   Remove the windshield washer tank and coolant reservoir tank (see Chapter 1).

11   Disconnect the throttle linkage and, if equipped, the cruise control cable from the throttle linkage (see Chapter 4).

12   Clearly label, then disconnect all vacuum lines, coolant and emissions hoses, wiring harness connectors and ground straps. Masking tape and/or a touch up paint applicator work well for marking items **(see illustration 6.7 in Chapter 2C)**. Take instant photos or sketch the locations of components and brackets.

13   Remove the cooling fan(s) and shroud(s). Drain the coolant and remove the radiator and all coolant and heater hoses (see Chapter 3).

14   Disconnect the shift and select cables (see Section 2).

15   Raise the vehicle and support it securely on jackstands. Remove the wheels.

16   Detach the exhaust pipe(s) from the manifold(s) (see Chapter 4).

17   Remove the splash shields (see Chapter 2).

18   Drain the engine oil (see Chapter 1).

19   Remove all accessory drivebelts (see Chapter 1).

20   Drain the transaxle fluid (see Chapter 1).

21   Remove the driveaxles (see Chapter 8).

22   On models with power steering, unbolt the power steering pump (see Chapter 10). It's unnecessary to disconnect the power steering fluid hoses. Swing the pump aside and suspend it out of the way with a piece of wire; don't allow the pump to hang by the hoses.

23   On models with air conditioning, unbolt the compressor and set it aside **(see illustration 6.16 in Chapter 2C)**. Do not disconnect the refrigerant hoses.

24   On four-cylinder models equipped with an oil cooler (small canister mounted between the oil filter and the block), remove the oil filter, hoses connected to the cooler, and the oil cooler **(see illustration 6.18 in Chapter 2C)**.

25   Remove the clutch release cylinder, hydraulic line and hydraulic line clamp (see Chapter 8). On 1992 models, remove the clutch accumulator, the hydraulic line, the hydraulic line clamp and the clutch release cylinder bracket. (see Chapter 8).

26   On four-cylinder models, remove the stiffener plate (see Chapter 2).

27   Attach a lifting sling to the engine. Position a hoist and connect the sling to it. Take up the slack until there is slight tension on the hoist.

28   Remove the right (passenger side) engine mount, the engine front mount, the transaxle shock absorber, the left (driver's side) transaxle mount (located underneath the left end of the transaxle, between the transaxle and the engine cradle) and the rear (firewall-side) engine mount bracket (see Chapter 2). Remove the center bearing support from the block.

29   Recheck to be sure nothing except the mounts are still connecting the engine to the vehicle or to the transaxle. Disconnect and label anything still remaining.

30   Slowly lift the engine/transaxle assembly out of the vehicle. It may be necessary to pry the mounts away from the frame brackets **(see illustration 6.26 in Chapter 2C)**. **Caution:** *Do not depress the clutch pedal while the transaxle is removed from the vehicle.*

31   *Move the engine/transaxle assembly away from the vehicle and carefully lower the hoist until the engine/transaxle assembly is near the floor. Leave enough room for a floor jack underneath the transaxle.* **Warning:** *Do not place any part of your body under the engine/transaxle assembly when it's supported only by a hoist or other lifting device.*

32   Remove the starter motor (see Chapter 5).

33   Support the transaxle with a floor jack. Place a block of wood on the jack head to prevent damage to the transaxle. Safety chains will help steady the transaxle on the jack.

34   Remove the transaxle-to-engine bolts and the engine-to-transaxle bolt.

35   Move the transaxle and jack away from the engine until the transaxle is clear of the engine. Keep the transaxle level as you're separating it from the engine to prevent damage to the input shaft. Once the input shaft is clear, lower the transaxle to the floor.

36   The clutch components can now be inspected (see Chapter 8). In most cases, new clutch components should be routinely installed whenever the transaxle is removed.

37   Check the engine and transaxle mounts and the transaxle shock absorber. If any of these components are worn or damaged, replace them.

Installation

38   If removed, install the clutch components (see Chapter 8). Apply a dab of high temperature grease to the pilot bearing.

39   With the transaxle secured to the jack as on removal, raise it into position and then carefully slide it forward, engaging the input shaft with the clutch splines. Do not use excessive force to install the transaxle - if the input shaft does not slide into place, readjust the angle of the transaxle so it is level and/or turn the input shaft so the splines engage properly with the clutch. **Caution:** *Do NOT use transaxle-to-engine bolts to force the engine and transaxle into alignment. Doing so could crack or damage major components. If you experience difficulties, have an assistant help you line up the dowel pins on the block with the transaxle. Some wiggling of the engine and/or the transaxle will probably be necessary to secure proper alignment of the two.*

40   Install the transaxle-to-engine bolts and the engine-to-transaxle bolt. Tighten the bolts to the torque listed in this Chapter's Specifications.

41   Lift the engine/transaxle assembly with the engine hoist and carefully lower the assembly into the engine compartment. Tighten all nuts and bolts securely.

42   Install the right engine mount, the front engine mount, the transaxle shock absorber, the left transaxle mount and the rear engine mount. Install the center bearing support on the rear of the block. Tighten all mounting bolts and nuts securely.

43   Reinstall the remaining components in the reverse order of removal.

44   Remove the jack and hoist and lower the vehicle. Tighten the wheel lug nuts to the torque listed in the Chapter 1 Specifications.

45   Add the specified amounts of coolant, oil and transmission fluid (see Chapter 1).

46   Connect the negative battery cable. Start the engine and check for proper operation and leaks.

47   Shut off the engine and recheck the fluid levels. Road test the vehicle to check for proper transaxle operation and check for leakage.

6   Manual transaxle overhaul - general information

Refer to illustrations 6.4a through 6.4i

1   Overhauling a manual transaxle is a difficult job for the do-it-yourselfer. It involves the disassembly and reassembly of many small

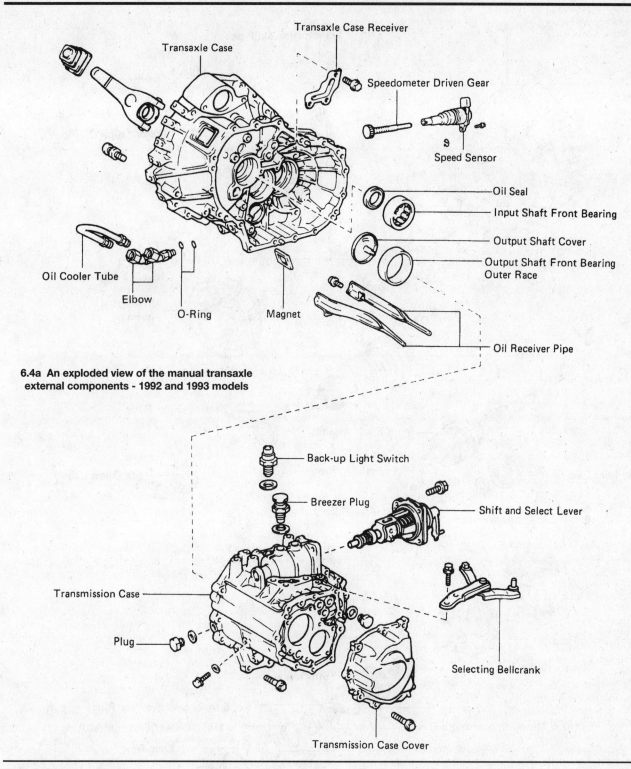

6.4a An exploded view of the manual transaxle external components - 1992 and 1993 models

7A

parts. Numerous clearances must be precisely measured and, if necessary, changed with select fit spacers and snap-rings. As a result, if transaxle problems arise, it can be removed and installed by a competent do-it-yourselfer, but overhaul should be left to a transmission repair shop. Rebuilt transaxles may be available - check with your dealer parts department and auto parts stores. At any rate, the time and money involved in an overhaul is almost sure to exceed the cost of a rebuilt unit.

2   Nevertheless, it's not impossible for an inexperienced mechanic to rebuild a transaxle if the special tools are available and the job is done in a deliberate step-by-step manner so nothing is overlooked.

3   The tools necessary for an overhaul include internal and external snap-ring pliers, a bearing puller, a slide hammer, a set of pin punches, a dial indicator and possibly a hydraulic press. In addition, a large, sturdy workbench and a vise or transaxle stand will be required.

4   During disassembly of the transaxle, make careful notes of how each component was removed, where it fits in relation to other components and what holds it in place. Exploded views are included to illustrate the correct transaxle assembly **(see illustrations)** - but actually noting how they are installed when you remove the components will make it much easier to get the transaxle back together correctly.

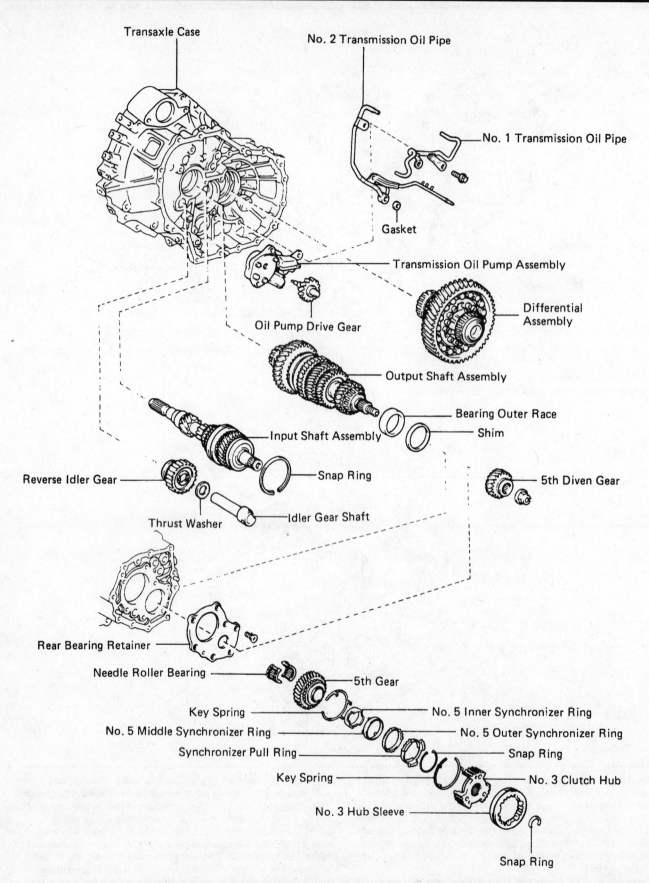

6.4b   An exploded view of the manual transaxle internal components - 1992 and 1993 models

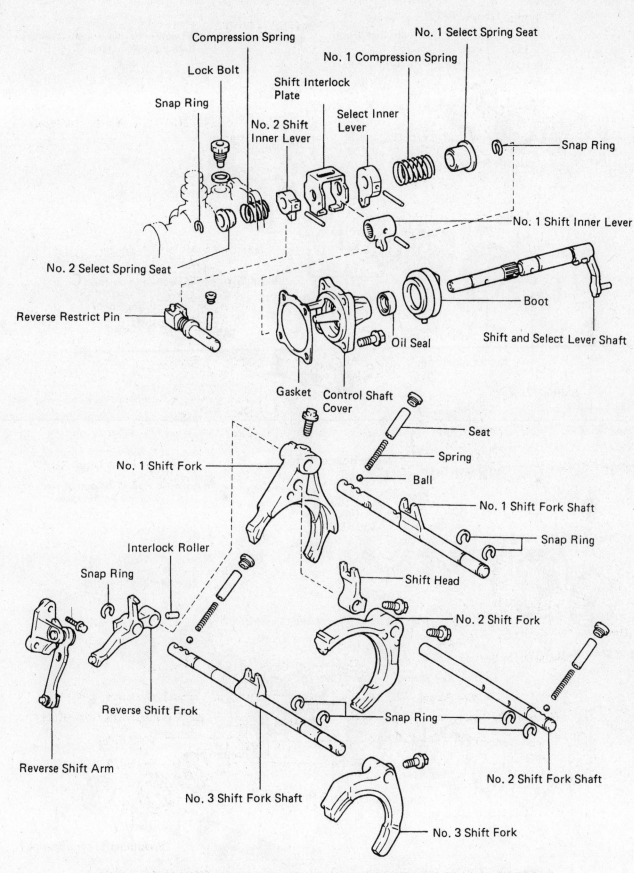

6.4c An exploded view of the manual transaxle shift fork components - 1992 and 1993 models

7A

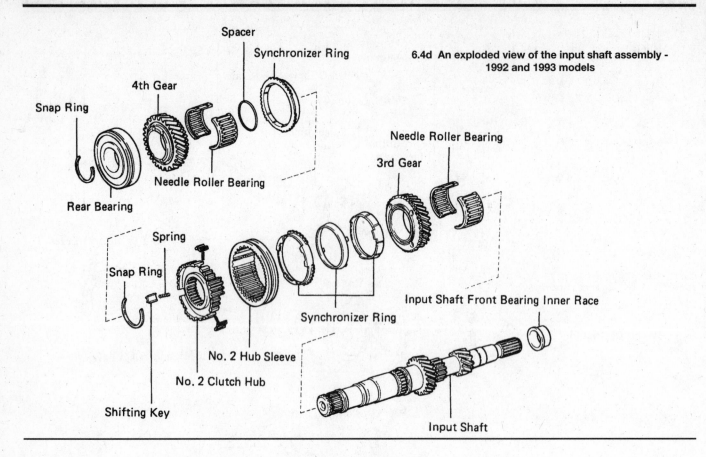

6.4d An exploded view of the input shaft assembly - 1992 and 1993 models

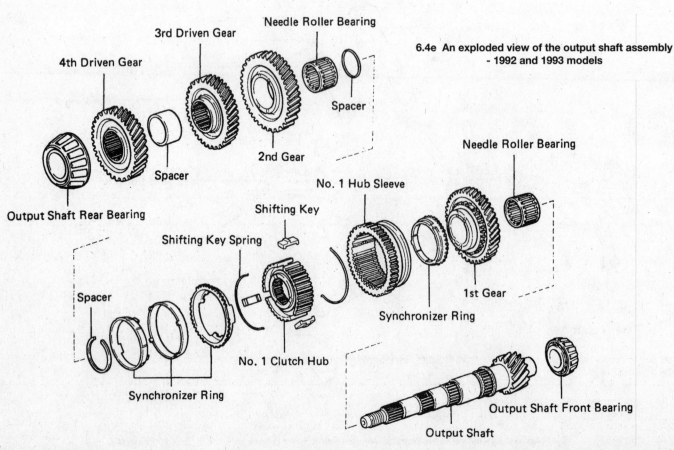

6.4e An exploded view of the output shaft assembly - 1992 and 1993 models

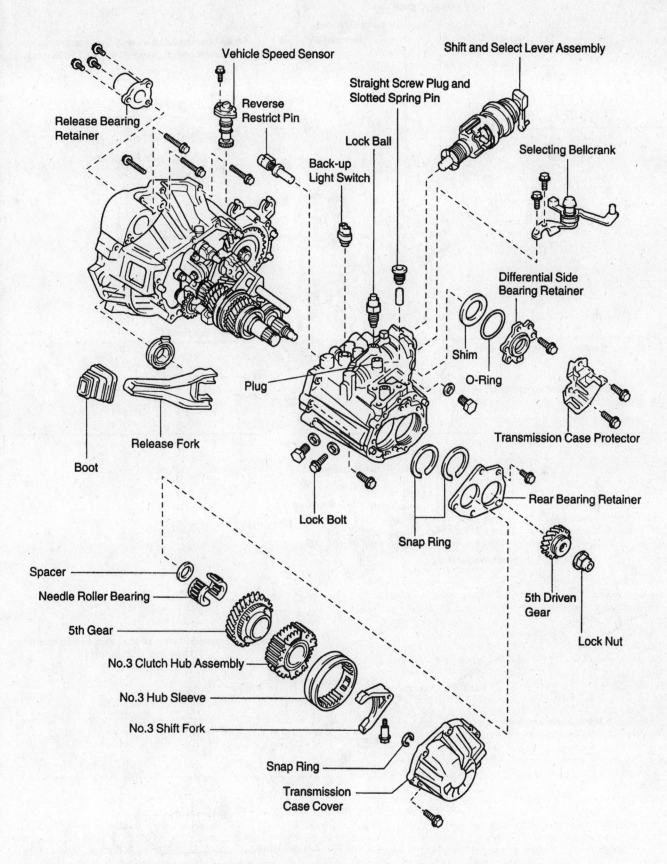

Vehicle Speed Sensor

Shift and Select Lever Assembly

Release Bearing Retainer

Reverse Restrict Pin

Straight Screw Plug and Slotted Spring Pin

Lock Ball

Back-up Light Switch

Selecting Bellcrank

Differential Side Bearing Retainer

Plug

Shim

O-Ring

Boot

Release Fork

Transmission Case Protector

Lock Bolt

Snap Ring

Rear Bearing Retainer

Spacer

Needle Roller Bearing

5th Driven Gear

5th Gear

No.3 Clutch Hub Assembly

Lock Nut

No.3 Hub Sleeve

No.3 Shift Fork

Snap Ring

Transmission Case Cover

6.4f An exploded view of the manual transaxle external components - 1994 and later models

7A

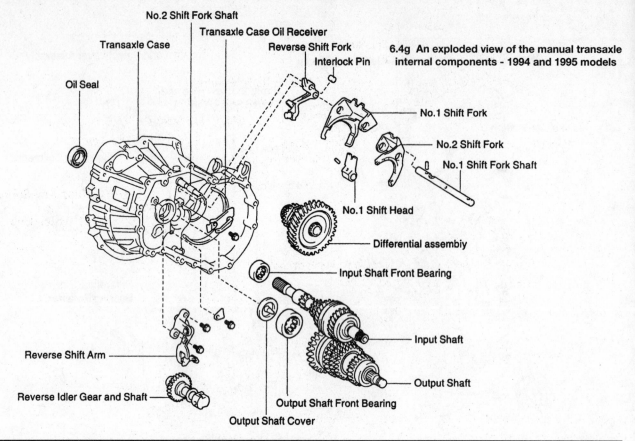

6.4g An exploded view of the manual transaxle internal components - 1994 and 1995 models

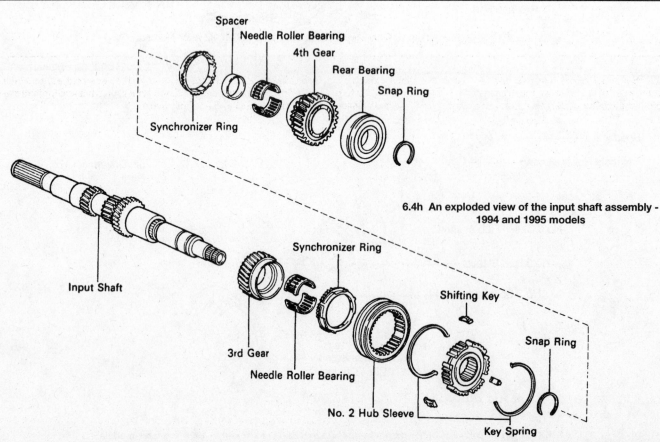

6.4h An exploded view of the input shaft assembly - 1994 and 1995 models

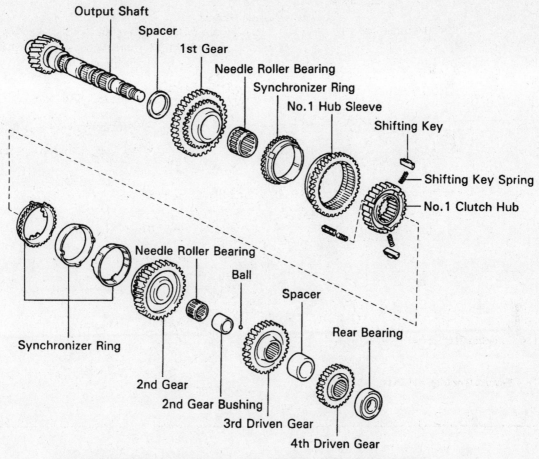

6.4i An exploded view of the output shaft assembly - 1994 and later models

5   Before taking the transaxle apart for repair, it will help if you have some idea what area of the transaxle is malfunctioning. Certain problems can be closely tied to specific areas in the transaxle, which can make component examination and replacement easier. Refer to the *Troubleshooting* section at the front of this manual for information regarding possible sources of trouble.

7A

Notes

Chapter 7 Part B
Automatic transaxle

Contents

7B

Specifications

Throttle valve outer cable end-to-stopper	0 to 3/64-inch
Shift lock system	
Shift lock solenoid resistance	21 to 27 ohms
Key interlock solenoid resistance	12.5 to 16.5 ohms
Shift solenoid resistance	10 to 15 ohms
Lock-up solenoid resistance	10 to 15 ohms

Torque specifications

Ft-lbs (unless otherwise indicated)

Torque converter to driveplate bolts	20
Transaxle-to-engine mounting bolts	
10 mm	32
12 mm	47
Vehicle speed sensor hold-down bolt	156 in-lbs

1　General information

All vehicles covered in this manual are equipped with either a 5-speed manual or a 4-speed automatic transaxle. All information on the automatic transaxle is included in this Part of Chapter 7. Information for the manual transaxle can be found in Part A of this Chapter.

Due to the complexity of the automatic transaxles covered in this manual and to the specialized equipment necessary to perform most service operations, this Chapter contains only those procedures related to general diagnosis, routine maintenance, adjustment and removal and installation.

If the transaxle requires major repair work, it should be left to a dealer service department or an automotive or transmission repair shop. You can, however, remove and install the transaxle yourself and save the expense, even if the repair work is done by a transmission shop.

2　Diagnosis - general

Automatic transaxle malfunctions may be caused by five general conditions:

a) *poor engine performance*
b) *improper adjustments*
c) *hydraulic malfunctions*
d) *mechanical malfunctions*
e) *malfunctions in the computer or its signal network*

Diagnosis of these problems should always begin with a check of the easily repaired items: fluid level and condition (see Chapter 1), shift linkage adjustment and throttle linkage adjustment. Next, perform a road test to determine if the problem has been corrected or if more diagnosis is necessary. If the problem persists after the preliminary tests and corrections are completed, additional diagnosis should be done by a dealer service department or transmission repair shop. Refer to the *Troubleshooting* section at the front of this manual for information on symptoms of transaxle problems.

Preliminary checks

1　Drive the vehicle to warm the transaxle to normal operating temperature.
2　Check the fluid level as described in Chapter 1:

a) *If the fluid level is unusually low, add enough fluid to bring the level within the designated area of the dipstick, then check for external leaks (see below).*
b) *If the fluid level is abnormally high, drain off the excess, then check the drained fluid for contamination by coolant. The presence of engine coolant in the automatic transmission fluid indicates that a failure has occurred in the internal radiator walls that separate the coolant from the transmission fluid (see Chapter 3).*
c) *If the fluid is foaming, drain it and refill the transaxle, then check for coolant in the fluid, or a high fluid level.*

3　Check the engine idle speed. **Note:** *If the engine is malfunctioning, do not proceed with the preliminary checks until it has been repaired and runs normally.*
4　Check the throttle valve cable for freedom of movement. Adjust it if necessary (see Section 4). **Note:** *The throttle cable may function properly when the engine is shut off and cold, but it may malfunction once the engine is hot. Check it cold and at normal engine operating temperature.*
5　Inspect the shift control linkage (see Section 3). Make sure that it's properly adjusted and that the linkage operates smoothly.

Fluid leak diagnosis

6　Most fluid leaks are easy to locate visually. Repair usually consists of replacing a seal or gasket. If a leak is difficult to find, the following procedure may help.
7　Identify the fluid. Make sure it's transmission fluid and not engine oil or brake fluid (automatic transmission fluid is a deep red color).

8　Try to pinpoint the source of the leak. Drive the vehicle several miles, then park it over a large sheet of cardboard. After a minute or two, you should be able to locate the leak by determining the source of the fluid dripping onto the cardboard.
9　Make a careful visual inspection of the suspected component and the area immediately around it. Pay particular attention to gasket mating surfaces. A mirror is often helpful for finding leaks in areas that are hard to see.
10　If the leak still cannot be found, clean the suspected area thoroughly with a degreaser or solvent, then dry it.
11　Drive the vehicle for several miles at normal operating temperature and varying speeds. After driving the vehicle, visually inspect the suspected component again.
12　Once the leak has been located, the cause must be determined before it can be properly repaired. If a gasket is replaced but the sealing flange is bent, the new gasket will not stop the leak. The bent flange must be straightened.
13　Before attempting to repair a leak, check to make sure that the following conditions are corrected or they may cause another leak. **Note:** *Some of the following conditions cannot be fixed without highly specialized tools and expertise. Such problems must be referred to a transmission shop or a dealer service department.*

Gasket leaks

14　Check the pan periodically. Make sure the bolts are tight, no bolts are missing, the gasket is in good condition and the pan is flat (dents in the pan may indicate damage to the valve body inside).
15　If the pan gasket is leaking, the fluid level or the fluid pressure may be too high, the vent may be plugged, the pan bolts may be too tight, the pan sealing flange may be warped, the sealing surface of the transaxle housing may be damaged, the gasket may be damaged or the transaxle casting may be cracked or porous. If sealant instead of gasket material has been used to form a seal between the pan and the transaxle housing, it may be the wrong sealant.

Seal leaks

16　If a transaxle seal is leaking, the fluid level or pressure may be too high, the vent may be plugged, the seal bore may be damaged, the seal itself may be damaged or improperly installed, the surface of the shaft protruding through the seal may be damaged or a loose bearing may be causing excessive shaft movement.
17　Make sure the dipstick tube seal is in good condition and the tube is properly seated. Periodically check the area around the speedometer gear or sensor for leakage. If transmission fluid is evident, check the O-ring for damage.

Case leaks

18　If the case itself appears to be leaking, the casting is porous and will have to be repaired or replaced.
19　Make sure the oil cooler hose fittings are tight and in good condition.

Fluid comes out vent pipe or fill tube

20　If this condition occurs, the transaxle is overfilled, there is coolant in the fluid, the case is porous, the dipstick is incorrect, the vent is plugged or the drain-back holes are plugged.

3　Shift cable - adjustment and replacement

Adjustment

Refer to illustrations 3.3 and 3.4

1　When the shift lever inside the vehicle is moved from the Neutral position to other positions, it should move smoothly and accurately to each position and the gear position indicator should indicate the correct gear position. If the indicator isn't aligned with the correct position, adjust the shift cable as follows:
2　Raise the vehicle and support it securely on jackstands. Remove the splash shields that cover the area between the front of the vehicle

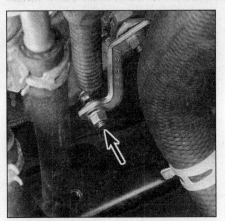

3.3 Before adjusting the shift cable, loosen the swivel nut (arrow) that connects the shift cable to the manual lever

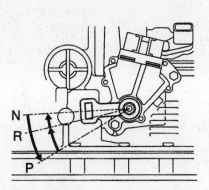

3.4 To adjust the shift cable, push the manual lever all the way down, return it two positions to the Neutral position, place the shift lever inside the vehicle at the Neutral position and tighten the swivel nut

3.8 To disconnect the shift cable from the transaxle, remove the large C-clip retainer (arrow) from the bracket on the front of the transaxle

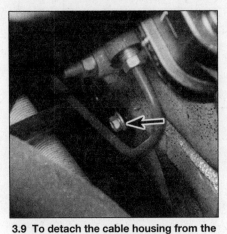

3.9 To detach the cable housing from the firewall, remove this bolt (arrow)

3.11 To detach the shift cable from the shift lever base, pry off this C-clip retainer (arrow)

3.12 To disconnect the shift cable from the shift lever, remove the retaining clip and pull out the clevis pin (arrow)

and the lower crossmember (see Chapter 11).

3   Loosen the swivel nut on the manual shift lever at the transaxle **(see illustration)**.

4   Push the lever down all the way, then return it two notches to the Neutral position **(see illustration)**.

5   Move the shift lever inside the vehicle to the Neutral position.

6   While holding the lever with a slight pressure toward the Reverse position, tighten the swivel nut securely.

7   Check the operation of the transaxle in each shift lever position (try to start the engine in each gear - the starter should operate in the Park and Neutral positions only).

Replacement

Refer to illustrations 3.8, 3.9, 3.11 and 3.12

8   Disconnect the cable from the manual lever **(see illustration 3.3)** and remove the large C-clip cable retainer **(see illustration)** from the bracket above the manual lever.

9   Remove the bolts from the cable housing retainer on the firewall **(see illustration)**.

10   Remove the center console (see Chapter 11).

11   Pry off the large C-clip cable retainer **(see illustration)**.

12   Remove the retaining clip **(see illustration)**, pull out the clevis pin and disconnect the cable from the shift lever.

13   Pull the cable through the firewall.

14   Installation is the reverse of removal.

15   Be sure to adjust the cable when you're done.

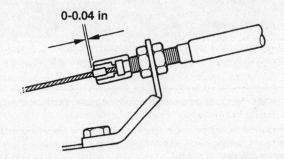

4.2 Throttle valve (TV) cable housing-to-stopper gap details

0-0.04 in

4   Throttle valve (TV) cable - check and adjustment

Refer to illustration 4.2

1   Have an assistant hold the throttle pedal down while you verify that the throttle valve linkage opens all the way.

2   If the linkage does not open all the way, ask your assistant to hold the pedal down while you loosen the adjusting nuts and adjust the cable until the mark or stopper is the specified distance from the boot end **(see illustration)**.

3   Tighten the adjusting nuts securely, recheck the clearance and make sure the link opens all the way when the throttle is depressed.

7B

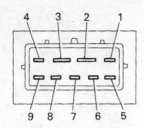

Terminal Range	2	3	6	1	5	7	8	9	4
P	O—O		O—	—O					
R			O—		—O				
N	O—O		O—			—O			
D			O—				—O		
2			O—					—O	
L			O—						—O

5.4a Park/Neutral position switch terminal guide and continuity table (1992 and 1993 models)

5.8 Remove the manual lever retaining nut (arrow), detach the manual lever and remove the switch retaining bolts (arrow)

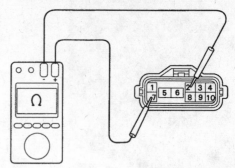

O——O Continuity

Terminal Shift Position	5	6	2	7	8	9	10	3	4
P	O—	—O	O—	—O					
R			O—		—O				
N	O—	—O	O—			—O			
D			O—				—O		
2			O—					—O	
L			O—						—O

5.4b Park/Neutral position switch terminal guide and continuity table (1994 and later models)

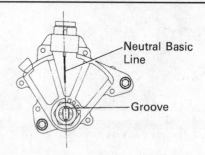

Neutral Basic Line

Groove

5.12 Park/Neutral position switch alignment details

Replacement

6   Raise the front of the vehicle and place it securely on jackstands.
7   Disconnect the electrical connector.
8   Remove the manual lever retaining nut **(see illustration)**.
9   Remove the switch retaining bolts.
10   Remove the switch.
11   Installation is the reverse of removal. Be sure to adjust the switch.

Adjustment

Refer to illustration 5.12

12   Loosen the switch retaining bolts and rotate the switch until the groove and the neutral basic line are aligned **(see illustration)**. Hold the switch in this position and tighten the bolts.

6   Shift lock system - description, check and component replacement

Description

Refer to illustrations 6.1a and 6.1b

1   The shift lock system **(see illustrations)** prevents the shift lever from being shifted out of Park until the brake pedal is applied. The

5   Park/Neutral position switch - check, replacement and adjustment

1   The Park/Neutral position switch prevents the engine from starting in any gear other than Park or Neutral. If the engine starts with the shift lever in any position other than Park or Neutral, adjust the switch. The Park/Neutral position switch is also an information sensor for the Electronic Controlled Transaxle (ECT) Electronic Control Unit (ECU). When the shift lever is placed in position, the Park/Neutral position switch sends a voltage signal to the ECU.

Check

Refer to illustrations 5.4a and 5.4b

2   Raise the front of the vehicle and place it securely on jackstands.
3   Disconnect the electrical connector from the Park/Neutral position switch.
4   Using an ohmmeter, check continuity between the indicated terminals for each switch position **(see illustrations)**.
5   If the switch continuity isn't as specified, replace it.

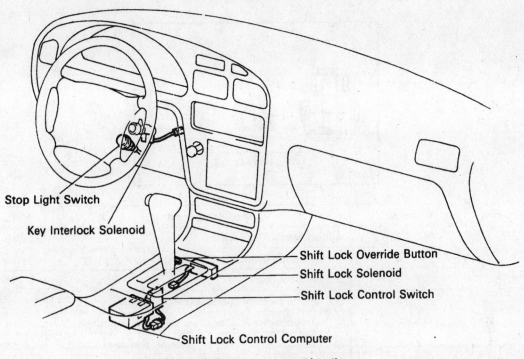

6.1a Shift lock system component location

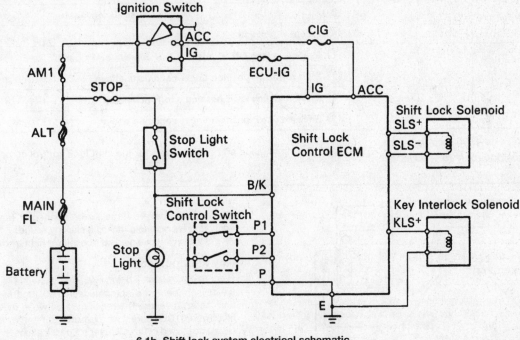

6.1b Shift lock system electrical schematic

system consists of a stop light switch, a key interlock solenoid, a shift lock override button, a shift lock solenoid, a shift lock control switch and a shift lock control computer. If the shift lock system doesn't perform as described, check the following components.

Check

Shift lock control computer

Refer to illustration 6.3

2   Remove the console (see Chapter 11).

3   Using a digital voltmeter, bridge the indicated terminals of each of the three computer connectors; measure the voltage with the ignition switch, brake pedal and/or shift lever in the indicated positions **(see illustration)**. Note: *Because these are running voltages, the connectors must be backprobed, i.e. they must be bridged from the back side of the connector. Do not attempt to push the probes of your voltmeter into the back side of the connector terminals; they're big enough to damage the connector. Instead, use a pair of long sharp pins, then clip onto them with a pair of alligator clips.*

4   If the computer doesn't operate as described, replace it.

7B

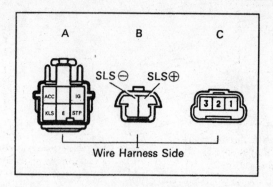

Wire Harness Side

Connector	Terminal	Measuring condition		Voltage (V)
A	ACC – E	Ignition switch ACC position		10 – 14
	IG – E	Ignition switch ON position		10 – 14
	B/K – E	Depress brake pedal		10 – 14
	KLS – E	① Ignition switch ACC position and P position		0
		② Ignition switch ACC position and except P position		10 – 14 *
		③ (Approx-after one second)		6 – 9
B	SLS + – SLS-	① Ignition switch ON position and P position		0
		② Depress brake pedal		8.5 – 13.5
		③ (Approx-after 20 seconds)		5.5 – 9.5 **
		④ Except P position		0
C	P_1 – P	① Ignition switch ON, P position and depress brake pedal		0
		② Shift except P position under conditions above		9 – 13.5
	P_2 – P	① Ignition switch ACC position and P position		9 – 13.5
		② Shift except P position under condition above		0

* *7.5-11 on 1995 models*
** *Does not apply to 1995 models*

6.3 Terminal guide and voltage table for the shift lock control computer

---

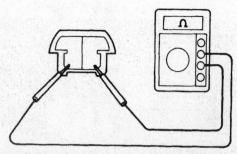

6.5 Check the resistance between the terminals of the electrical connector for the shift lock solenoid and compare your measurement to the resistance listed in this Chapter's Specifications

Shift lock solenoid

Refer to illustrations 6.5 and 6.6

5   Disconnect the solenoid electrical connector and, using an ohmmeter, measure the resistance between the two terminals **(see illustration)**. Compare your measurement to the shift lock solenoid resistance listed in this Chapter's Specifications.

6   Apply battery voltage to the connector **(see illustration)** and verify that the solenoid makes a clicking sound.

7   If the shift lock solenoid doesn't perform as described, replace it.

Key interlock solenoid

Refer to illustrations 6.8 and 6.9

8   Disconnect the solenoid electrical connector and, using an ohmmeter, measure the resistance between the two terminals **(see illustration)**. Compare your measurement to the key interlock solenoid resistance listed in this Chapter's Specifications.

9   Apply battery voltage to the connector **(see illustration)** and verify that the solenoid makes a clicking sound.

10   If the key interlock solenoid doesn't perform as described, replace it.

Shift lock control switch

Refer to illustration 6.11

11   Disconnect the shift lock control switch electrical connector and, using a continuity tester or an ohmmeter, verify that there's continuity between each of the indicated terminals when the shift lever is placed in the indicated positions **(see illustration)**.

12   If the shift lock control switch doesn't perform as described, replace it.

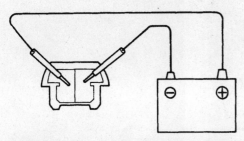

6.6 Apply battery voltage to the terminals of the electrical connector for the shift lock solenoid and verify that the solenoid makes a clicking sound

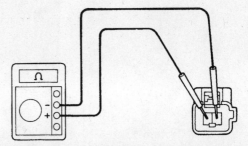

6.8 Check the resistance between the terminals of the electrical connector for the key interlock solenoid and compare your measurement to the resistance listed in this Chapter's Specifications

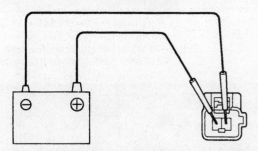

6.9 Apply battery voltage to the terminals of the electrical connector for the key interlock solenoid and verify that the solenoid makes a clicking sound

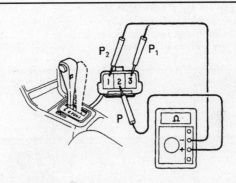

	Terminal		
Shift Position	P	P₁	P₂
P range (Release button is not pushed)	O————	————O	
P Range (Release button is pushed)	O———— O	————O	————O
R, N, D, 2, L range	O————		————O

6.11 Terminal guide and continuity table for the shift lock control switch

6.14a The shift lock control computer (arrow) is located behind the shift lever base; the shift lock control switch (not visible in this photo) is located just ahead of the computer, within the shift lever base

Component replacement

Refer to illustrations 6.14a and 6.14b

13   Remove the center console (see Chapter 11).

14   The shift lock control computer **(see illustration)** is located to the rear of the shift lever base. The shift lock control switch is located in front of the computer, within the shift lever base, immediately behind and below the shift lever. The shift lock solenoid **(see illustration)** is located at the front of the shift lever base. To replace one of these units, simply disconnect the electrical connector and unclip or unscrew the device from its mounting bracket.

15   The key interlock solenoid is located near the ignition switch (see Chapter 12).

7B

6.14b The shift lock solenoid (arrow) is located at the front of the shift lever base

7.4 Carefully pry out the old driveaxle seal with a prybar, screwdriver or a special seal removal tool; make sure you don't gouge or nick the surface of the seal bore

7.6 Drive in the new driveaxle seal with a large socket or a special seal installer

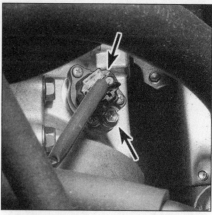

7.9 To remove the vehicle speed sensor from the transaxle, disconnect the electrical connector and remove the sensor hold-down bolt (arrows)

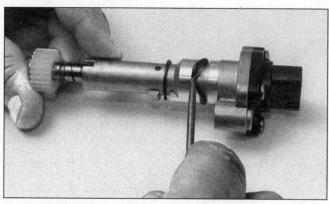

7.10 Remove the O-ring from the speedometer driven gear

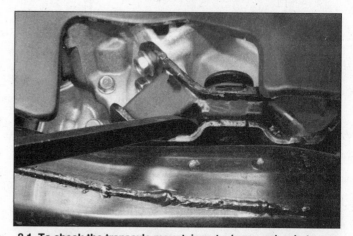

8.1 To check the transaxle mount, insert a large prybar between the rubber portion of the mount and the engine cradle, and try to lever the transaxle up and down; if the mount allows the transaxle to move considerably, or if the rubber portion is cracked or torn, replace the mount

7   Oil seal replacement

Refer to illustrations 7.4, 7.6, 7.9 and 7.10

1   Oil leaks frequently occur due to wear of the driveaxle oil seals and/or the speedometer drive gear oil seal and O-rings. Replacement of these seals is relatively easy, since the repairs can usually be performed without removing the transaxle from the vehicle.

Driveaxle seals

2   The driveaxle oil seals are located in either sides of the transaxle, where the driveaxle shaft is splined into the differential. If leakage at the seal is suspected, raise the vehicle and support it securely on jackstands. If the seal is leaking, lubricant will be found on the side of the transaxle.

3   Remove the driveaxle assembly (see Chapter 8). If you're replacing the right seal on models equipped with four-cylinder engines, remove the intermediate shaft and the driveaxle assembly as a single unit. On models equipped with V6 engines, you'll have to remove the side-gear shaft (left side) or the intermediate shaft (right side) along with the driveaxle, so don't remove the bolts that attach the driveaxle assembly to the side-gear shaft or intermediate shaft. Remove the entire assembly as a single unit.

4   Using a screwdriver or prybar, carefully pry the oil seal out of the transaxle bore **(see illustration)**.

5   If the oil seal cannot be removed with a screwdriver or prybar, a special oil seal removal tool (available at auto parts stores) will be required.

6   Using a large section of pipe or a large deep socket as a drift, install the new oil seal. Drive it into the bore squarely and make sure

that it is completely seated **(see illustration)**. Lubricate the lip of the new seal with multi-purpose grease.

7   Install the driveaxle assembly (see Chapter 8). Be careful not to damage the lip of the new seal.

Speedometer driven gear seal

8   The vehicle speed sensor and speedometer driven gear housing is located on the differential (rear) part of the transaxle housing. Look for lubricant around the sensor housing to determine if the O-ring is leaking.

9   Disconnect the electrical connector from the vehicle speed sensor and remove the sensor and speedometer driven gear housing from the transaxle **(see illustration)**.

10   Remove the O-ring **(see illustration)**.

11   Install a new O-ring on the driven gear housing and reinstall the speedometer driven gear and vehicle speed sensor housing. Tighten the hold-down bolt to the torque listed in this Chapter's Specifications.

8   Transaxle mount - check and replacement

Refer to illustration 8.1

1   Insert a large screwdriver or prybar between the mount bracket and the rubber portion of the mount and pry up **(see illustration)**.

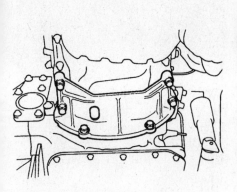

9.25a To gain access to the driveplate-to-torque converter bolts on models equipped with four-cylinder engines, remove this plate, which is retained by six bolts

9.25b To gain access to the driveplate-to-torque converter bolts on models equipped with V6 engines, remove this small plate, which is retained by two bolts (arrows)

9.25c Rotate the crankshaft to bring each of the six driveplate-to-torque converter bolts into the access area where it can be removed

2   The transaxle should not move excessively away from the mount. If it does, or if the rubber is torn or badly cracked, replace the mount.
3   To replace a mount, support the transaxle with a jack, remove the nuts and bolts and remove the mount. It may be necessary to raise the transaxle slightly to provide enough clearance to remove the mount.
4   Installation is the reverse of removal.

9   Automatic transaxle - removal and installation

Removal

Refer to illustrations 9.25a, 9.25.b and 9.25c
Note: *Read through the entire Section before beginning this procedure. The manufacturer recommends detaching the engine cradle and removing the transaxle from below. However, that method is difficult and dangerous without a vehicle hoist. We recommend removing the engine and transaxle out the top as a unit, then separating the transaxle from the engine on the shop floor.*
1   Place protective covers on the fenders and cowl and remove the hood (see Chapter 11).
2   Relieve the fuel system pressure (see Chapter 4).
3   Disconnect the negative cable from the battery. **Caution:** *If the stereo in your vehicle is equipped with an anti-theft system, make sure you have the correct activation code before disconnecting the battery.* **Note:** *On 1993 and later models, the airbag system will be disabled if the battery is disconnected for more than a brief period. If the airbag light comes on and stays on after the battery is reconnected, the vehicle must be taken to a dealer to have the system reset with a special tool.*
4   Remove the cruise control actuator cover, if equipped. Disconnect the electrical connector for the actuator and remove the actuator.
5   Remove the battery and the battery tray (see Chapter 5).
6   Remove the air intake duct and the air cleaner housing (see Chapter 4).
7   Release the residual fuel pressure in the tank by removing the gas cap, then disconnect the fuel lines connecting the engine to the chassis (see Chapter 4). Plug or cap all open fittings.
8   Remove the fuel filter and fuel filter mounting bracket (see Chapter 1).
9   Remove the charcoal canister and the canister mounting bracket (see Chapter 6).
10   Remove the windshield washer tank and coolant reservoir tank (see Chapter 1).
11   Disconnect the throttle cable and, on models with an automatic transaxle, the throttle valve (TV) cable from the throttle linkage (see

Chapter 4). Disconnect the cruise control cable (if equipped) from the throttle linkage (see Chapter 12).
12   Clearly label, then disconnect all vacuum lines, coolant and emissions hoses, wiring harness connectors and ground straps. Masking tape and/or a touch up paint applicator work well for marking items. Take instant photos or sketch the locations of components and brackets.
13   Remove the cooling fan(s) and shroud(s). Drain the coolant and remove the radiator and all coolant and heater hoses (see Chapter 3).
14   Disconnect the shift cable from the manual lever (see Section 3).
15   Raise the vehicle and support it securely on jackstands. Remove the wheels.
16   Detach the exhaust pipe(s) from the manifold(s) (see Chapter 4).
17   Remove the splash shields (see Chapter 2).
18   Drain the engine oil (see Chapter 1).
19   Remove all accessory drivebelts (see Chapter 1).
20   Drain the transaxle fluid (see Chapter 1).
21   Remove the driveaxles (see Chapter 8).
22   On models with power steering, unbolt the power steering pump (see Chapter 10). It's unnecessary to disconnect the power steering fluid hoses. Swing the pump aside and suspend it out of the way with a piece of wire; don't allow the pump to hang by the hoses.
23   On models with air conditioning, unbolt the compressor and set it aside. Do not disconnect the refrigerant hoses.
24   Disconnect the transaxle oil cooler hoses and plug them immediately to prevent leakage and to keep dirt and moisture out. On four-cylinder models equipped with an oil cooler, remove the oil filter and the oil cooler **(see illustration 6.18 in Chapter 2C).**
25   Remove the torque converter access plate **(see illustrations).** Remove the six driveplate-to-torque converter bolts **(see illustration).**Turn the crankshaft to gain access to each bolt.
26   On four-cylinder models, remove the stiffener plate.
27   Attach a lifting sling to the engine. Position a hoist and connect the sling to it. Take up the slack until there is slight tension on the hoist.
28   Remove the right (passenger side) engine mount, the engine front mount, the transaxle shock absorber, the left (driver's side) transaxle mount (located underneath the left end of the transaxle, between the transaxle and the engine cradle) and the rear (firewall-side) engine mount bracket. Remove the center bearing support from the block.
29   Recheck to be sure nothing except the mounts are still connecting the engine to the vehicle or to the transaxle. Disconnect and label anything still remaining.
30   Slowly lift the engine/transaxle assembly out of the vehicle **(see illustration 6.26a in Chapter 2C).** It may be necessary to pry the mounts away from the frame brackets. **Caution:** *Do not depress the clutch pedal while the transaxle is removed from the vehicle.*

7B

31   Move the engine/transaxle assembly away from the vehicle and carefully lower the hoist until the engine/transaxle assembly is near the floor. Leave enough room for a floor jack underneath the transaxle. **Warning**: *Do not place any part of your body under the engine/transaxle assembly when it's supported only by a hoist or other lifting device.*
32   Remove the starter motor (see Chapter 5).
33   Support the transaxle with a floor jack. Place a block of wood on the jack head to prevent damage to the transaxle. Safety chains will help steady the transaxle on the jack.
34   Remove the transaxle-to-engine bolts and the engine-to-transaxle bolt.
35   Move the transaxle and jack away from the engine until the transaxle is clear of the engine. Keep the transaxle level as you're separating it from the engine to prevent the torque converter from sliding off the transaxle input shaft. It's a good idea to have an assistant hold the converter in place until the transaxle is on the floor.
36   Slide the torque converter off the transaxle input shaft and have it inspected by a dealer service department or an automotive transmission shop.
37   Check the engine and transaxle mounts and the transaxle shock absorber. If any of these components are worn or damaged, replace them.

Installation

38   If removed, install the torque converter on the transaxle input shaft. Make sure the converter hub splines are properly engaged with the splines on the transaxle input shaft.
39   With the transaxle secured to the jack as on removal, and with an assistant holding the torque converter in place, raise the transaxle into position and turn the converter to align the bolt holes in the converter with the bolt holes in the driveplate. Do not use excessive force to install the transaxle - if something binds and the transaxle won't mate with the engine, alter the angle of the transaxle slightly until it does mate. **Caution**: *Do NOT use transaxle-to-engine bolts to force the engine and transaxle into alignment. Doing so could crack or damage major components. If you experience difficulties, have an assistant help you line up the dowel pins on the block with the transaxle. Some wiggling of the engine and/or the transaxle will probably be necessary to secure proper alignment of the two.*
40   Install the transaxle-to-engine bolts and the engine-to-transaxle bolt. Tighten the bolts to the torque listed in this Chapter's Specifications.
41   Lift the engine/transaxle assembly with the engine hoist and carefully lower the assembly into the engine compartment. Tighten all nuts and bolts securely.
42   Install the right engine mount, the front engine mount, the transaxle shock absorber, the left transaxle mount and the rear engine mount. Install the center bearing support on the rear of the block. Tighten all mounting bolts and nuts securely.
43   Reinstall the remaining components in the reverse order of removal.
44   Remove all jacks and hoists and lower the vehicle. Tighten the wheel lug nuts to the torque listed in the Chapter 1 Specifications.
45   Add the specified amounts of coolant, oil and transmission fluids (see Chapter 1).
46   Connect the negative battery cable. Road test the vehicle to check for proper transaxle operation and check for leakage.
47   Run the engine and check for proper operation and leaks. Shut off the engine and recheck the fluid levels.

10   Electronic control system

Trouble codes

1   The electronic-control system for the transaxle has some self-diagnostic capabilities. If certain kinds of system malfunctions occur, the ECM stores the appropriate diagnostic trouble code in its memory and the O/D OFF (overdrive off) indicator light flashes to inform the driver. You can display the diagnostic trouble code(s) stored in memory by following the procedure below.

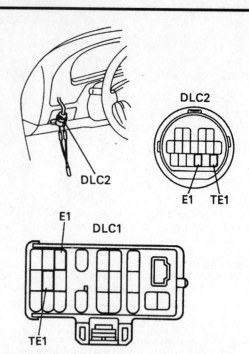

10.7 To put the ECM into diagnostic mode, bridge terminals E1 and TE1 either at the diagnostic connector under the dash (above) or at the diagnostic connector inside the engine compartment (below)

O/D OFF indicator light check

2   Turn the ignition switch to On.
3   Verify that the O/D OFF indicator light comes on when the O/D main switch is in the Off (up) position, and goes out when the O/D main switch is pushed to the On position.
4   If the O/D OFF indicator light does not light up, or remains on all the time, have the circuit checked out by a dealer service department. If the O/D OFF indicator light flashes, a trouble code is stored in the ECM memory.

Diagnostic trouble code check

Refer to illustration 10.7
Note: *The following procedure does not apply to 1994 and 1995 models with the 1MZ-FE V6 engine. The trouble codes for those models can be accessed only with a special Toyota tester.*
5   Turn the ignition switch to On. Do NOT start the engine.
6   Push in the O/D main switch to its On position. (diagnostic trouble codes can be accessed only when the O/D main switch is in the On position; if the switch is Off, the O/D OFF indicator will light continuously and won't flash.)
7   Using a jumper wire, bridge terminals E_1 and T_{E1} of the diagnostic connector **(see illustration)**.
8   To read the diagnostic trouble code(s), count the number of times the O/D OFF indicator light flashes. If the system is operating normally, the light will flash on and off continuously. If a code is stored, the light will flash the same number of times as the number to which it corresponds. For example, a Code 42 would flash four times, pause, then flash two more times. When two or more trouble codes are stored in memory, the numerically lower code is displayed first separated by a longer pause in-between codes.
9   Write down all codes stored in memory and refer to the accompanying trouble code chart to determine the trouble area.
10   After the trouble area has been repaired, the diagnostic trouble code retained in the ECM memory must be erased. Remove the EFI fuse for 10 seconds or more with the ignition switch turned to Off. After installing the fuse, road test the vehicle to verify that the normal code is the only code displayed by the O/D OFF light.

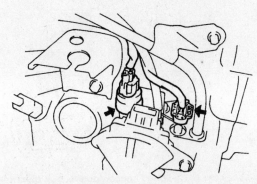

10.17 The solenoid electrical connectors are located right above the Park/Neutral position switch on the front of the transaxle

Trouble code	Trouble area
42	Defective no. 1 speed sensor, speedometer gauge, open in wiring harness or short circuit
61	Defective no. 2 speed sensor, open in wiring harness or short circuit
62	Defective no. 1 shift solenoid, open in wiring harness or short circuit
63	Defective no. 2 shift solenoid, open in wiring harness or short circuit
64	Defective lock-up solenoid, open in wiring harness or short circuit

Preliminary check

11   Check the fluid level and condition. If the fluid smells burned, replace it (see Chapter 1).

12   Check and, if necessary, replace the differential fluid (see Chapter 1).
13   Adjust the shift cable (see Section 3).
14   Check and, if necessary, adjust the throttle valve (TV) cable (see Section 4).
15   Adjust the Park/Neutral position switch (see Section 5).

Manual shifting test

Refer to illustration 10.17
16   This test can determine whether the trouble lies is in the electronic control system or is a mechanical problem inside the transaxle.
17   Disconnect the solenoid connectors **(see illustration)**.
18   Drive the vehicle, shifting through the "L," "2" and "D" ranges manually and verify that the gear changes correspond to the shift lever positions.
19   If the transaxle does not perform as described above, the problem is in the transaxle itself and is not an electronic control system problem.
20   Connect in the solenoid connectors.
21   Cancel the diagnostic trouble code (see Step 10).

Component check and replacement

Note: *Most electronic control system tests are beyond the scope of this manual. The following procedures are tests you can do at home. Aside from these procedures, diagnosis of the electronic control system should be handled by a dealer service department.*

Solenoids

Refer to illustrations 10.22 and 10.26
22   The accompanying chart **(see illustration)** shows the location of the system components.
23   To check a solenoid, disconnect the electrical connector from the solenoid harness at the transaxle **(see illustration 10.17)**. Measure the resistance on the transaxle-side of the connector with an ohmmeter. The

7B

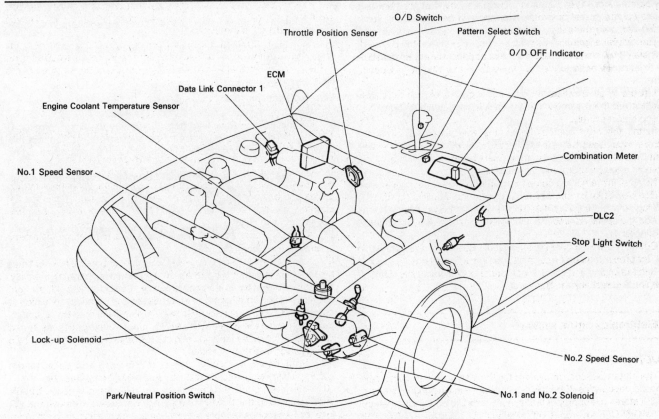

10.22 Electronic control system component locations

No.1 and No.2 Solenoid Valves

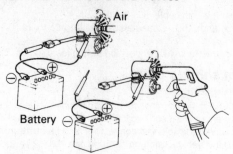

10.26 To check the solenoid valves, apply battery voltage to the terminals of each solenoid and verify that it makes a clicking sound; then apply about 65 psi of compressed air to each solenoid and verify that it doesn't pass air; finally, apply battery voltage to each solenoid and verify that the valve opens

resistance of each solenoid should be between 10 and 15 ohms. If the resistance is less than 8 ohms, there's a short circuit in the solenoid winding; if the resistance is more than 100 k-ohms, there's an open circuit in the solenoid windings. If the resistance of any solenoid is too high or too low, replace it. **Caution:** *Do NOT contact any pins on the ECM side of this electrical connector with the ohmmeter leads. Most ohmmeters use a 9-volt battery which could damage the ECM circuitry.*
24   The solenoids may also be bench tested for proper operation and obstructions, which would restrict fluid flow.
25   Remove the transaxle pan (see Chapter 1). Disconnect the solenoid from the harness and remove the solenoid from the valve body.
26   Apply battery voltage to each solenoid terminal and verify that the solenoids are working **(see illustration)**. When energized, they should make a clicking sound.
27   Apply no more than 65 psi of compressed air to each solenoid and verify that it doesn't pass air. Now apply battery voltage to each solenoid and verify that the valve opens.
28   The lock-up solenoid valve may be checked in the same manner.
29   If a solenoid doesn't operate as described, replace it. Installation is the reverse of removal.

Park/Neutral position switch

30   Refer to Section 5 and check the Park/Neutral position switch.

Throttle Position Sensor

31   Refer to Chapter 6 and check the TPS. A malfunctioning TPS can cause shift related problems.

No. 2 Speed sensor

Refer to illustration 10.33
32   Raise the left front corner of the vehicle and support it securely on a jackstand. **Note:** *If you raise the entire front end of the vehicle, you must immobilize the right front wheel to prevent it from turning.*

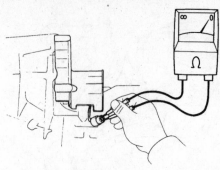

10.33 To check the No. 2 speed sensor, connect an ohmmeter between the terminals, spin the wheel and verify that the meter needle deflects back and forth between zero and infinite ohms

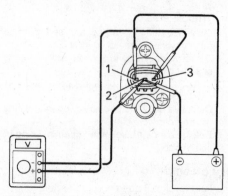

10.36 No. 1 speed sensor terminal guide

33   Connect an ohmmeter to the speed sensor terminals **(see illustration)**.
34   Spin the wheel and verify that the meter needle deflects from zero to infinite ohms.

No. 1 speed sensor

Refer to illustration 10.36
35   Remove the vehicle speed sensor (see Section 7).
36   Connect the positive lead from the battery to sensor terminal 1 and the negative lead to terminal 2 **(see illustration)**. Connect the positive lead from the voltmeter to terminal 3 and the negative lead to terminal 2.
37   Revolve the shaft and verify that the voltage changes from about zero volts to 11 volts or more between terminals 2 and 3. This voltage should occur about 20 times per each revolution of the speed sensor shaft.
38   If the No. 1 speed sensor doesn't perform as described, replace it (see Section 7).

Chapter 8
Clutch and driveaxles

Contents

Specifications

Clutch

Fluid type..	See Chapter 1
Pedal freeplay...	See Chapter 1
Pedal height..	See Chapter 1

Driveaxle length (standard)

Models with a 5S-FE engine
  Toyota type
Left side	23-15/16 inches (608 mm)
Right side...	34-7/64 inches (866 mm)

  GKN type
Left side	23-63/64 inches (609 mm)
Right side	
1992 through 1994	34-43/64 inches (880 mm)
1995 on	34-9/64 inches (867 mm)

Models with a 3VZ-FE or 1MZ-FE engine
Toyota type (left and right sides)..	17-61/64 inches (456 mm)
GKN type (left and right sides)	17-13/16 inches (452 mm)

8

Torque specifications

Ft-lbs (unless otherwise indicated)

Clutch master cylinder mounting nuts	58 in-lbs
Clutch pressure plate-to-flywheel bolts	168 in-lbs
Clutch release cylinder	
Mounting bolts	108 in-lbs
Hydraulic line threaded fitting	132 in-lbs
Banjo bolt	18
Driveaxle/hub nut	217
Driveaxle inner CV joint-to-intermediate shaft flange...........................	48
Right driveaxle center bearing lock bolt	24
Wheel lug nuts	See Chapter 1

1   General information

The information in this Chapter deals with the components from the rear of the engine to the front wheels, except for the transaxle, which is dealt with in Chapter 7A and 7B. For the purposes of this Chapter, these components are grouped into two categories: Clutch and driveaxles. Separate Sections within this Chapter offer general descriptions and checking procedures for both groups.

Since nearly all the procedures covered in this Chapter involve working under the vehicle, make sure it's securely supported on sturdy jackstands or a hoist where the vehicle can be easily raised and lowered.

2   Clutch - description and check

Refer to illustration 2.1

1   All vehicles with a manual transaxle use a single dry plate, diaphragm spring type clutch **(see illustration)**. The clutch disc has a splined hub which allows it to slide along the splines of the transaxle input shaft. The clutch and pressure plate are held in contact by spring pressure exerted by the diaphragm in the pressure plate.

2   The clutch release system is operated by hydraulic pressure. The hydraulic release system consists of the clutch pedal, a master cylinder and fluid reservoir, the hydraulic line, a slave cylinder which actuates the clutch release lever and the clutch release (or throw-out) bearing.

3   When pressure is applied to the clutch pedal to release the clutch, hydraulic pressure is exerted against the outer end of the clutch release lever. As the lever pivots, the shaft fingers push against the release bearing. The bearing pushes against the fingers of the diaphragm spring of the pressure plate assembly, which in turn releases the clutch plate.

4   Terminology can be a problem regarding the clutch components because common names have in some cases changed from that used by the manufacturer. For example, the driven plate is also called the clutch plate or disc, the pressure plate assembly is sometimes referred to as the clutch cover, the clutch release bearing is sometimes called a throw-out bearing, and the release cylinder is sometimes called the operating or slave cylinder.

5   Other than replacing components that have obvious damage, some preliminary checks should be performed to diagnose a clutch system failure.

a) *The first check should be of the fluid level in the clutch master cylinder (see Chapter 1). If the fluid level is low, add fluid as necessary and inspect the hydraulic clutch system for leaks. If the master cylinder reservoir has run dry, bleed the system (see Section 7) and re-test the clutch operation.*

b) *To check "clutch spin-down time," run the engine at normal idle speed with the transaxle in Neutral (clutch pedal up - engaged). Disengage the clutch (pedal down), wait several seconds and shift the transaxle into Reverse. No grinding noise should be heard. A grinding noise would most likely indicate a problem in the pressure plate or the clutch disc.*

c) *To check for complete clutch release, run the engine (with the parking brake applied to prevent movement) and hold the clutch pedal approximately 1/2-inch from the floor. Shift the transaxle between 1st gear and Reverse several times. If the shift is not smooth, component failure is indicated. Check the release cylinder pushrod travel. With the clutch pedal depressed*

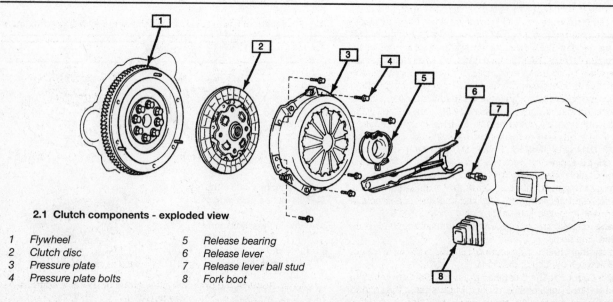

2.1 Clutch components - exploded view

1   Flywheel
2   Clutch disc
3   Pressure plate
4   Pressure plate bolts
5   Release bearing
6   Release lever
7   Release lever ball stud
8   Fork boot

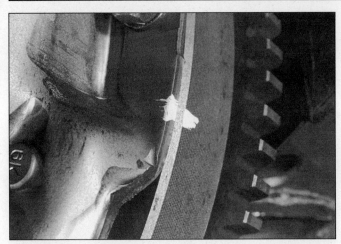

3.6 Mark the relationship of the pressure plate to the flywheel (in case you are going to re-use the same pressure plate)

3.10 Examine the clutch disc for evidence of excessive wear, such as smeared friction material, chewed-up rivets, worn hub splines and distorted damper cushions or springs

completely the release cylinder pushrod should extend substantially. If it doesn't, check the fluid level in the clutch master cylinder.

d) *Visually inspect the clutch pedal bushing at the top of the clutch pedal to make sure there is no sticking or excessive wear.*

e) *Under the vehicle, check that the clutch release lever is solidly mounted on the ball stud.*

3   Clutch components - removal, inspection and installation

Warning: *Dust produced by clutch wear and deposited on clutch components may contain asbestos, which is hazardous to your health. DO NOT blow it out with compressed air and DO NOT inhale it. DO NOT use gasoline or petroleum based solvents to remove the dust. Brake system cleaner should be used to flush the dust into a drain pan. After the clutch components are wiped clean with a rag, dispose of the contaminated rags and cleaner in a labeled, covered container.*

Removal

Refer to illustration 3.6

1   Access to the clutch components is normally accomplished by removing the transaxle, leaving the engine in the vehicle. If, of course, the engine is being removed for major overhaul, then the opportunity should always be taken to check the clutch for wear and replace worn components as necessary. However, the relatively low cost of the clutch components compared to the time and labor involved in gaining access to them warrants their replacement any time the engine or transaxle is removed, unless they are new or in near-perfect condition. The following procedures assume that the engine will stay in place.

2   Remove the release cylinder (see Section 6). Hang it out of the way with a piece of wire - it's not necessary to disconnect the hose.

3   Remove the transaxle from the vehicle (see Chapter 7A). Support the engine while the transaxle is out. Preferably, an engine hoist should be used to support it from above. However, if a jack is used underneath the engine, make sure a piece of wood is used between the jack and oil pan to spread the load. **Caution:** *The pick-up for the oil pump is very close to the bottom of the oil pan. If the pan is bent or distorted in any way, engine oil starvation could occur.*

4   The release fork and release bearing can remain attached to the transaxle for the time being.

5   To support the clutch disc during removal, install a clutch alignment tool through the clutch disc hub.

6   Carefully inspect the flywheel and pressure plate for indexing marks. The marks are usually an X, an O or a white letter. If they cannot be found, scribe marks yourself so the pressure plate and the flywheel

will be in the same alignment during installation **(see illustration)**.

7   Slowly loosen the pressure plate-to-flywheel bolts. Work in a diagonal pattern and loosen each bolt a little at a time until all spring pressure is relieved. Then hold the pressure plate securely and completely remove the bolts, followed by the pressure plate and clutch disc.

Inspection

Refer to illustrations 3.10, 3.12a and 3.12b

8   Ordinarily, when a problem occurs in the clutch, it can be attributed to wear of the clutch driven plate assembly (clutch disc). However, all components should be inspected at this time.

9   Inspect the flywheel for cracks, heat checking, score marks and other damage. If the imperfections are slight, a machine shop can resurface it to make it flat and smooth. Refer to Chapter 2 for the flywheel removal procedure.

10   Inspect the lining on the clutch disc. There should be at least 1/16-inch of lining above the rivet heads. Check for loose rivets, distortion, cracks, broken springs and other obvious damage **(see illustration)**. As mentioned above, ordinarily the clutch disc is replaced as a matter of course, so if in doubt about the condition, replace it with a new one.

11   The release bearing should be replaced along with the clutch disc (see Section 4).

12   Check the machined surface and the diaphragm spring fingers of

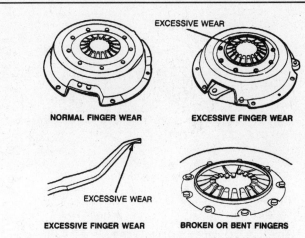

3.12a Replace the pressure plate if any of these conditions are noted

3.12b Examine the pressure plate friction surface for score marks, cracks and evidence of overheating (blue spots)

3.14 Center the clutch disc in the pressure plate with a clutch alignment tool

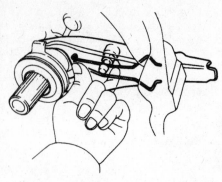

4.3 Reach behind the release lever and disengage the lever from the ball stud by pulling on the retention spring, then remove the lever and bearing

the pressure plate **(see illustrations)**. If the surface is grooved or otherwise damaged, replace the pressure plate assembly. Also check for obvious damage, distortion, cracking, etc. Light glazing can be removed with emery cloth or sandpaper. If a new pressure plate is indicated, new or factory rebuilt units are available.

Installation

Refer to illustration 3.14

13   Before installation, carefully wipe the flywheel and pressure plate machined surfaces clean. It's important that no oil or grease is on these surfaces or the lining of the clutch disc. Handle these parts only with clean hands.

14   Position the clutch disc and pressure plate with the clutch held in place with an alignment tool **(see illustration)**. Make sure it's installed properly (most replacement clutch plates will be marked "flywheel side" or something similar - if not marked, install the clutch disc with the damper springs or cushion toward the transaxle).

15   Tighten the pressure plate-to-flywheel bolts only finger-tight, working around the pressure plate.

16   Center the clutch disc by ensuring the alignment tool is through the splined hub and into the recess in the crankshaft. Wiggle the tool up, down or side-to-side as needed to bottom the tool. Tighten the pressure plate-to-flywheel bolts a little at a time, working in a crisscross pattern to prevent distortion of the cover. After all of the bolts are snug, tighten them to the torque listed in this Chapter's Specifications. Remove the alignment tool.

17   Using high-temperature grease, lubricate the inner groove of the

release bearing (see Section 4). Also place grease on the release lever contact areas and the transaxle input shaft bearing retainer.

18   Install the clutch release bearing (see Section 4).

19   Install the transaxle, release cylinder and all components removed previously, tightening all fasteners to the proper torque specifications.

---

4   Clutch release bearing and lever - removal, inspection and installation

---

Warning: *Dust produced by clutch wear and deposited on clutch components may contain asbestos, which is hazardous to your health. DO NOT blow it out with compressed air and DO NOT inhale it. DO NOT use gasoline or petroleum-based solvents to remove the dust. Brake system cleaner should be used to flush it into a drain pan. After the clutch components are wiped clean with a rag, dispose of the contaminated rags and cleaner in a labeled, covered container.*

Removal

Refer to illustration 4.3

1   Disconnect the negative cable from the battery. **Caution:** *If the stereo in your vehicle is equipped with an anti-theft system, make sure you have the correct activation code before disconnecting the battery.* **Note:** *On 1993 and later models, the airbag system will be disabled if the battery is disconnected for more than a brief period. If the airbag light comes on and stays on after the battery is reconnected, the vehicle must be taken to a dealer to have the system reset with a special tool.*

2   Remove the transaxle (see Chapter 7).

3   Remove the clutch release lever from the ball stud, then remove the bearing from the lever **(see illustration)**.

4.4 To check the operation of the bearing, hold it by the outer race and rotate the inner race while applying pressure - the bearing should turn smoothly - if it doesn't, replace it

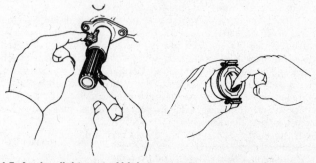

4.5 Apply a light coat of high-temperature grease to the transaxle bearing retainer and also fill the release bearing groove

Inspection

Refer to illustration 4.4

4   Hold the bearing by the outer race and rotate the inner race while applying pressure **(see illustration)**. If the bearing doesn't turn smoothly or if it's noisy, replace the bearing/hub assembly with a new one. Wipe the bearing with a clean rag and inspect it for damage, wear and cracks. Don't immerse the bearing in solvent - it's sealed for life and to do so would ruin it. Also check the release lever for cracks and bends.

Installation

Refer to illustrations 4.5 and 4.6

5   Fill the inner groove of the release bearing with high-temperature grease. Also apply a light coat of the same grease to the transaxle input shaft splines and the front bearing retainer **(see illustration)**.

6   Lubricate the release lever ball socket, lever ends and release cylinder pushrod socket with high-temperature grease **(see illustration)**.

7   Attach the release bearing to the release lever.

8   Slide the release bearing onto the transaxle input shaft front bearing retainer while passing the end of the release lever through the opening in the clutch housing. Push the clutch release lever onto the ball stud until it's firmly seated.

9   Apply a light coat of high-temperature grease to the face of the release bearing where it contacts the pressure plate diaphragm fingers.

10   The remainder of installation is the reverse of the removal procedure.

---

5   Clutch master cylinder - removal, overhaul and installation

Note: *Before beginning this procedure, contact local parts stores and dealer service departments concerning the purchase of a rebuild kit or a new master cylinder. Availability and cost of the necessary parts may dictate whether the cylinder is rebuilt or replaced with a new one. If you decide to rebuild the cylinder, inspect the bore as described in Step 12 before purchasing parts.*

Removal

Refer to illustration 5.2

1   Disconnect the negative cable from the battery. **Caution:** *If the*

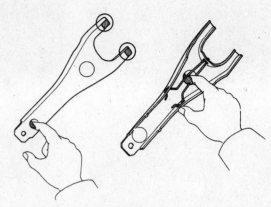

4.6 Apply high-temperature grease to the release lever in the areas indicated

stereo in your vehicle is equipped with an anti-theft system, make sure you have the correct activation code before disconnecting the battery. **Note:** *On 1993 and later models, the airbag system will be disabled if the battery is disconnected for more than a brief period. If the airbag light comes on and stays on after the battery is reconnected, the vehicle must be taken to a dealer to have the system reset with a special tool.*

2   Under the dashboard, disconnect the pushrod from the top of the clutch pedal. It's held in place with a clevis pin **(see illustration)**.

3   Disconnect the hydraulic line at the clutch master cylinder. If available, use a flare-nut wrench on the fitting, which will prevent the fitting from being rounded off. Have rags handy as some fluid will be lost as the line is removed. **Caution:** *Don't allow brake fluid to come into contact with paint, as it will damage the finish.*

4   From under the dash, remove the nut which secures the master cylinder to the engine firewall. Remove the master cylinder, again being careful not to spill any of the fluid.

Overhaul

Refer to illustrations 5.5, 5.6 and 5.8

5   Remove the reservoir cap and drain all fluid from the master cylinder. Drive out the spring pin with a hammer and punch, then carefully pry the reservoir off **(see illustration)**.

8

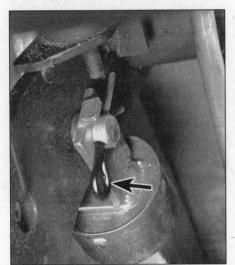

5.2 To release the clutch pushrod from the clutch pedal, remove the clip and clevis pin from the clutch pedal

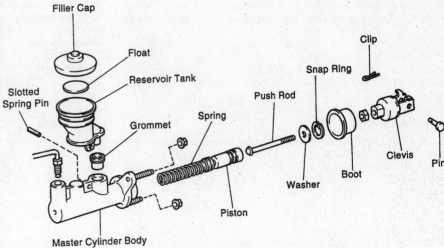

5.5 An exploded view of the clutch master cylinder assembly

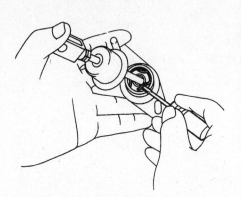

5.6 Use a small screwdriver to pry the snap-ring from the cylinder bore

5.8 Invert the cylinder and tap it against a block of wood to eject the piston

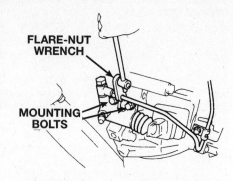

6.3 To remove the release cylinder, disconnect the hydraulic line threaded fitting from the banjo fitting with a flare-nut wrench and remove the two mounting bolts (arrows)

6   Pull back the dust cover on the pushrod and remove the snap-ring **(see illustration)**. On some models the snap-ring can be pried-out with a screwdriver. On other models, snap-ring pliers must be used.

7   Remove the retaining washer and the pushrod from the cylinder.

8   Tap the master cylinder on a block of wood to eject the piston assembly from inside the bore **(see illustration)**. **Note:** *If the rebuild kit supplies a complete piston assembly, ignore the steps which don't apply.*

9   Separate the spring from the piston.

10   Remove the spring support, seal and shim from the pushrod.

11   Carefully remove the seal from the piston.

12   Inspect the bore of the master cylinder for deep scratches, score marks and ridges. The surface must be smooth to the touch. If the bore isn't perfectly smooth, the master cylinder must be replaced with a new or factory rebuilt unit.

13   If the cylinder will be rebuilt, use the new parts contained in the rebuild kit and follow any specific instructions which may have accompanied the rebuild kit. Wash all parts to be re-used with brake cleaner, denatured alcohol or clean brake fluid. DO NOT use petroleum-based solvents.

14   Attach the seal to the piston. The seal lips must face away from the pushrod end of the piston.

15   Assemble the shim, spring support and spring on the other end of the piston.

16   Lubricate the bore of the cylinder and the seals with plenty of fresh brake fluid (DOT 3).

17   Carefully guide the piston assembly into the bore, being careful not to damage the seals. Make sure the spring end is installed first, with the pushrod end of the piston closest to the opening.

18   Position the pushrod and retaining washer in the bore, compress the spring and install a new snap-ring.

19   Apply a liberal amount of Girling Rubber Grease or equivalent to the inside of the dust cover and attach it to the master cylinder. Install the fluid reservoir.

Installation

20   Position the master cylinder on the firewall, installing the mounting nut(s) finger-tight.

21   Connect the hydraulic line to the master cylinder, moving the cylinder slightly as necessary to thread the fitting properly into the bore. Don't cross-thread the fitting as it's installed.

22   Tighten the mounting nut(s) and the hydraulic line fitting securely.

23   Connect the pushrod to the clutch pedal.

24   Fill the clutch master cylinder reservoir with brake fluid conforming to DOT 3 specifications and bleed the clutch system (see Section 7).

25   Check the clutch pedal height and freeplay and adjust if necessary, following the procedure in Chapter 1.

6   Clutch release cylinder - removal, overhaul and installation

Note: *Before beginning this procedure, contact local parts stores and dealer service departments concerning the purchase of a rebuild kit or a new release cylinder. Availability and cost of the necessary parts may dictate whether the cylinder is rebuilt or replaced with a new one. If you decide to rebuild the cylinder, inspect the bore as described in Step 8 before purchasing parts.*

Removal

Refer to illustration 6.3

1   Disconnect the negative cable from the battery. **Caution:** *If the stereo in your vehicle is equipped with an anti-theft system, make sure you have the correct activation code before disconnecting the battery.* **Note:** *On 1993 and later models, the airbag system will be disabled if the battery is disconnected for more than a brief period. If the airbag light comes on and stays on after the battery is reconnected, the vehicle must be taken to a dealer to have the system reset with a special tool.*

2   Raise the vehicle and support it securely on jackstands.

3   To disconnect the hydraulic line from the release cylinder, unscrew the threaded fitting from the banjo fitting. If available, use a flare-nut wrench on the fitting, which will prevent the fitting from being rounded off **(see illustration)**. Have a small can and rags handy, as some fluid will be spilled as the line is removed.

4   Remove the release cylinder mounting bolts and remove release cylinder.

Overhaul

Refer to illustration 6.5

5   Remove the banjo bolt, banjo fitting and washers from the release cylinder **(see illustration)**. Discard the old washers and install new ones during reassembly.

6   Remove the pushrod and the boot.

7   Tap the cylinder on a block of wood to eject the piston and seal. Remove the spring from inside the cylinder.

8   Carefully inspect the bore of the cylinder. Check for deep scratches, score marks and ridges. The bore must be smooth to the touch. If any imperfections are found, the release cylinder must be replaced with a new one.

9   Using the new parts in the rebuild kit, assemble the components using plenty of fresh brake fluid for lubrication. Note the installed direction of the spring and the seal. Be sure to use new washers for the banjo fitting and tighten the banjo bolt to the torque listed in this Chapter's Specifications.

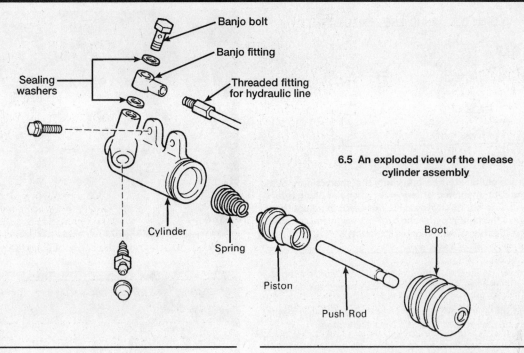

6.5 An exploded view of the release cylinder assembly

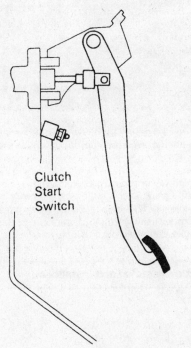

8.4 The clutch start switch is located on a bracket just ahead of the clutch pedal

Installation

10   Connect the hydraulic line to the banjo fitting. Install the release cylinder on the clutch housing, making sure the pushrod is seated in the release fork pocket. Tighten the bolts to the torque listed in this Chapter's Specifications.

11   Tighten the hydraulic line threaded fitting securely.

12   Fill the clutch master cylinder with brake fluid (conforming to DOT 3 specifications).

13   Bleed the system (see Section 7).

14   Lower the vehicle and connect the negative battery cable.

7   Clutch hydraulic system - bleeding

1   The hydraulic system should be bled of all air whenever any part of the system has been removed or if the fluid level has been allowed to fall so low that air has been drawn into the master cylinder. The procedure is very similar to bleeding a brake system.

2   Fill the master cylinder with new brake fluid conforming to DOT 3 specifications. **Caution:** *Do not re-use any of the fluid coming from the system during the bleeding operation or use fluid which has been inside an open container for an extended period of time.*

3   Raise the vehicle and place it securely on jackstands to gain access to the release cylinder, which is located on the left side of the clutch housing.

4   Remove the dust cap which fits over the bleeder valve and push a length of plastic hose over the valve. Place the other end of the hose into a clear container with about two inches of brake fluid in it. The hose end must be submerged in the fluid.

5   Have an assistant depress the clutch pedal and hold it. Open the bleeder valve on the release cylinder, allowing fluid to flow through the hose. Close the bleeder valve when fluid stops flowing from the hose. Once closed, have your assistant release the pedal.

6   Continue this process until all air is evacuated from the system, indicated by a full, solid stream of fluid being ejected from the bleeder valve each time and no air bubbles in the hose or container. Keep a close watch on the fluid level inside the clutch master cylinder reservoir; if the level drops too low, air will be sucked back into the system and the process will have to be started all over again.

7   Install the dust cap and lower the vehicle. Check carefully for proper operation before placing the vehicle in normal service.

8   Clutch start switch - check and adjustment

Refer to illustrations 8.4 and 8.5

1   Check the pedal height, pedal freeplay and pushrod play (see Chapter 1).

2   Verify that the engine will not start when the clutch pedal is released.

3   Verify that the engine will start when the clutch pedal is depressed all the way.

4   The clutch start switch is located on a bracket forward of the clutch pedal **(see illustration)**. Using a small flashlight, trace the

8

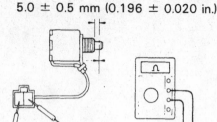

5.0 ± 0.5 mm (0.196 ± 0.020 in.)

8.5 To check the clutch start switch, verify that there's continuity between the switch connector terminals when the plunger is depressed and no continuity when it's released; to adjust the switch, depress the clutch pedal and turn the switch in or out to achieve the indicated distance

10.3 Remove the cotter pin and the nut lock

switch leads from the switch to the electrical connector, unplug the connector and pull it down so that you can see the connector terminals.

5   Verify that there is continuity between the clutch start switch terminals when the switch is On (pushed) **(see illustration)**.

6   Verify that no continuity exists between the switch terminals when the switch is Off (released).

7   If the switch fails either of the tests, replace it. This is accomplished by removing the nut nearest the plunger end of the switch and unscrewing the switch. Disconnect the wire harness. Installation is the reverse of removal.

8   To adjust the clutch start switch, depress the clutch pedal completely and turn the switch in or out to achieve the distance shown in **illustration 8.5**.

9   Verify again that the engine doesn't start when the clutch pedal is released.

9   Driveaxles - general information and inspection

1   Power is transmitted from the transaxle to the wheels through a pair of driveaxles. The inner end of each driveaxle is connected to the transaxle either by a side gear shaft (flanged stub axle) or directly splined to the differential side gears. The side gear shafts (on models so equipped) can be pulled out to replace the oil seals (see Chapter 7A). The outer ends of the driveaxles are splined to the axle hubs and locked in place by a large nut.

2   The inner ends of the driveaxles are equipped with sliding constant velocity joints, which are capable of both angular and axial motion. Each inner joint assembly consists of either a tripod bearing and a joint tulip (housing) or a ball and cage type constant velocity joint in which the joint is free to slide in-and-out as the driveaxle moves up-and-down with the wheel. The joints can be disassembled and cleaned in the event of a boot failure, but if any parts are damaged, the joints must be replaced as a unit (see Section 11).

3   Each outer joint, which consists of ball bearings running between an inner race and an outer cage, is capable of angular but not axial movement.

4   The boots should be inspected periodically for damage and leaking lubricant. Torn CV joint boots must be replaced immediately or the joints can be damaged. Boot replacement involves removal of the driveaxle (see Section 10). **Note:** *Some auto parts stores carry "split" type replacement boots, which can be installed without removing the driveaxle from the vehicle. This is a convenient alternative; however, the driveaxle should be removed and the CV joint disassembled and cleaned to ensure the joint is free from contaminants such as moisture and dirt which will accelerate CV joint wear.* The most common symptom of worn or damaged CV joints, besides lubricant leaks, is a clicking noise in turns, a clunk when accelerating after coasting and

10.4 You'll need a large breaker bar to loosen the driveaxle nut

vibration at highway speeds. To check for wear in the CV joints and driveaxle shafts, grasp each axle (one at a time) and rotate it in both directions while holding the CV joint housings, feeling for play indicating worn splines or sloppy CV joints. Also check the driveaxle shafts for cracks, dents and distortion.

10   Driveaxle - removal and installation

Removal

Refer to illustrations 10.3, 10.4, 10.6, 10.8, 10.11, 10.12, 10.14a, 10.14b, 10.14c, 10.14d and 10.15

Note: *Not all of the steps in this procedure apply to all models. Read through the procedure carefully and determine which steps apply to the vehicle being worked on before actually beginning any work.*

1   Disconnect the cable from the negative terminal of the battery. **Caution:** *If the stereo in your vehicle is equipped with an anti-theft system, make sure you have the correct activation code before disconnecting the battery.* **Note:** *On 1993 and later models, the airbag system will be disabled if the battery is disconnected for more than a brief period. If the airbag light comes on and stays on after the battery is reconnected, the vehicle must be taken to a dealer to have the system reset with a special tool.*

2   Set the parking brake.

3   Remove the cotter pin and the bearing nut lock from the driveaxle/hub nut **(see illustration)**.

4   Break loose the driveaxle/hub nut, but don't remove it yet **(see illustration)**.

10.6 On 3VZ-FE and 1MZ-FE models, the left inner CV joint housing is attached to the side gear shaft flange with six Allen bolts (arrows); the right inner CV joint on these models is bolted to a flange as well, but the side gear shaft (known as the intermediate shaft) is longer and is supported at its outer end by a bearing support bracket

10.8 Using a hammer and a brass punch, sharply strike the end of the driveaxle - it should move noticeably (don't push it in too far, though; only until it's loose)

5   Loosen the front wheel lug nuts, raise the vehicle and support it securely on jackstands. Remove the wheel. Remove any engine splash shields that are in the way (see Chapter 11). Remove the driveaxle/hub nut.

6   If you're removing the left driveaxle to replace the CV joint boots on models with a 3VZ-FE or 1MZ-FE engine, loosen (but do not remove) the six bolts securing the inner CV joint to the differential side gear shaft flange or the intermediate shaft flange **(see illustration)**. To prevent the driveaxle from turning, wedge a prybar between two of the wheel studs and allow the prybar to rest against the ground or the floor pan of the vehicle. **Note:** *This step doesn't apply to the right driveaxle assembly on these models; Toyota recommends removing the entire right driveaxle assembly as a single unit before attempting to disassemble it because, although you could disassemble it, reattaching the outer driveaxle assembly to the intermediate shaft on the vehicle would be extremely difficult. If you're removing the left driveaxle assembly to replace the left driveaxle oil seal, do not remove these six Allen bolts; the side gear shaft must also be removed.*

7   Remove the nuts and bolt securing the balljoint to the control arm, then pry the control arm down to separate the components (see Chapter 10).

8   To loosen the driveaxle from the hub splines, tap the end of the driveaxle with a soft-faced hammer or a hammer and a brass punch **(see illustration)**. If the driveaxle is stuck in the hub splines and won't move, it may be necessary to remove the brake disc (see Chapter 9) and push it from the hub with a two-jaw puller.

9   If you're working on a model with a splined left inner CV joint, or if you're working on a right driveaxle assembly, place a drain pan underneath the transaxle just in case lubricant leaks out.

10   If the transaxle has a case protector (the small plastic hood bolted to the transaxle) over the inner CV joint, remove it.

11   Pull out on the steering knuckle and detach the driveaxle from the hub **(see illustration)**.

12   On models with 3VZ-FE or 1MZ-FE engines, remove the six retaining bolts which attach the inner CV joint housing to the flange and remove the driveaxle. **Note:** *This step doesn't apply to the right driveaxle assembly on these models; the side gear shaft and driveaxle assembly must be removed as a single unit. If you're removing the driveaxle assembly to replace the left driveaxle oil seal, carefully pry the side gear shaft out of the transaxle* **(see illustration)**.

13   If you're removing the left driveaxle on a model with a 5S-FE engine, carefully pry the inner CV joint out of the transaxle **(see illustration 10.12)**.

14   If you're removing the right driveaxle on any model, remove the center bearing lock bolt **(see illustration)**, remove the snap-ring **(see**

10.11 Pull the steering knuckle out and slide the end of the driveaxle out of the hub. There is a sharp ring around the CV joint just behind the stub axle - wrap a rag around it so you don't cut your hand

10.12 Prying out the splined end of the left driveaxle side gear shaft (3VZ-FE and 1MZ-FE models, shown) or the inner CV joint (5S-FE models)

10.14a To release the intermediate shaft bearing from the bearing support bracket, remove this lock bolt (arrow) . . .

8

10.14b . . . and remove this snap-ring (arrows) with a pair of pliers

10.14c To remove the snap-ring from the bearing support bracket, pinch the ends together as shown and pull it out of its groove in the bracket (driveaxle assembly and bearing support bracket removed from the vehicle for clarity)

10.14d To detach the intermediate shaft from the differential side gear, grasp the shaft firmly and pull

illustrations), grasp the intermediate shaft as shown **(see illustration)** and pull the splined inner end of the shaft out of the differential side gear.

15   Should it become necessary to move the vehicle while the driveaxle is out, place a large bolt with two large washers (one on each side of the hub) through the hub and tighten the nut securely **(see illustration)**.

16   Refer to Chapter 7 for the driveaxle seal replacement procedure. On models with flanged left inner CV joints, remove the side gear shaft with a slide hammer.

Installation

17   Installation is the reverse of the removal procedure, but with the following additional points:

   a) *On models with 3VZ-FE and 1MZ-FE engines, tighten the inner CV joint-to-differential side gear shaft (or intermediate shaft) bolts to the torque listed in this Chapter's Specifications.*

   b) *When installing the left driveaxle on models with splined inner CV joints, or when installing the intermediate shaft on any model, push the driveaxle sharply inward to seat the retaining ring on the inner CV joint in the groove in the differential side gear.*

   c) *When installing the right driveaxle/intermediate shaft assembly, be sure to tighten the center bearing lock bolt to the torque listed in this Chapter's Specifications.*

   d) *Tighten the driveaxle/hub nut to the torque listed in this Chapter's Specifications, then install the nut lock and a new cotter pin.*

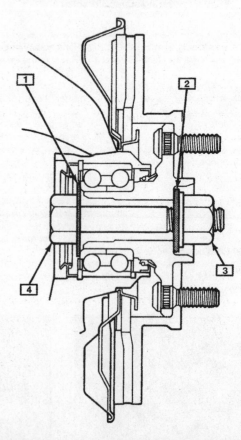

10.15 It isn't a good idea to move the vehicle with a driveaxle removed, but if you must, first install a bolt and a pair of washers through the hub and tighten them securely

1 2-inch (O.D.) washer	3 9/16-inch nut
2 1-3/4 inch (O.D.) washer	4 9/16-inch bolt

   e) *Install the wheel and lug nuts, lower the vehicle and tighten the lug nuts to the torque listed in the Chapter 1 Specifications.*

   f) *Check the transaxle or differential lubricant and add, if necessary, to bring it to the proper level (see Chapter 1).*

18   Check the intermediate shaft bearing for smooth operation. If it

11.3 Cut the old boot clamps off and discard them (if you're planning to re-use the boot, make sure you don't accidentally cut the boot itself)

11.4 Remove the boot from the inner CV joint and slide the tripod from the joint housing

11.6 Remove the snap-ring with a pair of snap-ring pliers

feels rough or sticky it should be replaced. Take it to a dealer service department or other repair shop, as special tools are needed to perform this job.

11   Driveaxle boot replacement and CV joint overhaul

Note: *If the CV joints must be overhauled (usually due to torn boots), explore all options before beginning the job. Complete rebuilt driveaxles are available on an exchange basis, which eliminates much time and work. Whichever route you choose to take, check on the cost and availability of parts before disassembling the vehicle.*

1   Remove the driveaxle (see Section 10).
2   Mount the driveaxle in a vise with wood lined jaws (to prevent damage to the axleshaft). Check the CV joint for excessive play in the radial direction, which indicates worn parts. Check for smooth operation throughout the full range of motion for each CV joint. If a boot is torn, the recommended procedure is to disassemble the joint, clean the components and inspect for damage due to loss of lubrication and possible contamination by foreign matter.

Models with a 5S-FE engine

Disassembly
Refer to illustrations 11.3, 11.4, 11.6 and 11.7
3   Using diagonal cutters, cut the boot clamps **(see illustration)**,

remove the clamps and discard them. **Note:** *Various types of boot clamps are used on these vehicles. Another typical clamp is shown in the illustrations accompanying Step 13.*
4   Using a screwdriver, carefully pry up on the edge of the outer boot and push it away from the CV joint. Old and worn boots can be cut off. Pull the inner CV joint boot back from the housing and slide the housing from the tripod **(see illustration)**. Set the housing and the intermediate shaft aside.
5   Mark the tripod and axleshaft to ensure that they are reassembled properly.
6   Remove the tripod joint snap-ring with a pair of snap-ring pliers **(see illustration)**.
7   Use a hammer and a brass punch to drive the tripod joint from the driveaxle **(see illustration)**.
8   If you haven't already cut them off, remove both boots.

Check
Refer to illustration 11.9
9   Thoroughly clean all components, including the outer CV joint assembly, with solvent until the old CV joint grease is completely removed. Inspect the bearing surfaces of the inner tripods and housings for cracks, pitting, scoring and other signs of wear. It's not possible to inspect the bearing surfaces of the inner and outer races of the outer CV joint, but you can at least check the surfaces of the ball bearings themselves **(see illustration)**. If they're in good shape, the races probably are, too; if they're not, neither are the races. If the inner

11.7 Drive the tripod joint from the driveaxle with a brass punch and hammer; be careful not to damage the bearing surfaces or the splines on the shaft

11.9 Clean the outer CV joint thoroughly with solvent and, working the joint through its entire range of motion, inspect the bearing surfaces of the balls; if they're worn or damaged, so are the bearing races

8

11.10a Wrap the splined area of the axleshaft with tape to prevent damage to the boots when removing or installing them

CV joint is worn, you can buy a new inner CV joint and install it on the old axleshaft; if the outer CV joint is worn, you'll have to purchase a new outer CV joint *and* axleshaft (they're sold preassembled). Check the condition of the bearing for the intermediate shaft **(see illustration 11.23)**. It should turn freely and smoothly. If it's difficult to turn, or makes a grinding noise when rotated, take the intermediate shaft to an automotive machine shop and have a new bearing installed on the shaft.

Reassembly

Refer to illustrations 11.10a, 11.10b, 11.10c, 11.10d, 11.10e, 11.12a, 11.12b and 11.12c

10   Wrap the splines on the inner end the axleshaft with electrical or duct tape to protect the boots from the sharp edges of the splines **(see illustration)**. Slide the clamps and boots onto the axleshaft, outer boot first, then place the tripod on the shaft. Apply grease to the tripod assembly and inside the housing. Insert the tripod into the housing and pack the remainder of the grease around the tripod. **(see illustrations)**.

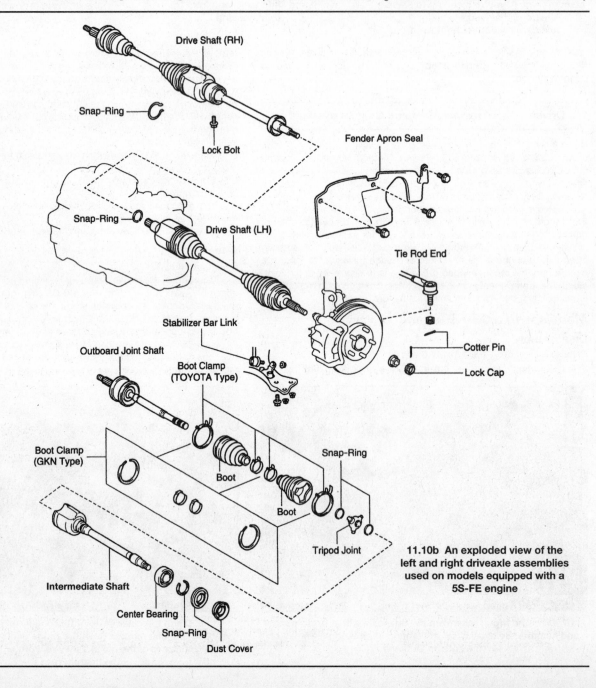

11.10b An exploded view of the left and right driveaxle assemblies used on models equipped with a 5S-FE engine

11.10c Install the tripod with the recessed portion of the splines facing the axleshaft

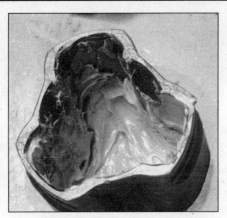

11.10d Place grease at the bottom of the CV joint housing

11.10e Install the boot and clamps onto the axleshaft, then insert the tripod into the housing, followed by the rest of the grease

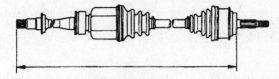

11.12a Measure between the points indicated and move the inner CV joint in or out to set the driveaxle to the length listed in this Chapter's Specifications (models with a 5S-FE engine)

If you're repacking the outer joint, be sure to work the entire tube of CV joint grease (included with the boot kit) into the bearing assembly.

11   Slide the boots into place, making sure the ends of both boots seat in their respective grooves in the axleshaft.

12   Adjust the driveaxle to the standard length listed in this Chapter's Specifications, then equalize the pressure in the boot and tighten the boot clamps **(see illustrations)**. The driveaxle is now ready for installation (see Section 10).

Models with a 3VZ-FE or 1MZ-FE engine

Disassembly

Refer to illustrations 11.14, 11.15, 11.16, 11.17a, 11.17b, 11.18, 11.19, 11.20a, 11.20b, 11.21 and 11.22

13   Cut off the old boot clamps **(see illustration 11.3).**

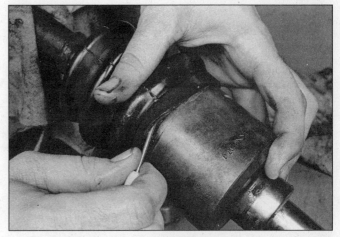

11.12b Equalize the pressure inside the boot by inserting a small, dull screwdriver between the boot and the outer race

14   Remove the six Allen bolts **(see illustration)** that attach the inner CV joint cover, the inner CV joint assembly and the intermediate shaft flange. Don't lose the three curved "joint" washers.

15   Knock the inner CV joint cover loose with a brass punch **(see illustration)**. **Caution:** *Do NOT use a steel punch or any other hard or*

11.12c You'll need a special boot clamp installation tool like this one to tighten the new clamps; follow the instructions provided by the manufacturer

11.14 Remove these six 10 mm Allen bolts to separate the side gear shaft or intermediate shaft flange, the inner CV joint and the inner joint cover

11.15 Mark the side gear shaft or intermediate shaft flange, the inner CV joint and the inner joint cover, then use a brass drift punch to tap the inner joint cover loose

8

sharp tool to remove the cover. If the cover is damaged, it must be replaced.

16   Separate the intermediate shaft and the inner CV joint assembly **(see illustration)**.

17   Remove the snap-ring **(see illustrations)** that retains the inner CV joint assembly on the axleshaft.

18   Pull the boot back from the inner CV joint assembly **(see illustration)**. Old and worn boots can be cut off.

19   Use a couple of the curved "joint" washers, four of the 10 mm Allen bolts and four 10 mm nuts of the appropriate thread pitch to hold the inner CV joint together. Reverse the curved washers **(see illustration)** to prevent the cage and the inner and outer races from coming apart while the axleshaft is being driven out.

20   Obtain a three-inch long piece of 1-1/4 or 1-1/2 PVC tubing, cut a slit down one side and pop it onto the axleshaft **(see illustrations)**.

21   Place the driveaxle assembly in a bench vise as shown, with the PVC tubing collar positioned so that it supports the inner race and is itself supported by the vise jaws **(see illustration)**.

22   Mark the relationship of the inner race, cage and outer race, then carefully drive the axleshaft from the inner race with a hammer and brass punch **(see illustration)**.

Check

Refer to illustration 11.23

23   Thoroughly clean all components, including the outer CV joint

11.16 Separate the side gear shaft or intermediate shaft flange from the inner CV joint

assembly, with solvent until the old CV joint grease is completely removed. Inspect the bearing surfaces of the inner tripods and housings for cracks, pitting, scoring and other signs of wear. It's not possible to inspect the bearing surfaces of the inner and outer races of

11.17a Remove the inner joint snap-ring with a pair of snap-ring pliers

11.17b If the snap-ring proves difficult to remove from its groove with snap-ring pliers, use a small screwdriver and a pick to work it out

11.18 Remove the boot from the inner joint cover

11.19 Before driving the axleshaft out of the inner race, install two of the curved washers in a reversed position to hold the CV joint assembly together; use four of the Allen bolts and four 10 mm nuts of the appropriate thread diameter to retain the washers

11.20a Obtain a three-inch long piece of 1-1/4 or 1-1/2 PVC tubing and cut it down one side . . .

11.20b . . . then pop it onto the axleshaft; make sure the tubing is slightly smaller in diameter than the inner race

the outer CV joint, but you can at least check the surfaces of the ball bearings themselves **(see illustration 11.9)**. If they're in good shape, so are the races; if they're not, neither are the races. If the inner CV joint is worn, you can buy a new inner CV joint and install it on the old axleshaft; if the outer CV joint is worn, you'll have to purchase a new outer CV joint *and* axleshaft (they're sold preassembled). Check the condition of the bearing for the intermediate shaft **(see illustration)**. It should turn freely and smoothly. If it's difficult to turn, or makes a grinding noise when rotated, take the intermediate shaft to an automotive machine shop and have a new bearing installed on the shaft. (Purchase a pair of new dust covers and have them installed at the same time.)

Reassembly

Refer to illustrations 11.24, 11.25a, 11.25b, 11.26a, 11.26b and 11.31

24   Install the new CV joint dust boots, outer boot first **(see illustration)**. It's a good idea to wrap the splined inner end of the axleshaft with tape to protect the new boots **(see illustration 11.10a)**. Do not install the new boot clamps at this time.

25   Attach the inner CV joint cover. Be sure to clean off any old sealant residue from the cover and from the mating surface of the inner

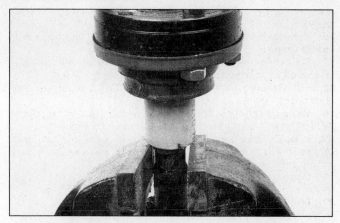

11.21 Place the driveaxle assembly in a bench vise with the PVC tubing collar positioned between the inner race of the inner CV joint and the bench vise jaws; note that the jaws are supporting the lower end of the tubing, but are not clamped up against the axleshaft

11.22 Mark the relationship of the axleshaft, the inner race, the cage and the outer race, then carefully tap the axleshaft out of the inner CV joint assembly with a brass drift punch

11.23 Check the condition of the center support bearing on the intermediate shaft. Make sure it turns freely, quietly and smoothly; if the bearing is hard to turn, is noisy or feels rough, have it replaced by an automotive machine shop (be sure to have a pair of new dust covers installed too)

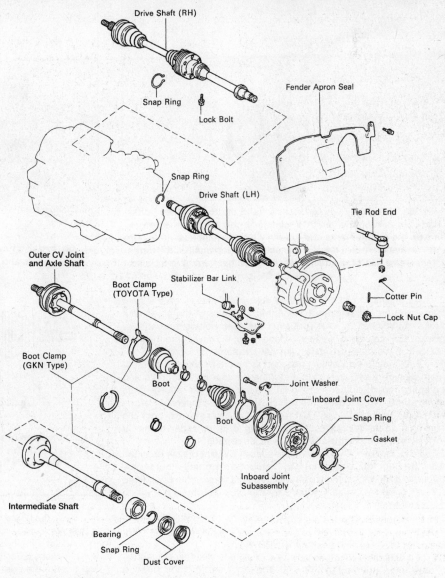

11.24 Exploded view of the driveaxle assembly (models with a 3VZ-FE or 1MZ-FE engine)

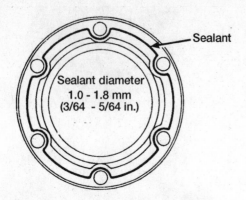

11.25a Apply a bead of RTV sealant to the area shown on the mating surface of the inner CV joint cover

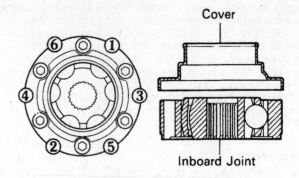

11.25b Align the holes in the cover and the inner CV joint assembly, then carefully tap the cover into place against the joint; use the Allen bolts as guides to ensure that the holes are lined up. Tap the circumference of the cover in a criss-cross pattern in the sequence shown

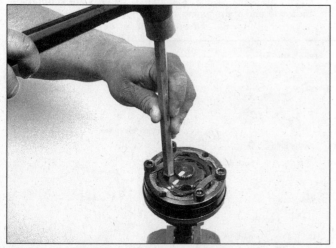

11.26a Using the reversed washers and the 10 mm Allen bolts and nuts to keep the inner CV joint assembly together as before, line up the match marks and carefully tap the joint assembly onto the axleshaft; use a criss-cross pattern to tap against the inner race - and don't tap against any other component or you could damage the CV joint

11.26b Install a new snap-ring, then remove the reversed 10 mm nuts and Allen bolts and the curved washers

CV joint against which it is attached. Apply RTV sealant on the inner joint cover **(see illustration)**. Align the bolt holes of the cover with those of the inner CV joint and insert the Allen bolts temporarily as guides. Using a plastic hammer, tap the rim of the cover onto the inner CV joint, in the sequence shown **(see illustration)**.

26   With the curved washers attached as before to hold the inner CV joint assembly and cover together, line up your match marks and carefully tap the inner race onto the axleshaft as shown **(see illustration)**. Keep moving the drift around the circumference of the race as you drive it on; don't just tap in one place or you may cock the race on the axleshaft splines. Also, don't strike any other part of the CV joint assembly. Install the snap-ring **(see illustration)**.

27   Pack the inner CV joint with the special CV joint grease provided with the boot kit. Make sure you distribute the grease thoroughly throughout the joint; if there's any left over, put it inside the boot. (If no CV joint grease is included with the boot kit, you can obtain it any auto parts store.)

28   Reattach the cover/inner CV joint assembly to the side gear shaft flange or to the intermediate shaft flange. Tighten the six Allen bolts to the torque listed in this Chapter's Specifications.

29   If you're repacking the outer joint, be sure to work the entire tube of CV joint grease (included with the boot kit) into the bearing assembly.

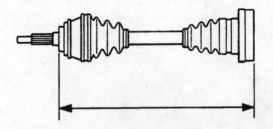

11.31 Measure between the points indicated and move the inner CV joint in or out to set the driveaxle to the length listed in this Chapter's Specifications (models with a 3VZ-FE or 1MZ-FE engine)

30   Slide the boots into place. Make sure the ends of both boots seat in their respective grooves in the axleshaft.

31   Adjust the driveaxle to the standard length listed in this Chapter's Specifications **(see illustration)**, then equalize the pressure in the boot and tighten the boot clamps **(see illustrations 11.12b and 11.12c)**. The driveaxle assembly is now ready for installation (see Section 10).

Chapter 9 Brakes

Contents

Specifications

General

Brake fluid type	See Chapter 1
Brake pedal specifications	See Chapter 1
Power brake booster pushrod-to-master cylinder piston clearance	0.0 inch
Brake light switch plunger (dimension A)	1/32 to 3/32 inch

Disc brakes

Minimum brake pad thickness	See Chapter 1
Front disc thickness	
Standard	1.102 inch
Minimum*	1.024 inch
Rear disc thickness (models with rear disc brakes)*	
Standard	0.394 inch
Minimum*	0.354 inch
Disc runout limit (front and rear)	0.0020 inch
Parking brake shoe minimum thickness	1/32 inch

Drum brakes

Brake shoe minimum lining thickness	1/16 inch
Drum inside diameter	
Standard	9.000 inch
Maximum*	9.079 inch

* **Note:** *If different specifications are cast into the disc or drum, they supersede information printed here.*

Torque specifications

	Ft-lbs (unless otherwise indicated)
Disc brake caliper mounting bolts	
Front caliper	25
Rear caliper	14
Caliper torque plate bolts	
Front torque plate	79
Rear torque plate	34
Brake hose-to-caliper banjo bolt	22
Wheel cylinder mounting bolts	84 in-lbs
Master cylinder-to-brake booster nuts	108 in-lbs
Power brake booster mounting nuts	108 in-lbs
Wheel lug nuts	See Chapter 1

9

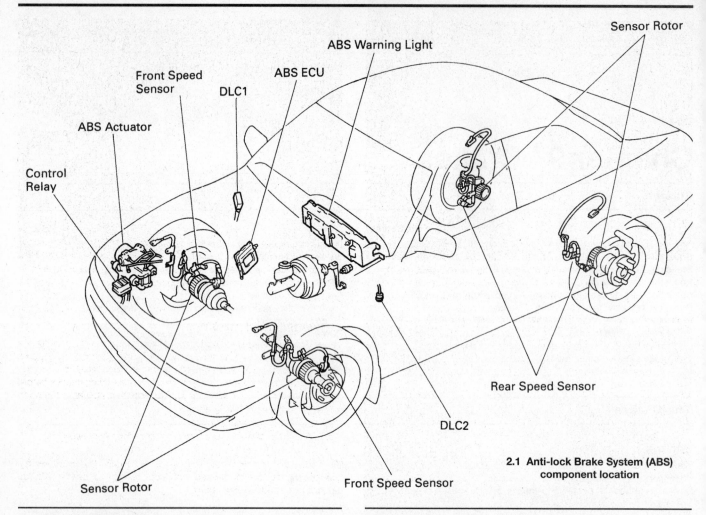

**2.1 Anti-lock Brake System (ABS)
component location**

1   General information

The vehicles covered by this manual are equipped with hydrauli-cally operated front and rear brake systems. The front brakes are disc type and the rear brakes are either drum or disc type. Both the front and rear brakes are self adjusting. The disc brakes automatically compensate for pad wear, while the drum brakes incorporate an adjustment mechanism which is activated as the parking brake is applied.

Hydraulic system

The hydraulic system consists of two separate circuits. The master cylinder has separate reservoirs for the two circuits, and, in the event of a leak or failure in one hydraulic circuit, the other circuit will remain operative. A dual proportioning valve on the firewall provides brake balance between the front and rear brakes.

Power brake booster

The power brake booster, utilizing engine manifold vacuum and atmospheric pressure to provide assistance to the hydraulically operated brakes, is mounted on the firewall in the engine compartment.

Parking brake

The parking brake operates the rear brakes only, through cable actuation. It's activated by a lever mounted in the center console or a pedal mounted on the left side kick panel.

Service

After completing any operation involving disassembly of any part of the brake system, always test drive the vehicle to check for proper braking performance before resuming normal driving. When testing the brakes, perform the tests on a clean, dry, flat surface. Conditions other than these can lead to inaccurate test results.

Test the brakes at various speeds with both light and heavy pedal pressure. The vehicle should stop evenly without pulling to one side or the other. Avoid locking the brakes, because this slides the tires and diminishes braking efficiency and control of the vehicle.

Tires, vehicle load and wheel alignment are factors which also affect braking performance.

2   Anti-lock Brake System (ABS) - general information

Refer to illustration 2.1

1   The anti-lock brake system **(see illustration)** is designed to maintain vehicle steerabilty, directional stability and optimum deceleration under severe braking conditions and on most road surfaces. It does so by monitoring the rotational speed of each wheel and controlling the brake line pressure to each wheel during braking. This prevents the wheel from locking up.

Components
Actuator assembly

2   The actuator assembly consists of the master cylinder, an electric hydraulic pump and four solenoid valves.

   a) *The electric pump provides hydraulic pressure to charge the reservoirs in the actuator, which supplies pressure to the braking system. The pump and reservoirs are housed in the actuator assembly.*
   b) *The solenoid valves modulate brake line pressure during ABS operation. The body contains four valves - one for each wheel.*

3.5 Before removing the front caliper, be sure to depress the piston into its bore in the caliper with a large C-clamp to make room for the new pads

3.6a Always wash the brakes with brake cleaner before disassembling anything

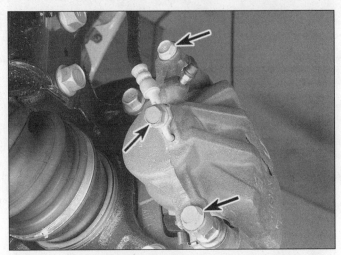

3.6b To remove the caliper, remove the bolts indicated by the upper and lower arrows (the center arrow points to the brake fitting bolt, which shouldn't be unscrewed unless the caliper is being completely removed)

Speed sensors

3   These sensors are located at each wheel and generate small electrical pulsations when the toothed sensor rings are turning, sending a signal to the electronic controller indicating wheel rotational speed.

4   The front speed sensors are mounted on the steering knuckles in close relationship to the toothed sensor rings, which are integral with the front hub assemblies. The rear speed sensors are bolted to the axle carriers. The sensor rings are integral with the rear hub assemblies.

ABS computer

5   The ABS computer is mounted behind the right kick panel. The computer is the "brain" of the ABS system. The function of the computer is to accept and process data from the wheel speed sensors and to control the hydraulic line pressure, avoiding wheel lock up. The computer also constantly monitors the system, even under normal driving conditions, to find faults within the system.

6   If a problem develops within the system, an "ANTI-LOCK" or "ABS" light will glow on the dashboard. A diagnostic code will also be stored in the computer, which, when retrieved by a service technician, will indicate the problem area or component.

Diagnosis and repair

7   If a dashboard warning light comes on and stays on while the vehicle is in operation, the ABS system requires attention. Although a special electronic ABS diagnostic tester is necessary to properly diagnose the system, you can perform a few preliminary checks before taking the vehicle to a dealer service department or other repair shop which is equipped with a tester.

    a) Check the brake fluid level in the reservoir.
    b) Check that all electrical connectors are securely connected.
    c) Check the fuses.

8   If the above preliminary checks do not rectify the problem, the vehicle should be diagnosed and repaired by a dealer service department or other repair shop.

3   Disc brake pads - replacement

Refer to illustrations 3.5, 3.6a through 3.6t and 3.7a through 3.7l
Warning: *Disc brake pads must be replaced on both front or rear wheels at the same time - never replace the pads on only one wheel. Also, the dust created by the brake system may contain asbestos, which is harmful to your health. Never blow it out with compressed air and don't inhale any of it. An approved filtering mask should be worn when working on the brakes. Do not, under any circumstances, use petroleum-based solvents to clean brake parts. Use brake system cleaner only!*
Note: *This procedure applies to both the front and rear disc brakes.*

1   Remove the cap from the brake fluid reservoir.

2   Loosen the wheel lug nuts, raise the front or rear of the vehicle and support it securely on jackstands. Block the wheels at the opposite end.

3   Remove the wheels. Work on one brake assembly at a time, using the assembled brake for reference if necessary.

4   Inspect the brake disc carefully as outlined in Section 5. If machining is necessary, follow the information in that Section to remove the disc, at which time the pads can be removed as well.

5   Push the piston back into its bore to provide room for the new brake pads. A C-clamp can be used to accomplish this **(see illustration)**. As the piston is depressed to the bottom of the caliper bore, the fluid in the master cylinder will rise. Make sure that it doesn't overflow. If necessary, siphon off some of the fluid.

6   If you're replacing the front brake pads, follow the accompanying photos, beginning with **illustration 3.6a**. Be sure to stay in order and read the caption under each illustration.

9

3.6c Remove the caliper . . .

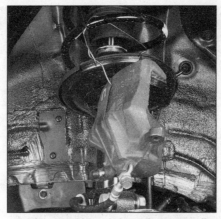

3.6d . . . and hang it from the strut coil spring with a piece of wire; do not allow the caliper to hang by the flexible brake hose

3.6e Remove the upper anti-squeal spring . . .

3.6f . . . and the lower anti-squeal spring (1994 and 1995 models)

3.6g Remove the outer shim . . .

3.6h . . . and the inner shim from the outer brake pad

3.6i Remove the outer brake pad

3.6j Remove the outer shim . . .

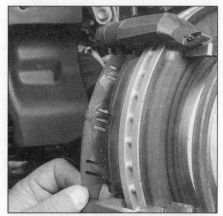

3.6k . . . and the inner shim from the inner brake pad

7   If you're replacing the rear brake pads, follow the accompanying photos, beginning with **illustration 3.7a**. Be sure to stay in order and read the caption under each illustration.

8   When reinstalling the caliper, be sure to tighten the mounting bolts to the torque listed in this Chapter's Specifications. After the job has been completed, firmly depress the brake pedal a few times to bring the pads into contact with the disc. Check the level of the brake fluid, adding some if necessary. Check the operation of the brakes carefully before placing the vehicle into normal service.

3.6l Remove the inner brake pad

3.6m Remove all four pad support plates; inspect them for damage and replace as necessary (the plates should "snap" into place in the torque plate; if they're weak or distorted, they should be replaced)

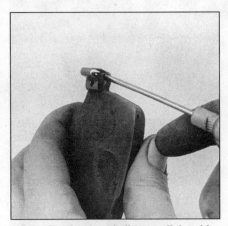

3.6n Pry the wear indicator off the old inner brake pad and transfer it to the new inner pad (if the wear indicator is worn or bent, replace it)

3.6o Install the pad support plates, the new inner brake pad and the shims; make sure the ears on the pad are properly engaged with the pad support plates as shown

3.6p Install the pad support plates, the outer pad and the shims

3.6q Install the upper and lower anti-squeal springs; make sure both springs are properly engaged with the pads as shown

3.6r Pull out the upper and lower sliding pins and clean them off (if either rubber boot is damaged, remove it by prying the flange of the metal bushing that retains the boot) . . .

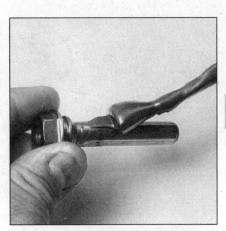

3.6s . . . apply a coat of high-temperature grease to the pins and install them

9

3.6t Install the caliper and tighten the caliper bolts to the torque listed in this Chapter's Specifications

3.7a Remove the caliper retaining bolt (lower arrow); the upper arrow points to the brake hose banjo fitting bolt, which shouldn't be unscrewed unless the caliper is being removed from the vehicle

3.7b Pivot the caliper up as shown, slide it off the upper pivot pin and suspend it from the strut coil spring with a piece of wire as shown in illustration 3.6d

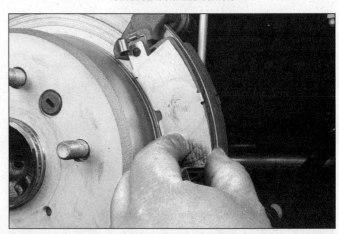

3.7c Remove the outer shim . . .

3.7d . . . and the inner shim from the outer brake pad

3.7e Remove the outer brake pad

4   Disc brake caliper - removal, overhaul and installation

Warning: *Dust created by the brake system may contain asbestos, which is harmful to your health. Never blow it out with compressed air and don't inhale any of it. An approved filtering mask should be worn when working on the brakes. Do not, under any circumstances, use petroleum-based solvents to clean brake parts. Use brake system cleaner only!*

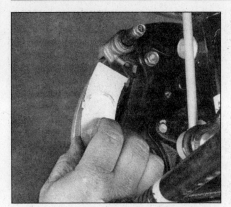

3.7f Remove the outer shim . . .

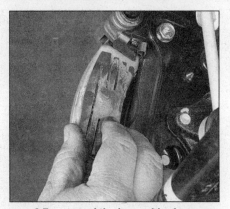

3.7g . . . and the inner shim from
the inner brake pad

3.7h Remove the inner brake pad

3.7i Remove the pad support plates;
inspect them for wear and replace as
necessary (the plates should "snap"
into place in the torque plate; if they're
weak or distorted, replace them)

3.7j Install the pad support plates, the
inner brake pad and the shims; make sure
both shims are properly engaged with the
inner brake pad and with each other

3.7k Install the pad support plates, the
outer brake pad and the shims; make sure
both shims are properly engaged with the
outer brake pad and with each other

3.7l Slide the caliper onto the upper pivot pin and swing it down
over the new pads. Install the caliper retaining bolt and tighten it
to the torque listed in this Chapter's Specifications

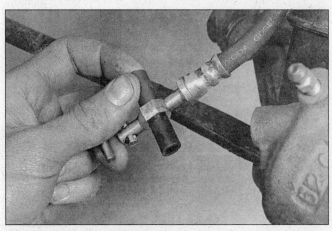

4.2 Using a piece of rubber hose of the appropriate size, plug the
brake line banjo fitting to prevent brake fluid from leaking
out and to prevent dirt and moisture from contaminating
the fluid in the hose

Note 1: *This procedure applies to both front and rear brake calipers.*
Note 2: *If an overhaul is indicated (usually because of fluid leakage),
explore all options before beginning the job. New and factory rebuilt
calipers are available on an exchange basis, which makes this job quite
easy. If you decide to rebuild the calipers, make sure a rebuild kit is
available before proceeding. Always rebuild the calipers in pairs - never
rebuild just one of them.*

Removal

Refer to illustration 4.2

1   Remove the bolt and disconnect the brake hose from the caliper
(see illustration 3.6b, front caliper; or illustration 3.7a, rear caliper).
2   Plug the brake hose to keep contaminants out of the brake
system and to prevent losing any more brake fluid than is necessary
(see illustration).

9

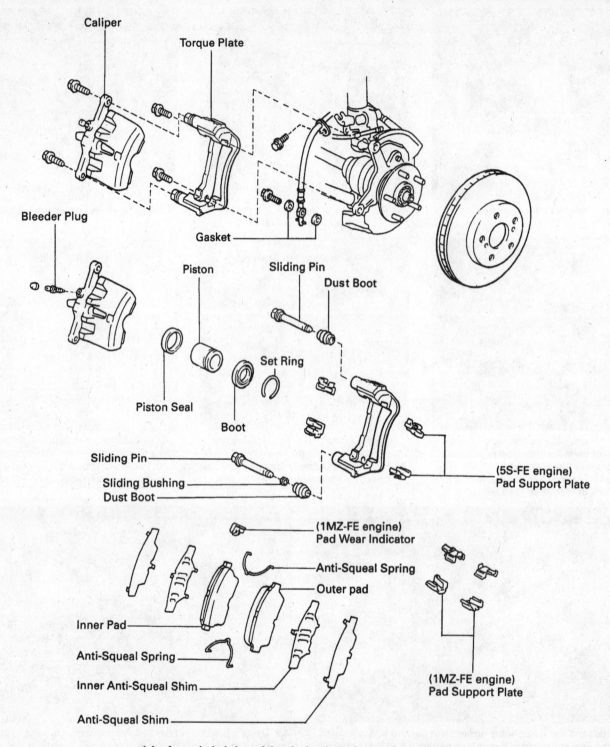

4.4a An exploded view of the single-piston front caliper assembly

3   Refer to Section 3 for either front or rear caliper removal procedures (it's part of the brake pad replacement procedure).

Overhaul

Refer to illustrations 4.4a, 4.4b, 4.4c, 4.4d, 4.5 and 4.7

4   To overhaul the caliper, remove the boot set ring and the boot **(see illustrations)**.
5   Before you remove the piston, place a wood block between the piston and caliper to prevent damage as it is removed. To remove the piston from the caliper, apply compressed air to the brake fluid hose connection on the caliper body **(see illustration)**. Use only enough pressure to ease the piston out of its bore. **Warning:** *Be careful not to place your fingers between the piston and the caliper as the piston may come out with some force.*

6   Inspect the mating surfaces of the piston and caliper bore wall. If there is any scoring, rust, pitting or bright areas, replace the complete caliper unit with a new one.

7   If these components are in good condition, remove the piston

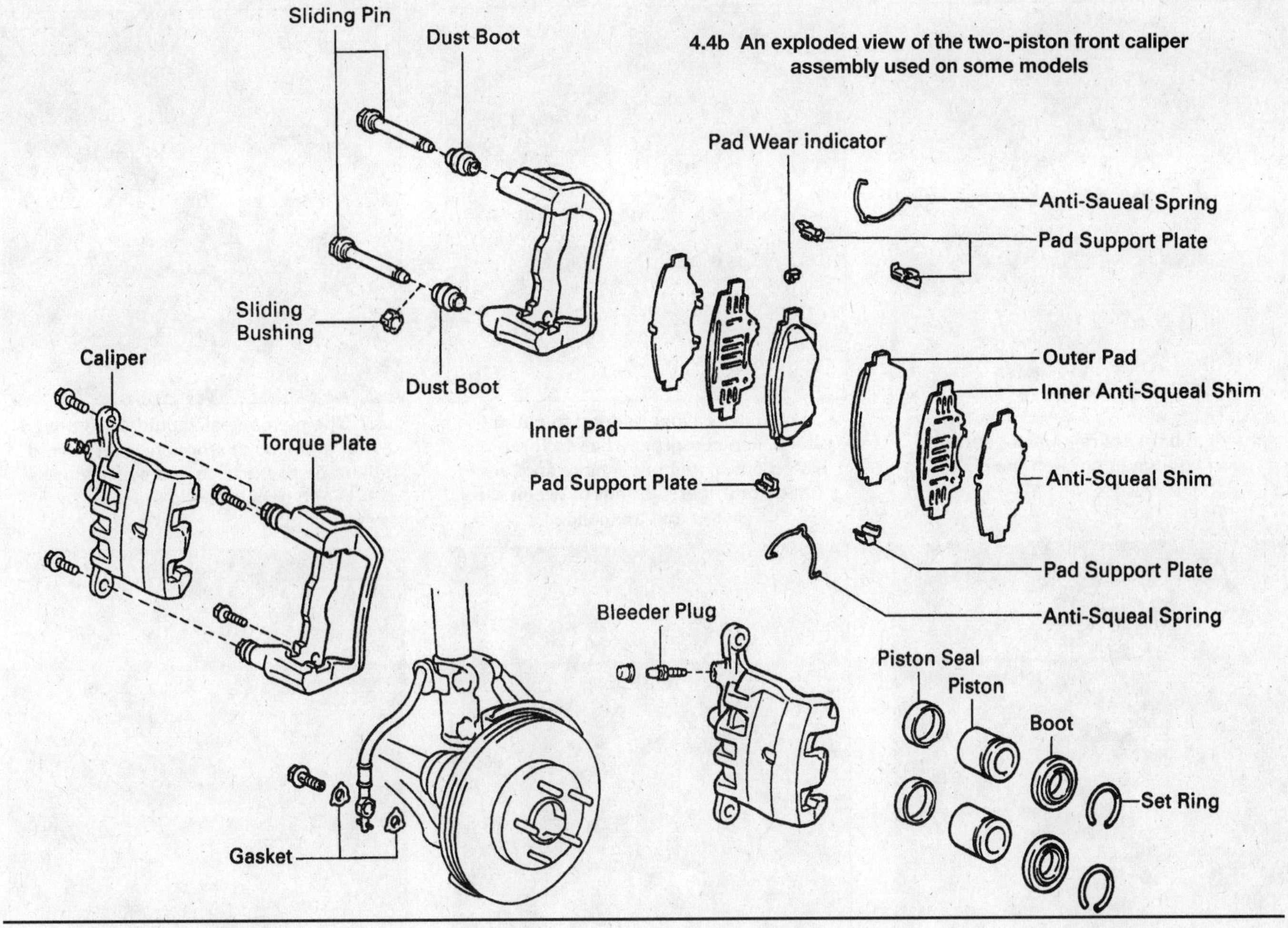

Sliding Pin

Dust Boot

4.4b An exploded view of the two-piston front caliper assembly used on some models

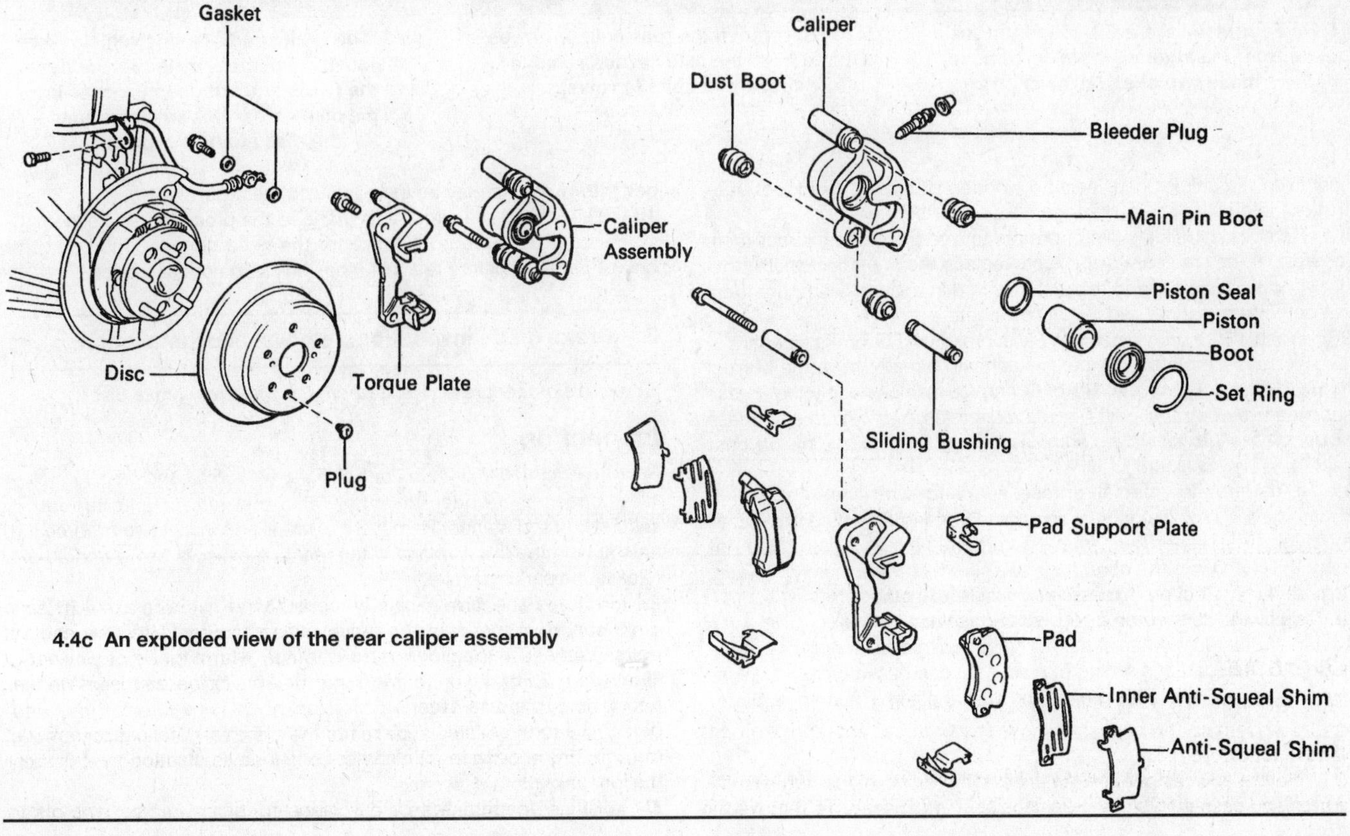

Pad Wear indicator

Anti-Saueal Spring

Pad Support Plate

Sliding Bushing

Dust Boot

Caliper

Torque Plate

Outer Pad

Inner Anti-Squeal Shim

Inner Pad

Anti-Squeal Shim

Pad Support Plate

Pad Support Plate

Anti-Squeal Spring

Bleeder Plug

Piston Seal

Piston

Boot

Set Ring

Gasket

4.4c An exploded view of the rear caliper assembly

Gasket

Caliper

Dust Boot

Bleeder Plug

Caliper Assembly

Main Pin Boot

Piston Seal

Piston

Boot

Set Ring

Disc

Torque Plate

Sliding Bushing

Plug

Pad Support Plate

Pad

Inner Anti-Squeal Shim

Anti-Squeal Shim

9

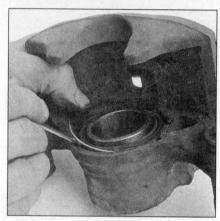

4.4d   Using a small screwdriver, remove the dust boot set ring; make sure you don't gouge or scratch the piston

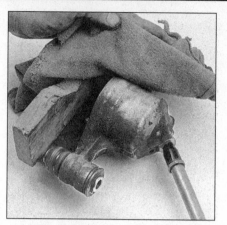

4.5   With the caliper padded to catch the piston, use compressed air to force the piston out of its bore - make sure your hands or fingers are not between the piston and the caliper

4.7   The piston seal should be removed with a plastic or wooden tool to avoid damage to the bore and seal groove - a pencil will do the job

5.2a   To remove the front-caliper torque plate from the steering knuckle, remove these two bolts (arrows)

5.2b   To remove the rear-caliper torque plate from the axle carrier, remove these two bolts (arrows)

5.3   The brake pads on this vehicle were obviously neglected, as they wore down to the rivets and cut deep grooves into the disc - wear this severe means the disc must be replaced

seal from the caliper bore using a wooden or plastic tool **(see illustration)**. Metal tools may damage the cylinder bore.

8   Remove the sliding pins from the torque plate and inspect them for wear. If they're scored or rusted, replace them. Inspect the rubber dust boots for cracks and tears. If they're damaged or worn, pry them out of the torque plate and install new boots.

9   Wash all the components in clean brake fluid or brake cleaner.

10   To reassemble the caliper, you should already have the correct rebuild kit for your vehicle. **Note:** *During reassembly, apply the grease supplied with the rebuild kit (Toyota recommends a "lithium soap base glycol grease") to all sliding surfaces (piston seal, piston, piston dust seal lip, sliding pins, etc.).*

11   If there's no special grease supplied with the rebuild kit, submerge the new piston seal and the piston in brake fluid and install them into the caliper bore. make sure the seal isn't twisted. Do not force the piston into the bore, but make sure that it is squarely in place, then apply firm (but not excessive) pressure to install it.

12   Install the new piston dust boot and set ring.

13   Install the dust boots. If there's no special grease supplied with the rebuild kit, lubricate the sliding pins with silicone-based grease or high-temperature multi-purpose grease and push them into the torque plate.

Installation

14   Install the caliper by reversing the removal procedure. Remember to replace the sealing washers with the brake hose-to-caliper banjo

bolt (new washers may be included with the rebuild kit).

15   Bleed the brake circuit according to the procedure in Section 10. Make sure there are no leaks from the hose connections. Test the brakes carefully before returning the vehicle to normal service.

5   Brake disc - inspection, removal and installation

Note: *This procedure applies to both front and rear brake discs.*

Inspection

Refer to illustrations 5.2a, 5.2b, 5.3, 5.4a, 5.4b, 5.5a and 5.5b

1   Loosen the wheel lug nuts, raise the vehicle and support it securely on jackstands. Remove the wheel and install two or three lug nuts to hold the disc in place. If the rear brake disc is being worked on, release the parking brake.

2   Remove the brake caliper as outlined in Section 4. It isn't necessary to disconnect the brake hose. After removing the caliper bolts, suspend the caliper out of the way with a piece of wire **(see illustration 3.6d)**. If you're removing the front brake disc, remove the two torque plate-to-steering knuckle bolts **(see illustration)** and detach the torque plate; if you're removing the rear brake disc, remove the two torque plate-to-axle carrier bolts **(see illustration)** and detach the torque plate.

3   Visually inspect the disc surface for score marks and other

5.4a Use a dial indicator to check disc runout; if the reading exceeds the maximum allowable runout limit, the disc will have to be machined or replaced

5.4b Using a swirling motion, remove the glaze from the disc surface with sandpaper or emery cloth

5.5a The minimum wear dimension is cast into the back side of the disc

5.5b Use a micrometer to measure disc thickness

5.6a If the rear disc is difficult to remove, remove this plug . . .

5.6b . . . insert a screwdriver through the hole (the hole must be at the 6 o'clock position, because that's where the adjuster is located) . . .

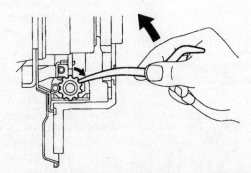

5.6c . . . and rotate the adjuster wheel in a clockwise direction (as seen from the front of the vehicle) to back off the parking brake shoes

damage. Light scratches and shallow grooves are normal after use and may not always be detrimental to brake operation, but deep scoring - over 0.039-inch (1.0 mm) - requires disc removal and refinishing by an automotive machine shop. Be sure to check both sides of the disc (see illustration). If pulsating has been noticed during application of the brakes, suspect disc runout.

4   To check disc runout, place a dial indicator at a point about 1/2-inch from the outer edge of the disc (see illustration). Set the indicator to zero and turn the disc. The indicator reading should not exceed the specified allowable runout limit. If it does, the disc should be refinished

by an automotive machine shop. **Note:** *The discs should be resurfaced regardless of the dial indicator reading, as this will impart a smooth finish and ensure a perfectly flat surface, eliminating any brake pedal pulsation or other undesirable symptoms related to questionable discs. At the very least, if you elect not to have the discs resurfaced, remove the glaze from the surface with emery cloth using a swirling motion* (see illustration).
5   It's absolutely critical that the disc not be machined to a thickness under the specified minimum allowable refinish thickness. The minimum wear (or discard) thickness is cast into the inside of the disc (see illustration). The disc thickness can be checked with a micrometer (see illustration).

Removal
Refer to illustrations 5.6a, 5.6b and 5.6c
6   Remove the lug nuts which were put on to hold the disc in place and remove the disc from the hub. If the rear disc is stuck to the hub and won't come off, remove the plug (see illustration) and rotate the adjuster as shown (see illustrations) to back the parking brake shoes away from the drum surface within the disc.

Installation
7   Place the disc in position over the threaded studs.
8   Install the torque plate and caliper assembly over the disc and position it on the steering knuckle. Tighten the torque plate bolts to the torque listed in this Chapter's Specifications.
9   Install the wheel, then lower the vehicle to the ground. Tighten the

9

6.4a Mark the relationship of the drum to the hub to insure that the dynamic balance is unaltered

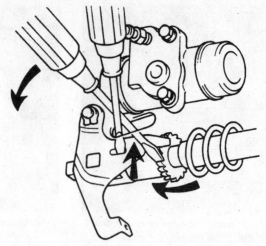

6.4b If the brake shoes hang up on the drum because of excessive wear, insert two screwdrivers through the hole in the backing plate to push the adjuster lever off the star wheel and turn the star wheel to retract the brake shoes

lug nuts to the torque listed in the Chapter 1 Specifications. Depress the brake pedal a few times to bring the brake pads into contact with the disc. Bleeding won't be necessary unless the brake hose was disconnected from the caliper. Check the operation of the brakes carefully before driving the vehicle.

6   Drum brake shoes - replacement

Refer to illustrations 6.4a through 6.4x and 6.5

Warning: *Drum brake shoes must be replaced on both wheels at the same time - never replace the shoes on only one wheel. Also, the dust created by the brake system may contain asbestos, which is harmful to your health. Never blow it out with compressed air and don't inhale any of it. An approved filtering mask should be worn when working on the brakes. Do not, under any circumstances, use petroleum-based solvents to clean brake parts. Use brake system cleaner only!*

Caution: *Whenever the brake shoes are replaced, the return and hold-down springs should also be replaced. Due to the continuous heating/cooling cycle the springs are subjected to, they lose tension over a period of time and may allow the shoes to drag on the drum and wear at a much faster rate than normal.*

1   Loosen the wheel lug nuts, raise the rear of the vehicle and support it securely on jackstands. Block the front wheels to keep the vehicle from rolling.
2   Release the parking brake.
3   Remove the wheel. **Note:** *All four rear brake shoes must be replaced at the same time, but to avoid mixing up parts, work on only one brake assembly at a time.*
4   Follow the accompanying illustrations for the brake shoe replacement procedure **(see illustrations 6.4a through 6.4x)**. Be sure to stay in order and read the caption under each illustration. **Note:** *If*

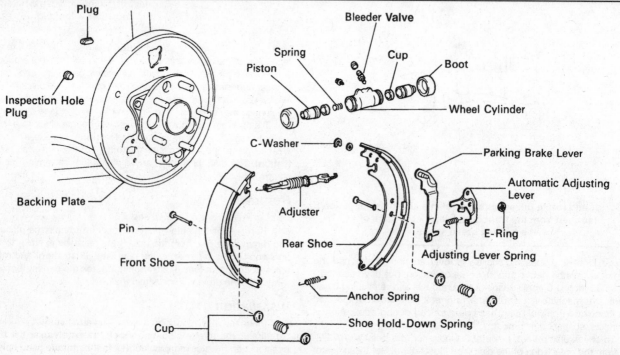

6.4c An exploded view of the rear drum brake assembly

6.4d Before removing anything, clean the brake assembly with brake cleaner and allow it to dry (position a drain pan under the brake to catch the fluid and residue); DO NOT USE COMPRESSED AIR TO BLOW OFF BRAKE DUST!

6.4e Unhook the return spring from the front brake shoe. Use a pair of locking pliers to stretch the spring and pull the end out of the hole in the shoe

6.4f Depress the hold-down spring and turn the retainer 90-degrees, then release it; a pair of pliers will work, but a special hold-down spring removal tool makes the job easier (these inexpensive tools are available at most auto parts stores)

6.4g Remove the front shoe from the backing plate and unhook the anchor spring from the end of the shoe

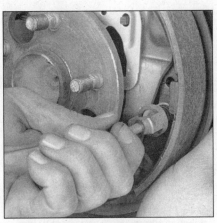

6.4h Remove the hold-down spring from the rear shoe

6.4i Remove the rear shoe and adjuster assembly from the backing plate

6.4j Hold the end of the parking brake lever with a pair of pliers and pull it out of the parking brake lever

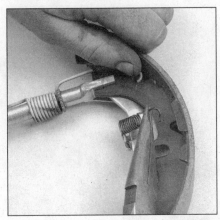

6.4k Remove the adjusting lever spring

6.4l Unhook the return spring from the shoe and slide the adjuster and spring off

9

the brake drum cannot be easily pulled off the axle and shoe assembly, make sure the parking brake is completely released. If the drum still cannot be pulled off, the brake shoes will have to be retracted. This is done by first removing the plug from the backing plate. With the plug removed, push the lever off the adjuster star wheel with a narrow screwdriver while turning the adjuster wheel with another screwdriver, moving the shoes away from the drum (see illustration 6.4b). *The drum should now come off.*

5   Before reinstalling the drum, it should be checked for cracks, score marks, deep scratches and hard spots, which will appear as small discolored areas. If the hard spots cannot be removed with fine emery cloth or if any of the other conditions listed above exist, the drum must be taken to an automotive machine shop to have it resurfaced. **Note:** *Professionals recommend resurfacing the drums each time a brake job is done. Resurfacing will eliminate the possibility of out-of-round drums. If the drums are worn so much that they can't be resurfaced without exceeding the maximum allowable diameter (stamped into the drum), then new ones will be required* (see illustration). *At the very least, if you elect not to have the drums resurfaced, remove the glaze from the surface with emery cloth using a swirling motion.*

6   Install the brake drum on the axle flange.

7   Mount the wheel, install the lug nuts, then lower the vehicle.

8   Make a number of forward and reverse stops and operate the

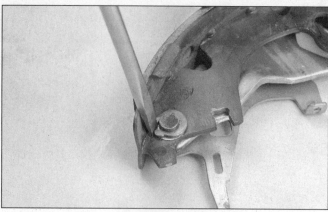

6.4m Pry the C-washer apart and remove it to separate the parking brake lever and adjuster lever from the rear shoe

parking brake to adjust the brakes until satisfactory pedal action is obtained.

9   Check the operation of the brakes carefully before driving the vehicle.

6.4n Assemble the parking brake lever and adjuster lever to the new rear shoe and crimp the C-washer closed with a pair of pliers (always use a new C-washer)

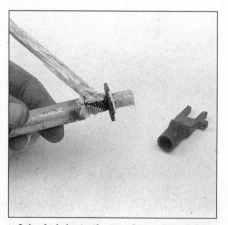

6.4o Lubricate the moving parts of the adjuster screw with a light coat of high-temperature grease; the screw portion of the adjuster will need to be threaded in further than before to allow the drum to fit over the new shoes

6.4p Install the adjuster assembly on the rear shoe (make sure the end fits properly into the slot in the shoe and hook the spring into the opening in the shoe)

6.4q Install the adjuster lever spring

6.4r Lubricate the brake shoe contact area with high-temperature grease

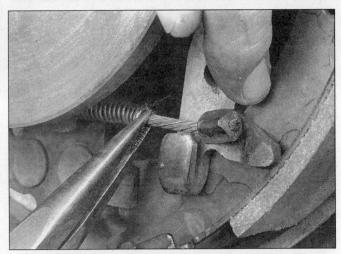

6.4s Pull the parking brake cable spring back and hold it there with a pair of pliers, then place the cable into the hooked end of the parking brake lever

6.4t Place the rear shoe assembly against the backing plate and push the hold-down spring pin through the shoe. Install the cups (one on each end of the spring) and lock the outer cup to the pin by turning it 90-degrees after the spring has been compressed

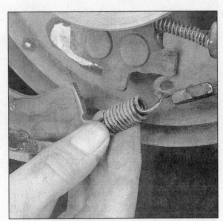

6.4u Connect the anchor spring to the bottom of each shoe and mount the front shoe to the backing plate, then install the hold-down spring and cups

6.4v Using a screwdriver, stretch the return spring into its hole in the front shoe

6.4w Pry the parking brake lever forward and verify that the return spring hasn't come unhooked from the rear shoe

6.4x Wiggle the assembly to make sure it's seated properly against the backing plate

6.5 The maximum drum diameter is cast into the inside of the rear drums

9

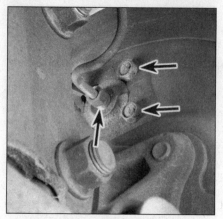

7.4 To remove the wheel cylinder assembly, unscrew the hydraulic line-to-wheel cylinder threaded fitting, then remove the mounting bolts (arrows)

8.1 Unplug the electrical connector for the brake fluid level warning switch

8.4 Loosen the threaded fittings (arrows) on the brake fluid hydraulic lines

7   Wheel cylinder - removal, overhaul and installation

Note: *If an overhaul is indicated (usually because of fluid leaks or sticky operation), explore all options before beginning the job. New wheel cylinders are available, which makes this job quite easy. If you decide to rebuild the wheel cylinder, make sure a rebuild kit is available before proceeding. Never overhaul only one wheel cylinder - always rebuild both of them at the same time.*

Removal

Refer to illustration 7.4

1   Raise the rear of the vehicle and support it securely on jackstands. Block the front wheels to keep the vehicle from rolling.

2   Remove the brake shoe assembly (see Section 6).

3   Remove all dirt and foreign material from around the wheel cylinder.

4   Disconnect the brake line with a flare-nut wrench, if available **(see illustration)**. Don't pull the brake line away from the wheel cylinder.

5   Remove the wheel cylinder mounting bolts.

6   Detach the wheel cylinder from the brake backing plate and place it on a clean workbench. Immediately plug the brake line to prevent fluid loss and contamination.

Overhaul

7   Remove the bleeder screw, cups, pistons, boots and spring assembly from the wheel cylinder body **(see illustration 6.4c)**.

8   Clean the wheel cylinder with brake fluid or brake system cleaner. **Warning:** *Do not, under any circumstances, use petroleum-based solvents to clean brake parts!*

9   Use compressed air to dry the wheel cylinder and blow out the passages.

10   Check the bore for corrosion and score marks. Crocus cloth can

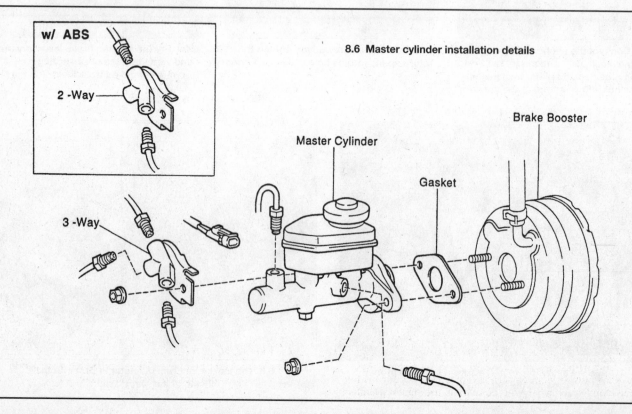

8.6 Master cylinder installation details

w/ ABS

2 -Way

3 -Way

Master Cylinder

Gasket

Brake Booster

8.8a The brake fluid reservoir is retained by a set screw

8.8b After the reservoir has been removed, pull the grommets from the cylinder body. If they're cracked, torn or hard, or appear to have been leaking, replace them

be used to remove light corrosion and stains, but the cylinder must be replaced with a new one if the defects cannot be removed easily, or if the bore is scored.

11   Lubricate the new cups with brake fluid.

12   Assemble the brake cylinder components. Make sure the cup lips face in.

Installation

13   Place the wheel cylinder in position and install the bolts finger tight. Connect the brake line to the cylinder, being careful not to cross-thread the fitting. Tighten the wheel cylinder bolts to the torque listed in this Chapter's Specifications.

14   Tighten the brake line and install the brake shoe assembly.

15   Bleed the brakes (see Section 10).

16   Check the operation of the brakes carefully before driving the vehicle.

8   Master cylinder - removal, overhaul and installation

Note: *Before deciding to overhaul the master cylinder, check on the availability and cost of a new or factory rebuilt unit and also the availability of a rebuild kit.*

Removal

Refer to illustrations 8.1, 8.4 and 8.6

1   Unplug the electrical connector for the brake fluid level warning switch **(see illustration)**.

2   Remove as much fluid as possible from the reservoir with a syringe.

3   Place rags under the fittings and prepare caps or plastic bags to cover the ends of the lines once they're disconnected. **Caution:** *Brake fluid will damage paint. Cover all body parts and be careful not to spill fluid during this procedure.*

4   Loosen the fittings at the ends of the brake lines where they enter the master cylinder **(see illustration)**. To prevent rounding off the flats, use a flare-nut wrench, which wraps around the fitting hex.

5   Pull the brake lines away from the master cylinder and plug the ends to prevent contamination.

6   Remove the nuts attaching the master cylinder to the power booster **(see illustration)**. Pull the master cylinder off the studs to remove it. Again, be careful not to spill the fluid as this is done.

Overhaul

Refer to illustrations 8.8a, 8.8b, 8.9, 8.10, 8.11a, 8.11b and 8.11c

7   Before attempting the overhaul of the master cylinder, obtain the proper rebuild kit, which will contain the necessary replacement parts and also any instructions which may be specific to your model.

8   Remove the reservoir retaining screw, pull off the reservoir and remove the grommets **(see illustrations)**.

9   Place the cylinder in a vise and use a punch or Phillips screwdriver to depress the pistons until they bottom against the other end of the master cylinder. Hold the pistons in this position and remove the stopper bolt from the master cylinder **(see illustration)**.

10   Carefully remove the snap-ring at the end of the master cylinder **(see illustration)**.

8.9 Using a Phillips screwdriver, depress the pistons, then remove the stopper bolt; be sure to replace the copper washer on the stopper bolt when you reassemble the master cylinder

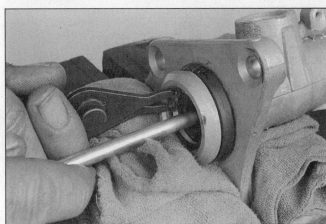

8.10 Depress the pistons again and remove the snap-ring with a pair of snap-ring pliers

9

11   The internal components can now be removed from the bore (see illustrations). Make a note of the proper order of the components so they can be returned to their original locations. **Note:** *The two springs are different, so pay particular attention to their installed order.*

12   Carefully inspect the bore of the master cylinder. Any deep score marks or other damage will mean a new master cylinder is required. DO NOT attempt to hone the bore.

13   Replace all parts included in the rebuild kit, following any instructions in the kit. Clean all re-used parts with new brake fluid or brake system cleaner. **Warning:** *Do not use any petroleum-based solvents.*

During reassembly, lubricate all parts liberally with clean brake fluid.

14   Push the assembled components into the bore, bottoming them against the end of the master cylinder, then install the stopper bolt.

15   Install the new snap-ring, making sure it's seated properly in the groove.

16   Install the reservoir grommets, reservoir and screw.

17   Before installing the master cylinder, it should be bench bled. Since you'll have to apply pressure to the master cylinder piston and, at the same time, control flow from the brake line outlets, the master cylinder should be mounted in a vise, with the jaws of the vise

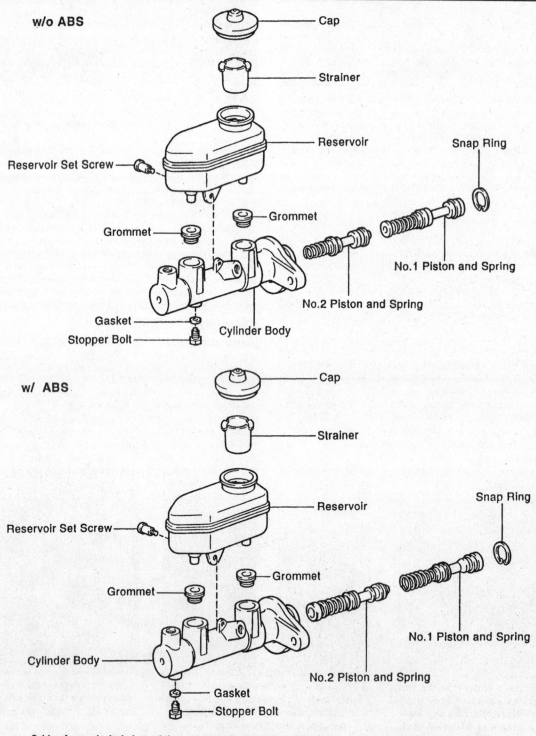

8.11a An exploded view of the master cylinder assembly (upper, without ABS; lower, with ABS)

clamping on the mounting flange.

18   Insert threaded plugs into the brake line outlet holes and snug them down so no air will leak past them, but not so tight that they can't be easily loosened.

19   Fill the reservoir with brake fluid of the recommended type (see Chapter 1).

20   Remove one plug and push the piston assembly into the bore to expel the air from the master cylinder. A large Phillips screwdriver can be used to push on the piston assembly.

21   To prevent air from being drawn back into the master cylinder, the plug must be replaced and snugged down before releasing the pressure on the piston.

22   Repeat the procedure until only brake fluid is expelled from the brake line outlet hole. When only brake fluid is expelled, repeat the procedure at the other outlet hole and plug. Be sure to keep the master cylinder reservoir filled with brake fluid to prevent the introduction of air into the system.

23   Since high pressure isn't involved in the bench bleeding procedure, an alternative to the removal and replacement of the plugs with each stroke of the piston assembly is available. Before pushing in on the piston assembly, remove the plug as described in Step 20. Before releasing the piston, however, instead of replacing the plug, simply put your finger tightly over the hole to keep air from being drawn back into the master cylinder. Wait several seconds for brake fluid to be drawn from the reservoir into the bore, then depress the piston again, removing your finger as brake fluid is expelled. Be sure to

put your finger back over the hole each time before releasing the piston, and when the bleeding procedure is complete for that outlet, replace the plug and tighten it before going on to the other port.

Installation

Refer to illustration 8.27

24   Install the master cylinder over the studs on the power brake booster and tighten the nuts only finger-tight at this time.

25   Thread the brake line fittings into the master cylinder. Since the master cylinder is still a bit loose, it can be moved slightly so the fittings thread in easily. Don't strip the threads as the fittings are tightened.

26   Tighten the mounting nuts and the brake line fittings.

27   Fill the master cylinder reservoir with fluid, then bleed the master cylinder (only if hasn't been bench bled) and the brake system (see Section 10). To bleed the master cylinder on the vehicle, have an assistant depress the brake pedal and hold it down. Loosen the fitting to allow air and fluid to escape. Tighten the fitting, then allow your assistant to return the pedal to its rest position. Repeat this procedure on both fittings until the fluid is free of air bubbles **(see illustration)**. Check the operation of the brake system carefully before driving the vehicle.

---

9   Brake hoses and lines - inspection and replacement

Inspection

1   About every six months, with the vehicle raised and supported securely on jackstands, the rubber hoses which connect the steel brake lines with the front and rear brake assemblies should be inspected for cracks, chafing of the outer cover, leaks, blisters and other damage. These are important and vulnerable parts of the brake system and inspection should be complete. A light and mirror will be helpful for a thorough check. If a hose exhibits any of the above conditions, replace it with a new one.

Replacement

Front brake hose

Refer to illustrations 9.3 and 9.4

2   Loosen the wheel lug nuts, raise the vehicle and support it securely on jackstands. Remove the wheel.

3   At the frame bracket, unscrew the brake line fitting from the hose **(see illustration)**. Use a flare-nut wrench to prevent rounding off the corners.

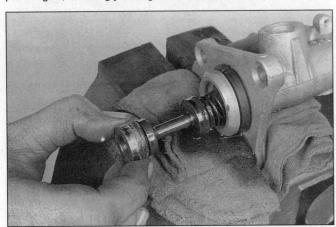

8.11b After the snap-ring has been removed, the primary (No. 1) piston assembly can be removed

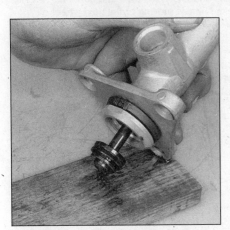

8.11c Remove the cylinder from the vise and tap it against a block of wood until the secondary (No. 2) piston is exposed. Pull the piston assembly STRAIGHT out; if it becomes even slightly cocked, the bore may be damaged

8.27 Have an assistant depress the brake pedal and hold it down, then loosen the fitting nut, allowing the air and fluid to escape; repeat this procedure on both fittings until the fluid is clear of air bubbles

9.3 Unscrew the brake line threaded fitting with a flare-nut wrench to protect the fitting corners from being rounded off

9

4   Remove the U-clip from the female fitting at the bracket with a pair of pliers **(see illustration)**, then pass the hose through the bracket.

5   At the caliper end of the hose, remove the banjo fitting bolt **(see illustration 3.6b)**, then separate the hose from the caliper. Note that there are two copper sealing washers on either side of the fitting - they should be replaced with new ones during installation.

6   Remove the U-clip from the strut bracket, then feed the hose through the bracket.

7   To install the hose, pass the caliper fitting end through the strut bracket, then connect the fitting to the caliper with the banjo bolt and copper washers. Make sure the locating lug on the fitting is engaged with the hole in the caliper, then tighten the bolt to the torque listed in this Chapter's Specifications.

8   Push the metal support into the strut bracket and install the U-clip. Make sure the hose isn't twisted between the caliper and the strut bracket.

9   Route the hose into the frame bracket, again making sure it isn't twisted, then connect the brake line fitting, starting the threads by hand. Install the clip and E-ring, if equipped, then tighten the fitting securely.

10   Bleed the caliper (see Section 10).

11   Install the wheel and lug nuts, lower the vehicle and tighten the lug nuts to the torque specified in Chapter 1.

Rear brake hose

12   Perform Steps 2, 3 and 4 above, then repeat Steps 3 and 4 at the other end of the hose. Be sure to bleed the wheel cylinder (or caliper) (see Section 10).

Metal brake lines

13   When replacing brake lines, be sure to use the correct parts. Don't use copper tubing for any brake system components. Purchase steel brake lines from a dealer or auto parts store.

14   Prefabricated brake line, with the tube ends already flared and fittings installed, is available at auto parts stores and dealer parts departments. These lines are also bent to the proper shapes.

15   When installing the new line, make sure it's securely supported in the brackets and has plenty of clearance between moving or hot components.

16   After installation, check the master cylinder fluid level and add fluid as necessary. Bleed the brake system (see Section 10) and test the brakes carefully before driving the vehicle in traffic.

---

10   Brake hydraulic system - bleeding

Refer to illustration 10.8

Warning: *Wear eye protection when bleeding the brake system. If the fluid comes in contact with your eyes, immediately rinse them with water and seek medical attention.*

Note: *Bleeding the hydraulic system is necessary to remove any air that manages to find its way into the system when it's been opened during removal and installation of a hose, line, caliper or master cylinder.*

1   You'll probably have to bleed the system at all four brakes if air has entered it due to low fluid level, or if the brake lines have been disconnected at the master cylinder.

2   If a brake line was disconnected only at a wheel, then only that caliper or wheel cylinder must be bled.

3   If a brake line is disconnected at a fitting located between the master cylinder and any of the brakes, that part of the system served by the disconnected line must be bled.

4   Remove any residual vacuum from the brake power booster by applying the brake several times with the engine off.

5   Remove the master cylinder reservoir cover and fill the reservoir with brake fluid. Reinstall the cover. **Note:** *Check the fluid level often during the bleeding operation and add fluid as necessary to prevent the fluid level from falling low enough to allow air bubbles into the master cylinder.*

9.4 Remove the brake hose-to-brake line U-clip with a pair of pliers

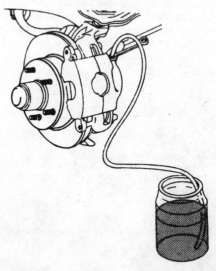

10.8 When bleeding the brakes, a hose is connected to the bleeder valve at the caliper or wheel cylinder and then submerged in brake fluid. Air will be seen as bubbles in the tube and container. All air must be expelled before moving to the next wheel

---

6   Have an assistant on hand, as well as a supply of new brake fluid, a clear plastic container partially filled with clean brake fluid, a length of 3/16-inch plastic, rubber or vinyl tubing to fit over the bleeder valve and a wrench to open and close the bleeder valve.

7   Beginning at the right rear wheel, loosen the bleeder valve slightly, then tighten it to a point where it's snug but can still be loosened quickly and easily.

8   Place one end of the tubing over the bleeder valve and submerge the other end in brake fluid in the container **(see illustration)**.

9   Have the assistant pump the brakes slowly a few times to get pressure in the system, then hold the pedal down firmly.

10   While the pedal is held down, open the bleeder valve just enough to allow a flow of fluid to leave the valve. Watch for air bubbles to exit the submerged end of the tube. When the fluid flow slows after a couple of seconds, close the valve and have your assistant release the pedal.

11   Repeat Steps 9 and 10 until no more air is seen leaving the tube, then tighten the bleeder valve and proceed to the left front wheel, the left rear wheel and the right front wheel, in that order, and perform the same procedure. Be sure to check the fluid in the master cylinder reservoir frequently.

12   Never use old brake fluid. It contains moisture which will

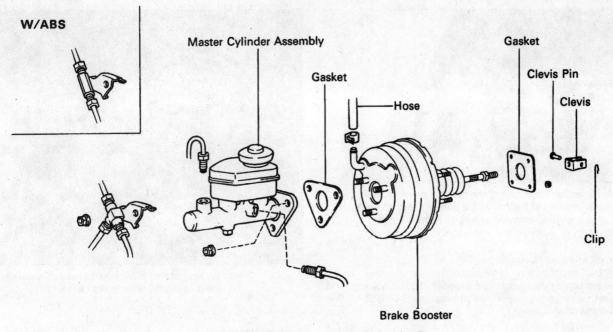

11.11 Power brake booster installation details

deteriorate the brake system components.

13   Refill the master cylinder with fluid at the end of the operation.

14   Check the operation of the brakes. The pedal should feel solid when depressed, with no sponginess. If necessary, repeat the entire process. **Warning:** *Do not operate the vehicle if you're in doubt about the effectiveness of the brake system.*

11   Power brake booster - check, removal and installation

Operating check

1   Depress the brake pedal several times with the engine off and make sure there's no change in the pedal reserve distance.

2   Depress the pedal and start the engine. If the pedal goes down slightly, operation is normal.

Airtightness check

3   Start the engine and turn it off after one or two minutes. Depress the brake pedal slowly several times. If the pedal depresses less each time, the booster is airtight.

4   Depress the brake pedal while the engine is running, then stop the engine with the pedal depressed. If there's no change in the pedal reserve travel after holding the pedal for 30 seconds, the booster is airtight.

Removal

Refer to illustration 11.11

5   Power brake booster units shouldn't be disassembled. They require special tools not normally found in most automotive repair stations or shops. They're fairly complex and, because of their critical relationship to brake performance, should be replaced with a new or rebuilt one.

6   Remove the brake master cylinder (see Section 8).

7   On 1992 and 1993 models, remove the wire harness clamp below the brake booster.

8   Loosen the clamp screw and push the charcoal canister down slightly (see Chapter 6).

9   Disconnect the vacuum hose from the brake booster. Be careful not to damage the hose when removing it from the booster fitting.

10   Inside the vehicle, remove the steering column cover pad (see Chapter 11).

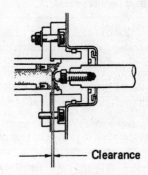

11.14a There should be no clearance between the booster pushrod and the master cylinder pushrod, but no interference either; if there is interference between the two, there will be excessive brake pedal travel

11   Using a flashlight or a drop light, locate the clevis which connects the booster pushrod to the top of the brake pedal. Remove the clevis pin retaining clip with pliers and pull out the pin **(see illustration)**.

12   Remove the four nuts and washers holding the brake booster to the firewall (you may need a light to see them). Slide the booster straight out from the firewall until the studs clear the holes.

Installation

Refer to illustrations 11.14a and 11.14b

13   Installation procedures are basically the reverse of removal. Tighten the clevis locknut securely and the booster mounting nuts to the torque listed in this Chapter's Specifications.

14   If the power booster unit is being replaced, the clearance between the master cylinder piston and the pushrod in the vacuum booster must be measured and, if necessary, adjusted. Using a depth micrometer or vernier calipers, measure the distance from the seat (recessed area) in the master cylinder to the master cylinder mounting flange. Next, measure the distance from the end of the vacuum booster pushrod to the mounting face of the booster (including gasket) where the master cylinder mounting flange seats. The measurements should be the same **(see illustration)**. If not, turn the adjusting screw on the end of the power booster pushrod until the clearance is within

9

11.14b To adjust the length of the booster pushrod, hold the serrated portion of the rod with a pair of pliers and turn the adjusting screw in or out, as necessary, to achieve the desired setting

the specified limit **(see illustration)**.

15   After the final installation of the master cylinder and brake hoses and lines, the brake pedal height and freeplay must be adjusted and the system must be bled. See the appropriate Sections of this Chapter for the procedures.

12   Parking brake shoes (rear disc brakes only) - inspection and replacement

Refer to illustrations 12.4 and 12.5a through 12.5v

Warning 1: *Dust created by the brake system may contain asbestos, which is hazardous to your health. Never blow it out with compressed air and don't inhale any of it. An approved filtering mask should be worn when working on the brakes. Do not, under any circumstances, use petroleum-based solvents to clean brake parts. Use brake system cleaner only!*

Warning 2: *Parking brake shoes must be replaced on both wheels at the same time - never replace the shoes on only one wheel.*

12.4 Before disassembling it, be sure to wash the parking brake assembly with brake cleaner

Caution: *Whenever the brake shoes are replaced, the return and hold-down springs should also be replaced. Due to the continuous heating/cooling cycle the springs are subjected to, they lose tension over a period of time and may allow the shoes to drag on the drum and wear at a much faster rate than normal.*

1   Remove the brake disc (see Section 5).

2   Inspect the thickness of the lining material on the shoes. If the lining has worn down to 1/32-inch or less, the shoes must be replaced.

3   Remove the hub and bearing assembly (see Chapter 10).

4   Wash off the brake parts with brake system cleaner **(see illustration)**.

5   Follow the accompanying illustrations for the brake shoe replacement procedure **(see illustrations 12.5a through 12.5)**. Be sure to stay in order and read the caption under each illustration.

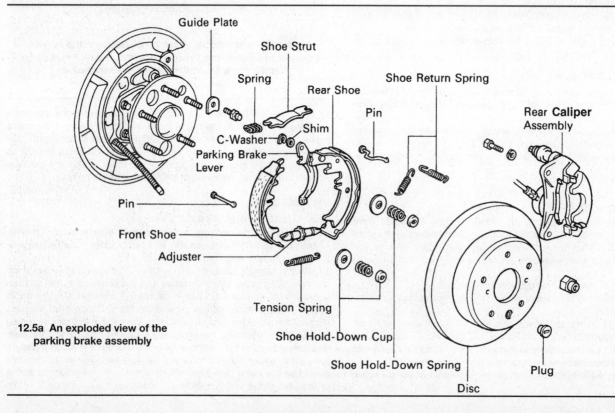

12.5a An exploded view of the parking brake assembly

12.5b Remove the rear parking brake shoe return spring from the anchor pin . . .

12.5c . . . and unhook it from the rear shoe

12.5d Remove the front parking brake shoe return spring from the anchor pin . . .

6   Install the brake disc. Temporarily thread three of the wheel lug nuts onto the studs to hold the disc in place.

7   Remove the hole plug from the brake disc. Adjust the parking brake shoe clearance by turning the adjuster star wheel with a brake adjusting tool or screwdriver until the shoes contact the disc and the disc can't be turned **(see illustrations 5.6a, 5.6b and 5.6c)**. Back-off the adjuster eight notches, then install the hole plug.

8   Install the torque plate **(see illustration 5.2b)** and brake caliper

(see Section 4). Be sure to tighten the bolts to the torque listed in this Chapter's Specifications.

9   Install the wheel and tighten the lug nuts to the torque specified in Chapter 1.

10   If the vehicle is equipped with a parking brake lever, pull up on the lever and count the number of clicks that it travels. It should be between five and eight clicks - if it's not, adjust the parking brake as described in the next Section.

12.5e . . . and unhook it from the front shoe

12.5f Remove the rear shoe hold-down spring, pull out the pin and put it in a plastic bag

12.5g Remove the shoe strut from between the shoes

12.5h Remove the front shoe hold-down spring, pull out the pin and put it in a plastic bag

12.5i Remove the adjuster and the tension spring (the tension spring, which is not visible in this photo, is behind the adjuster and is attached to both shoes

12.5j Pop the C-washer off the pivot pin on the back of the rear shoe . . .

9

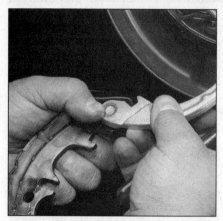

12.5k . . . and pull the parking brake lever off the pivot pin

12.5l Apply a thin coat of high-temperature grease to the contact surfaces of the backing plate

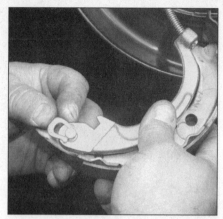

12.5m Slide the parking brake lever onto the pivot pin and install a new C-washer

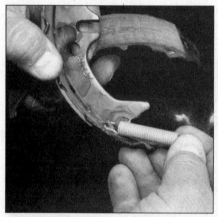

12.5n Attach the tension spring to the back side of the rear shoe . . .

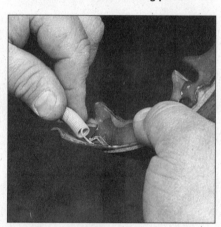

12.5o . . . and to the back side of the front shoe

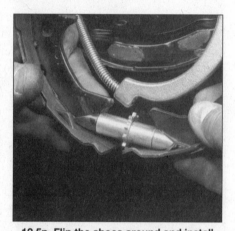

12.5p Flip the shoes around and install the adjuster; make sure both ends of the adjuster are properly engaged with the shoes as shown

11   To bed the shoes to the drum, drive the vehicle at approximately 30 mph on a dry, level road. If the vehicle has a parking brake lever, push in on the parking brake release button and pull up slightly on the lever with about 20 pounds of force; if the vehicle has a pedal-type parking brake system, apply the pedal with about 33 pounds of

force. Drive the vehicle with the parking brake applied like this for 1/4-mile. Repeat this procedure two or three times, allowing the brakes to cool between applications.

13   Parking brake - adjustment

Lever type

1   The parking brake lever, when properly adjusted, should travel five to eight clicks when a moderate pulling force is applied. If it travels less than five clicks, there's a chance the parking brake might not be releasing completely and might be dragging on the drum or disc. If the lever can be pulled up more than eight clicks, the parking brake may not hold adequately on an incline, allowing the car to roll.
2   To gain access to the parking brake cable adjuster, remove the center console (see Chapter 11).
3   Loosen the locknut (the upper nut) while holding the adjusting nut (lower nut) with a wrench **(see illustration 13.7)**. Tighten the adjusting nut until the desired travel is attained. Tighten the locknut.
4   Install the console.

Pedal type

Refer to illustration 13.7

5   Slowly depress the parking brake pedal all the way and count the number of clicks. It should take about three to six clicks to apply the parking brake. If it travels less than three clicks, there's a chance the parking brake might not be releasing completely and might be

12.5q Place the shoes in position and install the strut and spring as shown; make sure the ends of the strut are properly engaged with the shoes as shown

12.5r Install the front shoe return spring . . .

12.5s . . . and the rear shoe return spring

12.4t Install the rear shoe hold-down spring

12.5u . . . and the front shoe hold-down spring

dragging on the drum or disc. If it travels more than six clicks, the parking brake may not hold adequately on an incline, allowing the car to roll.

6   Remove the center console (see Chapter 11).

7   Loosen the locknut (the upper nut) while holding the adjusting nut (lower nut) with a wrench **(see illustration)**. Tighten the adjusting nut until the desired travel is attained. Tighten the locknut.

8   Install the console.

12.5v This is how the parking brake assembly should look when you're done!

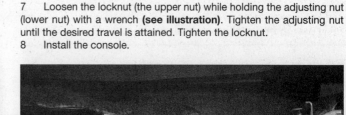

13.7 Parking brake cable locknut (upper nut) and adjuster nut (lower nut) for pedal-type parking brake cable systems (same setup is used on models with a parking brake lever)

9

14.4 To detach either parking brake cable housing from the brake backing plate, remove these two bolts (disc brake backing plate shown, drum brake setup similar)

14.5 This parking brake bracket is located near the forward end of the strut rod (but there may be others, depending on the year and model)

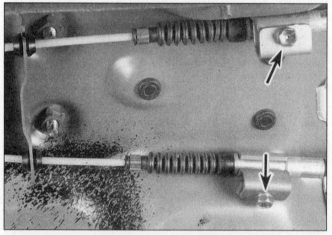

14.7 To release either parking brake cable from its cable clamp, loosen the clamp bolt (arrows) and slide the cable housing out of the clamp

14.8 To detach either parking brake cable from the equalizer, align the cable with the slot in the top of the equalizer and slide the cable end out of the hole

14 Parking brake cables - replacement

Equalizer-to-parking brake cable

Refer to illustrations 14.4, 14.5, 14.7 and 14.8

1   Loosen the rear wheel lug nuts, raise the rear of the vehicle and support it securely on jackstands. Block the front wheels. Remove the wheel.

2   Make sure the parking brake is completely released, then remove the brake drum or disc.

3   On models with rear drum brakes, remove the brake shoes and disconnect the cable from the parking brake lever (see Section 6); on models with rear disc brakes, remove the parking brake shoes and disconnect the parking brake lever (see Section 12).

4   Unbolt the cable housing from the backing plate **(see illustration)**.

5   Unbolt all cable brackets **(see illustration)**.

6   Remove the center exhaust pipe, or lower it enough to get at the forward part of the cables (see Chapter 4).

7   Trace the cable forward and locate the cable clamp **(see illustration)**. Loosen the clamp bolt and slide the cable housing out of the clamp.

8   Disconnect the cable end from the equalizer by aligning the cable with the slot in the top of the equalizer. Slide the cable end out of the hole **(see illustration)**.

9   Installation is the reverse of removal.

10   Adjust the parking brake (see Section 13).

Intermediate lever-to-equalizer lever cable

Refer to illustration 14.14

11   Remove the center console (see Chapter 11).

12   With the parking brake cable released, remove the locknut and the adjusting nut (see Section 13) and detach the cable.

13   Working under the vehicle, pull the cable to the rear, turn it 90-degrees and pass it through the center of the equalizer **(see illustration 14.17)**. Pull the cable through the hole in the floorpan.

14   Installation is the reverse of the removal procedure **(see illustration)**. Apply a light coat of grease to the portion of the cable end that contacts the equalizer. Adjust the parking brake cable as outlined previously (see Section 13).

Parking brake pedal-to-intermediate lever cable

Refer to illustration 14.17

15   Remove the center console (see Chapter 11).

16   Disconnect the cable from the intermediate lever **(see illustration 13.7)**.

17   Disconnect the parking brake switch **(see illustration)**.

18   Remove the clip, pull out the clevis pin and disconnect the parking brake cable from the parking brake pedal assembly.

19   Installation is the reverse of removal.

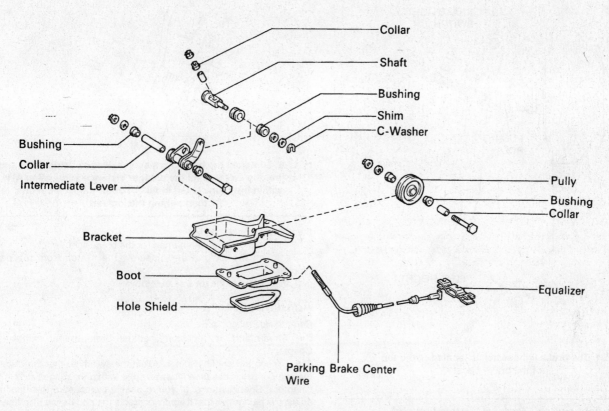

14.14 An exploded view of the intermediate lever and lever-to-equalizer cable assembly

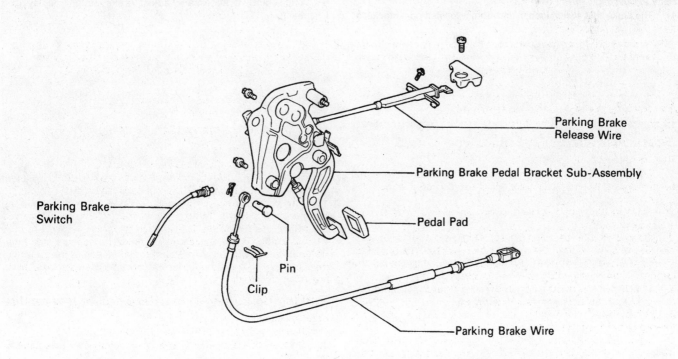

14.17 An exploded view of the parking brake pedal and pedal-to-intermediate lever cable assembly

9

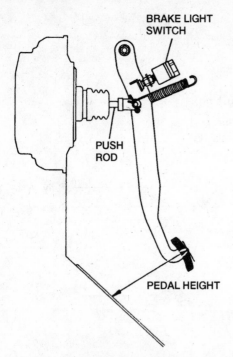

**15.1 The brake light switch is located at the top
of the brake pedal**

---

15   Brake light switch - removal, installation and adjustment

Removal and installation

Refer to illustration 15.1

1   The brake light switch **(see illustration)** is located on a bracket at

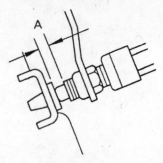

**15.6 To adjust the brake light switch, loosen the locknut and
rotate the switch until the plunger distance (dimension A) is
within the range listed in this Chapter's Specifications,
then tighten the locknut**

---

the top of the brake pedal.

2   Disconnect the wiring harness at the brake light switch.

3   Loosen the locknut and unscrew the switch from the pedal bracket.

4   Installation is the reverse of removal.

Adjustment

Refer to illustration 15.6

5   Check and, if necessary, adjust brake pedal height (see Chapter 1).

6   Loosen the switch locknut, adjust the switch so that the distance the plunger protrudes **(see illustration)** is within the range listed in this Chapter's Specifications. (If you're unable to measure this distance, adjust the plunger so that it lightly contacts the pedal stop.) Tighten the locknut.

7   Plug the electrical connector into the switch and reconnect the battery. Make sure the brake lights come on when the brake pedal is depressed and go off when the pedal is released. If not, repeat the adjustment procedure until the brake lights function properly

8   Check and, if necessary, adjust brake pedal freeplay (see Chapter 1).

Chapter 10
Suspension and steering systems

Contents

Specifications

Torque specifications

Ft-lbs (unless otherwise indicated)

Front suspension

Balljoint
Balljoint-to-steering knuckle nut	90
Balljoint-to-control arm nuts and bolts	94

Control arm
Front bolts	152
Rear bolt..	152

Stabilizer bar
Stabilizer bar link-to-control arm bracket nut
1992 and 1993...	47
1994 and later	29
Stabilizer bushing/retainer bolts..	168 in-lbs

Strut
Strut upper mounting nuts	59
Strut-to-suspension support (damper shaft) nut.............................	36
Strut-to-steering knuckle bolts/nuts	156

Rear suspension

Hub and bearing assembly
Bearing-to-axle carrier bolts	59
Hub-to-bearing retaining nut	90
LSPV spring-to-rear suspension arm nut (station wagon).....................	48 in-lbs

Strut
Strut upper mounting nuts	29
Strut-to-suspension support (damper shaft) nut.............................	36
Strut-to-axle carrier nuts/bolts	188

10

Torque specifications (continued)

Rear suspension

Suspension arms

Ft-lbs (unless otherwise indicated)

No. 1/No. 2 arm-to-body through-bolt nut	134
No. 1/No. 2 arm-to-axle carrier through-bolt nut	134
Strut rod-to-body bolt	83
Strut rod-to-axle carrier bolt	83

Steering system

Airbag module retaining screws	78 in-lbs
Steering wheel nut	26
Steering gear mounting bolts/nuts	134
Steering shaft universal joint pinch bolt	26
Tie-rod end-to-steering knuckle nut	36
Power steering pump	
Adjuster and pivot bolts	32
Fluid line threaded fitting	33
Fluid line banjo bolt	38
Wheel lug nuts	See Chapter 1

1   General information

Refer to illustrations 1.1 and 1.2

The front suspension is a Macpherson strut design. The upper end of each strut is attached to the vehicle's body strut support. The lower end of the strut is connected to the upper end of the steering knuckle. The steering knuckle is attached to a balljoint mounted on the outer end of the suspension control arm **(see illustration)**.

The rear suspension also utilizes strut/coil spring assemblies. The upper end of each strut is attached to the vehicle body by a strut support. The lower end of the strut is attached to an axle carrier. The carrier is located by a pair of suspension arms on each side, and a longitudinally mounted strut rod between the body and each knuckle **(see illustration)**.

The power-assisted rack-and-pinion steering gear, which is located behind the engine/transaxle assembly, is mounted on the engine cradle. The steering gear actuates the tie-rods, which are attached to the steering knuckles. The steering column is designed to collapse in the event of an accident.

Frequently, when working on the suspension or steering system components, you may come across fasteners which seem impossible to loosen. These fasteners on the underside of the vehicle are continually subjected to water, road grime, mud, etc., and can become rusted or "frozen," making them extremely difficult to remove. In order to unscrew these stubborn fasteners without damaging them (or other

1.1 Front steering and suspension components

1 Steering gear assembly	*3 Balljoint nuts and bolt*	*5 Stabilizer bar link*
2 Control arm	*4 Strut assembly*	

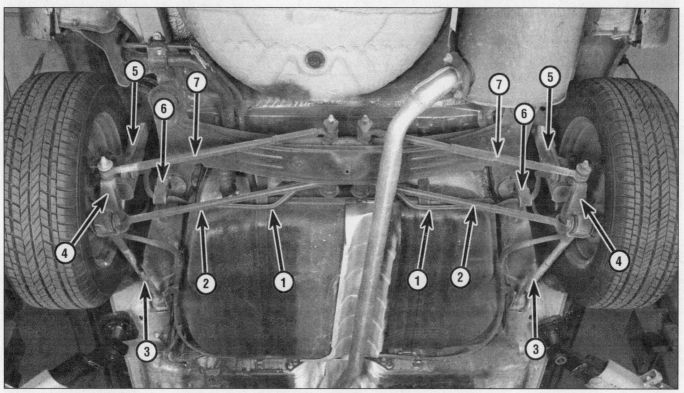

1.2 Rear suspension components

1	Stabilizer bar	4	Rear axle carrier	6	Stabilizer bar bushing retainer
2	Suspension arm (front)	5	Strut assembly	7	Suspension arm (rear)
3	Strut rod				

components), be sure to use lots of penetrating oil and allow it to soak in for a while. Using a wire brush to clean exposed threads will also ease removal of the nut or bolt and prevent damage to the threads. Sometimes a sharp blow with a hammer and punch will break the bond between a nut and bolt threads, but care must be taken to prevent the punch from slipping off the fastener and ruining the threads. Heating the stuck fastener and surrounding area with a torch sometimes helps too, but isn't recommended because of the obvious dangers associated with fire. Long breaker bars and extension, or "cheater," pipes will increase leverage, but never use an extension pipe on a ratchet - the ratcheting mechanism could be damaged. Sometimes tightening the nut or bolt first will help to break it loose. Fasteners that

require drastic measures to remove should always be replaced with new ones.

Since most of the procedures dealt with in this Chapter involve jacking up the vehicle and working underneath it, a good pair of jackstands will be needed. A hydraulic floor jack is the preferred type of jack to lift the vehicle, and it can also be used to support certain components during various operations. **Warning:** *Never, under any circumstances, rely on a jack to support the vehicle while working on it. Whenever any of the suspension or steering fasteners are loosened or removed they must be inspected and, if necessary, replaced with new ones of the same part number or of original equipment quality and design. Torque specifications must be followed for proper reassembly and component retention. Never attempt to heat or straighten any suspension or steering components. Instead, replace any bent or damaged part with a new one.*

2   Stabilizer bar and bushings (front) - removal and installation

Removal

Refer to illustrations 2.4, 2.5 and 2.9

1   Loosen the front wheel lug nuts. Raise the front of the vehicle and support it securely on jackstands. Apply the parking brake and block the rear wheels to keep the vehicle from rolling off the stands. Remove the front wheels.

2   Remove the left and right fender apron seals. Each seal is retained by three bolts.

3   Disconnect the left and right tie-rod ends from the steering knuckles (see Section 17).

4   Disconnect the stabilizer bar links from the bar **(see illustration)**. If the ballstud turns with the nut, use a hex wrench to hold the stud.

2.4 To detach the stabilizer bar link from the bar, remove the nut (arrow); if the ballstud turns with the nut, use a hex wrench to hold the stud

10

2.5 To detach the stabilizer bar from the engine cradle, remove these bushing retainer bolts (arrows) and remove the retainer

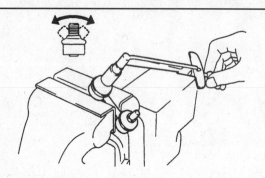

2.9 To check the balljoint in the stabilizer bar link, flip the balljoint stud side to side five or six times as shown, install the nut and, using an inch-pound torque wrench, turn the nut continuously one turn every two to four seconds, then note the torque reading on the fifth turn. It should be about 0.4 to 8.7 in-lbs; if it isn't, replace the link assembly

5   Detach both stabilizer bar bushing retainers from the engine cradle **(see illustration)**.
6   Remove the front exhaust pipe (see Chapter 4).
7   Remove the steering gear mounting bolts (see Section 19).
8   Lift the steering gear assembly and remove the stabilizer bar by working it out through the left wheel housing.
9   While the stabilizer bar is off the vehicle, slide off the retainer

bushings and inspect them. If they're cracked, worn or deteriorated, replace them. It's also a good idea to inspect the stabilizer bar link. To check it, flip the balljoint stud side to side five or six times as shown **(see illustration)**, then install the nut. Using an inch-pound torque wrench, turn the nut continuously one turn every two to four seconds and note the torque reading on the fifth turn. It should be about 0.4 to 8.7 in-lbs. If it isn't, replace the link assembly.
10   Clean the bushing area of the stabilizer bar with a stiff wire brush to remove any rust or dirt.

Installation

11   Lubricate the inside and outside of the new bushing with vegetable oil (used in cooking) to simplify reassembly. **Caution:** *Don't use petroleum or mineral-based lubricants or brake fluid - they will lead to deterioration of the bushings.*
12   Installation is the reverse of removal.

---

3   Strut assembly (front) - removal, inspection and installation

---

Removal

Refer to illustrations 3.2, 3.4 and 3.6
1   Loosen the wheel lug nuts, raise the vehicle and support it securely on jackstands. Remove the wheel. Support the control arm with a floor jack.
2   Remove the brake hose bracket from the strut **(see illustration)**.
3   If the vehicle is equipped with ABS, detach the speed sensor wiring harness from the strut by removing the clamp bracket bolt.
4   Remove the strut-to-knuckle nuts **(see illustration)** and knock the bolts out with a hammer and punch.
5   Separate the strut from the steering knuckle. Be careful not to overextend the inner CV joint. Also, don't let the steering knuckle fall outward, as the brake hose could be damaged.
6   Support the strut and spring assembly with one hand and remove the three strut-to-shock tower nuts **(see illustration)**. Remove the assembly out from the fenderwell.

Inspection

7   Check the strut body for leaking fluid, dents, cracks and other obvious damage which would warrant repair or replacement.
8   Check the coil spring for chips or cracks in the spring coating (this can cause premature spring failure due to corrosion). Inspect the spring seat for cuts, hardness and general deterioration.
9   If any undesirable conditions exist, proceed to the strut disassembly procedure (see Section 4).

3.2 Remove the brake hose bracket from the strut

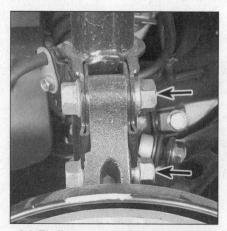

3.4 To disconnect the lower end of the strut from the steering knuckle, remove these two nuts (arrows) and knock out the bolts with a hammer and punch

3.6 To disconnect the upper end of the strut from the vehicle body, remove these three nuts (arrows)

4.3 Install the spring compressor in accordance with the manufacturer's instructions and compress the spring until all pressure is relieved from the upper spring seat

4.4 Remove the damper shaft nut

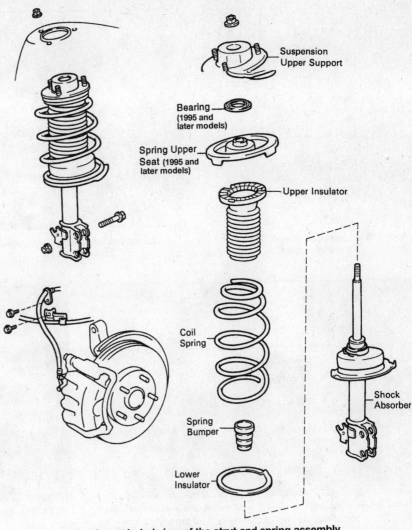

Suspension Upper Support

Bearing (1995 and later models)

Spring Upper Seat (1995 and later models)

Upper Insulator

Coil Spring

Spring Bumper

Lower Insulator

Shock Absorber

4.5a An exploded view of the strut and spring assembly

Installation

10   Guide the strut assembly up into the fenderwell and insert the three upper mounting studs through the holes in the shock tower. Once the three studs protrude from the shock tower, install the nuts so the strut won't fall back through. This is most easily accomplished with the help of an assistant, as the strut is quite heavy and awkward.

11   Slide the steering knuckle into the strut flange and insert the two bolts. Install the nuts and tighten them to the torque listed in this Chapter's Specifications.

12   Reattach the brake hose bracket to the strut. If the vehicle is equipped with ABS, install the speed sensor wiring harness bracket.

13   Install the wheel and lug nuts, then lower the vehicle and tighten the lug nuts to the torque listed in the Chapter 1 Specifications.

14   Tighten the three upper mounting nuts to the torque listed in this Chapter's Specifications.

15   Drive the vehicle to an alignment shop to have the front end alignment checked, and if necessary, adjusted.

4   Strut/coil spring assembly - replacement

1   If the struts or coil springs exhibit the telltale signs of wear (leaking fluid, loss of damping capability, chipped, sagging or cracked coil springs) explore all options before beginning any work. The strut/shock absorber assemblies are not serviceable and must be replaced if a problem develops. However, strut assemblies complete with springs may be available on an exchange basis, which eliminates much time and work. Whichever route you choose to take, check on the cost and availability of parts before disassembling your vehicle.
Warning: *Disassembling a strut assembly is a potentially dangerous undertaking and utmost attention must be directed to the job, or serious injury may result. Use only a high-quality spring compressor and carefully follow the manufacturer's instructions furnished with the tool. After removing the coil spring from the strut assembly, set it aside in a safe, isolated area.*

Disassembly

Refer to illustrations 4.3, 4.4, 4.5a, 4.5b, 4.6 and 4.7

2   Remove the strut and spring assembly following the procedure described in the previous Section. Mount the strut assembly in a vise. Line the vise jaws with wood or rags to prevent damage to the unit and don't tighten the vise excessively.

3   Following the tool manufacturer's instructions, install the spring compressor (which can be obtained at most auto parts stores or equipment yards on a daily rental basis) on the spring and compress it sufficiently to relieve all pressure from the upper spring seat **(see illustration)**. This can be verified by wiggling the spring.

4   Loosen the damper shaft nut **(see illustration)**.

5   Remove the nut and suspension support **(see illustrations)**. Inspect the bearing in the suspension support for smooth operation. If it doesn't turn smoothly, replace the suspension support. Check the

10

4.5b Lift the suspension support off the damper shaft

4.6 Remove the spring seat from the damper shaft

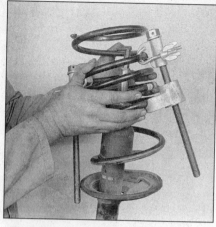

4.7 Remove the compressed spring assembly - keep the ends of the spring pointed away from your body

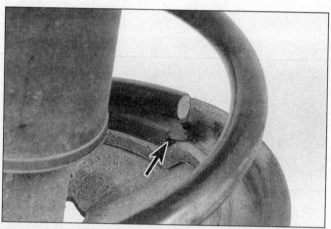

4.11 When installing the spring, make sure the end fits into the recessed portion of the lower seat (arrow)

4.12 The flats on the damper shaft (arrow) must match up with the flats in the spring seat

rubber portion of the suspension support for cracking and general deterioration. If there is any separation of the rubber, replace it.

6   On 1995 models, remove the upper spring seat from the damper shaft **(see illustration)**. Check the spring seat for cracking and hardness; replace it if necessary. On all models, remove the upper insulator from the damper shaft.

7   Carefully lift the compressed spring from the assembly **(see illustration)** and set it in a safe place. **Warning:** *Never place your head near the end of the spring!*

8   Slide the rubber bumper off the damper shaft.

9   Check the lower insulator for wear, cracking and hardness and replace it if necessary.

Reassembly

Refer to illustrations 4.11, 4.12, 4.13a and 4.13b

10   If the lower insulator is being replaced, set it into position with the dropped portion seated in the lowest part of the seat. Extend the

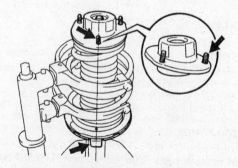

4.13a On 1992 through 1994 models, be sure to rotate the upper support so that the lowest bolt on the upper support is aligned with the projection part of the spring lower seat

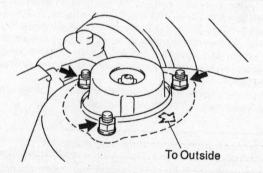

To Outside

4.13b On 1995 and later models, make sure that the arrow on the spring seat faces toward the lower bracket, where the steering knuckle fits

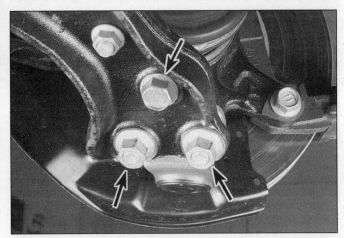

5.3a Remove these nuts and this bolt to disconnect the control
arm from the balljoint

5.3b Separate the control arm from the steering knuckle
with a prybar

5.4 To detach the front end of the control arm from the engine
cradle, remove these two bolts (arrows)

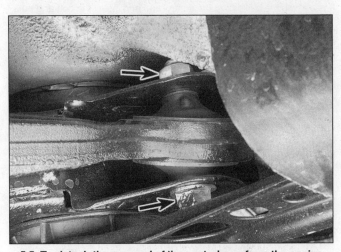

5.5 To detach the rear end of the control arm from the engine
cradle, remove this nut and bolt (arrows)

damper rod to its full length and install the rubber bumper.

11   Carefully place the coil spring onto the lower insulator, with the
end of the spring resting in the lowest part of the insulator (see
illustration).

12   Install the upper insulator and spring seat, making sure that the
flats in the hole in the seat match up with the flats on the damper shaft
(see illustration).

13   On 1992 through 1994 models, be sure to rotate the upper
support so that the lowest bolt on the upper support is aligned with the
projection part of the spring lower seat (see illustration). On 1995 and
later models, make sure the arrow on the spring seat faces toward the
lower bracket, where the steering knuckle fits (see illustration).

14   Install the dust seal and suspension support to the damper shaft.

15   Install the nut and tighten it to the torque listed in this Chapter's
Specifications.

16   Install the strut/spring assembly following the procedure outlined
previously (see Section 3).

5   Control arm - removal, inspection and installation

Removal

Refer to illustrations 5.3a, 5.3b, 5.4 and 5.5

1   Loosen the wheel lug nuts on the side to be dismantled, raise the

front of the vehicle, support it securely on jackstands and remove the
wheel.

2   Disconnect the stabilizer bar link from the control arm (see
Section 2).

3   Remove the balljoint retaining bolt and nuts (see illustration).
Use a prybar to disconnect the control arm from the steering knuckle
(see illustration).

4   Remove the two bolts that attach the front of the control arm to
the engine cradle (see illustration).

5   Remove the bolt and nut that attach the rear of the control arm to
the engine cradle (see illustration).

6   Remove the control arm.

Inspection

7   Make sure the control arm is straight. If it's bent, replace it. Do not
attempt to straighten a bent control arm.

8   Inspect the bushings. If they're cracked, torn or worn out, replace
the control arm.

Installation

9   Installation is the reverse of removal. Be sure to tighten all
fasteners to the torque listed in this Chapter's Specifications.

10   Install the wheel and lug nuts, lower the vehicle and tighten the
lug nuts to the torque listed in the Chapter 1 Specifications.

11   It's a good idea to have the front wheel alignment checked, and if
necessary, adjusted after this job has been performed.

10

6   Balljoints - replacement

1   Loosen the wheel lug nuts, raise the vehicle and support it securely on jackstands. Remove the wheel.

Picklefork method

Caution: *The following procedure is the quickest way to detach a balljoint from the steering knuckle, but it will very likely damage the balljoint boot. If you want to save the boot, proceed to Step 9.*

2   Remove the cotter pin from the balljoint stud and loosen the nut (but don't remove it yet).

3   Separate the balljoint from the steering knuckle with a picklefork-type balljoint separator. Lubricate the rubber boot with grease and work carefully so as not to tear the boot. Remove the balljoint stud nut.

4   Remove the bolt and nuts securing the balljoint to the control arm **(see illustration 5.3a)**. Separate the balljoint from the control arm with a prybar **(see illustration 5.3b)**.

5   To install the balljoint, position it on the steering knuckle and install the nut, but don't tighten it yet.

6   Attach the balljoint to the control arm and install the bolt and nuts, tightening them to the torque listed in this Chapter's Specifications.

7   Tighten the balljoint stud nut to the torque listed in this Chapter's Specifications and install a new cotter pin. If the cotter pin hole doesn't line up with the slots on the nut, tighten the nut additionally until it does line up - don't loosen the nut to insert the cotter pin.

8   Install the wheel and lug nuts. Lower the vehicle and tighten the lug nuts to the torque listed in the Chapter 1 Specifications.

Puller method

Refer to illustration 6.12

9   Separate the control arm from the balljoint (see Section 5).

10   Pull the outer end of the driveaxle from the steering knuckle (see Chapter 8) and suspend the driveaxle with a piece of wire.

11   Remove the cotter pin from the balljoint stud and loosen the nut (but don't remove it yet).

12   Install a small puller **(see illustration)** and pop the balljoint stud from the steering knuckle.

13   Remove the nut and remove the balljoint.

14   Insert the outer end of the driveaxle through the steering knuckle, install the nut and tighten it to the torque listed in the Chapter 8 Specifications. Install the lock washer and cotter pin.

15   Refer to Steps 5 through 8 above.

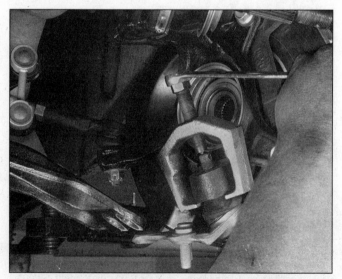

6.12 To separate the balljoint from the steering knuckle, install a small puller and pop the balljoint stud loose

7   Steering knuckle and hub - removal and installation

Warning: *Dust created by the brake system may contain asbestos, which is harmful to your health. Never blow it out with compressed air and don't inhale any of it. Do not, under any circumstances, use petroleum-based solvents to clean brake parts. Use brake system cleaner only.*

Removal

1   Loosen the hub nut (see Chapter 8). Loosen the wheel lug nuts, raise the vehicle and support it securely on jackstands. Remove the wheel.

2   Remove the brake caliper and support it with a piece of wire as described in Chapter 9. Remove the caliper torque plate and separate the brake disc from the hub.

3   Loosen, but do not remove the strut-to-steering knuckle bolts **(see illustration 3.4)**.

4   Separate the tie-rod from the steering knuckle arm (see Section 17).

5   Remove the balljoint-to-lower arm bolt and nuts **(see illustration 5.3a and 5.3b)**. The strut-to-knuckle bolts can now be removed.

6   Push the driveaxle from the hub as described in Chapter 8. Support the end of the driveaxle with a piece of wire.

7   Carefully separate the steering knuckle from the strut and lower arm.

Installation

8   Guide the knuckle and hub assembly into position, inserting the driveaxle into the hub.

9   Push the knuckle into the strut flange and install the bolts and nuts, but don't tighten them yet.

10   Connect the balljoint to the control arm and install the bolt and nuts (don't tighten them yet).

11   Attach the tie-rod to the steering knuckle arm (see Section 17). Tighten the strut bolt nuts, the balljoint-to-control arm bolt and nuts and the tie-rod nut to the torque values listed in this Chapter's Specifications.

12   Place the brake disc on the hub and install the caliper as outlined in Chapter 9.

13   Install the hub nut and tighten it securely (final tightening will be carried out when the vehicle is lowered).

14   Install the wheel and lug nuts.

15   Lower the vehicle and tighten the lug nuts to the torque listed in the Chapter 1 Specifications. Tighten the driveaxle/hub nut and tighten it to the torque listed in the Chapter 8 Specifications)

8   Hub and bearing assembly (front) - removal and installation

Due to the special tools and expertise required to press the hub and bearing from the steering knuckle, this job should be left to a professional mechanic. However, the steering knuckle and hub may be removed and the assembly taken to a dealer service department or other repair shop. See Section 7 for the steering knuckle and hub removal procedure.

9   Stabilizer bar and bushings (rear) - removal and installation

Refer to illustrations 9.2 and 9.3

1   Loosen the rear wheel lug nuts. Raise the rear of the vehicle and place it securely on jackstands. Remove the rear wheels.

2   Detach the stabilizer bar links from the bar **(see illustration)**. If the ballstud turns with the nut, use a hex wrench to hold the stud.

9.2 Remove the nut (arrow) and detach the link from the stabilizer bar (do this on each side)

9.3 To detach the stabilizer bar from the suspension member lower supports, remove the bushing retainer bolts (arrows) from both the left and right retainers (left retainer shown)

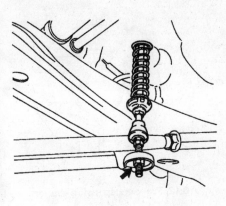

10.3 On station wagon models, disconnect the load sensing proportioning valve (LSPV) spring from the lower arm by removing this nut (arrow)

3   Unbolt the stabilizer bar bushing retainers from the body **(see illustration)**.

4   The stabilizer bar can now be removed from the vehicle. Pull the retainers off the stabilizer bar (if they haven't fallen off already) using a rocking motion.

5   Check the bushings for wear, hardness, distortion, cracking and other signs of deterioration, replacing them if necessary. Also check the link bushings for these signs.

6   Using a wire brush, clean the areas of the bar where the bushings ride. Installation is the reverse of the removal procedure. If necessary, use a light coat of vegetable oil to ease bushing and U-bracket installation (don't use petroleum-based products or brake fluid, as these will damage the rubber).

7   Installation is the reverse of removal.

10   Strut assembly (rear) - removal, inspection and installation

Removal

Refer to illustrations 10.3, 10.7 and 10.8

1   On coupe and sedan models, remove the rear seat and package tray trim panel; on station wagon models, remove the rear side seatback and tonneau side cover (see Chapter 11).

2   Loosen the rear wheel lug nuts, raise the rear of the vehicle and support it securely on jackstands. Remove the wheel.

3   On station wagon models, detach the load sensing proportioning valve (LSPV) spring from the lower arm **(see illustration)**.

4   Detach the brake hose from the strut **(see illustration 3.2)**. If the vehicle is equipped with ABS, detach the ABS sensor wire from the strut.

5   Disconnect the stabilizer bar link from the strut **(see illustration 9.2b)**.

6   Support the axle carrier with a floor jack. Place a block of wood between the jack head and the carrier.

7   Loosen the strut-to-axle carrier bolt nuts **(see illustration)**.

8   Remove the three upper strut-to-body mounting nuts **(see illustration)**.

9   Lower the axle carrier with the jack and remove the two strut-to-axle carrier bolts.

10   Remove the strut assembly.

Inspection

Refer to illustration 10.12

11   Follow the inspection procedures described in Section 3. If you

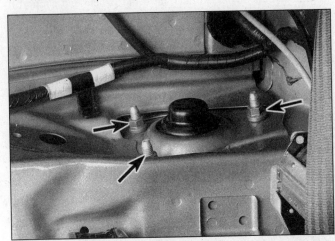

10.7 To disconnect the lower end of the strut from the rear axle carrier, remove these nuts (arrows) and knock out the bolts (but don't remove the bolts until after the upper strut nuts are removed and the axle carrier is supported by a floor jack - the strut assembly is heavy, so it's a good idea to have an assistant standing by to lend a hand if necessary)

10.8 To disconnect the upper end of the strut from the vehicle, remove these three nuts (arrows) (this part of the vehicle is accessible only by removing the back seat on coupes and sedans, or the rear side seat back and tonneau side cover on station wagons)

10

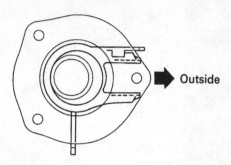

10.12 Proper suspension support-to-strut relationship

determine that the strut assembly must be disassembled for replacement of the strut or the coil spring, refer to Section 4.

12   When reassembling the strut, make sure the suspension support is aligned as shown, with the pointed part of the support facing out, with the hole centered on the strut bracket **(see illustration)**.

Installation

13   Maneuver the assembly up into the fenderwell and insert the mounting studs through the holes in the body. Install the nuts, but don't tighten them yet.

14   Push the axle carrier into the strut lower bracket and install the bolts and nuts, tightening them to the torque listed in this Chapter's Specifications.

15   Connect the stabilizer bar link to the strut bracket.

16   Attach the brake hose bracket to the strut. If the vehicle is equipped with ABS, attach the ABS wire to the strut.

17   Install the wheel and lug nuts, lower the vehicle and tighten the lug nuts to the torque listed in the Chapter 1 Specifications.

18   Tighten the three strut upper mounting nuts to the torque listed in this Chapter's Specifications.

19   Install the package tray trim and seat (coupe or sedan) or the rear side seatback and tonneau side cover (station wagon).

11   Strut rod - removal and installation

Refer to illustrations 11.2 and 11.3

1   Loosen the wheel lug nuts, raise the vehicle and support it securely on jackstands. Remove the wheel.

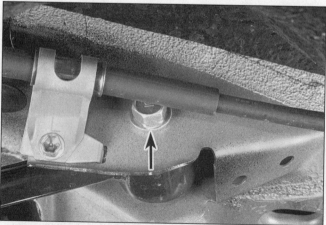

11.3 To disconnect the forward end of the strut rod from the vehicle body, remove this bolt (arrow)

11.2 To disconnect the strut rod from the rear axle carrier, remove the bolt indicated by the lower arrow; to disconnect the suspension arms from the carrier, remove the nut and long through bolt

2   Remove the strut rod-to-axle carrier bolt **(see illustration)**. It isn't necessary to hold the nut with a wrench, because the nut has a tang attached to it to prevent rotation.

3   Remove the strut rod-to-body bracket bolt **(see illustration)** and detach the rod from the vehicle.

4   Installation is the reverse of the removal procedure. Be sure to tighten the bolts to the torque listed in this Chapter's Specifications.

12   Suspension arms - removal and installation

Removal

Refer to illustrations 12.5

1   Raise the rear of the vehicle and support it securely on jackstands. Block the front wheels.

2   Disconnect the strut rod from the axle carrier **(see illustration 11.2)**.

3   On station wagon models, disconnect the load sensing proportioning valve (LSPV) spring **(see illustration 10.3)**.

4   Remove the suspension arm-to-rear axle carrier bolt and nut **(see illustration 11.2)**.

5   Remove the suspension arm-to-suspension member lower support nut and bolt **(see illustration)**.

12.5 To disconnect the inner ends of the suspension arms from the suspension member lower support, remove these nuts (arrows) and drive out the bolts

13.3 To remove the four bolts which attach the hub and bearing assembly to the rear axle carrier, rotate the hub flange and align one of the holes in the flange with each of the bolts

6   Remove the No. 2 (rear) suspension arm.
7   Remove the left and right stabilizer bar bushing retainers **(see illustration 9.3)**.
8   Remove the exhaust center pipe and tail pipe (see Chapter 4).
9   Remove the No. 1 (front) suspension arm.

Installation

10   Installation is the reverse of removal. Be sure to tighten all fasteners to the torque listed in this Chapter's Specifications.
11   Install the wheel and lug nuts, then lower the vehicle to the ground. Tighten the wheel lug nuts to the torque listed in the Chapter 1 Specifications.
12   Have the rear wheel alignment checked by a dealer service department or an alignment shop.

13   Hub and bearing assembly (rear)- removal and installation

Warning: *Dust created by the brake system may contain asbestos, which is harmful to your health. Never blow it out with compressed air and don't inhale any of it. Do not, under any circumstances, use petroleum-based solvents to clean brake parts. Use brake system cleaner only.*
Note: *Due to the special tools required to replace the bearing, the hub and bearing assembly should not be disassembled by the home mechanic. The assembly can be removed, however, and taken to a dealer service department or other repair shop to have the bearing replaced.*

Removal

Refer to illustrations 13.3 and 13.5
1   Loosen the wheel lug nuts, raise the vehicle and support it securely on jackstands. Remove the wheel.
2   On models with rear disc brakes, remove the caliper (see Chapter 9). Pull the brake drum or disc from the hub (see Chapter 9).
3   Remove the four hub-to-axle carrier bolts, accessible by turning the hub flange so that the large circular cutout exposes each bolt **(see illustration)**.
4   Remove the hub and bearing assembly from its seat, maneuvering it out through the brake assembly.
5   Remove the old O-ring from the hub seat **(see illustration)**.
6   Take the hub and bearing assembly to an automotive machine shop and have the old bearing pulled off the hub and a new bearing pressed on (you can re-use the hub itself, as long as it's in good

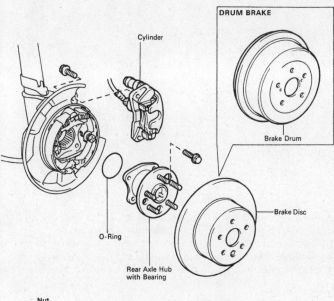

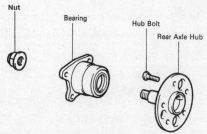

13.5 An exploded view of the rear hub and bearing assembly

condition). Make sure the hub retaining nut is tightened to the torque listed in this Chapter's Specifications.

Installation

7   Position the hub and bearing assembly on the axle carrier and align the holes in the backing plate. Install the bolts. A magnet is useful in guiding the bolts through the hub flange and into position. After all four bolts have been installed, tighten them to the torque listed in this Chapter's Specifications.
8   Install the brake drum, or disc and caliper, and the wheel. Lower the vehicle and tighten the lug nuts to the torque listed in the Chapter 1 Specifications.

14   Rear axle carrier - removal and installation

Warning: *Dust created by the brake system may contain asbestos, which is harmful to your health. Never blow it out with compressed air and don't inhale any of it. Do not, under any circumstances, use petroleum-based solvents to clean brake parts. Use brake system cleaner only.*

Removal

Refer to illustration 14.5
1   Loosen the wheel lug nuts, raise the vehicle and support it on jackstands. Block the front wheels and remove the rear wheel.
2   Remove the rear brake drum, or caliper and disc (see Chapter 9). On models with rear drum brakes, disconnect the brake line from the wheel cylinder (see Chapter 9).
3   Remove the rear hub and bearing assembly (see Section 13).

10

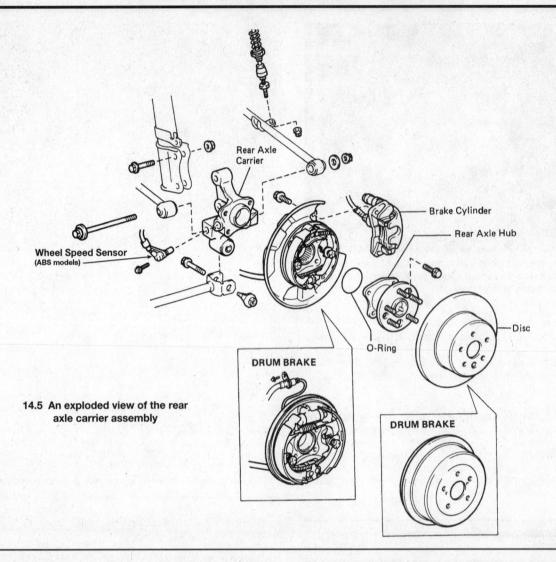

14.5 An exploded view of the rear axle carrier assembly

4   It isn't necessary to disassemble the brake shoe assembly or disconnect the parking brake cable from the backing plate. On models with rear drum brakes, detach the backing plate and rear brake assembly from the axle carrier; on models with rear disc brakes, detach the backing plate and rear parking brake assembly from the axle carrier. Suspend the backing plate and brake assembly from the coil spring with a piece of wire.
5   On models with ABS, remove the wheel speed sensor from the axle carrier **(see illustration)**.
6   On station wagon models, disconnect the load sensing proportioning valve (LSPV) spring from the rear suspension arm **(see illustration 10.3)**.
7   Loosen, but don't remove the strut-to-axle carrier bolts **(see illustration 10.6)**.
8   Remove the suspension arm-to-axle carrier bolt, nut and washers and remove the rear strut rod-to-axle carrier bolt **(see illustration 11.2)**.
9   Remove the loosened strut-to-axle carrier bolts while supporting the carrier so it doesn't fall and detach the axle carrier from the strut bracket.

Installation

10   Inspect the carrier bushing for cracks, deformation and signs of wear. If it is worn out, take the carrier to a dealer service department or other repair shop to have the old one pressed out and a new one pressed in.
11   Push the axle carrier into the strut bracket, aligning the two bolt

holes. Insert the two strut-to-carrier bolts and tighten them finger tight.
12   Install the suspension arm-to-axle carrier bolt (from the front), washers and nut. Tighten the nut by hand.
13   Place a jack under the carrier and raise it to simulate normal ride height.
14   Tighten the strut-to-carrier bolts to the torque listed in this Chapter's Specifications.
15   Connect the strut rod and tighten the bolt to the torque listed in this Chapter's Specifications.
16   Tighten the suspension arm bolt/nut to the torque listed in this Chapter's Specifications.
17   On station wagon models, reattach the LSPV spring to the rear suspension arm and tighten the nuts to the torque listed in this Chapter's Specifications.
18   On models with ABS, reattach the wheel speed sensor to the axle carrier.
19   Attach the brake backing plate to the axle carrier, install the hub and tighten the four bolts to the torque listed in this Chapter's Specifications.
20   On models with rear drum brakes, connect the brake line to the wheel cylinder (see Chapter 9). Be careful not to damage the line when bending it back into place.
21   Install the rear brake drum or disc and caliper (see Chapter 9).
22   Install the wheel and lug nuts.
23   Bleed the wheel cylinder or caliper (see Chapter 9).
24   Lower the vehicle and tighten the lug nuts to the torque listed in the Chapter 1 Specifications.

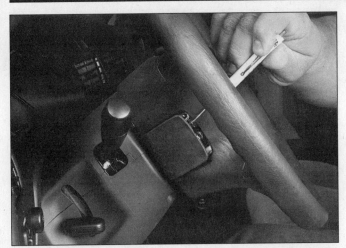

16.2a Pry open the small covers on either side of the steering wheel (left side shown, right cover is identical)

16.2b Remove these two T30 Torx screws (arrows) and the single Torx screw on the other side of the wheel (this is a TMC design; the TMM design has only one screw on this side instead of two

15 Steering system - general information

All models are equipped with rack-and-pinion steering. The steering gear is bolted to the engine cradle and operates the steering knuckles via tie-rods. The inner ends of the tie-rods are protected by rubber boots which should be inspected periodically for secure attachment, tears and leaking lubricant.

The power assist system consists of a belt-driven pump and associated lines and hoses. The fluid level in the power steering pump reservoir should be checked periodically (see Chapter 1).

The steering wheel operates the steering shaft, which actuates the steering gear through universal joints. Looseness in the steering can be caused by wear in the steering shaft universal joints, the steering gear, the tie-rod ends and loose retaining bolts.

16 Steering wheel - removal and installation

Warning: *These models are equipped with airbags. The airbag is armed and can deploy (inflate) anytime the battery is connected. To prevent accidental deployment (and possible injury), turn the ignition key to LOCK and disconnect the negative battery cable whenever working near airbag components. After the battery is disconnected, wait at least 90 seconds before beginning work (the system has a back-up capacitor that must fully discharge). For more information see Chapter 12.*

Note: *On 1993 and later models, the airbag system will be disabled if the battery is disconnected for more than a brief period. If the airbag light comes on and stays on after the battery is reconnected, the vehicle must be taken to a dealer to have the system reset with a special tool.*

Removal

Refer to illustrations 16.2a, 16.2b, 16.3a, 16.3b, 16.3c, 16.4 and 16.6

1   Turn the ignition key to Off, then disconnect the cable from the negative terminal of the battery. If the vehicle is equipped with an airbag system, wait at least 90 seconds before proceeding. **Caution:** *If the stereo in your vehicle is equipped with an anti-theft system, make sure you have the correct activation code before disconnecting the battery.*

2   Turn the steering wheel so that the wheels are pointing straight ahead, then pry off the small covers on either side of the steering wheel and loosen the T30 Torx screws that attach the airbag module to the steering wheel **(see illustrations)**. Loosen each screw until the groove in the circumference of the screw catches on the screw case **(see illustrations)**. Note that the two designs differ slightly: The TMC design has two screws on the left and one screw on the right; the TMM design has one screw on each side.

3   Pull the airbag module off the steering wheel **(see illustration)** and disconnect the module electrical connector **(see illustration)**.

16.3a Remove the airbag module . . .

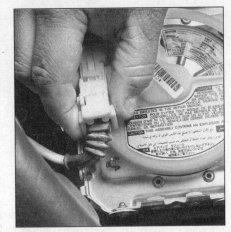

16.3b . . . flip up the lock for the module electrical connector . . .

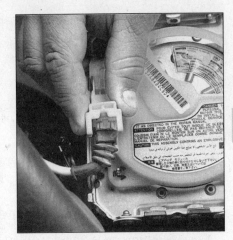

16.3c . . . and unplug the electrical connector

10

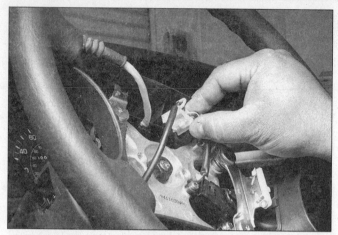

16.4 Unplug the electrical connector for the horn and cruise control

16.6 Use a steering wheel puller to remove the steering wheel

16.7 To align the spiral cable, turn the cable counterclockwise until it's harder to turn, rotate the cable clockwise three turns and align the two red marks (the cable should be able to rotate about three turns in either direction when it's properly centered)

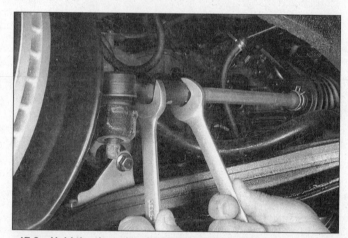

17.2a Hold the tie-rod end with a wrench and break the jam nut loose with another wrench

17.2b Back off the jam nut and mark the exposed threads to ensure that the new tie-rod end is threaded on the same number of turns

4   Unplug the electrical connector for the horn and cruise control system **(see illustration)**.
5   Remove the steering wheel retaining nut, then mark the relationship of the steering shaft to the hub (if marks don't already exist or don't line up) to simplify installation and ensure steering wheel alignment.
6   Use a puller to disconnect the steering wheel from the shaft **(see illustration)**.

Installation

Refer to illustration 16.7

7   Make sure that the front wheels are facing straight ahead. Turn the spiral cable counterclockwise by hand until it becomes harder to turn the cable. Rotate the cable clockwise about three turns and align the two red pointers **(see illustration)**.
8   To install the wheel, align the mark on the steering wheel hub with the mark on the shaft and slip the wheel onto the shaft. Install the nut and tighten it to the torque listed in this Chapter's Specifications.
9   Plug in the horn and cruise control connector.
10   Plug in the electrical connector for the airbag module.
11   Install the airbag module and tighten the Torx retaining screws to the torque listed in this Chapter's Specifications.
12   Connect the negative battery cable.

17   Tie-rod ends - removal and installation

Removal

Refer to illustrations 17.2a, 17.2b and 17.4

1   Loosen the wheel lug nuts. Raise the front of the vehicle, support it securely on jackstands, block the rear wheels and set the parking brake. Remove the front wheel.

17.4 Install a small puller as shown to separate the tie-rod from the steering knuckle

18.3 Remove the outer clamp (arrow) from the steering gear boot with a pair of pliers; the inner clamp (not visible in this photo) must be cut off with a pair of diagonal cutters

19.2 Disconnect the power steering fluid line fittings (arrows) from the steering gear assembly

2   Hold the tie-rod with a pair of locking pliers or wrench and loosen the jam nut enough to mark the position of the tie-rod end in relation to the threads **(see illustrations)**.
3   Remove the cotter pin and loosen the nut on the tie-rod end stud.
4   Disconnect the tie-rod from the steering knuckle arm with a puller **(see illustration)**. Remove the nut and separate the tie-rod.
5   Unscrew the tie-rod end from the tie-rod.

Installation

6   Thread the tie-rod end on to the marked position and insert the tie-rod stud into the steering knuckle arm. Tighten the jam nut securely.
7   Install the castle nut on the stud and tighten it to the torque listed in this Chapter's Specifications. Install a new cotter pin.
8   Install the wheel and lug nuts. Lower the vehicle and tighten the lug nuts to the torque listed in the Chapter 1 Specifications.
9   Have the alignment checked by a dealer service department or an alignment shop.

18 Steering gear boots - replacement

Refer to illustration 18.3
1   Loosen the lug nuts, raise the vehicle and support it securely on jackstands. Remove the wheel.
2   Remove the tie-rod end and jam nut (see Section 17).
3   Remove the steering gear boot clamps **(see illustration)** and slide off the boot.
4   Before installing the new boot, wrap the threads and serrations on the end of the steering rod with a layer of tape so the small end of the new boot isn't damaged.
5   Slide the new boot into position on the steering gear until it seats in the groove in the steering rod and install new clamps.
6   Remove the tape and install the tie-rod end (see Section 17).
7   Install the wheel and lug nuts. Lower the vehicle and tighten the lug nuts to the torque listed in the Chapter 1 Specifications.

19 Steering gear - removal and installation

Warning: *These models are equipped with airbags. Make sure the steering shaft is not turned while the steering gear is removed or you could damage the airbag system. To prevent the shaft from turning, turn the ignition key to the lock position before beginning work or run*

19.3 Remove the U-joint pinch bolt and nut (arrows)

the seat belt through the steering wheel and clip the seat belt into place. Due to the possible damage to the airbag system, we recommend only experienced mechanics attempt this procedure.

Removal

Refer to illustrations 19.2, 19.3 and 19.6
1   Park the vehicle with the front wheels pointing straight ahead. Loosen the front wheel lug nuts, raise the front of the vehicle and support it securely on jackstands. Apply the parking brake and remove the wheels. Remove the engine under-covers on models so equipped.
2   Place a drain pan under the steering gear. Detach the power steering pressure and return lines **(see illustration)** and cap the ends to prevent excessive fluid loss and contamination. Detach the bracket from the top of the steering gear assembly.
3   Mark the relationship of the lower universal joint to the steering gear input shaft. Remove the lower intermediate shaft pinch bolt **(see illustration)**.
4   Separate the tie-rod ends from the steering knuckle arms (see Section 17).
5   Remove the stabilizer bar bushing retainer bolts (see Section 2). (You can't remove the steering gear mounting bolts until the stabilizer is lifted up out of the way.)

10

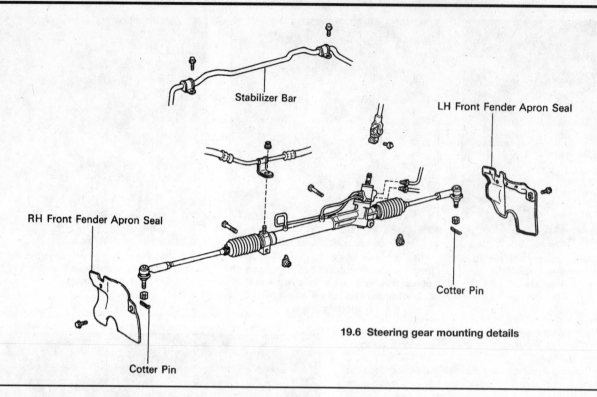

Stabilizer Bar

LH Front Fender Apron Seal

RH Front Fender Apron Seal

Cotter Pin

19.6 Steering gear mounting details

Cotter Pin

6   Remove the steering gear mounting nuts **(see illustration)**, lift up the stabilizer bar assembly and knock out the steering gear mounting bolts.
7   Separate the intermediate shaft from the steering gear input shaft and pull the steering gear assembly out from the right side.
8   Check the steering gear mounting grommets for excessive wear or deterioration, replacing them if necessary.

Installation

9   Raise the steering gear into position and connect the U-joint, aligning the marks.
10   Install the mounting bolts and nuts and tighten them to the torque listed in this Chapter's Specifications.
11   Connect the tie-rod ends to the steering knuckle arms (see Section 17).

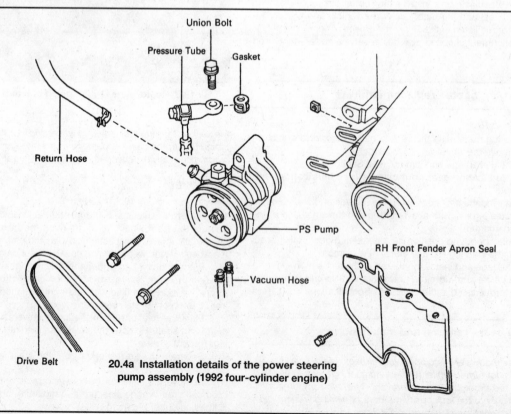

Union Bolt

Pressure Tube

Gasket

Return Hose

PS Pump

RH Front Fender Apron Seal

Vacuum Hose

Drive Belt

20.4a Installation details of the power steering pump assembly (1992 four-cylinder engine)

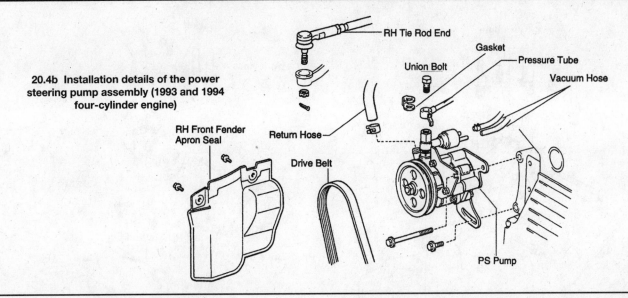

20.4b Installation details of the power steering pump assembly (1993 and 1994 four-cylinder engine)

12   Install the U-joint pinch bolt and tighten it to the torque listed in this Chapter's Specifications.
13   Connect the power steering pressure and return hoses to the steering gear and fill the power steering pump reservoir with the recommended fluid (see Chapter 1). Reattach the bracket to the top of the steering gear assembly.
14   Install the stabilizer bar bushing retainer bolts and tighten them to the torque listed in this Chapter's Specifications.
15   Lower the vehicle and bleed the steering system (see Section 21).

20   Power steering pump - removal and installation

Removal

Refer to illustrations 20.4a, 20.4b, 20.4c, 20.4d, 20.4e and 20.4f
1   Disconnect the cable from the negative battery terminal. **Caution:**

If the stereo in your vehicle is equipped with an anti-theft system, make sure you have the correct activation code before disconnecting the battery. **Note:** *On 1993 and later models, the airbag system will be disabled if the battery is disconnected for more than a brief period. If the airbag light comes on and stays on after the battery is reconnected, the vehicle must be taken to a dealer to have the system reset with a special tool.*
2   Using a large syringe or suction gun, suck as much fluid out of the power steering fluid reservoir as possible. Place a drain pan under the vehicle to catch any fluid that spills out when the hoses are disconnected.
3   Loosen the right front wheel lug nuts, raise the vehicle and support it securely on jackstands. Remove the right front wheel.
4   Remove the right front fender apron seal **(see illustrations)**.
5   Loosen the clamp and disconnect the fluid return hose from the pump.
6   Remove the pressure line-to-pump union bolt and separate the

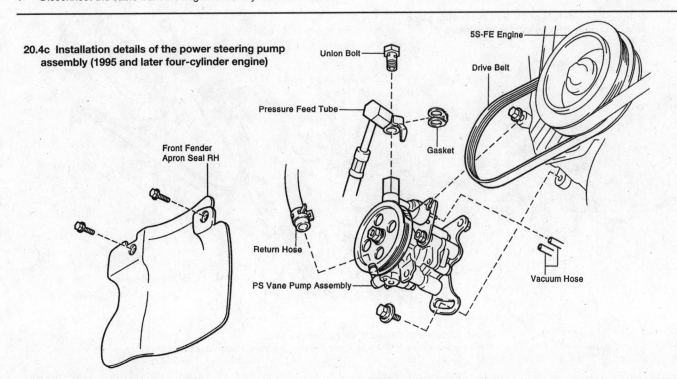

20.4c Installation details of the power steering pump assembly (1995 and later four-cylinder engine)

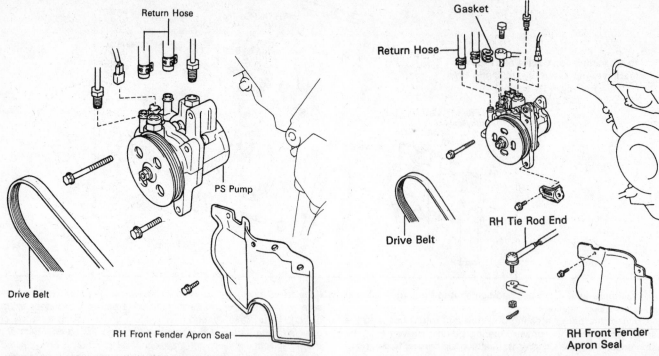

20.4d Installation details of the power steering pump assembly (1992 V6 engine)

20.4e Installation details of the power steering pump assembly (1993 and 1994 V6 engine)

line from the pump. Remove the copper sealing washers on each side of the fitting - these should be replaced when installing the pump.
7   Loosen the adjuster and pivot bolts and remove the drivebelt.
8   Remove the pivot, adjuster and any other mounting bolts, and remove the pump.

Installation

9   Installation is the reverse of removal. Be sure to tighten the fluid line threaded fitting or banjo bolt and the adjuster and pivot bolts to the torque listed in this Chapter's Specifications. Adjust the drivebelt tension (see Chapter 1).

20.4f Installation details of the power steering pump assembly (1995 and later V6 engine)

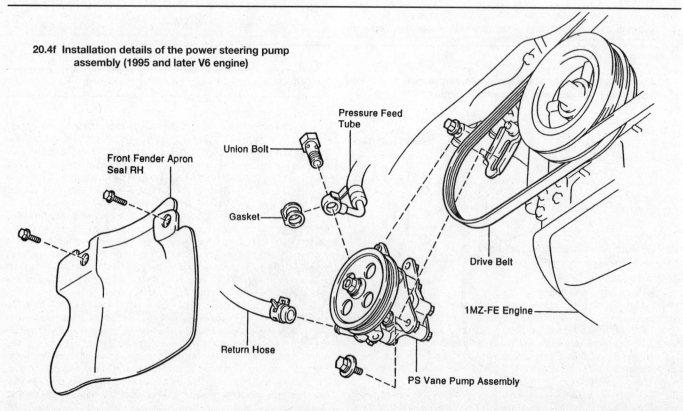

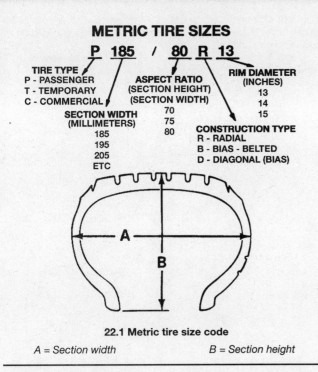

22.1 Metric tire size code

A = Section width   *B = Section height*

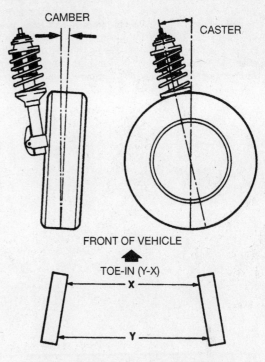

23.1 Camber, caster and toe-in angle

10   Top up the fluid level in the reservoir (see Chapter 1) and bleed the system (see Section 21).

21   Power steering system - bleeding

1   Following any operation in which the power steering fluid lines have been disconnected, the power steering system must be bled to remove all air and obtain proper steering performance.
2   With the front wheels in the straight ahead position, check the power steering fluid level and, if low, add fluid until it reaches the Cold mark on the dipstick.
3   Start the engine and allow it to run at fast idle. Recheck the fluid level and add more if necessary to reach the Cold mark on the dipstick.
4   Bleed the system by turning the wheels from side to side, without hitting the stops. This will work the air out of the system. Keep the reservoir full of fluid as this is done.
5   When the air is worked out of the system, return the wheels to the straight ahead position and leave the vehicle running for several more minutes before shutting it off.
6   Road test the vehicle to be sure the steering system is functioning normally and noise free.
7   Recheck the fluid level to be sure it is up to the Hot mark on the dipstick while the engine is at normal operating temperature. Add fluid if necessary (see Chapter 1).

22   Wheels and tires - general information

Refer to illustration 22.1
1   All vehicles covered by this manual are equipped with metric-sized fiberglass or steel belted radial tires **(see illustration)**. Use of other size or type of tires may affect the ride and handling of the vehicle. Don't mix different types of tires, such as radials and bias belted, on the same vehicle as handling may be seriously affected. It's recommended that tires be replaced in pairs on the same axle, but if only one tire is being replaced, be sure it's the same size, structure and tread design as the other.
2   Because tire pressure has a substantial effect on handling and wear, the pressure on all tires should be checked at least once a month or before any extended trips (see Chapter 1).
3   Wheels must be replaced if they are bent, dented, leak air, have elongated bolt holes, are heavily rusted, out of vertical symmetry or if the lug nuts won't stay tight. Wheel repairs that use welding or peening are not recommended.
4   Tire and wheel balance is important in the overall handling, braking and performance of the vehicle. Unbalanced wheels can adversely affect handling and ride characteristics as well as tire life. Whenever a tire is installed on a wheel, the tire and wheel should be balanced by a shop with the proper equipment.

23   Wheel alignment - general information

Refer to illustration 23.1
A wheel alignment refers to the adjustments made to the wheels so they are in proper angular relationship to the suspension and the ground. Wheels that are out of proper alignment not only affect vehicle control, but also increase tire wear. The alignment angles normally measured are camber, caster and toe-in **(see illustration)**. Toe-in is the only adjustable angle on the front or the rear. The other angles should be measured to check for bent or worn suspension parts.
Getting the proper wheel alignment is a very exacting process, one in which complicated and expensive machines are necessary to perform the job properly. Because of this, you should have a technician with the proper equipment perform these tasks. We will, however, use this space to give you a basic idea of what is involved with a wheel alignment so you can better understand the process and deal intelligently with the shop that does the work.
Toe-in is the turning in of the wheels. The purpose of a toe specification is to ensure parallel rolling of the wheels. In a vehicle with zero toe-in, the distance between the front edges of the wheels will be the same as the distance between the rear edges of the wheels. The actual amount of toe-in is normally only a fraction of an inch. On the front end, toe-in is controlled by the tie-rod end position on the tie-rod. On the rear end, it's controlled by a cam on the inner end of the rear (number two) suspension arm. Incorrect toe-in will cause the tires to

10

wear improperly by making them scrub against the road surface.

Camber is the tilting of the wheels from vertical when viewed from one end of the vehicle. When the wheels tilt out at the top, the camber is said to be positive (+). When the wheels tilt in at the top the camber is negative (-). The amount of tilt is measured in degrees from vertical and this measurement is called the camber angle. This angle affects the amount of tire tread which contacts the road and compensates for changes in the suspension geometry when the vehicle is cornering or traveling over an undulating surface.

Caster is the tilting of the front steering axis from the vertical. A tilt toward the rear is positive caster and a tilt toward the front is negative caster.

Chapter 11   Body

Contents

1   General information

These models feature a "unibody" layout, using a floor pan with front and rear frame side rails which support the body components, front and rear suspension systems and other mechanical components. Certain components are particularly vulnerable to accident damage and can be unbolted and repaired or replaced. Among these parts are the body moldings, bumpers, hood and trunk lids and all glass.

Only general body maintenance practices and body panel repair procedures within the scope of the do-it-yourselfer are included in this Chapter.

2   Body - maintenance

1   The condition of your vehicle's body is very important, because the resale value depends a great deal on it. It's much more difficult to repair a neglected or damaged body than it is to repair mechanical components. The hidden areas of the body, such as the wheel wells, the frame and the engine compartment, are equally important, although they don't require as frequent attention as the rest of the body.

2   Once a year, or every 12,000 miles, it's a good idea to have the underside of the body steam cleaned. All traces of dirt and oil will be removed and the area can then be inspected carefully for rust, damaged brake lines, frayed electrical wires, damaged cables and other problems. The front suspension components should be greased after completion of this job.

3   At the same time, clean the engine and the engine compartment with a steam cleaner or water soluble degreaser.

4   The wheel wells should be given close attention, since undercoating can peel away and stones and dirt thrown up by the tires can cause the paint to chip and flake, allowing rust to set in. If rust is found, clean down to the bare metal and apply an anti-rust paint.

5   The body should be washed about once a week. Wet the vehicle thoroughly to soften the dirt, then wash it down with a soft sponge and plenty of clean soapy water. If the surplus dirt is not washed off very carefully, it can wear down the paint.

6   Spots of tar or asphalt thrown up from the road should be removed with a cloth soaked in solvent.

7   Once every six months, wax the body and chrome trim. If a chrome cleaner is used to remove rust from any of the vehicle's plated parts, remember that the cleaner also removes part of the chrome, so use it sparingly.

11

3   Vinyl trim - maintenance

Don't clean vinyl trim with detergents, caustic soap or petroleum-based cleaners. Plain soap and water works just fine, with a soft brush to clean dirt that may be ingrained. Wash the vinyl as frequently as the rest of the vehicle.

After cleaning, application of a high quality rubber and vinyl protectant will help prevent oxidation and cracks. The protectant can also be applied to weatherstripping, vacuum lines and rubber hoses, which often fail as a result of chemical degradation, and to the tires.

4   Upholstery and carpets - maintenance

1   Every three months remove the carpets or mats and clean the interior of the vehicle (more frequently if necessary). Vacuum the upholstery and carpets to remove loose dirt and dust.
2   Leather upholstery requires special care. Stains should be removed with warm water and a very mild soap solution. Use a clean, damp cloth to remove the soap, then wipe again with a dry cloth. Never use alcohol, gasoline, nail polish remover or thinner to clean leather upholstery.
3   After cleaning, regularly treat leather upholstery with a leather wax. Never use car wax on leather upholstery.
4   In areas where the interior of the vehicle is subject to bright sunlight, cover leather seats with a sheet if the vehicle is to be left out for any length of time.

5   Body repair - minor damage

See photo sequence

Repair of minor scratches

1   If the scratch is superficial and does not penetrate to the metal of the body, repair is very simple. Lightly rub the scratched area with a fine rubbing compound to remove loose paint and built-up wax. Rinse the area with clean water.
2   Apply touch-up paint to the scratch, using a small brush. Continue to apply thin layers of paint until the surface of the paint in the scratch is level with the surrounding paint. Allow the new paint at least two weeks to harden, then blend it into the surrounding paint by rubbing with a very fine rubbing compound. Finally, apply a coat of wax to the scratch area.
3   If the scratch has penetrated the paint and exposed the metal of the body, causing the metal to rust, a different repair technique is required. Remove all loose rust from the bottom of the scratch with a pocket knife, then apply rust inhibiting paint to prevent the formation of rust in the future. Using a rubber or nylon applicator, coat the scratched area with glaze-type filler. If required, the filler can be mixed with thinner to provide a very thin paste, which is ideal for filling narrow scratches. Before the glaze filler in the scratch hardens, wrap a piece of smooth cotton cloth around the tip of a finger. Dip the cloth in thinner and then quickly wipe it along the surface of the scratch. This will ensure that the surface of the filler is slightly hollow. The scratch can now be painted over as described earlier in this section.

Repair of dents

4   When repairing dents, the first job is to pull the dent out until the affected area is as close as possible to its original shape. There is no point in trying to restore the original shape completely as the metal in the damaged area will have stretched on impact and cannot be restored to its original contours. It is better to bring the level of the dent up to a point which is about 1/8-inch below the level of the surrounding metal. In cases where the dent is very shallow, it is not worth trying to pull it out at all.
5   If the back side of the dent is accessible, it can be hammered out

gently from behind using a soft-face hammer. While doing this, hold a block of wood firmly against the opposite side of the metal to absorb the hammer blows and prevent the metal from being stretched.
6   If the dent is in a section of the body which has double layers, or some other factor makes it inaccessible from behind, a different technique is required. Drill several small holes through the metal inside the damaged area, particularly in the deeper sections. Screw long, self-tapping screws into the holes just enough for them to get a good grip in the metal. Now the dent can be pulled out by pulling on the protruding heads of the screws with locking pliers.
7   The next stage of repair is the removal of paint from the damaged area and from an inch or so of the surrounding metal. This is done with a wire brush or sanding disk in a drill motor, although it can be done just as effectively by hand with sandpaper. To complete the preparation for filling, score the surface of the bare metal with a screwdriver or the tang of a file, or drill small holes in the affected area. This will provide a good grip for the filler material. To complete the repair, see the subsection on filling and painting later in this Section.

Repair of rust holes or gashes

8   Remove all paint from the affected area and from an inch or so of the surrounding metal using a sanding disk or wire brush mounted in a drill motor. If these are not available, a few sheets of sandpaper will do the job just as effectively.
9   With the paint removed, you will be able to determine the severity of the corrosion and decide whether to replace the whole panel, if possible, or repair the affected area. New body panels are not as expensive as most people think and it is often quicker to install a new panel than to repair large areas of rust.
10   Remove all trim pieces from the affected area except those which will act as a guide to the original shape of the damaged body, such as headlight shells, etc. Using metal snips or a hacksaw blade, remove all loose metal and any other metal that is badly affected by rust. Hammer the edges of the hole in to create a slight depression for the filler material.
11   Wire brush the affected area to remove the powdery rust from the surface of the metal. If the back of the rusted area is accessible, treat it with rust inhibiting paint.
12   Before filling is done, block the hole in some way. This can be done with sheet metal riveted or screwed into place, or by stuffing the hole with wire mesh.
13   Once the hole is blocked off, the affected area can be filled and painted. See the following subsection on filling and painting.

Filling and painting

14   Many types of body fillers are available, but generally speaking, body repair kits which contain filler paste and a tube of resin hardener are best for this type of repair work. A wide, flexible plastic or nylon applicator will be necessary for imparting a smooth and contoured finish to the surface of the filler material. Mix up a small amount of filler on a clean piece of wood or cardboard (use the hardener sparingly). Follow the manufacturer's instructions on the package, otherwise the filler will set incorrectly.
15   Using the applicator, apply the filler paste to the prepared area. Draw the applicator across the surface of the filler to achieve the desired contour and to level the filler surface. As soon as a contour that approximates the original one is achieved, stop working the paste. If you continue, the paste will begin to stick to the applicator. Continue to add thin layers of paste at 20-minute intervals until the level of the filler is just above the surrounding metal.
16   Once the filler has hardened, the excess can be removed with a body file. From then on, progressively finer grades of sandpaper should be used, starting with a 180-grit paper and finishing with 600-grit wet-or-dry paper. Always wrap the sandpaper around a flat rubber or wooden block, otherwise the surface of the filler will not be completely flat. During the sanding of the filler surface, the wet-or-dry paper should be periodically rinsed in water. This will ensure that a very smooth finish is produced in the final stage.
17   At this point, the repair area should be surrounded by a ring of

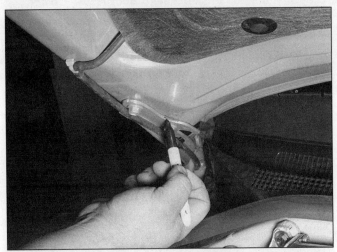

9.1 Before removing the hood, draw alignment marks around the hinge plate

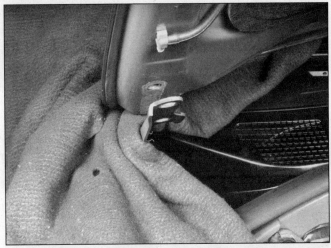

9.2 Cover the cowl and fenders with a blanket to protect the paint finish from accidental damage as the hood is removed

bare metal, which in turn should be encircled by the finely feathered edge of good paint. Rinse the repair area with clean water until all of the dust produced by the sanding operation is gone.

18   Spray the entire area with a light coat of primer. This will reveal any imperfections in the surface of the filler. Repair the imperfections with fresh filler paste or glaze filler and once more smooth the surface with sandpaper. Repeat this spray-and-repair procedure until you are satisfied that the surface of the filler and the feathered edge of the paint are perfect. Rinse the area with clean water and allow it to dry completely.

19   The repair area is now ready for painting. Spray painting must be carried out in a warm, dry, windless and dust free atmosphere. These conditions can be created if you have access to a large indoor work area, but if you are forced to work in the open, you will have to pick the day very carefully. If you are working indoors, dousing the floor in the work area with water will help settle the dust which would otherwise be in the air. If the repair area is confined to one body panel, mask off the surrounding panels. This will help minimize the effects of a slight mismatch in paint color. Trim pieces such as chrome strips, door handles, etc., will also need to be masked off or removed. Use masking tape and several thickness of newspaper for the masking operations.

20   Before spraying, shake the paint can thoroughly, then spray a test area until the spray painting technique is mastered. Cover the repair area with a thick coat of primer. The thickness should be built up using several thin layers of primer rather than one thick one. Using 600-grit wet-or-dry sandpaper, rub down the surface of the primer until it is very smooth. While doing this, the work area should be thoroughly rinsed with water and the wet-or-dry sandpaper periodically rinsed as well. Allow the primer to dry before spraying additional coats.

21   Spray on the top coat, again building up the thickness by using several thin layers of paint. Begin spraying in the center of the repair area and then, using a circular motion, work out until the whole repair area and about two inches of the surrounding original paint is covered. Remove all masking material 10 to 15 minutes after spraying on the final coat of paint. Allow the new paint at least two weeks to harden, then use a very fine rubbing compound to blend the edges of the new paint into the existing paint. Finally, apply a coat of wax.

6   Body repair - major damage

1   Major damage must be repaired by an auto body shop specifically equipped to perform unibody repairs. These shops have the specialized equipment required to do the job properly.

2   If the damage is extensive, the body must be checked for proper

alignment or the vehicle's handling characteristics may be adversely affected and other components may wear at an accelerated rate.

3   Due to the fact that all of the major body components (hood, fenders, etc.) are separate and replaceable units, any seriously damaged components should be replaced rather than repaired. Sometimes the components can be found in a wrecking yard that specializes in used vehicle components, often at considerable savings over the cost of new parts.

7   Hinges and locks - maintenance

Once every 3000 miles, or every three months, the hinges and latch assemblies on the doors, hood and trunk should be given a few drops of light oil or lock lubricant. The door latch strikers should also be lubricated with a thin coat of grease to reduce wear and ensure free movement. Lubricate the door and trunk locks with spray-on graphite lubricant.

8   Windshield and fixed glass - replacement

Replacement of the windshield and fixed glass requires the use of special fast-setting adhesive/caulk materials and some specialized tools. It is recommended that these operations be left to a dealer or a shop specializing in glass work.

9   Hood - removal, installation and adjustment

Refer to illustrations 9.1, 9.2, 9.10 and 9.11
Note: *The hood is heavy and somewhat awkward to remove and install - at least two people should perform this procedure.*

Removal and installation

1   Scribe or draw alignment marks around the hinge to ensure proper alignment during installation **(see illustration)**.

2   Use blankets or pads to cover the cowl area of the body and fenders. This will protect the body and paint as the hood is lifted off **(see illustration)**.

3   Disconnect any cables or wires that will interfere with removal.

4   Have an assistant support the hood and remove the support struts (see Section 12), then remove the hinge-to-hood bolts.

5   Lift off the hood.

6   Installation is the reverse of removal.

11

These photos illustrate a method of repairing simple dents. They are intended to supplement *Body repair - minor damage* in this Chapter and should not be used as the sole instructions for body repair on these vehicles.

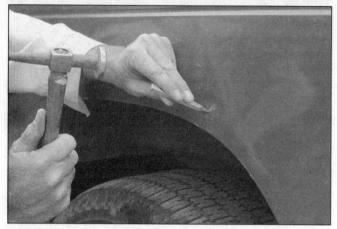

1   If you can't access the backside of the body panel to hammer out the dent, pull it out with a slide-hammer-type dent puller. In the deepest portion of the dent or along the crease line, drill or punch hole(s) at least one inch apart . . .

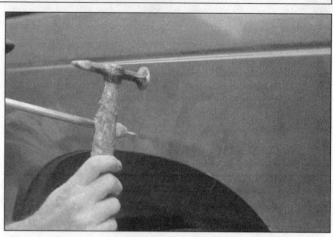

2   . . . then screw the slide-hammer into the hole and operate it. Tap with a hammer near the edge of the dent to help 'pop' the metal back to its original shape. When you're finished, the dent area should be close to its original contour and about 1/8-inch below the surface of the surrounding metal

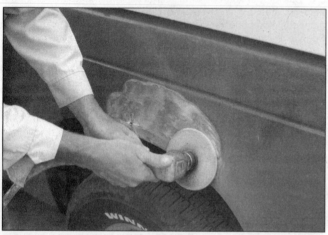

3   Using coarse-grit sandpaper, remove the paint down to the bare metal. Hand sanding works fine, but the disc sander shown here makes the job faster. Use finer (about 320-grit) sandpaper to feather-edge the paint at least one inch around the dent area

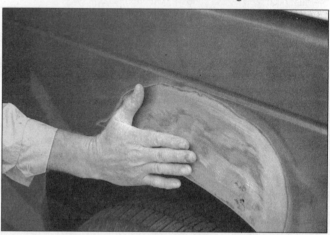

4   When the paint is removed, touch will probably be more helpful than sight for telling if the metal is straight. Hammer down the high spots or raise the low spots as necessary. Clean the repair area with wax/silicone remover

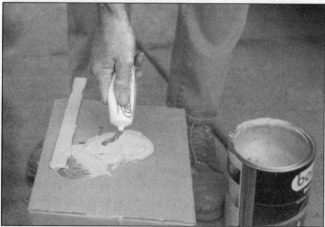

5   Following label instructions, mix up a batch of plastic filler and hardener. The ratio of filler to hardener is critical, and, if you mix it incorrectly, it will either not cure properly or cure too quickly (you won't have time to file and sand it into shape)

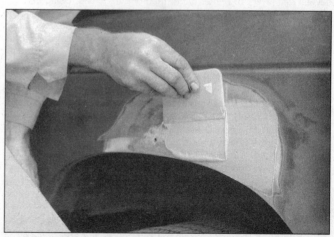

6   Working quickly so the filler doesn't harden, use a plastic applicator to press the body filler firmly into the metal, assuring it bonds completely. Work the filler until it matches the original contour and is slightly above the surrounding metal

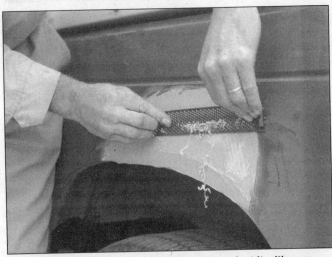

7   Let the filler harden until you can just dent it with your fingernail. Use a body file or Surform tool (shown here) to rough-shape the filler

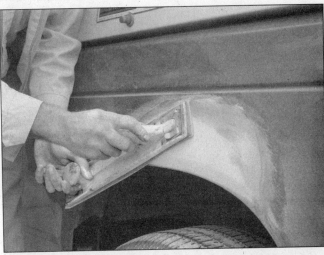

8   Use coarse-grit sandpaper and a sanding board or block to work the filler down until it's smooth and even. Work down to finer grits of sandpaper - always using a board or block - ending up with 360 or 400 grit

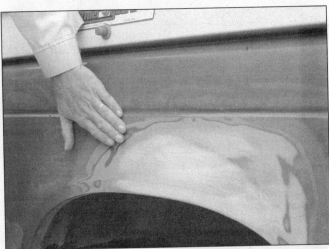

9   You shouldn't be able to feel any ridge at the transition from the filler to the bare metal or from the bare metal to the old paint. As soon as the repair is flat and uniform, remove the dust and mask off the adjacent panels or trim pieces

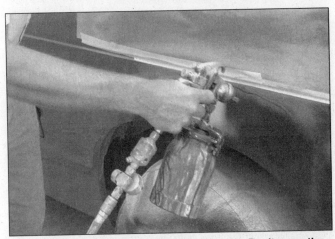

10   Apply several layers of primer to the area. Don't spray the primer on too heavy, so it sags or runs, and make sure each coat is dry before you spray on the next one. A professional-type spray gun is being used here, but aerosol spray primer is available inexpensively from auto parts stores

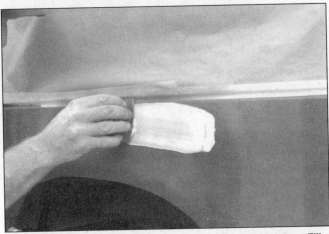

11   The primer will help reveal imperfections or scratches. Fill these with glazing compound. Follow the label instructions and sand it with 360 or 400-grit sandpaper until it's smooth. Repeat the glazing, sanding and respraying until the primer reveals a perfectly smooth surface

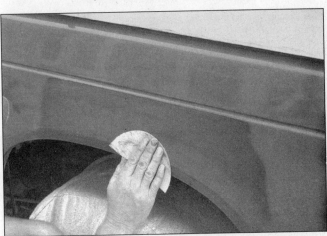

12   Finish sand the primer with very fine sandpaper (400 or 600-grit) to remove the primer overspray. Clean the area with water and allow it to dry. Use a tack rag to remove any dust, then apply the finish coat. Don't attempt to rub out or wax the repair area until the paint has dried completely (at least two weeks)

1

9.10 Loosen the hood latch bolts, move the latch and retighten bolts, then close the hood to check the fit - repeat the procedure until the hood is flush with the fenders

9.11 Adjust the hood closing by screwing the hood bumpers in-or-out

Adjustment

7   Fore-and-aft and side-to-side adjustment of the hood is done by moving the hood in the hinge plate slot after loosening the bolts or nuts.

8   Scribe or draw a line around the entire hinge plate so you can judge the amount of movement **(see illustration 9.1)**

9   Loosen the bolts or nuts and move the hood into correct alignment. Move it only a little at a time. Tighten the hinge bolts or nuts and carefully lower the hood to check the position.

10   If necessary after installation, the entire hood latch assembly can be adjusted up-and-down as well as from side-to-side on the radiator support so the hood closes securely and flush with the fenders. To make the adjustment, scribe or draw a line around the hood latch mounting bolts to provide a reference point, then loosen them and reposition the latch assembly, as necessary. Following adjustment, retighten the mounting bolts **(see illustration).**

11   Finally, adjust the hood bumpers on the radiator support so the hood, when closed, is flush with the fenders **(see illustration).**

12   The hood latch assembly, as well as the hinges, should be periodically lubricated with white, lithium-base grease to prevent binding and wear.

10   Trunk lid - removal and installation

Refer to illustrations 10.2, 10.4 and 10.8
Note: *The trunk lid is heavy and somewhat awkward to remove and install - at least two people should perform this procedure.*

1   Open the trunk lid and cover the edges of the trunk compartment with pads or cloths to protect the painted surfaces when the lid is removed.

2   Remove the plastic screws, pry out the retainers and detach the trim panel **(see illustration).**

3   Disconnect any cables or wire harness connectors attached to the trunk lid that would interfere with removal.

4   Scribe or draw alignment marks around the hinge bolt mounting bolts **(see illustration).**

5   While an assistant supports the lid, remove the lid-to-hinge bolts on both sides and lift it off.

6   Installation is the reverse of removal. **Note:** *When reinstalling the trunk lid, align the lid-to-hinge bolts with the marks made during removal.*

7   Forward-and-backward and side-to-side adjustments are made

10.2 Remove the trunk lid trim panel retainers

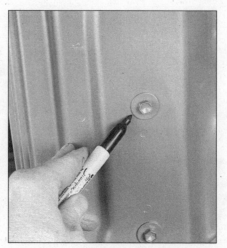

10.4 Scribe a mark around the bolt heads to help with lid realignment on installation

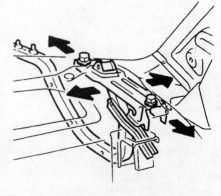

10.8 The trunk lid hinge position can be adjusted after loosening the bolts

11.8 Liftgate hinge adjustment details

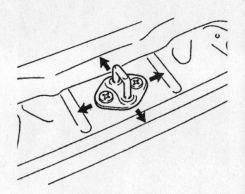

11.9 Loosen the liftgate striker screws and adjust its position by tapping with a hammer

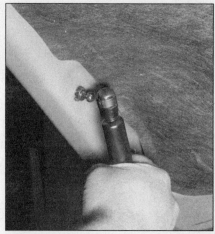

12.1 Grasp the strut securely and pull out sharply to detach it from the hood ballstud

by removing the rear seat, roof side inner garnish and package tray, then loosening the two hinge bolts and gently moving the lid into correct alignment. After adjustment tighten the bolts.

8   Adjust the latch position by removing the trunk lid trim panel and loosening the retaining bolts attaching the latch to the lid (**see illustration**).

9   Adjust the latch striker by loosening the mounting bolts and gently tapping it into position with a plastic hammer.

11   Rear liftgate - removal and installation

Refer to illustrations 11.8 and 11.9
Note: *The rear liftgate is heavy and somewhat awkward to remove and install - at least two people should perform this procedure.*

1   Open the liftgate and cover the edges of the body with pads or cloths to protect the painted surfaces when the lid is removed.
2   Disconnect any cables or wire harness connectors attached to the liftgate that would interfere with removal.
3   Make alignment marks around the hinge bolt mounting flanges.
4   Have an assistant support the rear liftgate and detach the support struts (see Section 12).
5   While an assistant supports the liftgate, remove the hinge bolts on both sides and lift it off.
6   Installation is the reverse of removal. **Note:** *When reinstalling the liftgate, align the lid-to-hinge bolts with the marks made during removal.*
7   After installation, close the liftgate and make sure it's aligned properly with the surrounding panels.
8   Forward-and-backward and side-to-side adjustments are made by removing the header trim and pulling down the headliner for access, then loosening the hinge to liftgate nuts and carefully moving the liftgate into correct alignment (**see illustration**).
9   Adjust the latch by loosening the striker mounting screws and gently tapping the striker into position with a plastic hammer (**see illustration**).

12   Support strut - replacement

Refer to illustrations 12.1 and 12.2
Warning: *The support strut is filled with pressurized gas - do not disassemble this component, if it is faulty replace it with a new one.*
Note: *The hood and rear liftgate are heavy and somewhat awkward to hold securely while replacing the struts - at least two people should perform this procedure.*

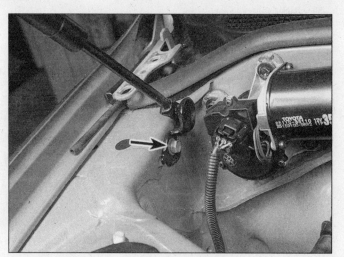

12.2 Remove the bolt (arrow) and detach the lower end of the strut

Hood

1   Grasp the upper end of the strut securely and pull out sharply to detach it from the ballstud (**see illustration**).
2   Remove the bolt from the lower end and remove the strut (**see illustration**).
3   Installation is the reverse of the removal procedure.

Liftgate

4   Remove the bolts from both ends of the strut and detach it from vehicle.
5   Installation is the reverse of the removal procedure.

13   Door trim panel - removal and installation

Refer to illustrations 13.2, 13.3, 13.4a, 13.4b, 13.4c, 13.6 and 13.7
Caution: *If the stereo in your vehicle is equipped with an anti-theft system, make sure you have the correct activation code before disconnecting the battery.*
Note: *On 1993 and later models, the airbag system will be disabled if the battery is disconnected for more than a brief period. If the airbag light comes on and stays on after the battery is reconnected, the vehicle must be taken to a dealer to have the system reset with a special tool.*

11

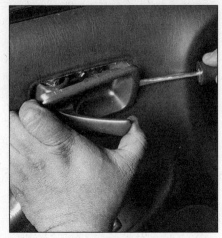

13.2 Pry the door handle bezel out and detach it

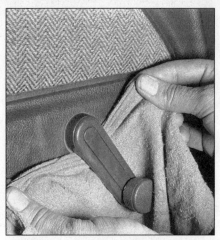

13.3 Work a cloth up behind the regulator handle and move it back-and-forth to detach the clip

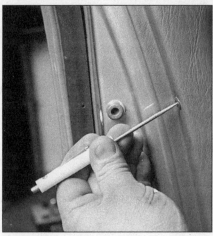

13.4a Use a small screwdriver to unscrew the center of the plastic retainer, then . . .

13.4b . . . pry the retainer out

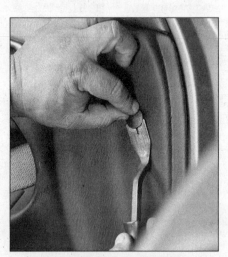

13.4c A tool like this one will make removing the larger clips easier

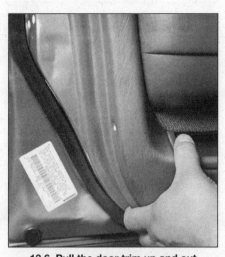

13.6 Pull the door trim up and out to remove it

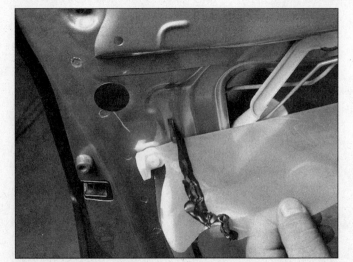

13.7 Carefully peel back the plastic watershield

1   Disconnect the cable from the negative battery terminal.
2   Remove the door handle bezel **(see illustration)**.
3   If equipped with a manual window regulator, remove the window crank by working a cloth back-and-forth behind the handle to dislodge the retainer **(see illustration)**. A special tool is available for this purpose but it's not essential. With the retainer removed, pull off the handle.
4   Remove the door trim panel retainers along the front and rear edge of the door panel **(see illustrations)**. Remove the door armrest assembly retaining screws.
5   Insert a wide putty knife or a thin pry bar between the trim panel and door to disengage the retaining clips along the bottom edge. Work around the outer edge until the panel is free.
6   Once all of the clips are disengaged, detach the trim panel, disconnect any electrical connectors and remove the trim panel from the vehicle by gently pulling it up and out **(see illustration)**.
7   For access to the inner door, peel back the plastic watershield, taking care not to tear it **(see illustration)**.
8   Prior to installation of the door panel, be sure to reinstall any clips in the panel which may have come out during the removal procedure and remained in the door. Press the watershield into place.
9   Plug in any electrical connectors and place the panel in position. Press it into place until the clips are seated and install the remaining retainers. Install the manual regulator window crank.

14.2 Use two jackstands padded with rags (to protect the paint) to support the door during the removal and installation procedures

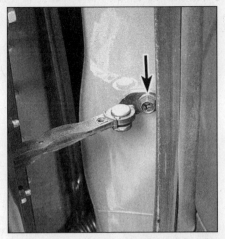

14.3 Remove the bolt (arrow) retaining the door stop strut

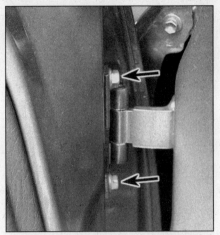

14.4 Draw alignment marks around the door bolt locations (arrows) with a marking pen

14 Door - removal, installation and adjustment

Removal and installation

Refer to illustrations 14.2, 14.3 and 14.4

1   Remove the door trim panel (see Section 13). Disconnect any electrical connectors and push them through the door opening so they won't interfere with removal.

2   Position a jack or jackstands under the door. Have an assistant on hand to support the door when the hinge bolts are removed **(see illustration)**. **Note:** *If a jack or stand is used, place a rag between it and the door to protect the paint.*

3   Remove the door stop strut bolt **(see illustration)**.

4   Scribe or draw alignment marks around the door bolts **(see illustration)**.

5   Remove the hinge-to-door bolts and carefully detach the door. Installation is the reverse of removal.

Adjustment

Refer to illustrations 14.6a, 14.6b and 14.6c

6   Following installation, make sure the door is aligned properly. Adjust it if necessary as follows:

a) *Forward, rearward and vertical adjustments are made by loosening the hinge-to-body bolts and moving the door, as necessary. A special offset tool may be required to reach some of the bolts* **(see illustration)**.

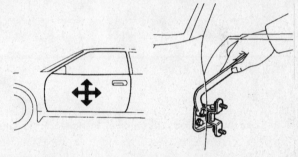

14.6a Loosen the hinge-to-body bolts to adjust the door forward, rearward and vertical - a special curved wrench may be required to reach the bolts

b) *Left, right and vertical adjustments are made by loosening the door-to-hinge bolts and moving the door as necessary* **(see illustration)**.

c) *The door lock striker can also be adjusted both up-and-down and sideways to provide a positive engagement with the locking mechanism. This is done by loosening the screws and moving the striker, as necessary* **(see illustration)**.

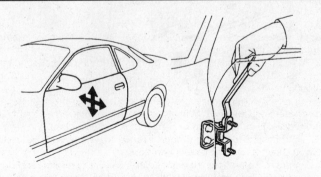

14.6b Adjust the door right, left and vertical after loosening the hinge-to-door bolts

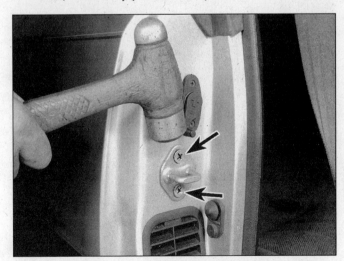

14.6c Adjust the door lock striker by loosening the mounting screws and gently tapping the striker in the desired direction

11

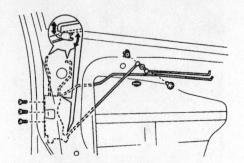

15.2 Door latch installation details

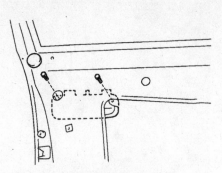

**15.6 Outside door handle
installation details**

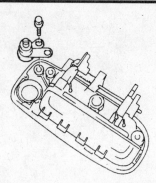

**15.7 Remove the screw and detach the
lock cylinder from the handle assembly**

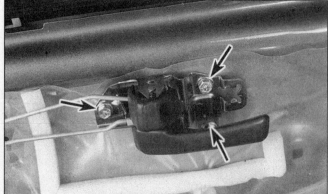

15.9 Remove the retaining bolts (arrows), then detach the links

15 Door latch, lock cylinder and handle - removal and installation

1   Remove the door trim panel and watershield (Section 13).

Door latch

Refer to illustration 15.2

2   Reaching through the access hole in the door panel, disconnect the links from the outside handle and the lock cylinder and remove the

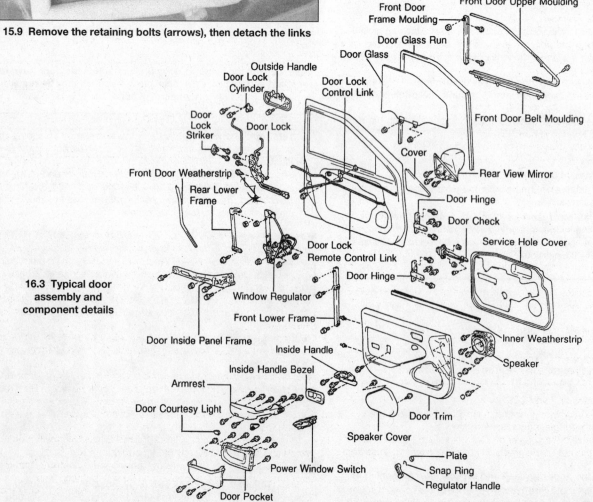

**16.3 Typical door
assembly and
component details**

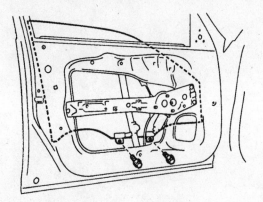

16.4 Remove the two mounting nuts or bolts to disconnect the glass from the window regulator

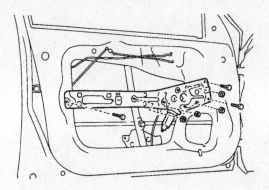

17.4 Remove the nut and bolts and detach the inside door panel frame

latch retaining screws from the end of the door **(see illustration)**.

3   Detach the door latch assembly.

4   Installation is the reverse of removal.

Lock cylinder and outside handle

Refer to illustrations 15.6 and 15.7

5   Disconnect the control links from the lock cylinder and outside handle.

6   Remove the outside handle retaining bolts and pull the handle assembly from the door **(see illustration)**.

7   Remove the screw and separate the lock cylinder from the handle **(see illustration)**.

8   Installation is the reverse of removal.

Inside handle

Refer to illustration 15.9

9   Remove the handle assembly retaining bolts **(see illustration)**.

10   Pull the handle out, disconnect the links and pull the handle free.

11   Installation is the reverse of removal.

16   Door window glass - removal and installation

Refer to illustrations 16.3 and 16.4

1   Remove the door trim panel and watershield (Section 13).

2   Lower the window glass.

3   Remove the door glass run by pulling the glass run upward. Pry out the retaining clips and remove the door belt molding. Remove the screws retaining the door frame moulding and the upper moulding. Pry out the retaining clips and remove the mouldings **(see illustration)**.

4   Remove the two glass mounting nuts or bolts and disconnect the glass from the window regulator **(see illustration)**.

5   Remove the glass by pulling it up and out of the door frame. Place rags inside the door frame to prevent scratching the glass, if necessary.

6   Installation is the reverse of the removal procedure.

17   Door glass regulator - removal and installation

Refer to illustrations 17.4 and 17.5

1   Remove the door trim panel and watershield (see Section 13).

2   Remove the door glass (see Section 16).

3   Carefully remove the clips and pull the weatherstrip free - do not pull strongly as this may damage the weatherstrip **(refer to illustration 16.3)**.

4   Remove the door inside panel frame **(see illustration)**.

5   Remove the mounting nuts, disconnect the power window electrical connector (if equipped) and remove the regulator through the

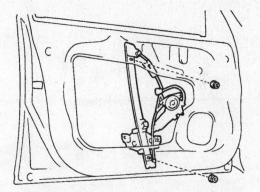

17.5 Door glass regulator installation details

service hole **(see illustration)**.

6   Installation is the reverse of removal. Apply multipurpose grease to the regulator rollers.

18   Front and rear bumper - removal and installation

Front bumper

Refer to illustration 18.4

Warning: *These models are equipped with airbags. The airbag is armed and can deploy (inflate) anytime the battery is connected. To prevent accidental deployment (and possible injury), turn the ignition key to LOCK and disconnect the negative battery cable whenever working near airbag components. After the battery is disconnected, wait at least 90 seconds before beginning work (the system has a back-up capacitor that must fully discharge). For more information see Chapter 12.*

Caution: *If the stereo in your vehicle is equipped with an anti-theft system, make sure you have the correct activation code before disconnecting the battery.*

Note: *On 1993 and later models, the airbag system will be disabled if the battery is disconnected for more than a brief period. If the airbag light comes on and stays on after the battery is reconnected, the vehicle must be taken to a dealer to have the system reset with a special tool.*

1   Apply the parking brake, block the rear wheels, lift the front of the vehicle and support it securely on jackstands.

2   Disconnect the cable from the negative battery terminal. Disconnect any wiring that would interfere with bumper removal.

3   Remove the radiator grille (see Section 26), headlight, clearance, side marker and turn signal lights (see Chapter 12).

11

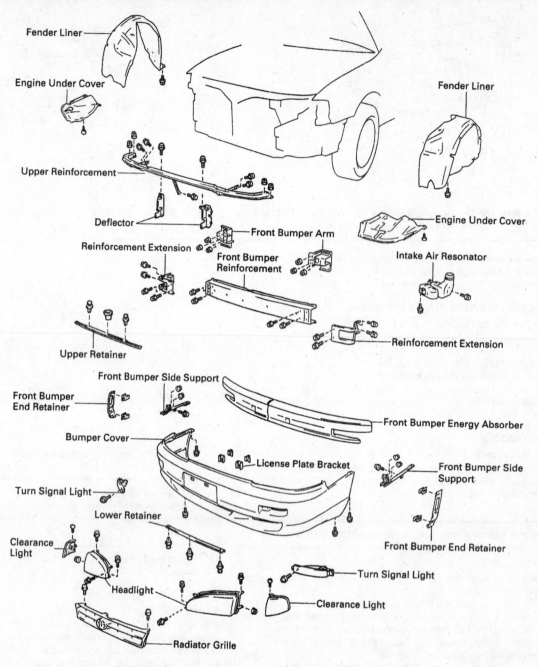

Fender Liner

Engine Under Cover

Fender Liner

Upper Reinforcement

Deflector

Front Bumper Arm

Engine Under Cover

Reinforcement Extension

Front Bumper Reinforcement

Intake Air Resonator

Reinforcement Extension

Upper Retainer

Front Bumper Side Support

Front Bumper End Retainer

Front Bumper Energy Absorber

Bumper Cover

License Plate Bracket

Front Bumper Side Support

Turn Signal Light

Lower Retainer

Front Bumper End Retainer

Clearance Light

Turn Signal Light

Headlight

Clearance Light

Radiator Grille

18.4 Typical front bumper assembly and related components

4   Remove the fender liner **(see illustration)**.
5   Remove the engine under cover, splash shield and intake air resonator.
6   Working under the vehicle, remove the upper and lower bumper cover nuts/bolts and detach the bumper cover and energy absorber assembly.
7   Remove the bolts attaching the front bumper bar to the frame and remove the bumper.
8   Installation is the reverse of the removal procedure.

Rear bumper

Refer to illustrations 18.9a and 18.9b
9   From inside the luggage compartment, remove the luggage trim

and floor finish plate **(see illustrations)**.
10   Remove the rear bumper cover bolts and nuts and detach the bumper cover and energy absorber assembly.
11   Remove the bolts attaching the rear bumper bar to the frame and remove the bumper.
12   Installation is the reverse of the removal procedure.

19   Outside mirror - removal and installation

Refer to illustration 19.2
1   Gently pry the mirror bracket cover off using a small screwdriver.

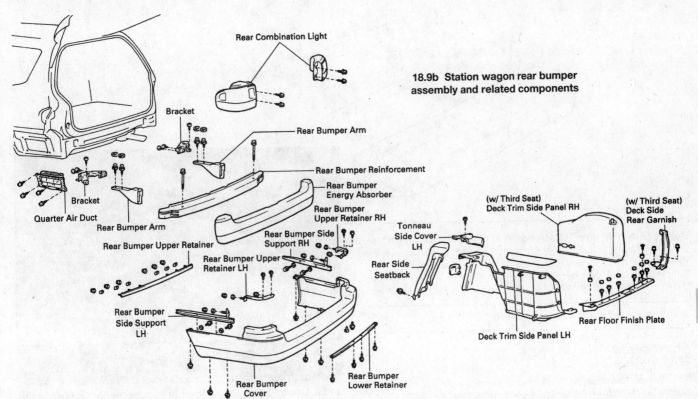

Rear Bumper Arm

Rear Bumper Arm

Rear Bumper Reinforcement

Rear Bumper Energy Absorber

Quarter Air Duct

Rear Bumper Upper Retainer

Rear Bumper Side Support

Rear Bumper Cover

Rear Bumper Side Support

License Plate Light

Lift Side Luggage Trim

Right Side Luggage Trim

Rear Luggage Trim

Rear Floor Finish Plate

18.9a Typical sedan/coupe rear bumper assembly and related components

Rear Combination Light

18.9b Station wagon rear bumper assembly and related components

Bracket

Rear Bumper Arm

Bracket

Quarter Air Duct

Rear Bumper Arm

Rear Bumper Reinforcement

Rear Bumper Energy Absorber

Rear Bumper Upper Retainer RH

Rear Bumper Side Support RH

Rear Bumper Upper Retainer

Rear Bumper Upper Retainer LH

Rear Bumper Side Support LH

(w/ Third Seat) Deck Trim Side Panel RH

(w/ Third Seat) Deck Side Rear Garnish

Tonneau Side Cover LH

Rear Side Seatback

Deck Trim Side Panel LH

Rear Floor Finish Plate

Rear Bumper Cover

Rear Bumper Lower Retainer

11

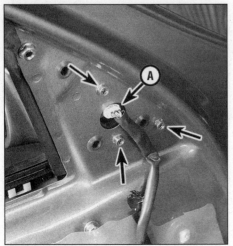

19.2 Disconnect the connector (A), remove the bolts (arrows) and detach the mirror

20.1 Typical front seat details

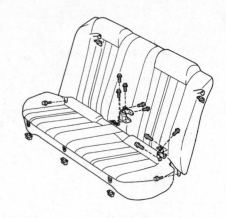

20.3 Rear bench seat details

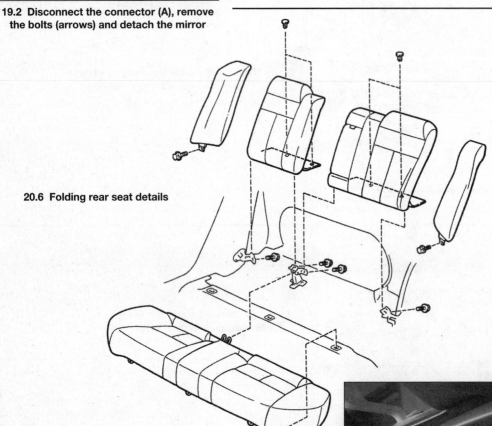

20.6 Folding rear seat details

Be sure to tape the tip of the screwdriver to prevent damaging the trim.

2   Disconnect the electrical connector (if equipped), remove the three retaining screws and detach the mirror **(see illustration)**.

3   Installation is the reverse of removal.

20   Seats - removal and installation

Front seats

Refer to illustration 20.1

1   Remove the retaining bolts, disconnect any electrical connectors and lift the seats from the vehicle **(see illustration)**.

2   Installation is the reverse of removal.

21.2a Use a Phillips screwdriver to remove the two screws at the top of the bezel

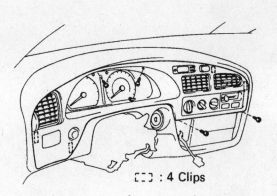

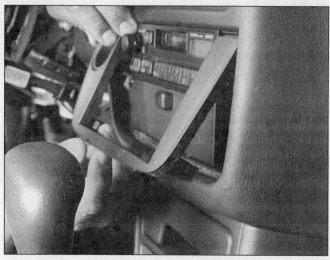

21.2c Remove the center bezel

: 4 Clips

21.2b Cluster bezel screw and retaining clip locations

Rear seats - fixed type

Refer to illustration 20.3

3   Pull the seat release tabs forward and lift the lower seat cushion up and free **(see illustration)**.

4   Remove the mounting bolts from the bottom of the seat back and pull the seat up to free the upper mounting slots **(see illustration 20.3)**.

5   Installation is the reverse of removal.

Rear seats - fold-down type

Refer to illustration 20.6

6   On split foldable type seats, pull up on the front edge of the seat cushion to disengage the clips, then rotate the cushion up and out **(see illustration)**.

7   Remove the bolts and detach the two shoulder bolsters.

8   Release the locks and pull the seat backs forward, then remove the rear seat hinge bolts and lift the seat backs out **(see illustration 20.6)**.

21   Instrument cluster bezel - removal and installation

Refer to illustrations 21.2a, 21.2b, 21.2c and 21.4

Warning: *These models are equipped with airbags. The airbag is armed and can deploy (inflate) anytime the battery is connected. To prevent accidental deployment (and possible injury), turn the ignition key to LOCK and disconnect the negative battery cable whenever working near airbag components. After the battery is disconnected, wait at least 90 seconds before beginning work (the system has a back-up capacitor that must fully discharge). For more information see Chapter 12.*

Caution: *If the stereo in your vehicle is equipped with an anti-theft system, make sure you have the correct activation code before disconnecting the battery.*

Note: *On 1993 and later models, the airbag system will be disabled if the battery is disconnected for more than a brief period. If the airbag light comes on and stays on after the battery is reconnected, the vehicle must be taken to a dealer to have the system reset with a special tool.*

1   Disconnect the cable from the negative battery terminal.

2   Remove the bezel retaining screws **(see illustrations)**. Remove the center cluster trim panel for access to the right side bezel screws **(see illustration)**.

3   Pull off the cluster dimmer switch knob and unscrew the switch retaining nut.

4   Grasp the bezel securely and detach it from the clips, then pull it out and disconnect the electrical connectors **(see illustration)**.

5   Installation is the reverse of the removal procedure.

21.4 After disconnecting the connectors, lift the bezel out

22   Steering column cover and lower pad - removal and installation

Refer to illustrations 22.2, 22.6a, 22.6b and 22.7

Warning: *These models are equipped with airbags. The airbag is armed and can deploy (inflate) anytime the battery is connected. To prevent accidental deployment (and possible injury), turn the ignition key to LOCK and disconnect the negative battery cable whenever working near airbag components. After the battery is disconnected, wait at least 90 seconds before beginning work (the system has a back-up capacitor that must fully discharge). For more information see Chapter 12.*

Caution: *If the stereo in your vehicle is equipped with an anti-theft system, make sure you have the correct activation code before disconnecting the battery.*

Note: *On 1993 and later models, the airbag system will be disabled if the battery is disconnected for more than a brief period. If the airbag light comes on and stays on after the battery is reconnected, the vehicle must be taken to a dealer to have the system reset with a special tool.*

1   Disconnect the cable from the negative battery terminal.

11

22.2 Remove the screws (arrows) and separate the steering column cover halves

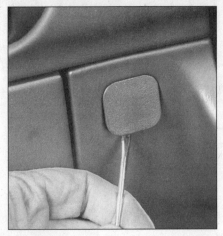

22.6a Use a small screwdriver to pry out the screw covers

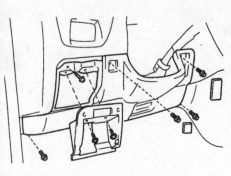

22.6b Steering column lower pad installation details

Steering column cover

2   Remove the steering column cover retaining screws **(see illustration)**.

3   Separate the cover halves and remove them from the steering column.

4   Installation is the reverse of removal.

Lower pad

5   Remove the coin box by squeezing the sides and rotating it out of the instrument panel

6   Remove the pad retaining screws **(see illustrations)**.

7   Disconnect any electrical connections and lower the pad from the instrument panel **(see illustration)**.

8   Installation is the reverse of the removal procedure.

23   Console - removal and installation

Refer to illustrations 23.2, 23.3a, 23.3b and 23.5

Warning: *These models are equipped with airbags. The airbag is armed and can deploy (inflate) anytime the battery is connected. To prevent accidental deployment (and possible injury), turn the ignition key to LOCK and disconnect the negative battery cable whenever working near airbag components. After the battery is disconnected,* wait at least 90 seconds before beginning work (the system has a back-up capacitor that must fully discharge). For more information see Chapter 12.

Caution: *If the stereo in your vehicle is equipped with an anti-theft system, make sure you have the correct activation code before disconnecting the battery.*

Note: *On 1993 and later models, the airbag system will be disabled if the battery is disconnected for more than a brief period. If the airbag light comes on and stays on after the battery is reconnected, the vehicle must be taken to a dealer to have the system reset with a special tool.*

1   Disconnect the cable from the negative battery terminal.

2   Use a small screwdriver to pry up on the rear edge of the shift bezel to detach it, then lift it off **(see illustration)**.

3   Remove the rear console retaining screws **(see illustrations)**.

4   Detach the rear console and lift it out.

5   Remove the front console retaining screws, detach the front console and lift it out **(see illustration)**.

6   Installation is the reverse of the removal procedure.

24   Glove compartment - removal and installation

Refer to illustration 24.2

Warning: *These models are equipped with airbags. The airbag is*

22.7 Detach the lower pad and lower it from the dash

23.2 Pry the clips free with a screwdriver, disconnect the electrical connector and remove the shift bezel

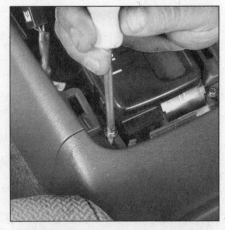

23.3a Remove the two screws from the front edge of the rear console

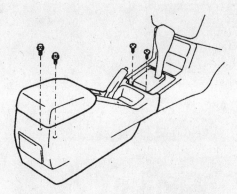

23.3b Rear console installation details

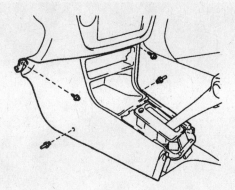

23.5 Front console installation details

armed and can deploy (inflate) anytime the battery is connected. To prevent accidental deployment (and possible injury), turn the ignition key to LOCK and disconnect the negative battery cable whenever working near airbag components. After the battery is disconnected, wait at least 90 seconds before beginning work (the system has a back-up capacitor that must fully discharge). For more information see Chapter 12.

Caution: *If the stereo in your vehicle is equipped with an anti-theft system, make sure you have the correct activation code before disconnecting the battery.*

Note: *On 1993 and later models, the airbag system will be disabled if the battery is disconnected for more than a brief period. If the airbag*

light comes on and stays on after the battery is reconnected, the vehicle must be taken to a dealer to have the system reset with a special tool.

1   Disconnect the cable from the negative battery terminal.
2   Remove the lower instrument panel on the passenger side **(see illustration)**.
3   Remove the nuts and the glove compartment door.
4   Remove screws and the glove compartment.
5   Installation is the reverse of removal.

25 Seat belts - check

1   Check the seat belts, buckles, latch plates and guide loops for any obvious damage or signs of wear.
2   Make sure the seat belt reminder light comes on when the key is turned on.
3   The seat belts are designed to lock up during a sudden stop or impact, yet allow free movement during normal driving. The retractors should hold the belt against your chest while driving and rewind the belt when the buckle is unlatched.
4   If any of the above checks reveal problems with the seat-belt system, replace parts as necessary.

26 Radiator grille - removal and installation

Refer to illustrations 26.1 and 26.2
1   Remove the bolt at each corner of the grille **(see illustration)**.

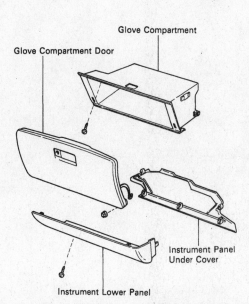

Glove Compartment

Glove Compartment Door

Instrument Panel Under Cover

Instrument Lower Panel

24.2 Glove compartment installation details

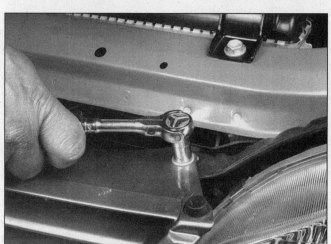

26.1 Remove the bolt at each corner of the grille

11

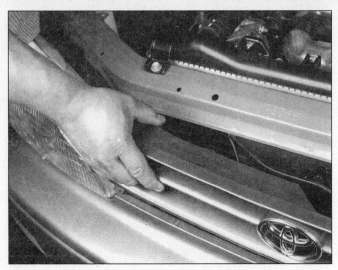

26.2 Lift the grille up and out to remove it

27.2 Remove the bolts (arrows) and detach the splash shields

2   Lift the grille straight up and remove it **(see illustration)**.
3   To install the grille, lower into position and install the bolts.

27 Splash shields - removal and installation

Refer to illustration 27.2

1   Raise the front of the vehicle and support it on jackstands.
2   Remove the bolts, detach the splash shields and lower them from the vehicle **(see illustration)**.
3   Installation is the reverse of removal.

Chapter 12   Chassis electrical system

Contents

1   General information

The electrical system is a 12-volt, negative ground type. Power for the lights and all electrical accessories is supplied by a lead/acid-type battery which is charged by the alternator.

This Chapter covers repair and service procedures for the various electrical components not associated with the engine. Information on the battery, alternator, distributor and starter motor can be found in Chapter 5.

It should be noted that when portions of the electrical system are serviced, the cable should be disconnected from the negative battery terminal to prevent electrical shorts and/or fires.

2   Electrical troubleshooting - general information

A typical electrical circuit consists of an electrical component, any switches, relays, motors, fuses, fusible links or circuit breakers related to that component and the wiring and electrical connectors that link the component to both the battery and the chassis. To help you pinpoint an electrical circuit problem, wiring diagrams are included at the end of this book.

Before tackling any troublesome electrical circuit, first study the appropriate wiring diagrams to get a complete understanding of what makes up that individual circuit. Trouble spots, for instance, can often be narrowed down by noting if other components related to the circuit

12

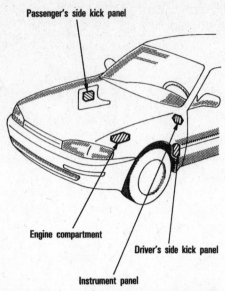

3.1a Typical U.S. model fuse block locations

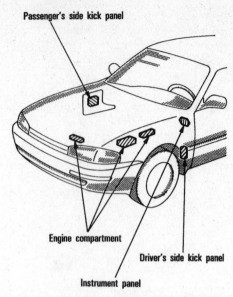

3.1b Canadian model fuse block locations

are operating properly. If several components or circuits fail at one time, chances are the problem is in a fuse or ground connection, because several circuits are often routed through the same fuse and ground connections.

Electrical problems usually stem from simple causes, such as loose or corroded connections, a blown fuse, a melted fusible link or a bad relay. Visually inspect the condition of all fuses, wires and connections in a problem circuit before troubleshooting it.

If testing instruments are going to be utilized, use the diagrams to plan ahead of time where you will make the necessary connections in order to accurately pinpoint the trouble spot.

The basic tools needed for electrical troubleshooting include a circuit tester or voltmeter (a 12-volt bulb with a set of test leads can also be used), a continuity tester, which includes a bulb, battery and set of test leads, and a jumper wire, preferably with a circuit breaker incorporated, which can be used to bypass electrical components. Before attempting to locate a problem with test instruments, use the wiring diagram(s) to decide where to make the connections.

Voltage checks

Voltage checks should be performed if a circuit is not functioning properly. Connect one lead of a circuit tester to either the negative battery terminal or a known good ground. Connect the other lead to a electrical connector in the circuit being tested, preferably nearest to the battery or fuse. If the bulb of the tester lights, voltage is present, which means that the part of the circuit between the electrical connector and the battery is problem free. Continue checking the rest of the circuit in the same fashion. When you reach a point at which no voltage is present, the problem lies between that point and the last test point with voltage. Most of the time the problem can be traced to a loose connection. **Note:** *Keep in mind that some circuits receive voltage only when the ignition key is in the Accessory or Run position.*

Finding a short

One method of finding shorts in a circuit is to remove the fuse and connect a test light or voltmeter in its place to the fuse terminals. There should be no voltage present in the circuit. Move the wiring harness from side to side while watching the test light. If the bulb goes on, there is a short to ground somewhere in that area, probably where the insulation has rubbed through. The same test can be performed on each component in the circuit, even a switch.

Ground check

Perform a ground test to check whether a component is properly grounded. Disconnect the battery and connect one lead of a self-powered test light, known as a continuity tester, to a known good ground. **Caution:** *If the stereo in your vehicle is equipped with an anti-theft system, make sure you have the correct activation code before disconnecting the battery.* Connect the other lead to the wire or ground connection being tested. If the bulb goes on, the ground is good. If the bulb does not go on, the ground is not good.

Continuity check

A continuity check is done to determine if there are any breaks in a circuit - if it is passing electricity properly. With the circuit off (no power in the circuit), a self-powered continuity tester can be used to check the circuit. Connect the test leads to both ends of the circuit (or to the "power" end and a good ground), and if the test light comes on the circuit is passing current properly. If the light doesn't come on, there is a break somewhere in the circuit. The same procedure can be used to test a switch, by connecting the continuity tester to the power in and power out sides of the switch. With the switch turned On, the test light should come on.

Finding an open circuit

When diagnosing for possible open circuits, it is often difficult to locate them by sight because oxidation or terminal misalignment are hidden by the electrical connectors. Merely wiggling an electrical connector on a sensor or in the wiring harness may correct the open circuit condition. Remember this when an open circuit is indicated when troubleshooting a circuit. Intermittent problems may also be caused by oxidized or loose connections.

Electrical troubleshooting is simple if you keep in mind that all electrical circuits are basically electricity running from the battery, through the wires, switches, relays, fuses and fusible links to each electrical component (light bulb, motor, etc.) and to ground, from which it is passed back to the battery. Any electrical problem is an interruption in the flow of electricity to and from the battery.

3   Fuses - general information

Refer to illustrations 3.1a, 3.1b, 3.1c, 3.1d and 3.3

1   The electrical circuits of the vehicle are protected by a combination of fuses, circuit breakers and fusible links. The fuse blocks on these models can be found in several locations **(see illustrations)**.

2   Each of the fuses is designed to protect a specific circuit, and the various circuits are identified on the fuse panel itself.

3.1c The main fuse block is located in the left side of the dash, under a cover

3.1d The engine compartment fuse block contains fuses, relays and fusible links - refer to the cover for information

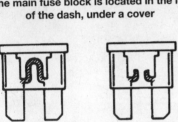

GOOD   BLOWN

3.3 The fuses used in these models can be visually checked to determine if they are blown

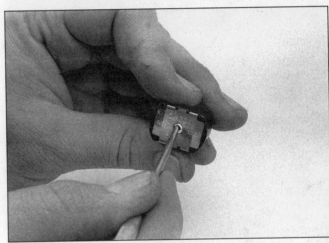

5.3 Insert a pin or paper clip into the circuit breaker reset hole and push it in to reset it

3   Miniaturized fuses are employed in the fuse block. These compact fuses, with blade terminal design, allow fingertip removal and replacement. If an electrical component fails, always check the fuse first. A blown fuse is easily identified through the clear plastic body. Visually inspect the element for evidence of damage (**see illustration**). If a continuity check is called for, the blade terminal tips are exposed in the fuse body.

4   Be sure to replace blown fuses with the correct type. Fuses of different ratings are physically interchangeable, but only fuses of the proper rating should be used. Replacing a fuse with one of a higher or lower value than specified is not recommended. Each electrical circuit needs a specific amount of protection. The amperage value of each fuse is molded into the fuse body.

5   If the replacement fuse immediately fails, don't replace it again until the cause of the problem is isolated and corrected. In most cases, this will be a short circuit in the wiring caused by a broken or deteriorated wire.

4   Fusible links - general information

Caution: *If the stereo in your vehicle is equipped with an anti-theft system, make sure you have the correct activation code before disconnecting the battery.*
Note: *On 1993 and later models, the airbag system will be disabled if the battery is disconnected for more than a brief period. If the airbag light comes on and stays on after the battery is reconnected, the vehicle must be taken to a dealer to have the system reset with a special tool.*

1   Some circuits are protected by fusible links. The links are used in circuits which are not ordinarily fused, such as the ignition circuit.

2   The fusible links on these models are similar to fuses in that they can be visually checked to determine if they are melted.

3   To replace a fusible link, first disconnect the negative cable from the battery. Disconnect the burned-out link and replace it with a new

one (available from your dealer or auto parts store). Always determine the cause for the overload which melted the fusible link before installing a new one.

5   Circuit breakers - general information

Refer to illustration 5.3

Circuit breakers protect components such as power windows, power door locks and headlights. Some circuit breakers are located in the fuse boxes.

Because on some models the circuit breaker resets itself automatically, an electrical overload in a circuit breaker protected system will cause the circuit to fail momentarily, then come back on. If the circuit does not come back on, check it immediately. Note, however, that some circuit breakers must be reset manually. Once the condition is corrected, the circuit breaker will resume its normal function.

To reset a manual circuit breaker, first disconnect the cable from the negative battery terminal. **Caution:** *If the stereo in your vehicle is equipped with an anti-theft system, make sure you have the correct activation code before disconnecting the battery.* Remove the circuit breaker, insert a pin into the reset hole and push in until you hear a click (**see illustration**). Once the circuit breaker is reset, its a good idea to use an ohmmeter to make sure there continuity between the terminal before reinstalling it.

12

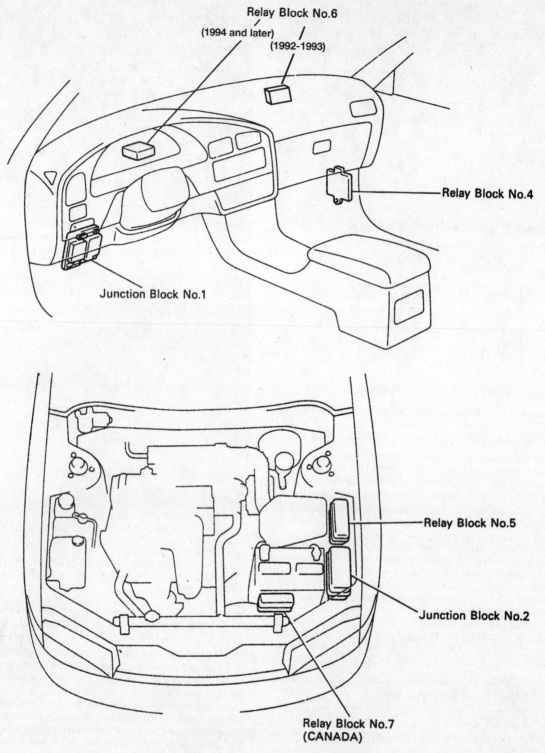

6.2 Typical relay and junction block locations

6 Relays - general information

Refer to illustration 6.2

1   Several electrical accessories in the vehicle use relays to transmit the electrical signal to the component. If the relay is defective, that component will not operate properly.

2   The various relays are mounted in several locations throughout the vehicle **(see illustration)**. Refer to the fuse/relay block cover for additional information.

3   If a faulty relay is suspected, it can be removed and tested by a dealer or other qualified shop. Defective relays must be replaced as a unit.

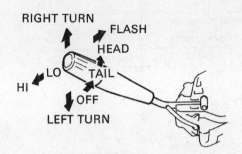

LIGHT CONTROL SWITCH

Terminal / Switch position	A2 or A11	A11 or A2	A13
OFF			
TAIL	O———	———O	
HEAD	O———	———O———	———O

HEADLIGHT DIMMER SWITCH

Terminal / Switch position	A3	A9	A12	A14
Flash			O———	———O———O
Low beam	O———	———O		
High beam			O———	———O

TURN SIGNAL SWITCH

Terminal / Switch position	A1	A5	A8
Left turn	O———	———O	
Neutral			
Right turn	O———	———O	———O

Connector "A"   Connector "B"

8.4a Lighting system switch terminal guide and continuity chart

7   Turn signal and hazard flashers - check and replacement

Warning: *These models are equipped with airbags. The airbag is armed and can deploy (inflate) anytime the battery is connected. To prevent accidental deployment (and possible injury), turn the ignition key to LOCK and disconnect the negative battery cable whenever working near airbag components. After the battery is disconnected, wait at least 90 seconds before beginning work (the system has a back-up capacitor that must fully discharge). For more information on the airbag system see Section 26.*

Caution: *If the stereo in your vehicle is equipped with an anti-theft system, make sure you have the correct activation code before disconnecting the battery.*

Note: *On 1993 and later models, the airbag system will be disabled if the battery is disconnected for more than a brief period. If the airbag light comes on and stays on after the battery is reconnected, the vehicle must be taken to a dealer to have the system reset with a special tool.*

1   Both the turn signal and hazard flashers are operated by a small canister shaped unit.
2   When the flasher unit is functioning properly, an audible click can be heard during its operation. If the turn signal lights fail on one side or the other and the flasher unit does not make its characteristic clicking sound, a faulty turn signal bulb is indicated.
3   If both turn signal lights fail to blink, the problem may be due to a blown fuse, a faulty flasher unit, a broken switch or a loose or open connection. If a quick check of the fuse box indicates that the turn signal fuse has blown, check the wiring for a short before installing a new fuse.
4   The flasher unit is located in the relay block under the right side of the dash on 1993 and earlier models and in the fuse block under the left side of the dash on later models.
5   Make sure that the replacement unit is identical to the original.

Compare the old one to the new one before installing it.
6   Installation is the reverse of removal.

8   Combination switch - check and replacement

Warning: *These models are equipped with airbags. The airbag is armed and can deploy (inflate) anytime the battery is connected. To prevent accidental deployment (and possible injury), turn the ignition key to LOCK and disconnect the negative battery cable whenever working near airbag components. After the battery is disconnected, wait at least 90 seconds before beginning work (the system has a back-up capacitor that must fully discharge). For more information on the airbag system see Section 26.*

Caution: *If the stereo in your vehicle is equipped with an anti-theft system, make sure you have the correct activation code before disconnecting the battery.*

Note: *On 1993 and later models, the airbag system will be disabled if the battery is disconnected for more than a brief period. If the airbag light comes on and stays on after the battery is reconnected, the vehicle must be taken to a dealer to have the system reset with a special tool.*

Check

Refer to illustrations 8.4a and 8.4b
1   Disconnect the cable from the negative battery terminal.
2   Remove the steering column cover and lower pad (see Chapter 11). .
3   Trace the wiring harness down the steering column to the large electrical connector.
4   Disconnect the electrical connector and using an ohmmeter, check for continuity between the indicated terminals with the various switches in each of the indicated positions **(see illustrations)**.
5   If the continuity is not as specified, replace the defective switch.

12

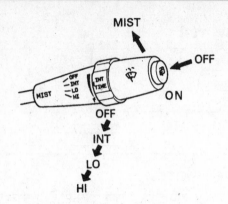

WIPER OFF

Switch position	Tester connection to terminal number	Specified value
MIST OFF	B4 — B7	Continuity
MIST ON	B4 — B7 B16 — B18	Continuity

WIPER INT

Switch position	Tester connection to terminal number	Specified value
MIST OFF	B4 — B7 B14 — B16	Continuity
MIST ON	B4 — B7 B14 — B16 — B18	Continuity

WIPER LO

Switch position	Tester connection to terminal number	Specified value
MIST OFF	B7 — B18	Continuity
MIST ON	B7 — B18	Continuity

Connector "A"   Connector "B".

**8.4b Wiper/washer switch terminal guide
and continuity chart**

Replacement

Refer to illustrations 8.7, 8.9 and 8.11

6   Remove the steering wheel (see Chapter 10).

7   Remove the combination switch retaining screws **(see illustration)**.

8   Release the wiring retainer clamps and slide the combination switch and wiring harness up off the column.

9   Remove the retaining screws from the switch being replaced and remove the defective switch from the switch body **(see illustration)**.

10   Separate the wiring harness of the switch being replaced from the main wiring harness and remove the terminals from the connector.

11   Release the tabs from the terminal cover at the rear of the connector. From the front of the connector, insert a small screwdriver or pick, pry down on the locking lug and remove the terminal from the rear **(see illustration)**.

12   Insert the terminals from the new switch into the connector, pushing in until they are securely locked in place.

13   The remainder or installation is the reverse of removal. Be sure to center the spiral cable before installing the steering wheel (see Chapter 10).

9   Ignition switch and key lock cylinder - removal and installation

Warning: *These models are equipped with airbags. The airbag is armed and can deploy (inflate) anytime the battery is connected. To prevent accidental deployment (and possible injury), turn the ignition key to LOCK and disconnect the negative battery cable whenever working near airbag components. After the battery is disconnected, wait at least 90 seconds before beginning work (the system has a back-up capacitor that must fully discharge). For more information on the airbag system see Section 26.*

Caution: *If the stereo in your vehicle is equipped with an anti-theft system, make sure you have the correct activation code before disconnecting the battery.*

Note: *On 1993 and later models, the airbag system will be disabled if the battery is disconnected for more than a brief period. If the airbag light comes on and stays on after the battery is reconnected, the vehicle must be taken to a dealer to have the system reset with a special tool.*

**8.7 Remove the four combination switch
mounting screws (arrows)**

Check

Refer to illustration 9.4

1   Disconnect the cable from the negative battery terminal.

2   Remove the steering column cover and lower pad (see Chapter 11).

3   Trace the wire from the ignition switch to the electrical connector and disconnect the connector.

4   Use an ohmmeter to check for continuity at the indicated terminals with the switch in each indicated position **(see illustration)**.

5   Replace the switch if continuity is not as specified.

Replacement

Ignition switch

Refer to illustration 9.7

6   Remove the ventilation duct running under the steering column.

7   Remove the screws retaining the switch to the rear of the lock cylinder housing and remove the switch **(see illustration)**.

8   Installation is the reverse of removal.

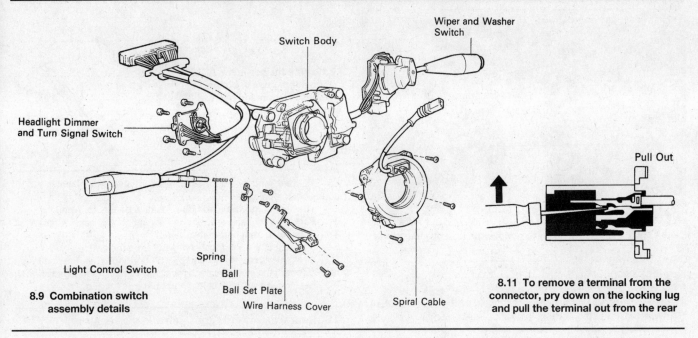

Wiper and Washer Switch

Switch Body

Headlight Dimmer and Turn Signal Switch

Light Control Switch

Spring

Ball

Ball Set Plate

Wire Harness Cover

Spiral Cable

Pull Out

8.9 Combination switch assembly details

8.11 To remove a terminal from the connector, pry down on the locking lug and pull the terminal out from the rear

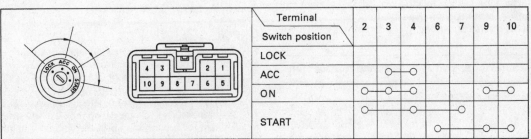

Terminal / Switch position	2	3	4	6	7	9	10
LOCK							
ACC		○	○				
ON	○	○	○			○	○
START	○		○		○		
START					○	○	○

9.4 Ignition switch terminal guide and continuity chart

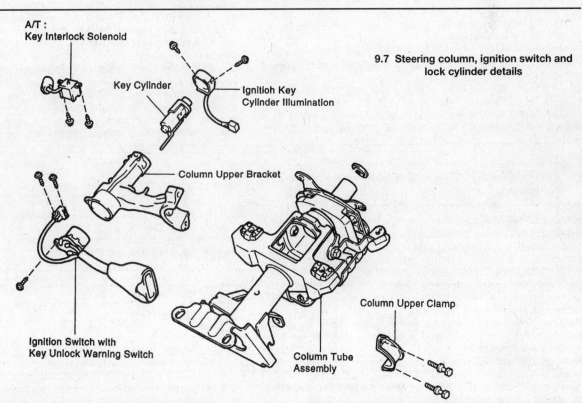

A/T : Key Interlock Solenoid

Key Cylinder

Ignitioh Key Cylinder Illumination

9.7 Steering column, ignition switch and lock cylinder details

Column Upper Bracket

Ignition Switch with Key Unlock Warning Switch

Column Tube Assembly

Column Upper Clamp

12

9.9 Use a small screwdriver to remove the lock cylinder cover

Key lock cylinder

Refer to illustrations 9.9 and 9.10

9   Remove the lock cylinder cover by prying it off **(see illustration)**.
10   With the key in the Accessory position, insert a small screwdriver (a hooked tool may be necessary on models where access is restricted) in the hole in the casting, pull the lock cylinder straight out and remove it from the steering column **(see illustration)**.
11   Installation is the reverse of removal.

10   Rear window defogger switch - check and replacement

Refer to illustrations 10.6a and 10.6b

Warning: *These models are equipped with airbags. The airbag is armed and can deploy (inflate) anytime the battery is connected. To prevent accidental deployment (and possible injury), turn the ignition key to LOCK and disconnect the negative battery cable whenever working near airbag components. After the battery is disconnected, wait at least 90 seconds before beginning work (the system has a back-up capacitor that must fully discharge). For more information on the airbag system see Section 26.*
Caution: *If the stereo in your vehicle is equipped with an anti-theft system, make sure you have the correct activation code before disconnecting the battery.*
Note: *On 1993 and later models, the airbag system will be disabled if the battery is disconnected for more than a brief period. If the airbag light comes on and stays on after the battery is reconnected, the vehicle must be taken to a dealer to have the system reset with a special tool.*

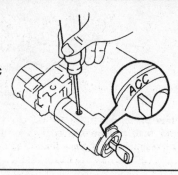

9.10 With the key in the ACC position. push in on the release button and pull the lock cylinder straight out

1   The rear window defogger switch is located on the heater and air conditioning control panel.
2   Disconnect the cable from the negative battery terminal.
3   Remove the heater and air conditioning control panel (Chapter 3).
4   Detach the switch from the panel.
5   Disconnect the electrical connector from the switch.
6   Use an ohmmeter to check for continuity at the indicated terminals with the switch in each indicated position **(see illustrations)**.
7   Replace the switch if continuity is not as specified.

11   Rear window defogger - check and repair

Refer to illustrations 11.4, 11.5 and 11.7

Check

1   The rear window defogger consists of a number of horizontal elements baked onto the glass surface.
2   Small breaks in the element can be repaired without removing the rear window.
3   Turn the ignition switch and defogger system switches to On.
4   When measuring voltage during the next two tests, wrap a piece of aluminum foil around the tip of the voltmeter negative probe and press the foil against the wire with your finger **(see illustration)**.
5   Check the voltage at the center of each heat wire **(see illustration)**. If the voltage is 5-volts, the wire is okay (there is no break). If the voltage is 10-volts, the wire is broken between the center of the element and the positive end of the element and ground.
6   Connect the negative lead to a good body ground. The reading should stay the same.
7   To find the break, place the voltmeter positive lead against the defogger positive terminal. Place the voltmeter negative lead with the foil strip against the heat wire at the positive terminal end and slide it toward the negative terminal end. The point at which the voltmeter deflects from zero to several volts is the point at which the heat element is broken **(see illustration)**. **Note:** *If the heat element is not*

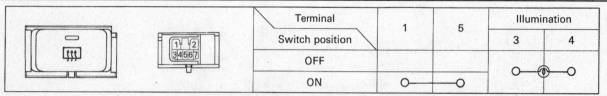

Terminal Switch position	1	5	Illumination	
			3	4
OFF			o—⊗—o	
ON	o——o			

10.6a 1993 and earlier model defogger switch terminal guide and continuity chart

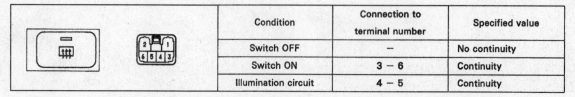

Condition	Connection to terminal number	Specified value
Switch OFF	—	No continuity
Switch ON	3 — 6	Continuity
Illumination circuit	4 — 5	Continuity

10.6b 1994 and later model defogger switch terminal guide and continuity chart

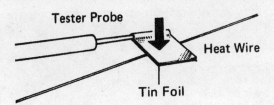

11.4 When measuring the voltage at the rear window defogger grid, wrap a piece of aluminum foil around the negative probe of the voltmeter and press the foil against the wire with your finger

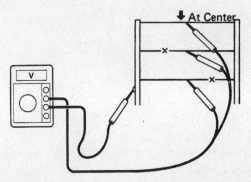

11.5 To determine if a wire has broken, check the voltage at the *center* of each wire - if the voltage is 5-volts, the wire is unbroken; if the voltage is 10-volts, the wire is broken between the center of the wire and the positive end; if the voltage is 0-volts, the wire is broken between the center of the wire and ground

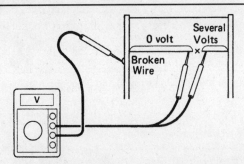

11.7 To find the break, place the voltmeter positive lead against the defogger positive terminal, place the voltmeter negative lead with the foil strip against the heat wire at the positive terminal end and slide it toward the negative terminal end - the point at which the voltmeter deflects from zero to several volts is the point at which the wire is broken

broken, the voltmeter will indicate no voltage at the positive end of the heat element but gradually increase to about 12-volts.

Repair

8   Repair the break in the element using a repair kit specifically recommended for this purpose, such as Dupont paste No. 4817 (or equivalent). Included in this kit is plastic conductive epoxy.
9   Prior to repairing a break, turn off the system and allow it to cool off for a few minutes.
10   Lightly buff the element area with fine steel wool, then clean it thoroughly with rubbing alcohol.
11   Use masking tape to mask off the area being repaired.
12   Thoroughly mix the epoxy, following the instructions provided with the repair kit.
13   Apply the epoxy material to the slit in the masking tape, overlapping the undamaged area about 3/4-inch on either end.
14   Allow the repair to cure for 24 hours before removing the tape and using the system.

12   Radio and speakers - removal and installation

Warning: *These models are equipped with airbags. The airbag is armed and can deploy (inflate) anytime the battery is connected. To prevent accidental deployment (and possible injury), turn the ignition key to LOCK and disconnect the negative battery cable whenever working near airbag components. After the battery is disconnected, wait at least 90 seconds before beginning work (the system has a back-up capacitor that must fully discharge). For more information on the airbag system see Section 26.*
Caution: *If the stereo in your vehicle is equipped with an anti-theft system, make sure you have the correct activation code before disconnecting the battery.*
Note: *On 1993 and later models, the airbag system will be disabled if the battery is disconnected for more than a brief period. If the airbag light comes on and stays on after the battery is reconnected, the vehicle must be taken to a dealer to have the system reset with a special tool.*

Radio

Refer to illustrations 12.3 and 12.4
1   Disconnect the cable from the negative battery terminal.
2   Remove the center cluster trim panel (see Chapter 11).
3   Remove the radio mounting screws **(see illustration)**.
4   Pull the radio out, reach behind it, disconnect the electrical connector and the antenna lead and lower the radio from the instrument panel **(see illustration)**.
5   Installation is the reverse of removal.

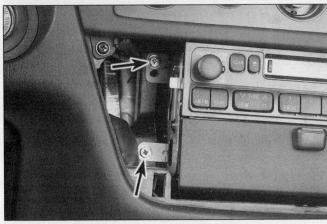

12.3 Remove the radio mounting screws (arrows) - there are two on each side

12.4 Pull the radio, disconnect the electrical connector and the antenna cable

12

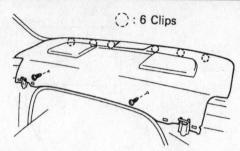

12.6 Remove the package shelf for access to the rear speakers

12.7 Remove the screws (arrows) and disconnect the speaker

Speakers

Refer to illustrations 12.6 and 12.7

6   Remove the door trim panel (see Chapter 11) or rear seat and package tray trim panel **(see illustration)**.

7   Remove the speaker retaining screws, pull the speaker out, disconnect the electrical connector and remove the speaker **(see illustration)**.

8   Installation is the reverse of removal.

13   Radio antenna - removal and installation

Refer to illustrations 13.2 and 13.3

Caution: *If the stereo in your vehicle is equipped with an anti-theft system, make sure you have the correct activation code before disconnecting the battery.*

Note: *On 1993 and later models, the airbag system will be disabled if the battery is disconnected for more than a brief period. If the airbag light comes on and stays on after the battery is reconnected, the vehicle must be taken to a dealer to have the system reset with a special tool.*

1   Disconnect the cable from the negative battery terminal.

2   Pull down the luggage compartment trim and disconnect the electrical connector at the antenna relay. Disconnect the antenna cable and remove the antenna mounting nuts **(see illustration)**.

3   Unscrew the antenna mast retaining nut, lower the antenna assembly and remove it from the vehicle **(see illustration)**.

4   Installation is the reverse of removal.

14   Headlight bulb - replacement

Refer to illustrations 14.3 and 14.4

Warning: *Some models are equipped with halogen gas-filled bulbs which are under pressure and may shatter if the surface is scratched or the bulb is dropped. Wear eye protection and handle the bulbs carefully, grasping only the base whenever possible. Do not touch the surface of the bulb with your fingers because the oil from your skin*

could cause it to overheat and fail prematurely. If you do touch the bulb surface, clean it with rubbing alcohol.

Caution: *If the stereo in your vehicle is equipped with an anti-theft system, make sure you have the correct activation code before disconnecting the battery.*

Note: *On 1993 and later models, the airbag system will be disabled if the battery is disconnected for more than a brief period. If the airbag light comes on and stays on after the battery is reconnected, the vehicle must be taken to a dealer to have the system reset with a special tool.*

1   Open the hood.

2   Disconnect the cable from the negative battery terminal.

3   Press the lock release and disconnect the bulb holder from the electrical connector **(see illustration)**.

4   Rotate bulb holder counterclockwise and withdraw it from the headlight housing **(see illustration)**.

5   Again, without touching the glass with your bare fingers, insert the new bulb holder assembly into the headlight housing, install and rotate it clockwise to lock it in place.

6   Connect in the electrical connector. Test the headlight operation, then close the hood.

15   Headlights adjustment

Refer to illustration 15.1

Note: *It is important that the headlights be correctly aimed. If incorrectly adjusted, they could blind the driver of an oncoming vehicle and cause a serious accident, or seriously reduce your ability to see the road. The headlights should be checked for proper aim every 12 months and any time a new headlight is installed or front-end body work is performed. It*

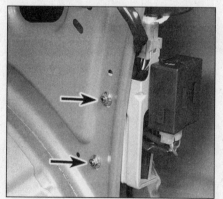

13.2 Disconnect the antenna electrical connector and remove the mounting nuts (arrows)

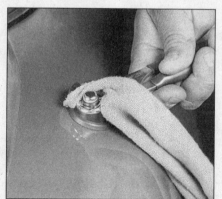

13.3 Use a rag and pliers to unscrew the antenna nut

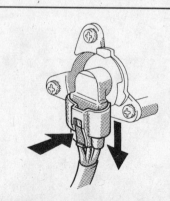

14.3 Press in on the clip and disconnect the headlight bulb connector

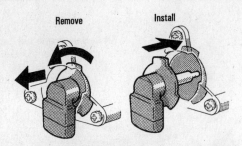

14.4 Headlight bulb replacement details

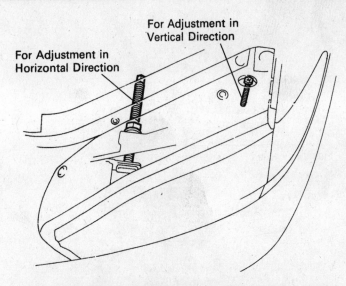

15.1 The headlight adjustment screws are located at the back and corner of the housing

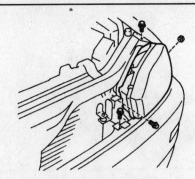

16.3 Remove the three bolts and one nut and remove the composite headlight housing

should be emphasized that the following procedure is only an interim step which will provide temporary adjustment until the headlights can be adjusted by a properly equipped shop.

1   Headlights have two adjusting screws, one at the top of the headlight housing controlling up-and-down movement, and one at the lower corner of the headlight controlling left-and-right movement **(see illustration)**.

2   There are several methods of adjusting the headlights. The simplest method requires a blank wall, masking tape and a level floor.

3   Position a strip of masking tape vertically on the wall in reference to the vehicle centerline and the centerline of both headlights.

4   Position a horizontal line in reference to the centerline of the headlights. **Note:** *It may be easier to position the tape on the wall with the vehicle parked only a few inches away.*

5   Adjustment should be made with the vehicle 25 feet from the wall, sitting level, the gas tank half-full and no unusually heavy load in the vehicle.

6   Starting with the low-beam adjustment, position the high-intensity zone so it is two inches below the horizontal line and two inches to the right of the headlight vertical line. Adjustment is made by turning the adjusting screw behind the headlight as necessary to raise or lower the beam **(see illustration 15.1)**. The other adjusting screw should be used in the same manner to move the beam left or right.

7   With the high beams on, the high-intensity zone should be

vertically centered with the exact center just below the horizontal line. **Note:** *It may not be possible to position the headlight aim exactly for both high and low beams. If a compromise must be made, keep in mind that the low beams are the most used and have the greatest effect on driver safety.*

8   Have the headlights adjusted by a dealer service department or service station at the earliest opportunity.

16   Composite headlight housing - removal and installation

Warning: *These models are equipped with airbags. The airbag is armed and can deploy (inflate) anytime the battery is connected. To prevent accidental deployment (and possible injury), turn the ignition key to LOCK and disconnect the negative battery cable whenever working near airbag components. After the battery is disconnected, wait at least 90 seconds before beginning work (the system has a back-up capacitor that must fully discharge). For more information on the airbag system see Section 26.*

Caution: *If the stereo in your vehicle is equipped with an anti-theft system, make sure you have the correct activation code before disconnecting the battery.*

Refer to illustration 16.3

Note: *On 1993 and later models, the airbag system will be disabled if the battery is disconnected for more than a brief period. If the airbag light comes on and stays on after the battery is reconnected, the vehicle must be taken to a dealer to have the system reset with a special tool.*

1   Disconnect the cable from the negative battery terminal.

2   Remove the parking light assembly (see Section 17) and the radiator grille (Chapter 11).

3   Remove the housing bracket nuts and bolts **(see illustration)**.

4   Disconnect the headlight bulb electrical connector, then withdraw the housing from the body and remove it from the vehicle.

5   Installation is the reverse of removal.

17   Bulb replacement

Parking/turn signal and marker lights

Refer to illustrations 17.1 and 17.2

1   Open the hood and remove the screw that secures the parking light housing to the fender, rotate the bulb holder counterclockwise and pull the bulb out **(see illustration)**.

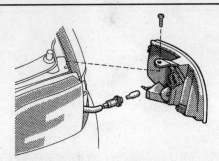

17.1 Parking light bulb replacement details

12

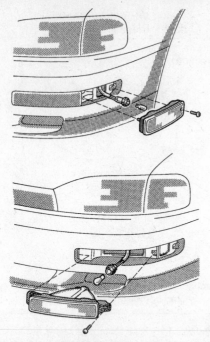

17.2 Side marker (top) and turn signal (bottom) bulb replacement details

2   Remove the screw(s) and detach the side marker or turn signal lens from the bumper **(see illustration)**. The bulb can then be pulled out of the socket (side marker) or pushed in and rotated counterclockwise (turn signal).
3   Installation is the reverse of removal.

Tail light

Refer to illustrations 17.4 and 17.5

4   On sedan/coupe models, remove screws and detach the tail light housing **(see illustration)**. Turn the bulb holder counterclockwise and remove it from the back of the housing. Push in and rotate the turn signal, stop and tail light bulbs counterclockwise to remove them from the holder. The side marker bulb pulls straight out of the holder.

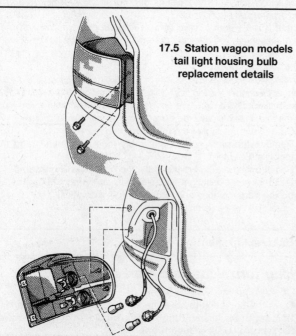

17.5 Station wagon models tail light housing bulb replacement details

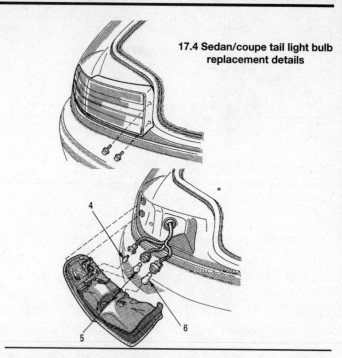

17.4 Sedan/coupe tail light bulb replacement details

5   On station wagon models, remove the screws and detach the light housing **(see illustration)**. Push in and rotate the bulbs counterclockwise to remove them from the holder.
6   Installation is the reverse of removal.

High-mounted brake light

Sedan/Coupe models

Refer to illustrations 17.7a and 17.7b

7   On earlier models, pry off the housing cover and replace the bulb by pulling it straight out **(see illustrations)**. On later models, pry off the

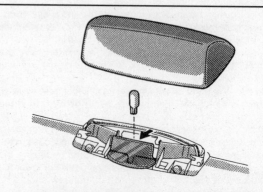

17.7a On 1993 and earlier model high-mounted brake lights, pry off the cover, then pull the bulb straight out of the holder

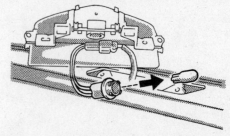

17.7b On 1994 and later models, pry off the high-mounted brake light cover, then remove the bolts and lift the housing out for access to the bulb

cover, remove the two bolts and lift the housing out and turn it over, then rotate bulb holder counterclockwise to remove it and pull the bulb straight out.

8   Installation is the reverse of removal.

Station wagon models

Refer to illustrations 17.9a and 17.9b

9   Pry out the clips and remove the housing cover **(see illustration)**. Rotate the bulb holder counterclockwise to remove it and pull the bulb straight out **(see illustration)**.

10   Installation is the reverse of removal.

Instrument cluster lights

Refer to illustration 17.12

11   To gain access to the instrument cluster illumination lights, the instrument cluster will have to be removed (see Section 19). The bulbs can then be removed and replaced from the rear of the cluster.

12   Rotate the bulb counterclockwise to remove it **(see illustration)**.

13   Installation is the reverse of removal.

License plate light

Refer to illustrations 17.14 and 17.15

14   On coupe and sedan models, remove the screws and pull out the lens, then remove the bulb by pulling it straight out **(see illustration)**.

15   On station wagon models, remove the screw and rotate the lens out, then rotate the bulb holder counterclockwise and withdraw it out for access to the bulb which pulls straight out **(see illustration)**.

16   Installation is the reverse of removal.

Interior lights

Refer to illustrations 17.18a, 17.18b and 17.18c

17   Pry the interior lens off.

18   Detach the bulb from the terminals. It may be necessary to pry the

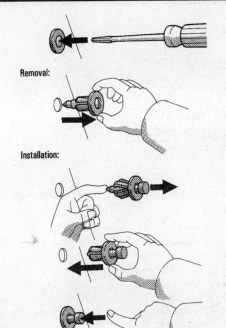

17.9a Station wagon high-mounted brake light cover clip retainer details

bulb out - if this is the case, pry only on the ends of the bulb (otherwise the glass may shatter **(see illustrations)**.

19   Installation is the reverse of removal.

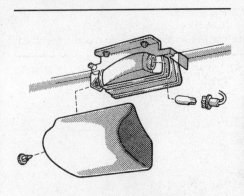

17.9b After removing the cover, pull out the holder and replace the bulb

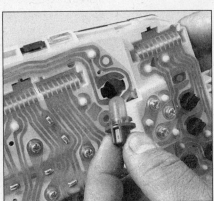

17.12 Rotate the instrument cluster bulb counterclockwise and lift it out

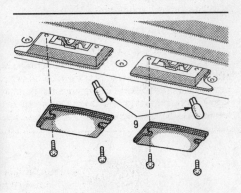

17.14 Sedan/coupe license plate bulb replacement details

17.15 Station wagon license plate light bulb replacement details

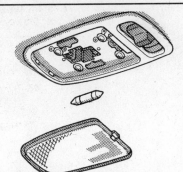

17.18a Interior light bulb replacement details

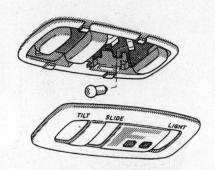

17.18b Personal light bulb replacement details

12

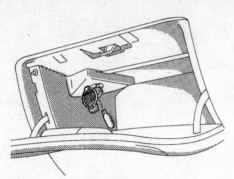

17.18c Glove compartment light bulb replacement details

18 Wiper motor - check and replacement

Refer to illustrations 18.3, 18.4 and 18.6
Warning: *These models are equipped with airbags. The airbag is armed and can deploy (inflate) anytime the battery is connected. To prevent accidental deployment (and possible injury), turn the ignition key to LOCK and disconnect the negative battery cable whenever working near airbag components. After the battery is disconnected, wait at least 90 seconds before beginning work (the system has a back-up capacitor that must fully discharge). For more information on the airbag system see Section 26.*
Caution: *If the stereo in your vehicle is equipped with an anti-theft system, make sure you have the correct activation code before disconnecting the battery.*

Note: *On 1993 and later models, the airbag system will be disabled if the battery is disconnected for more than a brief period. If the airbag light comes on and stays on after the battery is reconnected, the vehicle must be taken to a dealer to have the system reset with a special tool.*

Check

1   The windshield wiper motor is located on the right (passenger) side of the underhood compartment and the rear wiper motor is mounted in the liftgate on station wagon models. If a motor doesn't work or doesn't park properly and the switch checks out okay (see Section 8), the relay or the motor must be replaced.

Replacement

Windshield wiper motor
2   Disconnect the cable from the negative battery terminal.
3   Remove the wiper arms, weatherstrip and cowl louver assembly **(see illustration)**.
4   Disconnect the electrical connector, detach the wiper link from the motor shaft by prying it off with a screwdriver. Disconnect the electrical connector, remove the motor retaining bolts, then lower the wiper motor and remove it from the vehicle **(see illustration)**.
5   Installation is the reverse of removal.

Rear wiper motor
6   Remove the wiper arm from the motor **(see illustration)**
7   Open the liftgate and remove the trim panel (Chapter 11).
8   Use a screwdriver to detach the wiper link from the arm pivot.
9   Disconnect the electrical connector, remove the retaining bolts and lower the motor and link through the liftgate access hole as an assembly.
10   Installation is the reverse of removal.

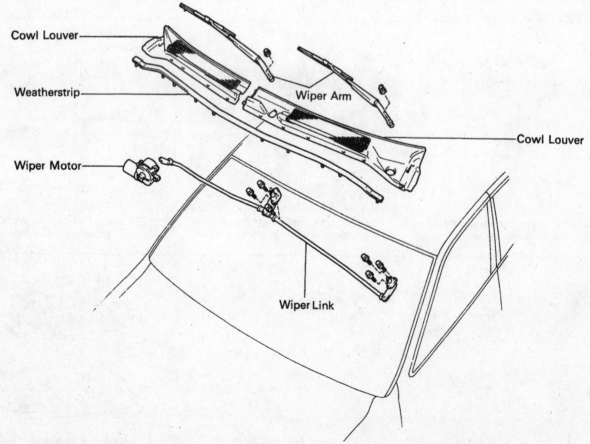

18.3 Remove the wiper arms and cowl louver for access to the wiper motor-to-arm link connection

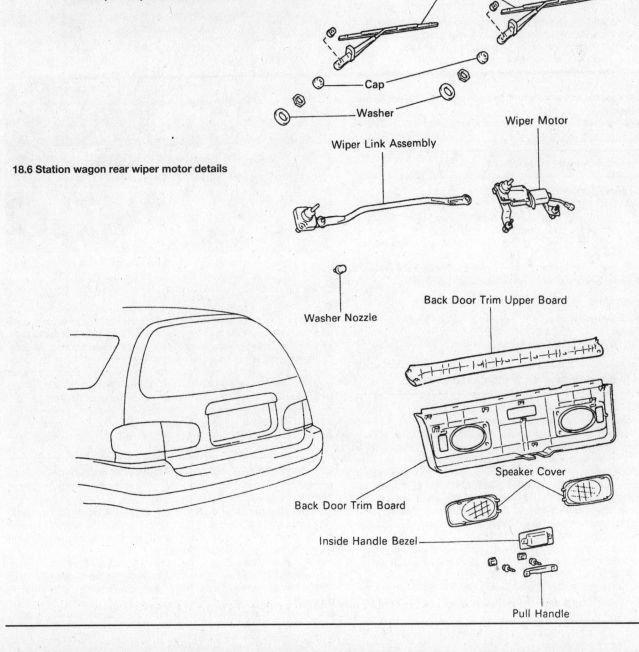

18.4 Disconnect the wiper motor connector (A), then remove the bolts (arrows) and detach the motor

19   Instrument cluster - removal and installation

Refer to illustrations 19.3 and 19.4

Warning: *These models are equipped with airbags. The airbag is armed and can deploy (inflate) anytime the battery is connected. To prevent accidental deployment (and possible injury), turn the ignition key to LOCK and disconnect the negative battery cable whenever working near airbag components. After the battery is disconnected, wait at least 90 seconds before beginning work (the system has a back-up capacitor that must fully discharge). For more information on the airbag system see Section 26.*

Caution: *If the stereo in your vehicle is equipped with an anti-theft system, make sure you have the correct activation code before disconnecting the battery.*

Note: *On 1993 and later models, the airbag system will be disabled if the battery is disconnected for more than a brief period. If the airbag light*

18.6 Station wagon rear wiper motor details

Wiper Arm

Cap

Washer

Wiper Link Assembly

Wiper Motor

Washer Nozzle

Back Door Trim Upper Board

Speaker Cover

Back Door Trim Board

Inside Handle Bezel

Pull Handle

12

19.3 Remove the instrument cluster screws (arrows)

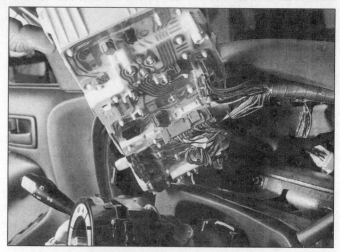

19.4 Rotate the cluster away and disconnect the electrical connectors

comes on and stays on after the battery is reconnected, the vehicle must be taken to a dealer to have the system reset with a special tool.

1   Disconnect the cable from the negative battery terminal.
2   Remove the instrument cluster bezel (see Chapter 11).
3   Remove the retaining screws and pull the cluster out **(see illustration)**.
4   Disconnect the connectors from the rear of the instrument cluster **(see illustration)**.
5   Installation is the reverse of the removal procedure.

20 Horn - check and replacement

Refer to illustration 20.4

Check

1   Disconnect the electrical connector from the horn.
2   Test the horn by connecting battery voltage to the two terminals with a pair of jumper wires.
3   If the horn doesn't sound, replace it. If it does sound, the problem lies in the switch, relay or the wiring between components.

Replacement

4   Disconnect the electrical connector and remove the bracket bolt **(see illustration)**.
5   Installation is the reverse of removal.

21 Cruise control system - description and check

Refer to illustrations 21.1 and 21.5

1   The cruise control system maintains vehicle speed with an actuator/servo motor located near the battery in the engine compartment. The actuator is connected to the throttle linkage by a cable or rod. Besides the actuator, the system consists of the brake switch, clutch switch, control switches, a relay and associated wiring and vacuum hoses **(see illustration)**. Some features of the system requires special testers and diagnostic procedures which are beyond the scope of the home mechanic. Listed below are some general procedures that may be used to locate common problems.
2   Locate and check the fuse (see Section 3).
3   Have an assistant operate the brake lights while you check their operation (voltage from the brake light and (if equipped) clutch switch deactivates the cruise control).
4   If the brake lights don't come on or don't shut off, correct the problem and retest the cruise control. Check the clutch switch (Chapter 8).

20.4 Disconnect the electrical connector and remove the bolts (arrows) and detach the horn

5   Visually inspect the vacuum hose (if equipped) connected to the servo and check the control linkage between the cruise control servo and the throttle linkage and replace as necessary **(see illustration)**.
6   Cruise control systems use a variety of speed sensing devices. On these models the speed sensor pickup is located in the transaxle. Remove the bolt and detach the sensor, rotate the sensor and check it with a digital voltmeter while it's rotating (see Chapter 7B). If the resistance doesn't vary as the cable rotates, the sensor is defective.
7   Test drive the vehicle to determine if the cruise control is now working. If it isn't, take it to a dealer service department or an automotive electrical specialist for further diagnosis and repair.

22 Power window system - description and check

Refer to illustrations 22.1, 22.7 and 22.10

1   The power window system operates the electric motors mounted in the doors which lower and raise the windows. The system consists of the control switches, the motors (regulators), glass mechanisms and associated wiring **(see illustration)**.
2   Power windows are wired so they can be lowered and raised from the master control switch by the driver or by remote switches located at the individual windows. Each window has a separate motor which is reversible. The position of the control switch determines the polarity and therefore the direction of operation. Some systems are equipped

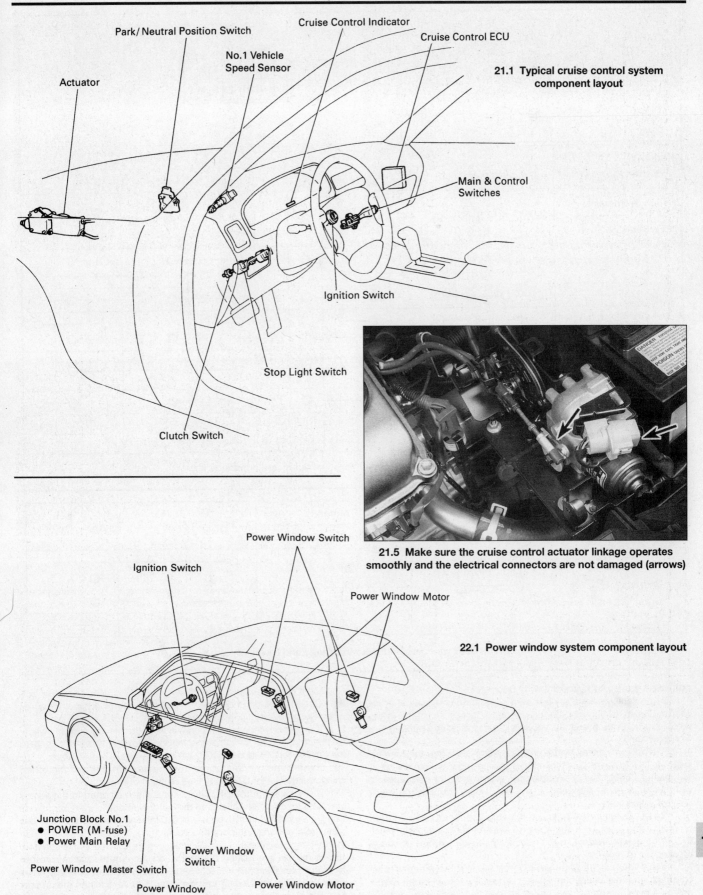

Actuator

Park/Neutral Position Switch

No.1 Vehicle Speed Sensor

Cruise Control Indicator

Cruise Control ECU

21.1 Typical cruise control system component layout

Main & Control Switches

Ignition Switch

Stop Light Switch

Clutch Switch

21.5 Make sure the cruise control actuator linkage operates smoothly and the electrical connectors are not damaged (arrows)

Power Window Switch

Power Window Motor

Ignition Switch

22.1 Power window system component layout

Junction Block No.1
● POWER (M-fuse)
● Power Main Relay

Power Window Master Switch

Power Window Switch

Power Window Motor

Power Window Motor

12

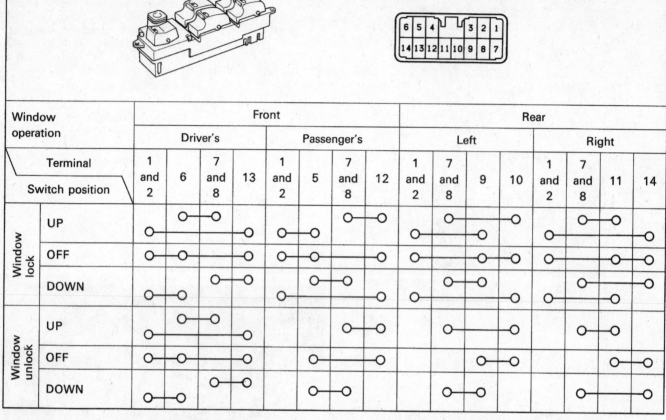

22.7 Power window master switch terminal guide and continuity chart

Window operation		Front								Rear							
		Driver's				Passenger's				Left				Right			
Terminal		1 and 2	6	7 and 8	13	1 and 2	5	7 and 8	12	1 and 2	7 and 8	9	10	1 and 2	7 and 8	11	14
Switch position																	
Window lock	UP																
	OFF																
	DOWN																
Window unlock	UP																
	OFF																
	DOWN																

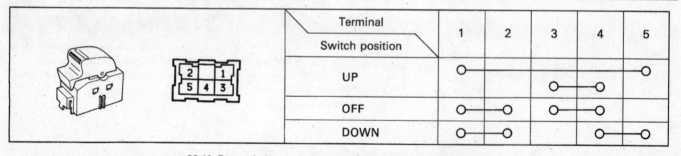

Terminal Switch position	1	2	3	4	5
UP					
OFF					
DOWN					

22.10 Door window switch terminal guide and continuity chart

with relays that control current flow to the motors.

3   Some vehicles are equipped with a separate circuit breaker for each motor in addition to the fuse or circuit breaker protecting the whole circuit. This prevents one stuck window from disabling the whole system.

4   The power window system will only operate when the ignition switch is ON. In addition, when activated the window lockout switch at the master control switch disables the switches at the passenger's window also. Always check these items before troubleshooting a window problem.

5   These procedures are general in nature, so if you can't find the problem using them, take the vehicle to a dealer service department.

6   If the power windows don't work at all, check the fuse or circuit breaker.

7   If only the rear windows are inoperative, or if the windows only operate from the master control switch, check the rear window lockout switch for continuity in the unlocked position **(see illustration)**.

Replace it if it doesn't have continuity.

8   Check the wiring between the switches and fuse panel for continuity. Repair the wiring, if necessary.

9   If only one window is inoperative from the master control switch, try the other control switch at the window. **Note:** *This doesn't apply to the drivers door window.*

10   If the same window works from one switch, but not the other, check the switch for continuity **(see illustration)**.

11   If the switch tests OK, check for a short or open in the wiring between the affected switch and the window motor.

12   If one window is inoperative from both switches, remove the trim panel from the affected door and check for voltage at the motor while the switch is operated.

13   If voltage is reaching the motor, disconnect the glass from the regulator (see Chapter 11). Move the window up and down by hand while checking for binding and damage. Also check for binding and damage to the regulator. If the regulator is not damaged and the

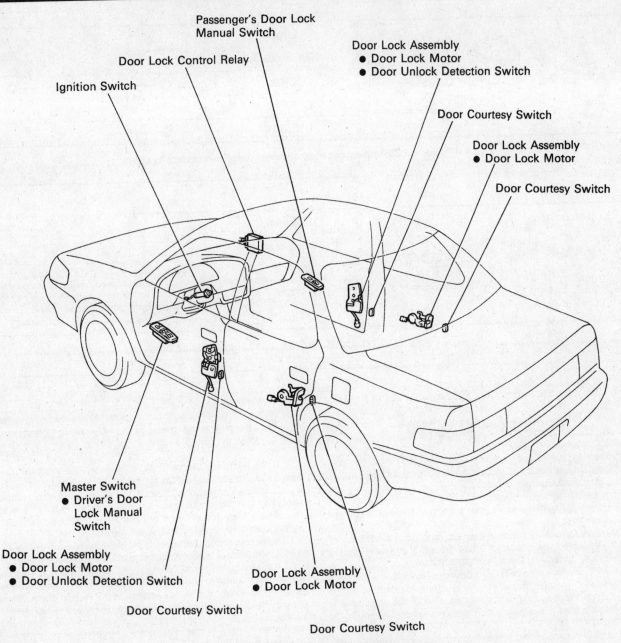

Passenger's Door Lock
Manual Switch

Door Lock Control Relay

Ignition Switch

Door Lock Assembly
● Door Lock Motor
● Door Unlock Detection Switch

Door Courtesy Switch

Door Lock Assembly
● Door Lock Motor

Door Courtesy Switch

Master Switch
● Driver's Door
Lock Manual
Switch

Door Lock Assembly
● Door Lock Motor
● Door Unlock Detection Switch

Door Courtesy Switch

Door Lock Assembly
● Door Lock Motor

Door Courtesy Switch

23.1 Power door lock system component layout

window moves up and down smoothly, replace the motor. If there's binding or damage, lubricate, repair or replace parts, as necessary.

14 If voltage isn't reaching the motor, check the wiring in the circuit for continuity between the switches and motors. You'll need to consult the wiring diagram for the vehicle. Some power window circuits are equipped with relays. If equipped, check that the relays are grounded properly and receiving voltage from the switches. Also check that each relay sends voltage to the motor when the switch is turned on. If it doesn't, replace the relay.

15 Test the windows after you are done to confirm proper repairs.

23 Power door lock system - description and check

Refer to illustrations 23.1, 23.7a and 23.7b

1 The power door lock system operates the door lock actuators mounted in each door. The system consists of the switches, actuators and associated wiring **(see illustration)**. Diagnosis can usually be limited to simple checks of the wiring connections and actuators for minor faults which can be easily repaired.

2 Power door lock systems are operated by bi-directional solenoids located in the doors. The lock switches have two operating positions: Lock and Unlock. These switches activate a relay which in turn connects voltage to the door lock solenoids. Depending on which way the relay is activated, it reverses polarity, allowing the two sides of the circuit to be used alternately as the feed (positive) and ground side.

3 Some vehicles may have anti-theft systems incorporated into the power locks. If you are unable to locate the trouble using the following general steps, consult your a dealer service department. **Note:** *Some models may also have control switches connected to the key locks in the doors which unlock all the doors when one is unlocked.*

4 Always check the circuit protection first. Some vehicles use a combination of circuit breakers and fuses.

5 Operate the door lock switches in both directions (Lock and

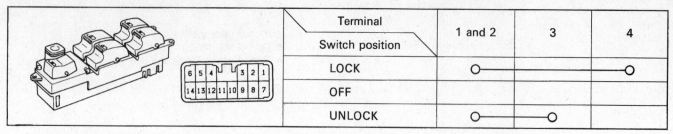

Terminal Switch position	1 and 2	3	4
LOCK	O————————————O		
OFF			
UNLOCK	O————————O		

23.7a   Power door lock master switch terminal guide and continuity chart

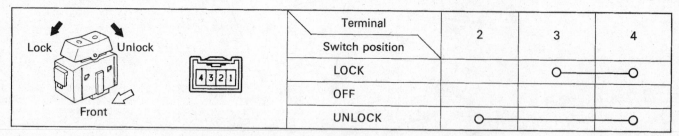

Terminal Switch position	2	3	4
LOCK		O————————O	
OFF			
UNLOCK	O————————————O		

23.7b   Power door lock switch terminal guide and continuity chart

Unlock) with the engine off. Listen for the faint click of the relay operating.

6   If there's no click, check for voltage at the switches. If no voltage is present, check the wiring between the fuse panel and the switches for shorts and opens.

7   If voltage is present but no click is heard, test the switch for continuity. Replace the switch if there's no continuity in both switch positions **(see illustrations)**.

8   If the switch has continuity but the relay doesn't click, check the wiring between the switch and relay for continuity. Repair the wiring if there's no continuity.

9   If the relay is receiving voltage from the switch but is not sending voltage to the solenoids, check for a bad ground at the relay case. If the relay case is grounding properly, replace the relay.

10   If all but one lock solenoids operate, remove the trim panel from the affected door (see Chapter 11). and check for voltage at the solenoid while the lock switch is operated. One of the wires should have voltage in the Lock position; the other should have voltage in the unlock position.

11   If the inoperative solenoid is receiving voltage, replace the solenoid.

12   If the inoperative solenoid isn't receiving voltage, check for an open or short in the wire between the lock solenoid and the relay.

Note: *It's common for wires to break in the portion of the harness between the body and door (opening and closing the door fatigues and eventually breaks the wires).*

24   Power seats - description and check

1   Power seats allow you to adjust the position of the seat with little effort. These models feature a six-way seat that goes forward and backward, up and down and tilts forward and backward.

2   The seats are powered by three reversible motors mounted in one housing that are controlled by switches on the side of the seat. Each switch changes the direction of seat travel by reversing polarity to the drive motor.

3   Diagnosis is a simple matter, using the following procedures.

4   Look under the seat for any object which may be preventing the

seat from moving.

5   If the seat won't work at all, check the fuse or circuit breaker.

6   With the engine off to reduce the noise level, operate the seat controls in all directions and listen for sound coming from the seat motors.

7   If the seat won't work at all, check the fuse or circuit breaker. **Note:** *The ignition must be ON for the power seats to work.*

8   If the motor runs or clicks but the seat doesn't move, check the seat drive mechanism for wear or damage and correct as necessary.

9   If the motor doesn't work or make noise, check for voltage at the motor while an assistant operates the switch.

10   If the motor is getting voltage but doesn't run, test it off the vehicle with jumper wires. If it still doesn't work, replace it.

11   If the motor isn't getting voltage, check for voltage at the switch. If there's no voltage at the switch, check the wiring between the fuse panel and the switch. If there's voltage at the switch, check the switch for continuity in all its operating positions. Replace the switch if there's no continuity.

12   If the switch is OK, check for a short or open in the wiring between the switch and motor. If there's a relay between the switch and motor, check that it's grounded properly and there's voltage to the relay. Also check that there's voltage going from the relay to the motor when the when the switch is operated. If there's not, and the relay is grounded properly, replace the relay.

13   Test the completed repairs.

25   Electric rear view mirrors - description and check

Refer to illustrations 25.1, 25.7a, 25.7b and 25.7c

1   The electric rear view mirrors use two motors to move the glass; one for up and down adjustments and one for left-right adjustments **(see illustration)**.

2   The control switch has a selector portion which sends voltage to the left or right side mirror. With the ignition key in the ACC position, roll down the windows and operate the mirror control switch through all functions (left-right and up-down) for both the left and right side mirrors.

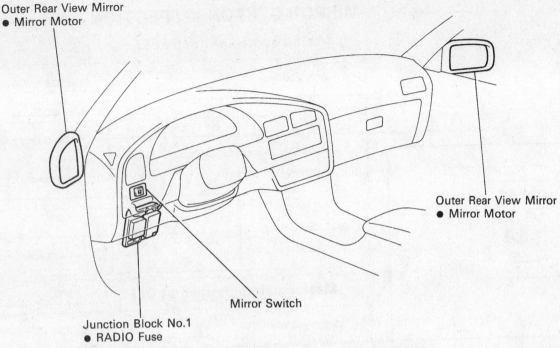

Outer Rear View Mirror
● Mirror Motor

Outer Rear View Mirror
● Mirror Motor

Mirror Switch

Junction Block No.1
● RADIO Fuse

25.1 Electric mirror system component layout

**25.7a Press in on the clips and push the mirror switch
out of the cluster bezel**

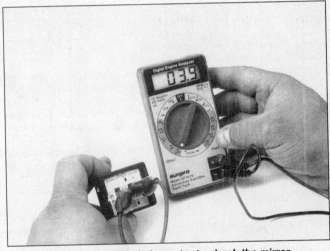

**25.7b Use a digital ohmmeter to check the mirror
switch for continuity**

3   Listen carefully for the sound of the electric motors running in the mirrors.
4   If the motors can be heard but the mirror glass doesn't move, there's probably a problem with the drive mechanism inside the mirror. Remove and disassemble the mirror to locate the problem.
5   If the mirrors don't operate and no sound comes from the mirrors, check the Radio fuse in the fuse block located under the left side of the dash (see Section 3).
6   If the fuse is OK, remove the instrument cluster bezel (see Chapter 11) for access to the back of the mirror control switch without disconnecting the wires attached to it. Turn the ignition ON and check for voltage at the switch. There should be voltage at one terminal. If there's no voltage at the switch, check for an open or short in the wiring between the fuse panel and the switch.
7   If there's voltage at the switch, disconnect it. Check the switch for

continuity in all its operating positions **(see illustrations)**. If the switch does not have continuity, replace it.
8   Re-connect the switch. Locate the wire going from the switch to ground. Leaving the switch connected, connect a jumper wire between this wire and ground. If the mirror works normally with this wire in place, repair the faulty ground connection.
9   If the mirror still doesn't work, remove the mirror and check the wires at the mirror for voltage. Check with ignition ON and the mirror selector switch on the appropriate side. Operate the mirror switch in all its positions. There should be voltage at one of the switch-to-mirror wires in each switch position (except the neutral "off" position).
10   If there's no voltage in each switch position, check the wiring between the mirror and control switch for opens and shorts.
11   If there's voltage, remove the mirror and test it off the vehicle with jumper wires. Replace the mirror if it fails this test.

1

MIRROR SWITCH INSPECTION

Master switch position at L:

Switch position	Tester connection to terminal number	Specified condition
OFF	—	No continuity
UP	2 — 5 6 — 8	Continuity
DOWN	2 — 6 5 — 8	Continuity
LEFT	1 — 8 2 — 5	Continuity
RIGHT	1 — 2 5 — 8	Continuity

Master switch position at OFF:

Switch position	Tester connection to terminal number	Specified condition
OFF	—	No continuity
UP	2 — 5	Continuity
DOWN	5 — 8	Continuity
LEFT	2 — 5	Continuity
RIGHT	5 — 8	Continuity

Master switch position at R:

Switch position	Tester connection to terminal number	Specified condition
OFF	—	No continuity
UP	2 — 5 3 — 8	Continuity
DOWN	2 — 3 5 — 8	Continuity
LEFT	2 — 5 7 — 8	Continuity
RIGHT	2 — 7 5 — 8	Continuity

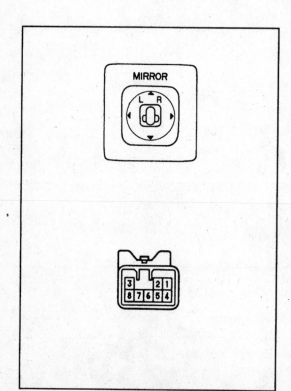

25.7c Power mirror switch terminal guide and continuity chart

26 Airbag - general information

Refer to illustration 26.1

Later models are equipped with a Supplemental Restraint System (SRS), more commonly known as an airbag. This system is designed to protect the driver from serious injury in the event of a head-on or frontal collision. It consists of an airbag module in the center of the steering wheel, two crash sensors mounted at the front of the vehicle and a diagnostic module which also contains a crash sensor located inside the passenger compartment **(see illustration)**.

Airbag module

The airbag module contains a housing incorporating the cushion (airbag) and inflator unit. The inflator assembly is mounted on the back of the housing over a hole through which gas is expelled, inflating the bag almost instantaneously when an electrical signal is sent from the system. The specially wound wire that carries this signal to the module is called a spiral cable **(see illustration 26.1)**. The spiral cable is a flat, ribbon-like electrically conductive tape which is wound many times so that it can transmit an electrical signal regardless of steering wheel position.

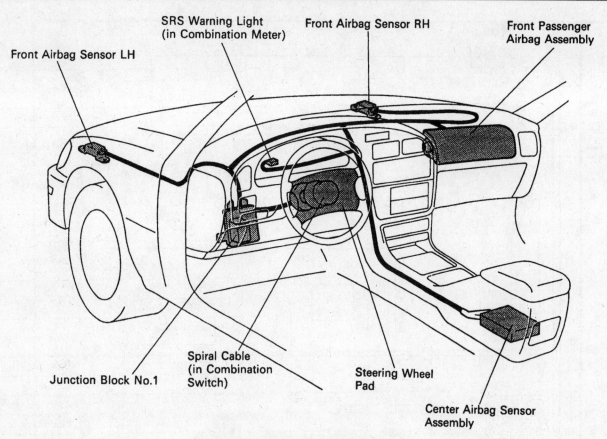

Front Airbag Sensor LH

SRS Warning Light
(in Combination Meter)

Front Airbag Sensor RH

Front Passenger
Airbag Assembly

Junction Block No.1

Spiral Cable
(in Combination
Switch)

Steering Wheel
Pad

Center Airbag Sensor
Assembly

26.1 Airbag system component layout

Sensors

The system has three sensors: two crash sensors at the front of the vehicle behind the bumper and above the wheel arches and a "safing" sensor in the center airbag sensor assembly located in the center console.

The front crash sensors are basically pressure sensitive switches that complete an electrical circuit during an impact of sufficient G force. The electrical signal from the crash sensors is sent to the safing sensor in the center airbag sensor assembly, which then completes the circuit and inflates the airbag.

Center Airbag Sensor Assembly (CASA)

The CASA contains the safing sensor and an on-board microprocessor which monitors the operation of the system. It checks this system every time the vehicle is started, causing the "AIRBAG" light to go on **(see illustration 26.1)**, then off, if the system is operating properly. If there is a fault in the system, the light will go on and stay on and the CASA will store fault codes indicating the nature of the fault. If the AIRBAG light goes on and stays on, the vehicle should be taken to your dealer immediately for service.

27   Wiring diagrams - general information

Refer to illustration 27.4

Since it isn't possible to include all wiring diagrams for every year covered by this manual, the following diagrams are those that are typical and most commonly needed.

Wire colors are indicated by an alphabetical code.

B	= Black	L	= Blue	R	= Red
BR	= Brown	LG	= Light Green	V	= Violet
G	= Green	O	= Orange	W	= White
GR	= Gray	P	= Pink	Y	= Yellow

The first letter indicates the basic wire color and the second letter indicates the color of the stripe.

Example: L—Y

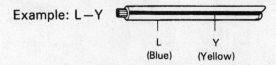

L
(Blue)

Y
(Yellow)

27.4 Wiring diagram color code chart

Prior to troubleshooting any circuits, check the fuse and circuit breakers (if equipped) to make sure they are in good condition. Make sure the battery is properly charged and has clean, tight cable connections (see Chapter 1).

When checking the wiring system, make sure that all electrical connectors are clean, with no broken or loose pins. When disconnecting an electrical connector, do not pull on the wires, only on the connector housings themselves.

Refer to the **accompanying illustration** for the wire color codes applicable to your vehicle.-

12

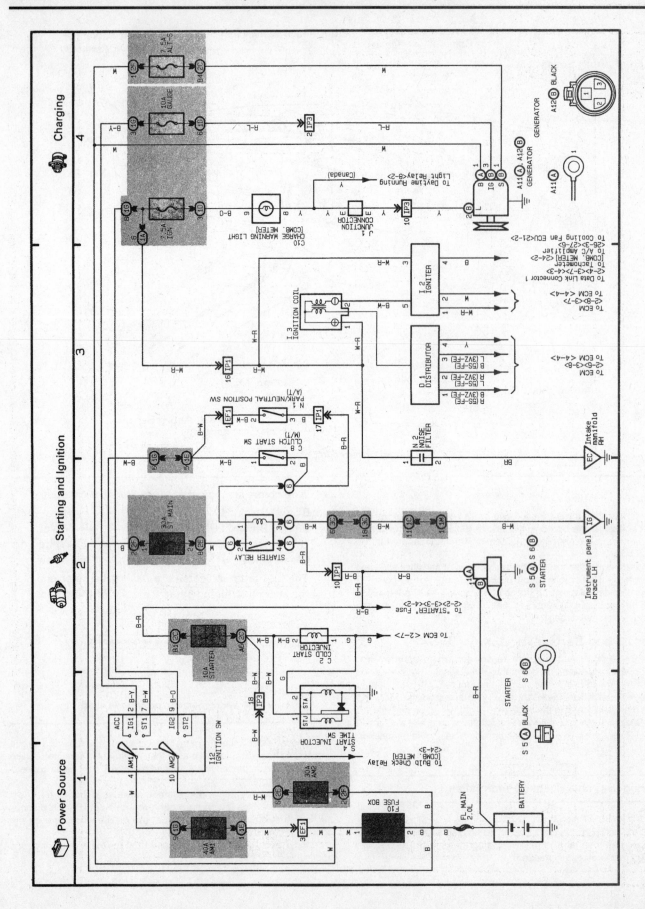

Typical starting and charging system wiring diagram (1993 and earlier models)

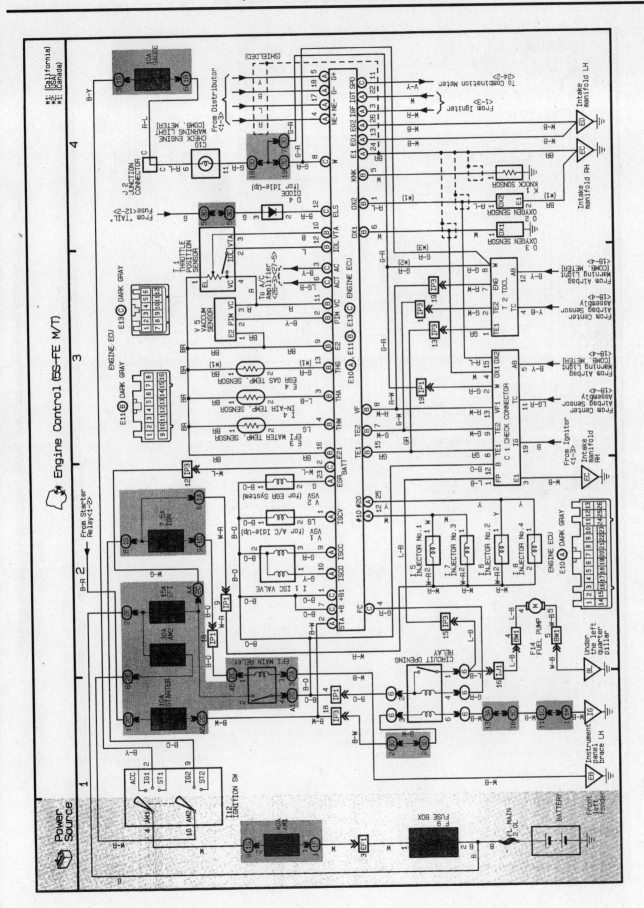

Typical 5S-FE four-cylinder engine control system wiring diagram (1993 and earlier models)

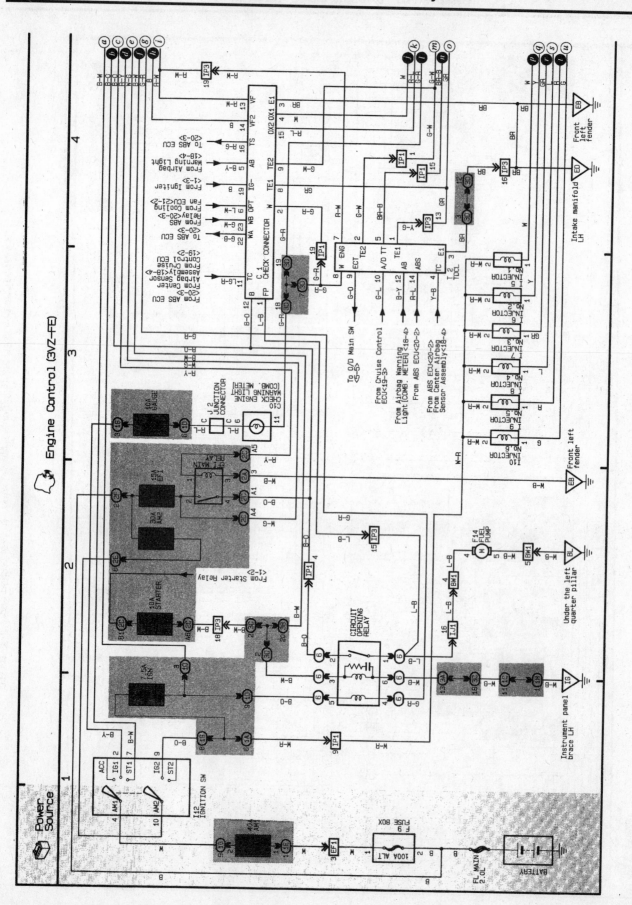

Typical 3VZ-FE V6 engine control system wiring diagram (1993 and earlier models) (1 of 2)

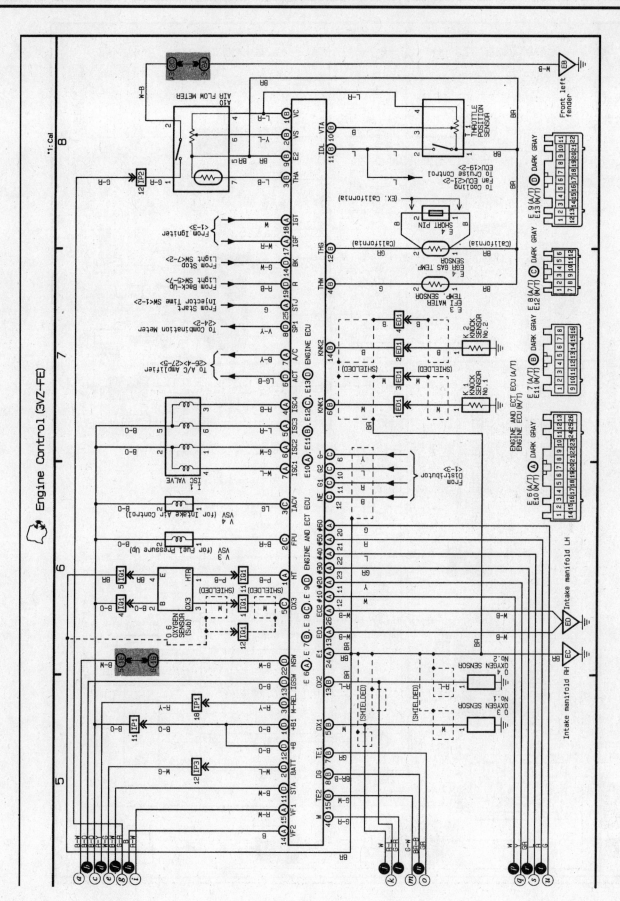

Typical 3VZ-FE V6 engine control system wiring diagram (1993 and earlier models) (2 of 2)

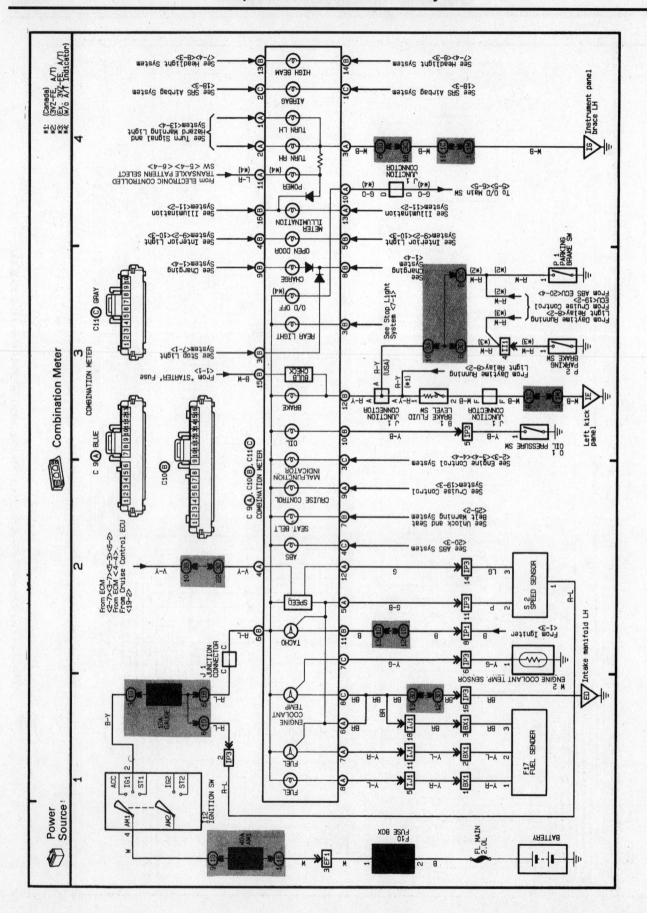

Typical instrument cluster (combination meter) wiring diagram (1993 and earlier models)

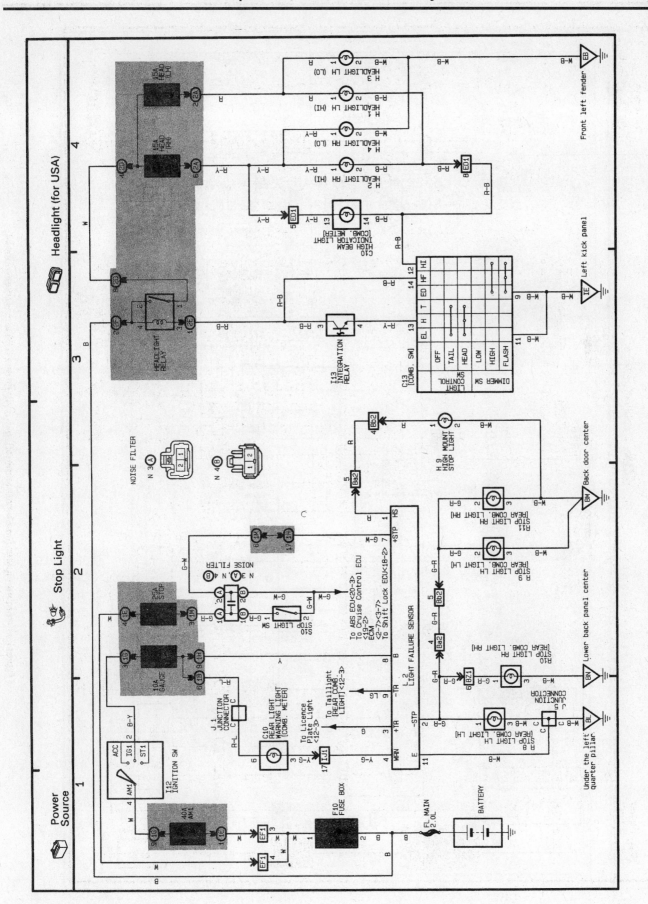

Typical stoplight and headlight system wiring diagram (1993 and earlier U.S. models)

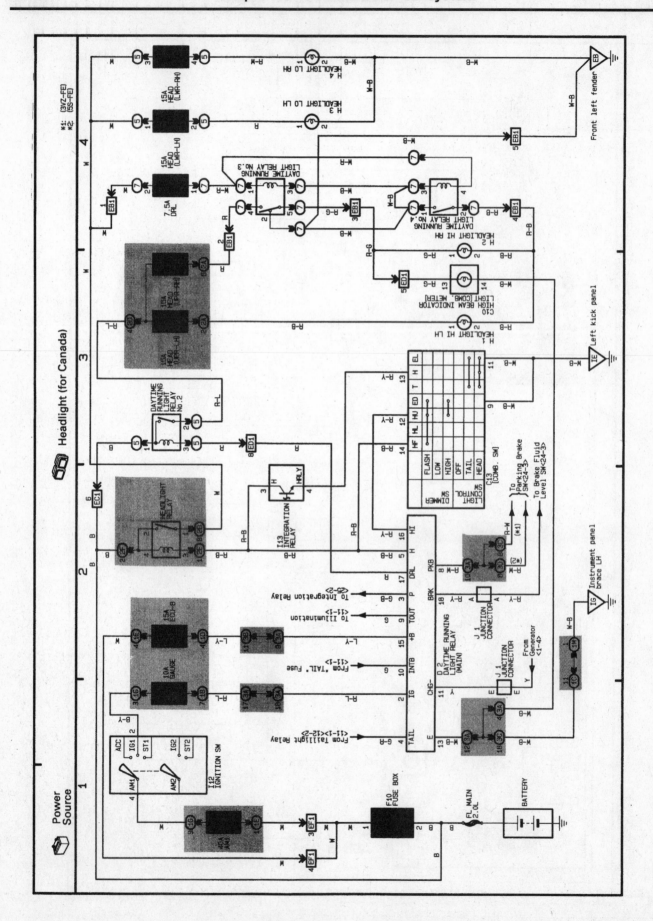

Typical stoplight and headlight system wiring diagram (1993 and earlier Canadian models)

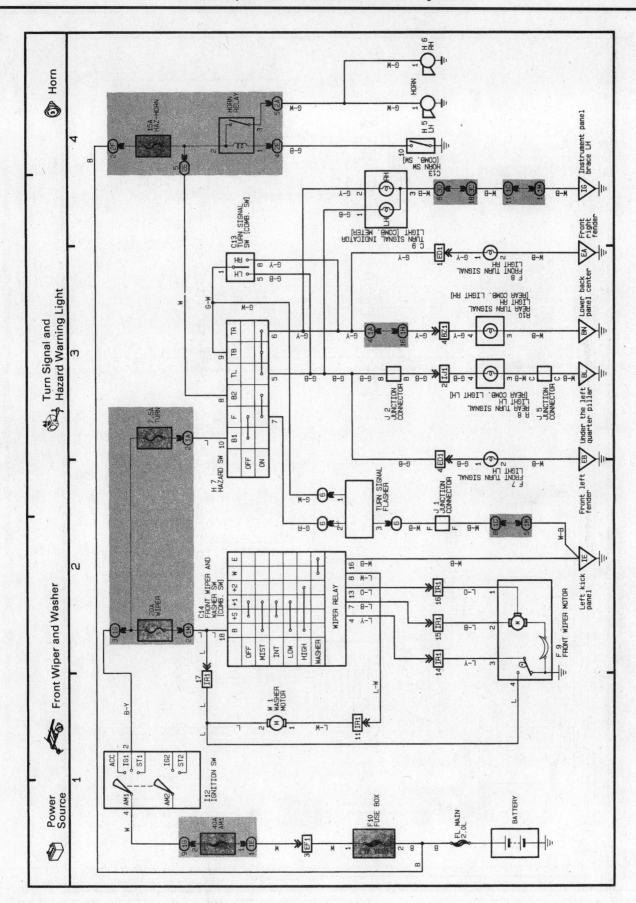

Typical front wiper/washer, turn signal/hazard warning light system wiring diagram (1993 and earlier models)

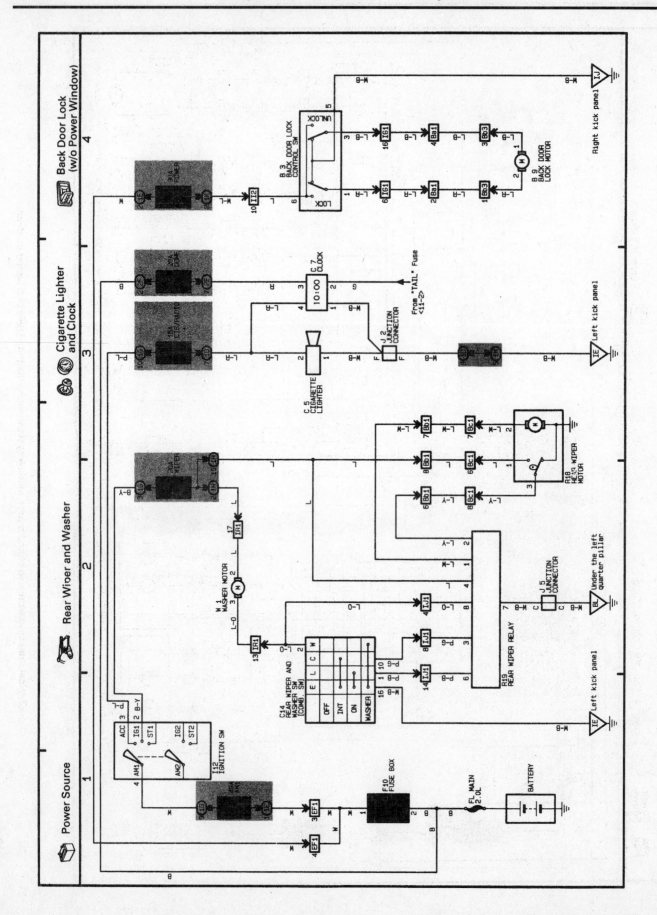

Typical rear wiper/washer, cigarette lighter/clock and rear door lock system wiring diagram (1993 and earlier models)

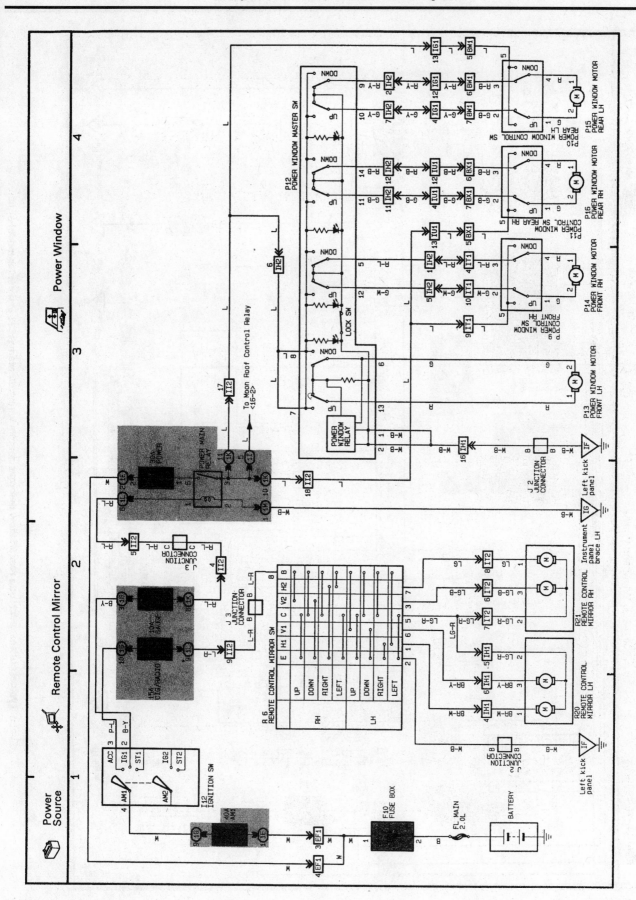

Typical remote control mirror and power window system wiring diagram (1993 and earlier models)

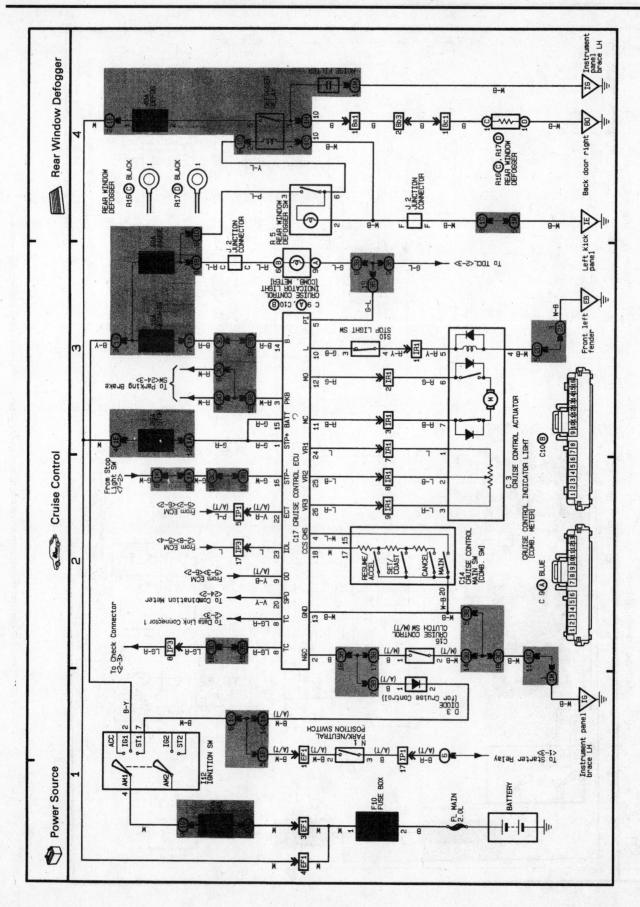

Typical cruise control and rear window defogger system wiring diagram (1993 and earlier models)

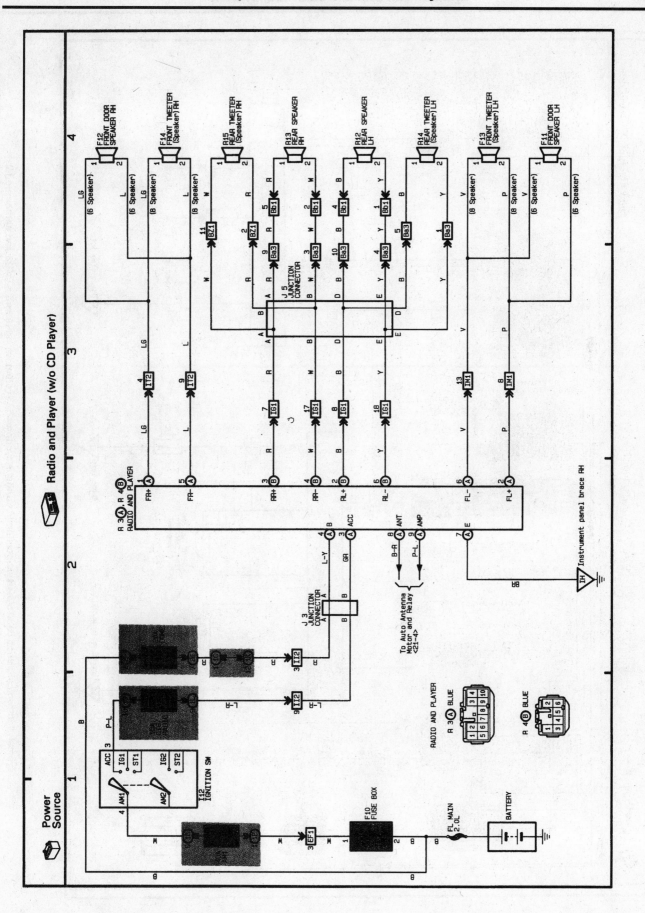

Typical radio and speaker system wiring diagram (1993 and earlier models)

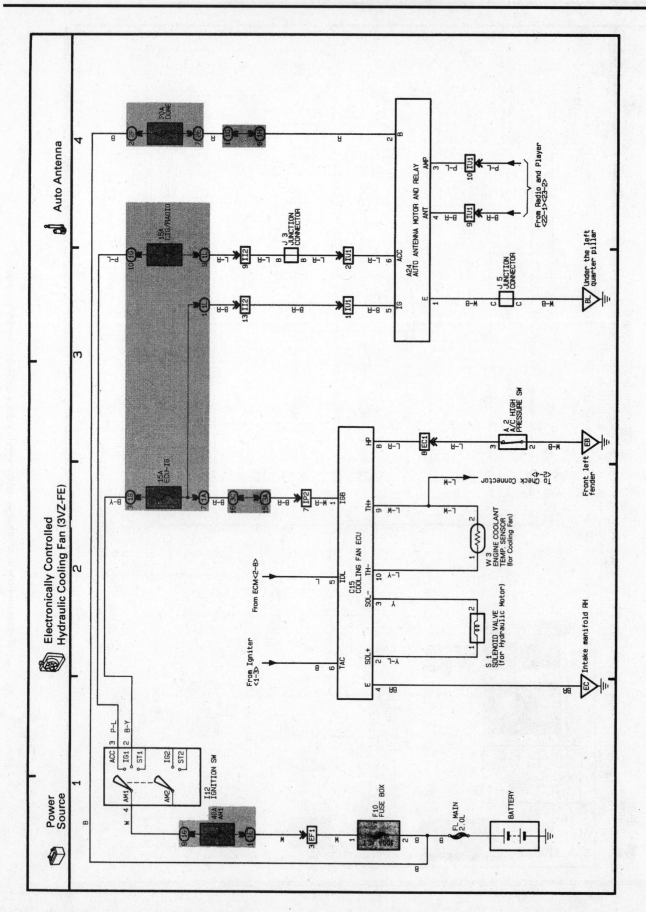

Typical electronically controlled hydraulic cooling fan and power antenna system wiring diagram (1993 and earlier models)

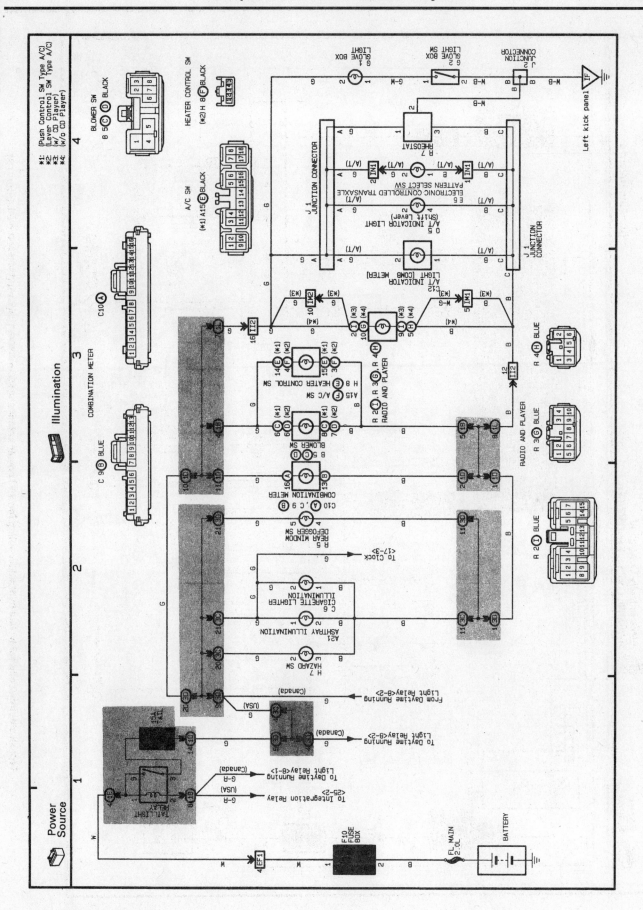

Typical instrument panel lighting system wiring diagram (1993 and earlier models)

12

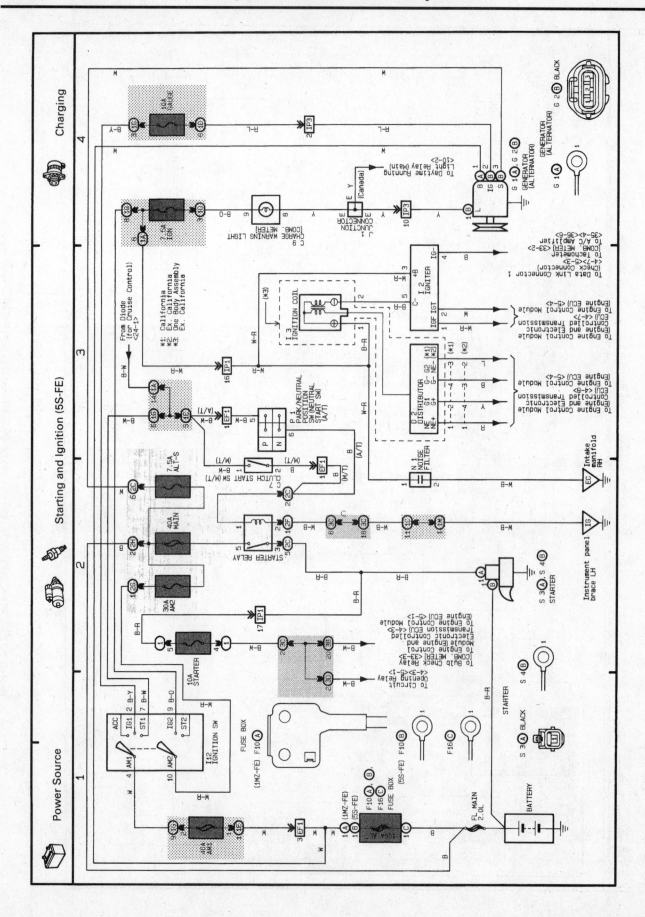

Typical 5S-FE four-cylinder engine starting and charging system wiring diagram (1994 and later models)

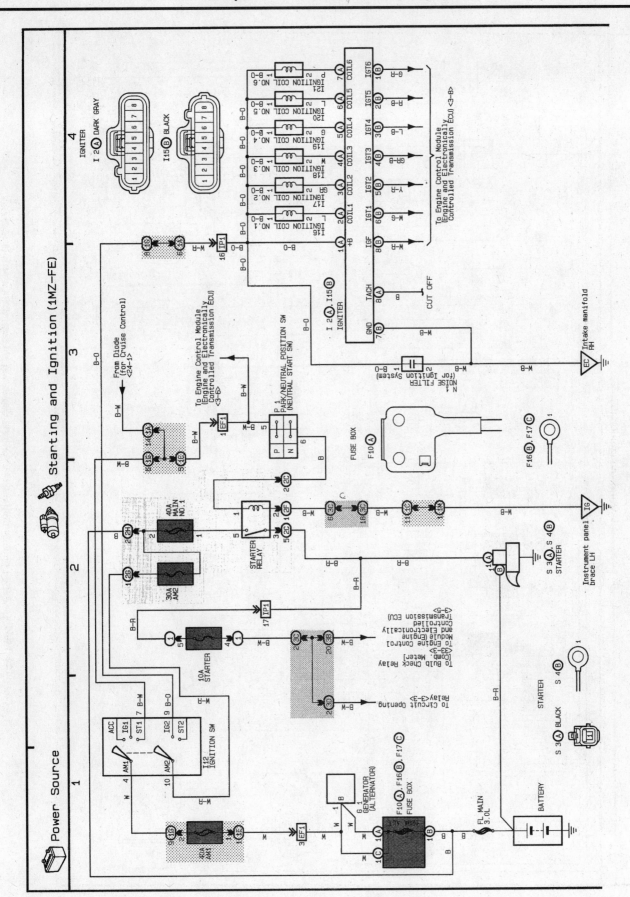

Typical 1MZ-FE V6 engine starting and charging system wiring diagram (1994 and later models)

12

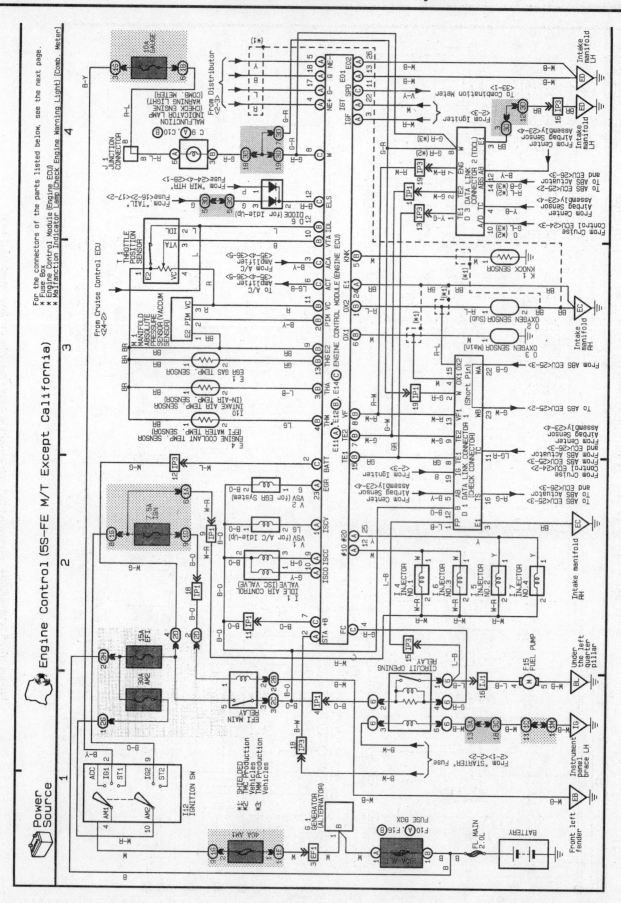

Typical 5S-FE four-cylinder engine control system wiring diagram (1994 and later models) (1 of 2)

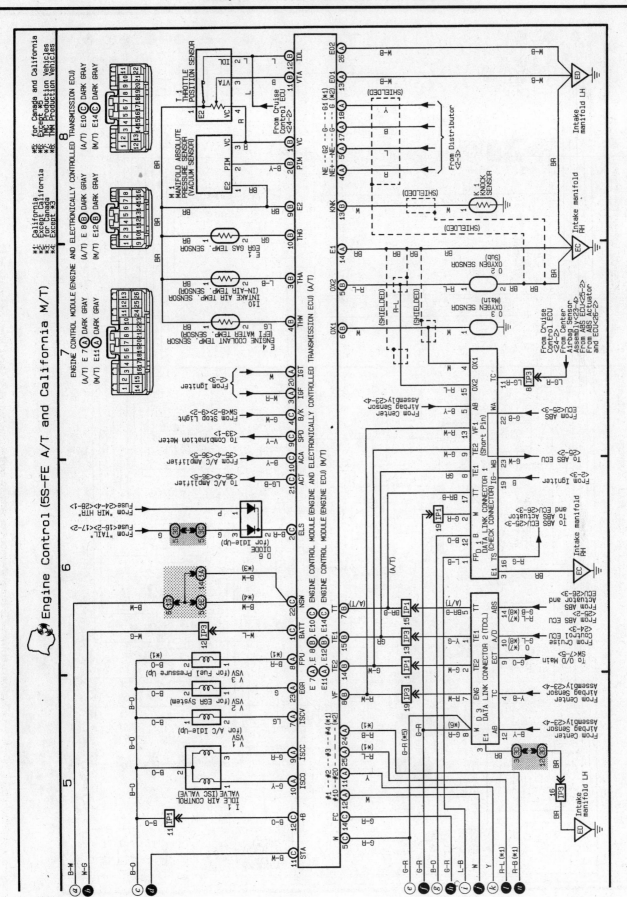

Typical 5S-FE four-cylinder engine control system wiring diagram (1994 and later models) (2 of 2)

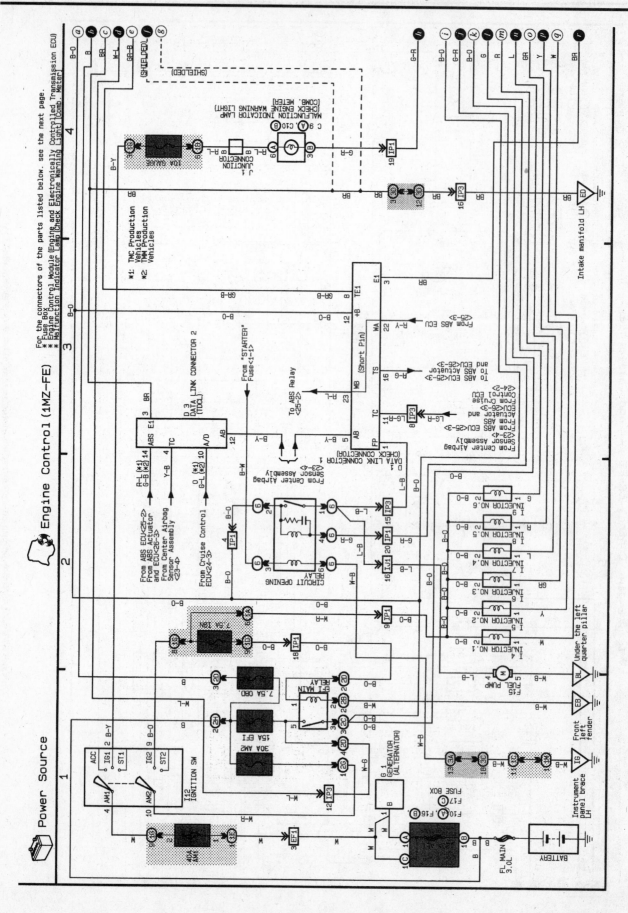

Typical 1MZ-FE V6 engine control system wiring diagram (1994 and later models) (1 of 2)

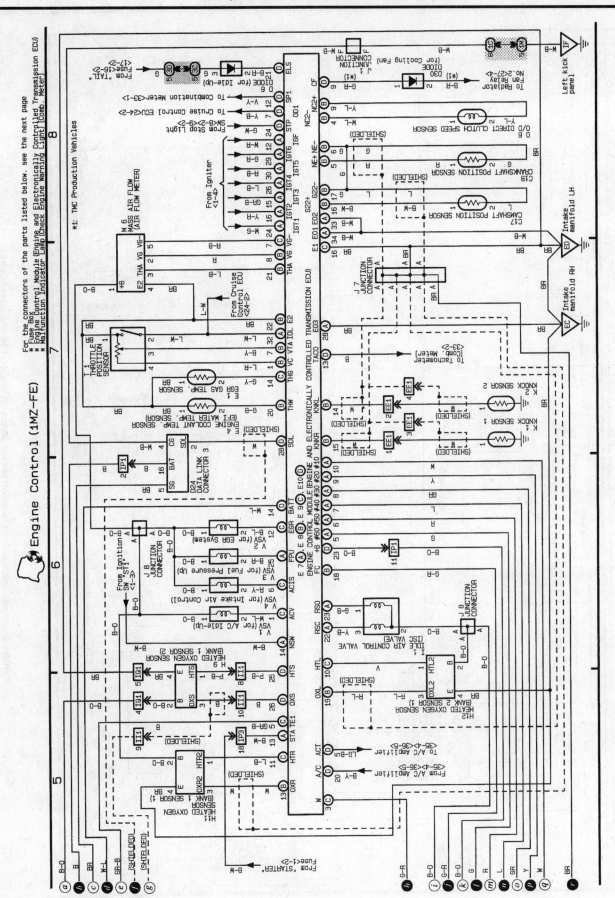

Typical 1MZ-FE V6 engine control system wiring diagram (1994 and later models) (2 of 2)

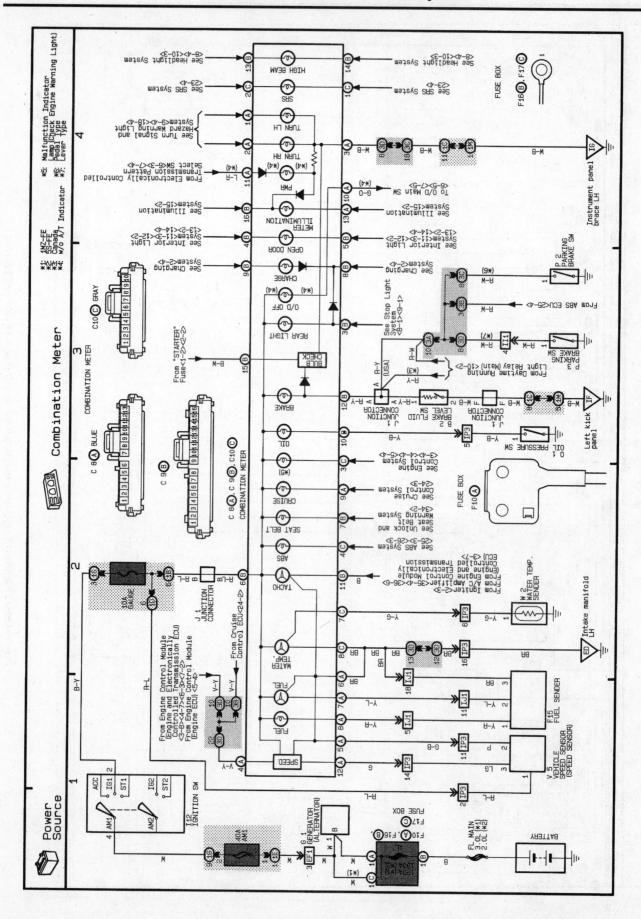

Typical instrument cluster (combination meter) wiring diagram (1994 and later models)

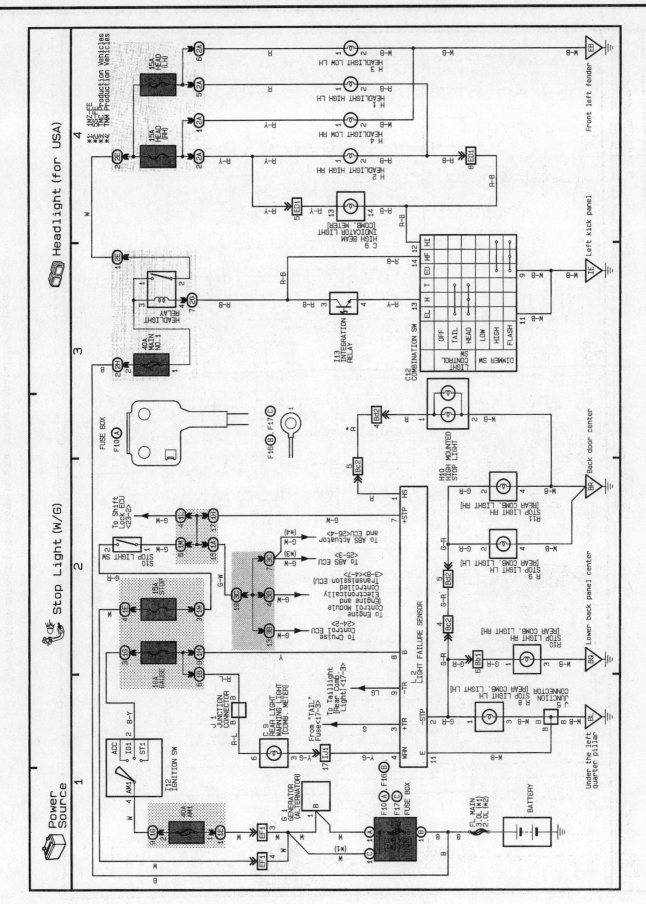

Typical stoplight and U.S. model headlight system wiring diagram (1994 and later)

12

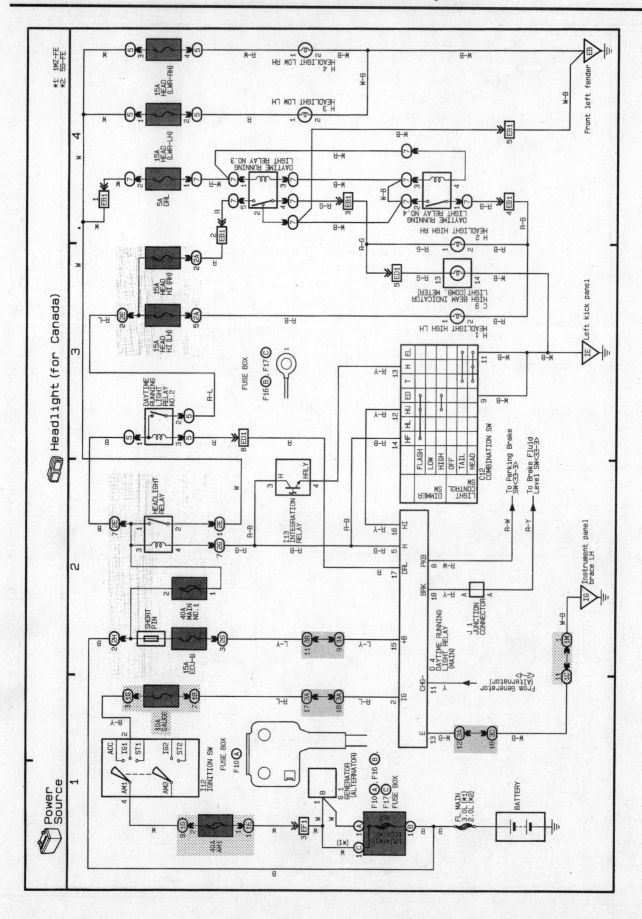

Typical headlight system wiring diagram (1994 and later Canadian models)

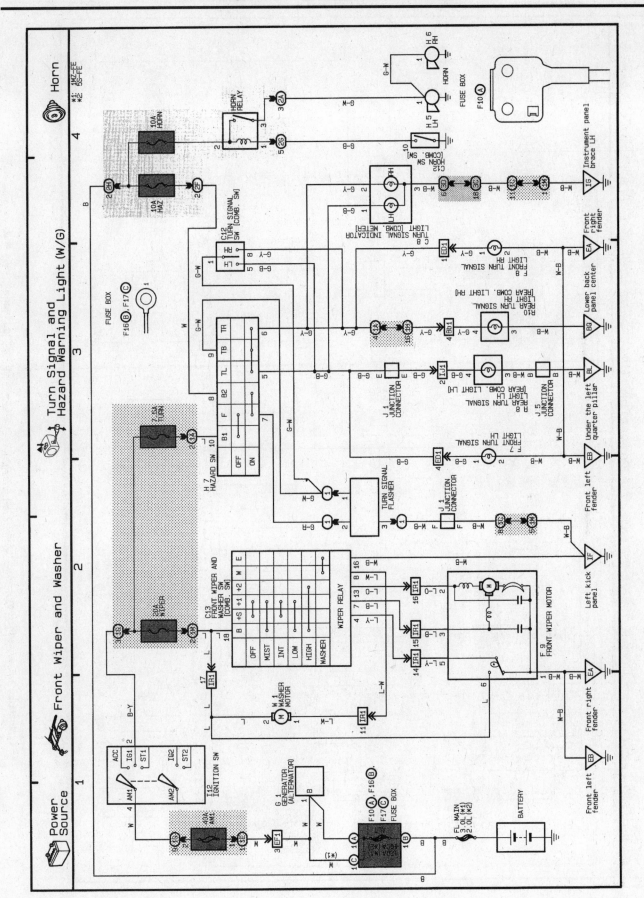

Typical front wiper/washer, turn signal/hazard warning light system wiring diagram (1994 and later models)

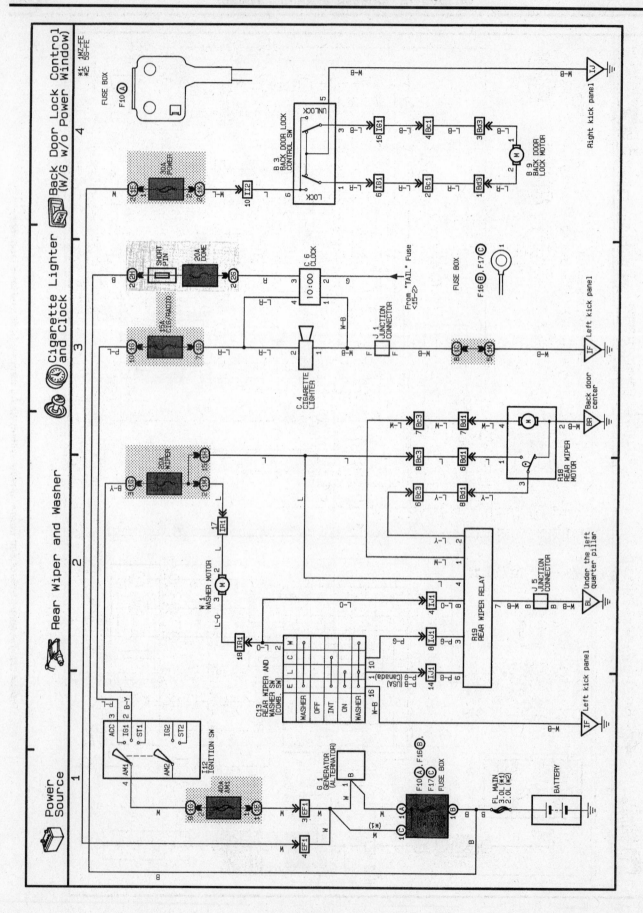

Typical rear wiper/washer, cigarette lighter/clock and rear door lock system wiring diagram (1994 and later models)

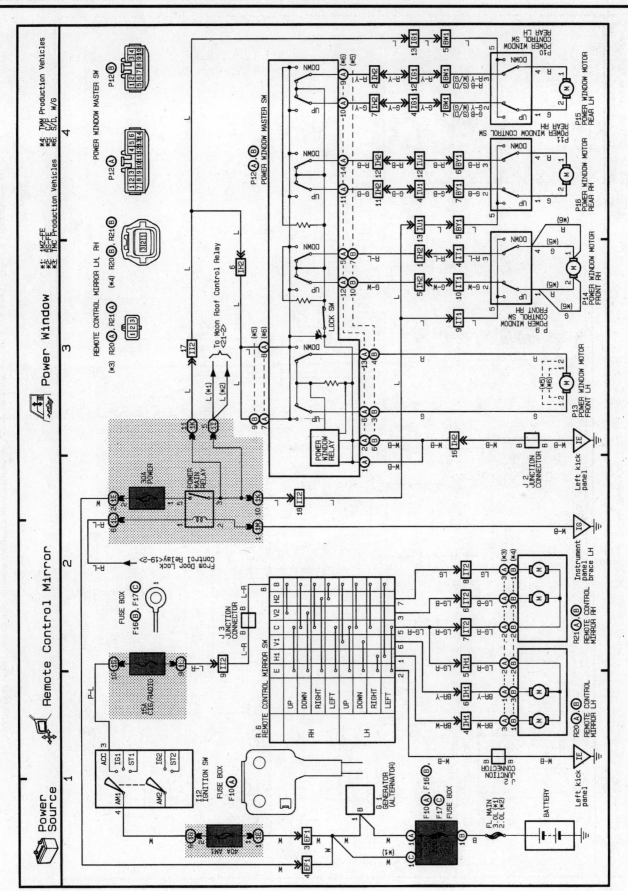

Typical remote control mirror and power window system wiring diagram (1994 and later models)

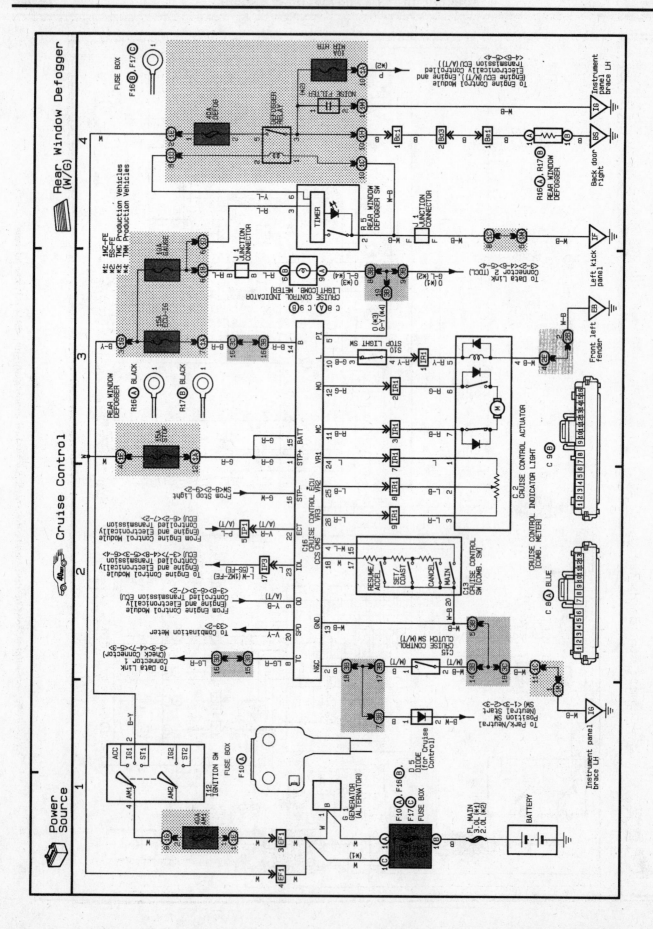

Typical cruise control and station wagon rear window defogger system wiring diagram (1994 and later models)

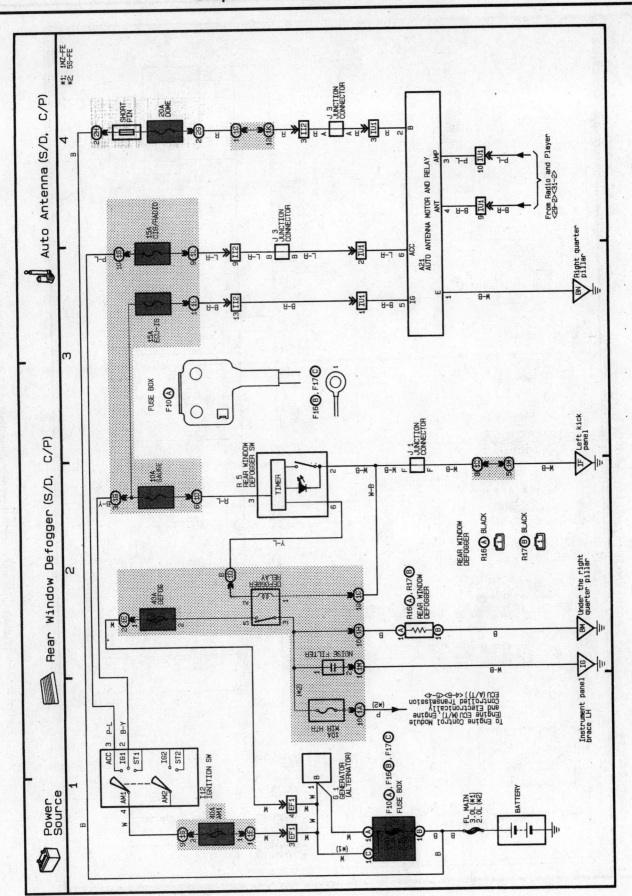

Typical power antenna and coupe and sedan rear window defogger system wiring diagram (1994 and later models)

12

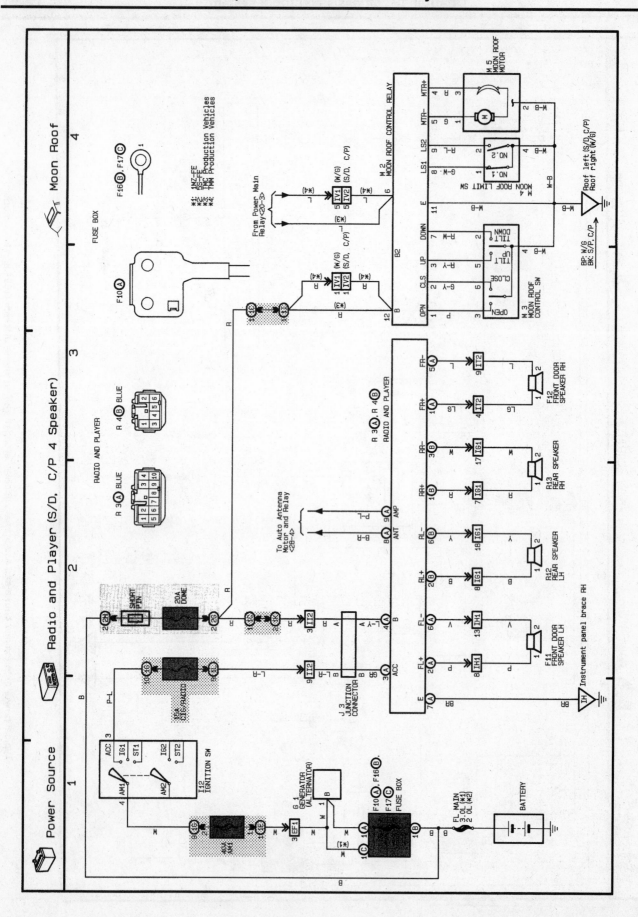

Typical radio and moof roof system wiring diagram (1994 and later models)

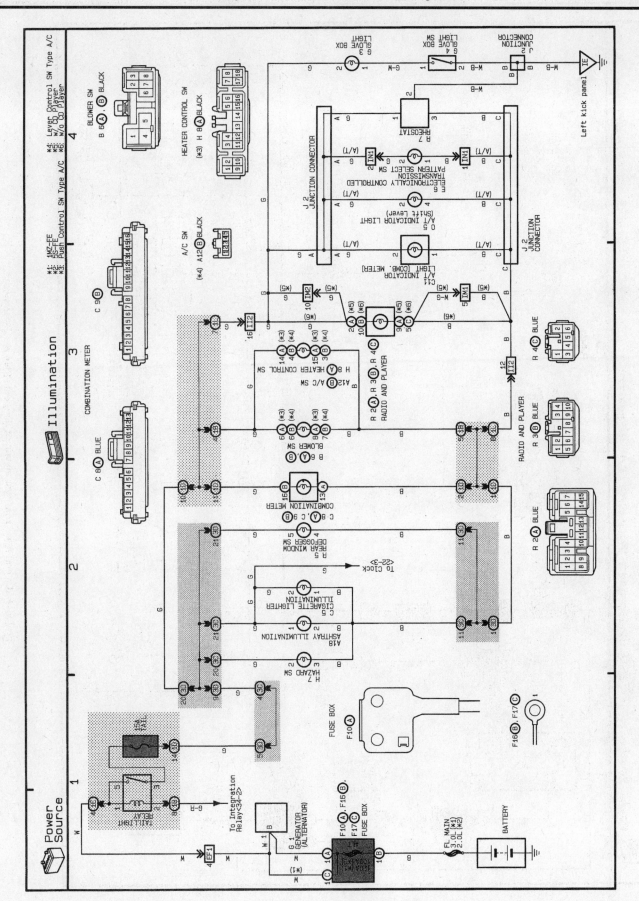

Typical instrument panel lighting system wiring diagram (1994 and later models)

Notes

Index

Haynes Automotive Manuals

NOTE: New manuals are added to this list on a periodic basis. If you do not see a listing for your vehicle, consult your local Haynes dealer for the latest product information.

ACURA
- *1776 **Integra** '86 thru '89 & **Legend** '86 thru '90

AMC
- **Jeep CJ** - see JEEP (412)
- 694 **Mid-size models,** Concord, Hornet, Gremlin & Spirit '70 thru '83
- 934 **(Renault) Alliance & Encore** '83 thru '87

AUDI
- 615 **4000** all models '80 thru '87
- 428 **5000** all models '77 thru '83
- 1117 **5000** all models '84 thru '88

AUSTIN-HEALEY
- **Sprite** - see MG Midget (265)

BMW
- *2020 **3/5 Series** not including diesel or all-wheel drive models '82 thru '92
- 276 **320i** all 4 cyl models '75 thru '83
- 632 **528i & 530i** all models '75 thru '80
- 240 **1500 thru 2002** except Turbo '59 thru '77

BUICK
- **Century (front wheel drive)** - see GM (829)
- *1627 **Buick, Oldsmobile & Pontiac Full-size (Front wheel drive)** all models '85 thru '95
  Buick Electra, LeSabre and Park Avenue; **Oldsmobile** Delta 88 Royale, Ninety Eight and Regency; **Pontiac** Bonneville
- 1551 **Buick Oldsmobile & Pontiac Full-size (Rear wheel drive)**
  Buick Estate '70 thru '90, Electra '70 thru '84, LeSabre '70 thru '85, Limited '74 thru '79 **Oldsmobile** Custom Cruiser '70 thru '90, Delta 88 '70 thru '85, Ninety-eight '70 thru '84 **Pontiac** Bonneville '70 thru '81, Catalina '70 thru '81, Grandville '70 thru '75, Parisienne '83 thru '86
- 627 **Mid-size Regal & Century** all rear-drive models with V6, V8 and Turbo '74 thru '87
  Regal - see GENERAL MOTORS (1671)
  Riviera - see GENERAL MOTORS (38030)
  Skyhawk - see GENERAL MOTORS (766)
  Skylark '80 thru '85 - see GM (38020)
  Skylark '86 on - see GM (1420)
  Somerset - see GENERAL MOTORS (1420)

CADILLAC
- *751 **Cadillac Rear Wheel Drive** all gasoline models '70 thru '93
  Cimarron - see GENERAL MOTORS (766)
  Eldorado - see GENERAL MOTORS (38030)
  Seville '80 thru '85 - see GM (38030)

CHEVROLET
- *1477 **Astro & GMC Safari Mini-vans** '85 thru '93
- 554 **Camaro V8** all models '70 thru '81
- 866 **Camaro** all models '82 thru '92
  Cavalier - see GENERAL MOTORS (766)
  Celebrity - see GENERAL MOTORS (829)
- 24017 **Camaro & Firebird** '93 thru '96
- 625 **Chevelle, Malibu & El Camino** all V6 & V8 models '69 thru '87
- 449 **Chevette & Pontiac T1000** '76 thru '87
- 550 **Citation** all models '80 thru '85
- *1628 **Corsica/Beretta** all models '87 thru '96
- 274 **Corvette** all V8 models '68 thru '82
- *1336 **Corvette** all models '84 thru '91
- 1762 **Chevrolet Engine Overhaul Manual**
- 704 **Full-size Sedans** Caprice, Impala, Biscayne, Bel Air & Wagons '69 thru '90
  Lumina - see GENERAL MOTORS (1671)
  Lumina APV - see GENERAL MOTORS (2035)
- 319 **Luv Pick-up** all 2WD & 4WD '72 thru '82
- 626 **Monte Carlo** all models '70 thru '88

- 241 **Nova** all V8 models '69 thru '79
- *1642 **Nova and Geo Prizm** all front wheel drive models, '85 thru '92
- 420 **Pick-ups '67 thru '87** - Chevrolet & GMC, all V8 & in-line 6 cyl, 2WD & 4WD '67 thru '87; Suburbans, Blazers & Jimmys '67 thru '91
- *1664 **Pick-ups '88 thru '95** - Chevrolet & GMC, all full-size pick-ups, '88 thru '95; Blazer & Jimmy '92 thru '94; Suburban '92 thru '95; Tahoe & Yukon '95
- 831 **S-10 & GMC S-15 Pick-ups** '82 thru '93
- *24071 **S-10 & GMC S-15 Pick-ups** '94 thru '96
- *1727 **Sprint & Geo Metro** '85 thru '94
- *345 **Vans - Chevrolet & GMC,** V8 & in-line 6 cylinder models '68 thru '96

CHRYSLER
- 25025 **Chrysler Concorde, New Yorker & LHS, Dodge** Intrepid, **Eagle** Vision, '93 thru '96
- 2114 **Chrysler Engine Overhaul Manual**
- *2058 **Full-size Front-Wheel Drive** '88 thru '93
  K-Cars - see DODGE Aries (723)
  Laser - see DODGE Daytona (1140)
- *1337 **Chrysler & Plymouth Mid-size** front wheel drive '82 thru '95
  Rear-wheel Drive - see Dodge (2098)

DATSUN
- 647 **200SX** all models '80 thru '83
- 228 **B - 210** all models '73 thru '78
- 525 **210** all models '79 thru '82
- 206 **240Z, 260Z & 280Z** Coupe '70 thru '78
- 563 **280ZX** Coupe & 2+2 '79 thru '83
  300ZX - see NISSAN (1137)
- 679 **310** all models '78 thru '82
- 123 **510 & PL521 Pick-up** '68 thru '73
- 430 **510** all models '78 thru '81
- 372 **610** all models '72 thru '76
- 277 **620 Series Pick-up** all models '73 thru '79
  720 Series Pick-up - see NISSAN (771)
- 376 **810/Maxima** all gasoline models, '77 thru '84
  Pulsar - see NISSAN (876)
  Sentra - see NISSAN (982)
  Stanza - see NISSAN (981)

DODGE
- **400 & 600** - see CHRYSLER Mid-size (1337)
- *723 **Aries & Plymouth Reliant** '81 thru '89
- 1231 **Caravan & Plymouth Voyager Mini-Vans** all models '84 thru '95
- 699 **Challenger/Plymouth Saporro** '78 thru '83
  Challenger '67-'76 - see DODGE Dart (234)
- 610 **Colt & Plymouth Champ (front wheel drive)** all models '78 thru '87
- *1668 **Dakota Pick-ups** all models '87 thru '96
- 234 **Dart, Challenger/Plymouth Barracuda & Valiant** 6 cyl models '67 thru '76
- *1140 **Daytona & Chrysler Laser** '84 thru '89
  Intrepid - see CHRYSLER (25025)
- *30034 **Neon** all models '94 thru '97
- *545 **Omni & Plymouth Horizon** '78 thru '90
- *912 **Pick-ups** all full-size models '74 thru '93
- *30041 **Pick-ups** all full-size models '94 thru '96
- *556 **Ram 50/D50 Pick-ups & Raider and Plymouth Arrow Pick-ups** '79 thru '93
- 2098 **Dodge/Plymouth/Chrysler** rear wheel drive '71 thru '89
- *1726 **Shadow & Plymouth Sundance** '87 thru '94
- *1779 **Spirit & Plymouth Acclaim** '89 thru '95
- *349 **Vans - Dodge & Plymouth** V8 & 6 cyl models '71 thru '96

EAGLE
- **Talon** - see Mitsubishi Eclipse (2097)
- **Vision** - see CHRYSLER (25025)

FIAT
- 094 **124 Sport Coupe & Spider** '68 thru '78
- 273 **X1/9** all models '74 thru '80

FORD
- 10355 **Ford Automatic Trans. Overhaul**
- *1476 **Aerostar Mini-vans** all models '86 thru '96

- 268 **Courier Pick-up** all models '72 thru '82
- 2105 **Crown Victoria & Mercury Grand Marquis** '88 thru '96
- 1763 **Ford Engine Overhaul Manual**
- 789 **Escort/Mercury Lynx** all models '81 thru '90
- *2046 **Escort/Mercury Tracer** '91 thru '96
- *2021 **Explorer & Mazda Navajo** '91 thru '95
- 560 **Fairmont & Mercury Zephyr** '78 thru '83
- 334 **Fiesta** all models '77 thru '80
- 754 **Ford & Mercury Full-size,** Ford LTD & Mercury Marquis ('75 thru '82); Ford Custom 500, Country Squire, Crown Victoria & Mercury Colony Park ('75 thru '87); Ford LTD Crown Victoria & Mercury Gran Marquis ('83 thru '87)
- 359 **Granada & Mercury Monarch** all in-line, 6 cyl & V8 models '75 thru '80
- 773 **Ford & Mercury Mid-size,** Ford Thunderbird & Mercury Cougar ('75 thru '82); Ford LTD & Mercury Marquis ('83 thru '86); Ford Torino, Gran Torino, Elite, Ranchero pick-up, LTD II, Mercury Montego, Comet, XR-7 & Lincoln Versailles ('75 thru '86)
- 231 **Mustang II** 4 cyl, V6 & V8 models '74 thru '78
- 357 **Mustang V8** all models '64-1/2 thru '73
- *654 **Mustang & Mercury Capri** all models Mustang, '79 thru '93; Capri, '79 thru '86
- *36051 **Mustang** all models '94 thru '97
- 788 **Pick-ups & Bronco** '73 thru '79
- *880 **Pick-ups & Bronco** '80 thru '96
- 649 **Pinto & Mercury Bobcat** '75 thru '80
- 1670 **Probe** all models '89 thru '92
- *1026 **Ranger/Bronco II** gasoline models '83 thru '92
- *36071 **Ranger** '93 thru '96 & **Mazda Pick-ups** '94 thru '96
- *1421 **Taurus & Mercury Sable** '86 thru '95
- *1418 **Tempo & Mercury Topaz** all gasoline models '84 thru '94
- 1338 **Thunderbird/Mercury Cougar** '83 thru '88
- *1725 **Thunderbird/Mercury Cougar** '89 and '96
- 344 **Vans** all V8 Econoline models '69 thru '91
- *2119 **Vans** full size '92-'95

GENERAL MOTORS
- *10360 **GM Automatic Transmission Overhaul**
- *829 **Buick Century, Chevrolet Celebrity, Oldsmobile Cutlass Ciera & Pontiac 6000** all models '82 thru '96
- *1671 **Buick Regal, Chevrolet Lumina, Oldsmobile Cutlass Supreme & Pontiac Grand Prix** front wheel drive models '88 thru '95
- *766 **Buick Skyhawk, Cadillac Cimarron, Chevrolet Cavalier, Oldsmobile Firenza & Pontiac J-2000 & Sunbird** '82 thru '94
- 38020 **Buick Skylark, Chevrolet Citation, Olds Omega, Pontiac Phoenix** '80 thru '85
- 1420 **Buick Skylark & Somerset, Oldsmobile Achieva & Calais and Pontiac Grand Am** all models '85 thru '95
- 38030 **Cadillac Eldorado** '71 thru '85, **Seville** '80 thru '85, **Oldsmobile Toronado** '71 thru '85 & **Buick Riviera** '79 thru '85
- *2035 **Chevrolet Lumina APV, Olds Silhouette & Pontiac Trans Sport** all models '90 thru '95
  General Motors Full-size Rear-wheel Drive - see BUICK (1551)

GEO
- **Metro** - see CHEVROLET Sprint (1727)
- **Prizm** - '85 thru '92 see CHEVY Nova (1642), '93 thru '96 see TOYOTA Corolla (1642)
- *2039 **Storm** all models '90 thru '93
  Tracker - see SUZUKI Samurai (1626)

GMC
- **Safari** - see CHEVROLET ASTRO (1477)
- **Vans & Pick-ups** - see CHEVROLET (420, 831, 345, 1664 & 24071)

(Continued on other side)

---

* Listings shown with an asterisk (*) indicate model coverage as of this printing. These titles will be periodically updated to include later model years - consult your Haynes dealer for more information.

Haynes North America, Inc., 861 Lawrence Drive, Newbury Park, CA 91320 • (805) 498-6703

Haynes Automotive Manuals (continued)

NOTE: New manuals are added to this list on a periodic basis. If you do not see a listing for your vehicle, consult your local Haynes dealer for the latest product information.

HONDA
351	**Accord CVCC** all models '76 thru '83
1221	**Accord** all models '84 thru '89
2067	**Accord** all models '90 thru '93
42013	**Accord** all models '94 thru '95
160	**Civic 1200** all models '73 thru '79
633	**Civic 1300 & 1500 CVCC** '80 thru '83
297	**Civic 1500 CVCC** all models '75 thru '79
1227	**Civic** all models '84 thru '91
*2118	**Civic & del Sol** '92 thru '95
*601	**Prelude CVCC** all models '79 thru '89

HYUNDAI
*1552	**Excel** all models '86 thru '94

ISUZU
*1641	**Trooper & Pick-up**, all gasoline models Pick-up, '81 thru '93; Trooper, '84 thru '91
	Hombre - *see CHEVROLET S-10 (24071)*

JAGUAR
*242	**XJ6** all 6 cyl models '68 thru '86
*49011	**XJ6** all models '88 thru '94
*478	**XJ12 & XJS** all 12 cyl models '72 thru '85

JEEP
*1553	**Cherokee, Comanche & Wagoneer Limited** all models '84 thru '96
412	**CJ** all models '49 thru '86
50025	**Grand Cherokee** all models '93 thru '95
50029	**Grand Wagoneer & Pick-up** '72 thru '91 Grand Wagoneer '84 thru '91, Cherokee & Wagoneer '72 thru '83, Pick-up '72 thru '88
*1777	**Wrangler** all models '87 thru '95

LINCOLN
2117	**Rear Wheel Drive** all models '70 thru '96

MAZDA
648	**626** (rear wheel drive) all models '79 thru '82
*1082	**626/MX-6** (front wheel drive) '83 thru '91
370	**GLC Hatchback** (rear wheel drive) '77 thru '83
757	**GLC** (front wheel drive) '81 thru '85
*2047	**MPV** all models '89 thru '94
	Navajo - *see Ford Explorer (2021)*
267	**Pick-ups** '72 thru '93
	Pick-ups '94 thru '96 - *see Ford Ranger (36071)*
460	**RX-7** all models '79 thru '85
*1419	**RX-7** all models '86 thru '91

MERCEDES-BENZ
*1643	**190 Series** four-cyl gas models, '84 thru '88
346	**230/250/280** 6 cyl sohc models '68 thru '72
983	**280 123 Series** gasoline models '77 thru '81
698	**350 & 450** all models '71 thru '80
697	**Diesel 123 Series** '76 thru '85

MERCURY
See FORD Listing

MG
111	**MGB** Roadster & GT Coupe '62 thru '80
265	**MG Midget, Austin Healey Sprite** '58 thru '80

MITSUBISHI
*1669	**Cordia, Tredia, Galant, Precis & Mirage** '83 thru '93
*2097	**Eclipse, Eagle Talon & Plymouth Laser** '90 thru '94
*2022	**Pick-up** '83 thru '96 & **Montero** '83 thru '93

NISSAN
1137	**300ZX** all models including Turbo '84 thru '89
*72015	**Altima** all models '93 thru '97
*1341	**Maxima** all models '85 thru '91
*771	**Pick-ups** '80 thru '96 **Pathfinder** '87 thru '95
876	**Pulsar** all models '83 thru '86
*982	**Sentra** all models '82 thru '94
*981	**Stanza** all models '82 thru '90

OLDSMOBILE
	Achieva - *see GENERAL MOTORS (1420)*
	Bravada - *see CHEVROLET S-10 (831)*
	Calais - *see GENERAL MOTORS (1420)*
	Custom Cruiser - *see BUICK RWD (1551)*
*658	**Cutlass V6 & V8** gas models '74 thru '88
	Cutlass Ciera - *see GENERAL MOTORS (829)*
	Cutlass Supreme - *see GM (1671)*
	Delta 88 - *see BUICK Full-size RWD (1551)*
	Delta 88 Brougham - *see BUICK Full-size FWD (1551), RWD (1627)*
	Delta 88 Royale - *see BUICK RWD (1551)*
	Firenza - *see GENERAL MOTORS (766)*
	Ninety-eight Regency - *see BUICK Full-size RWD (1551), FWD (1627)*
	Ninety-eight Regency Brougham - *see BUICK Full-size RWD (1551)*
	Omega - *see GENERAL MOTORS (38020)*
	Silhouette - *see GENERAL MOTORS (2035)*
	Toronado - *see GENERAL MOTORS (38030)*

PEUGEOT
663	**504** all diesel models '74 thru '83

PLYMOUTH
	Laser - *see MITSUBISHI Eclipse (2097)*
	For other PLYMOUTH titles, see DODGE.

PONTIAC
	T1000 - *see CHEVROLET Chevette (449)*
	J-2000 - *see GENERAL MOTORS (766)*
	6000 - *see GENERAL MOTORS (829)*
	Bonneville - *see Buick FWD (1627), RWD (1551)*
	Bonneville Brougham - *see Buick (1551)*
	Catalina - *see Buick Full-size (1551)*
1232	**Fiero** all models '84 thru '88
555	**Firebird** V8 models except Turbo '70 thru '81
867	**Firebird** all models '82 thru '92
	Firebird '93 thru '96 - *see CHEVY Camaro (24017)*
	Full-size Front Wheel Drive - *see BUICK, Oldsmobile, Pontiac Full-size FWD (1627)*
	Full-size Rear Wheel Drive - *see BUICK Oldsmobile, Pontiac Full-size RWD (1551)*
	Grand Am - *see GENERAL MOTORS (1420)*
	Grand Prix - *see GENERAL MOTORS (1671)*
	Grandville - *see BUICK Full-size (1551)*
	Parisienne - *see BUICK Full-size (1551)*
	Phoenix - *see GENERAL MOTORS (38020)*
	Sunbird - *see GENERAL MOTORS (766)*
	Trans Sport - *see GENERAL MOTORS (2035)*

PORSCHE
*264	**911** except Turbo & Carrera 4 '65 thru '89
239	**914** all 4 cyl models '69 thru '76
397	**924** all models including Turbo '76 thru '82
*1027	**944** all models including Turbo '83 thru '89

RENAULT
141	**5 Le Car** all models '76 thru '83
	Alliance & Encore - *see AMC (934)*

SAAB
247	**99** all models including Turbo '69 thru '80
*980	**900** all models including Turbo '79 thru '88

SATURN
2083	**Saturn** all models '91 thru '96

SUBARU
237	**1100, 1300, 1400 & 1600** '71 thru '79
*681	**1600 & 1800** 2WD & 4WD '80 thru '89

SUZUKI
*1626	**Samurai/Sidekick & Geo Tracker** '86 thru '96

TOYOTA
1023	**Camry** all models '83 thru '91
92006	**Camry** all models '92 thru '95
935	**Celica Rear Wheel Drive** '71 thru '85
*2038	**Celica Front Wheel Drive** '86 thru '93
1139	**Celica Supra** all models '79 thru '92
361	**Corolla** all models '75 thru '79
961	**Corolla** all rear wheel drive models '80 thru '87
1025	**Corolla** all front wheel drive models '84 thru '92
*92036	**Corolla & Geo Prizm** '93 thru '96
636	**Corolla Tercel** all models '80 thru '82
360	**Corona** all models '74 thru '82
532	**Cressida** all models '78 thru '82
313	**Land Cruiser** all models '68 thru '82
*1339	**MR2** all models '85 thru '87
304	**Pick-up** all models '69 thru '78
*656	**Pick-up** all models '79 thru '95
*2048	**Previa** all models '91 thru '95
2106	**Tercel** all models '87 thru '94

TRIUMPH
113	**Spitfire** all models '62 thru '81
322	**TR7** all models '75 thru '81

VW
159	**Beetle & Karmann Ghia** '54 thru '79
238	**Dasher** all gasoline models '74 thru '81
96017	**Golf & Jetta** all models '93 thru '97
*884	**Rabbit, Jetta, Scirocco, & Pick-up** gas models '74 thru '91 & Convertible '80 thru '92
451	**Rabbit, Jetta & Pick-up** diesel '77 thru '84
082	**Transporter 1600** all models '68 thru '79
226	**Transporter 1700, 1800 & 2000** '72 thru '79
084	**Type 3 1500 & 1600** all models '63 thru '73
1029	**Vanagon** all air-cooled models '80 thru '83

VOLVO
203	**120, 130 Series & 1800 Sports** '61 thru '73
129	**140 Series** all models '66 thru '74
*270	**240 Series** all models '76 thru '93
400	**260 Series** all models '75 thru '82
*1550	**740 & 760 Series** all models '82 thru '88

TECHBOOK MANUALS
2108	**Automotive Computer Codes**
1667	**Automotive Emissions Control Manual**
482	**Fuel Injection Manual, 1978 thru 1985**
2111	**Fuel Injection Manual, 1986 thru 1996**
2069	**Holley Carburetor Manual**
2068	**Rochester Carburetor Manual**
10240	**Weber/Zenith/Stromberg/SU Carburetors**
1762	**Chevrolet Engine Overhaul Manual**
2114	**Chrysler Engine Overhaul Manual**
1763	**Ford Engine Overhaul Manual**
1736	**GM and Ford Diesel Engine Repair Manual**
1666	**Small Engine Repair Manual**
10355	**Ford Automatic Transmission Overhaul**
10360	**GM Automatic Transmission Overhaul**
1479	**Automotive Body Repair & Painting**
2112	**Automotive Brake Manual**
2113	**Automotive Detailing Manual**
1654	**Automotive Eelectrical Manual**
1480	**Automotive Heating & Air Conditioning**
2109	**Automotive Reference Manual & Dictionary**
2107	**Automotive Tools Manual**
10440	**Used Car Buying Guide**
2110	**Welding Manual**
10450	**ATV Basics**

SPANISH MANUALS
98903	**Reparación de Carrocería & Pintura**
98905	**Códigos Automotrices de la Computadora**
98910	**Frenos Automotriz**
98915	**Inyección de Combustible 1986 al 1994**
99040	**Chevrolet & GMC Camionetas** '67 al '87 Incluye Suburban, Blazer & Jimmy '67 al '91
99041	**Chevrolet & GMC Camionetas** '88 al '95 Incluye Suburban '92 al '95, Blazer & Jimmy '92 al '94, Tahoe y Yukon '95
99042	**Chevrolet & GMC Camionetas Cerradas** '68 al '95
99055	**Dodge Caravan & Plymouth Voyager** '84 al '95
99075	**Ford Camionetas y Bronco** '80 al '94
99077	**Ford Camionetas Cerradas** '69 al '91
99083	**Ford Modelos de Tamaño Grande** '75 al '87
99088	**Ford Modelos de Tamaño Mediano** '75 al '86
99095	**GM Modelos de Tamaño Grande** '70 al '90
99118	**Nissan Sentra** '82 al '94
99125	**Toyota Camionetas y 4-Runner** '79 al '95

* Listings shown with an asterisk (*) indicate model coverage as of this printing. These titles will be periodically updated to include later model years - consult your Haynes dealer for more information.

 Over 100 Haynes motorcycle manuals also available

5-97

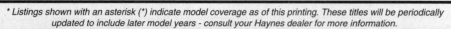

Haynes North America, Inc., 861 Lawrence Drive, Newbury Park, CA 91320 • (805) 498-6703